FORENSIC PSYCHOLOGY

Joanna Pozzulo   Craig Bennell   Adelle Forth

FIFTH EDITION

EDITORIAL DIRECTOR: Claudine O'Donnell
ACQUISITIONS EDITOR: Darcey Pepper
MARKETING MANAGER: Leigh-Anne Graham
PROGRAM MANAGER: Madhu Ranadive
PROJECT MANAGER: Susan Johnson
MANAGER OF CONTENT DEVELOPMENT: Suzanne Schaan
DEVELOPMENT EDITOR: Cheryl Finch
PRODUCTION SERVICES: Cenveo® Publisher Services, Inc.

PERMISSIONS PROJECT MANAGER: Kathryn O'Handley
PHOTO PERMISSIONS RESEARCH: iEnergizerAptara®
TEXT PERMISSIONS RESEARCH: iEnergizerAptara®
ART DIRECTOR: Cenveo Publisher Services, Inc.
COVER DESIGNER: Cenveo Publisher Services, Inc.
COVER IMAGE: Adrian Niederhäuser/Fotolia
VICE-PRESIDENT, CROSS MEDIA AND PUBLISHING
SERVICES: Gary Bennett

Pearson Canada Inc., 26 Prince Andrew Place, Don Mills, Ontario M3C 2T8.

ISBN 978-0-13-430806-7

Library and Archives Canada Cataloguing in Publication

Pozzulo, Joanna, author
   Forensic psychology / Joanna Pozzulo, Craig Bennell, Adelle
Forth. — Fifth edition.

Includes bibliographical references and index.
ISBN 978-0-13-430806-7 (hardback)

   1. Forensic psychology—Textbooks.   I. Bennell, Craig, author
I. Forth, Adelle Elizabeth, 1961-, author   III. Title.

RA1148.P68 2016   614'.15   C2016-904437-8

This book is dedicated to our many students who challenge our thinking and inspire us, and to our dear colleagues Don Andrews, Grant Harris, and Marnie Rice, who paved the way for us.

Brief Contents

Contents

Preface

We are excited about the continued interest in our textbook. We never expected that we would be going into our fifth edition when we first gathered in Adelle's office almost thirteen years ago. We are pleased to have seen the field expand dramatically in this timeframe and we hope that this new edition captures the innovations and the diversity of research now being conducted by our colleagues around the world.

As in previous editions, we have taken a broad-based perspective that incorporates both experimental and clinical topics. The text covers topics that might otherwise be discussed in social and cognitive psychology courses—including eyewitness testimony, jury decision making, and police procedures—as well as topics that are clinical in nature and might otherwise be discussed in personality or mental health psychology courses—such as the meaning of being unfit to stand trial, mentally disordered offenders, and psychopathy. Our goal in this edition was to update important ideas, issues, and research in a way that students will understand and enjoy, and in some cases find useful in their professional careers. We hope that the academic community will find this textbook a valuable teaching tool that provides a comprehensive and current coverage of forensic psychology.

NEW TO THE FIFTH EDITION

- **Increased coverage** on Aboriginal issues.
- Each chapter now includes a box on myths and realities related to forensic psychology.
- Updated relevant court cases in each chapter.
- **Reorganization** of chapters to allow for easier delivery of course material and to decrease the overlap between chapters.
- **Updated**—All chapters have been updated to reflect the expanding field of forensic psychology, including recent changes to Canadian legislation and reference to the *DSM-5*.
- **New profiles** of prominent Canadian researchers:

  Dr. Tara Burke, Ryerson University

  Dr. Mary Ann Campbell, University of New Brunswick

  Dr. Leanne ten Brinke, University of Denver

  Dr. Laura Melnyk Gribble, King's University College at the University of Western

  Dr. Leena Augimeri, Child Development Institute

  Dr. Karl Hanson, Public Safety Canada

  Dr. Joseph Eastwood, University of Ontario Institute of Technology

  Dr. Eric Beauregard, Simon Fraser University

RETAINED FEATURES

The pedagogical aids are designed to promote student learning and assist instructors in presenting key material. Important features include the following:

- **Learning Objectives and End-of-Chapter Summaries.** Each chapter starts with a list of learning objectives to guide students' learning of the material and closes with a summary linked to the learning objectives.

- **Vignettes.** Chapter-opening vignettes provide students with a context for the key concepts they will encounter in each chapter. These engaging vignettes present real-world scenarios in which students, or people they know, could potentially find themselves.

- **Boxes.** Boxed features within the chapters provide interesting asides to the main text. Some detail current Canadian cases and legal rulings **(Cases in Forensic Psychology boxes)**, while others highlight "hot" topics in the news **(In the Media boxes)** that have not yet been the subject of much psychological research. These boxes will develop students' consciousness of current issues and spark some research ideas.

- **Profiles of Canadian Researchers.** To expose students to the varied and excellent research in forensic psychology being conducted by Canadians, each chapter includes a profile of a key Canadian researcher whose work is relevant to the chapter topic. These profiles highlight educational background, current position, and research interests, along with a little about the researcher's personal life, so students realize the researchers featured are people too.

- **Research Methodology.** Research methodology specific to forensic topics is described in the relevant chapters, with the goal of helping students understand how studies in forensic psychology are conducted.

- **Research Studies.** Data reported in original studies are cited throughout the textbook, often in graph or table form for easy interpretation. Diagrams of psychological models and flow charts demonstrate key processes that occur through the criminal justice system.

- **Theoretical Perspectives.** Theories that provide accounts for specific topic areas are discussed in each chapter. The discussion of the various theories emphasizes a multidisciplinary approach, showing the interplay among cognitive, biological, and social factors in understanding the different forensic psychology areas.

- **Law.** *Forensic Psychology* provides the student with information on current Canadian law relevant to the psychological issues discussed. At times, Canadian law is contrasted with U.S. and/or British law; however, it is important to remember that the emphasis is on Canadian case law, statutes, regulations, and so on. We do not provide full coverage of law that is not Canadian, so students who are interested in the laws of other countries should refer to other resources.

- **Research Questions.** At the end of case boxes, a set of questions are provided to aid students' thinking about the material. These questions do not necessarily contain a "correct" answer but rather allow the student to consider alternative views of the issues.

- **Discussion Questions.** Several discussion questions are offered at the end of each chapter. Instructors can assign these questions for group discussion, or students can use the questions to examine their comprehension and retention of the chapter material. We hope these questions will inspire critical thought in students.

- **Key Terms and Glossary.** Throughout the chapters, keywords with which students in forensic psychology should be familiar appear in bold type and are defined in marginal notes. These key terms and their definitions are also provided in a glossary at the end of the book for easy reference.

SUPPLEMENTS FOR INSTRUCTORS

The following supplements specific to *Forensic Psychology*, Fifth Edition, can be downloaded by instructors from a password-protected location on Pearson Education Canada's online catalogue. Contact your local sales representative for further information.

- **Instructor's Manual.** The instructor's manual is a comprehensive resource that provides chapter outlines, class activities, and summaries of select cases cited. We hope our colleagues will use the textbook and instructor's manual as foundations that they can build on in the classroom lecture.

- **Test Item File.** This test bank, offered in Microsoft Word format, contains multiple-choice and short-answer questions. Each question is classified according to difficulty level and is keyed to the appropriate page number in the textbook.

- **MyTest.** The new edition test bank comes with MyTest, a powerful assessment generation program that helps instructors easily create and print quizzes, tests, and exams, as well as homework or practice handouts. Questions and tests can all be authored online, allowing instructors ultimate flexibility and the ability to efficiently manage assessments at any time, from anywhere.

- **PowerPoint Presentations.** PowerPoint slides highlight the key concepts in each chapter of the text.

Learning Solutions Managers

Pearson's Learning Solutions Managers work with faculty and campus course designers to ensure that Pearson technology products, assessment tools, and online course materials are tailored to meet your specific needs. This highly qualified team is dedicated to helping schools take full advantage of a wide range of educational resources, by assisting in the integration of a variety of instructional materials and media formats. Your local Pearson Education sales representative can provide you with more details on this service program.

peerScholar

Firmly grounded in published research, peerScholar is a powerful online pedagogical tool that helps develop students' critical and creative thinking skills through creation, evaluation, and reflection. Working in stages, students begin by submitting written assignments. peerScholar then circulates their work for others to review, a process that can be anonymous or not, depending on instructors' preferences. Students immediately receive peer feedback and evaluations, reinforcing their learning and driving development of higher-order thinking skills. Students can then re-submit revised work again depending on instructors' preferences.

ACKNOWLEDGMENTS

This book would never have come to fruition had we not been mentored by outstanding forensic researchers. Joanna Pozzulo is indebted to Rod Lindsay at Queen's University for his unfailing support, his rich insights, and his commitment to academic excellence that she aspires to achieve. Craig Bennell is grateful to David Canter at the University of Liverpool for providing a stimulating intellectual environment in which to study and for teaching him how to think critically. Adelle Forth wishes to express her admiration, respect, and gratitude to Robert Hare at the University of British Columbia, who nurtured her interest in the area of psychopathy and who has provided consistent support and guidance.

We would like to acknowledge that the forensic program at Carleton University, of which we are part, would not exist without our colleagues Julie Blais, Shelley Brown, Kevin Nunes, Ralph Serin, and Evelyn Maeder.

We are thankful to the exceptional researchers we profiled in this textbook for giving us their time and insight into their lives, specifically: Stephen Wormith, Dorothy Cotton, Joseph Eastwood, Leanne ten Brinke, Rod Lindsay, Laura Melynk Gribble, Tara Burke, Mary Ann Campbell, Ralph Serin, Karl Hanson, Robert Hare, Leena Augimeri, Don Dutton, Martin Lalumière, and Eric Beauregard. All have made significant contributions to the field of forensic psychology.

We thank our many undergraduate and graduate students who over the years have challenged our thinking and who have influenced the ideas expressed in this book. In particular, we wish to thank the following students for their help in researching the book: Emily Pica, Andrei Mesesan, Chelsea Sheahan, Mary Ritchie, Becky Grace, and Kristopher Brazil.

We would like to thank the great staff at Pearson Education Canada. Madhu Ranadive and Cheryl Finch (developmental editor) deserve special mention—this book would not exist without their enthusiasm, expertise, and dedication. Susan Johnson, Darcey Pepper, and Lisa Gillis also played important roles in making *Forensic Psychology*, Fifth Edition, become a reality.

Finally on a personal note, Joanna Pozzulo would like to thank her partner David for his patience and support during the writing process. She also would like to thank Craig and Adelle for being great collaborators and dear friends. Craig Bennell would like to thank his wife, Cindy, for her love, patience, and support during the long hours of writing, and his sons, Noah and Elijah, for making him always remember what is most important. Adelle Forth would like to thank her partner, colleague, and friend, John Logan, for his insights, suggestions, and feedback that improved the book, as well as his understanding and support while preparing the book. She would also like to acknowledge the contribution of her numerous four-legged furry friends for keeping her sane.

Chapter 1

An Introduction to Forensic Psychology

Learning Objectives

- Identify some of the major milestones in the history of forensic psychology.
- Provide a narrow and a broad definition of forensic psychology.
- Describe the differences between clinical and experimental forensic psychology.
- List the three ways in which psychology and the law can interact.
- List the criteria used in Canada to decide when expert testimony is admissible.

Sarah Henderson has just finished watching her favourite television show, *Criminal Minds*. She has her heart set on a career that will allow her to do what the characters in her favourite show do for a living—profiling serial arsonists, rapists, and killers. Sarah thinks that becoming a forensic psychologist is the right path for her. Fortunately, Sarah's neighbour works as a probation officer and has regular contact with forensic psychologists. This neighbour has repeatedly told Sarah that forensic psychology isn't necessarily what she sees on the television. Sarah finally decides to find out for herself what forensic psychology is all about and enrolls in a course at her local university, much like the one you are currently taking.

Although you may not appreciate it yet, **forensic psychology** is all around you. Every time you pick up the newspaper, there are stories that relate directly to the field of forensic psychology. Hollywood has also gotten in on the act. More and more often, television shows and blockbuster movies focus on issues that are related to the field of forensic psychology—profiling serial killers, selecting jury members, or determining someone's sanity. Unfortunately, the way in which the media portrays forensic psychology is frequently inaccurate. Although forensic psychologists often carry out the sorts of tasks depicted in the media, the way in which they carry them out is typically very different from the typical Hollywood image. One of our primary goals throughout this book is to provide you with a more accurate description of what forensic psychology is and to encourage you to think more critically about the things you see and hear in the media. See the In the Media box for further discussion on the role of the media in shaping our attitudes about the criminal justice system.

Like all psychologists, forensic psychologists are interested in understanding the mechanisms that underlie people's thoughts, feelings, and actions. However, as you will

Forensic psychology: A field of psychology that deals with all aspects of human behaviour as it relates to the law or legal system

The Reality of Reality TV

Crime has always been a popular topic for television shows, and researchers are interested in understanding the role that television plays in shaping the attitudes of viewers towards crime-related matters. With the introduction of crime-based reality television, even more attention is being been paid to this issue (Doyle, 2003).

No crime-based reality show has been more popular than the award-winning *Cops*, which has been on the air since 1989. If shows like *Cops* are influencing the attitudes of viewers (e.g., their attitudes towards the police), one obvious question to ask is whether this is problematic. Perhaps it isn't if *Cops* presents an accurate portrayal of crime and our legal system's response to it. But, what if these shows are biased and present a distorted view of policing (or of crime)?

A colleague of ours at Carleton University, Dr. Aaron Doyle, explored these types of issues in his 2003 book *Arresting Images: Crime and Policing in Front of the Television Camera*. Some of what he found in his research might surprise you. For example, despite the fact that its producers have referred to the show as "unfiltered television," Doyle's analysis of *Cops* indicates quite the opposite. In contrast to how the show is pitched to viewers, Doyle argued that *Cops* "offers a very particular and select vision of policing" (p. 34). Rather than reality television, Doyle suggests the show is reality fiction, a "constructed version of reality with its own biases, rather than a neutral record" (p. 35). Once one understands how shows such as *Cops* are actually produced, Doyle's argument becomes more convincing.

Consider the following examples, which were highlighted by Doyle (2003):

- While the producers of *Cops* state that the show allows viewers to share a cop's point of view in "real time," this is not actually true. As Doyle showed, while each of the seven- to eight-minute vignettes that make up a *Cops* episode does tend to unfold in a linear fashion, the sequence of events is not typically presented in real time. Instead, the various parts of the vignette that are ultimately aired have often taken place over many hours, only to be edited together later. In fact, according to Doyle, each hour of *Cops* airtime is typically edited down from between 50 and 60 hours of actual footage.

- Clever techniques for giving the illusion of real-time flow are also regularly used by the editors of *Cops*. For example, as Doyle revealed, although it appears as if the visual and sound elements of *Cops* are both captured simultaneously, this is often not the case. Rather, "sound is edited to overlap cuts in the visuals . . . [with the continuing sound suggesting] continuity in time, as if the viewer has simply looked in a different direction during continuous action . . . although in fact an hour's worth of action and dialogue could have been omitted between the cuts" (p. 36).

- *Cops* is also made more realistic by ensuring that the camera crew is never seen, even during those segments of the episode when police officers are driving the camera crew to and from incidents. As Doyle says, this involves considerable editing (e.g., of civilians reacting to the cameras) and ensures that viewers are never left with the impression that what they are watching could ever have been affected by television cameras.

- Unsurprisingly, the stories selected for airing on a *Cops* episode are also delivered in a way that ensures certain audience reactions. As pointed out by Doyle, various storytelling techniques are used to encourage viewers to identify with the police, but not with suspects. For example, most *Cops* vignettes are hosted by a particular officer whom we get to know. Suspects in all vignettes remain nameless; they are criminals who have given their consent to be shown, but otherwise remain anonymous.

As you proceed through this course, take some time to think about the television shows that you watch. Think also about how these shows may have an impact on your attitudes towards the topics we cover in this textbook and whether this is a good thing. Of course, reality fiction can make for great television, but perhaps it should not shape our attitudes about crime-related matters as much as it sometimes does.

Criminal profiling is a task that some forensic psychologists are involved in. However, much of what is seen in the show *Criminal Minds* is an exaggeration of what actually occurs and is possible in the field of criminal profiling.

Collection Christophel/Alamy Stock Photo

see throughout this book, forensic psychologists get involved in activities that other psychologists rarely do. This is because forensic psychologists are interested in understanding how people function within a very particular context—a legal context. In this first chapter, we will introduce you to the exciting field of forensic psychology. We will provide a more formal definition of what forensic psychology is, try to paint an accurate picture of what forensic psychologists do, and discuss some of the challenges that forensic psychologists face. But, before we do all these things, we will examine the history of this field to determine where it came from and where it might be heading.

A BRIEF HISTORY OF FORENSIC PSYCHOLOGY

Compared with some other areas of psychology, forensic psychology has a relatively short history, dating back roughly to the late nineteenth century. In the early days of the field, this type of psychology was actually not even referred to as forensic psychology, and most of the psychologists conducting research in the area or carrying out applied work did not identify themselves formally as forensic psychologists. However, their contributions formed the building blocks of an emerging field of forensic psychology that continues to be strong today.

Early Research on Testimony and Suggestibility

The field of forensic psychology arguably began with research taking place in both the United States and Europe that had serious implications for the legal system. Some of the first experiments were those of James Cattell at Columbia University in

New York (Bartol & Bartol, 2013). After developing an expertise in the study of human cognitive processes while working with Wilhelm Wundt in Leipzig, Germany, Cattell conducted experiments looking at what would later be called the psychology of eyewitness testimony. For example, in a paper entitled *Measurements of the Accuracy of Recollection*, Cattell (1895) asked 56 university students in psychology to recall things they had witnessed in their everyday lives (e.g., "What was the weather a week ago today?"). Cattell found not only that his students' answers were often inaccurate, but also that the relationship between participants' accuracy and their confidence (i.e., that their recollection was accurate) was far from perfect. In Cattell's view, these findings had the potential to assist in "courts of justice" (p. 765).

Around the same time, a number of other psychologists began studying testimony and suggestibility (see Ceci & Bruck, 1993, for a review). For example, in his classic work, *La Suggestibilité* (1900), the famous French psychologist Alfred Binet presented numerous studies in which he showed that the testimony provided by children was highly susceptible to suggestive questioning techniques. In one study discussed by Ceci and Bruck (1993), Binet presented children with a series of objects for a short period of time (e.g., a button glued to poster board). After viewing an object, some of the children were told to write down everything that they saw while others were asked questions. Some of these questions were direct (e.g., "How was the button attached to the board?"), others were mildly leading (e.g., "Wasn't the button attached by a thread?"), and still others were highly misleading (e.g., "What was the color of the thread that attached the button to the board?"). As found in numerous studies since this experiment, Binet demonstrated that asking children to report everything they saw (i.e., free recall) resulted in the most accurate answers. Highly misleading questions resulted in the least accurate answers.

Shortly after Binet's study, a German psychologist named William Stern also began conducting studies examining the suggestibility of witnesses (Ceci & Bruck, 1993). The "reality experiment" that is now commonly used by eyewitness researchers to study eyewitness recall and recognition can in fact be attributed to Stern. Using this research paradigm, participants are exposed to staged events and are then asked to provide information about the event. In one of Stern's first experiments, which he conducted with the famous German criminologist Franz von Liszt in 1901, participants in a law class were exposed to a scenario that involved two students arguing in a classroom (Stern, 1939). The scenario ended with one of the students drawing a revolver; the observers were then asked questions about the event. Consistent with the findings of Cattell and Binet, Stern found that the testimony of participants was often incorrect. In addition, he found that recall was the worst for portions of the event that were particularly exciting (i.e., when the revolver was drawn). This led him to conclude that emotional arousal can have a negative impact on the accuracy of a person's testimony.

Court Cases in Europe

Around the same time that this research was being conducted, psychologists also started to appear as experts in court. This was particularly the case in Europe. Unsurprisingly, given the research being conducted at the time, some of the testimony that these experts provided dealt with issues involving the accuracy of testimony.

Albert von Schrenck-Notzing, a German physician, was probably one of the first expert witnesses to provide testimony in court about the effect of pretrial publicity on memory (Bartol & Bartol, 2013). The date was 1896 and the case involved a series of three sexual murders. The crimes attracted a great deal of attention from the press of the time, and Schrenck-Notzing testified that this extensive pretrial press coverage could influence the testimony of people by causing what he called *retroactive memory falsification*. According to Bartol and Bartol (2013), this term was used to refer to a process whereby people confused actual memories of events with the events described by the media. Schrenck-Notzing supported his expert testimony with laboratory research, which revealed findings that are in line with more contemporary research on the topic (e.g., Ogloff & Vidmar, 1994).

Following this case, Julian Varendonck, a Belgian psychologist, was called on to be an expert witness in a 1911 case involving the murder of a young girl, Cecile. Ceci and Bruck (1993) described the case:

> Two of Cecile's friends who had played with her on the day of her murder were awakened that night by Cecile's mother to ask of her whereabouts. One of the children replied that she did not know. Later that night, she led the police to the spot where the children had played, not far from where Cecile's body was found. In the next month, the two children were repeatedly interviewed by authorities who asked many suggestive questions. The children quickly changed their original testimony of not knowing about Cecile's actions on the day of her murder. They provided details of the appearance of the murderer as well as his name. Because of an anonymous letter, the police arrested the father of one of the playmates for the murder of Cecile. On the basis of the details of the case, Varendonck was convinced of the defendant's innocence. He quickly conducted a series of studies with the specific intent of demonstrating the unreliability of children's testimony. (p. 406)

According to Ceci and Bruck (1993), in one of his studies, Varendonck (1911) asked a group of children to describe a person who had supposedly approached him in front of the children earlier that morning. Although this person did not exist, Varendonck was able to demonstrate that many of the children were easily led by suggestive questioning. Based on these findings, the conclusion Varendonck offered to the court was that the testimony provided by the children in this case was likely inaccurate and that children were prone to suggestion.

Advocates for Forensic Psychology in North America

Similar sorts of legal issues were also being debated in courts throughout the United States in the early 1900s. Most notably, Hugo Munsterberg, another student of Wilhelm Wundt who came from Germany to Harvard University in 1892, was involved in several criminal cases, but not as an expert witness. One case, in 1906, concerned a young intellectually disabled man from Chicago, Richard Ivens, who had confessed to raping and murdering a woman. On the request of the man's lawyer, Munsterberg (along with fellow Harvard psychologist William James) reviewed the interrogation records. Based on his analysis, Munsterberg concluded that "the so-called confessions of Ivens are untrue, and that he had nothing to do with the crime" (Golan, 2004, p. 217). Another case, one year later, involved a confession by Harry Orchard that he had killed the former governor of Idaho and, on the orders of a well-known union boss, had killed several others. On the request of the prosecution in the trial of the union boss, Munsterberg tested Orchard and found that what he was saying was true. In both cases, the courts appeared to pay little attention to Munsterberg's findings, evidenced by the fact that Ivens was found guilty and executed, and the union boss in the second trial was acquitted.

Munsterberg's contributions to these cases were not ignored by all, however. The press strongly objected to his involvement. For example, one news story presented psychology as the "new scientific fad for 'cheating justice'" (Golan, 2004, p. 217). In another story about the Ivens case, the contributions by Munsterberg and James were said to "have no effect except to make themselves and their science ridiculous" (Golan, 2004, p. 217). The legal community also took a stance against Munsterberg.

Perhaps in response to these strong negative reactions, Hugo Munsterberg published his classic book, *On the Witness Stand* (Munsterberg, 1908). In this book, Munsterberg argued that psychology had much to offer the legal system. Through a collection of his essays, he discussed how psychology could assist with issues involving eyewitness testimony, crime detection, false confessions, suggestibility, hypnotism, and even crime prevention. Unfortunately, Munsterberg presented his ideas in a way that led to even more criticism, especially from the legal profession. This is perhaps unsurprising given his writing style. Consider the following quotation from the introduction of his book:

> The lawyer and the judge and the juryman are sure that they do not need the experimental psychologist. They do not wish to see that in this field pre-eminently applied experimental psychology has made strong strides. . . . They go on thinking that their legal instinct and their common sense supplies them with all that is needed and somewhat more . . . if the time is ever to come when even the jurist is to show some concession to the spirit of modern psychology, public opinion will have to exert some pressure. (Munsterberg, 1908, pp. 10–11)

Considered by many to be the father of forensic psychology, Hugo Munsterberg is best known for his controversial book *On the Witness Stand,* which helped push North American psychologists into the legal arena.

Response to Munsterberg's book from the legal community was swift. One of Munsterberg's biggest critics was John Henry Wigmore, a well-respected law professor at Northwestern University in Chicago. Through a series of fabricated "transcripts," Wigmore (1909) put Munsterberg on "trial," where he was "sued" and found guilty of "claiming more than he could offer" (Brigham, 1999, p. 276). Poking fun at Munsterberg, Wigmore declared that the case was tried by the "Supreme Court of Wundt County" on "April Fool's Day" (Golan, 2004, p. 237). In the trial, Wigmore criticized Munsterberg for the lack of relevant research publications to back up his claims and, more generally, for the lack of applied research in the field of forensic psychology as a whole.

Perhaps because of Wigmore's comprehensive attack on Munsterberg's work, little progress was made by psychologists working in areas of relevance to the law in the very early 1900s. However, the field of forensic psychology in the United States would soon catch up to what was happening in Europe. Indeed, psychological research gradually began to be practically applied in a wide range of criminal justice settings across America. For example, according to Bartol and Bartol (2013), psychologists were instrumental in opening the first clinic for juvenile delinquents in 1909, in developing laboratories to conduct pretrial assessments in 1916, and in establishing psychological testing for law enforcement selection purposes in 1917.

Psychologists also began to focus on theory development. New theories of crime were being proposed by psychologists (and researchers from other fields) at a rapid rate, especially around the mid-1900s (see Box 1.1).

Box 1.1 Forensic Psychology in the Spotlight

Biological, Sociological, and Psychological Theories of Crime

While an in-depth discussion of crime theories is beyond the scope of this book, efforts to develop such theories are clearly an important part of the history of forensic psychology. Over the last century, a variety of biological, sociological, and psychological theories of crime have been proposed and tested. Many have been used to develop intervention or management programs for offenders. Below are brief descriptions of some of the most popular theories.

Biological Theories of Crime

- *Sheldon's (1949) constitutional theory*. Sheldon proposed that crime is largely a product of an individual's body build, or somatotype, which is assumed to be linked to an individual's temperament. According to Sheldon, endomorphs (obese) are jolly, ectomorphs (thin) are introverted, and mesomorphs (muscular) are bold. Sheldon's studies indicated that, because of their aggressive nature, mesomorphs were most likely to become involved with crime.
- *Jacobs, Brunton, Melville, Brittain, and McClemont's (1965) chromosomal theory*. Jacobs and her colleagues proposed that chromosomal irregularity is linked to criminal behaviour. A normal female has two X chromosomes, whereas a normal male has one X and one Y chromosome. However, it was discovered that there were men with two Y chromosomes, which, it was proposed, made them more masculine and, therefore, more aggressive. According to Jacobs et al., this enhanced aggressiveness would result in an increased chance that these men would commit violent crimes.
- *Nevin's (2000) theory of lead exposure.* Nevin was one of the first researchers to propose a link between childhood lead exposure (e.g., from paint and gasoline) and criminal behaviour. Although it was unclear *why* lead exposure and crime were related in his early research, more recent studies using neuroimaging technology suggest that lead exposure may impact brain development, including regions that are responsible for emotional regulation and impulsive control. Such deficits may increase the probability that one exhibits anti-social behaviour.

Sociological Theories of Crime

- *Merton's (1938) strain theory.* Merton proposed that crime is largely a product of the strain felt by certain individuals in society, typically the lower class, who have restricted access to legitimate means (e.g., education) of achieving valued goals of success (e.g., status). Merton argued that while some of these individuals will be happy with lesser goals that are achievable, others will turn to illegitimate means (e.g., crime) in an attempt to achieve these valued goals.
- *Sutherland's (1939) differential association theory.* Sutherland proposed that criminal behaviour is learned through social interactions in which people are exposed to values that can be either favourable or unfavourable to violations of the law. More specifically, Sutherland maintained that people are likely to become involved in criminal activity when they learn more values (i.e., attitudes) that are favourable to violations of the law than values that are unfavourable to it.
- *Becker's (1963) labelling theory.* Becker proposed that deviance (e.g., antisocial behaviour) is not inherent to an act but a label attached to an act by society. Thus, a "criminal" results primarily from a process of society labelling an individual as a criminal. This labelling process is thought to promote the individual's deviant behaviour through a self-fulfilling prophecy.

Psychological Theories of Crime

- *Eysenck's (1964) biosocial theory of crime.* Eysenck believed that some individuals (e.g., extraverts and neurotics) are born with nervous systems that influence their ability to learn from the consequences of their behaviour, especially the negative consequences experienced in childhood as part of the socialization and conscience-building process. Because of their poor

(continued)

(continued)

"conditionability," it is assumed that individuals who exhibit high levels of extraversion and neuroticism will develop strong antisocial inclinations.

- *Akers's (1973) social learning theory.* Akers suggested that crime is learned in the same way that noncriminal behaviour is learned. According to Akers, the likelihood of becoming a criminal increases when one interacts with individuals who favour antisocial attitudes; when one is exposed to role models, either in person or symbolically,

who disproportionally exhibit antisocial behaviour; when one defines antisocial behaviour as justified in a particular situation; and when one has received (and expects to receive) a greater degree of rewards versus punishments for antisocial behaviour.

- *Gottfredson and Hirschi's (1990) general theory of crime.* Gottfredson and Hirschi argued that low self-control, internalized early in life, in the presence of criminal opportunities explains an individual's propensity to commit crimes.

Landmark Court Cases in the United States

In the early to mid-1900s, psychologists in the United States began to be more heavily involved in the judicial system as expert witnesses. The first time this happened was in the case of *State v. Driver* in 1921. According to Bartol and Bartol (2013), the *Driver* case was only a partial victory for forensic psychology in America. The West Virginia case involved the attempted rape of a young girl and the court accepted expert evidence from a psychologist in the area of juvenile delinquency. However, the court rejected the psychologist's testimony that the young girl was a "moron" and, therefore, could not be believed. In its ruling the court stated, "It is yet to be determined that psychological and medical tests are practical, and will detect the lie on the witness stand" (quoted in Bartol & Bartol, 2013, p. 14).

Other important cases in the United States expanded the role of psychologists in court, with rulings that allowed psychologists to provide opinions on matters that were traditionally reserved for physicians. In *People v. Hawthorne* (1940), for example, a psychologist was permitted, on appeal, to provide an opinion about the mental state of the defendant at the time of his offence (Viljoen, Roesch, Ogloff, & Zapf, 2003). The view that psychologists could provide an admissible opinion regarding a defendant's mental health was strongly reinforced in *Jenkins v. United States* (1962). The *Jenkins* trial involved charges of breaking and entering, assault, and intent to rape. The defendant, Jenkins, pleaded not guilty by reason of insanity. Three psychologists supported this defence on the basis that the defendant was suffering from schizophrenia at the time of the crimes. However, the trial judge instructed the jury to disregard the testimony from the psychologists because "psychologists were not qualified to give expert testimony on the issue of mental disease" (American Psychological Association [APA], 2016). The case was appealed. As part of the appeal, the APA provided a report to the court stating their view that psychologists are competent to provide opinions concerning the existence of mental illness (APA, 1962). The court reversed the conviction and ordered a new trial, stating that "some psychologists are qualified to render expert testimony on mental disorders" (APA, 2016).

Currently in the United States, it is common for psychologists to testify on matters such as fitness to stand trial and criminal responsibility (Viljoen et al., 2003), in addition to a wide range of other issues, including risk assessment, treatment of traumatic brain injury, factors affecting eyewitness memory and jury decision making, the impact of hostile work environments, etc. (Cutler & Kovera, 2011).

Progress in Canada

Although it is difficult to pinpoint exactly when the field of forensic psychology began in Canada, it has been growing since at least the mid-1900s. Indeed, since that time, Canadian psychologists have made many important contributions to this field. Some examples of major developments are listed in Figure 1.1. As you can see from

1940s—Inmate classification officers begin to be employed in federal correctional facilities in Canada, many of whom have training in the social sciences (often psychology).

1955—The first federal correctional psychologist is hired at St. Vincent de Paul Penitentiary (later renamed Laval Institution) in the province of Quebec.

1970s—Vernon Quinsey helps establish phalometry as a tool for assessing sex offenders in Canada.

Late 1970s—Significant advances are made in the area of sex offender treatment by Bill Marshall and his colleagues, including approaches to eliminate arousal to sexually deviant stimuli.

1980—Robert Hare publishes the first version of the Psychopathy Checklist. The revised version of this checklist, published in 2003, has become the gold standard for assessing psychopathy.

1980s—Under the direction of psychologist Robert Loo, the Royal Canadian Mounted Police's (RCMP) first manager of Psychological Services, the RCMP develops its own in-house health services to prevent psychological distress in its officers and provide them with treatment.

1985—The Criminal Justice Section of the Canadian Psychological Association (CPA) is formed.

1990—Don Andrews and his colleagues publish a meta-analysis in *Criminology* that describes several principles of effective correctional intervention. These principles are now being incorporated into treatment programs around the world.

1990s—Canadian psychologists develop important new risk-assessment tools, including the Violent Risk Appraisal Guide, the Level of Service Inventory, the Spousal Assault Risk Assessment Guide, the Historical/Clinical/Risk Management 20 Scale, and the Static-99.

1994—In *R. v. Mohan*, the Canadian Supreme Court defines criteria for determining when the testimony of expert witnesses, including psychologists, will be admitted in court.

1996—Jury researcher Regina Schuller and her colleague publish a study on battered women syndrome, which examines how expert testimony on the issue can influence jury verdicts.

1999—Psychologists Rod Lindsay and John Turtle co-author, with several American colleagues, an important report that provides recommendations for how best to collect eyewitness evidence.

2001—Regina Schuller and James Ogloff publish the first Canadian textbook on psychology and law.

2001—Paul Gendreau and his colleagues publish work that demonstrates the ineffectiveness of several get-tough-on-crime strategies, including long terms of imprisonment.

2001—The American Psychological Association (APA) recognizes forensic psychology as a specialty discipline, which has an impact on the status of the field in both the United States and Canada.

2004—Don Andrews, Jim Bonta, and Stephen Wormith introduce the Level of Service/Case Management Inventory, an assessment tool that moves beyond traditional risk assessment to integrate the assessment of risk with a case management plan.

2009–2011—A framework for structuring parole decisions developed by Ralph Serin and his colleagues is formally incorporated into policy at the Parole Board of Canada.

2015—Julia Shaw and Stephen Porter show that innocent adult research participants can be convinced, over a relatively short time period, that they have perpetrated serious crimes.

Figure 1.1 The History of Forensic Psychology in Canada

this figure, some of the significant advances in this country, much like in the United States, have emerged from research on eyewitness testimony and jury decision making. However, the most significant contributions by psychologists in Canada have, arguably been in the area of corrections (e.g., constructing better risk-assessment tools and developing effective treatment approaches). One person who has played a particularly important role in developing this area of research and practice is Dr. Stephen Wormith. He is profiled in Box 1.2.

Despite the rapid growth of forensic psychology in Canada since the 1940s, Canadian courts have arguably been slower than courts in the United States to open their doors to psychologists (at least when it comes to certain topics). For example, compared to the United States, where psychologists have been permitted to conduct assessments of fitness to stand trial and criminal responsibility since the mid-1900s, Canadian courts have tended to rely upon physicians (primarily psychiatrists) for this purpose (Viljoen et al., 2003). Why the difference? There may be multiple explanations, but part of the answer probably relates to educational standards (Viljoen et al., 2003). As you will see below, while the majority of the U.S. states require doctoral-level training before one can become a licensed psychologist, several Canadian provinces and territories still require only a master's degree. Canadian courts may perceive this to be an inadequate level of training to qualify as an expert in some circumstances, especially when compared to the medical degree held by forensic psychiatrists. That being said, Canadian courts have allowed forensic psychologists to provide testimony on a wide range of other issues. As forensic psychology continues to develop in Canada, it is likely that the value of this field for the courts will continue to increase.

A Legitimate Field of Psychology

Although the field of forensic psychology has perhaps not come as far as some forensic psychologists would have hoped in its relatively short history, it has now become a recognized and legitimate field of study within psychology. Indeed, forensic psychology now appears to have many of the markings of an established discipline. As highlighted by Schuller and Ogloff (2001), this is reflected in numerous ways.

First, a growing number of high-quality textbooks in the area provide the opportunity to teach students about forensic psychology. The availability of textbooks is particularly evident in the United States, but several also exist in Canada. Second, numerous academic journals are now dedicated to various aspects of the field, and more mainstream psychology journals publish research from the forensic domain at a regular rate. This speaks to the large number of psychologists currently conducting research in this area. Third, a number of professional associations have been developed to represent the interests of forensic psychologists and to promote research and practice in the area. The largest of these is the American Psychology-Law Society (AP-LS), founded in 1968–1969, in which Canadian forensic psychologists have played a crucial role. Other countries have developed similar professional associations, such as the Criminal Justice Section of the CPA, which was founded in 1985. Fourth, new training opportunities in forensic psychology, at both the undergraduate and graduate level, are being established in North America and existing training

Box 1.2

Canadian Researcher Profile: Dr. Stephen Wormith

Courtesy of Stephen Wormith

Like many of his colleagues in the 1970's, Dr. Wormith fell into the field of correctional psychology quite by accident because it had not yet developed into the strong specialty field that it has become. Having completed his undergraduate degree at Brown University, he moved to Carleton University, where he pursued his interests in child development. At Carleton, he met Dr. Donald Andrews, who was teaching an undergraduate course in criminal behavior, and they began working together. This might seem like an odd transition, but for Stephen and his mentor, Dr. Andrews, it made a great deal of sense. Applying the principles of reinforcement, behavioural analysis, and Albert Bandura's social learning theory to offenders was a natural fit. It was also consistent with the concept of risk, which emerged later in their correctional work, but was common in discussions about "at risk" children even then.

Dr. Wormith completed his PhD at the University of Ottawa where he designed, delivered, and studied an offender treatment program for his dissertation, and then carried out a follow-up evaluation of participants' recidivism some years later (Wormith, 1984). The study was based on his observations at the Rideau Correctional Centre (RCC) and found that some offenders sincerely did not want to return to a life of crime, but six months later they would show up again in the institution, while other offenders seemed to have numerous intellectual and social skills, but no real motivation to change and they, too, would return to prison in short order. These observations are consistent with what is now called "the will and the skill" perspective of offender rehabilitation. Hence, the list of offender risk factors that he and colleagues noted began to take shape.

Following his graduation, Dr. Wormith moved to a clinical position at Stony Mountain Penitentiary in Manitoba, followed by research positions at the Regional Psychiatric Centre (RPC) in Saskatoon and then the Ministry of the Solicitor General of Canada (now Public Safety Canada). This was followed by a move into administration, first as the Deputy Superintendent (Treatment) at what had become the Rideau Correctional and Treatment Centre and then as Psychologist-in-Chief of the Ontario Ministry of Correctional Services.

From his position in provincial corrections, Wormith began to work with Dr. Andrews and Dr. James Bonta to update and extend their risk assessment tool, the *Level of Service Inventory-Revised* (Andrews & Bonta, 1995), first for the Ontario Ministry of Correctional Services, and then for a more general group of users with the *Level of Service/Case Management Inventory* (Andrews, Bonta, & Wormith, 2004). This latter version was developed to meet the increasing demands of clinicians and probation officers for a more sophisticated tool, one that not only addressed static and dynamic risk (criminogenic need), but also considered client strengths, other noncriminogenic factors, and offender responsivity, then forged a link between offender assessment, case planning, and service delivery. His background, research, and clinical experience have made Dr. Wormith a strong advocate for the risk/need/responsivity (RNR) model of offender rehabilitation, which will be discussed more thoroughly in Chapter 9 (Andrews, Bonta, & Wormith, 2011).

Dr. Wormith returned to Saskatoon to take a faculty position in psychology at the University of Saskatchewan. Currently, he is Director of the Centre for Forensic Behavioural Science and Justice Studies, where he is active in community engaged scholarship, conducting criminal justice research and program evaluation, often for government and nongovernmental organizations (Nilson et al., 2015). His favourite course to teach is the one that triggered his interest in correctional psychology back in 1973—Criminal Behaviour. He feels it is crucial for students to get out of the classroom and into the complex world of criminal justice agencies, and encourages future researchers to take a multidisciplinary approach to the understanding of criminal behaviour. To balance his busy academic life, he enjoys being both a participant and fan of team sports, but increasingly the latter as time goes by.

opportunities are being improved. A growing number of training programs exist in Canada (Helmus, Babchishin, Camilleri, & Olver, 2011). Fifth, and perhaps most importantly, the APA formally recognized forensic psychology as a specialty discipline in 2001 (it was recertified by the APA in 2008).

FORENSIC PSYCHOLOGY TODAY

Given the historical overview of forensic psychology that was just provided, and the fact that this discipline is now recognized as a distinct field within psychology, it may surprise you to learn that debate continues about how forensic psychology should be defined in modern times. It is fair to say that, currently, there is no generally accepted definition of the field. Indeed, experts in this area still don't agree on what the field should be called, let alone how it should be defined (Otto & Ogloff, 2013). For example, you will often see forensic psychology being referred to as legal psychology or criminological psychology in some parts of the world. Much of the ongoing debate concerning the definition of forensic psychology centres on whether the field should be defined narrowly or more broadly (Otto & Ogloff, 2013).

Narrow definitions of forensic psychology focus on certain aspects of the field while ignoring other, potentially important, aspects. For example, a narrow definition might focus on clinical aspects of the field, while ignoring the experimental research that many psychologists who refer to themselves as forensic psychologists conduct. Many leading psychologists, and the professional associations to which they belong, prefer to define the discipline in this way. Consider the petition made to the APA in 2001 to recognize forensic psychology as a specialization. As Otto and Heilbrun (2002) stated, "It was ultimately decided that the petition . . . should define forensic psychology narrowly, to include the primarily clinical aspects of forensic assessment, treatment, and consultation" (p. 8). According to this definition, the only individuals who should call themselves forensic psychologists are those individuals engaged in clinical practice (i.e., assessing, treating, or consulting) within the legal system. Psychologists who spend all their time conducting forensic research would not technically be considered forensic psychologists.

For reasons such as these, many psychologists prefer to define the field of forensic psychology more broadly. For example, Bartol and Bartol (2013) define the discipline as "(1) the *research endeavor* that examines aspects of human behavior directly related to the legal process . . . and (2) the *professional practice* of psychology within or in consultation with a legal system that embraces both criminal and civil law and the numerous areas where they intersect" (p. 4). Thus, unlike narrow definitions of forensic psychology that may focus solely on the *application* of psychology, the definition provided by Bartol and Bartol does not restrict forensic psychology to applied issues. The definition also focuses on the *research* that is required to inform applied practice in the field of forensic psychology.

Throughout this textbook, we adopt a broad definition of forensic psychology. Although we will often focus on the application of psychological knowledge to various aspects of the Canadian legal system, our primary goal is to demonstrate that this application of knowledge must always be based on a solid grounding of psychological research. In line with a broad definition of forensic psychology, this research frequently originates in areas of psychology that are often not obviously connected with the forensic area, such as social, personality, cognitive, organizational, and developmental psychology. The fact that forensic psychology is such an eclectic field is just one of the reasons why it is such an exciting area of study.

The Roles of a Forensic Psychologist

Another aspect of contemporary forensic psychology that makes it so exciting is that forensic psychologists can play different roles. While all forensic psychologists will be interested in issues that arise at the intersection between psychology and the law, the specific issues that an individual focuses on will be determined largely by his or her role. Three roles in particular are important to discuss: the forensic psychologist as clinician, the forensic psychologist as researcher, and the forensic psychologist as legal scholar.

The Forensic Psychologist as Clinician **Clinical forensic psychologists** are broadly concerned with mental health issues as they pertain to the legal system (Otto & Heilbrun, 2002). Clinical forensic psychologists currently work in a variety of settings, including private practices, prisons, and hospitals. A frequent task for this type of forensic psychologist might involve the assessment of an offender to determine if he or she is likely to pose a risk to the community if released from prison. Other issues that clinical forensic psychologists are currently interested in include, but are certainly not limited to, the following:

- Conducting divorce and child custody mediation
- Providing expert testimony on questions of a psychological nature
- Carrying out personnel selection (e.g., for law enforcement agencies)
- Running critical incident stress debriefings with police officers
- Facilitating treatment programs for offenders

A clinical forensic psychologist practising in Canada must be a licensed clinical psychologist who has specialized in the forensic area. The educational requirements to obtain a licence currently vary across provinces and territories, but some form of graduate-level training is always required (CPA, 2016). In Alberta, Saskatchewan, Newfoundland and Labrador, Nova Scotia, New Brunswick, the Northwest Territories, and Nunavut, the requirement is a master's degree in psychology, whereas in British Columbia, Manitoba, Ontario, Quebec, and Prince Edward Island, a PhD in psychology is required (Yukon currently has no legislation governing the practice of psychology; CPA, 2016). The forensic specialization typically takes the form of an intense period of supervised practice, before and/or after completion of the required degree, in an applied forensic setting under the watchful eye of an experienced clinical supervisor. The last step of the licensing process is a comprehensive exam, which often involves an oral component.

Students often wonder what the difference is between clinical forensic psychology and **forensic psychiatry**. In fact, many people often confuse these two fields.

Clinical forensic psychologists: Psychologists who are broadly concerned with the assessment and treatment of mental health issues as they pertain to the law or legal system

Forensic psychiatry: A field of medicine that deals with all aspects of human behaviour as it relates to the law or legal system

Box 1.3   Forensic Psychology in the Spotlight

Other Forensic Disciplines

Nowadays, people are bombarded by media portrayals of various forensic disciplines, beyond just forensic psychology and forensic psychiatry. Although this does much to promote the respective specialties, it can also be the source of a lot of confusion. Listed below are brief descriptions of just a few forensic specialty areas.

- *Forensic anthropology.* Forensic anthropologists examine the remains of deceased individuals to help determine their identity and how they might have died.

- *Forensic biology.* Forensic biologists apply their knowledge of the life sciences (e.g., entomology, genetics, botany, etc.) to legal investigations. For example, forensic entomologists are concerned with how insects can assist with criminal investigations. They can help determine when someone died based on an analysis of insect presence/development on a decomposing body.

- *Forensic odontology.* Forensic odontologists study the dental aspects of criminal activity. For example, they might assist the police in identifying deceased individuals through an examination of dental records, or they might help determine who left bite marks on an individual.

- *Forensic pathology.* Sometimes referred to as coroners, forensic pathologists are medical doctors who examine injuries or the remains of dead bodies in an attempt to determine the time and cause of death through physical autopsy.

- *Forensic toxicology.* Forensic toxicologists study the effects of drugs and other chemicals on people within the context of the law. For example, they might be consulted to determine if drugs played a part in a person's death.

Sources: Based on Types of Forensic Scientists: Disciplines of AAFS, published by American Academy of Forensic Sciences, 2016.

To some extent in Canada, clinical forensic psychology and forensic psychiatry are more similar than they are different. For example, both clinical forensic psychologists and forensic psychiatrists are trained to assess and treat individuals experiencing mental health problems who come into contact with the law, and you will see psychologists and psychiatrists involved in nearly every component of the criminal justice system. However, the two disciplines are also different in many ways. The most obvious difference is that forensic psychiatrists are medical doctors. Therefore, forensic psychiatrists undergo training that is quite different from the training clinical forensic psychologists receive. Forensic psychiatrists also have certain privileges that forensic psychologists do not have, such as their ability to prescribe medication to treat mental illnesses.

Other forensic disciplines, especially disciplines associated with forensic science, are also frequently confused with the field of forensic psychology. We discuss some of these disciplines in Box 1.3.

The Forensic Psychologist as Researcher   A second role for the contemporary forensic psychologist is that of experimenter or researcher. Although this role does not necessarily have to be separate from the clinical role, it often is. As with clinical forensic psychologists, **experimental forensic psychologists** are concerned with mental health issues as they pertain to the legal system, and they can be found in a variety of criminal justice settings. However, researchers in the forensic area are

Experimental forensic psychologists: Psychologists who are broadly concerned with the study of human behaviour as it relates to the law or legal system

usually concerned with much more than just mental health issues. Indeed, they can be interested in any research issue that relates to the law or legal system. The list of research issues that are of interest to this type of forensic psychologist is far too long to present here, but they include the following:

- Examining the effectiveness of risk-assessment strategies
- Determining what factors influence jury decision making
- Developing and testing better ways to conduct eyewitness lineups
- Evaluating offender and victim treatment programs
- Studying the effect of stress management interventions on police officers

Not only do clinical forensic psychologists differ from experimental forensic psychologists in terms of what they do, they also differ in terms of their training. The forensic psychologist who is interested primarily in research will have undergone PhD-level graduate training in one of many different types of experimental graduate programs (no internship is typically required). Only some of these graduate programs will be devoted solely to the study of forensic psychology. Others will be programs in social, personality, cognitive, organizational, or developmental psychology, although the program will have a faculty member associated with it who is conducting research in a forensic area. Regardless of the type of graduate program chosen, the individual's graduate research will be focused primarily on a topic related to forensic psychology (e.g., the malleability of child eyewitness memory). As can be seen in the short list of topics provided above, research in forensic psychology is eclectic and may require expertise in areas such as memory processing, decision making, and organizational issues. This is one of the reasons why training for experimental forensic psychology is more varied than the training for clinical forensic psychology.

The Forensic Psychologist as Legal Scholar   A third role for the forensic psychologist, which is far less common than the previous two, is that of legal scholar. Because this role is less common, we will not deal with it as much in this textbook, but it is important to discuss this role briefly, especially because of the attention it has received in Canada. Two initiatives at Simon Fraser University (SFU) in Burnaby, British Columbia, are particularly important to mention. The first was SFU's Psychology and Law Program, originally established in 1991. This program has partnered with the University of British Columbia to allow students to obtain both their PhD in psychology and their LLB in law. The program produces forensic psychologists who are more informed about the legal process and the legal system than was the case previously. The second initiative was the formation, also in 1991, of the Mental Health, Law, and Policy Institute (MHLPI) at SFU. The purpose of the MHLPI is to "promote interdisciplinary collaboration in research and training in areas related to mental health law and policy" (MHLPI, 2016). According to Brigham (1999), forensic psychologists in their role as legal scholars "would most likely engage in scholarly analyses of mental health law and psychologically oriented legal movements," whereas their applied work "would most likely center around policy analysis and legislative consultation" (p. 281).

The Relationship Between Psychology and Law

Not only is the field of forensic psychology an exciting field to be in today because of the diversity of roles that a forensic psychologist can play, but it is also exciting because forensic psychologists can now be involved in such a wide range of activities. One useful way of thinking about these various activities is to consider an idea proposed by Craig Haney, a professor of psychology at the University of California, Santa Cruz. Haney (1980) suggested that there are three primary ways in which psychology and the law can relate to each other. He called these relationships **psychology and the law**, **psychology in the law**, and **psychology of the law**. Within each of these relationships, certain activities can be emphasized. While each relationship is important, we will focus most of our attention here (and throughout the rest of this book) on the first two relationships, psychology and the law and psychology in the law. Clinical and experimental forensic psychologists are typically involved in these areas much more often than in the third. Psychology of the law is largely the domain of the legal scholar role and, therefore, we will touch on it only briefly.

Psychology and the law: The use of psychology to examine the operation of the legal system

Psychology in the law: The use of psychology in the legal system as that system operates

Psychology of the law: The use of psychology to examine the law itself

Psychology and the Law   In this relationship, "psychology is viewed as a separate discipline [to the law], examining and analysing various components of the law [and the legal system] from a psychological perspective" (Bartol & Bartol, 1994, p. 2). Frequently, research that falls under the category of psychology *and* the law examines assumptions made by the law or our legal system, asking questions such as "Are eyewitnesses accurate?" "Do certain interrogation techniques cause people to falsely confess?" "Are judges fair in the way they hand down sentences?" and "Is it possible to accurately predict whether an offender will be violent when released from prison?" When working within the area of psychology *and* the law, forensic psychologists attempt to answer these sorts of questions so that the answers can be communicated to the legal community. Much of forensic psychology deals with this particular relationship. Therefore, research issues that fall under the general heading of "psychology and the law" will be thoroughly discussed throughout this textbook.

Psychology in the Law   Once a body of psychological knowledge exists in any of the aforementioned areas of study, that knowledge can be used in the legal system by psychologists, lawyers, judges, and others. As the label indicates, psychology *in* the law involves the use of psychological knowledge in the legal system (Haney, 1980). As with psychology and the law, psychology in the law can take many different forms. It might consist of a psychologist in court providing expert testimony concerning some issue of relevance to a particular case. For example, the psychologist might testify, based on his or her understanding of eyewitness research, how certain factors can influence the accuracy of identifications from a police lineup. Alternatively, psychology in the law might consist of a psychologist using his or her knowledge in a police investigation to assist the police in developing an effective (and ethical) strategy for interrogating a suspect. Many of the research applications that we focus on in this textbook fit nicely with the label "psychology in the law."

Psychology of the Law   Psychology *of* the law involves the use of psychology to study the law itself (Haney, 1980), and it addresses questions such as "Does the law reduce the amount of crime in our society?" "Why is it important to allow for discretionary decision making in the Canadian criminal justice system?" and "What impact should court rulings have on the field of forensic psychology?" (see Box 1.4 for a description of several Canadian court cases that have dealt with issues directly relevant to the field of forensic psychology). Although often not considered a core topic in forensic psychology, there does appear to be a growing interest in the area

There are a large number of Canadian court cases that have had an impact on the field of forensic psychology. A brief discussion of some of these cases is presented here. Several of these cases will be expanded upon in upcoming chapters to demonstrate how they have influenced the activities of Canadian forensic psychologists, in terms of research and practice.

■ *R. v. Hubbert* (1975). The Ontario Court of Appeal states that jurors are presumed to be impartial (i.e., unbiased) and that numerous safeguards are in place within the Canadian judicial system to ensure this (e.g., limitations can be imposed on the press regarding what they can report before the start of a trial).

■ *R. v. Sophonow* (1986). The Manitoba Court of Appeal overturns the murder conviction of Thomas Sophonow because of errors in law, many of which related to problems with the eyewitness evidence collected by the police as part of their investigation.

■ *R. v. Lavallee* (1990). The Supreme Court of Canada (SCC) sets guidelines for when and how expert testimony should be used in cases involving battered women syndrome. Since this ruling, expert testimony in cases of battered women who kill has increased.

■ *Wenden v. Trikha* (1991). The Alberta Court of Queen's Bench rules that mental health professionals have a duty to warn a third party if they have reasonable grounds to believe that their client intends to seriously harm that individual.

■ *R. v. Swain* (1991). The SCC makes a ruling that results in changes to the insanity defence standard in Canada, including the name of the defence, when the defence

can be raised, and for how long insanity acquittees can be detained.

■ *R. v. Levogiannis* (1993). The SCC rules that children are allowed to testify in court behind screens that prevent them from seeing the accused.

■ *R. v. Mohan* (1994). The SCC establishes formal criteria for determining when expert testimony should be admitted into court.

■ *R. v. Williams* (1998). The SCC formally acknowledges that jurors can be biased by numerous sources, ranging from community sentiment on a particular issue to direct involvement with a case (e.g., being related to the accused).

■ *R. v. Gladue* (1999). The SCC rules that prison sentences are being relied on too often by judges as a way of dealing with criminal behaviour, especially for Aboriginal offenders, and that other sentencing options should be considered.

■ *R. v. Oickle* (2000). The SCC rules that police interrogation techniques, which consist of various forms of psychological coercion, are acceptable and that confessions extracted through their use can be admissible in court.

■ *R. v. L.T.H.* (2008). The SCC makes a ruling that, when determining the admissibility of a statement made by a young person to the police, the prosecution does not have to prove that the young person understood his or her legal rights as explained by police, but they do have to prove that these rights were explained to the young person using language appropriate to his or her age and understanding.

of psychology of the law. The challenge in this case is that in order to address the sorts of questions posed above, a set of skills from multiple disciplines (e.g., psychology, criminology, sociology, law) is often important and sometimes crucial. The new focus in North America and elsewhere on the role of forensic psychologist as legal scholar will no doubt do much to assist in this endeavour. We are confident that in the future more research in the area of forensic psychology will focus on issues surrounding psychology of the law.

MODERN-DAY DEBATES: PSYCHOLOGICAL EXPERTS IN COURT

Since the field of forensic psychology has become more widely accepted, forensic psychologists have increasingly been asked to provide expert testimony in court. While the rate at which psychologists have been permitted to do so varies from country to country, the variety of topics that forensic psychologists can now testify about is very broad indeed, including custody issues, malingering and deception, the accuracy of eyewitness identification, the effects of crime on victims, and the assessment of dangerousness (to name a few). In order for contemporary forensic psychologists to increase the extent to which they can contribute to the judicial system in this way, it is important for them to become more knowledgeable about the law and the legal system (Ogloff & Cronshaw, 2001). They need to become more aware of the role of an expert witness, the various ways in which psychology and the law differ from each other, and the criteria that courts consider when determining whether psychological testimony should be admitted.

The Function of the Expert Witness

Expert witness: A witness who provides the court with information (often an opinion on a particular matter) that assists the court in understanding an issue of relevance to a case

According to Cutler and Kovera (2011), the role of an **expert witness** "is to provide assistance to the triers of fact – either the judge or a jury – in the form of an opinion based on some type of specialized knowledge, education, or training" (p. 53). Understanding this function is important because it is what separates the expert witness from other witnesses who regularly appear in court (e.g., eyewitnesses). To be clear on this issue, in contrast to the other witnesses in court who can testify only about what they have directly observed, expert witnesses can provide the court with their personal opinion on matters relevant to the case. As indicated above, these opinions must always fall within the limits of expert witnesses' areas of expertise and the testimony must be deemed reliable and helpful to the court. In addition, it is important to point out that, when providing testimony to the courts, the expert witness is supposed to be there as an educator to the judge and jury, not as an advocate for the defence or the prosecution (Cutler & Kovera, 2011).

The Challenges of Providing Expert Testimony

Providing expert testimony to the courts in an effective way is not a simple task, which probably explains why numerous manuals have been published to assist psychologists with the task of preparing for court (e.g., Brodsky, 1991; 1999). Even judges have provided suggestions on how forensic psychologists can increase their chances of being effective witnesses in court (e.g., Saunders, J. W. S., 2001).

In part, providing expert testimony is challenging because there is simply so much for the expert witness to know, not only about their own testimony, but about their role in the court proceedings and what those proceedings involve. As Otto, Kay, and Hess (2013) argue, "It is the witness who is knowledgeable about and/or skilled in his or her area of expertise, in relevant rules of legal procedure, in direct and cross-examination strategies, and in effective ways of communicating who will be persuasive and helpful to the legal decision maker" (p. 755).

Providing effective testimony is also challenging because of the inherent differences (often conflicts) that exist between the fields of psychology and law. Numerous individuals have discussed these differences, but we will focus on one particular attempt to describe them. According to Hess (2006), psychology and law differ along at least seven different dimensions:

1. *Epistemology*. Psychologists assume that it is possible to uncover hidden objective truths if the appropriate experiments are conducted. Truth in the law is defined subjectively and is based on who can provide the most convincing story of what really happened that is consistent with the law.

2. *Nature of law*. The goal in psychology is to describe how and why people behave the way they do (i.e., psychology is descriptive). Law, however, is prescriptive. It tells people how they should behave and provides the means to punish people for not behaving in the prescribed way.

3. *Knowledge*. Knowledge in psychology is based on the empirical, nomothetic (group-based) data collected using various research methodologies. In the law, knowledge comes from the idiographic analysis of court cases and the rational application of logic to establish the facts of a case and connections to other cases that have set legal precedent.

4. *Methodology*. Methodological approaches in psychology are predominantly nomothetic and experimental with an emphasis on controlling for confounding variables and replicating results. In contrast, the law operates on a case-by-case basis, with a focus on constructing compelling narratives that adequately cover the details of a specific case while being consistent with the law.

5. *Criterion*. Psychologists are relatively cautious in terms of their willingness to accept something as true. To accept a hypothesis, for example, conservative statistical criteria are used (e.g., the use of $p<.05$ in significance testing). A more expedient approach is adopted in the law, whereby guilt is determined using various criteria established for a particular case (e.g., beyond a reasonable doubt).

6. *Principles*. Psychologists take an exploratory approach that encourages the consideration of multiple explanations for research findings. Ideally, the correct explanation is identified through experimentation. Lawyers adopt a much more conservative approach. An explanation surrounding a case predominates based on its coherence with the facts and with precedent-setting cases.

7. *Latitude of courtroom behaviour*. The behaviour of the psychologist when acting as an expert witness is severely limited by the court. For example, testimony

provided by a psychologist is restricted by rules of evidence. The law imposes fewer restrictions on the behaviour of lawyers (though they are also restricted in numerous ways). For example, so long as they act within the rules, lawyers can present a wide range of evidence, call on various types of witnesses, and present their case in the way they see fit.

Understanding these differences help us appreciate why the courts are sometimes reluctant to admit testimony provided by psychological experts. For example, after considering how psychology and the law differ with respect to their methodological approach, it may not be surprising that judges often have difficulty seeing how psychologists can assist in court proceedings. Indeed, numerous legal scholars have questioned whether the general patterns and trends that result from a nomothetic psychological approach should ever be used in court. As Sheldon and Macleod (1991) stated:

> The findings derived from empirical research are used by psychologists to formulate norms of human behavior. From observations and experiments, psychologists may conclude that in circumstance X there is a likelihood that an individual . . . will behave in manner Y. . . . [N]ormative data of this sort are of little use to the courts. The courts are concerned to determine the past behavior of accused *individuals* [emphasis added], and in carrying out that function, information about the past behavior of *other individuals* [emphasis added] is wholly irrelevant. (p. 815)

Criteria for Accepting Expert Testimony

In order for forensic psychologists to provide expert testimony in court, they must meet certain criteria (Cutler & Kovera, 2011). In the United States, criteria of one sort or another have been in place since the early twentieth century. For example, until quite recently, the admissibility of expert testimony in the United States was based on a decision handed down by the courts in *Frye v. United States* (1923). Frye was being tried for murder and the court rejected his request to admit the results from a polygraph exam he had passed. On appeal, the court also rejected requests to allow the polygraph expert, William Marston, to present evidence on Frye's behalf (Bartol & Bartol, 1994). In the ruling, the court spoke specifically to the issue of when expert testimony should be admitted into court. The court indicated that for novel scientific evidence to be admissible in court, it must be established that the procedure(s) used to arrive at the testimony is (are) generally accepted in the scientific community. More specifically, the court stated that "while courts will go a long way in admitting expert testimony deduced from a well-recognized scientific principle or discovery, the thing from which the deduction is made must be sufficiently established to have gained general acceptance in the particular field in which it belongs" (*Frye v. United States*, 1923, p. 1).

General acceptance test: A standard for accepting expert testimony, which states that expert testimony will be admissible in court if the basis of the testimony is generally accepted within the relevant scientific community

This criterion came to be called the **general acceptance test**, and although it formed the basis of admissibility decisions in the United States for a long time (and still does in some states), it has been criticized. One criticism centres on the vagueness of the term *general acceptance* and whether trial judges are able to make this determination. Consider a case where a lawyer would like to have a criminal profiler provide expert testimony in court (as you will see in Chapter 3, a profiler is someone who attempts to predict the characteristics of an unknown offender based on how that offender's crimes were committed). How should the trial judge decide whether the profiler's testimony is based on procedures that are "generally accepted"? Profiling is certainly a commonly used investigative technique, but members of the scientific community disagree strongly about whether criminal profiling is sufficiently grounded in valid research (e.g., Dern, Dern, Horn, & Horn, 2009; Snook, Cullen, Bennell, Taylor, & Gendreau, 2008). So, whom should the judge turn to and believe?

This issue of vagueness was addressed in the U.S. Supreme Court decision handed down in *Daubert v. Merrell Dow Pharmaceuticals, Inc.* (1993). Daubert sued Merrell Dow because he believed a morning sickness drug his mother ingested while pregnant, which was produced by the company, led to his birth defects. At trial, Merrell Dow presented experts who provided evidence that the use of the drug Bendectin does not result in birth defects. In turn, Daubert provided evidence from experts who claimed that Bendectin could lead to birth defects. The state court and the appeal court both rejected the testimony provided by Daubert's experts on the basis that the methods they used to arrive at their results were not generally accepted by the scientific community. On appeal before the U.S. Supreme Court, Daubert's lawyers challenged the state and appeal courts' interpretation of "general acceptance."

In addressing this issue, the U.S. Supreme Court stated that for scientific evidence to be admitted into court, it must: (1) be provided by a qualified expert, (2) be relevant, and (3) be reliable. To assist judges in making the decision as to whether evidence is in fact reliable, the U.S. Supreme Court laid out four specific criteria, now commonly referred to as the **Daubert criteria**. Scientific evidence is considered reliable if the following criteria are met:

Daubert criteria: An American standard for accepting expert testimony, which states that scientific evidence is valid if the research on which it is based has been peer reviewed, is testable, has a recognized rate of error, and adheres to professional standards

1. The research has been peer reviewed.
2. The research is testable (e.g., falsifiable through experimentation).
3. The research has a recognized rate of error.
4. The research adheres to professional standards.

Similar criteria are currently being used in Canada. The rules for admissibility in Canada were laid out in *R. v. Mohan* (1994). Mohan was a pediatrician charged with sexually assaulting several of his teenage female patients. At trial, Mohan wanted to provide expert testimony from a psychiatrist who was prepared to testify that the typical offender in such a case would be a pedophile and, in his opinion, Mohan was not a pedophile. The trial judge ruled that the testimony was inadmissible and, on appeal before the Supreme Court of Canada, the court agreed and established the standard for admitting expert testimony in Canada. The standard is now referred to as the **Mohan criteria**. In addition to requiring that the testimony being offered by the expert is reliable, four other admissibility criteria were highlighted, some of which are similar to the *Daubert* criteria:

Mohan criteria: A Canadian standard for accepting expert testimony, which states that expert testimony will be admissible in court if the testimony is relevant, is necessary for assisting the trier of fact, does not violate any exclusionary rules, and is provided by a qualified expert

1. The evidence must be relevant, in that it makes a fact at issue in the case more or less likely. Returning to our criminal profiling example, consider a serial rape case involving a white defendant and black victims. If an expert in the area of profiling concludes, as a result of reliable research, that 95% of all rapes are intraracial, it is

possible that this testimony may be deemed relevant by the court since it makes it less likely that the defendant is guilty (Ormerod, 1999).

2. The evidence must be necessary for assisting the trier of fact. In other words, the testimony must be about something that goes beyond the common understanding of the court. For example, testimony from a profiler might suggest that the offender who committed a series of rapes is likely to have been unemployed or a shift worker at the time of the crimes. If that testimony were based on the fact that many of the rapes were committed during the day, it is doubtful that the testimony would be deemed admissible by the court because jurors applying their common sense will likely come to the same conclusion (Ormerod, 1999).

3. The evidence must not violate any other rules of exclusion (i.e., rules that would otherwise exclude the admissibility of the evidence). For example, even in cases where testimony was deemed relevant, it can still be ruled inadmissible if its potential prejudicial effect (on jurors) outweighs its probative value. Consider a trial where the defendant allegedly raped very young girls. In this case, it would be relevant that the defendant has previously been convicted of similar crimes in the past, and therefore testimony about this fact has probative value. However, the prejudicial effect associated with this testimony is so great that it may lead jurors to convict the defendant, not because they are convinced of his guilt, but because "he did it before so he deserves to be punished anyways" (Ormerod, 1999, p. 218).

4. The testimony must be provided by a qualified expert. Expertise in a court of law is typically determined by considering the type and amount of training and experience a witness possesses. Thus, if the testimony being considered relates to a criminal profile of the offender who committed a series of rapes, the witness must possess expertise in this specific domain for the testimony to be admissible. While determining this issue is usually straightforward, difficulties sometimes arise in determining what type of training and/or experience is valid, especially in cases where the testimony is based not in science but on "art" (as is arguably the case with profiling; Ormerod, 1999).

Since the *Mohan* ruling, additional criteria have been added to the list of issues that judges can or should consider when ruling on the admissibility of expert testimony. For example, in *White Burgess Langille Inman v. Abbott and Haliburton Co.* (2015), the Supreme Court of Canada ruled that, in addition to the *Mohan* criteria, experts must also be independent and impartial. The threshold to determine this is "whether the expert's opinion would not change regardless of which party retained him or her."

Using the above information, read the scenario described in the You Be the Judge box and see what challenges you might encounter as a judge when trying to apply the *Mohan* criteria.

Although *Mohan*-type criteria probably make the judge's job of deciding when to admit expert testimony easier, they do not eliminate all possible problems. In large part, these problems occur because the assessment of each criterion still relies heavily on the discretion of the judge. An example of one potential problem is illustrated by the case of *R. v. D.D* (2000), which is discussed in Box 1.5.

YOU BE THE JUDGE

You are a judge. The case before you involves a defendant who allegedly committed two sexual assaults against young women. The prosecutor on the case is trying to introduce testimony from an "expert" who will present evidence that the defendant can be linked to the two crimes in question. Specifically, the witness plans to testify that the crimes were committed in such a similar fashion that the same individual must have committed them: Not only did both crimes occur in the same general geographic area, but the way the crimes were committed was also broadly similar (e.g., in terms of how the offender approached the victims, the type of weapon used, the sexual acts committed, and the level of violence exhibited).

Your Turn . . .

Your task as the judge in this case is to determine whether this witness should be allowed to present her testimony in court. What are the major issues that you would consider when making this decision? How would you go about determining whether the evidence that the witness plans to introduce is relevant and necessary for assisting the court in understanding the case? How would you go about determining whether the evidence is reliable and whether the witness should in fact be considered an expert? Would you have concerns related to the independence or impartiality of the testimony? How would you determine if those were valid concerns?

Box 1.5   Cases in Forensic Psychology

The Challenges of Applying the *Mohan* Criteria: The Case of *R. v. D.D.* (2000)

R. v. D.D. (2000) is a case that highlights some of the challenges judges encounter when applying the *Mohan* criteria. The case involved a young girl who claimed that she was sexually assaulted by the accused (who was living with the girl's mother at the time) on a number of occasions when the girl was 5–6 years old. Central to the case is the fact that the girl didn't report the abuse at the time the alleged assaults occurred; the accusations came to light two and a half years later, with the trial commencing when the girl was 10 years old (paragraphs 3–4).

The defence lawyers in the case argued that the delay in reporting the assaults indicated that the young girl was not telling the truth. The Crown hoped to introduce expert testimony from a child psychologist who would testify that delays in reporting abuse happen for a variety of reasons and do not necessarily suggest that the allegations are false (paragraph 4). For example, based on his knowledge of the scientific literature, the psychologist planned to testify that a range of factors can discourage children from reporting abuse (e.g., embarrassment, fear of getting themselves or others in trouble, bribery or threats by the perpetrator, etc.).

The trial judge admitted the expert evidence and the jury found the accused guilty. However, the case was

(continued)

(continued)

appealed and the Court of Appeal determined that the expert testimony of the psychologist should not have been admitted at trial. The Court argued that the testimony was not relevant to the case (it related to the girl's credibility, which the Court of Appeal argued was not a fact in issue; paragraph 9). Importantly, with respect to the *Mohan* criteria, the Court also argued that the testimony was not necessary for assisting the triers of fact (paragraph 9). The Court of Appeal set aside the verdict for these and other reasons, ordered a new trial, and directed that the expert testimony not be admitted in the new trial.

While the Crown agreed that a new trial was warranted based on the Court of Appeal's other reasons, they appealed the finding that the expert testimony was inadmissible. The Supreme Court of Canada (SCC) heard the case. The central point debated by the Supreme Court Justices related to the *Mohan* criteria of necessity: Specifically, was the evidence presented by the psychologist necessary for the triers of fact in that it went beyond their common understanding? The SCC Justices were split on this issue.

Writing in support of the Court of Appeal's decision, four of the Supreme Court judges felt that the testimony was not necessary, and that the matter could have been dealt with through simple jury instructions given by the judge:

. . . one statement of principle emerges from the expert evidence: the timing of disclosure signifies nothing; not all children immediately disclose sexual abuse; and the timing of disclosure depends upon the circumstances of the particular victim. The content of this evidence had no technical quality sufficient to require an expert's testimony. It was neither unique nor scientifically puzzling but was rather the proper subject for a simple jury instruction. . . . A trial judge should instruct a jury that there is no inviolable rule on how people who are the victims of trauma like a sexual assault will behave.

In their dissenting opinion, the other three Supreme Court judges disagreed and argued that:

With respect to the necessity requirement, the psychologist's evidence provided information likely to be outside the ordinary experience and knowledge of the jury. . . . it was open to the trial judge to conclude that the psychologist's evidence would assist the jurors by giving them an understanding of the issue of delay in reporting that their ordinary knowledge and experience might not provide. . . . while the need for expert evidence may be diminished if the same objective can be met with a warning to the jury, a warning in this case would not have been a complete substitute for the psychologist's evidence.

The result of the SCC decision was that the Appeal Court decision was upheld and the expert evidence tendered by the Crown was deemed inadmissible.

Despite having access to the same information not only did the Court of Appeal disagree with the trial judge's interpretation of the *Mohan* necessity criterion, the Supreme Court Justices also disagreed with one another regarding how this criterion should be interpreted. Thus, while the *Mohan* criteria may be useful for assisting judges with admissibility decisions, there remain challenges when applying these criteria.

Questions

1. Do you feel that judges are qualified to determine whether expert testimony meets the *Mohan* criteria?

2. What could be put in place to allow judges to make better decisions regarding the admissibility of expert testimony? For example, do you think there is a role for additional training for judges, or could outside experts (e.g., forensic psychologists) be used to assist judges in making these decisions?

Source: From *R. v. D.D.*, [2000] 2 S.C.R. 275.

This case not only showcases some of the issues that judges consider when determining whether to admit testimony from psychological experts, it also highlights the degree of subjectivity associated with the *Mohan* criteria and the disagreements that can occur between judges as a result of this subjectivity.

Now that you have finished reading this introductory chapter, we hope that you are more familiar with the field of forensic psychology and the sorts of activities that forensic psychologists get involved in. In each of the remaining chapters, we will provide you with accurate and up-to-date information about specific topics that are studied by forensic psychologists. Our goal is to make you more informed about forensic psychology. By doing so, we hope to eliminate many of the myths associated with this exciting field of research and practice, some of which are discussed in Box 1.6.

Box 1.6   Myths and Realities

Myths Associated with the Field of Forensic Psychology

Given how popular forensic psychology has become, certain myths have developed around this field, many of which are perpetuated by popular books, television shows, and Hollywood films. Thankfully, attempts are also being made to provide people with correct information about this exciting field (as we are trying to do with this textbook). Below is a list of some common myths associated with forensic psychology, along with factual information from this chapter that helps to dispel these myths.

Myth 1. Forensic psychologists and forensic scientists perform the same tasks.
Fact. Forensic psychologists and forensic scientists are not the same. Forensic psychologists, like forensic scientists, examine issues that are relevant to the law or legal system. However, forensic psychologists use their knowledge of the behavioural or social sciences to do this, whereas forensic scientists rely on their knowledge of the "hard" sciences (e.g., biology, chemistry, physics, etc.). The sorts of issues that forensic psychologists and forensic scientists examine are usually very different, and they require very different types of training and expertise.

Myth 2. Forensic psychologists spend much of their time helping the police with criminal investigations.
Fact. While some forensic psychologists do assist the police with their investigations, very few spend a significant amount of time doing this (and even fewer are involved with specific investigative activities, such as criminal profiling). While there is no typical job profile for a forensic psychologist, it would be much more common in Canada to see forensic psychologists conducting research in a university or government setting, assessing or treating offenders in prisons and the community, or consulting with the courts and other correctional agencies.

Myth 3. To become a researcher in the field of forensic psychology, one must earn a graduate degree in forensic psychology.
Fact. Most full-time researchers in the field of forensic psychology will possess a graduate degree in psychology (a master's degree or PhD), but not necessarily in forensic psychology. In fact, forensic psychology graduate programs are still quite rare in Canada. Despite their degree not being labelled as a "forensic psychology degree," most researchers will have taken forensic coursework and conducted research during their graduate degree on a forensic topic. As graduate students, these people will usually have been supervised by individuals with expertise in forensic psychology.

Myth 4. For you to be admitted as an expert witness in court, you require a law degree.
Fact. Although it is helpful for expert witnesses to understand trial procedures and the role of experts in court proceedings, there is no requirement that expert witnesses have a law degree or even possess any legal knowledge. Psychologists (and other professionals) without formal legal training regularly present expert evidence in courts. Expert witnesses must possess expertise in areas related to their specific testimony and be able to meet the other criteria that the courts use to assess the admissibility of expert testimony (e.g., the testimony needs to be relevant to the case).

SUMMARY

1. The history of forensic psychology is marked by many important milestones, in both the research laboratory and the courtroom. Early research included studies of testimony and suggestibility, and some of the early court cases in Europe where psychologists appeared as experts dealt with similar issues. Hugo Munsterberg played a significant role in establishing the field of forensic psychology in North America, and by the early 1900s, forensic psychologists were active in many different parts of the North American criminal justice system, including in Canada. Currently, forensic psychology is viewed as a distinct and specialized discipline, with its own textbooks, journals, educational programs, and professional associations.

2. Forensic psychology can be defined in a narrow or broad fashion. Narrow definitions usually focus only on the clinical *or* experimental aspects of the field, whereas broad definitions are less restrictive and encompass both aspects.

3. Forensic psychologists can play different roles. Clinical forensic psychologists are primarily interested in mental health issues as they pertain to law. Experimental forensic psychologists are interested in studying any aspect of human behaviour that relates to the law (e.g., eyewitness memory, jury decision making, risk assessment).

4. Psychology can relate to the field of law in three ways. Psychology and the law refers to the use of psychology to study the operation of the legal system. Psychology in the law refers to the use of psychology within the legal system as it operates. Psychology of the law refers to the use of psychology to study the legal system itself.

5. Expert witnesses differ from regular witnesses in that expert witnesses can testify about their opinions, whereas other witnesses can testify only as to what they know to be fact. In Canada, the criteria for determining whether an expert's testimony will be admitted into court relate to whether the testimony (1) is relevant, (2) goes beyond the common understanding of the court, (3) does not violate any exclusionary rules, and (4) comes from a qualified expert.

Discussion Questions

1. The majority of forensic psychologists have no formal training in law. Do you think this is appropriate given the extent to which many of these psychologists are involved in the judicial system?

2. Put yourself in the shoes of an expert witness providing testimony in a murder trial where the victim was a young child. You are supposed to act as an educator to the judge and the jury, not as an advocate for the defence or the prosecution. To what extent do you think you could do this? Do you think there is anything that can be done to ensure that experts do not act as advocates?

Chapter 2
Police Psychology

Learning Objectives

- Outline the major steps in developing a valid police selection procedure.
- Describe the various instruments that are used to select police officers.
- Define what is meant by the term *police discretion*.
- List some key decisions in policing that require the use of discretion.
- Outline some of the major sources and consequences of stress in policing.
- Describe various strategies for dealing with police stress.

It's Friday night, just after 12:00 a.m., and Constable Jeremy Li is performing a routine patrol in the entertainment district of his town. It's a popular area with the local university students, and it gets particularly crowded on Friday nights. As he is about to head back to the station, Constable Li receives a call from dispatch that a fight has broken out between two groups of males in a crowded bar. As he is closest to the scene, Constable Li responds to the call. He parks his cruiser in front of the bar and makes his way inside with another officer who just arrived on scene. Upon seeing the police enter the bar, most of the students run outside. However, two men continue fighting in the corner of the bar. Constable Li carefully approaches the individuals, identifies himself as a police officer, and orders the men to stop fighting. Without any warning, one of the men pulls out a knife and starts swinging it in front of himself. Despite repeated requests to drop his weapon, the man continues to hold on to the knife, becoming increasingly agitated. Believing the man to be dangerous, Constable Li must quickly decide how to respond. He must protect the other man, while also protecting himself. What should he do?

The scenario described above raises many questions about police officers and the nature of the work they do. We might ask whether Constable Li is well suited to deal with this sort of situation. Is he the type of person who can think clearly under pressure, and if not, why was he hired as a police officer? Alternatively, we might be curious about what Constable Li should do in this case. What options are available to him? How can he de-escalate the situation? How much force, if any, should he use to subdue the individual? Finally, we might be interested in how Constable Li is reacting to the events that are unfolding. Is he experiencing serious stress reactions, and if so, what are they and how might they have an impact on his immediate decisions and his well-being in the future? This chapter will provide some of the answers to these questions by examining a number of issues being studied in the area of police psychology, including police selection, police discretion, and police stress.

POLICE SELECTION

As part of ongoing recruitment efforts, the Vancouver Police Department (VPD) posts information about the policing profession on its recruitment web page:

> A police officer is expected to be many things to many different people. In the course of a shift you might conduct an investigation and make an arrest, and just hours later console a family over the death of a loved one. . . . You'll be autonomous in how you handle calls, while being guided by the law, the VPD's policies, and your own common sense. . . . No two calls will ever be the same, and at the start of a shift you never know what your day will hold. . . . To be an effective police officer, you're going to need a sound knowledge of the law and modern policing methods. . . . In some cases, you will need to exercise discretion and tact in persuading people to comply with directions so that an arrest is not necessary. At crime scenes, you'll pay close attention to detail and make observations on suspects and the crime scene itself. You will gather relevant physical evidence and ensure that it remains safe and uncontaminated. Often, you'll be required to visualize and recall an event after the fact so it can be documented accurately, possibly for court purposes. . . . Given the physical demand of police work, you must recognize the importance of maintaining a high level of fitness. . . . In addition to knowing arrest and control tactics, you will be trained to handle and care for a variety of firearms and to operate police vehicles in emergency situations. . . . Although high-stress and risky situations are the exception rather than the rule, you need to be prepared for the unexpected. Long periods of routine tasks can be suddenly interrupted by an urgent call requiring immediate intervention. . . . At times you will deal with people who are intoxicated, high on drugs or mentally unstable and, on occasion, people may direct their hostility at you. (Vancouver Police Department, 2016, "The Job")

As this excerpt clearly indicates, police work is a complex, demanding, stressful, and potentially dangerous occupation. It requires intelligent, creative, patient, ethical, caring, and hard-working individuals. The job may not be for everyone and, therefore, it is important for all those involved to ensure that the individuals who are accepted for the job have the highest potential for success. The purpose of police selection is to make sure this happens (Lough & Von Treuer, 2013). This requires the use of valid **police selection procedures** that allow police agencies to effectively screen out applicants who possess undesirable characteristics and/or select in applicants who possess desirable characteristics (Sanders, 2008). These characteristics may relate to a variety of features, including (but not limited to) an applicant's physical fitness, cognitive abilities, personality, and performance on various job-related tasks.

Police selection procedures: A set of procedures used by the police to either screen out undesirable candidates or select in desirable candidates

A Brief History of Police Selection

The task of selecting appropriate police officers is not a new one for police agencies, nor is it a new phenomenon in the world of psychology. Indeed, psychologists have

Table 2.1 U.S. Police Agency Selection Procedures

Selection Procedure	Percentage of Police Agencies*
Background checks	99.4
Medical exams	98.7
Selection interviews	98.1
Personality tests	91.6
Drug testing	88.4
Physical agility tests	80.0
Polygraph tests	65.8
Recommendation letters	46.5
Cognitive ability tests	46.5

* These data represent responses from 155 U.S. police agencies that responded to a survey sent out by Cochrane et al., 2003.
Source: Data from Cochrane, R.E., Tett, R.P., & Vandecreek, L. (2003). Psychological testing and the selection of police officers: A national survey. Criminal Justice and Behavior, 30, 511–537.

been involved in police selection since the early twentieth century. In what is considered one of the earliest examples, Lewis Terman used the Stanford-Binet Intelligence Test to assist with police selection in California in 1917 (Terman, 1917). Terman tested the intelligence of 30 police and firefighter applicants, which led him to recommend a minimum IQ score of 80 for future applicants. Following this, attempts were made to use personality tests to predict police performance in the mid-twentieth century (e.g., Humm & Humm, 1950). By the mid-1950s, psychological and psychiatric screening procedures of police applicants became a standard part of the selection process in several major police forces in the United States (Reiser, 1982). Since that time, key changes have involved the adoption of higher educational requirements for police officers and the introduction of formal tests to assess the cognitive abilities and personality features of applicants (Ho, 1999). As indicated in Table 2.1, police selection has now become a relatively formalized process, with police forces relying on a wide range of selection procedures (Cochrane, Tett, & Vandecreek, 2003).

Although police selection research is not as common in Canada as it is in the United States, many of the same selection procedures are used in both countries. For example, Canadian police agencies routinely conduct background checks of their applicants and require medical exams. In addition, most Canadian police agencies also use a range of cognitive ability and personality tests in their selection process, such as the RCMP's Police Aptitude Test and the Six Factor Personality Questionnaire, which measures conscientiousness (see Box 2.1 for a detailed description of the selection process in the RCMP, some of which involves the use of psychological assessment tools). In general, similar selection procedures are used by police agencies across Canada, although there are some differences across provincial and territorial borders. For example, while some police agencies (e.g., Edmonton Police Service) use polygraph tests for selection purposes, other police forces (e.g., Hamilton Police Service) do not.

Box 2.1   Forensic Psychology in the Spotlight

So, You Want to Be an RCMP Officer? The RCMP Regular Member Selection Process

Some of you may wish to apply for a position with the RCMP. As is the case for other police agencies, the process to become an RCMP officer is a rigorous one, with portions of it consisting of psychologically-based assessments of applicants. The approach the RCMP has adopted for selecting officers is commonly referred to as a hurdle approach—the applicant has to successfully jump over each successive hurdle to remain in the race. Below, we briefly describe the main hurdles you will encounter on your way to becoming a member of the RCMP. These are described in more detail on the RCMP's recruitment website (RCMP, 2016a).

Meet Job Requirements
Before one can apply to work as an officer with the RCMP the interested applicant must first ensure that they meet the requirements of the job. For example, to apply for officer positions, the applicant must be a Canadian citizen, be at least 19 years old, possess a valid driver's licence, be prepared to carry a firearm, and be willing to relocate anywhere within Canada (this is a partial list of requirements). Applicants must also not have any criminal convictions that have not been pardoned and they must not have been involved in any criminal activity within 1 year of their application date.

Physical Abilities Requirement Evaluation
Interested applicants must also successfully complete the Physical Abilities Requirement Evaluation (PARE), which assesses physical fitness, before they can apply to become an officer with the RCMP.

Vision and Hearing Assessments
Finally, before one can apply to work as an officer with the RCMP, the applicant must successfully pass vision and hearing tests.

Online Submission
After fulfilling the above requirements, interested applicants must complete an online application.

RCMP Entrance Exam
After submitting an application, some candidates will need to undergo the RCMP Entrance Exam (RPAB). This test battery consists of two separate assessments. The Six Factor Personality Questionnaire assesses personality qualities that have been deemed important for the job, such as conscientiousness. The RCMP Police Aptitude Test (RPAT) assesses cognitive aptitude, including composition, comprehension, judgement, observation, logic, and computation. Applicants who have received a Bachelor's degree from a recognized university are exempt from writing the RPAB.

Forms Package
If candidates rank highly enough on the RPAB they will be asked to fill in a variety of forms. Among the forms in this package will be the Applicant Questionnaire, which attempts to assess qualities such as honesty, integrity, and ethics.

Regular Member Selection Interview
After completing the required forms, applicants may be interviewed using the RCMP Member Selection Interview (RMSI). Using a range of questions, this interview is an attempt to determine whether applicants possess certain qualities that the RCMP feels are important for the policing profession. For example, through the interview, the RCMP will want to determine whether a candidate is a team player, has good communication skills, is an effective problem solver, etc.

Pre-employment Polygraph
Applicants who rank highly on their RMSI may undergo a pre-employment polygraph exam. The exam is designed to assess applicants' suitability for police work, and questions will focus on topics covered in the Applicant Questionnaire (e.g., driving history, drug and alcohol use, dealing with law enforcement, etc.).

Health Assessment
Beyond the initial vision and hearing tests, each applicant must now undergo a thorough health assessment. This includes a full physical and psychological assessment.

Field Investigation and Security Clearance
The applicant's background will be thoroughly checked in this phase of the application process. For example, the RCMP will contact references to investigate the candidate's previous employment, education, drug use, etc.

Cadet Training
Finally, applicants who successfully make it through the selection process will enroll in the cadet training program (CTP) at the RCMP Academy in Regina. This is a 24-week program that trains cadets to become police officers with the RCMP.

Source: From Royal Canadian Mounted Police (2016a). Published By RCMP, © 2016.

Developing Police Selection Instruments

There are two separate stages involved with the development of police selection instruments (Gowan & Gatewood, 1995). Stage one is referred to as the job analysis stage. Here, the knowledge, skills, and abilities (KSAs) of a "good" police officer must be identified and carefully defined. Stage two is referred to as the construction and validation stage. In this stage, an instrument must be developed for measuring the extent to which applicants possess a relevant KSA (or KSAs). An attempt must also be made to determine the instrument's validity, or the extent to which the scores on the instrument relate to measures of actual, on-the-job police performance.

Conducting a Job Analysis   As indicated above, a **job analysis** involves a procedure to identify and define relevant KSAs. An organizational psychologist, working in conjunction with a police agency, may conduct the job analysis. These psychologists could use a range of techniques for identifying relevant KSAs, including survey methods and observational techniques. At other times, a job analysis can be conducted more informally, simply by asking members of a police agency to list the qualities they feel are essential for their job.

> **Job analysis:** A procedure for identifying the knowledge, skills, and abilities that make a good police officer

Although it may seem straightforward, conducting a job analysis can be complicated. One of the major problems is that the KSAs of a good police officer may not be stable over time, which makes it difficult to determine what the selection procedures should actually be testing for. For example, Pugh (1985a, 1985b) found that, at two years of service, police officers who were enthusiastic and fit in well were rated as the best officers, while at four years of service officers who were stable and responsible were given the highest performance ratings. Another potentially related problem is that different types of police officers, or different policing jobs, will likely be characterized by different KSAs. The ideal police constable, for instance, possesses different KSAs than the ideal police manager (Ainsworth, 1993). Finally, the fact that individuals may disagree over which KSAs are important can be a challenge when trying to decide which KSAs should be assessed. For example, police constables have been known to rank sense of humour very highly when asked about important policing qualities (Ainsworth, 1993), yet this quality is rarely rated highly by senior police officials (Sanders, 2003). So, should sense of humour be focused on when selecting police officers or not?

Despite these problems, there does appear to be some agreement, even across police officers of varying ranks, on what type of person is "right for the job" (Sanders, 2003). For example, regardless of how the job analysis is conducted, the following KSAs are typically viewed as essential for policing: honesty, reliability, sensitivity to others, good communication skills, high motivation, problem-solving skills, and being a team player.

Constructing and Validating Selection Instruments   Recall that the goals in stage two of the police selection process are (1) to develop a selection instrument for measuring the extent to which police applicants possess relevant KSAs (construction) and (2) to ensure that this instrument relates to measures of police performance (validation). The validation measure that we are most interested in within this context is referred to as **predictive validity**. Predictive validity tells us if there is a relationship between scores obtained from a selection instrument and measures of actual job performance (Gowan & Gatewood, 1995). In the policing context, predictive validity

> **Predictive validity:** The extent to which scores on a test (e.g., a cognitive abilities test) predict scores on some other measure (e.g., supervisor ratings of police performance)

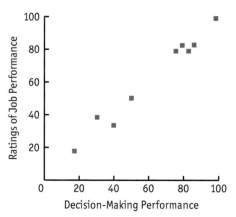

Figure 2.1 A Positive Relationship between Scores on a Selection Instrument and Job Performance Ratings

involves collecting data from police applicants using a selection instrument of some kind, such as scores on a test of decision making under stress. The results on this test are then compared with a measure of job performance, such as performance scores provided by supervisors. If the selection data accurately predict job performance, the selection instrument is said to have predictive validity.

A selection instrument's predictive validity can be determined by calculating validity coefficients, which range from +1.00 to –1.00. These coefficients indicate the strength and direction of the relationship between the scores on a selection instrument and the ratings of job performance. If a selection instrument is shown to have a validity coefficient near +1.00, then a very strong positive relationship exists, indicating that, as performance on the selection instrument increases (in this case, the instrument measures decision making performance under stress), ratings of job performance also increase (see Figure 2.1). Conversely, if a selection instrument is shown to have a validity coefficient near –1.00, a very strong negative relationship exists: As performance on the selection instrument increases, ratings of job performance decrease (see Figure 2.2).

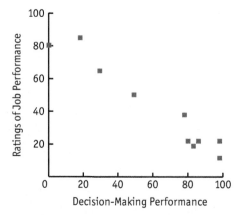

Figure 2.2 A Negative Relationship between Scores on a Selection Instrument and Job Performance Ratings

Any value between these two extreme values represents an intermediate level of predictive validity.

In addition to challenges that are encountered when trying to establish relevant KSAs, a number of major challenges have been identified at this validation stage. One challenge relates to how researchers measure the performance of police officers (Hargrave & Hiatt, 1987). How one measures police performance is crucial, since it will have a direct impact on the validity of any selection instrument. Unfortunately, it appears that no answer to this question currently exists (Sanders, 2008). This is not to say that researchers don't have access to a variety of performance measures. Indeed, many such measures exist, including the number of times an officer is tardy, the number of complaints against an officer, the number of commendations received by an officer, graduation from training academy, academy exam scores, performance ratings by supervisors, performance ratings by peers, and so forth. The problem is that there is little evidence to suggest that one of these measures is any better than another. Furthermore, research suggests that a different picture of performance can emerge depending on what measure is used. For example, measures of performance during training often do not generalize to on-the-job performance, presumably because "such data do not involve the officers' responses to the real job demands" (Burkhart, 1980, p. 123). In addition, ratings by different individuals (e.g., peers versus supervisors) can contradict one another (Gul & O'Connell, 2013).

The Validity of Police Selection Instruments

Now that we have discussed some of the problems with constructing and validating police selection instruments, we will describe some of the instruments that are currently in use and present some research on their validity. Although some of these instruments might be new to you, there are many others, such as the selection interview, that you will be familiar with. We will focus our attention on three specific selection instruments: the selection interview, psychological tests, and the assessment centre.

The Selection Interview In both Canada and the United States, the **selection interview** is one of the most common selection instruments used by the police. Typically, selection interviews take the form of a semi-structured interview. In a semi-structured interview, the interviewer has a preset list of questions that are asked of each applicant, thus ensuring a more objective basis for comparing applicants (Gowan & Gatewood, 1995). One of the main goals of the selection interview is to determine the extent to which the applicant possesses the KSAs that have been deemed important through a job analysis. To some extent, these qualities may vary from agency to agency and, as indicated above, they may depend on the job being applied for. As an example of the sort of KSAs that may be considered, the criteria evaluated by the Hamilton Police Service's Essential Competency Interview include analytical thinking, self-confidence, communication, flexibility, self-control, relationship building, achievement orientation, physical skills/abilities, and dealing with diversity (Hamilton Police Service, 2016).

Given its frequent use as a selection instrument, there is surprisingly little research examining the predictive validity of the selection interview in the policing

Selection interview: In recruiting police officers, an interview used by the police to determine the extent to which an applicant possesses the knowledge, skills, and abilities deemed important for the job context (Aamodt, 2004). The research that does exist seems to suggest that interviews can sometimes predict job performance (e.g., Hargrave & Hiatt, 1987), but not always (Annell, Lindfors, & Sverke, 2015). For example, drawing on a sample of Swedish police recruits, Annell et al. (2015) recently studied how well three types of interviews (a psychologist interview, a police interview, and a medical examination) predicted performance, satisfaction, occupational retention, and health across three different settings (at the academy, during field training, and on the job). Of the 36 validity coefficients that were reported, only 5 coefficients were significant, and the largest coefficient was 0.10.

These results are consistent with research from the general field of organizational psychology, where mixed results regarding the predictive validity of the selection interview are also reported (Dipboye, Macan, & Shahani-Denning, 2012; McDaniel, Whetzel, Schmidt, & Maurer, 1994). Given such findings, it seems clear that interviewing should be used with caution. It must also be remembered, however, that changing the way in which an interview is conducted can have an impact on its validity. For example, the more structured an interview is, the more likely that it will predict future job performance with some degree of success (Cortina, Goldstein, Payne, Davison, & Gilliland, 2000). For example, interviews are more likely to result in useful information for selection purposes when they consist of a standard, pre-determined list of questions that are asked of all applicants. Police psychologists should continue to examine how selection interviews in the policing context can be improved and the predictive validity of new interview procedures should be established.

Psychological Tests   In addition to the selection interview, psychological tests are also commonly used by police agencies to select suitable officers (Cochrane et al., 2003). Some of these tests have been developed to measure cognitive abilities, whereas others have been designed to assess an applicant's personality. In addition, some of these tests have been developed with police selection in mind, whereas others have been developed in other contexts, such as the mental health field. As with other selection instruments, there are still many unanswered questions when it comes to the use of psychological tests. However, there seems to be general agreement among police researchers that psychological tests are useful in deciding whether a person possesses certain attributes, and it is believed that this knowledge can be helpful, to some extent at least, in selecting applicants to become police officers.

Cognitive ability tests: Procedure for measuring verbal, mathematical, memory, and reasoning abilities

Cognitive Ability Tests   A wide variety of **cognitive ability tests** are available for police use. Although each test may emphasize something slightly different, they are typically used to measure verbal, mathematical, memory, and reasoning abilities. Such tests are used regularly when selecting police officers in Canada. For example, as indicated in Box 2.1, if you were to apply to become a police officer with the RCMP today, part of the selection procedure would require you to take the Electronic RCMP Police Aptitude Test (RPAT). The RPAT consists of multiple-choice questions designed to evaluate an applicant's potential aptitude for police work. More specifically, the test measures seven core skills that are considered essential in performing the duties of an RCMP officer: composition, comprehension, memory, judgment, observation, logic, and computation (RCMP, 2016b).

In general, the reliance on cognitive ability tests for police selection purposes is supported to some extent by empirical research. However, these tests tend to be better at predicting performance during police academy training compared with future on-the-job performance. For example, Hirsh, Northrop, and Schmidt (1986) conducted a meta-analysis of 40 validation studies involving cognitive ability tests. They found average validity coefficients of 0.36 and 0.13 for predicting training success and on-the-job performance, respectively. A more recent meta-analytic study reported similar results. More specifically, Aamodt (2004) found validity coefficients of 0.41 and 0.16 when examining the use of cognitive ability tests for predicting academy performance and on-the-job performance, respectively, where on-the-job performance was assessed via supervisor ratings.

There are a variety of potential explanations for why higher scores are found when cognitive ability tests are used to predict academy performance versus on-the-job performance, but one interesting possibility is that personality variables play a larger role in determining job success, above and beyond one's cognitive abilities (e.g., Forero, Gallardo-Pujol, Maydeu-Olivares, & Andres-Pueyo, 2009). Thus, it is worthwhile describing some of the personality tests used for police selection and the degree of validity associated with each.

Personality Tests   A number of personality tests are used for police selection, but only two of the most commonly used tests will be discussed here. Perhaps the most common test is an assessment instrument known as the **Minnesota Multiphasic Personality Inventory** (MMPI), now in its third iteration (Tellegen & Ben-Porath, 2008). According to Cochrane et al. (2003), of the 155 U.S. police agencies that responded to their 2003 survey, 71.9% of the agencies indicated that the MMPI was the personality test they used most often for selection purposes. Although similar data are not readily available in Canada, a search of recruitment websites for Canadian police agencies suggests that the MMPI is also a popular assessment tool in this country as well. Interestingly, the MMPI, originally designed in the 1940s, was not developed for selecting police officers. Neither was the MMPI-2 or the MMPI-2-RF (a recent version of the MMPI-2 that had some of its scales restructured). Rather, this assessment instrument was developed as a general inventory for identifying people with psychopathological problems (Tellegen & Ben-Porath, 2008). Currently, the MMPI-2 consists of 567 true-false questions that attempt to identify psychopathological problems, including depression, paranoia, and schizophrenia. The MMPI-2-RF retains 338 of the original 567 questions from the MMPI-2.

Although Aamodt's (2004) meta-analysis of the MMPI revealed that it possesses little power in predicting academy performance or on-the-job police behaviour, some research does suggest that the MMPI (and its more recent variations) can be associated with significant, but relatively low validity coefficients. This may be especially true when the tests are used to predict problematic police behaviours (Chibnall & Detrick, 2003; Sellbom, Fischler, & Ben-Porath, 2007; Weiss, Vivian, Weiss, Davis, & Rostow, 2013). For example, drawing on data from 291 male police officers, Sellbom et al. (2007) reported that the Restructured Clinical Scales in the MMPI-2 performed significantly better than the original MMPI Clinical Scales for predicting items such as internal affairs complaints and termination. Likewise, in a large study

Minnesota Multiphasic Personality Inventory: An assessment instrument for identifying people with psychopathological problems

of 4348 police officers, Weiss and his colleagues (2013) demonstrated that one particular scale on the MMPI-2—the so-called Lie scale, which assesses the degree to which the test taker is "faking good"—was a significant predictor of problematic police behaviour (as indicated by supervisor ratings of the police officers).

In part, the relatively low levels of predictive validity associated with the MMPI tests may be due to the fact that they were never developed as police selection instruments. If this is true, then it may be the case that personality tests developed for police selection purposes will be associated with higher levels of predictive validity. In fact, this does appear to be the case at least sometimes, as indicated by studies examining the **Inwald Personality Inventory** (IPI).

Unlike the MMPI tests, the IPI was developed specifically for the law enforcement community. According to Inwald (1992), the creator of the IPI, the purpose of this selection instrument is to identify police applicants who are most suitable for police work by measuring their personality attributes and behaviour patterns. The instrument consists of 310 true-false questions that measure factors such as stress reactions, interpersonal difficulties, and alcohol and other drug use. According to several researchers, the IPI appears to be slightly more predictive of police officer performance than the MMPI (e.g., Inwald & Shusman, 1984; Scogin, Schumacher, Gardner, & Chaplin, 1995; Varela, Boccaccini, Scogin, Stump, & Caputo, 2004). This has been confirmed in meta-analytic studies as well (e.g., Aamodt, 2004).

Assessment Centres   The last selection procedure we will discuss is the **assessment centre**. An assessment centre is a facility within which the behaviour of police applicants can be observed in a number of different ways by multiple observers (Pynes & Bernardin, 1992). The primary selection instrument used within an assessment centre is the **situational test**, which involves simulations of real-world policing tasks. Trained observers evaluate how applicants perform during these tasks, and the performance appraisals are used for the purpose of selection. As indicated in Box 2.2, these centres are now an integral part of police assessment and training in Canada.

Situational tests used in assessment centres attempt to tap into KSAs identified as part of a job analysis for the purpose of identifying candidates who will be successful police officers. Although there is not a great deal of research examining the validity of assessment centres for police selection, some research suggests that situational tests do have modest levels of predictive validity. For example, Pynes and Bernardin (1992) examined the scores given to applicants across four simulation exercises. These scores were then compared with training academy performance and future on-the-job performance. Overall, the correlation coefficients were 0.14 and 0.20 for training academy performance and future on-the-job performance, respectively. Similar results were presented by Aamodt (2004) in his meta-analysis of six studies where the predictive validity of assessment centres was examined.

Whether these coefficients are high enough to warrant the use of assessment centres will ultimately depend on whether assessment centres provide added value over cheaper, easier to implement alternatives. At least some research in the policing domain (e.g., Dayan, Fox, & Kasten, 2008), suggests that assessment centres might not provide added value (e.g., beyond what can be achieved through employment interviews) in terms of police selection decisions.

Inwald Personality Inventory: An assessment instrument used to identify police applicants who are suitable for police work by measuring their personality attributes and behaviour patterns

Assessment centre: A facility in which the behaviour of police applicants can be observed in a number of situations by multiple observers

Situational test: A simulation of a real-world policing task

Box 2.2   Forensic Psychology in the Spotlight

The Use of Assessment Centres in Canadian Policing

Across Canada, assessment centres are being used for training and assessment purposes. For example, the Police Academy Assessment Centre at the Justice Institute of British Columbia (JIBC) plays a key role in the assessment of police officers (of all ranks) in the province. Like all assessment centres, the centre at JIBC relies on trained observers to assess police candidates (or officers) in a wide range of carefully constructed situational tests.

Some of the scenarios that trainees are exposed to at the centre reflect the stressful events that police officers in Canada sometimes encounter. However, many of the scenarios reflect the more mundane, but no less important tasks that police officers must perform on a more routine basis, such as organizing and prioritizing a large volume of incoming information.

For example, one of the scenarios used in the assessment centre at JIBC is referred to as the Electronic In-Basket

Courtesy of The Justice Institute of British Columbia

Exercise (Whetzel, Rotenberry, & McDaniel, 2014). This is a particularly useful scenario for assessing police supervisors or managers. As stated by the JIBC,

> The In-Basket is designed to evaluate the candidate's administrative skills. Police agencies submit current operational information that is used to custom-design the electronic email exercise. Candidates are expected to digest, organize and prioritize their correspondence. They must then answer emails, "cc" the appropriate recipients and send new emails in response to the problems posed. All meetings and commitments can be

entered into the electronic calendar contained within the program. A marking site is available on the server that allows an administrator to both monitor the candidates while the exercise is in progress and mark their work. At a glance, the marker can determine the number of emails and calendar entries the student has entered and see what stage the candidate is at in the exercise. (JIBC, 2016, "Electronic In-Basket Exercise")

The potential benefits associated with assessment centres are obvious. In a job where people are regularly exposed to a wide range of events, many of which are dangerous,

(continued)

(continued)

assessment centres provide a means to simulate these events under relatively realistic, but safe conditions. People's performance can easily be observed in an assessment centre, which is not typically possible in naturalistic settings, and a wide variety of scenarios can be assessed. This provides centre staff with an opportunity to focus on the full range of KSAs that police agencies deem important when selecting officers.

Despite these benefits, however, there appears to be little published research demonstrating that assessment centres are useful for predicting on-the-job police performance, although anecdotal evidence from many police trainers suggests that the approach is effective. Indeed, surprisingly perhaps, the validity coefficients associated with situational tests (when they are used for the purpose of police selection) are usually quite modest, as reported above.

Source: The Justice Institute of British Columbia, 2016.

POLICE DISCRETION

As indicated through job analyses, many of the qualities deemed necessary for success as a police officer have to do with the applicant being adaptable, having common sense, possessing effective decision-making skills, and being a good problem solver (Sanders, 2003). In large part, these qualities are necessary because officers are required to use **police discretion** in much of their daily work (Walma & West, 2002). To appreciate the extent to which the police use discretion, consider the following decisions that need to be made routinely by police officers:

Police discretion: The freedom that a police officer often has for deciding what should be done in any given situation

- What street should I patrol tonight?
- Should I stop that vehicle for a traffic violation?
- What level of force is required to achieve my objective?
- Should I run after that suspect or wait for backup?
- Should I call an end to this investigation?
- Should I take this person to a psychiatric hospital or the police station?
- Should I arrest this individual for a law violation?

The list of situations requiring some degree of police discretion is endless and, therefore, police discretion is a topic of major concern to researchers. More specifically, researchers are interested in whether police discretion is really necessary, the sorts of situations in which discretion is used, the factors that influence police decision making in these situations, and ways of controlling the inappropriate use of police discretion. Each of these issues will be examined in this section.

Why Is Police Discretion Necessary?

Although some individuals and interest groups believe that police officers should have very limited discretion, others disagree. Currently, police officers have great latitude in how they make decisions (Bronitt & Stenning, 2011; McKenna, 2002). But is this discretion necessary?

The typical answers that researchers offer to such questions are based on the fact that it is impossible to establish laws or policies that adequately encompass all the possible situations an officer can encounter and, therefore, a degree of discretion is inevitable. For example, Walma and West (2002) argued the following:

> No manual or rule book can take into consideration every possible situation a police officer may face in doing his or her daily duties. No supervisor can follow a police officer around to monitor every decision he or she makes. As a result, police officers are entrusted with the discretion to apply their training and fulfill their duties in the manner they think is best. (p. 165)

Even when it comes to enforcing the law, there are many arguments for why police discretion is necessary. For example, Sheehan and Cordner (1989) provided the following important reasons for police discretion:

- A police officer who attempts to enforce all the laws all the time would be in the police station and in court all the time and, thus, of little use when serious problems arise in the community.
- Legislatures pass some laws that they clearly do not intend to have strictly enforced all the time.
- Legislatures pass some laws that are vague, making it necessary for the police to interpret them and decide when to apply them.
- Most law violations are minor in nature, such as driving slightly over the posted speed limit, and do not require full enforcement of the law.
- Full enforcement of all the laws all the time would alienate the public and undermine support for the police.
- Full enforcement of all the laws all the time would overwhelm the criminal justice system, including the prisons.
- The police have many duties to perform with limited resources. Good judgment must, therefore, be used in establishing enforcement priorities.

If police discretion is accepted as an inevitable part of policing, society has to deal with the consequences. Although the arguments put forward by researchers such as Sheehan and Cordner (1989) highlight some obvious advantages of police discretion, there are also potential disadvantages. For police discretion to be advantageous, officers must exercise discretion in a nondiscriminatory manner (Walma & West, 2002), and unfortunately this does not always happen; the police do, on occasion, use their discretion inappropriately. Perhaps the most commonly cited example of the inappropriate use of police discretion in Canada relates to racial profiling, or the initiation of police actions (e.g., traffic pullovers) based on the race of an individual rather than any evidence of wrongdoing (Ontario Human Rights Commission, 2003). However, other forms of inappropriate discretion also occur. We highlight an instance of inappropriate investigative discretion in Box 2.3.

Areas Where Police Discretion Is Used

Having now established that there are a variety of rationales for police discretion, it is important that we consider some of the situations in which it is used. As indicated above, there are relatively few decisions that a police officer has to make that do not

Box 2.3   Cases in Forensic Psychology

The Supreme Court of Canada Rules on Investigative Discretion in *Beaudry v. The Queen* (2007)

The accused in this case was Sergeant Beaudry. He was charged with obstructing justice when he deliberately failed to give a breathalyzer test to a fellow police officer (Constable Plourde) who he suspected was driving while impaired. During his trial, Sergeant Beaudry maintained that his decision was an example of proper police discretion. The Crown argued that Sergeant Beaudry's decision was based on preferential treatment toward Constable Plourde because he was a police officer. Agreeing with the Crown, the trial judge convicted Sergeant Beaudry. On appeal, the majority of the Court of Appeal upheld the conviction. The case was further appealed to the Supreme Court of Canada where the majority of Supreme Court Justices also upheld the conviction.

Central to the decision in the Supreme Court case was the view of police discretion held by some of the Justices. In their judgment, they state:

There is no question that police officers have a duty to enforce the law and investigate crimes . . . (paragraph 35)

However, they go on to say:

Nevertheless, it should not be concluded automatically . . . that this duty is applicable in every situation. Applying the letter of the law to the practical, real-life situations faced by police officers in performing their everyday duties requires that certain adjustments be made . . . The ability — indeed the duty — to use one's judgment to adapt the process of law enforcement to individual circumstances and to the real-life demands of justice is in fact the basis of police discretion . . . Thus, a police officer who has reasonable grounds to believe that an offence has been committed, or that a more thorough investigation might produce evidence that could form the basis of a criminal charge, may exercise his or her discretion to decide not to engage the judicial process. But this discretion is not absolute. Far from having *carte blanche*, police officers must justify their decisions rationally. (paragraph 37)

Outlining the justifications that are required for discretion to be appropriate, the Supreme Court Justices go on to say:

The required justification is essentially twofold. First, the exercise of the discretion must be justified subjectively, that is, the discretion must have been exercised honestly and transparently, and on the basis of valid and reasonable grounds . . . Thus, a decision based on favouritism . . . cannot constitute a proper exercise of police discretion. However, the officer's sincere belief that he properly exercised his discretion is not sufficient to justify his decision. (paragraph 38)

Hence, the exercise of police discretion must also be justified on the basis of objective factors. (paragraph 39)

Offence seriousness was one objective factor that was highlighted in the Supreme Court ruling:

In the case of a robbery, or an even more serious offence, the discretion can be exercised to decide not to arrest a suspect or not to pursue an investigation. However, the justification offered must be proportionate to the seriousness of the conduct and it must be clear that the discretion was exercised in the public interest. Thus, while some exercises of discretion are almost routine and are clearly justified, others are truly exceptional and will require that the police officer explain his or her decision in greater detail. (paragraph 40)

Arguing that impaired driving is indeed a very serious crime, the Supreme Court Justices found that the trial Judge was not wrong in rejecting Sergeant Beaudry's explanations for his conduct and finding him guilty. He had used his discretion inappropriately.

Questions

1. Do you agree with the Supreme Court decision that Officer's Beaudry's use of discretion was inappropriate in this case? Why or why not?

2. Do you have ideas for how we can minimize the use of inappropriate investigative discretion, while not restricting the appropriate use of police discretion?

Source: From R. v. Beaudry, [2007] 1 S.C.R. 190, 2007 SCC 5.

require at least some degree of discretion. However, four domains are worthy of a more in-depth discussion. Two of these domains—how the police interact with young offenders and how they intervene in cases of domestic violence—are dealt with thoroughly in later chapters (see Chapters 12 and 13, respectively) so we will not discuss them here. In this chapter, we will deal with two other domains where discretion is common. More specifically, we will look at how the police deal with mentally ill individuals and how they make decisions in use-of-force encounters.

Individuals with Mental Illnesses   Police officers in Canada frequently come into contact with individuals who suffer from mental illness. Most of these encounters are resolved without serious incident, but on rare occasions such encounters can be very serious indeed. One such example was the tragic 2008 Greyhound Bus incident, where a young man (Tim McLean) was stabbed to death and decapitated by Vince Li. In an extreme case of police discretion, RCMP officers who arrived at the scene decided not to intervene right away, but called instead for a negotiating team and a tactical unit. The decision was later criticized because Li reportedly cannibalized parts of McLean's body during the standoff ("Greyhound Suspect," 2008). Arrested by the RCMP when he attempted to escape the bus, Li was ultimately diagnosed as suffering from schizophrenia and was deemed not criminally responsible for the murder of McLean.

According to Cotton and Coleman (2008), several factors have increased the likelihood of encounters between the police and mentally ill individuals, but primary among these is the recent movement toward deinstitutionalizing individuals who have a mental illness. In an attempt to ensure these encounters are dealt with effectively, formal policies are often put in place specifying how police officers should deal with individuals who have a mental illness. These policies typically instruct police officers to apprehend the individual whenever he or she poses a danger to self or others or is causing some other kind of serious disturbance (Teplin, 2000). While these policies provide the police with the legal power to intervene, police officers must still rely on their discretion to choose the most appropriate action.

When police officers encounter an individual with a mental illness who is creating a disturbance there are generally three options available to them, depending on the circumstances: (1) they can transport that person to a psychiatric institution of some kind, (2) they can arrest the person and take him or her to jail, or (3) they can resolve the matter informally (Teplin, 2000). Although this decision may not seem difficult, in practice it is. For example, access to emergency hospitalization is sometimes barred (e.g., due to the dangerousness of the offender) and as a result, the police may be forced to take actions that are not in the long-term best interest of the individual in need, such as taking him or her to jail. This can lead to mentally ill individuals becoming criminalized (e.g., Crocker, Hartford, & Heslop, 2009). In other words, individuals who would have typically been treated within the mental health system are now dealt with by the criminal justice system.

This criminalization process appears to be at work in the study conducted by Hoch, Hartford, Heslop, and Stitt (2009). The aim of Hoch et al.'s study was to determine the rate at which individuals who suffered from a mental illness in the city of London, Ontario, came into contact with the police (and were charged and arrested) compared with individuals not identified as mentally ill. The data were restricted to a single year (January to December, 2001). In total, 817 people with a mental illness were

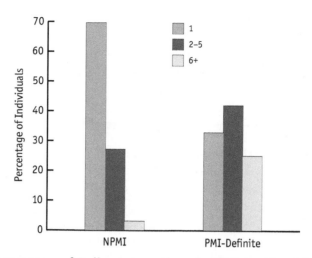

Figure 2.3 Percentage of Police Interactions in 2001 by Mental Illness Group

Source: Hoch et al., 2009, Figure 1 B (p. 54) Hoch, J.S., Hartford, K., Heslop, L., & Stitt, L. (2009). Mental illness and police interactions in a mid-sized Canadian city: What the data do and do not say. *Canadian Journal of Community Mental Health, 28,* 49–66. © Canadian Periodical for Community Studies. Reproduced with permission.

identified from the London Police Service database who had at least one interaction with the police, and 111 095 people were identified who did not have a mental illness. As you can see in Figure 2.3, the results from this study indicated that people who definitely had a mental illness (PMI-Definite) were more likely to interact with the police than people with no mental illness (NPMI). Similarly, people with a mental illness were more likely to be charged and arrested compared to people without a mental illness. More specifically, Hoch et al. found that "people with mental illness were arrested, charged, or both 10% more often than those without mental illness" (p. 55).

These figures raise many difficult questions. For example, do they reflect the discriminatory use of discretion on the part of the police, or do they reflect the fact that mentally ill offenders commit more serious crimes? Alternatively, could it be that these figures simply reflect the fact that the hands of the police are often tied, with arrests being one of the few options available to ensure that individuals with mental illnesses remain free from harm? To know what these figures actually mean, more systematic research clearly needs to be conducted. We are thankful that Canadian researchers have begun to conduct such research and that more training is now underway to better prepare Canadian police officers to deal effectively with mentally ill individuals (Bailey, 2013). One of the individuals who is responsible for much of the progress being made within this area in Canada is Dr. Dorothy Cotton, who is profiled in Box 2.4.

Use-of-Force Situations   Police officers in North America are granted the right to use force to protect the general public and themselves (Walma & West, 2002). However, police officers have a great deal of discretion when deciding when (and how) to use force. They can use force when it is necessary to suppress a situation, but only to the extent that is necessary to accomplish this goal. When a police officer uses force for any other purpose, or in excess of what is needed, that officer has made

Box 2.4

Canadian Researcher Profile: Dr. Dorothy Cotton

Courtesy of Dorothy Cotton

Dorothy Cotton came to Canada from Boston to study medicine at McGill University. She had no intention of studying psychology and certainly no intention of staying in Canada, but a second-year course in abnormal psychology piqued her interest and 30-something years after her arrival, she is still in Canada, having obtained her PhD in social psychology from Queen's University.

In the early days of her career, Dr. Cotton worked in a frontline psychology position at a provincial psychiatric hospital. She went on to become chief psychologist there as well as director of forensic services. Dr. Cotton subsequently was employed as a clinical neuropsychologist with the Correctional Service of Canada, where she worked with offenders with a variety of cognitive and neuropsychological problems. While she has done a variety of work in clinical and forensic psychology, her work with police services has been her professional passion. Dr. Cotton says her interest in policing issues happened quite by accident. As psychiatric services downsized over the years, she discovered that the police were spending more time with her patients than she was. Curious as to why, she set out to explore.

As an associate member of the Canadian Association of Chiefs of Police (CACP), Dr. Cotton has been integral to the development of programs linking police services and mental health services, in the interest of meeting the needs of people with mental illnesses. Her research and publications in this area have examined the attitudes and knowledge of police in regard to mental illness, the nature and extent of police training and education about mental illness, and best practices for police services in dealing with mentally ill offenders. She is co-author of the CACP's *Contemporary Policing Guidelines for Working with the Mental Health System.*

Dr. Cotton appears to have an affinity for unique and underserviced areas of psychology, as she is one of only a handful of clinical correctional neuropsychologists in Canada. She is also the first—and only—person in Canada to hold diplomate status in police psychology (the highest recognition that is currently available in this field).

Dr. Cotton is a past president of the College of Psychologists of Ontario, and is a fellow and a past board member of the Canadian Psychological Association. She has served as a member of the Mental Health and the Law Advisory Committee of the Mental Health Commission of Canada, which represents Canada's most significant attempt to address issues related to mental health and mental illness in Canada by developing a national mental health strategy—which, among other things, specifically addresses issues related to the interface between people with mental illnesses and the criminal justice system, including the police.

Known to cops across the country as the author of a "psychology for cops" column that appears in the national police magazine, *Blueline*, Dr. Cotton is one of a very rare species of people in the world who are bassoon-playing psychologists. In fact, she has been known to suggest that she practises psychology only to support her bassoon-playing habit.

The Death of Sammy Yatim

By now, all of you will have heard of the case of Sammy Yatim. He was shot and killed by Toronto police officer, Constable James Forcillo, and the case resulted in a media frenzy.

The tragic events began in the evening of July 26, 2013 when Sammy Yatim, an 18-year-old man, boarded a street car in Toronto. Once on the street car, Yatim reportedly drew a switchblade and started acting aggressively towards other passengers. He also exposed his genitals. Police soon arrived on the scene. One of these officers was Constable James Forcillo, who at the time of the incident had been an officer with the Toronto Police Service for six years.

Constable Forcillo was positioned at the front of the streetcar. At one point he called for a Taser believing that the situation could be contained, but one was not immediately available. Yatim was ordered to drop his knife and to refrain from moving towards the officers. When Yatim took a step forward, Forcillo fired nine shots at him—3 initially, followed by 6 more about five a half seconds later.

Forcillo later testified that he saw Yatim start sitting up after the first 3 shots to "renew his attack." But, according to surveillance video, Yatim was lying on the ground. Yatim was transported to hospital where he was pronounced dead.

On August 19, 2013, Forcillo was charged with second-degree murder, manslaughter, and attempted murder. After 35 hours of deliberation, the jury reached their verdict. They found Forcillo not guilty of second-degree murder or manslaughter, but guilty of attempted murder. Because jurors can't speak about their deliberations in Canada, it is difficult to know why the jury reached the verdicts they did. As reported in the media, the jurors presumably found it was reasonable for Constable Forcillo to shoot Yatim under the circumstances, but that the second round of gun shots was not justifiable given the lack of any immediate threat.

Sources: Based on Sammy Yatim shooting death on Toronto streetcar shown in court, Alamenciak, 2013; Hasham, 2016; Mehta, 2014.

---

inappropriate use of his or her discretionary power. When this happens, the result can be deadly. See the In the Media box for a recent case of police use-of-force in Canada that had tragic consequences.

In Canada, the authority to use force is laid out in our Criminal Code (Walma & West, 2002). For example, section 25 of the Criminal Code states, "Everyone who is required by law to do anything in the administration of enforcement of the law . . . is, if he acts on reasonable grounds, justified in doing what he is required or authorized to do and in using as much force as is necessary for that purpose." In court cases involving use-of-force decisions, difficulties can arise because of the ambiguity of terms such as *reasonable grounds* and *as is necessary*. Indeed, these terms are often hotly debated in cases such as the Forcillo trial described in the In the Media box. In some cases, an analysis of the facts will result in a decision that the force used by the police was inappropriate. This could occur because the use of force was viewed as unnecessary, in excess of what was needed, or based on factors that should not have been taken into account, such as the race of the suspect. In other cases, an analysis of the facts will find that the police used an appropriate amount of force that was justifiable under the circumstances.

Fortunately, police use of force in Canada is a relatively rare phenomenon. Perhaps the most comprehensive examination of police use of force in Canada is Hall and Votova's recent (2013) study. They examined use of force in 4 urban areas across the country (reflecting 7 municipal police agencies). Over their study period, from August 2006 to March 2013, 4992 use-of-force events (defined as anything more serious than soft-handed physical control techniques) occurred in a total of 3 594 812 police–public interactions (0.1% of all interactions). In addition to this result, which showed how infrequent use-of-force events are, Hall and Votova also reported the following:

- Single use-of-force modalities were used in 59.6% of all use-of-force events, whereas multiple use-of-force modalities (e.g., pepper spray and Taser) were used in the remainder of events.

- Physical strikes were by far the most common use-of-force modality used (77%). A Taser was used in 14.9% of cases, pepper spray was used in 3.6% of cases, and a police canine was used in 2.4% of cases.

- Subjects involved in use-of-force events were usually male (87%) and intoxication (drugs or alcohol) was the most frequent reason for police to be dispatched to the scene (22.5%).

- In terms of subject injuries, of the 4992 use-of-force incidents, 830 (16.6%) subjects were transported to hospital by police or an emergency medical service vehicle and had a retrievable medical record. Of these individuals, 57.3% were documented to have a physical injury of some type (ranging from bruises and lacerations to more serious injuries).

Controlling Police Discretion

In an attempt to ensure that police officers exercise their discretion appropriately, guidelines have been established that allow police discretion to be controlled. As indicated by Walma and West (2002), the Charter of Rights and Freedoms can, in a sense, be seen as a guideline to control police discretion because it makes clear that all people should be treated fairly and equally, but specific codes of conduct for police officers have also been developed that help to control the use of discretion (Walma & West, 2002). For example, in Canada, one section of the Police Services Act states that police officers commit misconduct if they fail to treat or protect a person without discrimination.

In this section, we will deal specifically with methods for controlling inappropriate police discretion in use-of-force situations. One reason for focusing on such situations is the public's widespread interest in this area. The other reason is that numerous attempts have been made, in Canada particularly, to develop innovative approaches for controlling the abuse of force by the police. One approach is the development of administrative policies within police agencies, which are specifically meant to control the use of force by police officers. Another approach is the development of use-of-force models that help to guide a police officer's decision-making process in use-of-force situations.

Departmental Policies Departmental policies for restricting use of force by police officers are not new, nor is research on the effectiveness of these policies. For example, Fyfe (1979) examined the impact of use-of-force policies put in place by the New York Police Department (NYPD) in 1972. He showed that, not only did the frequency of police shootings decrease in New York from 1971 to 1975, but the numbers of officers injured and killed during the same period also decreased. Similar findings have been reported in several other U.S. cities (e.g., Geller & Scott, 1992). In Canada, similar policies have been put in place for the purpose of restricting various use-of-force options available to the police. For example, following the case of Robert Dziekanski in 2007, who died shortly after he was Tasered by RCMP officers in the Vancouver International Airport, the RCMP introduced new policies for Taser use that restrict when officers can use the weapon (in addition to providing new requirements for training on the Taser).

Use-of-Force Models   Although use-of-force models may not directly restrict the use of force by police officers in the same way that departmental policies do, they may indirectly control force by increasing the likelihood that officers carefully assess and evaluate potential use-of-force situations when deciding upon the most appropriate course of action. In Canada, police agencies have invested a great deal of time and energy into developing use-of-force models. One such model is the RCMP's Incident Management/ Intervention Model (IMIM), which is described more fully in Box 2.5 (RCMP, 2016c). This model was developed to assist RCMP officers with their decision making in potential use-of-force situations and in articulating those decisions after the incident is over.

Box 2.5   Forensic Psychology in the Spotlight

The RCMP's Incident Management/Intervention Model

The use-of-force framework developed by the RCMP is referred to as the Incident Management/Intervention Model, or the IMIM. According to the RCMP, the IMIM "is a visual aid that helps the officer envision an event and explain why certain intervention methods were employed". More specifically, the IMIM model:

> . . . is the framework by which RCMP officers assess and manage risk through justifiable and reasonable intervention . . . it helps officers choose the appropriate intervention option, based on the subject's behavior and the totality of the situation. It promotes continuous risk assessment and centers on the RCMP problem solving model known as CAPRA (CAPRA stands for Clients/ Acquire & Analyze/Partnerships/Response/Assess). The IMIM also helps officers identify the subject's behavior and then select the best option to control the situation effectively. (RCMP, 2016c)

As you can see in Figure 2.4:

> The centre of the graphic depicts an officer. This officer uses the CAPRA problem solving model to assist in responding to an incident. The situational factors are a key element within the problem solving process. The situation is recognized as a constantly evolving event, represented by circular arrows, which requires continual risk assessment and evaluation by the

officer(s) involved . . . The area adjacent to the centre circle contains the various subject behaviour categories including cooperative, passive resistant, active resistant, assaultive, and grievous bodily harm or death. Perception and tactical considerations are interrelated and are therefore contained in the same ring . . . on the model . . . The outer ring of the graphic represents the officer's intervention options. These options range from officer presence to communication skills, physical control techniques, intermediate weapons, [and] lethal force . . . The outermost ring, tactical repositioning, represents the possibility that the officer may change or alter his or her position in an effort to gain a tactical advantage. This may occur at any point during the incident (RCMP, 2016c).

Even with this model, the decisions a police officer has to make when deciding whether to use force are not easy. For example, according to the RCMP (2016c), when assessing the unfolding situation, a police officer will have to consider, among many other factors, environmental conditions (lighting, location, hazards, etc.), subject characteristics (number, abilities, state of mind, etc.), and tactical issues (the number of subjects present, perceived subject abilities, threat cues, etc.). Based on an officer's continual assessment of the totality of the situation, the officer must develop a plan that involves selecting what he or she feels is an

(continued)

(continued)

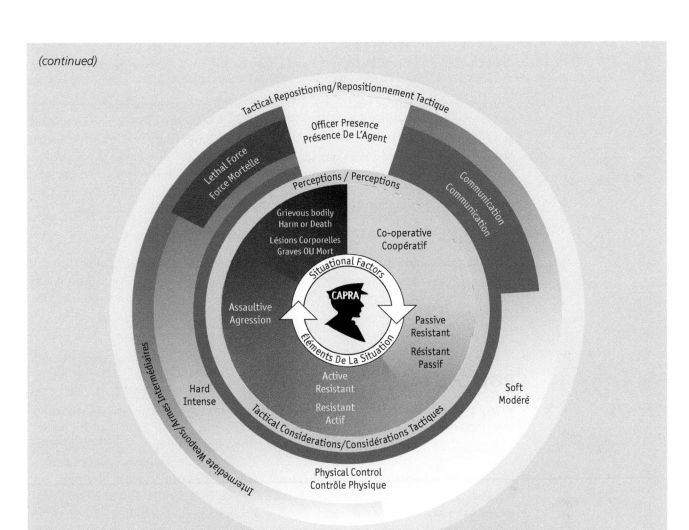

Figure 2.4 The RCMP's Incident Management/Intervention Model

Source: From Incident Management/Intervention Model. Copyright ©2009 by Royal Canadian Mounted Police. Used by permission of Royal Canadian Mounted Police.

appropriate response. As indicated in the diagram, there are five basic options. Officer presence is the least forceful option, followed by verbal and nonverbal communication, physical control, intermediate weapons, and, finally, use of lethal force. There is an approximate correspondence between the graphic's depiction of a subject's behaviour and the options available to the officer. For example, if a subject is being cooperative, effective communication may be sufficient to manage the situation. However, if the subject is exhibiting potentially lethal behaviour that can cause the officer grievous bodily harm, then it may be necessary for the police officer to use lethal force.

Source: From Incident Management/Intervention Model. Copyright © 2009 by Royal Canadian Mounted Police. Used by permission of Royal Canadian Mounted Police.

If you were a police officer, how would you make decisions in cases where use of force was involved? To experience some of the challenges you might face when making such decisions, see the You Be the Police Officer box.

YOU BE THE POLICE OFFICER

You are a police officer who has just received a call over your radio about a young man causing a disturbance on the side of the street. You arrive to see a man screaming at a large crowd that has gathered. He is waving what looks like a tree branch at them. He looks disheveled and is swearing. You approach him to de-escalate the situation. He starts swinging the branch at you and screams that he'll kill you if you come any closer. His words are slurred and you don't know if he's intoxicated, high on drugs, or mentally ill. You back off. He turns to the crowd again and starts yelling again.

Your Turn . . .

How do you handle this incident? What strategies would you use to de-escalate the situation? If the situation does not de-escalate and you decide to use force, how much force do you think is appropriate in this situation? What factors would you consider in making this decision?

POLICE STRESS

Many police psychologists, as well as police officers and their families, consider policing one of the most stressful occupations (Anshel, 2000). After our discussion of some of the dangerous situations police officers encounter, you will likely have come to a similar conclusion yourself. Even if this were debatable, we can all probably agree that police officers are exposed to many stressful events. Not only has research demonstrated that this is the case, it has also indicated that these stressful events can have a negative impact on police officers and their families, as well as the organizations they work for (Brown & Campbell, 1994). As discussed in Box 2.6, some of the most recent research to examine these issues has been conducted in Canada. In this section, we will discuss some of the sources of police stress and examine their potential consequences. In addition, we will briefly focus on what can be done to prevent and manage police stress.

Sources of Police Stress

As Finn and Tomz (1996) made clear, "different officers are likely to perceive different events as stressful, depending on their individual background, personalities, expectations, law enforcement experience, years on the job, type of law enforcement work they perform, and access to coping resources" (p. 6). However, research suggests that there are a number of common sources of police stress (Abdollahi, 2002). Although the labelling of these categories may differ depending on what article or book you read, the major sources of police stress tend to include organizational stressors (both within and between organizations), occupational stressors, criminal justice stressors, and public stressors. Finn and Tomz (1996) provided a list of specific stressors that fall into each of these categories, a partial listing of which is presented in Table 2.2.

Box 2.6   Forensic Psychology in the Spotlight

Work–Life Balance and Police Officer Well-Being in Canada

Although police stress research is not as common in Canada as it is in the United States, this is beginning to change. Interestingly, however, police psychologists are not taking the lead on this new research. Instead, two business professors are leading the charge, having now completed one of the largest studies of police stress in the world to date.

Linda Duxbury, a professor in the Sprott School of Business at Carleton University, and Christopher Higgins, a professor in the Richard Ivey School of Business at the University of Western Ontario, recently released their groundbreaking study entitled, *Caring For and About Those Who Serve: Work–Life Conflict and Employee Well-Being in Canada's Police Departments* (Duxbury & Higgins, 2012). Over 7000 officers and civilians from 25 Canadian police agencies responded to their survey.

In addition to the other sorts of police stressors that we focus on in this chapter (e.g., operational stressors, such as use-of-force encounters), the results reported by Duxbury and Higgins (2012) indicated that police officers in Canada often experience tremendous difficulty balancing their work and home life. This is not at all surprising when one considers some of the following findings from the report:

- 42% of the survey respondents work rotating shifts and 31% work four or more different shift patterns a month
- This can be difficult, especially considering that 85% of the respondents are married and 64% have two or more children
- On top of that, 33% of the respondents also have to care for three or more elderly dependents
- 78% of the respondents work more than 45 hours a week and 64% report that they can't get all their work done during regular works hours (and thus, they take their work home)
- 97% of the respondents spend time during the work day reading and responding to emails; however, 79% also do this on non-work days (on average an hour a day on days off)
- Given all these things, it shouldn't come as a surprise that a significant proportion of respondents (42%) report that their work seriously interferes with their family life

What impact do these things have on officers serving in our Canadian police agencies? Duxbury and Higgins's

(2012) study also speaks to these issues, and some of the results are alarming. Consider the following:

- 11% of respondents think of leaving their current police force several times a week or more
- Absenteeism from work is high, with two-thirds of the respondents indicating that they had missed a significant amount of work in the six months prior to the survey being conducted; reasons for missing work included health problems (51%), mental or emotional fatigue (28%), and issues with child care (27%)
- 22% of the respondents indicate that work–life challenges caused them to reduce work productivity in the 12 months prior to the survey being conducted
- One in five respondents report being in poor physical health, with 50% of the respondents reporting high levels of stress and 30% reporting high levels of depressed mood

Importantly, the study by Duxbury and Higgins (2012) also identified several things that can be done by police organizations to address these serious problems. Some of the recommendations included the following:

- The culture of policing needs to change so that work is not expected to take priority over family (e.g., the police culture needs to reflect the changing nature of Canadian society with respect to dual-career families and child/elder care responsibilities)
- Managers have to be supportive of their subordinates (e.g., they need to ask for more input before making decisions that affect the work of those who report to them)
- Police organizations need to commit to creating supportive managers and they need to provide managers with the necessary training and make available the tools that all good managers require
- Police organizations need to find a way to increase perceived flexibility on the part of their workers (i.e., the amount of control officers perceive they have over their work hours and work location)

Source: Based on Revisiting Work-Life Issues in Canada:The 2012 National Study on Balancing Work and Caregiving in Canada by Linda Duxbury, Christopher Higgins. © 2012.

Table 2.2 Sources of Police Stress

1. **Intra-organizational Stressors**
   - *Excessive paperwork.* The need for duplicate forms of every police transaction is often questioned.

2. **Inter-organizational Stress**
   - *Jurisdictional isolationism.* There is often an unfortunate lack of cooperation between neighbouring jurisdictions; sometimes an unhealthy competitive relationship exists.

3. **Occupational Stressors**
   - *Human suffering.* Officers are constantly exposed to the inequities and brutalities of life.

4. **Criminal Justice System Stressors**
   - *Unfavourable court decisions.* Many court decisions are viewed by officers as unfairly increasing the difficulty of police work.

5. **Public Stressors**
   - *Distorted press accounts.* Reports of incidents are often inaccurate and perceived as derogatory by officers, whether or not the inaccuracy is intentional.

Source: Based on Finn, P. & Tomz, J. E. (1996). *Developing a law enforcement stress program for officers and their families.* Washington, DC: National Institute of Justice, U.S. Department of Justice.

Although occupational stressors, such as making arrests, can cause a great deal of stress for many police officers, organizational stressors, such as perceptions of inadequate departmental support, can also result in harmful levels of stress.
Racheldonahue_82/Fotolia

Table 2.3 The Ten Highest-Ranked Police Stressors Among Ontario
Police Officers

The feeling that different rules apply to different people (4.78)*

Fatigue (4.47)

Feeling like you always have to prove yourself to the organization (4.41)

Inconsistent leadership style (4.36)

Dealing with the court system (4.17)

Bureaucratic red tape (4.14)

Not enough time available to spend with friends and family (4.09)

Shift work (4.04)

Finding time to stay in good physical condition (3.98)

Perceived pressure to volunteer free time (3.91)

* Numbers in parentheses are means out of 7.

Source: Based on Finn, P. & Tomz, J. E. (1996). Developing a law enforcement stress program for officers and their families. Washington, DC: National Institute of Justice, U.S. Department of Justice.

Although the majority of people assume that **occupational stressors** are the most stressful for police officers, officers indicate that they experience a degree of stress for each of the stressors described in Table 2.2. In fact, many police researchers believe they have evidence to show that **organizational stressors** more strongly affect officers than occupational stressors, especially intra-organizational stressors (Finn & Tomz, 1996). Such claims are backed up by anecdotal evidence. For example, as reported by Finn and Tomz, a wife of an officer who ended up resigning because of stress commented, "My husband came home more screwed up with department problems than with anything he ever encountered on the streets" (p. 7).

The stress associated with organizational issues is also revealed in surveys of officers. For example, Taylor and Bennell (2006) asked 154 officers in an Ontario police agency to fill out the Operational Police Stress Questionnaire and the Organizational Police Stress Questionnaire, both of which were developed by McCreary and Thompson (2006). More specifically, police officers were asked to rank 40 stressors from 1 to 7, with a score of 1 indicating that the event caused them no stress at all in the previous six months and a score of 7 indicating that the event caused them a lot of stress in the previous six months. For illustrative purposes, the ten highest-ranked stressors are provided in Table 2.3. As you can see, many of the stressors ranked highest are organizational stressors (e.g., the feeling that different rules apply to different people), although a number of occupational stressors (e.g., fatigue) also ranked very high.

Occupational stressors: In policing, stressors relating to the job itself

Organizational stressors: In policing, stressors relating to organizational issues

Consequences of Police Stress

When a police officer experiences a potentially life-threatening situation, the acute stress reactions that the officer experiences can have serious repercussions that last long after the actual event. Likewise, constant exposure to other police stressors, particularly organizational stressors, can affect police officers on a more chronic basis.

Without an effective prevention or management strategy (at both the individual and the organizational level) to deal with police stressors, police officers, their families, and the organizations they work for will suffer in numerous ways. Brown and Campbell (1994) categorized the general consequences of police stress into physical health problems, psychological and personal problems, and job performance problems.

Physical Health Problems One of the major consequences of police stress is the impact it can have on an officer's physical health. As McCraty, Tomasino, Atkinson, and Sundram (1999) explained, constant exposure to stressful events can result in the chronic activation of the body's stress response systems to a point where physiological breakdown occurs. The result of such a breakdown can take many different forms. For example, Kroes, Margolis, and Hurrell (1974) reported that more than 32% of the police officers they examined experienced digestive disorders, which was significantly higher than the prevalence rate in the civilian population. In a large-scale study of 2376 police officers, Violanti, Vena, and Marshall (1986) found that rates of death due to cancer were significantly higher among police officers than among the general population. Franke, Collins, and Hinz (1998) found that police officers are more than twice as likely as people in other occupations to develop cardiovascular disease, which is consistent with more recent research (e.g., Ramey, Downing, & Franke, 2009). In a study that examined 452 Detroit police retirees and 6873 Detroit city employees who had all retired, Brandl and Smith (2012) showed "that retired officers die significantly younger than other retired city employees and that officers have significantly shorter retirements prior to death than other city employees" (p. 113). Other physical health problems that have been studied include high blood pressure, high cholesterol, stomach ulcers, respiratory problems, weight gain, and diabetes. Unfortunately, the limited amount of research in the area makes it difficult to determine how many of these health problems are due to the stressful events that police officers are exposed to and how many of them are due to the lifestyle habits adopted by police officers (e.g., poor diet, alcohol consumption, etc.; Abdollahi, 2002; Fiedler, 2011). In addition, not all studies in this area have found convincing support for the findings cited above (e.g., Finkelstein, 1998; Franke, Ramey, & Shelley, 2002).

Psychological and Personal Problems Psychological and personal problems, including depression, post-traumatic stress disorder (PTSD), drug and alcohol abuse, marital problems, and suicide, can also emerge when police officers are exposed to stressful situations. However, as in the case of physical health problems, the research in this area can often be contradictory and caution must be used when interpreting the results of any single study. For example, although numerous studies have suggested that alcohol use may be particularly problematic among police officers (e.g., Violanti, Marshall, & Howe, 1985), Alexander, Innes, Irving, Sinclair, and Walker (1991) found that alcohol consumption by police officers was not statistically greater than consumption rates found for firefighters, prison officers, or nurses. Similarly, although some researchers have found indications of burnout among police officers (e.g., Anson & Bloom, 1988), other researchers have failed to find significant levels of burnout, especially among Canadian police managers (Loo, 1994). While some studies suggest that exposure to the sorts of stressors that officers encounter can lead to serious mental health problems like depression (Hartley, Violanti, Fekedulegn, Andrew, & Burchfiel, 2007), other research fails to find elevated levels of these problems in police officers compared to employees in low-risk occupations (e.g., banks, supermarkets; van der Velden, Rademaker, Vermetten, Portengen, Yzermans, & Grievink, 2013). Police-related suicide rates and divorce rates have also recently been examined. Here, as well, there are many contradictory findings. For example, in contrast to popular belief, studies of suicide in North American police agencies demonstrate that the rates are not significantly different from the suicide rates found in comparable male populations (Aamodt & Stalnaker, 2006). Likewise, despite the view voiced by some that the divorce rate is high in the police population (Territo & Sewell, 2007), recent research suggests that the divorce rate for law enforcement personnel in the United States is actually lower than that of the general population, even when controlling for demographic and various job-related variables (McCoy & Aamodt, 2010). These, and other myths associated with the field of police psychology are discussed in Box 2.7.

Job Performance Problems   Job performance problems are the third major category of stress consequences. Often as a direct result of the physical and psychological problems discussed above, the way a police officer performs on the job can suffer

Box 2.7   Myths and Realities

Myths Associated with Police Psychology

Myth 1. We can predict which applicant will become a successful police officer with a high degree of accuracy.
Fact. Meta-analyses that have examined the predictive validity of police selection tools actually suggest that it is very difficult to make selection decisions with a high degree of accuracy. Some tools, such as clinical interviews, are often very poor predictors of future on-the-job-performance. Not only is it difficult to adequately assess relevant KSAs, many things happen in an individual's life (post-hire) that will impact their performance as a police officer, and these things often can't be predicted at the time an individual is applying to become a police officer.

Myth 2. Police officers are required to enforce every law on the books.
Fact. Police officers often have a great deal of discretion when it comes to enforcing the law. In certain circumstances (e.g., when dealing with young offenders) officers are actually encouraged to use their discretion when a crime has been committed, and they will often handle the situation informally (e.g., by issuing a warning).

Myth 3. Police officers are much more likely than the general public to get divorced and commit suicide.
Fact. Although some research does support this view, high quality studies that compare police officers to relevant comparison samples do not support these statements. This research suggests that the divorce rate for law enforcement personnel in the U.S. is actually lower than the general population, and the suicide rate is no different from rates of suicide found for comparable males.

Myth 4. The effort that has been put into dealing with police stress in Canada has allowed police agencies to get the problem under control.
Fact. Many useful initiatives have been put in place in Canada to help prevent and manage police stress, and it appears that some of these initiatives are having a positive impact. However, many prevention and management initiatives have not yet been evaluated to determine the impact they are having on police stress, and police stress is still a serious problem in Canadian policing. Relatively high rates of stress continue to be reported by police officers.

greatly. As with other stress reactions, impaired job performance can take many forms, including a decrease in work efficiency and productivity, increased absenteeism and tardiness, and early retirement. Although these consequences may not seem as serious as the physical and psychological problems caused by police stress, from an organizational perspective they certainly are. For example, according to one recent news report from England, police officers around the UK are taking more and more sick days each year (250 000 days in the year preceding the publication of the article), with many arguing that this is due largely to stress (e.g., fewer officers doing the same amount of work; Baggot, 2014). While we do a poor job of tracking such information in this country, based on the research conducted by Duxbury and Higgins (2012), which was discussed above, we suspect that a very similar situation exists in Canada.

Preventing and Managing Police Stress

Most police officers and police agencies have now recognized the need to prevent and manage negative reactions to stressful events. Indeed, during the past 20 years, formal stress programs have been set up in most agencies to combat the effects of police stress. A variety of strategies are included in these programs, including informal support networks, physical fitness programs, professional counselling services, family assistance programs, and special assessments following exposure to critical events such as shootings or accidents (Brown & Campbell, 1994). A thorough discussion of each of these strategies is beyond the scope of this chapter. Here, we will simply focus on two particular strategies—one preventive strategy and one management strategy.

Resiliency training: Training delivered to police officers to improve their ability to effectively adapt to stress and adversity

Resiliency Training **Resiliency training** is one strategy that can be used to proactively minimize some of the harmful effects of police work. The goal of resiliency training is to allow police officers to "thrive in the face of adversity and to recover after exposure to extreme stress and trauma" (Andersen, Papazoglou, Nyman, Koskelainen, & Gustafsberg, 2015, p. 4). A key focus of resiliency training in the policing domain is facilitating mental preparedness. This is usually done through "psycho-education about the psychological and physiological aspects of extreme stress and potential trauma" and "techniques that allow officers to apply [and practice resilience] these techniques in their critical incident training and the real world . . . [so that] they become automatic physical and mental responses" (Andersen et al., 2015, p. 4). Although evaluative research is somewhat limited in this area (Andersen et al., 2015), a small number of studies have shown that evidence-based resiliency training can improve performance in job-related tasks and the health and general well-being of officers.

For example, Arnetz and his colleagues (Arnetz, Arble, Backman, Lynch, & Lublin, 2013; Arnetz, Nevedal, Lumley, Backman, & Lublin, 2009) tested the effectiveness of a resiliency training program that combined a relaxation exercise with mental skills rehearsal. Participants in both studies were Swedish police recruits. The recruits were presented with descriptions of stressful critical incident scenarios (e.g., a domestic violence incident) while applying relaxation techniques and visualizing themselves resolving the incident effectively. In both studies, training resulted in improved job performance in critical incident simulations and improved stress reactions, relative to the control group. Similar results have been reported in other recent studies (e.g., McCraty & Atkinson, 2012; Page, Asken, Zwemer, & Guido, 2015).

Psychological Debriefings   One of the most commonly used methods for managing police stress is the **psychological debriefing** (e.g., Mitchell, 1983), which often consists of a brief psychologically oriented intervention delivered to officers following exposure to an event that has resulted in psychological distress. Typically forming one part of a larger crisis intervention program, psychological debriefings revolve around a group or individual meeting aimed at mitigating emotional distress and preventing long-term psychopathology. Its key elements frequently involve social support and the ventilation of emotions through discussion, while facilitators educate participants about stress responses and coping mechanisms in an attempt to restore adaptive functioning (Everly, Flannery, & Mitchell, 2000; Raphael & Wilson, 2000).

Psychological debriefing: A psychologically oriented intervention delivered to police officers following exposure to an event that resulted in psychological distress and an impairment of normal functioning

Although numerous studies have examined the effectiveness of psychological debriefings, confusion still remains as to whether this stress management strategy actually works. For example, early meta-analytic research suggested that Mitchell's group-based Critical Incident Stress Debriefing (Mitchell, 1983) was effective (Everly & Boyle, 1999). A subsequent meta-analysis by Everly, Boyle, and Lating (1999), which examined a wider array of debriefing procedures, reported similar (although slightly more modest) results. However, two more recent meta-analytic studies concluded that psychological debriefings have only a small effect on reducing symptoms of PTSD (van Emmerik, Kamphuis, Hulsbosch, & Emmelkamp, 2002) or no effect at all (Mitte, Steil, & Nachtigall, 2005).

To some extent, these contrasting results can likely be attributed to the various forms of psychological debriefings that have been examined in these studies. For example, some of the debriefings were presented in a single session, whereas others took place over multiple sessions. The types of incidents encountered by the people being debriefed also varied from study to study, ranging from natural disasters to victims of crime. Furthermore, the person facilitating the debriefing is not constant across studies, and includes both peers (e.g., fellow police officers) and mental health professionals. Whether these (and other) factors are important is a hotly debated topic, and more research is clearly needed before we can determine conclusively whether psychological debriefings are an effective stress management tool (and how they should be delivered).

SUMMARY

1. The development of a useful police selection process requires two major steps: (1) an analysis of the knowledge, skills, and abilities that are required for the job, and (2) the construction and validation of selection instruments that measure these qualities and compare them with job performance.

2. Some of the most common police selection procedures are semi-structured interviews, psychological tests, and the use of assessment centres.

3. Police discretion refers to the power that police officers have to decide which laws apply to a given situation and whether to apply them. Many view police discretion as an inevitable part of police work, and, so long as it is used in an unbiased manner, police discretion can be very useful.

4. Nearly every decision that a police officer makes requires some degree of discretion. However, four of the most commonly studied areas of police discretion deal with youth crime, domestic violence, individuals with a mental illness, and use-of-force situations. A major effort has been made in Canada to develop policies to guide police decision making in each of these areas. One example is the RCMP's Incident Management/Intervention Model that provides guidelines to police officers with regard to what level of force is reasonable under various circumstances.

5. Policing is considered by many to be one of the most stressful occupations. Sources of stress include organizational stressors, occupational stressors, criminal justice stressors, and public stressors. These stressors can lead to serious physical health problems, psychological and personal problems, and job performance problems, if they are not dealt with appropriately.

6. To combat the negative effects of stress, police forces are developing and using a variety of prevention and management strategies. One prevention strategy that looks particularly promising involves teaching police officers how to use adaptive coping skills when faced with stressful events. A common management strategy is the use of psychological debriefings. Currently, there is disagreement as to whether this strategy is effective at reducing stress symptoms.

Discussion Questions

1. You are a member of a community group that has been put together to provide your local police agency with recommendations regarding police selection criteria. What do you, as a community citizen, feel are the most important characteristics of a good police officer? Do you think these characteristics should be considered when police forces select police officers? Why or why not?

2. Imagine you are a police officer who encounters a well-dressed woman walking down the street who is obviously intoxicated. She is yelling at bystanders that they should mind their own business if they don't want to die. What would you do? Would you arrest her and take her to jail, or would you drive her home? What factors would you consider when making your decision? Would your decision have been different if you had encountered an older man who was dressed in dirty and ripped clothes? Why or why not?

Chapter 3
The Psychology of Police Investigations

Learning Objectives

- Describe the Reid model of interrogation.

- Outline three potential problems with the Reid model of interrogation.

- Differentiate among false, retracted, and disputed confessions.

- Define the three major types of false confessions.

- Explain why police use criminal profiling and outline potential problems with its use.

- Explain what geographic profiling is and how it can be used in police investigations.

Mike Jackson was arrested for a late night robbery committed in a park near his residence. After his arrest, at approximately 11 p.m., he was taken to the police station for questioning. Two investigators interrogated Mike. At various points throughout his interrogation Mike declared his innocence, stating that he had never even met the person the officers say he robbed. Throughout the interrogation, the officers attempted to point out inconsistencies in Mike's story and repeatedly told Mike they didn't believe him—they knew he was involved in the robbery, so he should just "come clean" and "save everyone the pain of a long interrogation." All Mike had to do was confess, they said, and "all of this would end." Mike maintained his innocence and the interrogators left. Four hours later they returned. This time the interrogators said they had evidence of Mike's involvement in the crime, including several eyewitnesses who saw him in the park at the time of the robbery. In reality, none of the eyewitnesses existed. Throughout the second interrogation, the interrogators downplayed the seriousness of the crime. "The victim had it coming" the interrogators said; after all, "the guy was out late at night, in a secluded park, with over $500 in his wallet." They suggested the victim was probably a drug dealer and that Mike "did everyone a favour by teaching the guy a good lesson." Feeling anxious, tired, and desperate, Mike confessed after two more hours of questioning. In his mind it was clear he was never going to convince the investigators of his innocence. He just wanted to go back to his cell and sleep. Two days later, before Mike was to appear in court, the police discovered that he hadn't committed the robbery. Mike had given a false confession. The police found out that the victim of the robbery was in fact a drug dealer, but he was robbed by one of his regular customers who was desperate for money.

As seen in Chapter 2, forensic psychology plays an important role in many aspects of police work. One element we have yet to discuss is psychology's role in criminal investigations, such as the Mike Jackson investigation described above. Many people are aware that psychology is used during investigations, and recent movies and television shows have done much to promote this fact. However, as you will see throughout this chapter, psychology played an important role in the investigative process long before Hollywood became interested in the topic, and it continues to do so today.

Psychologists have identified a number of key investigative tasks where psychology is particularly relevant. One of these tasks relates to the collection and evaluation of investigative information—information that is often obtained from suspects through police interrogations. Another task relates to investigative decision making, especially decisions that require an in-depth understanding of criminal behaviour. This chapter will focus on how psychology contributes to these tasks by looking first at how the police interrogate suspects and some possible consequences of their interrogation practices, and then examining the practice of profiling the characteristics of criminals based on the way they commit their crimes.

POLICE INTERROGATIONS

Confession evidence is often viewed as a prosecutor's "most potent weapon" (Kassin & Gudjonsson, 2004, p. 35), and police officers will often go to great lengths to secure such evidence. In some countries, people may be convicted solely on the basis of their confession, although in North America a confession usually has to be backed up by some other form of evidence (Gudjonsson, 2003). Regardless of whether corroborative evidence is required, people who confess to a crime are more likely to be prosecuted and convicted than those who do not. Indeed, some legal scholars have gone so far as to claim that a confession makes other aspects of a trial unnecessary, because "the real trial, for all practical purposes, occurs when the confession is obtained" (McCormick, 1972, p. 316). Given the importance of confession evidence, it should come as no surprise that one of the main goals of a **police interrogation** is to obtain a confession of guilt from the suspect (Kassin, 1997).

Police interrogation: A process whereby the police interview a suspect for the purpose of gathering evidence and obtaining a confession

In the past, physically coercive tactics were often used to extract confessions from suspects. In the mid-twentieth century, for example, whipping was occasionally used to obtain confessions (e.g., *Brown v. Mississippi*, 1936). In a more recent example, a wide range of torture tactics were used by Chicago police officers throughout the 1970s and 80s to interrogate suspects, which has since resulted in the City of Chicago paying out millions of dollars in settlements (Taylor, 2013).

Although these overt acts of physical coercion have become less frequent with time, some people have argued that these tactics have been replaced with more subtle, psychologically based interrogation techniques, such as lying about evidence, promising lenient treatment, and implying threats to loved ones (Leo, 1992). While not all interrogators use these strategies, police officers sometimes view these techniques as a necessary evil to obtain confessions from guilty persons who are unlikely to cooperate with the police. Indeed, leading authorities in the field of interrogation training openly state that, because offenders are typically reluctant to confess, psychological coercion must often be used to secure confessions. For example, while condemning physically coercive interrogations, Inbau, Reid, Buckley, and Jayne (2013) state:

> We do approve...of psychological tactics and techniques that may involve deception; they are not only helpful but frequently indispensable in order to secure incriminating information from the guilty or to obtain investigative leads from otherwise uncooperative witnesses and informants. (p. xi)

See Box 3.1 for an example of how far Canadian police agencies will sometimes go in order to secure confessions from suspects.

Box 3.1   Forensic Psychology in the Spotlight

The Mr. Big Technique

Relatively recently it has become clear that some Canadian police forces will go to great lengths to secure a confession from suspects. In addition to the Reid model of interrogation, which is discussed in this chapter, another procedure that is sometimes used is the Mr. Big technique (Luther & Snook, 2016; Smith, Stinson, & Patry, 2009, 2010). Unlike the Reid model, the Mr. Big technique is a noncustodial procedure in that it happens outside of the interrogation room.

According to Smith et al. (2009), the procedure generally involves undercover police officers posing as members of a criminal organization who attempt to lure the suspect into the gang (e.g., by showing the suspect how lucrative gang involvement can be). Often the suspect is made to commit some minor crimes for which he may be rewarded, and once committed to the organization, the suspect is "interviewed" for a higher-level job. However, before the suspect can seal the deal with the boss, Mr. Big, he must confess to a serious crime (the one under investigation). Smith et al. (2009) found that one of several reasons is usually given to the suspect for why he needs to confess: "as a form of 'insurance' for the criminal gang, so they have something 'on' the suspect if he ever turns against them; so that Mr. Big can draw on his purported influence and connections to make the evidence or 'problem' disappear; or both" (p. 170). Once the confession is elicited, it is used against the suspect in his trial.

Although perhaps not used as frequently as other interrogation techniques, the Mr. Big technique does appear to be used quite often. For example, Smith et al. (2009) presented evidence that prior to 2004, the technique had been used at least 350 times in Canada. The technique also seems to be very effective, resulting in a 75% success rate and a 95% conviction rate (according to police statistics).

The use of the Mr. Big technique raises some interesting ethical and legal questions. For example, does this technique boil down to entrapment, where a person is induced to commit an illegal act he otherwise would not commit? And even if the Mr. Big technique doesn't constitute entrapment, are confessions that are extracted through the Mr. Big technique given voluntarily or are the confessions coerced, and thus potentially unreliable?

According to Smith et al.'s (2009) review of case law (e.g., *R. v. Mack*, 1988; *R. v. Mentuck*, 2001) the Mr. Big technique has historically been permitted by Canadian courts. For example, with respect to entrapment, Canadian courts have ruled that, "Because the Mr. Big operation is designed to elicit... a confession regarding an event that occurred before the operation started and not for criminal activity during the undercover operation, this type of sting operation falls outside of the Canadian definition of entrapment" (Smith et al., 2009, p. 179). And on the issue of coercion, once again Canadian courts have generally approved of the Mr. Big technique, stating that it is "a reasonable use of police trickery that would not bring the administration of justice into disrepute" (pp. 179–180).

Despite these previous rulings by Canadian courts, a recent ruling by the Supreme Court of Canada has taken a more critical approach, which will likely tighten the parameters of future Mr. Big operations (without forbidding their

(continued)

(continued)

use altogether). As Luther and Snook (2016) report, in *R. v. Hart* (2014) the Supreme Court has ruled that the burden of proof is on Crown prosecutors to show that the probative value of Mr. Big confessions outweighs their prejudicial effect; essentially, this means that "the risk of prejudice should only be ignored [by triers of fact] if the confession is deemed to have high probative value (i.e., the confirmatory evidence accompanying the confession outweighs the circumstances under which the confession was extracted)" (p. 7). The Supreme Court also ruled that "any action that causes a confession to be coerced from a suspect [e.g., through the use of violence, threats of violence, or preying on vulnerabilities] may be deemed unacceptable" (p. 7).

While the impact of this ruling is still unclear, it is likely that the ruling will limit the admissibility of confessions in Canadian courts when those confessions have been provided to Mr. Big.

The Reid Model of Interrogation

Police officers often receive specialized training in how to interrogate suspects. Depending on where this training is provided, different approaches are taught. For example, as discussed later in this chapter, police officers in England and Wales are trained to use interrogation techniques that are far less coercive than those used in North America (Kassin & Gudjonsson, 2004; Sear & Williamson, 1999; Snook, Eastwood, Stinson, Tedeschini, & House, 2010). These techniques are used primarily because courts in England and Wales have begun to recognize some of the potential problems associated with coercive interrogation practices, such as false confessions (Meissner & Russano, 2003). Before moving on to discuss these potential problems, let us look closely at the type of interrogation training provided to many police officers in North America.

One of the interrogation training programs offered to many North American police officers is based on a book written by Inbau et al. (2013) called *Criminal Interrogation and Confessions*. Within this manual, the authors described the well-known **Reid model** of interrogation, a technique originally developed by John E. Reid, a polygrapher from Chicago.

Reid model: A nine-step model of interrogation used frequently in North America to extract confessions from suspects

Although the Reid model of interrogation can take different forms, it generally consists of a three-part process. The first stage of the process is to gather evidence related to the crime and to interview witnesses and victims. The second stage is to conduct a non-accusatorial interview of the suspect to assess any evidence of deception (i.e., to determine whether the suspect is lying when he or she claims to be innocent). The third stage, which is the crux of the Reid technique, is to conduct an accusatorial interrogation of the suspect if he or she is perceived to be guilty. At this stage, a nine-step procedure is implemented, with the primary objective being to secure a confession from the suspect (Inbau et al., 2013).

This nine-step procedure in stage three generally consists of the following steps:

A police officer interrogating a suspect
Fisun Ivan/Shutterstock

1. The suspect is immediately confronted with his or her guilt. If the police do not have any evidence against the suspect at

this time, the interrogator can hide this fact and, if necessary, imply that such evidence exists.

2. Psychological themes are then developed that allow the suspect to rationalize or excuse the crime. For example, a murderer may be told that the interrogators understand why he committed the crime and that the crime was even justified (e.g., given that the victim was a known criminal "who had it coming").

3. The interrogator interrupts any statements of denial by the suspect to ensure the suspect does not get the upper hand in the interrogation.

4. The interrogator overcomes the suspect's objections to the charges.

5. If the suspect becomes withdrawn, the interrogator ensures that he or she has the suspect's attention and that the suspect does not tune out of the interrogation. A range of techniques can be used for this purpose, such as reducing the psychological distance between the interrogator and the suspect (e.g., by physically moving closer to the suspect).

6. The interrogator exhibits sympathy and understanding, and the suspect is urged to come clean (e.g., by appealing to the suspect's sense of decency).

7. The suspect is offered explanations for the crime, which makes self-incrimination easier to achieve. For example, rather than the suspect being involved in an intentional homicide, which would carry a very severe penalty, the interrogator may suggest to a murder suspect that the crime he or she committed was accidental (e.g., the result of an argument that simply went wrong).

8. Once the suspect accepts responsibility for the crime, typically by agreeing with one of the alternative explanations, the interrogator develops this admission into a full confession for the crime in question.

9. Finally, the interrogator gets the suspect to write and sign a full confession.

In addition to the techniques included in these nine steps, Inbau et al. (2013) provide many other suggestions for how to effectively interrogate suspects. These suggestions include things such as using a plainly decorated interrogation room to avoid distractions, having the evidence folder in your hand when beginning the interrogation, and making sure that the suspect is alone in the interrogation suite prior to the interrogator entering the room.

The Reid model of interrogation is based on the idea that "people make choices that they think will maximize their well-being given the constraints they face" (Kassin, 2015, p. 33). It is assumed during the accusatory phase of the interrogation that the suspect's fear of confessing outweighs their anxiety caused by remaining deceptive (about their involvement in the crime). The Reid model relies on psychologically based tactics that attempt to reverse this so that the consequences of confessing become more desirable than the anxiety related to the deception (Gudjonsson, 2003). For example, providing the suspect with a way to rationalize his or her behaviour (e.g., "the crime was just an accident") may reduce the perceived consequences of confessing and appealing to one's sense of morality (e.g., "taking responsibility for this is the right thing to do, for you and your family") can potentially increase the anxiety associated with deception.

These sorts of interrogation techniques can be broken down into two general categories (Kassin, 2014). These categories are often referred to by different names, but throughout this chapter, the labels *minimization* and *maximization* will be used. **Minimization techniques** refer to "soft sell" tactics used by police interrogators "to provide the weakening suspect with moral justification and face-saving excuses for the crime in question" (Kassin, 2014, p. 114). For example, when the interrogator in the opening scenario suggested to Mike Jackson that the victim "had it coming" because he was probably a drug dealer, and that Mike "did everyone a favour" by robbing the victim, that interrogator was using minimization techniques. In contrast to minimization techniques, **maximization techniques** refer to "scare tactics" that "convey the interrogator's certain belief that the suspect is guilty and that denials will fail" (Kassin, 2014, p. 114). According to Kassin (2014), these techniques can include "making an accusation, interrupting denials, overriding objections, and citing evidence, real or manufactured, to shift the suspect's mental state from confident to hopeless" (p. 114). Pointing out inconsistencies in Mike Jackson's story, repeatedly telling him that they don't believe him, and referring to nonexistent eyewitnesses could all be considered maximization tactics used by the interrogators in the opening scenario.

The Use of the Reid Model in Actual Interrogations

Simply because the Reid model of interrogation is commonly taught to police officers in North America does not necessarily mean that police officers actually rely on the model in practice. It is difficult to say with any degree of confidence how often police officers in North America use Reid interrogation techniques, but studies are beginning to shed some light on this issue.

For example, Kassin et al. (2007) conducted a survey of 631 police investigators about their interrogation practices. They had the officers rate how often they used different types of interrogation techniques. The results of the survey indicated that many of the techniques included in the Reid model of interrogation were used in actual police interrogations, although the frequency of use varied across techniques. For instance, interrogators almost always used techniques such as isolating suspects from friends and family and trying to establish rapport with suspects to gain their trust. Other common but less frequently used techniques included confronting suspects with their guilt and appealing to their self-interest. Less common still, but sometimes used, were techniques such as providing justifications for the crime and implying or pretending to have evidence. Very rare were instances of threatening the suspect with consequences for not cooperating and physically intimidating the suspect.

Given that Kassin et al.'s (2007) results were based on interrogators' self-reported behaviour, there is, of course, the chance that their responses were biased. Building on research by Leo (1996), King and Snook (2009) recently conducted a more objective analysis of police interrogations. They obtained 44 videotaped interrogations conducted by Canadian police officers and coded the various techniques the interrogators used. Their results, which are partially illustrated in Figure 3.1, provide the first glimpse into what goes on in Canadian interrogation rooms.

Minimization techniques:
Soft sell tactics used by police interrogators that are designed to lull the suspect into a false sense of security

Maximization techniques:
Scare tactics used by police interrogators that are designed to intimidate a suspect believed to be guilty

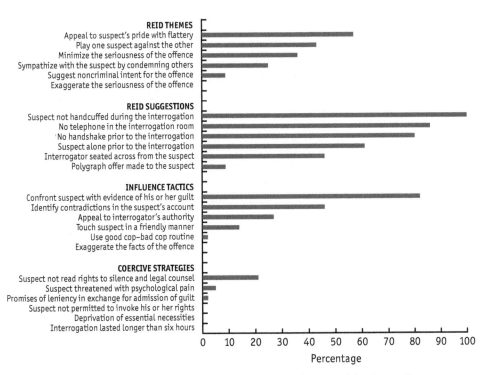

Figure 3.1 The Percentage of Interrogation Tactics Used in Canadian Interrogations (N = 44)

Source: Based on King and Snook, 2009, Tables 2-5.

Like Kassin et al.'s (2007) survey, the results indicate that the sampled interrogators did not always adhere to the core components of the Reid model of interrogation. Although some of the guidelines suggested by Inbau et al. (2013) were regularly observed, few coercive strategies were observed in the interrogations (although any evidence of coercion may be cause for concern). Interestingly, the number of Reid techniques used by the interrogators in this study did relate to interrogation outcomes, with more confessions being extracted when interrogations contained a greater proportion of Reid techniques. However, as King and Snook (2009) stated, this result does not necessarily prove the effectiveness of the Reid model, since there are many possible explanations for this finding (e.g., an interrogator could expend more effort when there is clearer evidence of a suspect's guilt and the number of interrogation techniques they use could reflect this effort).

Potential Problems with the Reid Model of Interrogation

Because many police officers appear to be trained to use the Reid model of interrogation, especially in North America, it has been the subject of much research. This research indicates that the technique is associated with a number of potential problems. Three problems in particular deserve our attention. The first two relate to the ability of investigators to detect deception (Memon, Vrij, & Bull, 2003) and to the biases that may result when an interrogator believes, perhaps incorrectly, that a suspect is guilty (Kassin, Goldstein, & Savitsky, 2003). The third problem has to do with the coercive and/or suggestive nature of certain interrogation practices and the possibility that these practices will result in various types of false confessions (Kassin, 2014). We will briefly discuss the first two problems here and reserve our discussion of false confessions for the next section of this chapter.

Deception detection: Detecting when someone is being deceptive

Detecting Deception   A more thorough discussion of **deception detection** will be provided in Chapter 4, so our discussion here will be limited to how deception detection relates to police interrogations. The issue of whether investigators are effective deception detectors is an important one, especially when using the Reid model of interrogation, because the actual interrogation of a suspect (stage three) begins only after an initial interview (stage two) has allowed the interrogator to determine whether the suspect is guilty (Inbau et al., 2013). The decision to commence a full-blown police interrogation, therefore, relies on an accurate assessment of whether the suspect is being deceptive when he or she claims to be innocent.

Despite Inbau et al.'s (2013) claim that training in the Reid model of interrogation provides police officers with the means to accurately detect deception, as you will see in Chapter 4, there is currently very little research to support the view that police officers, or anyone else for that matter, can detect deception with any degree of accuracy (Vrij, 2008). This finding often appears to be true even after people receive specialized training (Frank & Feeley, 2003), although there are some recent exceptions to this in Canada, where certain training programs appear to show some promise for improving lie detection accuracy (Porter, Juodis, ten Brinke, Klein, & Wilson, 2010; Porter, Woodworth, & Birt, 2000). Much of the deception detection training currently being offered, including Reid interrogation training, focuses on informing people about objective (i.e., empirically validated) cues to deception. However, recent meta-analyses suggest that this training approach will have limited utility because lie-catchers already tend to focus on these objective cues and the cues are simply too weak to be of any value when trying to distinguish between truth-tellers and liars (Hartwig & Bond, 2011). A more promising approach might be to teach people how to increase the behavioural differences between truth-tellers and liars so that deception cues become more pronounced (e.g., Levine, Shaw, & Shulman, 2010). Unfortunately, until such time as training exists that can significantly improve the accuracy of lie catchers, it is likely that the decision to interrogate a suspect when using the Reid model of interrogation could be based on an incorrect determination that the suspect is guilty (Kassin, 2015).

In addition to the myth of accurate lie detection, many other myths exist about police interrogations. Some of these are discussed in Box 3.2.

Of course, procedural safeguards are in place to protect an individual during the transition to the interrogation phase of the Reid model (Kassin & Gudjonsson, 2004). Most notable in the United States are an individual's *Miranda* rights (*Miranda v. Arizona*, 1966). In Canada, the rights of suspects are included in the Charter of Rights and Freedoms, and include the rights to silence and legal counsel (King & Snook, 2009). In both countries, it is only when suspects knowingly and voluntarily waive these rights that their statements can be used as evidence against them

Box 3.2   Myths and Realities

Myths About Police Interrogations

Myth 1. Police officers often use the sorts of physically coercive interrogation tactics that you see in good detective shows on TV.
Fact. While police officers have used physically coercive interrogation tactics to extract confessions from suspects, the use of these tactics is relatively rare in North America today.

Myth 2. By law, police officers aren't allowed to use trickery in their interrogations for the purpose of extracting a confession.
Fact. In Canada, police officers are in fact allowed to use psychologically based interrogation tactics, including a degree of trickery, to secure confessions from suspects (e.g., exaggerating evidence). Like research related to physically coercive tactics, research has shown that the use of psychologically coercive tactics can have negative consequences (e.g., encouraging false confessions).

Myth 3. There is no need for people to worry about being interrogated by the police; individuals in Canada must be read their legal rights and this provides all the protection they need.
Fact. In North America, there are indeed procedural safeguards in place to protect individuals during their interactions with the police. In Canada, these rights include the right to silence and the right to legal counsel. However, research has clearly and consistently shown that people don't often understand these rights and thus, they often cannot make an informed decision about whether they should waive their rights.

Myth 4. If someone confesses to a crime, that indicates that the person did in fact commit the crime.
Fact. Most confessions are valid and do indicate that the confessor committed the crime in question. However, false confessions do occur for a variety of reasons, some related to the interrogation tactics used by the police. Some research has suggested that false confessions account for up to 30% of wrongful conviction cases.

(Kassin & Gudjonsson, 2004; King & Snook, 2009). Research, however, has demonstrated that *Miranda*-type rights may not provide the protection that they are assumed to provide.

One significant problem is that many individuals do not understand their rights when they are presented to them (Kassin, 2015). This certainly appears to be the case in Canada, as evidenced by the work of Dr. Joseph Eastwood and his colleagues (Eastwood, Snook, & Luther, 2014). Dr. Eastwood, along with some of his research on the comprehension of legal rights, is profiled in Box 3.3.

Consider a recent Canadian study by Eastwood and Snook (2010). They sampled 56 undergraduate students, nearly half of whom were enrolled in a police recruitment program. Each participant was presented with the two legal cautions that are supposed to be presented to suspects in Canada—the right to silence and the right to legal counsel—first in verbal format and then in written format, one element at a time (e.g., the right to silence includes multiple elements, such as (1) you need not say anything, (2) you have nothing to hope from any promise or favour, and (3) you have nothing to fear from any threat). After each type of presentation, participants recorded their understanding of the caution and rated how confident they were with their answer. The researchers coded these responses for degree of accuracy, with points being provided for each element of the caution that the participants correctly understood.

The results of this study are consistent with previous research. In general, participants had difficulty understanding each of the cautions, particularly certain

Box 3.3

Canadian Researcher Profile: Dr. Joseph Eastwood

Courtesy of Joseph Eastwood

Dr. Joseph Eastwood is an assistant professor of forensic psychology at the University of Ontario Institute of Technology (UOIT) in Oshawa, Ontario. He holds a PhD in experimental social psychology from Memorial University of Newfoundland. His research aims to use psychological science to improve policing procedures, with a particular focus on investigative interviewing—all with the ultimate goal of improving the administration of justice in Canada.

One of Dr. Eastwood's primary research streams has been focused on increasing the comprehension of interrogation rights by interviewees. Across a set of studies with both laypeople and offenders, Dr. Eastwood and his colleagues have found that adult interrogation rights are written in a very complex manner and people struggle to understand them. However, by making linguistic and structural changes to these rights, such as simplifying the wording and repeating each right multiple times, he found that comprehension can be increased greatly. More recently, he has demonstrated similar problems with the wording of the interrogation rights delivered to youth, and that comprehension can be increased by simplifying the way the rights are delivered to youth. Ongoing research is examining further ways to increase comprehension and to ensure

the increases seen in past studies remain in more realistic situations (i.e., actual police interrogations).

Another research stream of Dr. Eastwood's has focused on enhancing the ability of interviewers to gather accurate and complete accounts from eyewitnesses. Most recently this has involved measuring the effectiveness of sketch procedures (i.e., drawing out the details of the event) to complement verbal recall of a witnessed event. Early results have shown that having interviewees draw out the account is effective in producing more details than simple verbal recall. Ongoing studies are examining ways of further improving the sketch technique, as well as other innovative memory recall procedures.

A third research stream is examining the role of alibis within the criminal justice system. This includes examining the factors that police officers attend to when trying to decide whether or not an alibi is true. Recent findings suggest that having multiple people available to corroborate an alibi, particularly when they have no personal connection to the suspect, leads to more believable alibis. Dr. Eastwood is currently conducting studies to uncover other aspects that result in believable alibis, as well as looking at the ability of innocent suspects to create an alibi that would be seen as more believable.

Throughout his career, Dr. Eastwood has been proactive in seeking opportunities to collaborate with police organizations to ensure his research findings reach practitioners. For example, he has published summaries of his research in Canada's national policing magazine (*Blue Line*), co-authored articles and book chapters with police officers, and conducted investigative interviewing training courses with police officers from across Canada. He is a strong believer that research can only have maximal impact when those impacted by the results of the research findings are engaged in the research process. He greatly enjoys the opportunity to work with police officers and law enforcement organizations to jointly improve policing practices.

Although he has recently hung up his rugby cleats, when he is not carrying out research Dr. Eastwood enjoys staying active and spending as much time as possible with his wife Joanna, daughter Chloe, and son Alex.

elements, but presenting the cautions in written format, one element at a time, allowed for a greater degree of comprehension. Importantly, self-reported confidence was not a good predictor of a participant's degree of comprehension, and demographic variables, such as group status (student versus police recruit), were not related to comprehension. Based on these results, Eastwood and Snook (2010) concluded that "Canadians facing an investigative interview situation will not fully comprehend their rights, and therefore are unable to make a fully informed decision regarding whether or not they should waive their rights" (p. 375). Not only does this mean that the rights and freedoms of Canadian suspects are not always being protected, but it also means that evidence collected by the police in their interviews could be deemed inadmissible in court.

Certain populations seem particularly vulnerable when it comes to misunderstanding their legal rights, including young people and those with impaired intellectual capacity (Eastwood, Snook, & Luther, 2015; Fulero & Everington, 2004). Eastwood et al. (2015), for example, demonstrated that Canadian high school students exhibit very low levels of comprehension when presented with Canadian youth waivers in oral format. In fact, in this particular study, high school students understood less than half the material (approximately 40%) contained in the waiver. In part this is because Canadian youth waivers are written in a relatively complex fashion (e.g., they are lengthy and contain difficult and infrequently used words; Eastwood et al., 2015).

Investigator Bias A second problem with the Reid model of interrogation occurs during the actual interrogation and results from the fact that when the police begin their interrogation they already believe the suspect to be guilty. The problem here is that when people form a belief about something before they enter a situation, they often unknowingly seek out and interpret information in that situation in a way that verifies their initial belief. A study by Kassin et al. (2003) demonstrated some of the potential dangers that can result from this particular form of **investigator bias**.

In a mock interrogation study, the researchers had students act as interrogators or suspects. Some of the interrogators were led to believe that the suspect was guilty of a mock crime (finding a hidden key and stealing $100 from a locked cabinet) while others were led to believe that the suspect was innocent. In reality, some of the suspects were guilty of the mock crime whereas others were innocent. Interrogators were instructed to devise an interrogation strategy to use on the suspects, and the suspects were told to deny any involvement in the crime and to convince the interrogator of their innocence. The interrogation was taped, and a group of neutral observers then listened to the recording and were asked questions about the interrogator and the suspect.

A number of important results emerged from this study:

1. Interrogators with guilty expectations asked more questions that indicated their belief in the suspect's guilt. For example, they would ask, "How did you find the key that was hidden behind the DVD player?" instead of "Do you know anything about the key that was hidden behind the DVD player?"

2. Interrogators with guilty expectations used a higher frequency of interrogation techniques compared with interrogators with innocent expectations, especially at the outset of the interrogation.

Investigator bias: Bias that can result when police officers enter an interrogation setting already believing that the suspect is guilty

3. Interrogators with guilty expectations judged more suspects to be guilty, regardless of whether a suspect was actually guilty.

4. Interrogators indicated that they exerted more pressure on suspects to confess when, unbeknownst to them, the suspect was innocent.

5. Suspects had fairly accurate perceptions of interrogator behaviour (i.e., innocent suspects believed their interrogators were exerting more pressure).

6. Neutral observers viewed interrogators with guilty expectations as more coercive, especially against innocent suspects, and they viewed suspects in the guilty expectation condition as more defensive.

In sum, these findings indicate that investigative biases led to coercive interrogations that caused suspects to appear guiltier to both the interrogator and neutral observers, even when the suspect had committed no crime. Similar sorts of investigator bias effects have also been reported in more recent studies (e.g., Hill, Memon, & McGeorge, 2008).

Interrogation Practices and the Courts

The decision to admit confession evidence into court rests on the shoulders of the trial judge. Within North America, the key issues a judge must consider when faced with a questionable confession are whether the confession was made voluntarily and whether the defendant was competent when he or she provided the confession (Wakefield & Underwager, 1998). The reason for using these criteria is that involuntary confessions and confessions provided when a person's mind is unstable are more likely to be unreliable.

While it is clear that confessions extracted through overt forms of coercion—such as physical force, prolonged isolation, or sleep deprivation—will be deemed inadmissible in North American courts (Kassin, 1997), the picture gets much muddier when the coercion being used is more subtle. Indeed, when subtler forms of psychological coercion are used to extract confessions, as is the case when using the Reid technique, what constitutes "voluntary" and "competent" becomes less clear. This might be why courts in Canada often appear to hand down rulings in cases involving questionable confessions that sometimes seem inconsistent or even contradictory.

Two examples of how Canadian courts have handled questionable confession evidence are discussed in Box 3.4.

An Alternative to the Reid Model

Because of the potential problems that can result from using coercive interrogation tactics, police agencies in several countries have introduced changes to their procedures. Perhaps more than anywhere else, these changes have been most obvious in England and Wales, where courts have restricted the use of many techniques found in the Reid model of interrogation (Gudjonsson, 2003).

Over the last 20 years, police agencies in England and Wales have gone through several phases of change in an attempt to reduce oppressive interrogation practices. Currently, these agencies use the so-called PEACE model to guide their interrogations.

Box 3.4   Cases in Forensic Psychology

The Admissibility of Confession Evidence: Court Rulings in *R. v. Oickle* (2000) *and R. v. Chapple* (2012)

One of the most important Canadian court cases to deal with questionable confessions is the Supreme Court case of *R. v. Oickle* (2000). Richard Oickle confessed to seven counts of arson occurring in and around Waterville, Nova Scotia, between 1994 and 1995. The confession was obtained after a police interrogation in which several questionable interrogation techniques were used. These tactics included exaggerating the infallibility of a polygraph exam, implying that psychiatric help would be provided if the defendant confessed, minimizing the seriousness of the crimes, and suggesting that a confession would spare Oickle's girlfriend from having to undergo a stressful interrogation.

After considering whether Oickle's confession was voluntarily given, the trial judge deemed the confession admissible and convicted him on all counts. The Court of Appeal subsequently deemed the confession evidence inadmissible and entered an acquittal. On appeal before the Supreme Court of Canada, a ruling was handed down, which stated that Oickle's confession was properly admitted by the trial judge, and therefore his conviction should stand, despite the interrogation techniques employed by the police. In their decision, the Supreme Court laid out a 4-point framework for determining whether a confession should be deemed voluntary: (1) the Court must consider whether the police made any threats or promises, (2) the Court must look for an atmosphere of oppression (unjust or inhumane treatment), (3) the Court must consider whether the suspect had an "operating mind" in that they were aware of what they were saying and who they were saying it to, and (4) the Court must consider the degree of police trickery that was used to extract the confession (while trickery is allowed it should not go so far as to "shock the community").

In contrast to the case of *R. v. Oickle* (2000), the judge in the more recent case of *R. v. Chapple* (2012) harshly criticized the interrogation tactics used by a Calgary interrogator and deemed the suspect's confession inadmissible. Christa Chapple was a self-employed daycare operator who was accused of being responsible for serious head injuries suffered by one of the children in her care. She was interrogated about her involvement in the case. Her interrogation lasted over 8 hours and despite asserting her right to remain silent on 24 separate occasions during the interrogation, the interrogator continued to question her. The interrogator also criticized the legal advice that was given to Chapple and suggested, untruthfully, that the medical evidence about the injuries supported only one conclusion that did not align with the version of events described by the accused.

Unlike the Supreme Court Justices in *Oickle*, the judge in this case found that Chapple's free will was compromised as a result of the interrogation tactics used and she simply told the police what they wanted to hear. In his ruling, the judge stated that "Although there is no law prohibiting the use of The Reid Technique, I find that it has the ability to extinguish the individual's sacred legal rights to be presumed innocent until proven guilty and to remain silent in the face of police questioning." (para. 121) He went on to say:

I denounce the use of this technique in the strongest terms possible and find that its use can lead to overwhelmingly oppressive situations that can render false confessions and cause innocent people to be wrongfully imprisoned. In this case, the police were convinced of the accused's guilt even though there was medical evidence available that was consistent with the accused's version of events. They pushed ahead with the interview with one goal in mind: a confession. And that confession had to fit their theory of the case. (para. 122)

Questions:

1. The courts in Canada have indicated that the police may use some level of trickery to extract confessions from suspects. Do you think this is appropriate? What would be the implications if we did not allow the police to use any coercive interrogation tactics?

2. To what extent do you believe that judges in Canada are qualified to determine the extent to which a confession was voluntary and the confessor was competent at the time of giving a confession? Are there alternative ways in which the courts could make these decisions?

PEACE is an acronym for *planning* and *preparation*, *engage* and *explain*, *account*, *closure*, and *evaluation*. According to Meissner and Russano (2003), this model provides an inquisitorial framework within which to conduct police interrogations (compared with the accusatorial framework used in the Reid model) and is based on an interview method known as conversation management, which encourages information gathering more than securing a confession.

In fact, police agencies in England and Wales have all but abandoned the term *interrogation* in favour of *investigative interviewing* to get away from the negative connotations associated with North American–style interrogation practices. Although relatively little research has been conducted to examine the impact of the PEACE model, some research has indicated that a decrease in the use of coercive interrogation tactics does not necessarily result in a substantial reduction in the number of confessions that can be obtained (Meissner & Russano, 2003). For example, one analysis showed that approximately 50% of all suspects confessed to crimes before and after the PEACE model was introduced (Milne & Bull, 1999).

Recently, a call has been made by Canadian researchers to replace current interrogation techniques in Canada with the PEACE model (e.g., Snook, Eastwood, & Barron, 2014; Snook, Eastwood, Stinson, et al., 2010). Such changes would shift the priorities of Canadian police interrogations. As highlighted above, rather than focusing on extracting confessions, the primary goal of a PEACE interview would be to obtain complete and accurate information about the crime in question—information that will ultimately allow investigators to conduct a more efficient and effective investigation.

It is clear at present that many Canadian interrogations are unlikely to achieve this goal. A recent study conducted by Snook, Luther, Quinlan, and Milne (2012), which involved an analysis of 80 Canadian police interviews with suspects, revealed that Canadian interrogators rarely rely on questioning practices that will allow them to maximize the amount of complete and accurate information that is collected. For example, open-ended questions were used much less frequently (<1% of all questions) than close-ended questions (approximately 40% of all questions) in the interviews analyzed by Snook et al., despite the fact that research consistently demonstrates that an interviewer can extract a higher quantity of information from suspects, as well as more accurate information, when they allow the interviewee to do most of the talking.

While it is still too early to know if the PEACE model of interviewing will be incorporated into Canadian policing, some change is occurring. At least one Canadian police force (the Royal Newfoundland Constabulary) is showing a commitment to reforming police interrogation practices (Royal Newfoundland Constabulary, 2010). They have recently adopted the PEACE model as their primary interview strategy. Despite these positive developments, however, examples still surface showing that police officers in Canada sometimes rely on coercive interrogation tactics that are likely to result in ethically and legally questionable outcomes, such as the confession given in the case of *R v. Chapple* (2012) that was discussed in Box 3.4.

FALSE CONFESSIONS

Perhaps the biggest problem that people have with the use of coercive interrogation tactics is that these techniques can contribute to the likelihood of suspects making

false confessions (Kassin 2014, 2015). False confessions can be defined in a number of ways. However, Ofshe (1989) provided a definition that appears to be well accepted. He suggested that a confession should be considered false "if it is elicited in response to a demand for a confession and is either intentionally fabricated or is not based on actual knowledge of the facts that form its content" (p. 13).

Before examining the extent and nature of this problem, it is important to define two additional terms that are often confused with false confessions: **retracted confessions** and **disputed confessions**. Retracted confessions consist of an individual declaring that the confession he or she made is false (regardless of whether it actually is) (Gudjonsson, 2003). Disputed confessions, however, are confessions that are disputed at trial, which does not necessarily mean the confession is false or that it was retracted. Instead, disputed confessions may arise because of legal technicalities, or because the suspect disputes the confession was ever made (Gudjonsson, 2003).

The Frequency of False Confessions

Most researchers readily admit that no one knows how frequently false confessions are made. One problem is that it can be difficult to determine whether a confession is actually false. The fact that a confession is coerced does not mean the confession is false, just as a conviction based on confession evidence does not mean the confession is true (Kassin, 1997). As a result of such problems, researchers come up with drastically different estimates of how frequently false confessions occur. For example, the incidence of self-reported false confessions among prison inmates has been found to vary substantially, with some studies providing very low estimates (e.g., 0.6%; Cassell, 1998) and others providing much higher estimates (e.g., 12%; Gudjonsson & Sigurdsson, 1994).

One approach that has become increasingly popular for estimating the false confession rate is to examine the causes of wrongful convictions. Using this approach, the files of people who have been exonerated for their crimes are examined to determine if a false confession was to blame for the wrongful conviction. Numerous studies have now used this approach, and while findings vary from study to study, they all suggest that false confessions are indeed a problem. For example, one recent study that examined 241 cases where prisoners were exonerated through DNA testing indicated that 24.48% of the cases contained false confessions as a contributing cause of the wrongful conviction (Kassin, Bogart, & Kerner, 2012). Regardless of the exact number of false confessions that occur, most researchers believe there are enough cases to treat the issue very seriously.

Different Types of False Confessions

One thing researchers do agree on is that there are different types of false confessions. While several different typologies exist for classifying false confessions (e.g., Gudjonsson, 2003; McCann, 1998), the most common typology still appears to be the one proposed by Kassin and Wrightsman (1985), which states that false confessions consist of voluntary false confessions, coerced-compliant false confessions, and coerced-internalized false confessions.

False confession: A confession that is either intentionally fabricated or is not based on actual knowledge of the facts that form its content

Retracted confession: A confession that the confessor later declares to be false

Disputed confession: A confession that is later disputed at trial

Voluntary False Confessions

Voluntary false confessions occur when someone voluntarily confesses to a crime he or she did not commit without any elicitation from the police. Research has indicated that people voluntarily false confess for a variety of reasons. For example, Gudjonsson (1992) suggested that such confessions may arise out of (1) a morbid desire for notoriety, (2) the person being unable to distinguish fact from fantasy, (3) the need to make up for pathological feelings of guilt by receiving punishment, or (4) a desire to protect somebody else from harm (which may be particularly prevalent among juveniles).

Although it may seem surprising, highly publicized cases do occasionally result in voluntary false confessions. Perhaps the most famous case was the kidnapping and murder of Charles Lindbergh's baby son, where it is estimated that 200 people falsely confessed to the crime (Kassin, 2014). Another more recent case involved the high-profile false confession made by John Mark Karr to the unsolved 1996

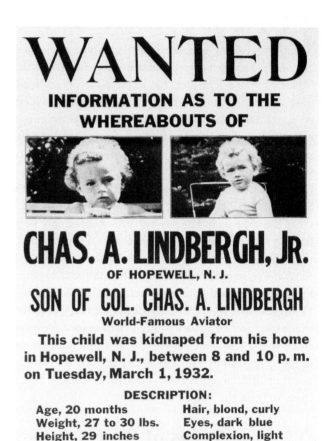

A plea for help in the famous Lindbergh baby kidnapping case. It is estimated that 200 people falsely confessed to the kidnapping and murder of 20-month-old Charles Lindbergh, Jr.

Bettmann/Corbis

murder of JonBenet Ramsey, the 6-year-old American beauty pageant queen. Karr was living in Thailand when he confessed to being with JonBenet when she died, but claimed that her death was an accident (Aglionby, 2006). He was released to the U.S. authorities and returned to Boulder, Colorado, where the murder had taken place. Shortly after his arrival, prosecutors announced that they would not pursue charges against Karr because his version of events did not match details of the case and because his DNA did not match samples found at the scene ("No DNA Match," 2006). However, Karr was quickly extradited to California on several child pornography charges.

Coerced-Compliant False Confessions   **Coerced-compliant false confessions** are those in which the suspect confesses to a crime, even though the suspect is fully aware that he or she did not commit it. This type of false confession is perhaps the most common (Gudjonsson & MacKeith, 1988). Unlike voluntary false confessions, these confessions are caused by the use of coercive interrogation tactics on the part of the police, such as the maximization and minimization techniques described earlier. Specifically, coerced-compliant confessions may be given so the suspect can (1) escape further interrogation, (2) gain a promised benefit, or (3) avoid a threatened punishment (Gudjonsson, 1992).

As with voluntary false confessions, there are a number of reported cases of coerced-compliant false confessions (Gudjonsson, 2003). Box 3.5 provides an example of a coerced-compliant false confession that occurred in Canada.

Coerced-compliant false confession: A confession that results from a desire to escape a coercive interrogation environment or gain a benefit promised by the police

---

Box 3.5   Forensic Psychology in the Spotlight

A Coerced-Compliant False Confession in a Canadian Child Abuse Case

In the case *R. v. M.J.S.* (2000), M.J.S. was accused of aggravated assault on his baby son (J.S.) and, after supplying the police with a written confession, was charged with the crime. But was M.J.S. responsible for the crime, or was this a case of a coerced-compliant false confession?

J.S. was one to three months old at the time the abuse was supposed to have happened. The boy had been admitted to the hospital for a suspected chest infection and vomiting problems. While J.S. was in the hospital, X-rays were taken, and it was later discovered that the baby had several rib fractures. The injuries were unusual for a baby so young, leading the baby's pediatrician to notify child welfare. The testimony of an expert suggested that the most likely cause of the fractures was that the baby was shaken.

A police investigation began. Both M.J.S. and his wife cooperated with the police throughout the investigation. On four occasions, the police interrogated the accused. During these interrogations, the police used techniques similar to those used in the Reid model of interrogation, which eventually led the accused to confess. Fortunately, all the interrogations were videotaped, which provided the courts with a means to determine whether the confession was coerced.

Much of the interrogation consisted of developing various psychological themes to justify the crime. For example, one of the interrogating officers stated, "No doubt it was probably accidental on your part.... I don't believe it was intentional.... Children's bones are so fragile.... You made a mistake" (para. 16). In addition, every time the accused denied his involvement in the crime, the officers

(continued)

interrupted him with statements such as "We are beyond that point—we know you did it" (para. 19).

The officers also lied to the accused, stating they had talked to everyone else who might have been involved with the incident and cleared them all. This had not happened. Furthermore, the interviewing officers appealed to the accused's sense of honour and decency, and stressed how much better he would feel if he confessed. For example, one officer stated, "You'll be able to say to yourself ... I'm going to sleep tonight, knowing that I told the truth" (para. 20). Still denying his involvement in any wrongdoing, the accused was presented with threatening statements. One interrogator stated, "If you run from this mistake, your family disintegrates, your family falls apart.... . If you want your kids to be raised in a foster home, or adopted somewhere, that is a decision that you have to make" (para. 25).

In ruling on the confession evidence, the judge stated that the alleged confession in this case was extracted by threats and implied promises. The judge decided that the techniques employed by the investigators were coercive and that the accused confessed to the crime to escape the oppressive atmosphere created by the interrogations. The judge concluded by stating, "This case is a classic illustration of how slavish adherence to a technique can produce a coerced-compliant false 'apology' [confession] even from an accused who has denied 34 times that he did anything wrong when caring for his child" (para. 45). As a result of these findings, the confession evidence was deemed inadmissible.

Source: "R. v. M. J. S". The Canadian Legal Information Institute, 2000.

Coerced-Internalized False Confessions   The third, and perhaps the most bizarre type of false confession proposed by Kassin and Wrightsman (1985) is the **coerced-internalized false confession**. Here, individuals recall and confess to a crime they did not commit, usually after they are exposed to highly suggestible questions, such as the minimization techniques described earlier in the chapter (Gudjonsson, 2003). In contrast to the coerced-compliant false confessor, however, these individuals actually end up believing they are responsible for the crime. According to Gudjonsson (1992), several vulnerability factors are associated with this type of false confession, including (1) a history of substance abuse or some other interference with brain function, (2) the inability of people to detect discrepancies between what they observed and what has been erroneously suggested to them, and (3) factors associated with mental state, such as severe anxiety, confusion, or feelings of guilt.

Examples of coerced-internalized false confessions are relatively rare, but such confessions do occur (Kassin, 2007). For example, Kassin (2007) retells the tragic case of 41-year-old Billy Wayne Cope from South Carolina who was convicted for the rape and murder of his 12-year-old daughter, Amanda. According to Kassin, Cope woke up to find his daughter dead, lying facedown on her bed. He immediately called 911, but was treated as a suspect by the police based on "an erroneous first impression that there was no sign of forced entry [to the home] and [a] belief that Cope showed 'too little emotion'" (Kassin, 2007, p. 169). Cope was taken to the police station where he underwent a lengthy interrogation. Cope persistently denied any involvement in the murder, he waived his rights, volunteered to be examined, and offered to take a polygraph test. The next morning, Cope was given a polygraph test and told that he failed (he actually didn't). In the words of Kassin, "Devastated by the result, Cope wondered aloud if a person could commit such a heinous act without knowing it—an idea suggested to him the previous night by his interrogators.

Coerced-internalized false confession: A confession that results from suggestive interrogation techniques, whereby the confessor actually comes to believe he or she committed the crime

According to the examiner, Cope broke down and admitted that 'I must have done it'" (p. 169). Following this, Cope provided a full narrative of how he molested and strangled his daughter. He even visited his house with the police where he reenacted the crime in a videotaped confession.

Eventually, DNA tests revealed that the semen found on Amanda's body was not from Cope, but from a sex offender who had raped and killed other young girls in the same way that Amanda was killed (Kassin, 2007). Following this, the police lied to Cope's wife and told her the semen was in fact Cope's and they persuaded her to visit Cope in jail to get him to confess again to the crime, which he didn't do (Cope's wife died shortly after this still believing that the semen found on her daughter was her husband's). When the DNA sample was finally matched to the offender responsible, the prosecutor on the case charged Cope with conspiracy, "arguing that he had pimped his daughter out to Sanders [the sex offender]" (p. 170). Some additional evidence was presented at this trial, which included testimony from a friend of Cope's wife who claimed that Cope had sent her two written confessions from jail. As Kassin reports, "Cope denied writing notes, which were penned on a paper he had no access to and in a handwriting that was likely not his own. As for the witness, she had once before been charged with forgery in another matter" (p. 170). Despite all of this, after a five-hour deliberation, the jury convicted Cope.

Studying False Confessions in the Lab

It is obviously difficult to study if, and how, false confessions occur. Even in the research laboratory it is not an easy task because of obvious ethical constraints (Kassin & Kiechel, 1996). Nowadays, no university ethics committee would allow research participants to be led to believe they had committed crimes of the sort that Billy Wanye Cope was accused of. As a result, researchers have attempted to develop innovative laboratory paradigms that allow them to study the processes that may cause false confessions to occur without putting their participants at risk.

In one classic study, Kassin and Kiechel (1996) tested whether individuals would confess to a "crime" they did not commit. They had participants take part in what they thought was a reaction time study. A co-conspirator read a list of letters out loud to a participant who had to type these letters into a computer. However, before each session began, the participant was warned that if he or she hit the ALT key on the keyboard while typing in the letters, all the data would be lost. Sixty seconds after beginning the task, the computer automatically crashed, which brought the head researcher into the lab with accusations that the participant had hit the key.

Kassin and Kiechel were specifically interested in how two factors would affect participant reactions to the allegations. Participant vulnerability (defined as the participant's certainty concerning his or her own innocence) was manipulated by varying the speed that participants had to type. In the "not vulnerable" condition, letters were read at a rate of 43 letters per minute; in the "vulnerable" condition, letters were read at a rate of 67 letters per minute. The researchers also varied whether false evidence was presented. In the "no false evidence" condition, the co-conspirator

Table 3.1 Compliance, Internalization, and Confabulation in Kassin and Kiechel's Study

	No False Evidence (No Witness)		False Evidence (Witness)	
	Not Vulnerable (Slow Pace)	*Vulnerable (Fast Pace)*	*Not Vulnerable (Slow Pace)*	*Vulnerable (Fast Pace)*
Compliance	35%	65%	89%	100%
Internalization	0%	12%	44%	65%
Confabulation	0%	0%	6%	35%

Source: Data from The Social Psychology of False Confessions: Compliance, Internalization, and Confabulation by Saul M. Kassin, Katherine L. Kiechel. Psychological Science, Vol 7, No. 3, May 1996. Copyright ©1996 by The American Psychological Society.

stated she did not see what happened; in the "false evidence" condition, she stated she saw the participant hit the ALT key. The results from the study are presented in Table 3.1.

To measure the degree to which participants exhibited **compliance** with the allegations, the researchers presented each participant with a written confession and recorded how many participants signed it. As indicated in Table 3.1, many participants accepted responsibility for the crime despite the fact that they were innocent, particularly the vulnerable participants presented with false evidence. To measure the degree to which participants internalized their confession, the researchers recorded comments made by participants to another co-conspirator outside the lab who asked them what had happened. If the participant accepted blame for the crime, he or she was recorded as exhibiting **internalization**. Based on the results from this study, many participants also internalized their confession. Again, this was especially true for vulnerable participants presented with false evidence. Finally, to measure the degree to which participants made up details to fit with their confession, known as **confabulation**, the researchers brought the participant back into the lab, read the list of letters again, and asked the participant to try to reconstruct where things had gone wrong. Vulnerable participants presented with false evidence were once again found to be particularly susceptible to confabulation.

Thus, Kassin and Kiechel's (1996) findings suggest that it is possible to demonstrate, under laboratory conditions, that people can admit to acts they are not responsible for and come to believe in their guilt to such a point that they can reconstruct details of an act that never occurred (Kassin & Kiechel, 1996). However, whether these findings can be generalized to actual police interrogations is unclear because the Kassin and Kiechel paradigm fails to capture a number of elements found in real-world interrogations: (1) while the participants in Kassin and Kiechel's study had nothing to lose if they couldn't convince others of their innocence, real suspects have much to lose if they are found guilty, (2) while all participants in Kassin and Kiechel's study were actually innocent of the crime, all suspects in real interrogations aren't, and (3) while the participants in Kassin and Kiechel's study could have easily been confused about their guilt (they may have accidentally hit the key), real suspects typically aren't confused about their involvement in a

Compliance: A tendency to go along with demands made by people perceived to be in authority, even though the person may not agree with them

Internalization: The acceptance of guilt for an act, even if the person did not actually commit the act.

Confabulation: The reporting of events that never actually occurred

crime (Russano, Meissner, Narchet, & Kassin, 2005). More recent research has helped to clarify these issues. Findings from newer studies suggest that, even when these sorts of issues are accounted for, people can still be coerced into confessing to "crimes" they didn't commit using the sorts of tactics that are commonly employed in police interrogations (e.g., Horselenberg, Merckelbach, & Josephs, 2003; Russano et al., 2005).

Recent Canadian research has found that it's even possible to convince university students that they committed crimes as a teenager that they didn't actually commit and to confess to those crimes (Shaw & Porter, 2015). Indeed, over the course of a few interviews where suggestive interviewing techniques were used, a relatively high percentage of participants developed false memories for crimes, even when those crimes were of a serious nature. For example, of the 30 participants who were told that they committed a crime as a teenager, 71% developed a false memory of the crime; false memories occurred for many participants even when the suggested crime was a serious one (e.g., assault with a weapon). Additionally, many participants were able to recount the events surrounding the crime with concrete and vivid details, of the sort that are seen in real-world cases of coerced false confessions.

The Consequences of Falsely Confessing

False confessions cause problems for both the person making the false confession and the police agencies tasked with investigating the crime. The obvious problem that the person making the false confession faces is that, if the confession is admitted in court, the jury could convict the suspect for a crime he or she did not commit (Leo & Ofshe, 1998). Importantly, recent laboratory studies have shown that jurors might be likely to convict a suspect based on confession evidence even when the jurors are aware that the suspect's confession resulted from a coercive interrogation. For example, in one study, Kassin and Sukel (1997) presented participants with transcripts of a mock murder trial. One group of participants received a transcript in which the defendant immediately confessed to the police during questioning (the low-pressure condition). A second group of participants received a transcript in which the defendant was coerced into confessing by having his hands handcuffed behind his back and by being threatened by the interrogator (the high-pressure condition). A third group of participants received a transcript in which the defendant never confessed to the murder (the control condition). The results of the study indicated that those participants presented with a confession obtained in the high-pressure condition recognized the confession was involuntary and said it would not affect their decisions. However, when actual verdicts were examined across the three groups, the presence of a confession was found to significantly increase the conviction rate, even for those participants in the high-pressure condition.

Unfortunately, research has also suggested that many genuine false confessions are likely to be viewed as evidence of guilt by potential jurors. Appleby, Hasel, and Kassin (2013) highlighted at least three reasons why jurors are unlikely to identify confessions by innocent people as false (and thus use them as the basis for guilty verdicts).

First, based purely on common sense, jurors are unlikely to believe that a person would be willing to make statements that counter self-interest, even in the context of a police interrogation. Second, due to problems with deception detection, people are unable to accurately distinguish between true and false confessions (e.g., see Kassin, Meissner, & Norwick, 2005). Third, and perhaps most interesting, false confessions are often very similar to true confessions with respect to their form and content. For example, in their analysis of 20 genuine false confessions, Appleby et al. found that, like true confessions, false confessions contained "specific visual and auditory details concerning the crime and victim(s) as well as references to the confessor's thoughts, feelings, and motives during and after committing the crime" (p. 1). When incorporated into confessions, these types of features were shown by Appleby et al. to increase confidence in mock jurors that the confessions were actually an indication of guilt.

Compounding the above matters even further are research findings which suggest that confession evidence, even false confessions, may taint other evidence presented in a trial, making the other evidence appear more corroborative than it really is (Kassin et al., 2012). In their archival analysis of DNA exoneration cases from the Innocence Project, Kassin and his colleagues found that multiple evidence errors—including the improper use of forensic science, eyewitness identifications, and snitches or informants—were more likely in cases involving false confessions. Furthermore, in cases involving multiple errors associated with evidence, the false confession was most likely to have been obtained first, suggesting perhaps that the confession skewed subsequent investigative and/or interpretative processes. While also highlighting other possible interpretations of this finding, Kassin et al. suggest that knowledge of a confession may have increased the motivation of subsequent witnesses to help police and prosecutors implicate the presumed guilty suspect.

A second, and less commonly recognized, consequence of false confessions involves the consequences for the police and, therefore, the public. When somebody makes a false confession, the police are diverted down a false trail that may waste valuable time, time that they could have used to identify and apprehend the real offender. Such was the case in both the Lindbergh kidnapping case and the Ramsey murder case, which were described above. Howitt (2002) also provided an example of this happening in the Yorkshire Ripper serial murder investigation that took place in England during the 1970s. At one point in the investigation, the police were sent several tape recordings supposedly from the Ripper himself. Howitt stated that senior police officers on the case, believing the tapes to be genuine, used up valuable resources investigating the tapes. However, the tapes were not genuine, and these actions probably delayed the eventual arrest of Peter Sutcliffe and allowed further murders to take place. Given the potential costs associated with false confessions—both financial and human—the police have to be very careful about confession evidence and they need to minimize the chance of false confessions occurring. Read the scenario in the You Be the Police Officer box and determine what you could do to reduce the likelihood of the suspect falsely confessing to the crime he is being questioned for.

YOU BE THE POLICE OFFICER

Jim Kowalski is a 68-year-old Polish immigrant who has just been picked up by the police on suspicion of murdering Emily Jones, a 30-year-old nurse who was killed when coming home from a late shift at the hospital where she worked. Jim fits the suspect descriptions that were given by several eyewitnesses and he has no alibi for the night when the murder took place. He also has a criminal record, which consists of several drug charges. He denies knowing the victim and says he had nothing to do with the murder. When he is brought into the police station for questioning, he appears very anxious and confused, shows potential signs of being slightly learning disabled, and does not write or speak fluent English.

Your Turn ...

As a police officer working on this case, what approach would you suggest be taken when interrogating Jim? What should be the primary goals of the interrogation? What would you be concerned with when developing the interrogation strategy? Would you be worried about Jim possibly confessing to the crime even if he didn't commit it? Why or why not? If you think a false confession is a possibility, what could you do to prevent this from happening?

CRIMINAL PROFILING

To conduct interrogations, police need to have a viable suspect in custody. In some instances, the identification of probable suspects is relatively straightforward, because in many crimes the victim and the offender know each other and there is often a clear motivation for the crime, such as passion, greed, or revenge. But what about those crimes in which it is more difficult to identify a suspect, crimes in which the victim and offender are strangers and there is no clear motive? In these cases, the police often rely on unconventional investigative techniques, such as criminal profiling.

What Is a Criminal Profile?

Perhaps more than any other investigative technique, criminal profiling has caught the attention of the public, and Hollywood depictions of criminal profiling are common (as illustrated in the In the Media box). But what is criminal profiling in reality? There is no single definition of *criminal profiling* (Alison et al., 2002). Indeed, there is even little agreement as to what the technique should be called (Wilson, Lincoln, & Kocsis, 1997). However, the definition proposed by John Douglas and his former colleagues from the Federal Bureau of Investigation (FBI) fairly accurately describes the procedure, despite the fact it was proposed some time ago: **criminal profiling** is "a technique for identifying the major personality and behavioral characteristics of an individual based upon an analysis of the crimes he or she has committed" (Douglas, Ressler, Burgess, & Hartman, 1986, p. 405).

Criminal profiling: An investigative technique for identifying the major personality and behavioural characteristics of an individual based upon an analysis of the crimes he or she has committed

Hollywood Depictions of Criminal Profiling

Countless television shows and films have profiling built into their plots, and there seems to be no end in sight to Hollywood portrayals of this topic. We are often asked by students about these media depictions: "Do profilers like this actually exist?" "Can they actually do in real life what they are seen to do on the screen?" And most often, "What do I need to do to get that kind of job?"

We are sometimes tempted to tell these students that these shows are all fake—after all, the chance of gaining full-time employment as a profiler is very small. However, the truth is that these shows are not entirely fake, even though many aspects of them are. Indeed, audiences have become too smart, and too demanding, for Hollywood to pull the wool over their eyes entirely. Audiences require a degree of realism in these shows to stay interested, although we also need to have directors spice things up a bit.

In fact, audiences have gotten so demanding that it is now common practice to have researchers attached to these shows and to even hire technical consultants (real-life profilers) who help make the shows appear more realistic. These individuals provide information about what terms to use, what places to go to, and what names to drop so that there is a ring of truth to what the actors are saying and doing. It is then up to Hollywood to make this all sound (and look) sexy so that the audience keeps coming back for more.

Consider the following examples:

The Silence of the Lambs

Adapted from Thomas Harris's book *The Silence of the Lambs,* much of this movie is set in Quantico, Virginia, where the FBI's Behavioral Science Unit (BSU) actually resides. In addition, parts of this film were largely based on the work of John Douglas, previous chief of the BSU. Indeed, Scott Glenn's character (Jack Crawford) was largely modelled after Douglas and Douglas served as a technical consultant on the film (Douglas, 2010). The serial killer depicted in the movie, Buffalo Bill, was also based loosely on a real-life killer. In particular, many of the things that Buffalo Bill did, such as the skinning of bodies, resemble the crimes of Ed Gein, a Wisconsin man who was a frequent grave robber. Interestingly, on some DVD versions of this film, Douglas provides a commentary informing the audience as to what parts of the movie are real and what parts are fake.

Numb3rs

The first episode of *Numb3rs* was broadcast on January 23, 2005. In that show, an FBI agent recruits his brother Charlie, who happens to be a mathematical genius, to help solve challenging crimes. One of the problems encountered in the first episode is to identify the residential location of an offender based on where he committed his crimes. Stumped, Charlie goes back to his university office and derives a formula for determining a "hot zone" where the offender is likely to live. The formula he writes on his blackboard was actually the work of Dr. Kim Rossmo, a former detective who helped to develop the field of geographic profiling while a PhD student at Simon Fraser University (Devlin & Lorden, 2007).

Although criminal profiling is now used in a range of contexts, it is most commonly used in cases involving violent serial crimes (Holmes & Holmes, 2002). Criminal profiling was originally intended to help the police identify the criminal in these sorts of cases, either by narrowing down a list of suspects or by providing new lines of inquiry. However, criminal profiling is now used for a number of purposes, including the following (Homant & Kennedy, 1998):

- To help set traps to flush out an offender
- To determine whether a threatening note should be taken seriously
- To give advice on how best to interrogate a suspect
- To tell prosecutors how to break down defendants in cross-examination

Because criminal profiling has evolved in this way, many agencies no longer refer to the work they do as "profiling." For example, the RCMP prefers to use the term *criminal investigative analysis*, which suggests a broader focus than *profiling* (Royal Canadian Mounted Police; RCMP, 2016). In many jurisdictions, agencies have also stopped using the term *criminal profiler* to describe the people involved in this line of work. Labels such as *behavioral investigative advisor* (Rainbow, 2008) or *criminal investigative analysts* (RCMP, 2016) are often used instead because this term more accurately describes the wide range of activities that "profilers" are now involved in, only some of which involve making predictions about an offender's background (i.e., what we generally think of as profiling).

Although every criminal profile will undoubtedly be different in terms of the information it contains, some of the most common personality, behavioural, and demographic characteristics that profilers try to predict include the offender's age, sex, race, level of intelligence, educational history, hobbies, family background, residential location, criminal history, employment status, psychosexual development, and post-offence behaviour (Holmes & Holmes, 2002). Sometimes these predictions are made by forensic psychologists and psychiatrists who have either clinical or research experience with offenders (e.g., Canter & Youngs, 2009; Wilson et al., 1997). In North America, however, the majority of profilers are experienced and specially trained law enforcement officers (Rossmo, 2000).

The Origins of Criminal Profiling

Criminal profiling is usually thought to have been developed by agents from the FBI in the 1970s. However, there are numerous examples of profiling techniques being used long before that time (Canter, 2000; Holmes & Holmes, 2002; Turvey, 2002; Woodworth & Porter, 2002). The investigation that you may be most familiar with is the famous case of Jack the Ripper (Harrison, 1993).

Early Attempts at Criminal Profiling   In 1888, a series of murders were committed in the east end of London, around an area known as Whitechapel. The victims were all women, and all were mutilated by the offender. At one point, the unknown offender sent a letter to the newspapers, and at the end of it he signed his name, Jack the Ripper (Holmes & Holmes, 2002). A police surgeon involved with the investigation of the murders engaged in a form of criminal profiling. As Woodworth and Porter (1999) revealed,

> Dr. George Phillips attempted to create a reconstruction of various crime scenes and describe the wounds of the victims for the purpose of gaining a greater insight into the offender's psychological make-up. In particular, Phillips believed that a circumspect examination of the wound patterns of murder victims could provide clues about both the behavior and personality of the offender who committed the crimes. (p. 244)

This instance is probably one of the first times that criminal profiling was used in a criminal investigation. Unfortunately, it assisted little, evidenced by the fact that we still have no idea who Jack the Ripper actually was.

A passage in Whitechapel, London where Jack the Ripper murdered his victims. The Ripper case is probably one of the first times criminal profiling was used as an investigative tool.

Peresanz/Shutterstock

Another well-known case, often cited as an example of how accurate some profilers can be, is the case of New York City's Mad Bomber. Starting in 1940, an unknown offender began detonating bombs in public places around New York (Wrightsman, 2001). Stumped, the New York City Police Department turned to a local forensic psychiatrist, Dr. James Brussel, for help with the case. By examining the actions of the bomber, Brussel began to develop a profile of the unknown offender. Dr. Brussel's profile included characteristics such as the following: The offender would be a middle-aged male, he would suffer from paranoia, he would be pathologically self-centred, he would be reasonably educated, he would be unmarried and possibly a virgin, he would be Roman Catholic, and he would wear buttoned-up double-breasted suits (Turvey, 2002). In 1957, almost 17 years after the bombings started, the police finally arrested George Metesky. Metesky fit most of the characteristics that Dr. Brussel had profiled, even down to the double-breasted suit he wore to the police station (Holmes & Holmes, 2002). Metesky was subsequently sent to a mental institution for the criminally insane. He was released in 1973 and died in 1994.

The FBI and Beyond   The next big milestone in the history of criminal profiling was the development of a criminal profiling program at the FBI in the 1970s (Turvey, 2002). Not only was this the first time that profiles were produced in a systematic way by a law enforcement agency, but it was also the first time that training was provided in how to construct criminal profiles. Subsequent to the development of the FBI's Behavioral Sciences Unit in 1972, the National Center for the Analysis of Violent Crime was opened for the purpose of conducting research in the area of criminal profiling and providing formal guidance to police agencies around the United States that were investigating serial crimes, serial murder in particular. Similar units have now sprung up in police agencies around the world, including Canada, Germany, and England. These outfits typically provide operational support to police agencies in cases in which profiling (and other forms of criminal investigative analysis) may be useful. Many also conduct their own research into criminal profiling. See Box 3.6 for an example of how the RCMP has been moving the criminal profiling field forward.

Investigative Psychology   Since the early 1990s, some of the most important advances in the area of criminal profiling have been made by David Canter, the founder of a relatively new field of psychology that he has named *investigative psychology*. The origins of this field can be traced back to Canter's involvement in the John Duffy (a.k.a., Railway Rapist) rape/murder case. Canter was called in by Scotland Yard to provide a profile of the unknown offender, and in doing so, he drew on knowledge of human behaviour that he had gained as an academic psychologist, especially in the area of environmental psychology (Canter, 1994). Since that early

Box 3.6   Forensic Psychology in the Spotlight

The RCMP's Violent Crime Linkage Analysis System (ViCLAS)

The RCMP has played a large role in developing the field of criminal profiling. To some extent, it has been able to do this by drawing on the best of modern computer technology. One of the RCMP's most significant advances has been the development in the mid-1990s of an automated system for linking serial crimes, the Violent Crime Linkage Analysis System, or **ViCLAS** (Martineau & Corey, 2008). One of the biggest problems the police encounter when they are faced with a possible crime series is **linkage blindness**, which refers to an inability on the part of the police to link geographically dispersed serial crimes committed by the same offender because of a lack of communication among police agencies (Egger, 2002). ViCLAS was developed, in part, to prevent such linkage blindness.

The backbone of ViCLAS is a booklet, now available in electronic form, that police officers fill out. The questions in this booklet are supposed to capture crucial information on crimes of a serious nature, including homicides, sexual assaults, missing persons, and non-parental abductions (Collins, Johnson, Choy, Davidson, & Mackay, 1998). The booklet contains more than a hundred questions about the offender's behaviour, the victim, and any available forensic information. This information is then entered into a computer and downloaded into a centralized database where it can be compared with other crimes. Specially trained ViCLAS analysts determine if there are any possible crime linkages. If any potential links are identified, then the crimes are highlighted as a series and the relevant police agencies are notified and encouraged to share information (Collins et al., 1998).

Recently, some of the assumptions underlying ViCLAS have been questioned by researchers (e.g., Bennell, Snook, MacDonald, House, & Taylor, 2012), and studies have raised potential concerns with some aspects of the system, such as the reliability of the data contained within it (Martineau & Corey, 2008; Snook, Luther, House, Bennell, & Taylor, 2012). However, anecdotal evidence suggests the system holds promise, and these successes have earned ViCLAS a reputation in the policing world as one of the best crime linkage analysis systems in existence. Indeed, police agencies from around the world, including England, Australia, and Germany, are currently using ViCLAS to help identify serial crimes.

---

successful contribution, Canter and his colleagues have spent the last 20 years developing the field of profiling into a scientific practice. These individuals have also made countless contributions to other areas of investigative psychology (Canter & Youngs, 2009). An example of how investigative psychologists might approach the profiling task is described in more detail below, when we discuss inductive criminal profiling.

How Is a Criminal Profile Constructed?

Profiles are constructed differently by different profilers. In fact, different "schools" of profiling now exist that guide the profile construction process (Hicks & Sales, 2006). However, regardless of what approach is taken to generate a profile, it is fair to say that, currently, relatively little is known about the profiling process. While some individuals have attempted to change this (e.g., Canter, 2000), such attempts are not common. Indeed, the descriptions of the profiling process provided by many researchers and profilers are still incredibly vague.

Despite the fact that it is not always entirely clear how criminal profilers construct their profiles, it is evident that they can draw on different types of profiling methods (Hicks & Sales, 2006). Two profiling methods are often talked about: the deductive profiling method and the inductive profiling method.

ViCLAS: The Violent Crime Linkage Analysis System, which was developed by the RCMP to collect and analyze information on serious crimes from across Canada

Linkage blindness: An inability on the part of the police to link geographically dispersed serial crimes committed by the same offender because of a lack of information sharing among police agencies

Deductive criminal profiling involves the prediction of an offender's background characteristics generated from a thorough analysis of the evidence left at the crime scenes by that particular offender (Holmes & Holmes, 2002). This method largely relies on logical reasoning, as indicated in an example provided by Canter (2000) in which the victim of an unidentified assailant noticed that the offender had short fingernails on his right hand and long fingernails on his left hand, resulting in the conclusion that the offender was likely to be a guitar player. While this is a very flexible approach in that it can be applied to all crimes, the disadvantage of this method is that the underlying logic of arguments can be faulty (e.g., the offender in Canter's example was not a guitar player, but someone who had a job repairing old tires).

In contrast to deductive profiling, **inductive criminal profiling** involves the prediction of an offender's background characteristics generated from a comparison of that particular offender's crimes with similar crimes committed by other, known offenders. This method is based on the premise that "if certain crimes committed by different people are similar, then the offenders must also share some common personality traits" (Holmes & Holmes, 2002, p. 5). The inductive method of profiling relies largely on a determination of how likely it is that an offender will possess certain background characteristics given the prevalence of these characteristics among known offenders who have committed similar crimes. An example of this method was provided by Aitken et al. (1996), who developed a statistical profile of a murderer of children. Based on their analysis of similar crimes committed by known offenders, they predicted that there was a probability of 0.96 that the offender would know the victim, a probability of 0.92 that the offender would have a previous criminal conviction, a probability of 0.65 that the offender would be under the age of 20, and so on. While arguably more objective than the deductive profiling method, it is unclear how this method could be used to profile offenders if the crimes being investigated are unique.

Of course, there is also the possibility of using both of these methods when developing a criminal profile. Indeed, profilers often combine these approaches to avoid as much as possible the disadvantages associated with either method when used in isolation. Such an approach allows for a degree of objectivity when preparing a profile, and it also allows the profiler to take into account particular aspects of the crimes being investigated that may be important. Combining these methods is somewhat similar to the structured professional judgment approach that has become popular when carrying out risk assessments (see Chapter 10).

The Organized-Disorganized Model Historically, many profilers have relied on an inductive profiling approach developed by the FBI in the 1980s (or at least a variation of this approach). This model was developed largely through interviews with incarcerated offenders and has come to be called the **organized-disorganized model** (Hazelwood & Douglas, 1980). The original model suggested that an offender's crime scene can be classified as either organized or disorganized. As seen in Table 3.2, organized crime scene behaviours reflect a well-planned and controlled crime, while disorganized behaviours reflect an impulsive crime, which is chaotic in nature. Similarly, it was thought that an offender's background can be classified as either organized or disorganized. As seen in Table 3.3, organized background characteristics

Table 3.2 Organized and Disorganized Crime Scene Behaviours

Organized Behaviours	Disorganized Behaviours
Planned offence	Spontaneous offence
Use of restraints on the victim	No restraints used on the victim
Ante-mortem sexual acts committed	Post-mortem sexual acts committed
Use of a vehicle in the crime	No use of a vehicle in the crime
No post-mortem mutilation	Post-mortem mutilation
Corpse not taken	Corpse (or body parts) taken
Little evidence left at the scene	Evidence left at the scene

Source: Based on Behavioral Sciences & the Law by John E. Douglas, Robert K. Ressler, Ann W. Burgess, Carol R. Hartman. Copyright © 1986 by John Wiley & Sons, Ltd.

reflect a methodical individual, while disorganized characteristics reflect a disturbed individual, who is usually suffering from some form of psychopathology.

The basic idea behind the model is that, when encountering a disorganized crime scene, the investigator should profile the background characteristics of a disorganized offender, and likewise for organized crime scenes and organized background characteristics. Although little research has examined whether the organized-disorganized model is actually valid, the research that does exist raises serious doubts (e.g., Canter, Alison, Alison, & Wentink, 2004). Indeed, even the FBI has refined this model to account for the many offenders who display mixtures of organized and disorganized features (Douglas, Burgess, Burgess, & Ressler, 1992).

Investigative Psychology Approaches to Profiling   More recently, other inductive approaches to profiling have been proposed by proponents of investigative psychology (see Canter & Youngs, 2009 for a review). These approaches are similar to previous inductive approaches, like the organized-disorganized model, in that they rely on previously solved cases to develop a framework for relating categories of crime scene behaviours to categories of background characteristics. However, unlike

Table 3.3 Organized and Disorganized Background Characteristics

Organized Behaviours	Disorganized Behaviours
High intelligence	Low intelligence
Skilled occupation	Unskilled occupation
Sexually adequate	Sexually inadequate
Lives with a partner	Lives alone
Geographically mobile	Geographically stable
Lives and works far away from crimes	Lives and works close to crimes
Follows crimes in media	Little interest in media
Maintains residence and vehicle	Does not maintain residence and vehicle

Source: Based on Behavioral Sciences & the Law by John E. Douglas, Robert K. Ressler, Ann W. Burgess, Carol R. Hartman. Copyright © 1986 by John Wiley & Sons, Ltd.

these other models, investigative psychologists tend to place more emphasis on rigorously testing the validity of the categories that are proposed and the degree of linkage between crime scene behaviours and the background characteristics.

A good example of this approach can be seen in a study by Goodwill, Lehmann, Beauregard, & Andrei (2016). They first used a statistical technique called cluster analysis to identify different ways that sex offenders searched for their victims, selected their victims, approached their victims, and assaulted their victims. For example, with respect to victim selection, their analysis identified three clusters: (1) offenders who predominantly target adult females with specific physical features (telio specific), (2) offenders who predominantly target child and adolescent victims with specific physical features (pedo/hebe specific), and (3) offenders who don't appear to have a preferred victim type (non-specific). Cluster analysis was also used to identify different clusters of background characteristics, which included (1) the socially competent offender, (2) the anti-social generalist offender, and (3) the sexually deviant offender.

After carrying out their cluster analyses, Goodwill and his colleagues used another statistical technique referred to as multiple correspondence analysis (MCA) to examine the inter-relationships between all of the clusters. As you can see from Figure 3.2, logical relationships were found, not only between the different clusters of crime scene behaviours, but between the clusters of crime scene behaviours and the clusters of background characteristics. These relationships could be used to inform profiling approaches with sex offenders. For example, in the top right corner of the plot, the

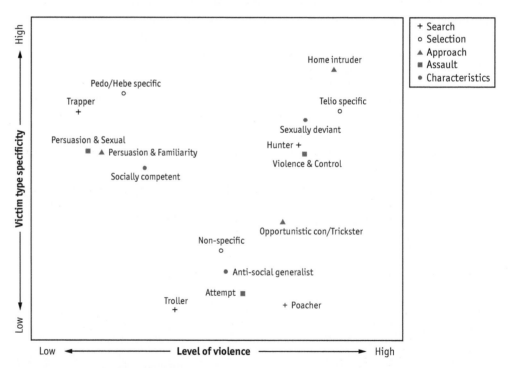

Figure 3.2 Multiple correspondence analysis showing the relationship between crime scene behaviours and background characteristics for a sample of serial sex offenders.

Source: From Legal and Criminological Psychology, © 2014. Reproduced with permission of John Wiley & Sons, Inc.

MCA shows that those offenders who adopt a hunter search strategy (actively seeking out victims within a short distance from their home), are telio specific (target adult females with specific physical features), use the home intruder approach style (often assaulting the victim in their home), and employ an assault strategy based on violence and control. Compared to other offenders (who exhibited other crime scene behaviours), these offenders are likely to be sexually deviant, characterized by the following background characteristics: socially isolated, persistent sexually deviant fantasies, voyeurism in adulthood, poor self-image in adulthood, etc. (all characteristics associated with the sexually deviant offender, as identified through the cluster analysis).

The Validity of Criminal Profiling

Because profiling is commonly used by the police, it is important to consider whether the technique is actually reliable and valid. Profilers certainly claim that they have experienced much success with their profiles (Woodworth & Porter, 1999), and it appears that police officers hold generally positive (although somewhat cautious) views of profiling (e.g., Copson, 1995; Jackson, van Koppen, & Herbrink, 1993; Snook, Haines, Taylor, & Bennell, 2007; Trager & Brewster, 2001). For example, Snook, Haines, et al. (2007) found that the majority of Canadian police officers they surveyed felt that profiling is a valuable investigative tool that can help to solve cases and further an investigator's understanding of a case. However, these officers also recognized the limitations of profiling, indicating that it shouldn't be used as evidence in court, that it shouldn't be used for all types of crimes, and that it does have the potential to seriously mislead an investigation.

Despite these findings indicating that criminal profiling may be useful, the practice is still often criticized. Several criticisms in particular have received attention from researchers:

1. Many forms of profiling appear to be based on a theoretical model of personality that lacks strong empirical support.

2. The core psychological assumptions underlying profiling currently lack strong empirical support.

3. Many profiles contain information that is so vague and ambiguous they can potentially fit many suspects.

4. Professional profilers may be no better than untrained individuals at constructing accurate profiles.

Let's now look at each of these criticisms in turn.

Does Profiling Have a Strong Theoretical Base?   There seems to be general agreement that many forms of profiling, especially those based on models such as the FBI's organized-disorganized approach, rely on a **classic trait model** of personality that was popular in psychology before the 1970s (Alison et al., 2002). In this model, the primary determinants of behaviour are stable, internal traits (Mischel, 1968). These traits are assumed to result in the expression of consistent patterns of behaviour over time and across situations. In the criminal context, this consistency is thought to persist across an offender's crimes and into the offender's noncriminal

Classic trait model: A model of personality that assumes the primary determinants of behaviour are stable, internal traits lifestyle, thus allowing him or her to be accurately profiled (Homant & Kennedy, 1998). Thus, an offender characterized by a trait of "organization" is expected to exhibit organized behaviours across his or her crimes, as well as organized features in his or her noncriminal life (Alison et al., 2002).

Although some researchers believe this classic trait model provides a solid basis for criminal profiling (e.g., Homant & Kennedy, 1998), other researchers disagree (e.g., Alison et al., 2002). Those who disagree draw on research from the field of personality psychology, which demonstrates that traits are not the only (or even primary) determinant of behaviour (Cervone & Shoda, 1999). Rather, situational influences are also known to be very important in shaping our behaviour. From a profiling perspective, the impact of situational factors (e.g., an extremely resistant victim) may create behavioural inconsistencies across an offender's crimes, and between different aspects of his or her life, making it very difficult to create an accurate profile (Woodhams & Bennell, 2015). Given the level of disagreement among researchers in this area, more empirical research is clearly needed before firm conclusions can be drawn about the theoretical support for traditional forms of profiling.

Is There Empirical Support for Profiling Assumptions?   Related to the first criticism is the question of whether empirical support exists for the key assumptions underlying criminal profiling. Two assumptions in particular have been tested by researchers: (1) that offenders behave in a stable fashion across the crimes they commit and (2) that reliable relationships exist between the way in which offenders commit their crimes and their background characteristics. Research has provided partial support for the first assumption. Consistent with the classic trait model, research has generally found moderate levels of behavioural consistency across the crimes committed by serial offenders, although consistency levels vary substantially as a function of the behaviours under examination (e.g., where offenders commit their crimes tends to be more consistent than how offenders interact with their victims, presumably because of situational factors; Bennell, Mugford, Ellingwood, & Woodhams, 2014). Research has provided even less support for the second assumption. In fact, a recent review of studies that examined this issue led the researchers to conclude that the majority of studies provide no support or little support for the assumption that crime scene behaviours can be used to reliably predict the background characteristics of offenders (Doan & Snook, 2008).

Despite these research findings, some recent Canadian research is beginning to reveal interesting results that provide some support for certain profiling assumptions (e.g., Goodwill & Alison, 2007; Goodwill, Alison, & Beech, 2009; Goodwill et al., 2013; Goodwill et al., 2016). Goodwill and Alison (2007), for example, have argued that previous profiling research may not have found results that were supportive of profiling assumptions because the studies oversimplified the profiling process. For instance, instead of simply testing whether it is possible to predict a background characteristic (offender age) from a crime scene variable (victim age), stable relationships may exist only when contextual factors are taken into account (a view that is more in line with contemporary models of personality that emphasize the importance of the situation). In support of this argument, Goodwill and Alison demonstrated that victim age can be a reliable predictor of offender age, but only under conditions where the offender has shown evidence of offence planning and/or when the offender acted in a particularly violent fashion. Research of this sort may eventually provide the support that is needed for profiling to be considered a reliable and valid investigative tool.

What Is the Impact of Ambiguous Profiles?   Another common criticism of criminal profiling is that many profiles are so ambiguous that they can fit many suspects. If one of the goals of profiling is to help to prioritize potential suspects, this concern clearly needs to be addressed. To examine this issue, Alison, Smith, Eastman, and Rainbow (2003) examined the content of 21 profiling reports developed for major investigations and found that almost a quarter (24%) of all the profiling opinions provided in these reports could be considered ambiguous (i.e., the opinion could be interpreted differently by different people). Of more direct relevance to the ambiguity criticism, however, is an interesting follow-up study conducted by Alison, Smith, and Morgan (2003), in which they examined whether ambiguous profiles could in fact be interpreted to fit more than one suspect.

Alison, Smith, and Morgan (2003) provided details of a genuine crime to two groups of forensic professionals, including senior detectives. The crime involved the murder of a young woman. Each group of participants was then provided with a criminal profile constructed for this case by the FBI. They were asked to read the profile and compare it with the description of a suspect. Unbeknownst to the participants, each group was provided with a different suspect description. One group was provided with the description of the genuine offender, while the other group was provided with a suspect constructed by the researchers, who was different from the genuine offender on a number of key points. After comparing the profile with his or her suspect, each participant was asked to rate the accuracy of the profile and to state if (and why) he or she thought the profile would be operationally useful. Despite the fact that each group received different suspect descriptions, both groups of participants rated the profile as fairly accurate, with no significant difference between the groups. In addition, both groups viewed the profile as generally useful and indicated they thought it would allow the police to narrow down the list of potential suspects and develop new lines of inquiry. This study, therefore, provides preliminary support for the criticism that ambiguous profiles can in fact be interpreted to fit more than one suspect, even when those suspects are quite different from each other.

Although such a finding could have serious implications, we must be careful when interpreting these results. For example, it would be important to know how closely the profile used in this study matches the typical criminal profile provided in the field. In addition, it should be emphasized that this study is far from realistic in that the crime scene details and suspect descriptions provided to the participants contained much less information than would be the case in an actual police investigation. Also important to note is that a more recent study revealed that a more up-to-date sample of profiles used in U.K. investigations did not contain the same degree of ambiguity (13% instead of 24%; Almond, Alison, & Porter, 2007). This result suggests that in certain jurisdictions at least this potential problem may be waning.

How Accurate Are Professional Profilers?   The last criticism that we will deal with here is the possibility that professional profilers may be no more accurate in their profiling predictions than individuals who have received no specialized training.

In early writings on criminal profiling, claims were even made that profilers may be no better than bartenders at predicting the characteristics of unknown offenders (Campbell, 1976). If this is in fact the case, the police must consider how much weight they will put on statements made by professional profilers. Unlike the previous criticisms, this issue has been examined on numerous occasions (e.g., Kocsis, 2003; Pinizzotto & Finkel, 1990).

Richard Kocsis, an Australian forensic psychologist, has conducted most of this research. In his studies, he compares the accuracy of various groups of individuals (e.g., profilers, psychologists, police officers, etc.) on profiling-related tasks. The standard task he uses involves providing participants with the details of a genuine crime to review. The participants are then given a series of questionnaires that deal with various aspects of the offender's background, including his or her physical characteristics, cognitions related to the offence, pre- and post-offence behaviours, social history, and personality characteristics. The participants' task is to select the alternatives that best describe the unknown offender, and accuracy is then determined for each group by comparing the responses from the participants with the correct answers (based on what is known about the genuine offender).

A reasonably large number of studies like this have now been conducted and a meta-analysis was recently published that summarized the results from some of the studies (Snook, Eastwood, Gendreau, Goggin, & Cullen, 2007). One set of analyses in this meta-analysis compared the performance of self-labelled profilers in previous studies to the comparison groups across a variety of prediction categories (e.g., cognitive processes, physical attributes, offence behaviours, history/habits). The results suggest that self-labelled profilers in previous studies performed better than the comparison groups across all the measures with the exception of predictions related to offence behaviours. However, the differences were relatively small. As stated by Snook, Eastwood, et al. (2007), this "demonstrates better performance [on the part of profilers], but not necessarily expert performance" (p. 447). In addition, given the preliminary nature of these sorts of studies and the artificial conditions under which these studies are conducted, it seems likely that the debate over whether professional profilers can provide substantially more accurate profiles than untrained individuals will continue (e.g., Bennell, Jones, Taylor, & Snook, 2006; Kocsis, Middledorp, & Karpin, 2008; Snook, Eastwood, Gendreau, & Bennell, 2010).

GEOGRAPHIC PROFILING

Geographic profiling: An investigative technique that uses crime scene locations to predict the most likely area where an offender resides

In addition to criminal profiling, another form of profiling is commonly used by the police: **geographic profiling**. In simple terms, geographic profiling uses crime scene locations to predict the most likely area where the offender resides (Rossmo, 2000). As is the case with criminal profiling, geographic profiling is used most often in cases involving very violent crimes, though it has also been used in cases of serial robbery, arson, and burglary (Emeno, Bennell, Snook, & Taylor, in press). Geographic profiling is used primarily for prioritizing potential suspects. This prioritization is accomplished by rank ordering the suspects based on how close they live to the predicted home location, so the suspect who lives closest to the predicted home location would be focused on first (Rossmo, 2000). This task is important, considering the number of suspects who can enter a serial crime investigation. For example, in the Green River serial murder case in Washington State, which was solved in 2001, the police collected more than 18 000 suspect names (Rossmo, 1995).

The basic assumption behind geographic profiling is that most serial offenders do not travel far from home to commit their crimes and, therefore, it should be possible to make a reasonably accurate prediction about where an offender lives. Fortunately for the geographic profiler, research supports this assumption. Perhaps surprisingly, it turns out that serial offenders tend to be consistent in their crime site selection choices, often committing their crimes very close to where they reside (Rossmo, 2000). Indeed, even many of the most bizarre serial killers commit their crimes close to home (Canter, Coffey, Huntley, & Missen, 2000). For travelling offenders, particularly those who travel in a particular direction to commit their crimes, geographic profiling is typically not a useful investigative strategy. However, for the majority of serial offenders who do commit their crimes locally, a number of profiling strategies can be used (Snook, Zito, Bennell, & Taylor, 2005).

One of the first cases in which geographic profiling techniques were used was the case of the Yorkshire Ripper in England. After five years of unsolved murders, an advisory team was set up to review the investigation. Although some of the investigators felt the offender lived in a different part of the country from where the crimes were happening, the advisory team believed the offender was a local man. To provide support for this claim, the team constructed a type of geographic profile (Kind, 1987). They plotted the 17 murders onto a map and calculated the centre of gravity for the points. That is, by adding up the x-y coordinates for each crime and dividing by the 17 crimes, they could calculate the x-y coordinate for the centre of gravity. In this case, the centre of gravity was near Bradford, a city close to where the majority of the murders had taken place. When Peter Sutcliffe was eventually arrested for the crimes, he was found to reside in a district of Bradford.

Since the time of the Yorkshire Ripper murders, a number of individuals have built computerized **geographic profiling systems** that can assist with the profiling task (Canter et al., 2000; Levine, 2007; Rossmo, 2000). In basic terms, the locations of linked crime sites are input into these systems and represented as points on a map. The systems then perform calculations by using mathematical models of offender spatial behaviour, which reflect the probability that the offender lives at particular points in the area where the offences have taken place. Every single location on the map is assigned an overall probability and these probabilities are designated a colour. For example, the top 10% of probabilities might be assigned the colour red, and so on. The eventual output is a coloured map, in which each colour band corresponds to the probability that the offender lives in the area (see Figure 3.3). The police use this map to prioritize their investigative activities. Geographic profilers also consider other factors that may affect an offender's spatial behaviour, such as the density of suitable victims in an area, but this probability map forms the basis of their prediction.

Unlike validation studies of criminal profiling, studies of computerized geographic profiling systems tend to show that they can make accurate profiling predictions and that these predictions are likely to assist the police. For example, using crimes committed by 15 serial killers, Rossmo (2000) calculated hit percentage values, which indicated the percentage of the entire prioritized activity space (defined by his Rigel profiling

Geographic profiling systems: Computer systems that use mathematical models of offender spatial behaviour to make predictions about where unknown serial offenders are likely to reside

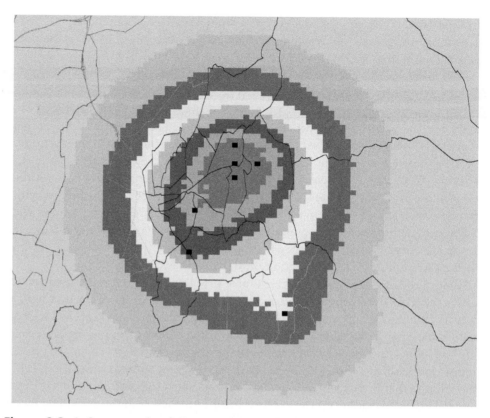

Figure 3.3 A Computerized Geographic Profile

The black dots represent the crime locations and the different coloured bands (represented here by different shades of grey) correspond to the probability that the offender resides in that particular geographic area. The high-priority search area in this case centres on the four crimes in the upper half of the map. This profile was constructed using Dragnet, a computerized geographic profiling system developed by David Canter.

Source: Based on Bennell, C., & Corey, S. (2007). Geographic profiling of terrorist attacks. In R. Kocsis (Ed.), *Criminal profiling: International theory, research, and practice* (pp. 189–203). Totowa, New Jersey: Humana Press.

system) that needed to be searched to locate the offender's home base. Rossmo found that using his system, an offender's residence could be found in 12% of the time it would take a completely random search. Similarly, when Canter et al. (2000) examined the accuracy of Dragnet using the crimes of 79 serial killers, 51% of offender residences that were profiled were located within the top 5% of the prioritized activity space and 87% of offender residences were located in the top 25% of the prioritized activity space.

SUMMARY

1. The primary goal of many police interrogations in North American is to obtain a confession from the suspect. Police officers sometimes use the Reid model of interrogation to accomplish this goal. This model advocates the use of psychologically based interrogation tactics to break down a suspect's resistance to telling the truth. The tactics used in the Reid model of interrogation can be broken down into minimization and maximization techniques.

2. The three potential problems with the Reid model of interrogation are (1) the inability of police officers to accurately detect deception, (2) biases that result from presuming a suspect is guilty, and (3) an increased likelihood that suspects will make false confessions.

3. False confessions must be differentiated from retracted confessions and disputed confessions. A false confession is one that is either intentionally fabricated or is not based on actual knowledge of the facts in a case. A retracted confession is simply an individual's statement that his or her confession is false. A disputed confession is one that is disputed at trial, often because of a legal technicality or because the suspect disputes the confession was ever made.

4. There are three types of false confessions, each having its own set of vulnerability factors. Voluntary false confessions occur when someone voluntarily confesses to a crime he or she did not commit without any elicitation from the police. Coerced-compliant false confessions are those in which the suspect confesses to a crime, even though the suspect is fully aware that he or she did not commit it. Coerced-internalized false confessions consist of individuals confessing to a crime they did not commit—and subsequently coming to the belief they committed the crime—usually after they are exposed to highly suggestible questions.

5. Criminal profiling is sometimes used by the police in serial crime investigations. They use it for prioritizing suspects, developing new lines of inquiry, setting traps to flush out offenders, determining whether an offender's actions should be taken seriously, giving advice on how to interrogate suspects, and developing courtroom strategies. Despite its use, criminal profiling is often criticized. One major criticism centres on the lack of a strong theoretical base underlying the approach. A second criticism relates to the lack of empirical support for certain profiling assumptions. A third criticism is that many profiles contain ambiguous information and this may cause problems when police officers are asked to interpret the profile. A fourth criticism is that professionally trained profilers may be no better than other individuals at constructing accurate profiles.

6. Another common form of profiling is geographic profiling, which is defined as any technique that uses crime scene locations to predict the most likely area where the offender resides. This form of profiling is often used to prioritize suspects, by rank ordering them based on the proximity of their residence to the predicted home location.

Discussion Questions

1. Many police agencies now videotape their interrogations, thus presenting potential advantages for the police, suspects, and the courts. Do you see any potential problems with using this procedure? What are some other possible ways to minimize the problems that result from modern-day interrogation practices?

2. You are a criminal profiler who uses the inductive approach to profiling. You encounter a series of crimes in which the offender consistently attacks elderly women in their apartments at night. How would you go about constructing a profile in this case? What sorts of problems would a deductive profiler have with your profile? How could you attempt to counter some of their arguments?

Chapter 4
Deception

Learning Objectives

- Describe the two types of polygraph tests.

- Describe the most common types of errors made by the Comparison Question Test (CQT) and the Concealed Information Test (CIT).

- Describe physiologically based alternatives to the polygraph, including event-related brain potentials and functional brain-imaging techniques.

- Outline the verbal and nonverbal characteristics of deception.

- Define malingering and list the three explanatory models of malingering.

- Differentiate between the types of studies used to examine malingering.

Dimitri Adonis is a 52-year-old offender serving 6 years for aggravated assault. He has a long history of criminal behaviour and this is his fourth prison sentence. He requests to see the prison psychiatrist complaining of increasing feelings of depression and suicidal ideation. He reports he does not have much of an appetite and is having problems falling asleep most nights. He states he needs to get meds for his depression immediately. Dimitri reports being annoyed by all the questions being asked by the psychiatrist and is very demanding. He is transferred to the behavioral health ward for observation. The nurses notice that as soon as the psychiatrist leaves the ward, Dimitri can be seen joking and laughing with the other offenders and nurses report he is constantly asking for snacks outside meal times. While socializing, Dimitri is overheard describing a situation where he was able to fake depression and get admitted into a hospital. When Dimitri is confronted by correctional staff about the differences between his complaints and the observations made on the ward, he becomes defensive and irritable.

How do we know whether someone is telling the truth or lying? A person may lie to the police about his or her involvement in a crime, lie to a psychologist about psychological symptoms, lie to a probation officer by claiming to be following conditional release requirements, or lie in a job interview. Several techniques have been developed to try to answer this question. As seen in Chapter 3, police attempt to detect whether someone is telling them the truth during an interrogation. Psychologists have participated in the development and testing of a variety of techniques to detect deception. In this chapter, we focus on several issues associated with deception, including the use of the polygraph and alternatives to the polygraph, the relationship between verbal and nonverbal cues to deception, and methods for detecting the malingering of mental disorders.

THE POLYGRAPH TECHNIQUE

Physiological measures have long been used in an attempt to detect deception. For example, at one time the Chinese forced suspects to chew on dry rice powder and then spit it out. If the powder was dry, the suspect was judged to be lying (Kleinmuntz & Szucko, 1984). The rationale for this technique was that anxiety causes a person's mouth to be dry. A person telling the truth would not be anxious and, therefore, would not have a dry mouth. In contrast, a person lying would be anxious and would have a dry mouth. Polygraphy relies on the same underlying principle: Deception is associated with physiological change. The origins of modern polygraphy date from 1917 when William Marston, a Harvard psychologist also trained as a lawyer, developed a systolic blood pressure test (Iacono & Patrick, 1999) and attempted to use this physiological response as evidence for a person's innocence (see Lykken, 1998). Marston's testimony was rejected by the courts in *Frye v. United States* (1923) because they felt the test had not gained acceptance by the scientific community, foreshadowing the debate associated with physiological measures that continues to the present day.

A **polygraph** (the word is a combination of two Greek words, *poly* = "many" and *grapho* = "write") is a device for recording an individual's autonomic nervous system responses. Measurement devices are attached to the upper chest and abdomen to measure breathing. The amount of sweat on the skin is measured by attaching electrodes to the fingertips. Sweat changes the conductance of the skin, which is known as the skin conductance response. Finally, heart rate is measured by a partially inflated blood pressure cuff attached to an arm. Each of these measures is amplified and stored on a computer to be analyzed. In a forensic context, a polygraph is used to measure a person's physiological responses to questions asked by an examiner.

Polygraph: A device for recording an individual's autonomic nervous system responses

In Canada, polygraph training is provided by the Canadian Police College. The polygraph course at the Canadian Police College is restricted to police officers. The college offers a 12-week intensive course that covers the various techniques, interviewing practices, and scoring.

Applications of the Polygraph Test

Polygraph tests are used for a range of purposes. In Canada, the police often use them to help in their criminal investigations. The police may ask a suspect to take a polygraph test as a means to resolve the case. If the

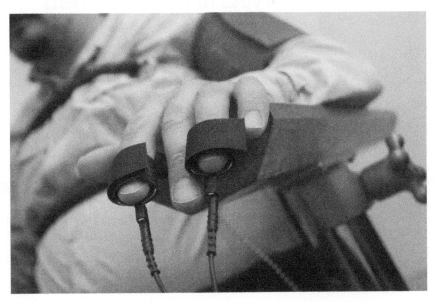

A suspect being given a polygraph test
Pefostudio5/Shutterstock

suspect fails the polygraph test, that person may be pressured to confess, thereby giving the police incriminating evidence. Although not common, police may ask alleged victims of crimes to take a polygraph test to help verify whether a crime has occurred. Insurance companies may request a polygraph test to verify the claims of the insured. More recently, the polygraph has been used in the United States to assess and monitor sexual offenders on probation. **Polygraph disclosure tests** are used to uncover information about an offender's past behaviour. Some sexual offender treatment programs require sexual offenders to take a polygraph to help uncover undetected offences. For example, Bourke and colleagues (2015) polygraphed 127 sexual offenders with no official history of hands-on offending. Prior to the polygraph, 5% admitted to sexually abusing a child, but during the polygraph procedure, 53% disclosed about hands-on sexual abuse. In addition, polygraph tests have been used to determine whether the offender is violating the conditions of probation or to test for evidence of risky behaviour, such as sexual fantasies about children.

At one time, the most widespread applications of polygraph testing in the United States were for the periodic testing of employees to identify those engaged in theft or using drugs at work and for the screening of prospective employees, to weed out those with criminal tendencies or substance-abuse problems. However, the Employee Polygraph Protection Act of 1988 restricted private companies from using the polygraph for these purposes and limited the use of the polygraph to specific investigations of job-related wrongdoing. Nonetheless, some governmental agencies in the United States and Canada still use the polygraph as a general screening tool. For example, some police departments require applicants to take a polygraph test, and the Canadian Security Intelligence Service (CSIS) also requires that its potential employees take a polygraph test to assess "the candidate's reliability and loyalty."

Types of Polygraph Tests

The polygraph is sometimes called a lie detector but the polygraph does not detect lies per se, since the physiological states associated with lying share much in common with many other states, including anxiety, anger, embarrassment, and fear. Instead, polygraph tests rely on measuring physiological responses to different types of questions. Some questions are designed to elicit a larger physiological response in guilty individuals than in those who are innocent. The two main types of polygraph tests are reviewed below.

The Comparison Question Test The **Comparison Question Test** (CQT; also known as the Control Question Test) is the most commonly used test to investigate criminal acts. First, the polygraph examiner becomes familiar with the case by reading the police file or speaking with the police investigator. Next, the examiner meets with the suspect and conducts a pretest interview in which the suspect is asked about the offense. During this stage the examiner develops a series of 'yes' or 'no' questions. During the testing phase, the examiner then connects the suspect to the polygraph and measures the suspect's physiological response to the questions. The questions are repeated three to five times in different order. The examiner then scores the physiological responses and ends the CQT with a post-test interview in which the test results are discussed.

Table 4.1 Typical Question Series Used in a Comparison Question Test

Type of Question	Questions
Irrelevant	Do you understand that I will be asking only questions we have discussed before?
Irrelevant	Do you live in Canada?
Comparison	Between the ages of 18 and 28, did you ever deliberatively plan to physically hurt someone?
Relevant	Did you stab Petunia Bottoms on the night of March 10?
Irrelevant	Is your first name Craig?
Comparison	Prior to 2010, did you ever verbally threaten to hurt anyone?
Relevant	Did you use a knife to stab Petunia Bottoms?
Irrelevant	Were you born in November?
Comparison	During the first 28 years of your life, did you ever do anything illegal?
Relevant	On March 10, did you participate, in any way, in the stabbing of Petunia Bottoms?

A critical component of this technique is the pretest interview. During the pretest interview, the polygraph examiner develops the comparison questions, learns about the background of the suspect, and attempts to convince the suspect of the accuracy of the polygraph test. The examiner will do this by quoting very high accuracy rates and conducting a stimulation test. For example, the suspect will pick a card with a number on it from a deck of cards, and the examiner will determine the number by examining the polygraph chart. The deck of cards is rigged so the examiner knows which card the suspect picked.

The examiner then asks ten questions to be answered with either "yes" or "no." Table 4.1 provides an example of a typical question series used in a CQT. Three types of questions are asked. Irrelevant questions, referring to the respondent's identity or personal background (e.g., "Is your first name *Beatrice*?"), are included as a baseline but are not scored. Relevant and comparison questions establish guilt or innocence. Relevant questions deal with the crime being investigated (e.g., "On June 12, did you stab your ex-wife?"). Probable-lie comparison questions (also known as control questions) are designed to be emotionally arousing for all respondents and typically focus on the person's honesty and past history prior to the event being investigated (e.g., "Before the age of 45, did you ever try to seriously hurt someone?"). Polygraph examiners assume they can detect deception by comparing reactions to the relevant and comparison questions. Guilty suspects are assumed to react more to relevant questions than comparison questions. In contrast, innocent suspects are assumed to react more to comparison questions than relevant questions. The reasoning behind these assumptions is that innocent people know they are telling the truth about the relevant question, so they will react more strongly to general questions about their honesty and past history.

Examiners in the past used global scoring, incorporating all available information—including physiological responses, the suspect's demeanour during the examination, and information in the case file—to make a decision about the guilt or the innocence of the suspect. Most examiners now numerically score the charts to ensure that decisions are based solely on the physiological responses. A polygraph test has three possible outcomes: truthful, deceptive, and inconclusive. During the post-test interview, the examiner tells the suspect the outcome, and if the outcome is deceptive the examiner attempts to obtain a confession.

Several psychologists have questioned the underlying rationale of the CQT (Cross & Saxe, 2001; Iacono, 2008). Imagine yourself being falsely accused of a serious crime and taking a polygraph exam. Being innocent, you might react more strongly to questions about a crime that you could get punished for (i.e., relevant questions) than about vague questions concerning your past behaviour (i.e., comparison questions). In contrast, guilty suspects might actually respond more to comparison questions because they are novel or because they believe they have other crimes to hide. In addition, the guilty suspect may no longer react to the crime-relevant questions because he or she may have been asked repeatedly about the crime. The validity of the CQT is discussed later in the chapter.

The Concealed Information Test   This test was developed by Lykken (1960) and was originally called the Guilty Knowledge Test but is currently known as the **Concealed Information Test** (CIT). The CIT does not assess deception but instead seeks to determine whether the suspect knows details about a crime that only the person who committed the crime would know. The general form of the CIT is a series of questions in multiple-choice format. Each question has one correct option (often called the critical option) and four options that are foils—alternatives that could fit the crime but that are incorrect. A CIT question in the context of a homicide might take the following form: "Did you kill the person with (a) a knife, (b) an axe, (c) a handgun, (d) a crowbar, or (e) a rifle?" The guilty suspect is assumed to display a larger physiological response to the correct option than to the incorrect options. An innocent person, conversely, who does not know the details of the crime, will show the same physiological response to all options.

Underlying the CIT is the principle that people will react more strongly to information they recognize as distinctive or important than to unimportant information. Suspects who consistently respond to critical items are assumed to have knowledge of the crime. The likelihood that an innocent person with no knowledge of the crime would react most strongly to the critical alternative is one in five for each question. If ten questions are asked, the odds that an innocent person will consistently react to the critical alternative are exceedingly small (less than 1 in 10 000 000). Critics of the CIT have warned that this test will work only if the suspect remembers the details of the crime (Honts & Schweinle, 2009). Criminals may not remember specific details from their crimes or may have memory interference from past crimes. The most common physiological response measured when administering the CIT is palmar sweating (i.e., skin conductance response).

Although law enforcement in Canada and the United States does not routinely use the CIT, it is used regularly in a limited number of other jurisdictions, such as Israel and Japan (Ben-Shakhar & Furedy, 1990). Iacono and Patrick (1999) suggested two reasons for the lack of widespread acceptance of the CIT. First, since polygraph examiners believe in the accuracy of the CQT, they are not motivated to

Concealed Information Test: A type of polygraph test designed to determine if the person knows details about a crime

use the more difficult-to-construct CIT. Second, for law enforcement to use the CIT, salient features of the crime must be known only to the perpetrator. If details of a crime appear in the media, the crime-related details given cannot be used to construct a CIT.

Validity of Polygraph Techniques

Types of Studies   How is the accuracy of polygraph tests assessed? Accuracy is determined under ideal circumstances by presenting information known to be true and false to individuals and measuring their corresponding physiological responses. In practice, studies assessing the validity of polygraph techniques vary in how closely they are able to achieve this ideal. Studies of the validity of polygraph techniques can be classified into two types: laboratory and field studies.

In laboratory studies, volunteers (often university students) simulate criminal behaviour by committing a mock crime. Volunteers come to a laboratory and are randomly assigned to one of two conditions: committing a mock crime or not committing a mock crime. The main advantage of these studies is that the experimenter knows **ground truth** (i.e., who is truly guilty or innocent). In addition, laboratory studies can also compare the relative merits of different types of polygraph tests and control for variables such as the time between the crime and the polygraph exam. However, because of the large motivational and emotional differences between volunteers in laboratory studies and actual suspects in real-life situations, the results of laboratory studies may have limited application to real life. In laboratory studies, guilty participants cannot ethically be given strong incentives to "beat" the polygraph, and both guilty and innocent participants have little to fear if they "fail" the polygraph exam.

Field studies involve real-life situations and actual criminal suspects, together with actual polygraph examinations. Field studies often compare the accuracy of "original" examiners to "blind" evaluators. Original examiners conduct the actual evaluation of the suspect. Blind evaluators are provided with only the original examiner's charts and are given no information about the suspect or the case. Original examiners are exposed to extra polygraph cues—information about the case in addition to that obtained via the polygraph, such as the case facts and the behaviour of the suspect during the examination. Although polygraph examiners are taught to ignore these cues, Patrick and Iacono (1991) found that examiners are nonetheless significantly influenced by them.

The largest problem with field studies is establishing ground truth. Indicators of guilt, such as physical evidence, eyewitness testimony, or DNA evidence, are often not available. In such situations, truth is more difficult to establish. To deal with this problem, two additional ways of establishing ground truth have been developed: judicial outcomes and confessions. Judicial outcomes are problematic because some people are falsely convicted and some guilty people are not convicted. Confessions are also problematic. Although rare, some people may falsely confess. More significant, however, is the problem that confessions are often not independent from the polygraph examiner's decisions. Confessions are often elicited because a person fails a polygraph exam. Moreover, cases in which a guilty suspect passes the polygraph are

Ground truth: As applied to polygraph research, the knowledge of whether the person is actually guilty or innocent

not included in research studies. Thus, reliance on confessions to establish ground truth likely inflates polygraph accuracy rates (Iacono & Patrick, 2006). Most field studies have used confessions to establish ground truth.

Polygraph Tests: Accurate or Not?   The accuracy of the polygraph for detecting lies is debatable. Numerous laboratory studies have assessed the accuracy of the CQT and the CIT (see Iacono & Patrick, 1999, for a review). However, as pointed out above, there are problems when relying on typical mock-crime scenarios to estimate real-life accuracy. As a consequence, only field studies of the CQT will be described here. The situation concerning the CIT is different. Since the CIT is almost never used in Canada or the United States, no relevant North American data are available. Thus, we will describe assessments of the CIT based on laboratory and field studies done in Israel.

Although the CQT has been investigated for more than 30 years, its ability to accurately measure deception remains controversial (Iacono, 2009; National Research Council, 2003). Most of the studies have used confessions to classify suspects as guilty or innocent, and as noted above, there are problems with using this as the criterion. Most guilty suspects (84% to 92%) are correctly classified as guilty (Patrick & Iacono, 1991; Raskin, Honts, & Kircher, 1997). However, the picture for innocent suspects is less optimistic, with accuracy rates ranging from 55% to 78% (Honts & Raskin, 1988; Patrick & Iacono, 1991). Many of the innocent suspects were classified as inconclusive. Between 9% and 24% of innocent suspects were falsely identified as guilty. Such a high false-positive rate indicates that innocent people respond more to relevant than comparison questions, suggesting that the premise underlying the CQT does not apply to all suspects.

Mock-crime laboratory studies evaluating the CIT indicate that it is very effective at identifying innocent participants (hit rates of up to 95%) and slightly less effective at identifying guilty participants (hit rates between 76% and 85%) (Gamer, Rill, Vossel, & Gödert, 2005; Iacono & Patrick, 1988; Jokinen, Santilla, Ravaja, & Puttonen, 2006; Lykken, 1998). A meta-analysis of 80 CIT studies examined what factors are associated with higher accuracies (Ben-Shakhar & Elaad, 2003). Correct outcomes were better in studies that included motives to succeed, verbal response to alternatives, five or more questions, and in laboratory mock-crime studies. Two published field studies, both done in Israel, have assessed the accuracy of the CIT. Elaad (1990) found that 98% of innocent suspects were correctly classified, but only 42% of guilty suspects were correctly classified. Elaad, Ginton, and Jungman (1992) measured both respiration and skin conductance and found that 94% of innocent and 76% of guilty suspects were correctly classified.

Based on the research described above, the CIT appears to be vulnerable to false-negative errors (falsely classifying guilty suspects as innocent), whereas the CQT is vulnerable to false-positive errors (falsely classifying innocent suspects as guilty). See Box 4.1 for a new way of measuring deception.

Can the Guilty Learn to Beat the Polygraph?

Countermeasures: As applied to polygraph research, techniques used to try to conceal guilt

Is it possible to use **countermeasures** to beat the polygraph? Honts, Raskin, and Kircher (1994) showed that 30 minutes of instruction on the rationale underlying the CQT was sufficient for community volunteers to learn how to escape detection in a

Box 4.1   Forensic Psychology in the Spotlight

Seeing Through the Face of Deception

If you travel by air, you will be subjected to intense scrutiny. Airport security officers have become increasingly vigilant in their attempts to detect passengers intent on harm. Technologies that can provide a rapid, accurate assessment of deceit are becoming more and more important.

Pavlidis, Eberhardt, and Levine (2002) examined whether high-definition thermal imaging of the face could be used to detect deceit. Thermal imaging measures the amount of facial warming, which is linked to regional blood flow. Imaging can be done quickly without the individual even knowing his or her facial temperature is being measured. Pavlidis and colleagues wanted to know whether facial warming was associated with deception. Individuals were randomly assigned to commit a mock crime (stab a mannequin and rob it of $20) or to a control condition in which they had no knowledge of the crime. Use of thermal imaging (in particular around the eyes) correctly classified 6 of the 8 (75%) guilty participants and 11 of the 12 (92%) innocent participants. This accuracy rate was similar to a polygraph exam administered to participants that correctly classified 6 of 8 guilty and 8 of 12

innocent participants. Pavlidis and colleagues claimed that this technique "has the potential for application in remote and rapid screening, without the need for skilled staff or physical contact" (p. 35).

Warmelink and colleagues (2011) questioned the claims made by Pavlidis et al. In a recent study, passengers at an international airport were randomly assigned to lie or tell the truth to an interviewer about their travel plans. Skin temperature was measured by a thermal-imaging camera with liars' facial skin temperature increasing during the interview whereas truth-tellers remained stable. Using skin temperature, 69% of the liars and 64% of the truth-tellers were identified. However, the interviewer did a better job at identifying deception, correctly classifying 77% of the liars and 74% of the truth-tellers. The researchers concluded from their findings that "it is unlikely that thermal imaging can be used effectively at airports as a general screening device" (p. 47). So unless there is more research supporting the use of thermal imaging, security or customs officers should still focus more on what you say than on how red your face gets.

mock-crime study. Participants were told to use either physical countermeasures (e.g., biting their tongue or pressing their toes on the floor) or mental countermeasures (e.g., counting backward by 7 from a number greater than 200) when asked a comparison question during the polygraph exam. Both countermeasures worked, with 50% of the guilty suspects beating the polygraph test. In addition, the polygraph examiners were not able to accurately detect which participants had used the countermeasures.

Iacono, Cerri, Patrick, and Fleming (1992) investigated whether anti-anxiety drugs would allow

Caraman/Getty Images

guilty subjects to appear innocent on the CIT. Undergraduate students were divided into one innocent group (who watched a noncrime videotape) and four guilty groups. Participants in the guilty groups watched a videotaped crime and then were given one of three drugs (diazepam, meprobamate, or propranolol) or a placebo prior to being administered a CIT. None of the drugs had an effect on the accuracy of the CIT. In addition, the polygraph examiner was able to identify 90% of the participants receiving drugs.

Scientific Opinion: What Do the Experts Say?

Most knowledgeable scientists are skeptical about the rationale underlying the CQT and its accuracy. But what does the public believe? Table 4.2 presents the results from two surveys: one done with 195 members of the Society for Psychophysiological Research and (Iacono & Lykken, 1997), and another done with 411 people from the general public (Myers, Latter, & Abdollahi-Arena, 2006). As you can see, both samples are not very supportive of the polygraph and using the results in courts. However, the public does have more positive beliefs concerning the accuracy of the polygraph. For example, experts are much less likely to agree that the CQT is 85% accurate at detecting a guilty person (27%) as compared to the general public (75%).

The United States National Research Council (NRC) established a panel of 14 scientists and 4 staff to review the validity of the polygraph (NRC, 2003). In a comprehensive report, the committee concluded the following:

- "The theoretical rationale for the polygraph is quite weak, especially in terms of differential fear, arousal, or other emotional states that are triggered in response to relevant and comparison questions" (NRC, 2003, p. 213).

Table 4.2 Comparing Expert and Nonexpert Opinion about the Polygraph

Question	Percent Who Agree	
Which one of the following statements best describes your opinion of the polygraph as evidence to be used in court to determine whether a suspect is, or is not, telling the truth? It is . . .	Expert	Nonexpert
(a) a sufficiently reliable method to be the sole determinant.	0	4
(b) a useful diagnostic tool when considered with other available information.	44	63
(c) of questionable usefulness, entitled to little weight against other available information.	54	25
(d) of no usefulness.	2	8

Source: Based on Iacono & Lykken, 1997; Myers et al., 2006.

- "The existing validation studies have serious limitations. Laboratory test findings on polygraph validity are not a good guide to accuracy in field settings. They are likely to overestimate accuracy in field practice, but by an unknown amount" (p. 210).

- "In summary, we were unable to find any field experiments, field quasi-experiments, or prospective research-oriented data collection specifically designed to assess polygraph validity and satisfying minimal standards of research quality" (p. 115).

- "What is remarkable, given the large body of relevant research, is that claims about the accuracy of the polygraph made today parallel those made throughout the history of the polygraph: practitioners have always claimed extremely high levels of accuracy, and these claims have rarely been reflected in empirical research" (p. 107).

Despite scientists' negative view of it, the CQT is still used by law enforcement as an investigative tool. To understand why, we have to know only that whatever its actual validity, the polygraph will cause many suspects to confess, thereby providing resolution of the criminal investigation.

Admissibility of Polygraph Evidence

Polygraph results were first submitted as evidence in court in the United States in *Frye v. United States* (1923). James Frye was denied the opportunity to have the results of a polygraph test conducted by William Marston admitted as evidence. This ruling led to the requirement that a technique must obtain "general acceptance" by the relevant scientific community before it can be admitted as evidence. Polygraph evidence is not admissible in Canadian criminal courts of law. The same concerns that U.S. courts have raised have been a focus of concern in Canadian courts. In *R. v. Beland* (1987), the Supreme Court of Canada ruled that polygraph evidence should not be admitted to help to determine whether a person is telling the truth. The court referred to the polygraph as being falsely imbued with the "mystique of science," thus causing jurors to give polygraph evidence more weight than it deserves when determining the verdict.

BRAIN-BASED DECEPTION RESEARCH

In the past decade, researchers have attempted to use brain-based responses to detect deception. **Event-related brain potentials** (ERPs) are a type of brain-based response that has been investigated for detecting deception. ERPs are measured by placing electrodes on the scalp and by noting changes in electrical patterns related to presentation of a stimulus. ERPs reflect underlying electrical activity in the cerebral cortex. One type of ERP that has shown promise is known as the P300. This ERP occurs in response to significant stimuli that occur infrequently. When using CIT procedures, guilty suspects should respond to crime-relevant events with a large P300 response, compared with their response to noncrime-relevant events. No difference in P300 responses to crime-relevant and irrelevant events should be observed in innocent suspects. One of the advantages of ERPs is that they have been proposed as a measure resistant to manipulation (Farwell, 2012).

Event-related brain potentials: Brain activity measured by placing electrodes on the scalp and by recording electrical patterns related to presentation of a stimulus

Several studies have been conducted to assess the validity of the P300 as a guilt detector (e.g., Abootalebi, Moradi, & Khalilzadeh, 2006; Farwell & Donchin, 1991; Rosenfeld, Angell, Johnson, & Qian, 1991; Rosenfeld, Nasman, Whalen, Cantwell, & Mazzeri, 1987; Verschuere, Rosenfeld, Winograd, Labkovsky, & Wiersema, 2009). Farwell and Donchin (1991) conducted one of the first studies on the use of the P300 to detect the presence of guilty knowledge. The study consisted of two experiments. In the first experiment, participants role-played one of two espionage scenarios that involved the exchange of information with a foreign agent, during which they were exposed to six critical details (e.g., the colour of the agent's hat). In the second experiment, participants were asked about details of minor offences they had committed in their day-to-day lives. In the first experiment, using P300 as the measure, 18 of 20 participants were correctly classified in the guilty condition, and 17 of 20 were correctly classified in the innocent condition. In the second experiment, all four of the guilty participants were correctly classified, and three of the four innocent participants were correctly classified. Although the results look impressive, there are several limitations to this study. First, guilty participants reviewed the crime-relevant details just prior to taking the CIT. In addition, there were no aversive consequences linked to performance in this study. Finally, the sample size, especially in the second experiment, was very small. Abootalebi and colleagues (2006) recently reported lower detection rates than previously reported (e.g., Rosenfeld et al., 1991) when employing the P300-CIT paradigm, with correct identification ranging from 74% to 80%, depending on the approach. More recently, Farwell (2012) described the P300-MERMER response, which is a longer ERP wave form. Farwell claims that this brainwave response is a more accurate measure of concealed knowledge in tasks that are more complex, such as actual criminal cases.

More recently, a possible new lie-detection technique using functional magnetic resonance imaging (fMRI) has been examined. fMRI measures the cerebral blood flow (a marker of neurological activity) in different areas of the brain. The appeal of using a brain-based lie detection approach is that instead of measuring emotional arousal, researchers hope that it measures the actual process of deception. Researchers have used fMRI to determine which areas of the brain are associated with deception in a variety of deception paradigms, including forced-choice lies (e.g., responding yes when the truth is no; Nuñez, Casey, Egner, Hare, &

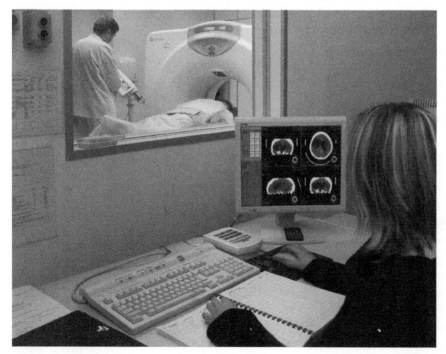

A suspect being given an fMRI exam
Andrzej Solnica/Fotolia

Hirsch, 2005), spontaneous lies (e.g., saying Vancouver when the true answer is Toronto; Ganis, Kosslyn, Stose, Thompson, & Yurgelun-Todd, 2003), rehearsed lies (Ganis et al., 2003), faking memory impairment (Lee et al., 2005), and concealed information tests (e.g., lying about hiding stolen money; Kozel et al., 2005; Mohamed et al., 2006). The most consistent finding from the studies is that the lie conditions produce greater activation in the prefrontal and anterior cingulate regions as compared to truth conditions. These findings and others indicate that brain-imaging techniques can differentiate which parts of the brain are involved in lying and may even indicate which areas are associated with different types of lying. fMRI laboratory studies have found that deceptive and honest responses can be detected at accuracies around 90% (Lee et al., 2009; Nose, Murai, & Taira, 2009). Ganis and colleagues (2011) investigated whether a simple covert movement (e.g., move your left toe) would impact the accuracy of the fMRI in a concealed information paradigm. When participants did not use this countermeasure, deception detection accuracy was 100%, but it was only 33% when the countermeasure was used. A limitation of this research, however, is that it is typically based on averaging fMRI data across multiple participants, which constrains its use for detecting deception in individuals. In addition, studies have used healthy volunteers who have been screened for neurological and psychiatric disorders, who have been instructed to lie, and who do not face any serious consequences. How well this technique will generalize to real-life cases remains to be investigated. Although there are already commercial companies such as No Lie MRI (established in 2006) encouraging the use of fMRI in legal proceedings, most scientists feel that it is premature to use fMRI to detect deception and that the results should not be admissible to court (Farah, Huchinson, Phelps, & Wanger, 2014; Greely & Illes, 2007; Simpson, 2008).

There are also concerns that brain-imaging evidence may have a particularly powerful influence on juror decision making. Simply seeing pictures of brain images makes people believe that scientific results are more valid compared to when other images (such as figures or tables) are presented (McCabe & Castel, 2008). McCabe, Castel, and Rhodes (2011) examined the influence of evidence from the polygraph, fMRI lie detection, or thermal imaging on verdicts in a mock juror trial. A sample of undergraduates read a court transcript in which a defendant was accused of killing his estranged wife and her lover. Students were randomly assigned to four conditions: control (no expert testified), polygraph (expert testified the defendant was lying when he denied killing his wife and her lover), thermal imaging (expert testified the temperature in defendant's face increased when he denied killing his wife and her lover), and fMRI (expert testified there was increased activation of the frontal brain areas when defendant denied killing his wife and her lover). Evidence from fMRI lie detection resulted in more guilty verdicts when compared with the other types of evidence being presented. Figure 4.1 presents the percentage of guilty verdicts across these conditions. However, the researchers found that if expert testimony that questioned the validity of fMRI lie detection was included, the number of guilty verdicts was reduced to a similar level as in the other conditions. There are clearly a number of practical, scientific, and ethical issues that need to be considered before fMRI evidence makes its way into the courtroom.

Box 4.2 describes the case of Terry Harrington, a man convicted of murder who attempted to use the results of brain-based deception testing to prove his innocence.

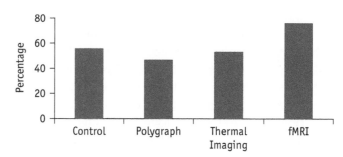

Figure 4.1 Percentage of Guilty Verdicts Across Conditions in the McCabe et al. (2011) Study

Source: Based on McCabe et al. (2011).

Box 4.2   Cases in Forensic Psychology

Brain Fingerprinting: Is This Admissible in Court?
Harrington v. State (2003)

The case that put brain fingerprinting in the news was *Harrington v. State* (2003). On July 22, 1977, retired police officer John Schweer was shot and killed while working as a security guard for a car dealership in Iowa. Seventeen-year-old Terry Harrington and Curtis McGhee were arrested for the murder. At his trial, Terry Harrington claimed he was not at the crime scene and several witnesses testified that Harrington had been at a concert on the night of the murder. The prosecution's key witness was another teenager, Kevin Hughes, who testified that he was with Harrington and McGhee on the night of the murder. According to Hughes, the three teenagers decided to steal a car. They went to the car dealership. Hughes testified that he waited in the car while Harrington, who first removed a shotgun from the trunk, and McGhee went around a building at the car dealership. Hughes claimed he heard a gunshot and Harrington and McGhee came running back to the car. Hughes testified that Harrington had stated he had just shot a cop. Both Terry Harrington and Curtis McGhee were convicted of first-degree murder and sentenced to life in prison without the possibility of parole.

Throughout his 25 years of imprisonment, Terry Harrington maintained his innocence, but all his attempts to appeal his conviction were unsuccessful. From his prison cell, Harrington heard about a new technology that might help his case. He contacted Lawrence Farwell, a cognitive psychophysiologist and head of Brain Fingerprinting Laboratories. On April 18 and 25, 2000, Farwell came to the

Iowa State Penitentiary to test Harrington to determine if he had knowledge of the crime scene and of details about his alibi (the concert he claimed he attended). Farwell measured the amplitude of Harrington's P300 brain potential to irrelevant and relevant crime scene and concert details. According to Farwell, Harrington's lack of P300 response to crime-relevant details indicated that Harrington had not participated in the murder. In contrast, Harrington showed a prominent P300 to alibi-relevant information.

Harrington's case received national attention in December 2001 when the CBS show *60 Minutes* featured Farwell's research and his testing of Harrington. In March 2002, Harrington's lawyer submitted a report describing the results of Farwell's testing to the Supreme Court of Iowa.

Although the results of the brain fingerprinting were entered as evidence, the judges relied on other evidence to overturn the murder conviction. During the hearing, three of the prosecution witnesses recanted their testimony. Kevin Hughes stated that he had made up the story about what happened the night of the murder. Hughes claimed that he lied to obtain the $5000 reward being offered about the murder and to avoid being charged with the crime. In addition, the police failed to turn over all the police reports to Harrington's defence lawyer. These reports documented the police investigation of an alternative suspect. On February 26, 2003, the Supreme Court of Iowa overturned the murder conviction of Terry Harrington and the case was remanded for a new trial. On October 24, 2003, the Pottawattamie

(continued)

(continued)

County Attorney announced that he was dropping the murder charges against Terry Harrington. Harrington and McGhee sued the prosecutor and the State of Iowa and received a joint $12 million out-of-court settlement.

Questions

1. What are the advantages of using brain-based deception-detection techniques?

2. Should psychologists be permitted to testify in court using these newly developed brain-based techniques to detect deception?

3. Do you think there are any ethical concerns with using brain-based techniques to identify deception?

Verbal and Nonverbal Behaviour Cues to Lying

On average, North Americans tell one to two lies per day (Serota, Levine, & Boster, 2010). However, a small number of people are prolific liars. The most common method of deception detection is through the analysis of verbal characteristics and nonverbal behaviours. The underlying assumption is the same as that for polygraphy: The act of deception produces a physiological change compared with telling the truth. The argument here is that it is more difficult for people to control aspects of their nonverbal behaviour than their verbal behaviour (DePaulo & Kirkendol, 1989). The typical experiment involves one group of participants (called the *message source*) who are told to provide either true or deceptive messages. For example, DePaulo, Lassiter, and Stone (1982) asked participants to honestly describe people they liked and disliked. They also asked participants to describe the same people dishonestly (i.e., to pretend to like the person they disliked and vice versa). Another group of participants was asked to detect when the message source participants were truthful or deceptive. Participants who were instructed to focus their attention on the message source participants' tone of voice were more successful at detecting deception than those participants given no special instructions.

Researchers have also assessed facial cues and other nonverbal cues to deception. For example, Ekman and Friesen (1974) showed student nurses a film of an ocean scene and videotaped them describing what they were seeing and how they felt while watching the film. They also watched a gruesome medical training film (e.g., the amputation of a hand or a severe industrial burn) and were videotaped while pretending that the film they were watching was pleasant. To motivate the nurses watching the gruesome film, the researchers told them that to be successful in nursing, they would have to be able to mask feelings when dealing with unpleasant events. Ekman and Friesen found that the nurses focused on controlling their facial expressions when attempting to deceive. Observers who watched videotapes of the nurses attempting to deceive were more likely to detect deception when they were shown a videotape of the nurses' bodies (with the faces blacked out) than when shown a videotape of their faces. Subsequent research on whether nonverbal cues can be used as an indicator of deception is mixed (Vrij, 2008). Nonverbal behaviours, such as gaze aversion, smiling, and self-manipulation (e.g., rubbing one's hands), are not reliable indicators of deception. See Box 4.3 for myths about detecting deception.

If a liar is not feeling excited, scared, or guilty, or when the lie is easy to fabricate, behavioural cues to deception will likely not be present. In a study of everyday lying, DePaulo, Kashy, Kirkendol, Wyer, and Epstein (1996) found that both college students

Box 4.3　Myths and Realities: Detection of Deception

What are valid cues to deception? There are several myths about what these are and who is able to successfully detect deception. Here is a list of these myths accompanied by facts that challenge these false beliefs.

Myth 1: Only antisocial people tell lies.
Fact. Most people are truthful most of the time but lying is also pretty common. On average we tell one to two lies a day. DePaulo and Kashy (1998) found that undergraduate students told fewer lies to closer friends and that lies to friends were more altruistic ("I told him I loved the food he ordered for me even though it wasn't great"), whereas lies to acquaintances and strangers were more self-serving ("I told the customer that if she likes her jeans that way, they weren't too tight").

Myth 2: Shifty eyes, avoidance of eye contact, or eyes looking to the left are signs of lying.
Fact. There is no scientific evidence that eye behaviours are reliable signs of lying. In 2006, a group of 90 researchers reported on stereotypes about liars in 75 countries (The Global Deception Team, 2006). The number one stereotype was that liars avoided eye contact. Avoidance of eye contact could be due to many different reasons, but it is not a reliable cue to lying. In contrast, Mann and colleagues (2013) reported that a liar is more likely to deliberate look at you in order to try and appear to be convincing and to monitor your reactions to their lies. Another concern is that in some cultures gaze aversion is a sign of respect when speaking to someone in authority.

Myth 3: It is easy to detect who is lying.
Fact. People are poor deception detectors and it is difficult to detect lies. People are accurate about 54 percent of the time at detecting lies (Bond & DePaulo, 2006). Even those whose job it is to detect lies, such as police officers, often perform at chance levels (Meissner & Kassin, 2002). However, more recent research has found higher accuracy rates when more ecologically valid or real-world stimulus materials are used. For example, Whelan, Wagstaff, and Wheatcroft (2015) asked 70 police officers to watch 36 videos of people lying or telling the truth in a high-stakes, real-life situation. Police officers obtained an accuracy of 72%, indicating that they are more accurate at detecting deception in real-life situations.

Myth 4: Liars fidget more.
Fact. Another stereotypic belief is that liars fidget more. Fidgeting is unrelated to lying. For example, Mann et al. (2004) examined the accuracy of 99 police officers to detect truths and lies by suspect during their police interviews. The researchers found that accuracy was negatively correlated with fidgeting.

Myth 5: Women are better at catching lies then men.
Fact. This myth is partially correct. Women are not any better at detecting the lies of strangers, but they are better than men at detecting the lies of friends and romantic partners. McCornack and Parks (1990), for example, found that women were better able than men to detect lies told by their romantic partners. Anderson, DePaulo, Ansfield, Tickle, and Green (1999) found that female friends were better at detecting lies after being friends for six months, whereas male friends were not any more accurate at detecting lies after six months.

and community members practised deception daily. Most of the deception was not considered serious, and the participants reported they were not concerned or worried about being caught. Participants lied about their opinions, feelings, achievements, reasons for doing things, and possessions. Most of the lies were told for psychological reasons, such as protecting the liar from embarrassment. For example, "I told her Ted and I still liked each other when really I don't know if he likes me at all." The reason this person lied was "because I'm ashamed of the fact that he doesn't like me anymore."

Ekman (1992) hypothesized that when people are attempting to conceal an emotion, the true emotion may be manifest as a microfacial expression. These microexpressions are brief facial expressions reflecting the true emotions the person is experiencing. In response to terrorists concerns, the United States has been training security officers at airports to use this technique (reading concealed emotions in people) to identify potential threats. Matsumoto, Hwang, Skinner, and Frank (2011) recommended that during interrogations investigators pay attention not only to what a suspect says but also to the suspect's facial expressions.

Strömwall, Hartwig, and Granhag (2006) explored the role of stress by creating a realistic deception scenario that used experienced police officers, employed long interrogations, and generated suspects who were motive driven and had adequate time to prepare their deception. Participants were offered $30 to tell a biographical story to a police officer and were randomly instructed to be honest or deceitful. To create motivation and higher risk, participants were offered an additional $20 if they were able to convince the officer that they were being truthful. Liars felt more anxious and stressed during the task when compared to truth-tellers. No differences in nonverbal behaviours were observed. For verbal strategies, the majority of truth-tellers claimed to "keep it real" (50%), whereas liars would "keep it simple" (46.7%). (For more on verbal cues to lying, see the next section.)

Table 4.3 describes the types of verbal and nonverbal indicators that have been researched as deception cues. Not all of these are valid indicators of deception. The verbal indicator that has been most strongly associated with deception is voice pitch. Liars tend to speak in a higher-pitched voice than those telling the truth. Most studies

Table 4.3 Potential Verbal and Nonverbal Characteristics of Deception

Verbal Characteristics

- Speech fillers (frequency of saying "ah" or "umm")
- Speech errors (word or sentence repetition, sentence change, sentence incompletion, or slips of the tongue)
- Pitch of voice (changes in pitch)
- Rate of speech (number of words spoken in a specific time period)
- Speech pauses (length of silence between question asked and answer given; number of noticeable pauses in speech)

Nonverbal Characteristics

- Gaze aversion (avoiding looking at the face of conversation partner or interviewer)
- Smiling (frequency of smiles or laughs)
- Blinking (frequency of eyeblinks)
- Fidgeting (scratching head, playing with jewellery)
- Illustrators (gestures to modify or supplement what is being said)
- Hand or finger movements
- Leg or foot movements
- Body movements
- Shrugs (frequency of shoulders raised in an "I-don't-know"–type gesture)
- Head movements (nodding or shaking head)
- Shifting positions

Source: Based on Nonverbal communication and credibility. In A. Memon, A. Vrij, & R. Bull, 2003 (Eds.), *Psychology and law: Truthfulness, accuracy, and credibility* (pp. 32–58). London, England: McGraw-Hill. Published by The McGraw-Hill Companies.

have found increased use of speech disturbances ("ah," "umm") and a slower rate of speech during deception (DePaulo et al., 1982; Fiedler & Walka, 1993; Sporer & Schwandt, 2006). In summary, it appears that cognitively more difficult lies (lies in which you have to fabricate an answer) may be associated with one pattern of speech disturbances, whereas cognitively simpler lies (lies in which you must conceal something) may be associated with a different pattern of speech disturbances.

Verbal Cues to Lying

In a comprehensive meta-analysis, DePaulo and colleagues (2003) coded 158 cues to deception from 120 samples of adults. Most of the verbal and nonverbal behaviours coded did not discriminate between liars and truth-tellers. One of the most reliable indicators was that liars provided fewer details than truth-tellers. Liars also told less compelling accounts compared with truth-tellers. For example, liars' stories were less likely to make sense (less plausible, lacking logical structure, had discrepancies), were less engaging, and were less fluent than truth-tellers' stories. Liars were also rated as less cooperative and more nervous and tense than truth-tellers. Finally, truth-tellers were more likely to spontaneously correct their stories and more likely to admit to a lack of memory than liars were. Deception cues were easier to detect when liars were motivated to lie or when they were attempting to cover up a personal failing or a transgression.

Can you detect a killer from a 911 call? Adams and Harpster (2008) analyzed a hundred 911 calls coding what the call was about, whom the call was from, and how the call was made. Fifty of the calls were from innocent people calling for help, whereas the other 50 were from the perpetrator or the person who had arranged the murder. Innocent callers were more likely to make requests for help for the victim, to correct any misperceptions during the call, to be rude and demanding of immediate assistance, and to cooperate with the 911 operator; they also displayed considerable emotion in their voices and spoke quickly. Callers who had committed or organized the killing were more likely to provide irrelevant details, blame or insult the victim, state that the victim was dead, and be polite and patient, with little emotion displayed in the voice. If future research replicates these findings, these cues may help police investigators plan how they will interview 911 callers.

What about online deception? Computer-mediated communication is extremely common, and researchers have begun to study when, where, and how people lie online. See Box 4.4 for an example of such research.

Are Some People Better at Detecting Deception?

If you believe what you see on the television, there are lie detection wizards out there. See the In the Media box for a description of popular recent television series. Across studies, the ability to distinguish lies from truth tends to be only slightly better than chance. For example, a meta-analysis by Aamodt and Custer (2006) found that on average the accuracy rate for detecting deception for "professional lie catchers," such as police officers, judges, and psychologists, was 55.5%, a rate that is not much more accurate than that of students and other citizens (who had 54.2% accuracy). Thus, the accuracy rate for both professionals and students is just barely above what

Box 4.4   Forensic Psychology in the Spotlight

Quest for Love: Truth and Deception in Online Dating

Approximately 20 million Americans have used online dating services. There are a range of different types of electronic dating sites. On some sites the participants provide a profile for others to read (e.g., Match.com), whereas at other sites participants pay a fee and complete a questionnaire about their personality traits, interests, attitudes, and beliefs (e.g., eHarmony). Using the Internet to find potential mates has become increasingly popular. Recently Canada was described as a "hotbed of online dating" (Oliveira, 2010). Canadians are heavy users of online dating sites, and Plenty of Fish, one of the more popular online dating sites, was developed and is run by a now very wealthy Canadian.

How Accurate Are Internet-Dating Profiles?

Most users of online dating sites believe that others misrepresent themselves (Gibbs, Ellison, & Heino, 2006), and some potential users avoid using these sites because of fear of deception. People who post profiles may embellish their profiles to attract potential mates. In contrast, users may want to ensure they present themselves accurately, quirks and all, since they are seeking a potential mate who will be compatible with their personality and interests. Do men and women engage in different types of impression management online? For example, are men more likely to enhance their occupations and earnings, and women their youthfulness and physical attractiveness?

Toma, Hancock, and Ellison (2008) invited online daters to participate in a study on self-presentation in online dating profiles. Participants needed to be a subscriber to popular dating sites in which the users create their own profile (this requirement excluded sites such as eHarmony, where subscribers are matched based on their responses to questionnaires). Forty men and 40 women were invited to the lab, and the accuracies of their dating profiles were examined.

Self-Reported Accuracy

Participants self-reported they were most accurate about their relationship information (e.g., married, divorced, single) and whether they had children. However, when photos were included in profiles, the participants rated them as less accurate than other information, such as their occupation, education, habits (e.g., smoking and drinking), and political and religious beliefs.

Observed Accuracy

In the study, the participants' height and weight were measured and their age was obtained from their driver's licence. The majority (81%) of the participants provided inaccurate information about height, weight, or age. Participants were more likely to lie about their weight than their age or height. Men were more likely overestimate their height, and women were more likely to underestimate their weight. Most of these deceptions were small in magnitude. However, in some cases they were larger in magnitude, such as a 7.5-centimetre difference in height, a 16-kilogram difference in weight, and an 11-year difference in age.

The authors concluded that "online daters in the present study used deception strategically as a resource in the construction of their online self-presentation and in the engineering of their romantic lives" (p. 1035).

Physical Attractiveness

In 2010, Toma and Hancock examined 69 of the participants who permitted their photograph to be taken in the lab. Online daters who were rated as less physically attractive were more likely to have enhanced their online photograph and lied about their height, weight, and age. Women were more likely to enhance their online photographs then men. The authors interpret their findings as being supportive of evolutionary theory that predicts physical attractiveness is very important when attempting to find a mate.

would be obtained by guessing (50%). Bond and DePaulo (2006) also compared the accuracy of "experts" (judges, police officers, psychiatrists, and auditors) with that of non-experts and found no differences in their abilities to accurately detect deception. This poor performance in deception detection has been explained in three ways. First, people tend to rely on behaviours that lack predictive validity (Fiedler & Walka, 1993).

TV and Lie Detection

Television shows about detecting deception are popular. In this box, we describe three shows whose underlying premise is using physiological, linguistic, or behavioural cues to detect deception.

Lie to Me

Lie to Me 's main character is Dr. Cal Lightman, a lie detection expert who has an uncanny ability to detect lies. He watches your face for microexpressions, reads your body language, listens to your voice, and monitors what you say. His only challenge is the stress caused by being able to detect all the lies told by those around him, even those told by his family and friends. This TV drama launched in 2009 and was an instant success. Although the accuracy of Dr. Lightman's abilities is unrealistic, a true expert on lie detection comments on each episode.

Lie Detector

You may also have heard of the reality TV show *Lie Detector*. The most recent version of this show was aired in 2005.

Its premise was to provide people who had been accused of lying with the opportunity to vindicate themselves. Dr. Ed Gelb, a forensic psychophysiologist and a trained polygraph examiner, would conduct a polygraph examination on the show. Guests on the show ranged from a woman claiming to have contact with extraterrestrials, to Paula Jones, who claimed Bill Clinton sexually harassed her. Although some reality shows maintain their popularity, *Lie Detector* was cancelled after only one season.

The Moment of Truth

In this game show, contestants were asked increasingly embarrassing personal questions that they had to answer honestly to win money. To determine whether the person was telling the truth, a polygraph test was administered prior to the show. The polygraph results were used to determine when the contestants were telling the truth or a lie. The show premiered in January 2008 and ended in August 2009.

Laypeople have a number of beliefs about lying. In a study that measured stereotypic beliefs about lying in 75 different countries, the Global Deception Research Team (2006) found that the most common stereotype about liars is that they avoid eye contact. Police officers share the widespread belief in these stereotypes: They believe that two cues indicative of deceit are eye gaze and fidgeting. Unfortunately, these two cues have not been found to be related to deception (Vrij, 2008). Second, most people have a **truth-bias**. Truth-bias refers to the tendency of people to judge more messages as truthful than deceptive (Bond & DePaulo, 2006). Third, there are only small differences between truth-tellers and liars. With so few cues to rely on, it is a challenging task for people to identify liars (Hartwig & Bond, 2011; Sporer & Schwandt, 2006).

Truth-bias: The tendency of people to judge more messages as truthful than deceptive

Are there lie detection wizards? O'Sullivan and Ekman (2004) claimed to have identified "wizards" of deception detection. They screened 12 000 professionals and discovered that a small group of 29 people were extremely accurate at detecting deception across three different deception tasks (90% accurate at detecting lies about opinions and 80% accurate at detecting lies about a mock crime and about emotions). According to these researchers, one practical implication would be for law enforcement agencies to consult with these wizards "on cases of extraordinary importance" (p. 284). Bond and Uysal (2007) critiqued O'Sullivan and Ekman's methodology and concluded that there is no evidence yet that detection wizards exist, the findings were statistical flukes, and it is certainly premature for any government officials to start relying on them (see O'Sullivan, 2008, for response to this critique).

Several studies by Ekman and colleagues have investigated the abilities of diverse professional groups to detect deception. In the 1991 study by Ekman and O'Sullivan, forensic psychiatrists, customs agents, FBI agents, and judges all performed around chance levels in detecting deception. The only group that performed better than chance (64% correct) were U.S. Secret Service agents. About a third of Secret Service agents were 80% accurate or better. The most accurate participants were those who relied on multiple cues to assess credibility rather than on any one cue.

In a review of 40 studies, Vrij (2000) found a 67% accuracy rate for detecting truths and a 44% accuracy rate for detecting lies. These results also showed that in most studies, truthful messages were identified with more accuracy than deceptive ones. Thus, most lie catchers have a truthfulness bias. In most of the studies, the lie catchers were not very accurate at detecting deception. One reason that people are not good at detecting lies is that they rely on the wrong cues. Table 4.4 presents the accuracy rates of professional lie catchers across two types of studies. In low-stakes studies, police officers were not very accurate at detecting deception in university students. However, in high-stakes studies, police officers' ability to detect deception by suspects during police interrogations is much better. There are two potential explanations for the higher-than-usual accuracy. First, the suspects were highly motivated to lie, and research has shown that high-stakes lies are easier to detect than low-stakes ones. Second, the police were more familiar with the setting and type of individual they were judging, namely suspects. Although police officers are better at detecting high-stakes lies, they still make many errors. Box 4.5 looks at police detection of high-stakes lies.

Two factors one might think would be related to deception-detection ability are level of job experience and confidence in judgment. DePaulo and Pfeifer (1986) compared the proficiency of deception detection of university students, new police

Table 4.4 Accuracy Rates of Professional Lie Catchers in Low and High Stakes Situations

Study	Accuracy Rate
Low Stakes	
DePaulo & Pfeifer, 1986 (Police officers)	52%
Köehnken, 1987 (Police officers)	45%
Ekman & O'Sullivan, 1991 (Robbery investigators)	56%
Porter, Woodworth, & Birt, 2000 (Parole officers)	52%
Meissner & Kassin, 2002 (Police officers)	50%
High Stakes	
Mann et al., 2004 (Police officers)	65%
Mann & Vrij, 2006 (Police officers)	68%
Mann, Vrij, & Bull, 2006 (Police officers)	69%
Whelan et al., 2015 (Police officers)	72%

recruits, and experienced police officers. None of the groups were better than others at detecting deception; however, the experienced police officers reported being more confident in their decisions. This finding is consistent with more recent research (Ekman & O'Sullivan, 1991; Leach, Talwar, Lee, Bala, & Lindsay, 2004; Porter, Woodworth, & Birt, 2000) indicating that neither level of experience nor confidence in deception-detection ability is associated with accuracy rates. For example, in a meta-analysis examining the relationship between judges' accuracy at detecting deception and their confidence in their own judgments, DePaulo, Charlton, Cooper, Lindsay, and Muhlenbruck (1997) found that the average correlation was .04. The reason that confidence is unrelated to accuracy may be that people rely on cues they believe are related to deception and when they see these cues, their confidence increases. However, since the cues people believe are related to deception are often not valid, their accuracy tends to be poor.

Detecting High-Stakes Lies

You are watching the news, and a mother is being interviewed outside her home, begging for the return of her two sons. She says that while she was stopped at a traffic light, a black man approached her car with a gun and demanded she get out of the car. Her two young sons were in the back seat. Frightened for her life, she got out of the car, and the carjacker jumped into the car and drove off with the children in the back. Over the next nine days, she is often on the news pleading with the carjacker to return her sons. Your initial reaction is concern for the mother and hope that the children will be found unharmed. On the ninth day, the mother confesses to police that there was no carjacker and that she had driven her car to a local lake, left the car on the boat ramp in neutral, got out, and watched as the car slowly rolled into the lake and sank. The two children's bodies were found in the car, still in their car seats.

This story is the true case of 23-year-old Susan Smith. Smith was convicted of first-degree murder of 3-year-old Michael and 14-month-old Alex. During the penalty phase of the trial, the assistant prosecutor, Keith Giese, stated, "We're going to go back over the nine days of lies, the nine days of deceit, the nine days of trickery, the nine days of begging this country to help her find her children, while the whole time they lay dead at the bottom of that lake" (Reuter, 1995).

Would you have been able to detect if Susan Smith was lying by what she said or by her behaviour during her numerous press conferences? Vrij and Mann (2001) asked a similar question. They asked 52 police officers to view videotaped press conferences of people who were asking for the public's help in locating their missing relatives or the murderers of their relatives. Vrij and Mann asked the officers to determine who was lying and who was telling the truth. What they didn't tell the officers was that every video showed people who had actually been found guilty of killing their own relatives. The officers were not very accurate at detecting the deception. Moreover, accuracy was not related to age, years of police work, level of experience interviewing suspects, or confidence.

More recently, ten Brinke, Porter, and Baker (2012) coded the faces of genuine or deceptive relatives pleading to the public for the return of their missing relatives. The deceptive relatives were those later convicted of murdering the missing person. The researchers wanted to determine if there were covert facial signs of emotional states that could distinguish the two groups. The "grief" facial muscles were more often identified in the genuine pleaders as compared to the deceptive pleaders. The next time you watch parents pleading for the return of their missing child, watch their faces closely for signs of genuine grief.

Research by Bond and DePaulo (2008) found that there are no specific traits related to detecting deception in others. They concluded that "deception judgments depend more on the liar than the judge" (p. 489).

Is it possible to improve professionals' deception-detection abilities? Although there have been only a few studies examining this, it appears that training programs can help professionals become more accurate. Porter, Woodworth, and Birt (2000) reported that a two-day workshop focusing on myth dissolution, knowledge of behavioural cues to deception, and performance feedback increased the detection accuracy of parole officers from below chance levels (40%) to 76.7%. More recently, Porter, Juodis, ten Brinke, Klein, and Wilson (2010) found that a brief three-hour training session increased the detection accuracy of health care professionals from chance levels of accuracy to 60.7%. Masip, Alonso, Garrido, and Herrero (2008) have recommended that training programs should focus on teaching not only deception cues but also truthfulness cues in order to counteract the tendency for professionals to judge people as deceptive. Thus, although detecting deception is difficult, it is possible to improve judgment accuracy through training. Future research is needed to design and evaluate what types of training programs are most effective at helping professionals become better at detecting deception.

See Box 4.6 to read about Dr. ten Brinke and her research.

Box 4.6

Canadian Researcher Profile: Dr. Leanne ten Brinke

Courtesy of Leanne ten Brinke

Dr. Leanne ten Brinke gravitated toward the field of forensic psychology as an undergraduate student at Dalhousie University. Always fascinated by the process of scientific discovery but originally intending to study microbiology, she served as a participant in a study conducted by Dr. Stephen Porter's forensic psychology lab and thought the research was so fascinating that she began volunteering in the lab as a Research Assistant. She was immediately hooked and continued to work with Dr. Porter throughout her research training. In 2007, she completed her Bachelor of Science with Honours in Psychology and a Certificate in Forensic Psychology. During this degree, Dr. ten Brinke examined the leakage of inconsistent emotional facial expressions as a cue to deception (Porter & ten Brinke, 2008) and completed her practica at the Halifax Parole Office and the East Coast Forensic Hospital.

Dr. ten Brinke received her doctoral degree from the University of British Columbia (UBC) in 2012, examining the behavioural consequences of emotional, high-stakes

(continued)

(continued)

deception. Specifically, she studied the behaviour of individuals pleading for the safe return of a missing relative—half of whom had perpetrated the murder of that person and were lying about their involvement in the disappearance. In this context, deception was characterized by the inappropriate expression of happiness (i.e., smiles) and the failure to display appropriate sadness (ten Brinke, Baker, & Porter, 2012; ten Brinke & Porter, 2012). Dr. ten Brinke is fascinated by what human faces and bodies reveal and how this behaviour can be used to detect deception and hidden emotions. Further, she is interested in how observers naturally interpret nonverbal behaviour and how it guides our social interactions. Methodologically, she strives to increase ecological validity by examining real, high-stakes interactions, complemented by rigorous, controlled laboratory research. She is driven by the excitement of scientific discovery—that moment when months of work produce data that reveal something entirely novel about the human experience.

Upon approaching the end of her Ph.D. program, Dr. ten Brinke had developed more broadly social interests in the same topics that she had been studying in the narrower context of forensic psychology. Telling lies is not exclusive to criminals; how do we detect lies in our everyday lives? Do psychopathic personality traits appear in contexts outside of prison walls? Are there professions in which psychopaths may thrive? She was fortunate to have a mentor—Dr. Paul Davies—who encouraged her to consider positions at business schools where social psychologists are increasingly studying these topics. In 2012, Dr. ten Brinke visited the London Business School where she examined the effect of inappropriate emotions in corporate apologies (i.e., smiles) on stock market performance with Dr. Gabrielle Adams (ten Brinke & Adams, 2015). Following graduation, Dr. ten Brinke moved to Berkeley, CA, where she began a Postdoctoral Fellowship under the tutelage of Drs. Dana Carney and Dacher Keltner.

In the Haas School of Business and the Department of Psychology at University of California, Berkeley, Dr. ten Brinke continued her research on behavioural cues to deception and deception detection, and began a program of research on theories of power. Her research has examined indirect detection of deception, including recent findings that observers experience physiological threat responses to deceptive pleaders and that attention to our bodies' natural responses can improve deception detection accuracy (ten Brinke, Lee, & Carney, under review). She has also examined the nonverbal behaviour of over 100 U.S. Senators, finding that those displaying behaviours consistent with psychopathic personality traits are poor leaders—unable to elicit support once they ascended to powerful positions (ten Brinke, Liu, Keltner, & Srivastava, 2016). Some of her current research examines how similar personality traits may be associated with financial success or failure for hedge fund managers.

This research has earned Dr. ten Brinke the CPA's New Investigator Award (2016) and an Assistant Professor position at the University of Denver, where she is the Director of the Truth and Trust Lab. She also provides training on deception detection to entrepreneurs and investment professionals. Dr. ten Brinke proudly hails from Antigonish, Nova Scotia, and currently resides in Denver, Colorado, with her husband.

ASSESSMENT OF MALINGERING AND DECEPTION

Disorders of Deception

Deception is a central component of some psychological disorders. The disorders described below vary on two dimensions: (1) whether the person intentionally or consciously produces the symptoms, and (2) whether the motivation is internal or external.

The *Diagnostic and Statistical Manual of Mental Disorders* (5th ed.; *DSM-5*; American Psychiatric Association [APA], 2013) created a new category titled *somatic symptom and related disorders*. There are many types of somatic symptoms and related disorders—most are rare. One of the disorders within this category is **factitious disorder**, which includes "falsification of physical or psychological signs or symptoms, or induction of injury or disease"; "individual presents himself or herself to others as ill,

Factitious disorder: A disorder in which the person's physical and psychological symptoms are intentionally produced and are adopted for no external rewards

impaired, or injured"; and "deceptive behavior is evident even in the absence of obvious external rewards" (p. 324). Eisendrath (1996) has suggested that patients with factitious disorders might be aware they are intentionally producing the symptoms, but they may lack insight into the underlying psychological motivation.

Meadow (1977) coined the term **Munchausen syndrome by proxy** (MBP; in *DSM-5* this is called *factitious disorder imposed on another*) to describe cases in which parents or caregivers falsified symptoms in their children. For example, a parent might purposely overdose a child with medicine and take the child to the hospital for treatment. The goal is for the parent to get the attention and sympathy of others. A study by Rosenberg (1987) evaluated 117 reported cases of MBP and found 98% of the individuals were the biological mother of the child; in almost 9% of the cases, the child died. In a more recent review of this syndrome, Sheridan (2003) analyzed the characteristics of 451 MBP cases. Although the most common perpetrator was the child's biological mother (77%), other perpetrators were also identified (the father in 7% of cases). Most the victims were young (age 4 or younger), with 6% of the victims dying and 7% suffering long-term physical injuries. Nearly a third (29%) of the perpetrators had some symptoms of Munchausen syndrome (or, as currently called, *factitious disorder imposed on self*).

Munchausen syndrome by proxy: A rare factitious disorder in which a person intentionally produces an illness in his or her child

The two key components to **malingering** are that (1) the psychological or physical symptoms are clearly under voluntary control and (2) there are external motivations for the production of symptoms. People typically malinger mental illness for one of the following external motivations:

Malingering: Intentionally faking psychological or physical symptoms for some type of external gain

- A criminal may attempt to avoid punishment by pretending to be unfit to stand trial, to have a mental illness at the time of a criminal act, or to have an acute mental illness to avoid being executed.

- Prisoners or patients may seek drugs, or prisoners may want to be transferred to a psychiatric facility to do easier time or escape.

- Malingerers may seek to avoid conscription to the military or to avoid certain military duties.

- Malingerers may seek financial gain from disability claims, workers' compensation, or damages from alleged injury.

- Malingerers may seek admission to a hospital to obtain free room and board.

Any psychiatric or physical disorder may be malingered. As new syndromes are developed, such as post-traumatic stress disorder, they provide new opportunities for people to use them to malinger. Malingering varies in terms of severity from benign (e.g., "Not tonight, honey; I have a headache.") to serious (e.g., "I heard a voice telling me to kill my neighbour, so I obeyed it.").

Individuals with factitious and somatoform disorders often encourage and even insist on having physical tests and invasive procedures, whereas malingerers will often refuse to cooperate with invasive procedures to determine the veracity of their symptoms. The incidence of malingering in the general population is unknown. Patients who malinger rarely admit it. Thus, individuals who successfully malinger are never included in the statistics. Moreover, mental health professionals are often reluctant to label a patient as a malingerer.

The prevalence rate of malingering is relatively high in forensic contexts. For example, Frederick, Crosby, and Wynkoop (2000) reported that 45% of patients evaluated for competency or mental state at the time of offence produced invalid psychological test profiles. Rogers, Ustad, and Salekin (1998) reported that 20% of emergency jail referrals feigned psychological symptoms. Rogers (1986) reported that 4.5% of defendants evaluated for mental state at the time of offence were definite malingerers and another 20% were suspected. More recently, Myers, Hall, and Tolou-Shams (2013) found that 17% of pretrial homicide offenders malingered psychological symptoms (e.g., delusions) or cognitive symptoms (e.g., memory impairment). Given these large numbers, it is clear that malingering should be considered in all forensic evaluations.

Defensiveness: Conscious denial or extreme minimization of physical or psychological symptoms

The opposite of malingering is called **defensiveness**. Defensiveness refers to the conscious denial or extreme minimization of physical or psychological symptoms. Patients or offenders of this sort seek to present themselves in a favourable light. Minimization of physical and psychological symptoms varies both in degree and motivation. Some people might want to appear to be functioning well to meet an external need, such as being a fit parent, or an internal need, such as unwillingness to acknowledge they are a "patient." Degree of defensiveness can range from mild, such as downplaying a minor symptom, to outright denial of a more serious psychological impairment, such as denying hearing command hallucinations.

Explanatory Models of Malingering

Based on motivations, Rogers (1990) described three explanatory models of malingering: pathogenic, criminological, and adaptational. The pathogenic model assumes that people are motivated to malinger because of an underlying mental disorder. According to this model, the patient attempts to gain control over his or her pathology by creating bogus symptoms. Over time, these patients experience more severe mental disorders and the true symptoms emerge. Little empirical support exists for this model.

The criminological model focuses on 'badness': "a bad person (Antisocial Personality Disorder), in bad circumstances (legal difficulties), who is performing badly (uncooperative)" (Rogers, 1997, p. 7). This definition is similar to the malingering definition described in the *DSM-5* (APA, 2013). According to this definition, malingering should be suspected in any forensic evaluation, when there are substantial differences between what a person reports and what others observe, when someone refuses to comply with an evaluation, and when the person is diagnosed with Antisocial Personality Disorder.

As with the pathogenic model, little empirical support exists for this model. No research indicates that persons with antisocial personality disorder are any more likely to malinger than other offenders (Rogers, 1990). In addition, many types of patients are uncooperative during evaluations, including those with eating disorders or substance-use problems. In contrast, some malingerers appear to be highly cooperative. Rogers (1990) found that *DSM-IV* indicators of malingering tended to overdiagnose malingering in a forensic sample. More recently, Berry and Nelson (2010) concluded that the criteria for malingering found in the *DSM-IV* is "terribly flawed on both conceptual and practical grounds" (p. 298). Despite these criticisms, the APA decided not to modify the criteria for malingering in the *DSM-5*.

According to the adaptational model, malingering is likely to occur when (1) there is a perceived adversarial context, (2) personal stakes are very high, and (3) no other viable alternatives are perceived. Research findings support this model in that there are higher rates of malingering in adversarial settings or when the personal stakes are high. This model provides the broadest and least pejorative explanation of malingering. Rogers, Sewell, and Goldstein (1994) asked 320 forensic psychologists to rate 32 items subdivided into pathogenic, criminological, and adaptational models on how important the item was to malingering. The adaptational model was rated as the most important and the pathogenic model as the least important.

How to Study Malingering

Research comprises three basic designs: case study, simulation, and known groups. Each of these designs has its associated strengths and weaknesses. Although case studies are not used as often as they once were, they are useful for generating a wide variety of hypotheses that can be tested by using designs with more experimental rigour. In addition, a case study is the only way to examine rare syndromes such as MBP syndrome.

Most research on malingering has used a **simulation design** (similar to polygraph laboratory studies). Participants are told to malinger a specific disorder and are typically compared with two groups: (1) a control group randomly selected from the same population as the malingerers and (2) a clinical comparison group representing the disorders or symptoms that are being feigned. These studies address whether measures can detect malingering in nonclinical samples. However, individuals with mental disorders may also malinger. Studies have begun to ask patients with mental disorders to feign a different mental disorder or to exaggerate the severity of their symptoms. These studies address how effectively participants with mental disorders can malinger. In an early study using a clinical sample, Rogers (1988) reported that nearly half of the psychiatric in-patients either did not remember or did not follow the instructions to malinger. To examine the relative efficacy of detection methods for disordered and nondisordered samples, the optimal simulation design would use four groups: nonclinical experimental, nonclinical-control, clinical-experimental, and clinical-control.

The primary strength of the simulation design is its experimental rigour. The main disadvantage is its limited generalizability to the real world. Simulation studies are often limited in their clinical usefulness because of the minimal levels of preparation and level of motivation by participants. Early studies used brief and nonspecific instructions, such as "Appear mentally ill." Instructions are now more specific, with some studies giving participants a scenario to follow: for example, "Imagine you have been in a car accident and you hit your head. You have decided to exaggerate the amount of memory problems you are having to obtain a larger monetary settlement from the car insurance company." In addition, participants may be given time to prepare.

Some studies have coached participants by providing information about genuine mental disorders or by telling them about detection strategies. Research suggests that telling participants about disorders does not help them, whereas information about

Simulation design: As applied to malingering research, people are told to pretend they have specific symptoms or a disorder

detection strategies does help them avoid detection (Baer, Wetter, & Berry, 1995; Storm & Graham, 2000). In contrast, Bagby, Nicholson, Bacchiochi, Ryder, and Bury (2002) found that providing students with information about validity scales designed to detect deception did not enhance their ability to feign successfully.

Ethical concerns have been raised about whether participants should be taught how to become skilled malingerers. Ben-Porath (1994) argued that such research does not "appear to have sufficient scientific justification to make up for the potential harm that might be caused by publishing such a study" (p. 150). A survey of lawyers and law students indicates that about 50% would provide information to clients about psychological testing, including whether the test had any validity scales to detect deception (Wetter & Corrigan, 1995).

When individuals engage in malingering in applied settings, the stakes are often high. For example, they may obtain funding for a disability or avoid a harsher sentence. Both the type and magnitude of incentives are typically limited in simulation studies. Studies that use incentives often offer monetary rewards to malingerers for being successful. The magnitude of the incentive ranges from very modest (e.g., $5) to more substantial (e.g., having their names placed in a lottery for the chance to win $100). Simulation studies have rarely used negative incentives. For example, the researcher could offer money for participating in a malingering study but take some of the money away if the participant is detected as unsuccessfully using deception.

Studies investigating malingering in applied settings would ideally use the known-groups design. The **known-groups design** involves two stages: (1) the establishment of the criterion groups (e.g., genuine patients and malingerers) and (2) an analysis of the similarities and differences between these criterion groups. The main strength of the known-groups design is its generalizability to real-world settings. Its chief limitation is the establishment of the criterion groups. Samples of the genuine patients likely include errors, and some of the classified malingerers may be genuine patients. Because of the difficulty with the reliable and accurate classification of criterion groups, this design is rarely used in malingering research.

Malingered Psychosis

How often people attempt to feign psychosis is unknown. Pope, Jonas, and Jones (1982) found nine patients with factitious psychosis in a sample of 219 consecutive admissions to a forensic psychiatric hospital. They followed these patients for seven years, and none went on to develop a psychotic disorder, although all were diagnosed with either borderline personality disorder (a personality disorder defined by instability in mood, self-image, and interpersonal relationships) or histrionic personality disorder (a personality disorder defined by excessive emotionality and attention-seeking behaviours). The presence of malingering does not negate the possibility that other psychiatric illnesses or psychological disorders are present. In fact, the term *instrumental psychosis* was developed to identify patients (many with psychiatric histories) attempting to feign symptoms to secure special accommodations (Waite & Geddes, 2006). Cornell and Hawk (1989) reported that 8% of 314 consecutive psychiatric admissions were diagnosed as malingering psychotic symptoms by experienced forensic psychologists. Box 4.7 describes one of the first studies of malingered psychosis.

Known-groups design: As applied to malingering research, involves comparing genuine patients and malingerers attempting to fake the disorder the patients have

Box 4.7   Forensic Psychology in the Spotlight

Being Sane in Insane Places

In 1973, David Rosenhan published a paper in the journal *Science* titled "Being Sane in Insane Places." Rosenhan's goal was to investigate the accuracy of psychiatric diagnoses and the consequences of diagnostic labels. In the first part of his study, eight individuals with no history of a mental disorder tried to gain admission to several mental hospitals. Imagine you are one of the pseudo-patients taking part in Rosenhan's study. You go to your local hospital complaining that you have been hearing voices. When asked what the voices are saying, you reply that it is sometimes unclear but you think they are saying "empty," "hollow," and "thud." You state that you do not recognize the voice. Other than falsifying your name and occupation, everything else about your personal history is true. Like the actual eight pseudo-patients in the study, you also have no history of any serious pathology. To your surprise, you are immediately admitted to the psychiatric in-patient ward with a diagnosis of schizophrenia. Once you are admitted, you tell the staff that your auditory hallucinations have disappeared. Like the real pseudo-patients, you are feeling somewhat apprehensive about what might happen to you. You are cooperative and friendly toward staff and patients. When the staff member asks you how you are feeling, you answer, "I am fine." You follow the rules in the hospital and pretend to take the medication given to you. You have been told that you have to get out of the hospital on your own. So you try to convince the staff you are "sane." To deal with the boredom, you pace up and down the hall, engage staff and patients in conversation, and write extensive notes about your daily activities. The staff members do not question you about this behaviour, although the other patients on the ward comment on your note-taking and accuse you of being "a journalist or a professor."

In the actual experiment, pseudo-patients were hospitalized from 7 to 52 days. Staff failed to recognize the lack of symptoms in the pseudo-patients. Not one of the pseudo-patients was identified as "normal" by staff. As noted by Rosenhan (1973), "once a person is designated abnormal, all of his other behaviors are colored by that label" (p. 253). For example, the nurses interpret your pacing behaviour as a manifestation of anxiety and your note-taking as a behavioural manifestation of your pathology. Pseudo-patients' attempts to initiate conversations with staff were not very successful, since the staff would "give a brief response while they were on the move and with head averted, or no response at all" (Rosenhan, 1973, p. 255). An example of one conversation was,

> **[Pseudo-patient]**: "Pardon me, Dr. X. Could you tell me when I am eligible for grounds privileges?"
> **[Physician]**: "Good morning, Dave. How are you today?" (Moves off without waiting for a reply.) (p. 255)

This study raises concerns about the use of labels and how such labels can influence the meaning of behaviours. What are the consequences of psychiatric diagnoses? As stated by Rosenhan (1973), "A diagnosis of cancer that has been found to be in error is cause for celebration. But psychiatric diagnoses are rarely found to be in error. The label sticks, a mark of inadequacy forever" (p. 257).

What Are the Indicators of Malingered Psychosis?   Table 4.5 provides a list of the potential indicators of malingered psychosis. Resnick (1997) provided a comprehensive description of these indicators. Malingerers often tend to overact, believing the more bizarre they are, the more psychotic they will appear. Early observers have also reported this. For example, Jones and Llewellyn (1917) stated the malingerer "sees less than the blind, he hears less than the deaf, and is more lame than the paralysed.... He ... piles symptom upon symptom and so outstrips madness itself" (p. 17). Malingerers are often willing to discuss their symptoms when asked, whereas actual patients with schizophrenia are often reluctant to discuss their symptoms. Some malingerers may attempt to control the assessment by behaving in an intimidating manner or by accusing the clinician of not believing them. In an

Table 4.5 Cues to Malingered Psychosis in Criminal Defendants

- Understandable motive for committing crime
- Presence of a partner in the crime
- Current crime fits pattern of previous criminal history
- Suspicious hallucinations
  - Continuous rather than intermittent
  - Vague or inaudible hallucinations
  - Hallucinations with no delusions
  - Inability to describe strategies to diminish voices
  - Claiming all command hallucinations are obeyed
  - Visual hallucinations in black and white
- Suspicious delusions
  - Abrupt onset or termination
  - Eagerness to discuss delusions
  - Conduct markedly inconsistent with delusions
  - Elaborate delusions that lack paranoid, grandiose, or religious themes
- Marked discrepancies in interview versus noninterview behaviour
- Sudden emergence of psychotic symptoms to explain criminal act
- Absence of any subtle signs of psychosis

Source: Based on Resnick, P.J. (1997). Malingered psychosis. In R. Rogers (Ed.), *Clinical assessment of malingering and deception* (2nd ed., pp. 47–67). New York, NY: Guilford Press.

interview, a malingerer may be evasive when asked to provide details, take a long time to answer, or answer, "I don't know." Malingerers often report rare or atypical symptoms, blatant symptoms, or absurd symptoms that are usually not endorsed by genuine patients. For example, a person attempting to malinger psychosis may claim to have seen "a large 60-foot Christ who told me to kill my mother."

Malingerers are more likely to report positive symptoms of schizophrenia, such as delusions (a false belief that is persistently held) or hallucinations (a perceptual experience in absence of external stimulation), as compared with negative or subtle symptoms of schizophrenia, such as blunted affect, concreteness, or peculiar thinking. Both auditory and visual hallucinations are common in psychotic patients. When a person is suspected of malingering auditory hallucinations, he or she should be asked the vocal characteristics (e.g., clarity, loudness, duration), source (inside or outside of the head), characteristics (e.g., gender, familiar or unfamiliar voice, command), and response (insight into unreality, coping strategies, obeying them). Comparing genuine and feigned auditory hallucinations is one way to detect a malingerer. For example, actual patients often report coping strategies to make the "voices go away," such as watching television, seeking out interpersonal contact, or taking medications (Kanas & Barr, 1984). The malingerer may report there is nothing that will make the voices go away. In other cases, malingerers may report atypical auditory

Jason King is a 30-year-old, single, white man charged with aggravated sexual assault. He is being assessed for fitness to stand trial at a pretrial jail. The police report indicated he acted alone and had stalked the victim prior to the sexual assault. The arresting police officers and correctional officers at the jail observed no signs of abnormal behaviour in Jason. During the psychological evaluation, Jason rocked back and forth and sang songs. He constantly interrupted the psychologist and claimed he had ESP powers and was being held as a political prisoner. He answered all the questions, although he refused to elaborate on some of his symptoms and would often say "I don't know." He claimed his lawyer was a communist and was out to convert him. He also stated the courtroom was actually a circus, with the judge being the ringmaster and the jury the audience.

Your Turn . . .

What are the clues that Jason might be malingering a mental disorder? If you were the forensic psychologist doing the assessment, which malingering tests would you use? Whom else might you want to interview to help your assessment?

command hallucinations (hallucinations telling people to act in a certain way), such as "Go commit a sex offence" or "Rob, rob, rob."

Genuine visual hallucinations are usually of normal-sized people seen in colour, and remain the same if eyes are open or closed. Atypical visual hallucinations, such as seeing "a green devil in the corner laughing," "a dog that would change in size when giving messages," or hallucinations only in black and white, are indicative of malingering.

If you were a forensic psychologist, how would you determine if someone was malingering a mental disorder? See the You Be the Forensic Psychologist box to develop some strategies you might use.

Assessment Methods to Detect Malingered Psychosis

Interview-Based Method   The Structured Interview of Reported Symptoms (SIRS) (Rogers, Bagby, & Dickens, 1992) was initially developed in 1985, and in its most recent version, it consists of 172 items that are scored from a structured interview. The items are organized into the following eight scales that represent different strategies that a person might employ when malingering:

1. Rare symptoms: symptoms that true patients endorse very infrequently
2. Symptom combinations: uncommon pairings of symptoms
3. Improbable or absurd symptoms: symptoms unlikely to be true, since true patients rarely endorsed them
4. Blatant symptoms: items that are obvious signs of mental disorder
5. Subtle symptoms: items that contain what most people consider everyday problems

6. Selectivity of symptoms: ratio of symptoms endorsed versus those not endorsed

7. Severity of symptoms: number of severe symptoms reported

8. Reported versus observed symptoms: discrepancy between self-report and observable symptoms

The SIRS has been extensively validated by using both simulation and known-groups designs, and research has consistently demonstrated differences in SIRS scores between honest and simulating samples, and between clinical samples and suspected malingerers (Rogers, 2008). A recent meta-analysis of 26 studies (Green & Rosenfeld, 2011) provided strong support for the accuracy of the SIRS as a measure of malingering mental disorders. The SIRS also correlates strongly with validity indices from the Minnesota Multiphasic Personality Inventory (MMPI-2; Boccaccini, Murrie, & Duncan, 2006; Edens, Poythress, & Watkins-Clay, 2007) and is used widely by clinical forensic psychologists (Archer, Buffington-Vollum, Stredny, & Handel, 2006). In 2010, Rogers, Sewell, and Gillard created the SIRS-2, which retained all the test items but added three new measures and a new decision-tree framework. Recent research comparing accuracy of the SIRS and SIRS-2 has been critical of the new decision-tree and these researchers recommend that it is premature of clinical professionals start using the SIRS-2 (Green, Rosenfeld, & Belfi, 2013; Tarescavage & Glassmire, 2016).

Self-Report Questionnaire   The most widely used personality inventory to assess nonoffenders and offenders is the MMPI-2 (Butcher, Dahlstrom, Graham, Tellegen, & Kaemmer, 1989). The MMPI-2 includes several clinical scales to assess psychopathology but also includes several scales specifically designed to test "faking-bad," or malingering. For example, the items on the Infrequency (F) scale and the Back F (Fb) scale were developed to detect unusual or atypical symptoms and consist of items endorsed by less than 10% of a normative sample.

A comprehensive meta-analysis of the MMPI-2 and malingering found that the F and Fb scales were the most useful at detecting malingerers (Rogers, Sewell, Martin, & Vitacco, 2003). However, the optimal cut-off score to use varies across the samples studied. A study by Storm and Graham (2000) examined whether the MMPI-2 validity scales would be able to correctly classify college students who have been coached on malingering strategies, students told to malinger but given no coaching, and psychiatric in-patients. Some validity indicators were more susceptible to coaching, whereas others, such as the Infrequency scale, could still discriminate coached malingerers from psychiatric in-patients. Recent research with criminal defendants classified as malingerers or not based on the SIRS has also supported the use of the Infrequency (F) scale to identify malingerers in forensic populations (Toomey, Kucharski, & Duncan, 2009).

The MMPI-2-RF (restructured form; Ben-Porath & Tellegen, 2008) has developed new validity scales to help detect malingering. Three studies have used known-groups design to investigate the validity of these new scales designed to identify malingerers (Rogers, Gillard, Berry, & Granacher, 2011; Sellbom & Bagby, 2010; Sellbom, Toomey, Wygant, Kurcharski, & Duncan, 2010). Across these studies, the MMPI-2-RF scales were effective at detecting feigned mental disorders, although future research is needed to clarify the optimal cut scores to use for different types of mental disorders.

This chapter focused on deception and how to detect deception. Over the centuries, humans have sought to identify liars and have developed many different methods for the detection of deception. Some measures, like the polygraph and fMRI, assess physiological responses, some focus on non-verbal behaviours, and others on the verbal content of speech. However, despite all these advances in measurement, spotting a liar is hard. More research is needed to determine the validity of the different methods under real-world conditions.

SUMMARY

1. The Comparison Question Test (CQT) is the most commonly used polygraph exam in North America. It consists of three types of questions: irrelevant, comparison (questions relating to past behaviours that are supposed to generate emotion), and relevant (questions relating to the crime being investigated). The Concealed Information Test (CIT) probes for whether the suspect has knowledge about the details of a crime that only the guilty person would have.

2. The CQT is quite accurate at detecting guilt but is not very good at determining a suspect's innocence (i.e., it has a high false-positive rate). The CIT is quite accurate in detecting innocence but is not very good at determining a suspect's guilt (i.e., it has a high false-negative rate).

3. Event-related brain potentials (ERPs) and brain-imaging techniques can be used to detect deception in laboratory settings. However, these techniques have not yet been used extensively in forensic settings.

4. Another method of attempting to detect whether someone is lying is through the analysis of verbal characteristics and nonverbal behaviours. The nonverbal indicator most strongly associated with deception is voice pitch. A verbal characteristic associated with deception is that liars provide fewer details when lying compared with those telling the truth.

5. The two key components to malingering are that the psychological or physical symptoms are clearly under voluntary control and that there are external motivations for the production of symptoms. Malingering should be considered in any forensic evaluation. Three explanatory models of malingering have been proposed: pathogenic, criminological, and adaptational. Only the adaptational model has received empirical support.

6. Malingering research uses three basic designs: case study, simulation, and known groups. The most common is the simulation design.

Discussion Questions

1. You have been wrongfully accused of stealing a laptop computer from the university library. Knowing what you now know about the polygraph, would you be willing to take a polygraph exam to prove your innocence?

2. You were recently hired as a customs agent. Knowing what you do about nonverbal and verbal cues to deception, what cues would you watch out for to catch someone smuggling?

Chapter 5
Eyewitness Testimony

Learning Objectives

- Describe two categories of independent variables and three general dependent variables found in eyewitness research.

- Describe and explain the misinformation effect.

- Outline the components of the cognitive interview.

- Describe lineup procedures and how they may be biased.

- Summarize the debate surrounding expert testimony on eyewitness issues.

- Outline the recommendations for collecting eyewitness identification evidence.

Amanda Ryder went to the local coffee house on her lunch hour. As she was deciding on her order, a man pushed by her trying to quickly exit. Seconds later, Amanda found out that the man had robbed the cashier. Amanda was an eyewitness. The police interviewed her along with the others in the coffee house. The witnesses were able to hear one another describe what they saw. Six months after the robbery, Amanda was asked to go to the police station to view a series of photographs. When she was asked whether the man who robbed the coffee house was pictured, Amanda very quickly pointed and said, "That's him, I'm certain."

Eyewitness evidence is one of the earliest and most widely studied topics in forensic psychology. As you read in Chapter 1, the German psychologist Albert von Schrenck-Notzing testified during a serial killer trial about the influence of pretrial media exposure on witnesses' memory. Today, both the police and the courts rely on eyewitness evidence. Eyewitness testimony is one of the most compelling types of evidence presented in criminal trials. Thus, information about the likelihood and types of mistakes made by eyewitnesses is vitally important. In this chapter, we will focus on how memory works when it comes to remembering in an eyewitness context. As well, we will examine the various factors and police procedures that can influence how accurate eyewitnesses can be.

EYEWITNESS TESTIMONY: THE ROLE OF MEMORY

A large part of eyewitness testimony rests on memory. The concept of memory can be viewed as a process involving several stages. The encoding stage occurs first, when you perceive and pay attention to details in your environment. For example, you are perceiving and paying attention when you look at a stranger's face and notice his big, bushy eyebrows. To some extent, the stranger's face and eyebrows have been encoded. The encoded information then passes into your short-term holding facility, known as your short-term memory. Your short-term memory has a limited capacity. Consequently, to make room for other, new information, information in your short-term memory passes into your longer-term holding facility, known as your long-term memory. Information from long-term memory can be accessed or retrieved as needed. For example, if you are asked to describe the stranger you saw, you will retrieve the information you stored in your long-term memory and report that the stranger had bushy eyebrows. It is important to remember that not every piece of information will go through all the memory stages and factors can affect each stage. For example, not all details from an event will be encoded, nor will all information in short-term memory move to long-term memory. Using our example of Amanda witnessing a robbery at the local cafe, consider the factors that are occurring to affect memory and retrieval.

Look at this scene for five seconds.
Mark Harvey/Alamy Stock Photo

Amanda is looking at the board listing all the varieties of coffee so she is ready to tell the cashier what she wants. She is not paying attention to her surroundings (factor: inattention). Unexpectedly, there is a brief interaction between her and an unfamiliar male (factors: unexpectedness; amount of time to view environmental details). Amanda is now a witness, and she is interviewed with several other people in the cafe by police (factor: hearing others describe the same environmental details she saw). The police officer asks Amanda a few brief questions (factor: the wording of the questions). Amanda is called six months after the crime to examine a lineup (factors: the amount of time elapsed between having witnessed the event and having to retrieve the information; type of lineup procedure used). Amanda is confident when she identifies the perpetrator (factor: relation between confidence and accuracy). Figure 5.1 delineates the stages of memory.

Before we discuss memory further, let's consider some myths you and others may have around eyewitness memory. See Box. 5.1 for a list of myths and what the research finds.

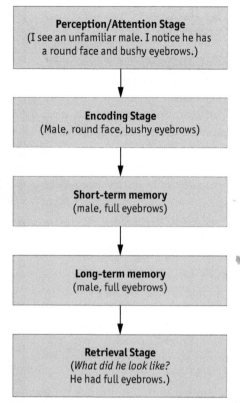

Figure 5.1 Stages of Memory

Box 5.1   Myths and Realities

Eyewitness Myths

Myth 1. Memory is like a videotape, that is, an exact representation of what occurred.
Fact. Memories can be influenced/changed by subsequent events; for example, subsequent interviews and the way questions are asked can influence what a person remembers. What is remembered though may sometimes be inaccurate (Wells & Loftus, 2003).

Myth 2. The wording of a question does not influence an eyewitness' response.
Fact. Suggestive/leading questioning can influence responses. Loftus and Zanni (1975) found that changing just one word in a question can lead to an increase in incorrect answers.

Myth 3. Greater stress improves an eyewitness' memory.
Fact. High stress levels can actually result in poorer memory for both the perpetrator's appearance and other crime details (Deffenbacher, Bornstein, Penrod & McGorty, 2004).

Myth 4. The race of the eyewitness and perpetrator has no impact on identification accuracy.
Fact. Eyewitnesses are better able to correctly identify a member of their own race compared to a member of a different race; this phenomenon is known as the cross-race effect (Meissner & Brigam, 2001).

Myth 5. The presence of a weapon does not impact an eyewitness' memory.
Fact. If a weapon is present, witnesses often focus on that (a term called "weapon focus") and therefore have a less reliable memory for other aspects of the crime (Saunders, 2009).

As you may have figured out by now, memory is not like a video recording in which an identical representation of the event is stored and then can be played back on request (Loftus, 1979a). Our memory can change each time we retrieve the event; some parts of the event may be embellished or guessed at because we cannot remember all the details. Often in our everyday life, our memory fallibilities are insignificant. For example, remembering that you bought a coffee at a Starbucks when actually it came from a Tim Hortons is harmless, most likely. In contrast, remembering whether the perpetrator was right- or left-handed may be critical if police are going to arrest the guilty suspect.

Eyewitness memory retrieval can be broadly partitioned into either recall or recognition memory. **Recall memory** refers to reporting details of a previously witnessed event or person. For example, describing what the perpetrator did and what the perpetrator looked like are both recall tasks. In contrast, **recognition memory** refers to determining whether a previously seen item or person is the same as what is currently being viewed. For example, hearing a set of voices and identifying the perpetrator's voice or identifying clothing worn by the perpetrator during the crime are both recognition tasks.

Sometimes being a witness or coming forward to report what you know may put you at risk for harm. See Box 5.2 for a discussion of Canada's witness protection program.

Recall memory: Reporting details of a previously witnessed event or person

Recognition memory: Determining whether a previously seen item or person is the same as what is currently being viewed

See Box 5.2 for a discussion of Canada's witness protection program.

Box 5.2   Forensic Psychology in the Spotlight

Canada's Witness Protection Program

Canada offers a federal witness protection program that is administered by the RCMP. The goal of the program is to protect individuals who provide police with information in the investigation and prosecution of crime. Some of these individuals provide information that places them at risk for harm, such as organized crime or terrorism informants. The program offers both short-term protection and permanent relocation, including identity changes.

At the end of 2012, Public Safety Minister Vic Toews introduced updated legislation for Canada's witness protection program. The Safer Witnesses Act is more far reaching and includes the following changes:

- It makes it easier for witnesses in provincial programs to obtain new identities.
- It imposes new restrictions on the disclosure of information, to help make the program more secure.
- It increases the amount of time emergency protection may be provided to witnesses.

- It makes the program available to individuals referred from National Defence and CSIS.

The impetus for the changes may have been a murder committed in 2007 by someone in the protection program. Some individuals in the program have sued for improper treatment, while others have been kicked out of the program. The Safer Witnesses Act came into force in late 2014 and amends the Witness Protection Program Act.

In 2013–2014, 34 individuals were granted protection under the program out of a total of 65 who were assessed.

Sources: Based on http://www.cbc.ca/news/politics/story/2012/12/11/ pol-cp-toews-witness-protection-program.html; http://www.theglobeandmail. com/news/politics/ottawa-set-to-expand-witness-protection-program/ article6190969/; http://www.ctvnews.ca/canada/bill-offers-witness-protection- to-defence-security-sources-1.1074467.

Statistics from https://www.publicsafety.gc.ca/cnt/rsrcs/pblctns/wtnss-prtctn- rprt-2013-14-eng.aspx.

HOW DO WE STUDY EYEWITNESS ISSUES?

Researchers interested in studying eyewitness issues can examine data from actual crimes. For example, they can use archival data such as police reports, or they can examine witnesses in naturalistic environments by accompanying police to crime scenes and interviewing witnesses after the police have done their job. Alternatively, they can conduct laboratory simulations. The laboratory simulation study is the most common paradigm used to study eyewitness issues.

The Laboratory Simulation

To study eyewitness memory by using a laboratory simulation, an unknowing participant views a critical event, such as a crime, through a slide sequence, a video recording, or live. The participant is unaware that he or she will be questioned about the event until after the event is witnessed. Now a witness, the participant is asked to describe what happened and the target/perpetrator involved. Following the descriptions of what was witnessed, the witness may be asked to examine a lineup. Many independent variables can be manipulated or examined; however, there are only three general dependent variables in eyewitness studies.

Estimator variables: Variables that are present at the time of the crime and that cannot be changed

Independent Variables   Numerous independent variables can be manipulated or examined within the laboratory simulation. Wells (1978) coined the terms *estimator variable* and *system variable* to help classify them. **Estimator variables** are those variables or factors that are present at the time of the crime and that cannot be changed. These can include the age of the witness, the amount of lighting, the presence of a weapon, and whether the witness was intoxicated. The criminal justice system cannot exert control over these variables. Thus, their effect on eyewitness accuracy can be estimated only after the crime. **System variables** are those variables or factors that can be manipulated to increase (or decrease) eyewitness accuracy, such as the type of procedure used by police to interview the witness or the type of lineup procedure used to present the suspect to the witness. These variables are under the control of the justice system. Both estimator and system variables can be manipulated in eyewitness laboratory studies.

System variables: Variables that can be manipulated to increase (or decrease) eyewitness accuracy

Open-ended recall: Witnesses are asked to either write or orally state all they remember about the event without the officer (or experimenter) asking questions. Also known as a *free narrative*

Dependent Variables   The three general dependent variables in eyewitness studies are (1) recall of the event/crime, (2) recall of the perpetrator, and (3) recognition of the perpetrator.

Recall of the crime or the perpetrator can take two formats. With **open-ended recall**, also known as a **free narrative**, witnesses are asked to either write or orally state all they remember about the event without the officer (or experimenter) asking questions. With this type of recall, the witness also may be asked to describe the perpetrator. With **direct question recall**, witnesses are asked a series of specific questions about the crime or the perpetrator. For example, the witness may be asked the colour of the getaway car or the length of the perpetrator's hair.

Free narrative: Witnesses are asked to either write or orally state all they remember about the event without the officer (or experimenter) asking questions. Also known as *open-ended recall*

Direct question recall: Witnesses are asked a series of specific questions about the crime or the perpetrator

A witness's recall of the crime or the perpetrator can be examined for the following:

- The amount of information reported. How many descriptors of the crime do witnesses report? How many descriptors of the perpetrator do witnesses report?
- The type of information reported. What is the proportion of peripheral details versus central details? What is the proportion of perpetrator details versus environment details?
- The accuracy of information reported. What is the proportion of correct descriptors reported? What is the proportion of omission errors (information the witness failed to report)? What is the proportion of commission errors (details falsely reported to be present)?

As for the recognition of the perpetrator, the typical recognition task is a lineup. A perpetrator **lineup** is a set of people presented to the witness, who in turn must identify the perpetrator if he or she is present. Another type of lineup takes the form of a set of voices, and the witness is asked to identify the perpetrator's voice. Clothing lineups, in which the witness examines clothing that may have been worn by the perpetrator, are sometimes also used.

A witness's recognition response can be examined for the following:

- Accuracy of decision. What is the rate of correctly identifying the perpetrator in the lineup? What is the rate of correctly stating that the perpetrator is not present in the lineup?
- *Types of errors made.* What is the rate of identifying an innocent person? What is the rate of stating that the perpetrator is not present when he or she is actually in the lineup?

Lineup: A set of people presented to the witness, who must state whether the perpetrator is present and, if so, which person it is

RECALL MEMORY

The primary goal for an officer interviewing an eyewitness is to extract from the witness a complete and accurate report of what happened (Fisher, Geiselman, & Raymond, 1987; Jackson, Sijlbing, & Thiecke, 1996). Insufficient information may provide the officer with few leads to pursue, resulting in a case that will not be solved. In this situation, the perpetrator will remain free to commit further crimes. If inaccurate information is supplied, then an officer may pursue innocent suspects, thus reducing the likelihood that the guilty person will be caught.

Now test your own recall. Without looking back at the crime scene photo on page 127, how many details can you remember?

Interviewing Eyewitnesses

Fisher et al. (1987) were curious about the techniques police were using to interview eyewitnesses. They analyzed 11 tape-recorded interviews from a police department in Florida. Eight detectives, who averaged 10.5 years of experience each, conducted these interviews. The researchers found a lot of variation in how the interviews were conducted. In general, however, the researchers found that the officers would introduce themselves, ask the eyewitnesses to report what they remembered by using an open-ended format, and then ask the witnesses a series of direct questions to determine specific information, such as the age or height of the perpetrator. The officers usually ended the interview by asking the eyewitnesses if there was any additional information that they could remember.

Fisher et al. (1987) found that the police officers' approach limited their ability to collect complete and accurate information in a number of ways. First, the researchers found that police often interrupted eyewitnesses when they were providing an open-ended recall report. The police may limit the amount of information eyewitnesses have in their conscious memory by preventing them from speaking or distracting them with questions.

Second, police questioned eyewitnesses with very short, specific questions. This type of question format uses a more superficial level of concentration than open-ended questions and tends to result in very short answers. The other problem with short, specific questions is that a police officer may not ask a relevant question that would provide critical information. For example, the perpetrator may have a tattoo, but if the officer does not ask about tattoos, the eyewitness may not report this feature. Thus, the police officer may miss a descriptor that could help in narrowing the suspect pool and arresting the perpetrator.

Third, police officers tended to ask questions in a predetermined or random order that was inconsistent with the information that witnesses were providing at the time. For example, a police officer may have asked a question about the perpetrator's voice while the witness was describing the perpetrator's clothing. Mixing visual and auditory questions has been found to decrease recall by approximately 19% (Fisher & Price-Roush, as cited in Fisher et al., 1987). Fourth, officers tended to ask questions that were "leading" or suggestive, which can be very dangerous when trying to collect accurate information.

A related issue is the contamination of co-witnesses. It is possible for crimes to have multiple witnesses. Witnesses can be "contaminated" if they know what other witnesses have reported. What one witness says about a crime can affect what another witness will say if those witnesses communicate with one another or come to learn what the other has reported. This phenomenon is referred to as **memory conformity** (Douglass & Pavletic, 2011). Thus, witnesses who have been influenced in this way produce reports that cannot be treated as if they were separate and independent.

Memory conformity: When what one witness reports influences what another witness reports

The Leading Question: The Misinformation Effect

Elizabeth Loftus, one of the most prominent researchers in the area of leading questions, has conducted many experiments demonstrating that a witness's recall report can be altered by the phrasing of a question. In one study, Loftus and Palmer (1974) had university students watch a videotape of a car accident. After viewing the accident, the participants were asked the identical question with a variation in one critical word, *hit*: "About how fast were the cars going when they hit each other?" *Hit* was replaced with either *smashed, collided, bumped,* or *contacted*. Even though all participants saw the same videotape, the speed reported by the participants varied depending on which critical word was used. Participants reported the highest rate of speed when the word *smashed* was used and the lowest rates of speed when the words *bumped* and *contacted* were used.

The experiment did not end there. The researchers called participants back a week later and asked whether they had seen any broken glass. Participants who were questioned with the word *smashed* were more likely to recall seeing broken glass than the other participants. However, there was no broken glass in the videotape. This study illustrates how the wording of a question can influence memory for the incident.

Loftus went on to demonstrate that simply introducing an inaccurate detail to witnesses could lead them to report that inaccurate detail when questioned later (Loftus, Altman, & Geballe, 1975). The **misinformation effect**, also called the **post-event information effect**, is a phenomenon in which a witness who is presented with inaccurate information after an event will incorporate that misinformation into a subsequent recall task (Loftus, 1975).

Past misinformation studies have used a common method or paradigm. Participants were exposed to an event via slides, video, or live action. They were then given a series of questions about the event, some of which contained misinformation. Later, the participants were asked a series of questions about the event, probing their response to the misinformation introduced. They were asked to respond from a forced-choice/multiple-choice set. That is, they were given a set of responses to choose from, with one response being correct, one response containing the misinformation, and one or two incorrect responses.

In one classic study, Loftus (1975) conducted four experiments demonstrating that how a question is worded can influence an eyewitness's recall at a later date. We'll discuss one of these experiments below.

Experiment   Forty university students watched a three-minute film clip of a class being interrupted by eight demonstrators. Following the clip, participants were given 20 questions. Half of the participants were asked, "Was the leader of the 4 demonstrators who entered the classroom a male?" The remaining participants were asked, "Was the leader of the 12 demonstrators who entered the classroom a male?" All other questions were the same for the two groups. After a one-week delay, the participants were asked 20 new questions about the film. The critical question in this new set was, "How many demonstrators did you see entering the classroom?" The participants who were asked a question about 12 demonstrators reported seeing an average of almost 9 demonstrators (8.85). Those who were asked about 4 demonstrators reported seeing an average of 6.40 demonstrators. Thus, incorporating the number of demonstrators into the question posed to witnesses affected the number of demonstrators witnesses recalled seeing later.

The misinformation effect occurs when a variety of different types of questions and methodology are used. But why does it occur?

Explaining the Misinformation Effect   Many studies have demonstrated that a witness's report can include misinformation that was previously supplied (Cole & Loftus, 1979; Loftus, 1979b), and these have fuelled debates on how and why this phenomenon occurs (Loftus, Miller, & Burns, 1978; McCloskey & Zaragoza, 1985). Were witnesses' memories changed? Were the participants just going along with the experimenter (or guessing) and providing the answer they thought was wanted? Or maybe the witness had two memories, a correct one and an incorrect one, and could not remember where

Misinformation effect:
Phenomenon where a witness who is presented with inaccurate information after an event will incorporate that misinformation into a subsequent recall task. Also known as the *post-event information effect*

Post-event information effect: Phenomenon where a witness who is presented with inaccurate information after an event will incorporate that misinformation into a subsequent recall task. Also known as the *misinformation effect*

each memory came from. Researchers have tried to advance or argue against these three general positions, each of which has different implications for memory:

1. With changes in the methodology, some studies have found support for guessing or experimenter pleasing. Some witnesses will guess at the answer they think the experimenter wants, resulting in the misinformation effect. This explanation is known as the **misinformation acceptance hypothesis** (McCloskey & Zaragoza, 1985).

2. Some studies have found that witnesses can recall both memories—the original, accurate one and the inaccurate one. However, witnesses cannot remember where each memory came from. When asked to recall what was seen, the witness chooses the incorrect memory. This explanation is called the **source misattribution hypothesis** (Lindsay, 1994).

3. Loftus is perhaps the biggest proponent of the **memory impairment hypothesis**. This hypothesis refers to the original memory being replaced or altered with the new, incorrect memory (Loftus, 1979a). The original memory is no longer accessible.

The debate on which explanation is responsible for the misinformation effect is far from over. Researchers continue to come up with methodologies that point to alternative explanations. One issue that has been put to rest, though, is whether the misinformation effect happens. The misinformation effect is a real phenomenon.

How can the misinformation effect happen in real life? A witness can be exposed to inaccurate information in a number of ways:

1. An officer may make assumptions about what occurred or what was witnessed and then inadvertently phrase a question consistent with his or her assumption. For example, the officer may ask the witness, "Did you see *the* gun?" rather than asking the more neutral question, "Did you see *a* gun?"

2. There may be more than one witness, and the witnesses overhear one another's statements. If there are discrepancies between the witnesses, then a witness may change his or her report to make it consistent.

3. A police officer may incorporate an erroneous detail from a previous witness's interview. For example, the officer may ask the witness, "What was the perpetrator with the scar wearing?" The witness may subsequently report that the perpetrator had a scar when in fact there was none.

PROCEDURES THAT HELP POLICE INTERVIEW EYEWITNESSES

Psychologists have been instrumental in developing procedures that can be beneficial at eliciting accurate information from witnesses.

Hypnosis

In some cases, eyewitnesses may be unable to recall very much that was witnessed, possibly because they were traumatized. With the help of hypnosis, they may be able to recall a greater amount of information. In a survey of ten forensic hypnosis

---

Misinformation acceptance hypothesis: Explanation for the misinformation effect where the incorrect information is provided because the witness guesses what the officer or experimenter wants the response to be

Source misattribution hypothesis: Explanation for the misinformation effect where the witness has two memories, the original and the misinformation; however, the witness cannot remember where each memory originated or the source of each

Memory impairment hypothesis: Explanation for the misinformation effect where the original memory is replaced with the new, incorrect information

experts, all felt that hypnosis could help witnesses remember crime details (Vingoe, 1995). It is assumed that a person under hypnosis is able to retrieve memories that are otherwise inaccessible. A hypnotized witness may be able to produce a greater number of details than a nonhypnotized witness; this phenomenon is termed *hypnotically refreshed memory* (Steblay & Bothwell, 1994).

According to Kebbell and Wagstaff (1998), two techniques that are often used in hypnosis are age regression and the television technique. With age regression, the witness goes back in time and re-experiences the original event. With the television technique, the witness imagines that he or she is watching an imaginary television screen with the events being played as they were witnessed. Further instructions stating that the eyewitness's memory will improve over time and in future sessions are provided once the witness has recalled the event. The witness is then awoken from the hypnosis.

Several reviews have examined the effectiveness of hypnosis in enhancing memory recall (e.g., Brown, Scheflin, & Hammond, 1998; Reiser, 1989; Steblay & Bothwell, 1994). These reviews found that individuals under hypnosis will provide more details, but those details are just as likely to be inaccurate as accurate (see also Fisher, 1995). Some researchers have suggested that one aspect of hypnosis that might help to increase recall of details is when individuals close their eyes. Both visual and auditory information is recalled to a greater degree when individuals close their eyes than when they keep their eyes open when trying to remember (Perfect et al., 2008). The hypnotized individual seems to be more suggestible to subtle cues by the interviewer than under normal conditions. The difficulty with using hypnosis is not being able to differentiate between the accurate and inaccurate details. In addition, witnesses recall both accurate and inaccurate details with the same degree of confidence (Sheehan & Tilden, 1984), and as we will see later, this confidence may be misleading.

Police are not interested in using hypnosis simply to collect more information; they are interested in collecting accurate information. For hypnosis to be useful in a forensic context, police need to know about the accuracy of the information recalled while under hypnosis. The Canadian courts are aware of the difficulties with hypnotically induced recall and typically do not permit information gained that way to be used as evidence. Hypnotically induced memories have recently been in the Canadian media. See the In the Media box to learn more about hypnotically refreshed memory.

The Cognitive Interview

Given the limitations of hypnosis, researchers have developed an interview procedure based on principles of memory storage and retrieval called the **cognitive interview** (Geiselman et al., 1984). The cognitive interview can be used with eyewitnesses, but it is not a procedure recommended for use with unwilling participants, such as suspects (see Chapter 3). The cognitive interview is based on four memory-retrieval techniques to increase recall: (1) reinstating the context, (2) reporting everything, (3) reversing order, and (4) changing perspective.

In an initial study, Geiselman, Fisher, MacKinnon, and Holland (1985) compared the "standard" police interview, hypnosis, and the cognitive interview to determine

Cognitive interview: Interview procedure for use with eyewitnesses based on principles of memory storage and retrieval

Hypnotically Refreshed Memory Goes to Court, or Not

On June 19, 1990, Elizabeth Bain was a 22-year-old student at the University of Toronto Scarborough campus studying psychology. She disappeared on her way to the university to check the tennis schedule. Two days later, Elizabeth's car was found with a bloodstain on the floor of the back seat. Her boyfriend, Robert Baltovich, was put under surveillance. Although a number of massive searches were undertaken, Elizabeth's body was not found. Investigators decided to hypnotize four witnesses who had seen Bain and Baltovich before Bain's disappearance to try to have the witnesses remember as much as possible. Baltovich was charged with first-degree murder five months later, and in 1992, he was convicted of the second-degree murder of his girlfriend. Baltovich's lawyers appealed the case and cited hypnotically refreshed memory as one of the reasons the conviction should be set aside. Baltovich spent almost nine years in prison until the Ontario Court of Appeal overturned his conviction in 2004 and ordered a new trial.

In 2007, the Supreme Court of Canada ruled that testimony elicited under hypnosis was inadmissible because individuals under hypnosis may be more suggestible and may have a difficult time distinguishing between accurate and fabricated memories. Moreover, there is no way of determining when the memories are accurate. So, in 2008, at the time of Baltovich's retrial, hypnotically refreshed memory was inadmissible in court and remains inadmissible.

Following several legal arguments in the Baltovich retrial, the Crown decided it would not call any evidence and Baltovich was acquitted of murder in April 2008. Some believe that Paul Bernardo was responsible for Elizabeth Bain's murder.

Sources: Based on Karl, S. (2009, December 21). On memory: Hypnotically refreshed memory. *National Post*. Retrieved from www.nationalpost.com/story.html?id=2368653; Robert Baltovitch: Not guilty. (2008, April 22). CBC News. Retrieved from www.cbc.ca/news/background/baltovich_robert/.

---

differences in the amount and accuracy of information recalled by witnesses. Participants watched a police training film of a crime. Forty-six hours after viewing the film, each participant was interviewed with one of the procedures by experienced law enforcement professionals. Compared with the "standard" police interview and hypnosis, the cognitive interview produced the greatest amount of accurate information without an increase in inaccurate details.

Over the years, Fisher and Geiselman (1992) expanded the cognitive interview into the **enhanced cognitive interview**, including various principles of social dynamics in addition to the memory retrieval principles used in the original cognitive interview. The additional components include the following:

Enhanced cognitive interview: Interview procedure that includes various principles of social dynamics in addition to the memory retrieval principles used in the original cognitive interview

1. *Rapport building.* An officer should spend time building rapport with the witness and make him or her feel comfortable and supported.

2. *Supportive interviewer behaviour.* A witness's free recall should not be interrupted; pauses should be waited out by the officer, who should express attention to what the witness is saying.

3. *Transfer of control.* The witness, not the officer, should control the flow of the interview; the witness is the expert—that is, the witness, not the officer, was the person who saw the crime.

4. *Focused retrieval*. Questions should be open-ended and not leading or suggestive; after free recall, the officer should use focused memory techniques to facilitate retrieval.

5. *Witness-compatible questioning*. An officer's questions should match the witness's thinking; if the witness is talking about clothing, the officer should be asking about clothing.

The enhanced cognitive interview, the original cognitive interview, and the standard police interview have been compared (Memon & Bull, 1991). Both cognitive interviews produced more accurate information, without an increase in inaccurate information, than standard interviews. Significant differences between the two cognitive interviews have not been found (Köehnken, 1995).

In a meta-analysis of the cognitive interview, reviewing 25 years of research, Memon, Meissner, and Fraser (2010) found that the cognitive interview produces a significant increase in accurate information with a small increase in errors. Both the original and modified versions of the cognitive interview produced these results. The question remains as to which components are responsible for the increase in accurate information (Kebbell & Wagstaff, 1998).

The cognitive interview has been tested in the United Kingdom with different-aged participants, including younger adults (age 17 to 31), older adults (age 60 to 74), and older-older adults (age 75 to 95) (Wright & Holliday, 2007). Compared with a "standard" police interview conducted in the United Kingdom, the cognitive interview increased the amount of accurate "person," "action," "object," and "surrounding" details for each age group without increasing the amount of inaccurate information recalled.

Although some officers in Canada (and in other countries, such as the United States and the United Kingdom) have been trained to conduct cognitive interviews, some are reluctant to use it, stating that it requires too much time to conduct and that the appropriate environment is not always available. However, trained officers report that they use some of the cognitive interview components on a regular basis when interviewing witnesses (see also Dando, Wilcock, & Milne, 2009).

RECALL OF THE PERPETRATOR

Along with a description of what happened, the witness will be asked to describe the perpetrator's appearance. Perusal of newspapers and news broadcasts finds that descriptions are vague and apply to many people. For example, a perpetrator may be described as white, male, between 1.75 metres and 1.83 metres tall, with short, brown hair. Think of how many people you know who fit this description.

Quantity and Accuracy of Descriptions

Research examining perpetrator descriptions provided by witnesses finds that descriptions are limited in detail and accuracy (Sporer, 1996). Lindsay, Martin, and Webber (1994) examined descriptions provided by adults in real and staged crimes.

Witnesses to staged crimes reported an average of 7.35 descriptors. In contrast, witnesses to real crimes reported significantly fewer descriptors—3.94 on average. Hair and clothing items were commonly reported descriptors.

In a study examining real-life descriptions, Fahsing, Ask, and Granhag (2004) examined, in an archival study, 250 offender descriptions made by witnesses to armed robberies of banks. Written descriptions from case files were compared to surveillance videos of the crimes. A total of 2348 attributes were described. All but one description included the gender of the perpetrator, and 90% included the upper body, clothing, and height. Witnesses usually included a description of the offender's build, weapon, pants, bag, and age. As has been found in previous studies, the descriptions, while usually reliable and accurate when compared to the videotaped offenders, were very general and non-specific. Witnesses reported an average of nine attributes each, which included at least four of gender, build, height, age, and ethnicity. Gender was always accurately reported. Age was the most inaccurately reported, followed by shoe descriptions and height estimates. In another archival study, Granhag, Ask, Rebelius, Öhman, and Giolla (2013) looked at witnesses' descriptions of the murderer of Anna Lindh, the Swedish Foreign Minister. Granhag et al. (2013) found that 42% of described attributes were incorrect, with witnesses being unreliable when describing basic features such as age and height, and more detailed features such as clothing. The number of errors was higher than that found in previous studies, which Granhag et al. suggested was due to the brief time the witnesses had to see the crime (12 to 14 seconds).

Wagstaff and colleagues (2003) found that hair colour and hairstyle were reported most accurately. Yarmey, Jacob, and Porter (2002) found that witnesses had difficulty correctly reporting weight (27% accuracy), eye colour (24% accuracy), and type of footwear (13% accuracy).

As you can see, perpetrator descriptions are limited in quantity and accuracy, which, in turn, limits their usefulness to the police in their investigation. Given the strides psychologists have made in other areas of police procedure, such as interviewing techniques, it would be worthwhile for psychologists to develop a technique or procedure that could be used to increase the amount and accuracy of witnesses' descriptions of perpetrators.

In one such attempt to increase the amount of descriptive information about an unfamiliar other, Kask, Bull, and Davies (2006) examined the effectiveness of having a "standard" for witnesses to use when answering questions about the target person. Participants saw an unfamiliar person interact with one of three experimenters. For half of the participants, the experimenter posed questions about the target stranger in reference to him- or herself (i.e., the experimenter functioned as a "standard" by which to be used as a reference). For example, when the experimenter was used as a standard, he or she would ask the participant, "My hair is this long; how long was his hair?" For the participants in the no-standard condition, the experimenter would ask the participant, "How long was his hair?" Unfortunately, the researchers found that the use of a standard did not help witnesses to recall accurate person information; however, it did aid somewhat when it came to recalling descriptors that are not typically remembered well (e.g., appearance of eyes, nose, or mouth).

A change in the modality of how a description is elicited from a witness can make a difference in the amount of information recalled. Sauerland and Sporer (2011) examined whether asking witnesses for a verbal description of a perpetrator differed from asking them to write down what they remembered. It was hypothesized that writing may produce less descriptive information because of the demands it puts on working memory in that writing is slower and less practised than speaking. Indeed, the researchers found that asking witnesses to write out their descriptions produced shorter and less accurate descriptions than when witnesses orally stated their descriptions.

RECOGNITION MEMORY

As defined at the beginning of the chapter, recognition memory involves determining whether a previously seen item or person is the one that is currently being viewed. A witness's recognition memory can be tested in a number of ways:

- Live lineups or photo arrays
- Video surveillance records
- Voice identification

Lineup Identification

"It's number 5; I'll never forget that face!" The typical method used to gain proof about the identity of the perpetrator is to conduct a lineup identification, in which a witness views a group of possible suspects and determines whether one is the perpetrator.

Why Conduct a Lineup?   A critical distinction needs to be made between the terms *suspect* and *perpetrator*. A **suspect** is a person the police "suspect" committed the crime. However, a suspect may be guilty or innocent of the crime in question. In contrast, a **perpetrator** is the guilty person who committed the crime.

A lineup identification reduces the uncertainty of whether a suspect is the perpetrator beyond the verbal description provided (Wells, 1993). A witness identifying the suspect increases the likelihood that the suspect is the perpetrator. In contrast, not identifying the suspect decreases the likelihood that the suspect is the perpetrator.

An alternative view of a lineup identification is that it provides police with information about the physical similarity between the lineup member chosen and the perpetrator (Navon, 1990). Police will have some notion of what the perpetrator looks like based on the person selected from the lineup.

Lineup Distractors   In addition to placing a suspect in a lineup, other lineup members may be included. These members are called **foils** or **distractors**, and they are known to be innocent of the crime in question. Police can use two types of strategies to decide on the physical appearance of the lineup distractors. A similarity-to-suspect strategy matches lineup members to the suspect's appearance. For example, if the

Suspect: A person the police "suspect" committed the crime, who may be guilty or innocent of the crime in question

Perpetrator: The guilty person who committed the crime

Foils: Lineup members who are known to be innocent of the crime in question. Also known as *distractors*

Distractors: Lineup members who are known to be innocent of the crime in question. Also known as *foils*

suspect had brown hair, blue eyes, and a moustache, then each lineup member would have these characteristics. A difficulty with this strategy, however, is that there are many physical features that could be matched, such as width of eyebrows, length of nose, and thickness of lips. If taken to the extreme, this strategy would produce a lineup of clones—everyone would look exactly like the suspect, making it virtually impossible to identify the perpetrator. In contrast, a match-to-description strategy sets limits on the number of features that need to be matched. With this strategy, distractors are matched only on the items that the witness provided in his or her description. For example, if a witness stated that the criminal had brown hair, blue eyes, a round face, and no facial hair, then those would be the features on which each lineup member is matched.

Lindsay et al. (1994) noted that some general characteristics that might not be mentioned would need to be included to produce a "fair" lineup. A **fair lineup** is one in which the suspect does not stand out from the other lineup members. For example, if skin colour was not mentioned, then a lineup could be constructed with one white face (the suspect) and five black faces. Thus, the lineup would be unfair or biased. Some characteristics, such as sex and race, are known as default values and should be matched even if not mentioned in the witness's description.

Also, to avoid a biased lineup, Luus and Wells (1991; Wells, Rydell, & Seelau, 1993) suggest that if a feature is provided in the witness's description but does not match the suspect's appearance, then the distractors should match the suspect's appearance on that feature. For example, if the perpetrator is described as having brown hair but the suspect has blond hair, then the distractors should have blond hair.

Estimating Identification Accuracy   When we are interested in finding out how often witnesses will make an accurate (or inaccurate) identification decision, we need to create the condition when police have arrested the right person, the guilty suspect. We also need to create the condition when police have arrested the wrong person, an innocent suspect. Thus, we create two lineups in our research. One lineup—the **target-present lineup**—contains a picture of the perpetrator. In the other lineup— the **target-absent lineup**—we substitute the perpetrator's picture with another photo. Identification decisions are different with each type of lineup. See Table 5.1 for the types of identification decisions possible as a function of type of lineup.

Three types of identification decisions can occur with a target-present lineup. The witness can identify the guilty suspect, which is a correct identification. If the

Fair lineup: A lineup where the suspect does not stand out from the other lineup members

Target-present lineup: A lineup that contains the perpetrator

Target-absent lineup: A lineup that does not contain the perpetrator but rather an innocent suspect

Table 5.1 Possible Identification Decisions as a Function of Lineup Type

Type of Lineup	Identification Decision				
	Correct Identification	False Rejection	Foil Identification	Correct Rejection	False Identification
Target-present	X	X	X	Not possible	Not possible
Target-absent	Not possible	Not possible	X	X	X

Source: Based on What do we know about eyewitness identification by Gary L. Wells. Published by American Psychological Association, © 1993.

witness identifies a foil, that is a foil identification. In addition, the witness may state that the perpetrator is not present, which is a false rejection.

Three types of identification decisions can occur with a target-absent lineup. The witness can state that the perpetrator is not present, which is a correct rejection. The witness can identify a foil, which is a foil identification. The witness can also identify an innocent suspect, in which case the witness makes a false identification. Sometimes, researchers will not make a distinction between false identifications and foil identifications from a target-absent lineup and will refer to these two errors simply as false positives.

Identification Decision Implications   The only correct decision with a target-present lineup is to make a correct identification. The only correct decision with a target-absent lineup is to make a correct rejection. The other decisions with each type of lineup are errors and have different implications for the witness and the justice system (Wells & Turtle, 1986):

- A foil identification (with either a target-present lineup or a target-absent lineup) is a known error to the police, so the person identified will not be prosecuted. The witness, however, may be perceived as having a faulty memory. Moreover, the other details provided by this witness may be viewed with some skepticism because a known recognition error was made.

- A false rejection is an unknown error and may result in the guilty suspect going free and possibly committing further crimes.

- A false identification also is an unknown error in real life and may result in the innocent suspect being prosecuted and convicted for a crime he or she did not commit. Moreover, with a false identification, the real criminal remains free to commit further crimes. False identifications may be the most serious type of identification error a witness can make.

Live Lineups or Photo Arrays?   Most often, police will use a set of photographs rather than live persons to assemble a lineup (Turtle, Lindsay, & Wells, 2003). *Photo array* is the term used for photographic lineups. Photo arrays are more common than lineups for a number of reasons:

- They are less time-consuming to construct. The police can choose foils from their mug shot (pictures of people who have been charged with crimes in the past) files rather than find live persons.

- They are portable. The police are able to bring the photo array to the witness rather than have the witness go to the police department.

- The suspect does not have the right to counsel being present when a witness looks at a photo array. This right is present with live lineups.

- Because photos are static, the police need not worry that the suspect's behaviour may draw attention to him- or herself, thus invalidating the photo array.

- A witness may be less anxious examining a photo array than a live lineup.

An alternative to photographs or live lineups is to use video-recorded lineups. Advantages to video lineups include the ability to enlarge faces or focus on particular features. Lineup members can be shown walking, turning, and talking. In a study by Cutler, Fisher, and Chicvara (1989), the researchers found that correct identification and correct rejection rates did not differ across live and video-recorded lineups. Havard, Memon, Clifford, and Gabbert (2010) examined whether children (7 to 9 year olds) and adolescents (13 to 15 year olds) performed differently with live versus videotaped lineups. They found, only for the adolescents, that the video lineup had a slight advantage when the target was not present (i.e., for correct rejections). There were no other differences found between the two lineup types. Video lineups are now the usual format in the United Kingdom (Horry, Memon, Wright, & Milne, 2012). These video lineups are shown sequentially (see below) to the witness and the witness views the lineup twice. Horry et al. (2012) examined the identification decisions from 1039 actual lineups in England. They found that witnesses requesting additional passes through the lineup were more likely to guess and that this occurred most often with foil identifications.

Lineup Presentation Procedures   Lineups can be presented in different formats or with different procedures to the witness. Perhaps most common is the procedure known as the **simultaneous lineup** (Wells, 1993). The simultaneous procedure presents all lineup members at one time to the witness. Wells (1993) suggested that this procedure encourages the witness to make a **relative judgment**, whereby lineup members are compared with one another and the person who looks most like the perpetrator is identified.

An alternative lineup procedure is the **sequential lineup**. This lineup procedure involves presenting the lineup members serially to the witness. The witness must make a decision as to whether the lineup member is the perpetrator before seeing the next lineup member (Lindsay & Wells, 1985). Also, with the sequential procedure, a witness cannot ask to see previously seen photos and the witness is unaware of the number of photos to be shown. Wells (1993) suggested that the sequential procedure reduces the likelihood that the witness can make a relative judgment. Instead, witnesses may be more likely to make an **absolute judgment**, whereby each lineup member is compared with the witness's memory of the perpetrator and the witness decides whether it is the perpetrator.

Lindsay and Wells (1985) compared the identification accuracy rate achieved with the simultaneous and sequential lineup procedures. University students witnessed a videotaped theft and were asked to identify the perpetrator from six photographs. Half the students saw a target-present lineup and the other half of students saw a target-absent lineup. Across target-present and target-absent conditions, the lineups were either presented using a simultaneous procedure or a sequential procedure.

Correct identification (target-present lineups) rates did not differ across lineup procedures. However, correct rejection rates were significantly different across lineup procedures. Only 42% of the participants made a correct rejection with a simultaneous lineup, whereas 65% of the participants made a correct rejection with a sequential lineup. In other words, if the perpetrator was not included in the lineup, witnesses were more likely to correctly indicate that he or she was not present if they were shown a sequential lineup rather than a simultaneous lineup. The higher correct

Simultaneous lineup: A common lineup procedure that presents all lineup members at one time to the witness

Relative judgment: Witness compares lineup members to one another and the person who looks most like the perpetrator is identified

Sequential lineup: Alternative lineup procedure where the lineup members are presented serially to the witness, and the witness must make a decision as to whether the lineup member is the perpetrator before seeing another member. Also, a witness cannot ask to see previously seen photos and is unaware of the number of photos to be shown

Absolute judgment: Witness compares each lineup member to his or her memory of the perpetrator to decide whether the lineup member is the perpetrator

rejection rate with the sequential procedure compared with the simultaneous procedure has been replicated numerous times (Steblay, Dysart, Fulero, & Lindsay, 2001; Steblay Dysart, & Wells, 2011). Two meta-analyses (Steblay et al., 2001; Steblay et al., 2011) also found that correct identification rates are somewhat lower for sequential lineups compared to simultaneous lineups, but this difference lessens as real-world conditions are considered. The sequential lineup is the procedure used in some Canadian jurisdictions, such as Ontario, and some U.S. states, such as New Jersey. Recent research, however, has called into question the "sequential superiority effect" (McQuiston-Surrett, Malpass, & Tredoux, 2006). The researchers suggest that when certain methodological factors are considered, the simultaneous procedure produces correct rejection rates similar to those of the sequential procedure without a drop in correct identifications. Thus, the debate continues (see also Malpass, Tredoux, & McQuiston-Surrett, 2009).

Dr. Rod Lindsay has been a key researcher in the area of lineup identification. See Box 5.3 to read about him and his research.

Box 5.3

Canadian Researcher Profile: Dr. Rod Lindsay

Courtesy of Rod Lindsay

Dr. Rod Lindsay recalls the fortuitous meeting that started his more than 30-year career researching eyewitness issues. While he was working in his office one day, during his time as a graduate student at the University of Alberta, a new faculty member walked in and introduced himself as Gary Wells. It was January 1978 and Dr. Wells was looking for graduate students who would be interested in working on a research project he was planning. The project was exam-

ining jurors' perceptions of eyewitness identification. In 1979, this project was published in the *Journal of Applied Psychology*, and it would be one of the first in a long list of articles that would follow for Dr. Lindsay.

In the early 1980s, Dr. Lindsay joined the faculty at Queen's University, where he continued conducting eyewitness research. Dr. Lindsay describes his favourite research questions as those that can lead to real-world applications. He prefers to use experimental methodology to investigate the research questions that intrigue him. Although he respects surveys, case studies, and many other forms of methodology, he likes how a good experiment can answer a very specific and narrowly defined question, such as "Which of two lineup procedures will generate more accurate identifications?"

Dr. Lindsay's extensive eyewitness expertise has led him to the courts as an expert witness in a number of cases. Perhaps one of the most emotionally difficult cases for him was a Rwandan war-crime trial. The defendants were charged with 20 000 counts of murder in a single afternoon.

Recently, Dr. Lindsay consulted on two Canadian cases that he found both professionally interesting and very frustrating. In one of the cases, a First Nations suspect was placed in a 12-person lineup in which no other lineup member was First Nations. In the other case, a Filipino

(continued)

suspect also was placed in a 12-person lineup; this time, all the other lineup members were First Nations! In each case, the court decided there was nothing wrong with the lineup—decisions that Dr. Lindsay did not agree with.

To deal with eyewitness issues on a practical level, Dr. Lindsay would like to see the Canadian government create something like the United Kingdom's Home Office. Such an organization could take responsibility for researching police procedures, then decide on the best practices and write and distribute this information through directives for law enforcement. Moreover, the courts would have the clout to back up a Home Office–type department by throwing out any evidence that resulted from procedures that did not meet the standards outlined.

In addition to informing the justice system on how to improve eyewitness evidence, Dr. Lindsay is committed to teaching and training future eyewitness researchers. He enjoys getting students excited about the eyewitness world: "If you love it, they will."

Eyewitness research is not the only thing Dr. Lindsay is passionate about. Often, he will escape the lab on a Friday afternoon only to re-emerge on Monday morning, having spent the time in between playing duplicate bridge and more duplicate bridge.

Dr. Lindsay has received numerous distinctions for his work. In 2002, Dr. Lindsay's contribution to the eyewitness field was recognized by the Canadian Psychological Association, with the Career Award for Distinguished Contributions to the Application of Psychology. More recently, in 2010, Dr. Lindsay's mentorship of graduate students was recognized with the Award for Excellence in Graduate Student Supervision.

Showup: Identification procedure that shows one person to the witness: the suspect

An alternative identification procedure to the lineup is a **showup**. This procedure shows one person to the witness: the suspect. The witness is asked whether the person is the perpetrator. Although an absolute judgment is likely with a showup, it has a number of other difficulties, making it a less-than-ideal procedure. Both courts and researchers have argued (*Stovall v. Denno*, 1967; Wells, Leippe, & Ostrom, 1979) that because there are no other lineup members shown, the witness is aware of whom the police suspect, and this knowledge may increase a witness's likelihood of making an identification that may be false.

Not everyone agrees with this view, however. In the early 1990s, a series of studies were conducted by Gonzalez, Ellsworth, and Pembroke (1993). They did not find false identifications to be higher with a showup than with a lineup. In fact, they found that witnesses were more likely to reject a showup than all members of a lineup. Gonzalez et al. concluded that witnesses are more cautious with their decision making when presented with a showup rather than a lineup, and as a result, they will err on making a rejection rather than an identification. Yarmey, Yarmey, and Yarmey (1996), however, reached a different conclusion. They found that lineups produced lower false-identification rates than showups. In a recent meta-analysis comparing showups and lineups, Steblay, Dysart, Fulero, and Lindsay (2003) found that false identifications were higher with showups than with lineups. Also, in an analysis of 271 actual police cases, the suspect was more likely to be identified in a field showup (76%) than in a photographic lineup (48%) (Behrman & Davey, 2001). These results are consistent with the notion that showups are suggestive (see also Agricola, 2009). Wetmore et al. (2015) had 1584 participants view a crime video and then perform a showup or simultaneous lineup identification, immediately or 2 days later. Showups never resulted in higher accuracy in comparison to a lineup, even when lineups were biased instead of fair. Further research is needed to understand the discrepancy in identification rates for showups across studies.

For now, there are only two acceptable uses of a showup. It may be used for deathbed identifications, when there is a fear that the witness will not be alive by the time a lineup is assembled (Wells, Malpass, Lindsay, Turtle, & Fulero, 2000). Also, police may use a showup if a suspect is apprehended immediately at or near the crime scene.

One other identification procedure that may precede a lineup identification is known as a **walk-by**. This identification occurs in a naturalistic environment. The police take the witness to a public location where the suspect is likely to be. Once the suspect is in view, the witness is asked whether he or she sees the perpetrator.

Walk-by: Identification procedure that occurs in a naturalistic environment. The police take the witness to a public location where the suspect is likely to be. Once the suspect is in view, the witness is asked whether he or she sees the perpetrator

In lineups with more than one person, the person administering the lineup will need to decide where to place the suspect's photo. Although this is usually done randomly (e.g., the witness can shuffle the photos before starting to look at them), it is interesting to consider whether the placement of the photos matters to identification accuracy. Megreya, Bindemann, Havard, and Burton (2012) examined the eye movements of witnesses examining a lineup. Faces that were on the left side were looked at first. Also, foils on the left side were more likely to be inaccurately identified as the target.

Lineup Biases   Constructing a fair lineup is a challenging task. **Biased lineups** suggest whom the police suspect and thereby whom the witness should identify. In some way, the suspect stands out from the other lineup members in a biased lineup. The following biases have been investigated and found to increase false positives:

Biased lineup: A lineup that "suggests" whom the police suspect and thereby whom the witness should identify

1. *Foil bias.* The suspect is the only lineup member who matches the description of the perpetrator. For example, the suspect has a beard and moustache while the other lineup members are clean-shaven (Lindsay, Lea, & Fulford, 1991).

2. *Clothing bias.* The suspect is the only lineup member wearing clothing similar to that worn by the perpetrator. For example, the perpetrator was described as wearing a blue baseball cap. The suspect is wearing a blue baseball cap while the foils are not (Dysart, Lindsay, & Dupuis, 2006; Lindsay et al., 1991; Lindsay, Wallbridge, & Drennan, 1987).

3. *Instruction bias.* The police fail to mention to the witness that the perpetrator may not be present; rather, the police imply that the perpetrator is present and that the witness should pick him or her out (Clark, 2005; Malpass & Devine, 1981; Steblay, 1997).

Voice Identification

Perhaps one of the first and most prominent cases involving voice identification (or "earwitness" identification) occurred in the United States in 1937. The infant son of Charles Lindbergh, a well-known doctor and aviator, was kidnapped and murdered (see Chapter 3). Lindberg identified Bruno Hauptmann's voice as the one he heard three years earlier when he

What is wrong with this lineup?
Jeremy Woodhouse/Alamy Stock Photo

paid the ransom. The kidnapper had said, "Hey, doctor, over here, over here." Hauptmann was convicted of kidnapping and murder. At the time, no studies on voice identification existed. Unfortunately, little has changed over the past 65 years, as very few studies have been conducted in this area.

In one study examining many key voice variables, Orchard and Yarmey (1995) had 156 university students listen to a taped voice of a mock kidnapper that varied in length—either 30 seconds or 8 minutes. The voice was varied such that the kidnapper either had a distinctive or nondistinctive voice. The researchers also varied whether the speaker spoke in a whisper or a normal tone. Voice-identification accuracy was tested using six-person voice lineups two days after the participants heard the taped voice. Here are some of the results:

- Identification accuracy was higher with longer voice samples.
- Whispering significantly decreased identification accuracy.
- Distinctiveness interacted with whispering, influencing identification accuracy.

Öhman, Eriksson, and Granhag (2011) conducted a study with 282 participants, consisting of 7 to 9 year olds, 11 to 13 year olds, and adults. Participants heard a 40-second recording of an unfamiliar voice. Approximately two weeks later, they were presented with a seven voice lineup, either target-present or target-absent. All conditions resulted in poor performance; the only condition in which participants performed above chance was the target present condition with 11 to 13 year olds, who had a 27% rate of correct identifications.

In a more recent study, Philippon, Randall, and Cherryman (2013) investigated whether laughter would influence the accuracy of voice identification. Participants were assigned to target-present and target-absent conditions. One-third of participants heard laughter only in the lineup, one-third heard speech and laughter, whereas the final third heard no laughter, just speech. Philippon et al. found that participants were more likely to recognize a voice when it was accompanied by laughter or only the laughter was heard. Overall, the two laughter conditions yielded similar accuracy. When the target was absent, laughter with speech resulted in higher accuracy while in target present situations, laughter alone resulted in more correct identifications.

Factors That Decrease the Likelihood of Correct Voice Identification Other studies have found that the likelihood of a correct identification is decreased if a voice is changed by whispering or muffling, or through emotion (Bull & Clifford, 1984; Saslove & Yarmey, 1980). Orchard and Yarmey (1995) stated that "when voices are disguised as whispers, or changed in tone between first hearing the perpetrator and the conduction of the voice lineup, identification evidence should be accepted with critical caution" (p. 259). In terms of target-voice position in a lineup, if the target voice occurs later in the lineup, correct identification decreases compared with an earlier presentation (Doehring & Ross, 1972).

Kersholt, Jansen, Van Amelsvoort, and Broeders (2006) examined the question of whether the perpetrator and witness having different accents would affect voice identification. There was a trend for participants to be more accurate when the speaker had a familiar versus a different accent: 41% correct identifications versus

34% correct identifications respectively, and 56% correct rejections versus 35% correct rejections respectively.

In a series of experiments, Pickel and Staller (2012) examined how a voice with an accent affected how witnesses described the perpetrator's appearance. Witnesses viewing a perpetrator who spoke with an accent reported less developed physical descriptions of the perpetrator and were less accurate in identifying the voice. If the message spoken by the perpetrator was more versus less detailed, the witnesses provided fewer accurate details about what the perpetrator looked like. Also, increasing the threatening nature of the message led to more inaccurate descriptions of the perpetrator's appearance.

Cook and Wilding (1997) reported that when the target's face was visible when participants originally heard the voice at encoding, correct identification decreased greatly. Also, as the number of foils increased from four to eight voices, correct identification decreased (Clifford, 1980).

Are Several Identifications Better Than One?

If identification decisions for different pieces of evidence were combined, would the decision regarding the suspect's guilt be more accurate? Pryke, Lindsay, Dysart, and Dupuis (2004) conducted two experiments examining the usefulness of multiple independent lineups to identify a perpetrator: for example, having the participants identify the clothing worn by the perpetrator in one lineup and identify the perpetrator's face in another lineup. If both of these identification decisions are of the suspect, then the likelihood that the suspect is the perpetrator should be greater than if just one identification decision implicates the suspect. In the first experiment, following exposure to a live target, participants were shown a face lineup, then a voice lineup, and lastly a body lineup (Pryke et al., 2004). In the second experiment, a clothing lineup was added to the other three lineups. The researchers found that exposing witnesses to more than one lineup, each consisting of a different aspect of the suspect, increased the ability to determine the reliability of an eyewitness's identification of the suspect. Thus, the likelihood of the suspect's guilt increased as the number of independent identifications of the suspect increased by any one witness. This research presents an interesting avenue for future research, with many questions still unanswered. For example, are certain types of lineups more diagnostic of a suspect's guilt than others?

Are Confident Witnesses Accurate?

In a landmark U.S. Supreme Court Case in 1972 (*Neil v. Biggers*), the court stated that the confidence of a witness should be taken as an indicator of accuracy. This assertion implies that witnesses who are certain in their identification of the perpetrator are likely to be accurate. Many studies, however, have investigated this relationship and found a different result (Cutler & Penrod, 1989a, 1989b; Penrod & Cutler, 1995; Sporer, Penrod, Read, & Cutler, 1995). Overall, there appears to be a small positive correlation between accuracy and confidence. There also are a number of moderator variables that can increase or decrease this relation.

When confidence is assessed at the time of initial identification, there appears to be a strong relationship between confidence and accuracy (Wixted, Mickes, Clark, Gronlund, & Roedinger, 2015). Dodson and Dobolyi (2016) found, in the case of correct identifications, confidence had a particularly strong relationship with accuracy when the decision is made very quickly, in which case high confidence was associated with 90% accuracy. However, Dodson and Dobolyi found there was not a relationship between confidence and accuracy when a 'not here' decision was made.

Odinot, Wolters, and van Geizen (2013) examined whether the confidence of an eyewitness's testimony should really be considered a gauge for its accuracy. All participants viewed a video depicting a complicated scenario. One group of the participants took part in cued recall tasks one week, three weeks, and five weeks after viewing the video, a second group only took part at three and five weeks, and the final group only took part five weeks after viewing the video. When the recall tasks were repeated, accuracy and confidence did not decline. A longer interval between viewing the video and answering questions was only associated with decreased confidence for incorrect answers, not correct answers. Accuracy decreased as the interval increased. A moderate to large relationship between confidence and accuracy was consistently found.

Wells and his colleagues have investigated post-lineup identification feedback and its effect on the confidence–accuracy relationship (Bradfield, Wells, & Olson, 2002; Luus & Wells, 1994; Wells & Bradfield, 1998). In one study (Semmler, Brewer, & Wells, 2004), after the witness made a lineup identification decision, the experimenter provided either confirming feedback ("This study has now had a total of 87 participants, 84 of them made the same decision as you!") or no feedback at all. In their first experiment, target-absent lineups were used and in the second target-present lineups were used.

Participants were asked to make a number of judgments following the feedback or lack thereof. Of key interest were the current confidence ratings the participants made regarding how confident they were that they identified the correct person on a percentage scale of 0 to 100 percent confident. Measures for current confidence are shown in Figure 5.2, as a function of feedback condition.

Participants who were informed that they had identified the perpetrator reported significantly higher confidence ratings than participants who received no feedback. Thus, confidence can be manipulated and inflated, thereby affecting the confidence–accuracy relation. A meta-analysis of post-identification feedback has shown it to be a reliable and robust effect, having an impact on a number of factors, including how certain witnesses feel and how much attention they think they paid to the perpetrator (Douglass & Steblay, 2006). Wright and Skagerberg (2007) interviewed eyewitnesses to actual crimes both before and after they were told they had identified a filler or the suspect. If they were told they had not picked the suspect, they believed the task was more difficult than if they were told they had picked a filler. This shows that post-identification feedback has an influence in real-life situations, and that confidence assessments should be taken prior to any feedback.

Research also indicates that the more often you express a decision, the greater your confidence in subsequent reports (Shaw, 1996; Shaw & McClure, 1996). You can imagine that by the time a witness testifies in court, he or she has been

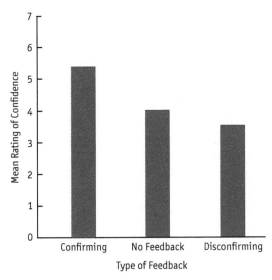

Figure 5.2 Mean Current Confidence Ratings as a Function of Feedback

	Mistaken ID (TP)	Incorrect Rejection (TP)	Correct ID (TP)	Mistaken ID (TA)	Correct Rejection (TA)
Feedback	63.68	77.23	76.15	70.71	75.77
No Feedback	47.14	57.07	63.23	53.33	70.71

Source: Gary L. Wells, Carolyn Semmler, Neil Brewer, Journal of Experimental Psychology: Applied Copyright 2004 by the American Psychological Association 2004, Vol. 10, No. 3, 139–147.

interviewed many times. Consequently, the confidence the witness expresses in the courtroom may be inflated. Inflated confidence may be problematic given that it is an indicator used by fact-finders (i.e., judges and juries) to assess accuracy. Moreover, mock jurors do not appear sensitive to "inflated confidence" (Bradfield & McQuiston, 2004). Wells et al. (1998) have recommended that police ask witnesses for their confidence rating immediately following their identification decision prior to any feedback and that this rating be used in court. This rating may be more informative with regard to accuracy. Also, it is recommended that the person administering the lineup not know who the suspect is to limit post-identification feedback.

Estimator Variable Research in Recognition Memory

Three estimator variables have received much attention in eyewitness research: age, race, and weapon focus.

Age Older adults (over age 60) appear less likely than younger adults to correctly identify the perpetrator from a target-present lineup; older adults are also more likely to make an incorrect decision from a target-absent lineup than younger adults (Wells & Olson, 2003). In other words, older adults make fewer correct identifications and fewer correct rejections than younger adults. Fitzgerald and Price (2015) found an increasing developmental trajectory for correct identifications and correct rejections, but also found that performance decreased for older adults.

Havard and Memon (2009) compared the identification abilities of younger adults (18 to 35 year olds) and older adults (61 to 83 year olds). They presented participants with two videos: one with a younger adult perpetrator and one with an older adult perpetrator. The lineups presented were 9-person video lineups in which all photos are presented sequentially, but no identification decision is made until all photos have been viewed. Havard and Memon found that the older adults made fewer correct identifications as well as fewer correct rejections. The younger adults made more correct rejections when the perpetrator was also a younger adult but the older adults did not show any own-age bias.

In their meta-analysis comparing the eyewitness identification performance of older and younger adults, Erickson, Lampinen, and Moore (2015) found that older adults consistently underperformed, i.e. made fewer correct decisions, in comparison to young adults. This was true regardless of the lineup procedure used, age of the perpetrator, as well as whether the lineup was target-present or target-absent.

Race The **cross-race effect**, also known as the **other-race effect** and the **own-race bias**, is the phenomenon of witnesses remembering faces of people of their own race with greater accuracy than they remember faces of people of other races. In a meta-analysis, Meissner and Brigham (2001) examined 30 years of research, including almost 5000 participants, on the topic of cross-race identification. They found that own-race faces produced higher correct identifications and lower false positives than other-race faces. In a Canadian study, the cross-race effect was examined by using Caucasian and First Nations samples (Jackiw, Arbuthnott, Pfeifer, Marcon, & Meissner, 2008). Similar to other studies, both Caucasian and First Nations participants were more accurate at recognizing faces from their own race compared with the "other" race. Intriguingly, both Caucasians and First Nations participants were more likely to choose a face when trying to identify a First Nations face compared to identifying a Caucasian face. The authors suggest that the potential for mistaken identification of First Nations people is high regardless of the race of the eyewitness. Moreover, it is important to note that many bands fit within the First Nations designation. Thus, individuals from different bands may be experiencing the cross-race effect.

It is not uncommon for criminal activity to occur when individuals are intoxicated. In a study by Hilliar, Kemp, and Denson (2010), alcohol intoxication and own-race bias were examined. Asian and European participants had to recognize Asian and European faces when they were either sober or somewhat intoxicated (mean breath alcohol concentration of .05). Being intoxicated had a larger negative effect when recognizing same-race faces compared to other-race faces.

A number of explanations for the cross-race effect have been suggested. Below are three of the more common explanations.

Attitudes One hypothesis to explain the other-race effect is based on attitudes. More specifically, people with fewer prejudicial attitudes may be more inclined to distinguish among members of other races. However, research to date does not

---

Cross-race effect: Phenomenon of witnesses remembering own-race faces with greater accuracy than faces from other races. Also known as the *other-race effect* and the *own-race bias*

Other-race effect: Phenomenon of witnesses remembering own-race faces with greater accuracy than faces from other races. Also known as the *cross-race effect* and the *own-race bias*

Own-race bias: Phenomenon of witnesses remembering own-race faces with greater accuracy than faces from other races. Also known as the *cross-race effect* and the *other-race effect*

support this explanation (Platz & Hosch, 1988; Slone, Brigham, & Meissner, 2000). Having said that, Meissner and Brigham (2001) did note that prejudicial attitudes may be related to the amount of contact a person has with other-race members, which, in turn, may help to explain the other-race effect (see page 150).

Physiognomic Homogeneity   An alternative hypothesis to explain the other-race effect suggests that some races have less variability in their faces—that is, "they all look alike." This hypothesis has not received much empirical support either. Goldstein (1979), for example, examined Japanese, black, and white faces and did not find that one group was more similar across members than the others were. Although physical similarity may not explain the other-race effect, some physical features may be more appropriate for discriminating among faces of certain races, such as hair colour (Deregowski, Ellis, & Shepherd, 1975; Shepherd, 1981; Shepherd & Deregowski, 1981). Thus, persons from other races may not pay attention or encode relevant features that distinguish between members of a particular race. For example, paying attention to hair colour for Asian faces may be less discriminating than hair colour for Caucasian faces. This explanation, however, does not seem adequate at explaining the cross-race phenomenon.

Interracial Contact   Perhaps the hypothesis receiving the most attention examines the amount or type of contact people have had with other races. This hypothesis states that the more contact you have with other races, the better you will be able to identify them. In the 1970s, some researchers examined children and adolescents living in integrated neighbourhoods versus those living in segregated neighbourhoods. It was predicted that participants from integrated neighbourhoods would be better at recognizing other-race faces than those living in segregated neighbourhoods. Some support for this prediction was found (Cross, Cross, & Daly, 1971; Feinman & Entwisle, 1976).

In another test of this hypothesis, Li, Dunning, and Malpass (as cited in Meissner & Brigham, 2001) examined the ability of white basketball "experts" (dedicated fans) and white basketball novices to recognize black faces. Given that the majority of U.S. professional basketball players are black, it was thought that the experts would have more experience distinguishing black faces because of their experience watching basketball. Indeed, the experts were better at identifying black faces than the novices.

It is important to note that not all studies that have investigated interracial contact have found the predicted effect. For example, Ng and Lindsay (1994) examined university students from Canada and Singapore and the other-race effect was not completely supported.

A definitive conclusion on the contact hypothesis and how it factors into the other-race effect remains unclear. Further work in this area is needed.

Weapon Focus   Weapon focus is the term used to describe the phenomenon of a witness's attention being focused on the perpetrator's weapon rather than on the perpetrator (Steblay, 1992). The witness will remember less about the crime and perpetrator when a weapon is present than when no weapon is present. It is clear that this phenomenon occurs, but why it occurs is less clear. There have been two primary explanations for the weapon focus effect: arousal and unusualness.

Weapon focus: Term used to describe the phenomenon of a witness's attention being focused on the perpetrator's weapon rather than on the perpetrator

Cue-utilization hypothesis:
Proposed by Easterbrook (1959) to explain why a witness may focus on the weapon rather than other details. The hypothesis suggests that when emotional arousal increases, attentional capacity decreases

Arousal   The **cue-utilization hypothesis** was proposed by Easterbrook (1959) to explain why a witness may focus on the weapon rather than other details. The hypothesis suggests that when emotional arousal increases, attentional capacity decreases. With limited attentional capacity, central details, such as the weapon, are more likely to be encoded than peripheral details, such as the colour of the perpetrator's hair. There is limited support for this hypothesis.

Unusualness   An alternative explanation for the weapon focus phenomenon has to do with unusualness, in that weapons are unusual and thus attract a witness's attention. Because a witness is not paying attention to and encoding other details, these other details are not remembered (Mitchell, Livosky, & Mather, 1998; Pickel, 1998). To follow this line of thinking, you would predict that not only weapons, but also other objects might produce a "weapon focus" effect, if they were unusual for the situation.

Pickel (1999) conducted two experiments to investigate the unusualness explanation. In one of the experiments, university students watched one of four videotapes in which a woman was approached by a man with a handgun. The scenarios differed in their location and the degree of threat posed to the witness. In one video, the interaction occurred at a baseball game in the stadium parking lot. In the other video, the interaction occurred at a shooting range. The handgun is unusual at the baseball game whereas the handgun is *not* unusual at the shooting range. In the low-threat condition, the man kept the gun pointed to the ground. In the high-threat condition, the man pointed the gun at the woman. Participants provided less accurate descriptions of the man if he was carrying a gun in the parking lot rather than at the shooting range. The degree of threat did not influence the descriptions of the man. These data suggest that unusualness can produce the weapon focus phenomenon. However, it should be noted that identification of the target was not affected.

In keeping with the notion of "unusualness," Carlson and Carlson (2012) examined whether a perpetrator with a distinctive facial feature would alter the weapon focus effect. A total of 600 participants watched a mock-crime video where the perpetrator used his fists, a beer bottle, or a shotgun in an apparent assault. The perpetrator either had a large sports sticker on his face or did not. Participants had more difficulty identifying the perpetrator when he had a shotgun that replicated the weapon focus effect, but only if the perpetrator did not have a sticker on his face. When the perpetrator had a sticker on his face, correct identifications increased and false-positive identifications decreased in the shotgun condition.

Thus, there is support for the unusualness explanation for the weapon focus effect, but it can be reversed depending on other "unusual" factors. More research is needed to definitively conclude why the weapon focus effect occurs. It may be encouraging to know that Pickel, Ross, and Truelove (2006) found that participants could be trained not to focus on a weapon, thus reducing the weapon focus effect.

In a recent meta-analysis of the weapon focus effect, Fawcett, Russell, Peace, and Christie (2013), found the effect occurred not only in lab studies but also in real-world investigations. Factors such as retention interval, exposure duration, and threat were found to influence the weapon focus effect. Expert testimony may be useful to jurors to understand the weapon focus effect and the factors that can influence it.

EXPERT TESTIMONY ON EYEWITNESS ISSUES

Eyewitness testimony is an area for which experts may be able to provide the courts with data that can help fact-finders with their decision making. However, not all eyewitness experts agree as to whether there is sufficient reliability across eyewitness studies and whether it is appropriate to apply the results of laboratory simulations to the real world. An additional criticism lodged against the testimony of eyewitness experts is that the information provided is common sense and, therefore, not necessary for the fact-finder.

Kassin, Tubb, Hosch, and Memon (2001; Kassin, Ellsworth, & Smith, 1989) surveyed researchers to determine which eyewitness issues they felt were reliable enough to provide expert testimony in court. Issues that were deemed sufficiently reliable included lineup procedures, interview procedures, and the confidence–accuracy relationship.

There are, however, some dissenters (e.g., Egeth, 1993; McCloskey & Egeth, 1983). In one critique, Ebbesen and Konecni (1997) argued that eyewitness experts are overconfident in their conclusions and have thus misled the courts about the validity, consistency, and generalizability of the data. The researchers took issue with the lack of theory in the eyewitness area and argued that the studies are too far removed from real-world eyewitness situations to be useful in predicting how "actual" witnesses would behave. They outlined a number of weaknesses in eyewitness research that should limit its usefulness to real-world application and experts testifying:

1. Studies examining the same issue produce different results.

2. Most of the studies use university students; real-life witnesses vary in age and other demographic variables.

3. Most studies allow a witness to view the perpetrator for approximately six seconds; in reality, witnesses may view the perpetrator for five or more minutes.

In defence of eyewitness research, Leippe (1995) noted that eyewitness research uses a number of methodologies and types of participants (see also Loftus, 1983). In addition, a number of studies are highly reliable. In support of the laboratory simulation using staged crimes, Wells (1993) asked, "If subjects believe that they are witnessing real crime, for instance, in what important way are they different from people who witness a real crime?" (p. 555). Perhaps the eyewitness field will always have critics on each side.

Overall, several studies have suggested that the lay public may not be sufficiently knowledgeable about eyewitness issues to evaluate this evidence in court (e.g., Benton, Ross, Bradshaw, Thomas, & Bradshaw, 2006; Brewer, Potter, Fisher, Bond, & Luszcz, 1999). Furthermore, Yarmey (2001) concluded that many results found with eyewitness studies are counterintuitive and contradict the common-sense beliefs of those in the community. In a Canadian survey by Read and Desmarais (2009), however, the researchers found that participants demonstrated a greater accuracy with regard to eyewitness issues than has been found in the past with the lay public. Moreover, these responses were similar to those provided by eyewitness experts.

YOU BE THE JUDGE

One Saturday evening in Vancouver during the holiday season, Kenji Hattori (a Japanese tourist) stopped at a bank machine on his way back to his hotel after having several drinks at a nearby bar. He withdrew $200 and left the bank. As he walked back to his car in a nearby parking lot, he was approached by a Caucasian man with a knife who robbed him of his wallet, watch, and cellphone. Unfortunately, the incident occurred outside the view of the bank's security cameras, and passersby didn't seem to notice.

At the police station, the police asked Kenji about the incident. Kenji stated that he was quite shaken by the incident, but he tried to provide as much information as he could about the appearance of the robber.

The police were certain they had the right man and asked Kenji to identify the robber from a simultaneous lineup. To ensure Kenji didn't make a mistake, they took a photo of the suspect standing outside the bank where Kenji was held up. Kenji identified the suspect as the man who had robbed him. He was certain he had selected the correct person. The police congratulated Kenji for picking out the robber.

Your Turn . . .

Based on Kenji's identification, the police arrested and charged the suspect.

What factors do you think influenced Kenji's identification? Should his identification be admissible in court? Why or why not? What recommendations would you make to police for future identifications?

Currently, the Canadian justice system tends to limit, and might not allow, the testimony of eyewitness experts on these issues in court. For example, the Ontario Court of Appeal in *R. v. McIntosh and McCarthy* (1997) ruled not to permit expert testimony on eyewitness-identification issues. However, in a recent murder case, *R. v. Henderson* (2009), a Manitoba judge allowed a jury to hear expert testimony on the limitations of eyewitness identification. The case involved several eyewitnesses who allegedly saw a barroom fight between Henderson and the victim several hours before the murder. It is unclear how the Canadian courts will respond to eyewitness experts providing testimony on the topic in the future. See the You Be the Judge box to see how you would evaluate eyewitness testimony.

PUBLIC POLICY ISSUES AND GUIDELINES

In the mid-1990s, then–U.S. attorney general Janet Reno commissioned a set of guidelines for the collection and preservation of eyewitness evidence. She was prompted by the large body of empirical literature on eyewitness issues. In addition, the more sensational factor that caught her attention involved a review of DNA exoneration cases (Wells et al., 2000). According to Turtle et al. (2003; also www. innocenceproject.org), in more than 75% of DNA exoneration cases, the primary

Table 5.2 DNA Exoneration Cases (United States)

Name	State	Crime	Years in Prison	Contributing Cause(s)
Steven Barnes	NY	Rape	19.5 years	Witness ID*, IFS**
Ronnie Bullock	IL	Sexual Assault	10.5 years	Witness ID
Willie Davidson	VA	Rape	12 years	Witness ID, IFS
Frederick Daye	CA	Rape	10 years	Witness ID, IFS
Anthony Gray	MD	Murder	7 years	False Confession
Clarence Harrison	GA	Rape	17.5 years	Witness ID, IFS
Ray Krone	AZ	Murder	10 years	IFS
Clark McMillan	TN	Rape	22 years	Witness ID
Vincent Moto	PA	Rape	8.5 years	Witness ID
Miguel Roman	CT	Murder	18.5 years	Snitches

* ID = identification
** IFS = improper forensic science
Source: Based on www.innocenceproject.org/know/Retrieved May 6, 2013.

evidence used to convict was eyewitness identification. See Table 5.2 for some of the cases that involved mistaken identification in the United States. In 1997, Osgoode Hall Law School at York University set up an Innocence Project for Canadians. This group often works with the Association for the Defence of the Wrongfully Convicted, a group of pro bono lawyers who worked to free Donald Marshall, David Milgaard, and Guy Paul Morin, all of whom were wrongfully convicted.

Eyewitness researchers, along with police officers and lawyers, constituted the Technical Working Group for Eyewitness Evidence (1999) that was commissioned in the United States to respond to Janet Reno's request. They developed a national set of guidelines known as *Eyewitness Evidence: A Guide for Law Enforcement*. In terms of lineup identification, Wells et al. (1998) proposed that the guidelines be limited to four recommendations:

1. The person who conducts the lineup or photo array should not know which person is the suspect.

2. Eyewitnesses should be told explicitly that the criminal may not be present in the lineup and, therefore, witnesses should not feel that they must make an identification.

3. The suspect should not stand out in the lineup as being different from the foils based on the eyewitness's previous description of the criminal or based on other factors that would draw extra attention to the suspect.

4. A clear statement should be taken from the eyewitness at the time of the identification and prior to any feedback as to his or her confidence that the identified person is the actual criminal.

Kassin (1998) added one more rule for lineup identification. He stated that the entire lineup procedure should be recorded on video to ensure accuracy in the process. In particular, the lineup and the interaction between the officer and the witness should be on video so that lawyers, the judge, and the jurors can later assess for themselves whether the reports of the procedure made by police are accurate.

Parallel guidelines have been developed in Canada. In the early 1980s, law professor Neil Brooks (1983) prepared Canadian guidelines titled *Police Guidelines: Pretrial Eyewitness Identification Procedures*. In addition, psychologists (eyewitness researchers) were asked to consult in the preparation of these guidelines. Thirty-eight recommendations were made with the goal of increasing the reliability of eyewitness identification. These recommendations, however, have not always been followed.

One Canadian case involving poor police techniques in collecting eyewitness identification was that of Thomas Sophonow (*R. v. Sophonow*, 1986). Sophonow was convicted of murdering Barbara Stoppel in Winnipeg, Manitoba. Sophonow spent four years in prison for a murder that he did not commit. DNA evidence exonerated him 15 years later. Supreme Court Justice Peter Cory requested a public inquiry into the case. Forty-three recommendations were made, including the following:

- The photo lineup procedure with the witness should be videotaped or audiotaped from the point the officer greets the witness to the completion of the interview.

- Officers should inform witnesses that it is just as important to clear innocent suspects as it is to identify guilty suspects.

- The photo lineup should be presented sequentially.

- Officers should not discuss a witness's identification decision with him or her.

See Box 5.4 to read more about the Sophonow case. It will be interesting to examine future cases to determine whether the recommendations from the inquiry are met.

Box 5.4   Cases in Forensic Psychology

How Does a Case Go Wrong? *R. v. Sophonow* (1986)

On the evening of December 23, 1981, Barbara Stoppel was working as a waitress at the Ideal Donut Shop in Winnipeg, Manitoba. At about 8:45 p.m., several patrons found her in the women's washroom of the shop, where she had been strangled and was close to death. Stoppel later died in hospital.

A number of eyewitnesses were available in this case. For example, Mrs. Janower worked at a drugstore in the same plaza as the doughnut shop. She went to the doughnut shop at about 8:20 p.m. She saw a man standing inside who had locked the door and headed toward the washroom. Mr. Doerksen was selling Christmas trees near the doughnut shop. He chased a man who walked out of the doughnut shop when Stoppel's body was found. Mr. McDonald sat in his parked truck as he waited for his wife to finish her shopping in the plaza. He could see into the doughnut shop and noticed a man talking to the waitress. He saw the man walk with the

(continued)

(continued)

waitress to the back of the shop. He then came out to lock the front door of the doughnut shop. In addition to eyewitness accounts, police accumulated much physical evidence.

Police discovered that Thomas Sophonow was in Winnipeg visiting his daughter on the night Stoppel was murdered. Sophonow was forthcoming with hair samples and so on. The police interview notes suggested that Sophonow might have been at the doughnut shop between 8:00 and 9:00 p.m. A few days later, Sophonow was interrogated for more than four hours. He was arrested in Vancouver and charged with Stoppel's murder on March 12, 1982.

Sophonow's first trial was a mistrial, but he was convicted in the second trial. The verdict was appealed, and the court of appeal overturned the guilty verdict from the second trial and ordered a new trial. After the third trial, the court of appeal overturned the guilty verdict and acquitted Sophonow. For the 15 years that followed, he sought his exoneration for the crime.

In 1998, the Winnipeg Police Service reopened the investigation into Stoppel's murder. On June 8, 2000, it was announced that Sophonow was not responsible for the murder and that another suspect had been identified. The Manitoba government issued a news release stating that the attorney general had made an apology to Sophonow, as he had endured three trials and two appeals, and spent 45 months in jail for an offence he did not commit. An inquiry was ordered into the police investigation and court proceedings to determine if mistakes were made and whether compensation should be provided.

The following are some of the issues that may have contributed to Sophonow's wrongful conviction:

- Detective notes when interviewing Sophonow were not verbatim, and a misquote was recorded. For example, Sophonow stated, "I could not have been in Ideal Donut Shop," but the statement recorded was "I could have been in Ideal Donut Shop."
- Winnipeg police did not inform Sophonow that he could call a lawyer at any time or inform him that the statements he made could be used against him. Sophonow stated that he asked for a lawyer on several occasions during the interrogation, but the officers did not allow him to call one.
- Sophonow was strip-searched and a search of his anal cavity was done to determine if he was carrying any

drugs, even though there was no reason to believe this was the case. Sophonow felt that there was nothing he could say that the police would believe and felt it best to keep quiet.

- Mr. Doerksen was hypnotized and asked to describe the assailant. Mr. Doerksen called the police when he thought he saw the perpetrator at a hotel. This man was quickly exonerated. Mr. Doerksen also identified a reporter as the perpetrator, who was also quickly exonerated. Mr. Doerksen failed to identify Sophonow from a lineup that the police assembled. The sergeant conducting the lineup told Mr. Doerksen to consider number 7—Sophonow was number 7.
- Sophonow had an alibi that was not considered seriously. He stopped at a Canadian Tire the night of the murder, where he spoke to a woman and her daughter waiting for their car repairs; went to a Safeway store, where he bought some red stockings; and went to hospitals to deliver the stockings for Christmas. These events occurred around 8:00 p.m. and, given the timeline of the killing, ruled Sophonow out as the murderer.
- Terry Arnold lived near the doughnut shop and reportedly had a crush on Stoppel. He fit the description and did not have an alibi. He was not fully investigated.

Dr. Elizabeth Loftus testified in the inquiry and noted a number of problems with the eyewitness evidence:

- When there is more than one witness, they can inadvertently influence one another.
- People under hypnosis are suggestible and often assume that what they retrieve under hypnosis is accurate, even though it may not be.
- The photo arrays shown to Mrs. Janower had Sophonow's picture stand out: His picture had a yellow background and his hat was off to the side, as was the suspect's hat in the composite drawing initially issued to the public. There also was a live lineup in which Sophonow stood out because of his height.

Questions

1. How should lineup identification be handled by police?
2. Should identification evidence be admissible in court?

Source: Based on "R. v. Sophonow" from Supreme Court of Canada, 1986.

SUMMARY

1. Independent variables in the eyewitness area can be categorized as estimator or system variables. The effect of estimator variables on eyewitness accuracy can be estimated only after the crime. In contrast, system variables can be manipulated by the criminal justice system to increase (or decrease) eyewitness accuracy. The three dependent variables in the eyewitness area are recall of the event, recall of the perpetrator, and recognition of the perpetrator.

2. The misinformation effect is a phenomenon in which a witness who is presented with inaccurate information after an event will incorporate that misinformation into a subsequent recall task. This effect could occur as a result of a witness guessing what the officer wants the response to be. Alternatively, this effect could occur because a witness has two memories—one for the correct information and one for the incorrect information—but cannot accurately remember how he or she acquired each piece of information. The misinformation effect could also occur because the inaccurate information replaces the accurate information in memory.

3. The cognitive interview is based on four memory-retrieval techniques to increase recall: reinstating the context, reporting everything that comes to mind, recalling the event in different order, and changing the perspective from which the information is recalled. In addition to these techniques, the enhanced cognitive interview includes five more techniques: building rapport, exhibiting supportive interviewer behaviour, transferring the control of the interview to the witness, asking for focused recall with open-ended questions, and asking the witness questions that match what the witness is recalling.

4. The simultaneous lineup, sequential lineup, showup, and walk-by are lineup procedures used by police to determine whether the suspect is the perpetrator. Biased lineups suggest whom the police suspect and thereby whom the witness should identify. In biased lineups, the suspect stands out from the other lineup members in some way. Foil bias, instruction bias, and clothing bias have been investigated and shown to increase false-positive responding.

5. Not all eyewitness experts agree on the reliability of research findings and whether we can apply the results of laboratory simulations to the real world. An additional criticism lodged against the eyewitness expert testifying is whether the information provided is common sense and therefore not necessary for the fact-finder.

6. Four rules were outlined to reduce the likelihood of false identification. First, the person who conducts the lineup should not know which member of the lineup is the suspect. Second, eyewitnesses should be told explicitly that the criminal may not be present in the lineup and, therefore, witnesses should not feel that they must make an identification. Third, the suspect should not stand out in the lineup as being different from the foils based on the

eyewitness's previous description of the criminal or based on other factors that would draw extra attention to the suspect. Fourth, a clear statement should be taken from the eyewitness at the time of the identification (and prior to any feedback) as to his or her confidence that the identified person is the actual criminal.

Discussion Questions

1. Imagine you are a judge and are allowing an eyewitness psychological expert to testify. What factors would you consider appropriate for the expert to testify about? What factors would you disallow testimony about?

2. There has been a considerable amount of research on the misinformation effect. Design an experiment to test whether the misinformation effect also occurs if participants witness a violent crime.

Chapter 6
Child Victims and Witnesses

Learning Objectives

- Differentiate between techniques that decrease versus increase the likelihood of accurate recall in child witnesses.

- Summarize children's ability to recall/describe people's appearances.

- Describe a lineup technique designed for children's identification.

- Outline the courtroom accommodations available for child witnesses.

- Explain child maltreatment categories and related consequences.

Suzie James lay asleep in the bed across from her older sister's when she heard something; someone was at the bedroom window. Suzie was 8 years old and Samantha (Sam) was 13 years old. They shared a bedroom with a large pullout window. In the summer it could get very warm in the city, so they kept their window open most nights. As Suzie opened her eyes, she saw a tall, thin, white man cover her sister's mouth and say, "Don't scream and I won't hurt you." Suzie pretended she was still asleep but tried to peek at the man so she could describe him later. In a few seconds, Sam was gone with this man who had come through the window. Suzie started yelling for help immediately. Her parents rushed in and asked what had happened and where Sam was. They called 911 and within minutes police arrived to interview Suzie.

Suzie sat on her mother's lap as she recounted what had happened moments earlier. Unfortunately, Suzie did not provide a lot of detail. Many questions remained regarding the identity of the man. The police officer started to ask Suzie direct questions, such as "Did you ever see this man before? Did he have a weapon? How old was he? How tall was he? Did he have any facial hair?" When the abduction occurred, the only light in the room came from a dim nightlight between the beds. Suzie could not see much in that light, but she provided answers to all the questions the officer asked.

A former gardener was arrested about three months after the crime, and his picture was placed in a lineup shown to Suzie. Suzie stared at his picture but could not make an identification. Almost a year after the abduction, Sam was spotted at a Quickie Mart with a man fitting the description her sister had provided. The store clerk quickly called police and tried to detain the two. Police arrived to arrest the abductor, who was the gardener, and bring Sam back home to her family. The abductor was charged with numerous offences.

How do we interview children? Should the justice system rely on children's memory? We will explore these questions and others in this chapter. We will focus on the historical legal context around children testifying in court, children's memory abilities, how best to tap into children's memory, and, lastly, the various forms of child abuse and their consequences.

Before we get started answering the above questions. Examine the myths on child eyewitnesses and victims in Box. 6.1. How many of these myths did you believe?

Box 6.1 Myths and Realities

Child Victims and Witnesses

Myth 1. Young children will not remember what they witnessed.
Fact. Younger children have been found to provide as much relevant, detailed information as older children when they had witnessed a homicide/manslaughter (Christianson, Azad, Leander & Selenius, 2013) and 3- to 16-year-old children have been found to have more accurate recall of a traumatic experience (i.e., sexual and/or physical abuse) compared to those who had not been abused (Eisen, Goodman, Qin, Davis, & Crayton, 2007).

Myth 2. People do not "forget" child abuse.
Fact. Research has found that it is not uncommon for victims of sexual abuse to suppress their memories of the abuse that can later influence their ability to recall those memories (e.g., Widom & Morris, 1997; Williams, 1994). Furthermore, research has found that those who did not report having been maltreated as a child were less likely to be substance abusers than if they reported the maltreatment; this suggests that being able to forget the maltreatment may mediate its impact on future mental health (Elywn & Smith, 2013).

Myth 3. Child abuse is rare.
Fact. MacMillan, Tanaka, Duku, & Vaillancourt (2013) analyzed results from the Ontario Child Health Study third wave (2000–2001) and found that 33.7% of males and 28.2% of females reported experiencing childhood physical abuse, and 8.3% of males and 22.1% of females reported experiencing childhood sexual abuse.

Myth 4. Anatomically detailed dolls are a good way of determining if a young child has been sexually abused.
Fact. Research on the use of anatomically detailed dolls with young children has been shown to contribute to errors of omission (i.e., not including relevant information) and/or commission (i.e., including things that did not happen) (Bruck, Ceci, & Francoeur, 2000; Dupree, Patterson, Nugent, & White, 2016).

Myth 5. Children usually tell someone if they are being abused.
Fact. Research has shown that people who experience sexual abuse during childhood usually do not tell anybody about the abuse until they are adults. Even if children do reveal they have been abused during childhood, it commonly happens after a delay. (McElvaney, 2015).

Myth 6. The same types of lineup procedures that work for adults will work for children.
Fact. Research has demonstrated that children are more likely than adults to incorrectly identify somebody when the suspect in the lineup is not guilty (e.g., Pozzulo & Lindsay, 1998). Therefore, two different lineups have been developed to help decrease children's false-positive responding: the elimination lineup procedure (Pozzulo & Lindsay, 1999) and the wildcard lineup procedure (Zajac & Karageorge, 2009).

Myth 7. The same types of interview procedures (e.g., cognitive interview) that work for adults will work for children.
Fact. Special care has to be taken when interviewing children. Some components of the Cognitive Interview, such as changing perspective, are useful with adults but are too confusing for children. Therefore, a modified version of the Cognitive Interview must be used with children (Larsson & Lamb, 2009).

HISTORY

The way in which child victims and witnesses have been viewed by the justice system has changed dramatically over the years. Some early views can be traced back to the Salem witch trials in 1692, when children told falsehoods and claimed to have witnessed the defendants perform supernatural feats (Ceci & Bruck, 1993). Several years following the execution of the defendants for witchcraft, some of the children recanted their testimonies. For the most part, the prevailing legal attitude toward child witnesses for the following 300 years was that of skepticism.

Research testing the validity of these negative attitudes toward child witnesses started in Europe in the early twentieth century. Reviews from this time seemed to conclude that young children were highly suggestible and had difficulty separating fact from fantasy, and thus were capable of providing inaccurate testimony, even if the testimony was of personal significance (Whipple, 1909, 1910, 1911, 1912). Unfortunately, little is known about the details of the research on which these conclusions were based. Also, the criminal justice system was not very interested in these reviews. As a result, few studies were conducted on children's competencies during the early and mid-twentieth century.

A flurry of research on children's witness abilities started in the 1970s and continues to this day. Ceci and Bruck (1993) outlined four factors that led to the renewed interest in child witnesses:

1. Expert psychological testimony was becoming more acceptable in the courtroom.
2. Social scientists were interested in research that could be applied to real-world problems.
3. Studies on adult eyewitness testimony were increasing.
4. The legal community became interested in behavioural science research regarding child witnesses.

This last point was in response to the increasing number of reported sexual and physical abuse cases where a child was a victim or witness. These cases, arising in both the United States and Canada, often involved numerous children and numerous defendants; not uncommon to these cases was the involvement of preschools. Box 6.2 describes a Canadian case in which children were the primary victims and witnesses.

How is it decided whether alleged child abuse cases move forward toward possible prosecution? Once police are contacted about alleged child abuse, a number of decisions must be made. Powell, Murfett, and Thomson (2010) noted that in numerous jurisdictions, the police officers were responsible for deciding whether a case would be referred for possible prosecution. The researchers examined the police documentation in 33 cases and conducted an analysis around the themes that emerged on whether a case would move forward for possible prosecution. As you have read in Chapter 5 and will read in this chapter, how (child) witnesses are interviewed and the questions asked can influence the accuracy of the information elicited. The researchers wanted to know the amount of influence police placed on the quality of interview

Box 6.2 Cases in Forensic Psychology

The Martensville Babysitting Case: *R. v. Sterling* (1995)

In the fall of 1991 in Martensville, Saskatchewan, Ms. L. noticed a rash on her 2.5-year-old daughter's bottom. Ms. L. suspected that child abuse had occurred at the babysitting service run by Linda Sterling. Following a medical examination of the child, a doctor concluded that the rash was not indicative of abuse.

The investigation continued, however, and several claims were made against Linda Sterling; her husband, Ronald; and her son Travis. The child in question was interviewed intensely and eventually stated that a man had touched her. Many more children were subsequently interviewed, some claiming that they had been confined in cages, penetrated with axe handles, forced to drink blood, whipped, and thrown naked into freezers. The children also claimed to have witnessed a ritual murder, a child's nipple being bitten off, a body dumped into an acid bath, and a dog stabbed to death.

Linda, Ronald, and Travis Sterling, along with one other woman and five other men, were arrested and charged. More than 40 charges, including sexual assault, sexual assault with a weapon, unlawful confinement, and intercourse with a minor, were laid against the Sterlings.

Dr. John Yuille from the University of British Columbia was an expert witness in the case. He noted that the interviews with the children were fraught with leading questions and that rewards were offered to children for giving the "right answer." Moreover, there was a lack of physical evidence consistent with the claims being made.

The investigation and trial spanned more than two and a half years. Linda and Ronald Sterling were acquitted, while Travis was convicted on several of the charges. Eventually, six of eight convictions were overturned because of the inappropriate interview techniques that were used with the children.

Questions

1. If you were the child's parent, how would you have proceeded following the conclusion of the medical examiner?

2. Would you have proceeded any differently than the police investigating the case?

Source: Based on "R. v. Steling" from Supreme Court of Canada, 1995.

---

questions when making their decisions on moving a case forward. The results revealed that whether there was corroborative evidence and whether the suspect denied the allegations were the two key themes. Intriguingly, questioning technique was *not* considered. Also important to note was that the questioning used often did not follow the best procedures for eliciting more accurate information.

RECALL FOR EVENTS

Are children able to recall events accurately? How does their performance compare with the recall of adults? The Martensville case and others similar to it may suggest that children do not make very reliable witnesses, even about events they supposedly experienced. However, studies have found that children are capable of accurately recalling forensically relevant details of events (e.g., Ceci & Bruck, 1993). Moreover, children are capable of recalling much that is accurate. The challenge, of course, is determining when children are recalling accurately and when they are **fabricating** (i.e., making false claims). Research suggests that the accuracy of children's reporting is highly dependent on how they are asked to report. Examine the You Be the Forensic Psychologist box. How would you interview children about an event that occurred?

Fabricating: Making false claims

YOU BE THE FORENSIC PSYCHOLOGIST

Five-year-old Caitlin attends Sunshine Daycare in the town of Minden, Ontario. One day when Caitlin's mother picked Caitlin up from daycare, Caitlin seemed upset. This mood was unusual for Caitlin—typically Caitlin would run into her mother's arms, overjoyed to see her. When Caitlin's mom asked what was wrong, the girl didn't reply.

That night when Caitlin was going into the tub for a bath, her mother noticed Caitlin had some red welts on her bottom. When Caitlin's mom asked, "Why is your bottom red?" Caitlin started crying. After calming Caitlin down, her mother asked, "Did something happen at daycare today?" Caitlin nodded "yes." After her mother asked her what happened, Caitlin said that Miss Mimi got angry with the kids and hit them with a wooden spoon. When her mother asked if all the children got hit, Caitlin nodded "yes."

After Caitlin went to bed, Caitlin's mom called some of the other mothers to find out whether their kids had red marks as well and whether their children's demeanour was unusual. The other mothers inspected their children and started asking them very specific questions. Some children had bruises, and some children had other marks. The next morning, the mothers kept their children home and called the police and the Children's Aid Society to report the physical abuse.

Children were interviewed by police officers and then again by social workers. Miss Mimi was ordered to close her daycare and was charged with the physical abuse of children.

Your Turn ...

What would you do if you were Caitlin's mother or father? How should children be interviewed to increase the likelihood of reporting reliable information?

Free Recall versus Directed Questioning

When children are asked to report all they can remember, using a free narrative approach, their accuracy in reporting is comparable with that of adults (Ceci & Bruck, 1993). Unfortunately, children tend to report very little information using a free narrative. Direct questions or probes, such as "What else do you remember?" or "Tell me more about what you remember" are often necessary to elicit the required information. The dilemma arises when we consider the accuracy of direct questioning.

As we have seen with adult eyewitnesses in Chapter 5, when children are asked leading, direct questions, they are also more likely to produce an erroneous response than when they are asked nonleading, direct questions (Roebers, Bjorklund, Schneider, & Cassel, 2002). Moreover, as we saw with adult eyewitnesses, an interviewer who provides approving statements to inaccurate information or disapproving statements to accurate information can elicit further inaccurate information from child witnesses (Sparling, Wilder, Kondash, Boyle, & Compton, 2011). A key Canadian researcher in the area of children's suggestibility is Dr. Laura Melnyk Gribble. In one study, the researchers found that the timing of suggestive interviewing also can be influential on children's responses such that repeated interviewing close in time to the event can heighten misinformation effects. To learn more about Dr. Melnyk Gribble see Box 6.3.

Box 6.3

Canadian Researcher Profile: Dr. Laura Melnyk Gribble

Courtesy of Reinhold Scherer

Dr. Laura Melnyk Gribble completed her Ph.D. at McGill University under the supervision of Dr. Maggie Bruck studying children's memory and suggestibility. Following graduation, she started her academic career at King's University College at the University of Western Ontario. King's is a liberal arts college affiliated with Western, with a focus on undergraduate education. Dr. Melnyk Gribble's expertise is in the area of forensic developmental psychology. She investigates issues in children's memory and suggestibility. She studies interviewing techniques to facilitate young children's autobiographical recall and lineup performance.

Dr. Melnyk Gribble recalls her research interests stemming from her undergraduate days as a student at McMaster. She states, "I had some fantastic professors that sparked my interest in studying memory and developmental psychology. I also enjoyed working with children in my 4th-year practicum placement and as a volunteer, and so I was considering further training in an applied field. When I was applying to graduate programs, Dr. Maggie Bruck gave a riveting, standing-room only talk at McMaster. This was in 1994, when research in the area of child witnesses was really taking off; indeed, I had read Dr. Bruck's recent papers and I saw her research featured on the television news program *20/20*. My undergraduate mentor, Dr. Betty Ann Levy, arranged for me to meet with Dr. Bruck after her talk. Her work was a perfect fit for my interests and background—it drew from research in cognitive and developmental psychology and had important applications. The rest is history."

Dr. Melnyk Gribble describes the "typical methodology" used in her studies…"My memory and suggestibility research with children uses a misinformation design. First, the children

participate in a special event at their school; a week or two later, we return and talk to the children about the event, and a week or two after that, we interview the children to assess the accuracy of their reports. This experimental design allows us to test interviewing variables, the timing of the interviews, the instructions we provide, and so forth."

Dr. Melnyk Gribble notes two of her favourite studies using this methodology. "My favourite study is probably Melnyk and Bruck (2004). We investigated how the timing of misinformation moderated the effects of suggestive interviewing on children's eyewitness memory. These experiments were a big undertaking—there were over 200 children, each participating in three or four sessions. The design was elegant and the data were clear and compelling. Another favorite is Bruck and Melnyk (2004). As part of my dissertation, I attempted to identify factors underlying individual differences in children's suggestibility. The data were rather uninteresting and were relegated to the dreaded file drawer. Later, Dr. Bruck and I talked about how so many researchers had been doing work into individual differences in the late 1990s, but how little of that work seemed to be published. So we contacted researchers who had published (and unpublished) data examining individual difference factors and children's suggestibility. We synthesized across 69 studies and some 500+ analyses. The resultant paper is my most-cited work and was selected to appear in the 25th anniversary *Applied Cognitive Psychology* special issue—a big honour".

Dr. Melnyk Gribble has testified as an expert witness in two cases and has consulted with police services in the London area on an informal basis. In terms of preparing future researchers in the area of forensic psychology, she would like to see coursework in the legal system and police practice included in the curricula: "It would give future researchers the opportunity to design better-informed studies that address issues in forensic psychology. For example, I've found that the kinds of things that police and lawyers are often interested in knowing are not necessarily studied by researchers. It's also useful for forensic researchers to have an understanding of the basics of criminal law, evidence, etc."

Outside Dr. Melnyk Gribble's rewarding work, her greatest joy is her young family with two children who keep her very busy. In her down time, she is a cycling enthusiast, logging many miles each summer on the lovely country roads surrounding London.

Generally, older children are more resistant to leading questions than younger children, and adults are even more resistant to leading questions (Ceci & Bruck, 1993).

Direct questions that require yes or no responses or use a forced-choice format are particularly problematic for preschoolers (Peterson & Biggs, 1997). For example, Waterman, Blades, and Spencer (2004) interviewed children between the ages of 5 and 9. First, a woman went into children's classrooms and engaged them in a discussion about familiar topics for approximately ten minutes. The woman showed children four photographs: two of pets and two of food items. After the woman had left, researchers then interviewed the children using questions that required yes or no answers—that is, *yes/no questions*—(e.g., "Did the lady show you a picture of a banana?") and *wh-* questions (e.g., "What was the lady's name?"). Half of both types of questions were unknown to the children (e.g., "How did the lady get to school this morning?). In these cases, the correct response should be "I don't know." Children performed similarly across both types of questions when they were answerable. However, when questions were unanswerable, children were more likely to say "I don't know" to *wh-* questions than yes/no questions. We see that yes/no questions are particularly problematic for children. Melnyk, Crossman, and Scullin (2006) suggested that this may be the case because these questions rely on recognition rather than recall, thus increasing the likelihood of error. Using recall (e.g., "Tell me everything you remember") may elicit brief responses, but those responses are more likely to be accurate. We will discuss recall and recognition in greater detail later in the chapter.

One particular question may be useful, however, in eliciting descriptions of emotional, cognitive, and physical reactions (i.e., evaluative information). A set of studies by Lyon, Scurich, Choi, Handmaker, and Blank (2012) examined transcripts from children's (ages 5 to 18 years) testimony in sexual abuse cases for the use and responses to *how* questions, *wh-* questions, *option-posing* questions that included yes/no questions and force-choice questions, and *suggestive* questions. "How" questions produced the most productive information compared to the other types of questions. More specifically, "How did you feel?" elicited the most evaluative information compared to direct and suggestive questions.

Why Are Children More Suggestible Than Adults?

Generally, two directions have been taken to understand children's greater propensity toward suggestibility (Bruck & Ceci, 1999). One focus has investigated the "social characteristics" of the interview. It has been argued that children respond to interviewers in the manner they feel the interviewer desires, a tendency known as *social compliance*. The alternative area researchers have concentrated on to understand children's responses has been the investigation of developmental changes in their cognitive or memory system.

Social Compliance or Social Pressure It has been argued that children may respond to suggestive influences because they trust and want to cooperate with adult interviewers, even if the children do not understand or have the knowledge to answer the question. Children may infer the desired response in keeping with the "gist" or general idea of the question (Brainerd & Reyna, 1996). In a study by Hughes and Grieve (1980), young children between the ages of 5 and 7 were asked nonsensical questions, such as "Is milk bigger than water?" and "Is red heavier than yellow?" Even though these questions are illogical and do not have correct responses, many children provided a yes or no answer rather than saying, "I don't know." It should be noted, however, that although children may respond according to a suggestion provided, their memory for the actual event may remain intact, and, if later questioned, they may report the accurate response (if asked about it in a nonsuggestive manner).

Changes to the Cognitive System   Some research has found developmental differences in the ways children and adults encode, store, and retrieve memories (Brainerd & Reyna, 2004). Moreover, differences between children and adults also have been found in forgetting and retention. Also related to memory is the notion that children "misattribute" where information came from (Parker, 1995). For example, children may report on an event that they heard about (e.g., through suggestive questioning from an interviewer) as if it were something they had experienced. For example, children may not remember that Ms. Z suggested that an event had occurred, and, when later asked about it, children report the "suggestion," believing that the event actually occurred.

Currently, researchers believe that an interaction of social and cognitive factors is likely responsible for children's suggestibility and their reporting of false information. The content and format of questions posed to child witnesses should be considered carefully. Interviewers need to balance asking direct questions with the risk of obtaining false information. Many researchers would recommend relying on free recall as much as possible to obtain accurate information.

A number of techniques, protocols, and procedures to aid child witnesses with recalling information have been investigated. Below, we describe some of these options for use with child witnesses and their efficacy for recalling accurate information.

Anatomically Detailed Dolls

If children have difficulty providing a verbal account of what they witnessed or experienced, props may be useful. When interviewing children suspected of being sexually abused, some mental health professionals may introduce **anatomically detailed dolls**. Just as the name implies, anatomically detailed dolls, sometimes like a rag doll, are consistent with the male or female anatomy. Dolls may be of an adult male or female or a young male or female. The assumption underlying the use of these dolls is that children may have difficulty verbalizing what occurred, and in their play with the dolls they will demonstrate the events they experienced (Vizard & Trantor, 1988). Is this assumption correct, though? The research provides some contradictory results (Aldridge, 1998).

Salmon, Pipe, Malloy, and MacKay (2012) wanted to assess the usefulness of interview aids, including anatomical dolls, in situations similar to that which would occur in the field. In Experiment 2, fifty-three 5- to 7-year-old children were involved

Anatomically detailed dolls: A doll, sometimes like a rag doll, that is consistent with the male or female anatomy

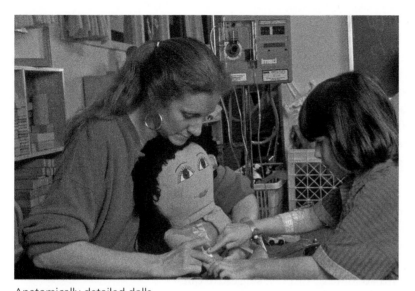

Anatomically detailed dolls being used in a therapy session

Will & Deni McIntyre/Science Source

in an activity during which a sticker, stamp, and badge were placed on their bodies. The children were randomly assigned to a verbal (i.e., no props used), Human Figure Drawing (HFD), or anatomical doll condition. The props were used either to clarify or confirm reports of previously verbally reported touch. The use of dolls did not significantly influence accuracy in comparison to the other two conditions. Salmon et al. (2012) concluded that the use of dolls was not warranted because their use did not add any benefit and, if used inappropriately, could have a negative effect.

Dupree, Patterson, Nugent, and White (2016) conducted a review of five studies, all of which were interested in how children would report the experience of a genital exam. Dupree et al. found that younger children were more likely to report erroneous information when using an anatomical doll, particularly when confronted with suggestive or leading questions.

Contrary to the above results, Goodman, Quas, Batterman-Faunce, Riddlesberger, and Kuhn (1997) found that 3- to 10-year-olds who had been touched during an examination were more likely to report such touching with dolls than when questioned orally. In another study, Melinder et al. (2010) compared the memory reports of a medical exam of 4-year-olds who were interviewed using either a verbal-type interview or a prop-assisted interview that included dolls and play material. On a final recall test, error rates were similar for the two types of interviews. It is important to note that other factors such as parental attachment (Chae, Ogle, & Goodman, 2009) may interact with interview style to influence accuracy in reporting.

Faller, Grabarek, Nelson-Gardell, and Williams (2011) also examined interview techniques, including the use of anatomical dolls, used by interviewers in the assessments of suspected sexual abuse for 137 children. Anatomical dolls were used the least frequently (14 times) out of all interview techniques. However, their use yielded the highest rate for confirming information (78.6%). The use of anatomical dolls, as well as anatomical drawings, was associated with higher ratings of 'sexual abuse being likely'. Faller et al. (2011) suggested that the higher confirmatory rate with the anatomical dolls might be due to the fact that evaluators had extensive time with the children and could therefore more accurately assess what specific techniques might be beneficial for each child in particular.

Should Anatomically Detailed Dolls Be Used?   A number of difficulties have been identified with using these dolls to determine if sexual abuse occurred (Koocher et al., 1995). For example, no specifications or guidelines are available for manufacturers of these dolls. Consequently, wide variation exists and some mental health professionals even make their own dolls. Not only is there no standardization for what the dolls should look like, but there are also no standard procedures for scoring the behaviours that children exhibit when interacting with the dolls. Research is not available to answer how nonabused versus abused children play with the dolls, and whether the groups of children play with the dolls differently. Thus, the use of anatomically detailed dolls for diagnosing sexual abuse can be inaccurate and dangerous (Dickinson, Poole, & Bruck, 2005). The APA Council Policy Manual recommends that psychologists using anatomically detailed dolls videotape their use of the dolls wherever possible, otherwise they should audiotape or write down the procedures used. Psychologists should be able to provide rationale, such as published research, for the way they used the dolls and the way in which they interpreted the results from the dolls' use ("The Use of Anatomically," 2016).

Other Techniques for Interviewing Children

Human Figure Drawings   The use of Human Figure Drawings (HFDs) when interviewing young children is popular. It is believed that children are able to understand the representational nature of a two-dimensional drawing at a younger age than the symbolic meaning of three-dimensional models such as anatomical dolls. Some of the controversy associated with dolls could perhaps be avoided, such as children's fantasy play with the dolls being misinterpreted as abuse indicators, with the use of HFDs. The main question is, while children as young as 2 may be able to correctly use two-dimensional representations in some circumstances, are they able to correctly and accurately use HFDs to indicate if they have been abused?

Brown, Pipe, Lewis, Lamb, and Orbach (2014) examined the use of HFDs in 5- to 7-year-old children in a staged incident involving seven incidents of physical touching (e.g., tickling feet or patting shoulder). Four to six weeks after the event, children were first verbally interviewed. A 'touch inquiry' period of questioning, accompanied by either no HFD, an HFD following instruction on how to use it, or an HFD following no instruction on how to use it. While children in all conditions usually provided extra information when asked specifically about touching, more incorrect touches were reported when the HFDs were used (either with or without instruction). Other research has had similar findings (e.g., Otgaar, Horselenberg, van Kampen, & Lalleman, 2012; Poole & Dickinson, 2011). This implies that the problems found when using anatomical dolls may also arise with HFDs. In their review of the use of external props, including dolls and HFDs, Poole and Bruck (2012) also express concern with their current use.

Criterion-Based Content Analysis   **Criterion-based content analysis** (CBCA) was developed in Germany in the 1950s by Udo Undeutsch (1989) to facilitate distinguishing truthful from false statements made by children. It has gone through some revision over the years by Stellar and Kohnken (1989) and Raskin and Esplin (1991) (Stellar, 1989). CBCA is part of a more comprehensive protocol called **statement validity analysis** (SVA) for credibility assessment for sexual abuse allegations. SVA consists of three parts: (1) a structured interview with the victim, (2) a systematic analysis of the verbal content of the victim's statements by using CBCA, and (3) the application of a statement validity checklist. Although some suggest the need to use

Criterion-based content analysis: Analysis that uses criteria to distinguish truthful from false statements made by children

Statement validity analysis: A comprehensive protocol to distinguish truthful or false statements made by children containing three parts: (1) a structured interview of the child witness, (2) a systematic analysis of the verbal content of the child's statements (criterion-based content analysis), and (3) the application of the statement validity checklist

Table 6.1 Partial List of Criterion-Based Content Analysis Criteria

General Characteristics

1. *Logical structure.* Is the statement coherent? Do the statements fit together?
2. *Unstructured production.* Is the account consistently organized?
3. *Quality of details.* Are there specific descriptions of place, time, person, etc.?

Specific Contents

4. *Contextual embedding.* Is the action connected to other daily routine events?
5. *Interactions.* Are there reports of conversation between the victim and the perpetrator?

…

8. *Unusual details.* Are there details that are unusual but meaningful?

…

10. *Accurately reported details misunderstood.* Did the child describe a detail accurately but interpret it incorrectly?

…

Motivation-Related Contents

14. *Spontaneous corrections or additions.* Were corrections offered or information added?
15. *Admitting lack of memory or knowledge.* Did the child indicate lack of memory or knowledge of an aspect of the incident?

…

18. *Pardoning the accused.* Did the child make excuses for or fail to blame the alleged perpetrator?

Source: From Statement validity assessment: Interview procedures and content analysis of children's statements of sexual abuse by D. C. Raskin; P. W. Esplin. Behavioral Assessment, 12, p. 279. Published by American Psychological Association (APA), © 1991.

the entire SVA system when assessing allegations, the CBCA is considered the most important part and is often used as a stand-alone protocol.

The underlying assumption of the CBCA is that descriptions of real events differ in quality and content from memories that are fabricated. Eighteen criteria were developed to discriminate between true and fabricated events of sexual abuse. See Table 6.1 for a partial list of CBCA criteria. It is assumed that true events are more likely to contain the CBCA criteria rather than fabricated events.

CBCA is not without its critics, however. For example, Ruby and Brigham (1997) noted a number of difficulties with CBCA, such as inconsistencies with the number of criteria that need to be present to conclude truthfulness and the different decision rules for reaching a conclusion. Research has shown that age of the interviewee is positively correlated with scores on the CBCA (e.g., Buck, Warren, Betman, & Brigham, 2002; Vrij, Akenhurst, Soukara, & Bull, 2002). Younger children do not possess the cognitive abilities and command of the language to provide statements as detailed as those of older children. As a result, truthful statements by younger interviewees may be judged as doubtful because the statements are missing certain CBCA criteria (Vrij, 2005). Also, results from Pezdek et al. (2004) and Blandon-Gitlin, Pezdek, Rogers, and Brodie (2005) raised concerns about the forensic suitability of the CBCA for discriminating between children's accounts of real and fabricated events. Authors of both studies noted that CBCA scores appear to be influenced by both how familiar the event is to the child and how old the child is.

Overall, CBCA scores are calculated by using a truth–lie classification that requires the assessor to classify the statement as truthful or untruthful based on his or her own interpretation of the statement. As a result, this method is highly subjective and does not ensure inter-rater reliability. Despite the criticisms, CBCA and SVA are being used in parts of Europe to distinguish between children's truthful and false reports. In a recent study, Roma, Martini, Sabatello, Tatarelli, and Ferracuti (2011) applied 14 criteria of the CBCA to 60 confirmed cases of sexual abuse and 49 unconfirmed cases. Nine of the fourteen CBCA criteria were more likely to be found in the confirmed cases than the unconfirmed cases. The best CBCA criteria that distinguished between the cases were quantity of details, interactions, and subjective experience. SVA has also been applied to adult statements to distinguish between truthful and false reports, and studies report great success (Parker & Brown, 2000).

Step-Wise Interview   An alternative procedure for interviewing children that aims to keep false claims at a minimum is the **step-wise interview** developed by Yuille and his colleagues (e.g., Yuille, Hunter, Joffe, & Zaparniuk, 1993). This interview protocol consists of a series of "steps" designed to start the interview with the least leading and directive type of questioning, and then proceed to more specific forms of questioning as necessary (see Table 6.2). The objective with this protocol is to provide the child with lots of opportunity to report by using a free narrative before other types of questioning are used.

Lindberg, Chapman, Samsock, Thomas, and Lindberg (2003) tested the step-wise procedure, along with a procedure they developed, the modified structured interview, and a procedure developed by Action for Child Protection in West Virginia that uses doll play. The three procedures are similar in terms of rapport building and the general question phases. The major difference is in terms of specific questioning. With the step-wise procedure, specific questioning occurs through progressively more focused questions and probes information obtained from the more general questions. With the modified structured interview, specific questioning occurs through the use of *wh-* questions. With the Action for Child Protection procedure, specific questioning occurs through doll play.

To test these three procedures, children in Grades 1 and 2 watched a video of a mother hitting her son. The children were then randomly assigned to be interviewed using one of the three procedures. The interviewers were blind to what the children witnessed on the video. Interviews were transcribed and then coded for correct and incorrect statements. The results indicated that the procedure developed by the Action for Child Protection group was less effective than the other two, and the step-wise and modified interviews produced a comparable amount of information during the free-narrative portions. The modified procedure was superior to the step-wise or the Action for Child Protection procedure for *wh-* questions.

Overall, the step-wise procedure is consistent with what we know about children's recall abilities and how to elicit accurate information. Four variations of the step-wise procedure were examined with 3- to 8-year-olds with variations producing comparable reports (Hardy & Van Leeuwen, 2004).

Step-wise interview: Interview protocol with a series of "steps" designed to start the interview with the least leading and directive type of questioning, and then proceed to more specific forms of questioning, as necessary

Table 6.2 The Step-Wise Interview

Step	Goal	How
1	Rapport building	Talk to the child about neutral topics, trying to make him or her feel comfortable.
2	Recall of two nonabuse events	Have the child describe two experienced events, such as a birthday party and going to the zoo.
3	Explanation of truth	Explain truth in general and have the child agree to tell the truth.
4	Introduction of critical topic	Start with open-ended questions, such as "Do you know why you are talking with me today?" Proceed to more specific questions if disclosure does not occur, such as "Who are the people you like/don't like to be with?"
5	Free-narrative	Ask the child to describe what happened by using a free-narrative approach.
6	General questions	Ask questions based on what the child said, in a manner the child understands.
7	Specific questions (if necessary)	Follow up and clarify inconsistencies with more specific questions.
8	Interview aids (if necessary)	Have the child draw if he or she is not responding. Dolls may be introduced only after disclosure has occurred.
9	Conclude	Thank the child for helping and explain what will happen next.

Source: Interviewing children in sexual abuse cases. In G. Goodman, & B. Bottoms, (Eds.), Child victims, child witnesses: Understanding and improving testimony (pp. 95–115). New York, NY: Guilford Press.

Narrative Elaboration   In the United States, Saywitz and Snyder (1996) developed an interview procedure called **narrative elaboration**. With this procedure, children learn to organize stories into relevant categories:

- Participants
- Settings
- Actions
- Conversation/affective states
- Consequences

A card containing a line drawing is available for each category (see Figure 6.1 for four of them). These visual cues help children remember to state all that they can. Children practise telling stories with each card before being questioned about the critical event. Then, they are asked for a free narrative about the critical event—for example, "What happened?" Lastly, children are presented with each card and asked, "Does this card remind you to tell something else?"

To test the narrative elaboration procedure, children in Grades 1 and 2 and children in Grades 4, 5, and 6 witnessed a staged event (Saywitz & Snyder, 1996). The

Narrative elaboration: An interview procedure whereby children learn to organize their story into relevant categories: participants, settings, actions, conversation/affective states, and consequences

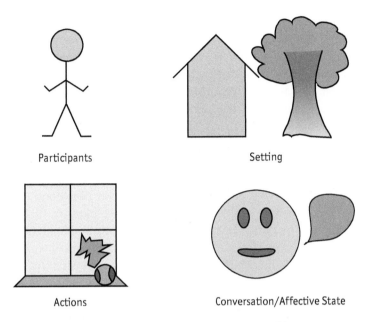

Participants

Setting

Actions

Conversation/Affective State

Figure 6.1 Line Drawings Appearing on Card Categories

Source: From Narrative Elaboration: Test of a new procedure for interviewing children by K.J Saywitz & L. Snyder. Journal of Consulting and Clinical Psychology, 64, 1347–1357. Published by American Psychological Association, © 1996.

children were then interviewed with either the narrative-elaboration procedure (involving training in the use of reminder cue cards), exposure to the cue cards without training, or a "standard" interview without training or cue cards. Children interviewed with the narrative elaboration procedure reported more accurate information but not more inaccurate information for the staged event compared with when just the cue cards were presented without training or the standard interview. Also, children did not fabricate more information with the narrative-elaboration procedure.

Given the positive effects of the narrative-elaboration procedure, Brown and Pipe (2003) considered whether they could further improve the procedure if it was coupled with mental reinstatement. The recall of 6- to 9-year-olds was compared when they received narrative-elaboration training, the narrative-elaboration training with mental reinstatement, or the control condition without training for narrative elaboration. Children trained in narrative elaboration reported almost twice as much information and were more accurate compared with the control group. Mental reinstatement did not increase accuracy. Moreover, research has found that simply asking children to report what they saw and heard, or to talk about information across categories was sufficient to produce increases in the amount of information recalled (Quas, Schaaf, Alexander, & Goodman, 2000). In a study examining the techniques used by forensic interviewers in 137 cases of sexual abuse, narrative elaboration was found to be used infrequently, in only about 12% of the cases (Faller, Grabarek, Nelson-Gardell, & Williams, 2011).

National Institute of Child Health and Human Development (NICHD) Interview Protocol   After examining a number of interviewing protocols for use with children, Dr. Michael Lamb and his colleagues at the National Institute of Child Health and Human Development (NICHD) developed an interviewing procedure that relies on open-ended questioning with two types of prompts available to interviewers (Sternberg, Lamb, Esplin, Orbach, & Hershkowitz, 2002). Interviewers can use time prompts to have the child fill in details and a timeline. For example, the interviewer may ask, "What happened next?" Also, interviewers can use cue question prompts where details that the child has reported are used in the question and children are asked to elaborate. For example, the interviewer may say, "You said the teacher took off his belt. Tell me more about that." This protocol also provides direction on how to start the interview and how to introduce the topic of abuse. For example, children are initially engaged to describe neutral events (e.g., the child's guitar lessons) in a nonleading manner. The topic of abuse may be introduced by asking the child why he or she has come to talk to you. A number of studies have been conducted investigating the NICHD protocol with positive results (Lamb, Hershkowitz, Orbach, & Esplin, 2008). A meta-analysis by Benia, Hauck-Filho, Dillenburg, and Stein (2015) found the protocol to be superior to standard interviewing procedures (i.e., interviews that were conducted by the same personnel as those conducted using the NICHD protocol, but prior to protocol training), particularly with school-aged children.

Hershkowitz, Lamb, and Katz (2014) tested a revised NICHD protocol in a study of 426 four- to thirteen-year-olds for whom abuse was suspected and corroborated independently. The revised protocol was designed to improve rapport-building as well as provide extra support in a non-suggestive manner for more reluctant suspected victims. When the revised protocol was used, Hershkowitz et al. found that children were more likely to report their abuse than when the standard NICHD protocol was used, highlighting the usefulness of supportive forensic interviewing practices with children.

One issue that appears problematic for children is a multipart prompt where interviewers ask two questions together, for example, "Can you tell me everything about how he caught you? When did it happen?" (Katz & Hershkowitz, 2012). The use of multipart prompts is not recommended.

Cognitive Interview   You may recall the cognitive interview from Chapter 5; this interview can be adapted and used with children (Geiselman & Padilla, 1988). A meta-analysis found that children interviewed with the cognitive interview reported more accurate information than children interviewed in control conditions (Kohnken, Milne, Memon, & Bull, 1999; also Holliday & Albon, 2004). A follow-up meta-analysis by Memon, Meissner, and Fraser (2010) replicated these findings.

As you can see, there are a number of protocols available to those who interview children. These protocols limit the use of direct questions and attempt to have the child provide as much information as possible by using a free-recall format (Larsson & Lamb, 2009). The interview protocols being used by police vary by jurisdiction.

RECALL MEMORY FOLLOWING A LONG DELAY

Is it possible to forget a traumatic event, such as abuse, only to recall it many years later? This question is at the centre of a heated debate about memory repression. Some argue that childhood sexual abuse memories are so traumatic for some individuals that they repress them in their unconscious. It is only as adults, with the help of therapy, that they come to recall the abuse, through what are known as recovered memories.

Others argue that it is only through therapy and the use of suggestive techniques that clients come to believe that they were sexually abused as children when in fact they were not; such recollections are known as false memories. Elizabeth Loftus (whose research is described in Chapter 5) is among the proponents of this second group. **False memory syndrome** was a term coined to describe a client's false belief that he or she was sexually abused as a child. Clients may have no memories of this abuse until they enter therapy to deal with some other psychological problem, such as depression or substance abuse (Read, 1999). See Box 6.4 for a case involving "delayed" memory.

False memory syndrome: Term to describe clients' false beliefs that they were sexually abused as children, despite having no memories of this abuse until they enter therapy to deal with some other psychological problem, such as depression or substance abuse

Box 6.4   Cases in Forensic Psychology

Delayed Memory Goes to Court: *R. v. Kliman* (1998)

On October 2, 1992, a 48-year-old teacher, Michael Kliman, from Richmond, B.C., was arrested and charged with the sexual abuse of two female students. The complainants (A and B) were in their late 20s when they made the allegations, but the abuse allegedly occurred in 1975, when the complainants were in Grade 6.

The complainants alleged that Kliman would take each of them out of class three or four times a week for up to 20 minutes at a time. It was alleged that Kliman would bring them to a small room in the school where he would sexually fondle them or they would fondle him. In addition, one of the complainants claimed that when she was on a class camping trip in Grade 7, Kliman took her to his tent and raped her. Both complainants alleged that they suffered from dissociative amnesia—that is, memory loss of an event because of the trauma of the event.

Both A and B testified that they had no memory of the abuse until many years later. A stated that she recovered the repressed memory after she was admitted to a hospital psychiatric ward for an eating disorder when she was 19. B stated that she recalled the past events after she was questioned by police following A's claim.

In A's hospital record for anorexia, Kliman's name was not mentioned. A testified that while she worked at an insurance company a superior sexually abused and harassed her. She also testified that she was repeatedly abused and stalked by a man between October 1990 and December 1991. She consulted a therapist as a result of this abuse in February 1991. The therapist specialized in adult survivorship of childhood sexual abuse, post-trauma reactions, dissociation, and memory. At the time A sought therapy, she had no memory of abuse at her elementary school. It was during the course of this therapy that A first identified Kliman as an abuser.

B was sexually abused by a foster brother and neighbour when she was 11 years old. She has a continuous memory of this abuse. B had no memory of abuse by Kliman until interviewed by the police officer following up A's allegation of abuse.

Dr. John Yuille and Dr. Elizabeth Loftus were called in to discuss memory and dissociative amnesia. The experts reached somewhat differing conclusions. Dr. Loftus noted that at present no scientific evidence supports the notion that several incidents of traumatic sexual abuse could cause memory of the events to be lost. She also testified that the use of leading questions and suggestive interviewing techniques could contaminate memory. Dr. Yuille testified that some literature, including some of his work, supports the notion of dissociative amnesia.

Kliman was tried three times. In the first trial, the jury convicted him. The decision was appealed and the court of appeal set aside the conviction because of inadequate disclosure. In the second trial, the jury was unable to reach a unanimous verdict. In the third trial, Kliman was acquitted on all counts. The trial judge noted that there were many improbabilities about the details of the complainants' testimony that made it difficult to believe, aside from the memory issues. For example, it is hard to imagine how Kliman could excuse himself from class several times a week.

Questions

1. Do you see any problems with the complainants' claims or testimony?

2. Based on the information presented, how would you have voted if you were a juror in the case? Why?

Source: Based on *R. v. Kliman*, 15078 (BC SC) From Supreme Court of British Columbia, 1998.

Can Traumatic Memories Be Forgotten?

Perhaps the greatest point of contention regarding false memory syndrome is whether traumatic memories can be completely forgotten only to be remembered many years later.

In a study by Porter and Birt (2001), university students were asked to describe their most traumatic experience and their most positive experience. A number of different experiences were reported in each condition. Approximately 5% of their sample of 306 participants reported sexual assault or abuse as their most traumatic experience. The majority of these participants stated that they had consciously forced the memory out of their minds rather than never having a memory of it. Hunter and Andrews (2002) compared the memories of 74 women who had self-reported experiences of childhood sexual abuse against those of 60 women who had not experienced childhood sexual abuse. Forty-two of the abused women reported having experienced a time period where they had forgotten the abuse. The women who had reported forgetting their abuse for a period of time were less able to remember semantic facts about their childhood, such as the names of teachers and friends, than the abused women who did not report a period of forgetting, as well as women who had not been abused.

Ghetti et al. (2006) interviewed young adults who had, as children, been involved in legal cases involving their childhood sexual abuse. For ethical reasons, only those who disclosed their prior abuse were asked questions about it. Sixteen percent of these remaining participants reported having had a period of amnesia (i.e., 'subjective forgetting'). Having a period of subjective forgetting was more common with males and with cases of more severe abuse. However, objective memory for details of the abuse did not differ between those who reported having a period of subjective forgetting versus those who had not. Ghetti et al. asked the people that reported forgetting if they could have remembered the abuse during the forgetting period if asked about it, and only 4% said that would have been unable to. This suggests that in most of the cases the abuse had not actually been forgotten, just actively not recalled.

Proponents of the false memory argument contend that not having any memory of abuse is different from preferring not to think about it. When there is absolutely no memory of abuse, and it is only through the use of suggestive techniques that the abuse is remembered, many argue that these memories should be interpreted cautiously.

Lindsay and Read (1995) suggested five criteria to consider when determining the veracity of a recovered memory:

1. *Age of complainant at the time of the alleged abuse.* It is unlikely that anyone would have a memory (of abuse or otherwise) prior to age 2.

2. *Techniques used to recover memory.* Techniques such as hypnosis and guided imagery heighten suggestibility and encourage fantasy.

3. *Similarity of reports across interview sessions.* Do the reports become increasingly more fantastic, or are they similar?

4. *Motivation for recall.* Is the client experiencing other psychological distress and wanting an answer to explain such feelings?

5. *Time elapsed since the alleged abuse.* It may be more difficult to recall abuse that occurred 25 years ago than abuse that took place 2 years ago.

Although some may "recover" memories of abuse and others never truly forget this traumatic experience, the courts are seeing a number of cases where there has been a delay in reporting the abuse, known as **historic child sexual abuse**. See Box 6.5 for a discussion of historic child sexual abuse.

Historic child sexual abuse: Allegations of child abuse having occurred several years, often decades, prior to when they are being prosecuted

---

Box 6.5   Forensic Psychology in the Spotlight

Delayed Prosecutions of Historic Child Sexual Abuse

Courts are having to deal with a relatively new phenomenon known as historic child sexual abuse (HCSA)—that is, allegations of child abuse having occurred several years, often decades, prior to the time at which they are being prosecuted (Connolly & Read, 2006). It should be noted that the vast majority of these cases involve memories of abuse that have been continuous. The alleged victim does not claim to have ever "forgotten" the abuse. From the results of a national survey in the United States, Smith et al. (2000) found that 47% of adults who reported having been abused as children delayed reporting the abuse for over five years. Even more intriguing is that approximately 27% of this sample noted that they reported the abuse for the first time on the survey. Being male seems to be a reliable predictor of delayed reporting (Finkelhor, Hotaling, Lewis, & Smith, 1990).

In Canada (as well as in the United Kingdom, Australia, and New Zealand), there is no time limit during which a victim must report sexual abuse. Connolly and Read (2006) examined 2064 criminal complaints of HCSA in Canada with the objective of describing these criminal prosecutions. "Historic abuse" was defined as abuse in which the last offence occurred two or more years prior to the time of trial. Connolly and Read (2006) stated that the "typical" HCSA case had the following characteristics:

> The complainant is probably female. On average, she was 9 years old when the abuse began, 12 years old when it ended, and 26 years old at trial. She is unlikely to be reported to have been in therapy, and she is very likely to report continuous memory for the offence. Her abuser is more likely than not to be a male relative and he is on average 23 years older than her. On average, he was 33 years old when the abuse began, 36 years old when it ended and 51 years old at trial. In the majority of cases, the complainant reports repeated abuse that was sustained over an

average period of almost 4 years. A threat is probably not reported to have accompanied the abuse, but if one is reported, it is likely to be against the complainant's or her family's physical safety. (p. 424)

Read, Connolly, and Welsh (2006) examined the factors that predicted the verdicts in actual HCSA cases between 1980 and 2002 in Canada. Four hundred and sixty-six cases were heard before a jury (434 cases resulted in a guilty verdict). Six hundred and forty-four cases were heard by a judge alone (442 cases resulted in a guilty verdict). In each case, the complainant was 19 years old or younger when the alleged offence began, and two or more years had elapsed from the end of the alleged offence to the trial date. Eleven independent variables were examined: (1) length of delay, (2) age of complainant at the time the alleged abuse began, (3) repressed memory testimony, (4) involvement in therapy, (5) expert testimony, (6) frequency of alleged abuse, (7) intrusiveness of alleged abuse, (8) duration of alleged abuse, (9) presence of threat, (10) complainant's gender, and (11) relationship of accused to complainant. The following section discusses the researchers' results, for both jury trials and judge-alone trials.

Results for Jury Trials

In 93% of the HCSAs prosecuted before a jury, a guilty verdict was reached. Guilty verdicts were lower with older-aged complainants (Mean [M] = 12.67 years) than with younger-aged complainants (M = 9.52 years). Fewer guilty verdicts were obtained when experts provided an opinion for one side or the other, but not when there was an expert on each side. Surprisingly, when an expert testified on behalf of the Crown, fewer guilty verdicts were obtained than when there was no expert testifying. An

(continued)

expert testifying for the defence also resulted in somewhat fewer convictions than when there was no expert. When the abuse was accompanied by threats (i.e., physical and/or emotional), guilty verdicts were more likely than when there were no threats. Also, guilty verdicts were higher for defendants who had a familial relationship with the complainant rather than a community connection to the complainant. Other independent variables did not differ significantly in their influence on the verdict.

Results for Judge-Alone Trials

In approximately 69% of the HCSAs prosecuted before a judge alone, a guilty verdict was reached. The increase in likelihood of acquittal corresponded with the increase in length of delay. The average delay period was 14.98 years for acquittals as compared with an average delay of 12.36 years for guilty verdicts. Guilty verdicts were more likely when a claim of repression was made than when no repression claim was made by the complainant. Guilty verdicts were more likely with more intrusive sexual abuse than with less intrusive sexual abuse, such as sexual exposure or

sexual touching. Judges were more likely to reach a guilty verdict when the defendant was a family member rather than someone in the community. When the defence had an unchallenged expert testify, guilty verdicts were less likely than if no expert testified.

Results for a Mock-Juror Trial

In a recent study examining historic child sexual abuse, Pozzulo, Dempsey, and Crescini (2010) had mock jurors read a trial transcript that manipulated the length of delay between the end of the alleged abuse and the time of reporting (2, 15, or 30 years), the relationship to the alleged victim (uncle or former coach), and abuse frequency (1 or 12 times). Compared to the longer delay, the shorter delay resulted in higher guilt ratings and longer sentence recommendations. Also, higher guilt ratings were found when the defendant was the uncle rather than the coach, but only when the abuse occurred once rather than 12 times. Lastly, mock jurors were more confident in their verdict decision when the defendant was the uncle versus the coach and the abuse occurred 12 times rather than once.

RECALL FOR PEOPLE

Not only must children report the events that happened, but it is likely they will have to describe the culprit, especially if he or she is a stranger. Culprit descriptions—also known as recall for people—by child witnesses have been examined in only a few studies relative to the number of studies that have examined recall for an event.

Describing the Culprit

In one study, Davies, Tarrant, and Flin (1989) asked for descriptions of a stranger from younger (age 6 to 7) and older (age 10 to 11) children. The younger children recalled fewer items (M = 1 descriptor) than the older children (M = 2.21 descriptors). The researchers also found that older children recalled more interior facial features, such as freckles and nose, than younger children. Hair was the most frequently mentioned feature by both younger and older children.

The exterior feature of hair seems to be a dominant descriptor focused on by both children and adults (Ellis, Shepherd, & Davies, 1980; Sporer, 1996). Pozzulo and Warren (2003) found that exterior facial descriptors such as hair colour and style were predominant and accurately reported by 10- to 14-year-olds and adults. Moreover, interior facial features were problematic for both youth and adults.

Height, weight, and age are descriptors commonly reported, and if they are not reported, police may ask about them directly. Unfortunately, children and youth may have considerable difficulty with their estimates of such characteristics. Davies, Stevenson-Robb, and Flin (1988) found that children/youth (age 7 to 12 years) were inaccurate when asked to report the height, weight, and age of an unfamiliar visitor. Pozzulo and Warren (2003) found that accuracy for body descriptors such as height and weight were consistently problematic for youth. One possible explanation for this result is that children and youth may not understand the relation between height and weight—that is, taller people are heavier than shorter people of similar girth. Alternatively, children and youth simply may lack experience with height and weight. It is only in later adolescence that people become body conscious and more familiar with weight (and height proportions).

Memon, Holliday, and Hill (2006) provided youngsters ages 5 to 6 with picture books of a man called Jim Step, who paints his house, bakes a cake, or goes to the zoo. There were three versions of each story:

- Jim was portrayed as a clumsy person.
- Jim was portrayed as a careful person.
- Jim was portrayed neutrally.

All children received post-storybook information that was consistent with the stereotype (e.g., Jim was described as clumsy in the book and then given stereotypical information about a clumsy person) and inconsistent with the stereotype (e.g., Jim was described as a careful person in the book and then given stereotypical information that is inconsistent with being a careful person) of Jim's character in the storybook.

The data revealed that children were more likely to accept positive, inaccurate information than negative, inaccurate information. Thus, negative information was more likely to be rejected and positive information was more likely to be accepted.

Candel, Hayne, Strange, and Prevoo (2009) investigated the influence of suggestive questioning techniques with 7- and 11-year-olds. Three days after a class presentation on China, the children were interviewed with one of three types of suggestive questions. In the 'commission errors' condition, it was suggested that details were present that actually weren't, in the 'omission errors' condition, it was suggested that details were missing that actually had been presented, and in the 'change errors' condition, it was suggested that the presentation of details was different than it actually was. The following day, the children took part in a recognition-memory activity that included the suggested information. The 7-year-old children were more suggestible than the 11-year-old children. Regardless of their age, the children were more easily misled by the change errors than the other types of errors, according to the recognition task results.

Kirk, Gurney, Edwards, and Dodimead (2015) were interested in whether misleading gestures made by an interviewer would influence children's responses. Children (ages 2 to 4 and 7 to 9) watched a video and were asked eight questions immediately afterwards. In half of the cases, the interviewer made gestures that agreed with the question being asked (i.e., if asking what the lady in the video wore, the interviewer would gesture putting on a hat, which was actually worn by the lady). In the other half of the cases, the interviewer made misleading gestures, such as asking what the lady was wearing while gesturing putting on gloves, which were not actually worn by the lady in the video. Kirk et al. (2015) found that regardless of age, misleading gestures resulted in significantly more misinformation being provided by the children.

As these studies illustrate, it is important for interviewers not to introduce their own biases or inaccurate information when interviewing children. Once again, the argument can be made that children should be asked to describe the culprit in terms of what he or she did and looked like by using a free narrative. Given the few descriptors children provide, it may be important to probe this information for detail. Some of the techniques described above for event recall may be helpful with person recall. More research is needed on how to elicit person descriptions from children (as well as adults).

RECOGNITION

One other task a child victim or witness may be asked to perform is an identification of the culprit from a lineup. In a meta-analysis comparing children's identification abilities to adults', Pozzulo and Lindsay (1998) found that children over age 5 produced comparable correct identification rates to adults, provided the culprit was present in the lineup (target-present lineup). However, when the culprit was not in the lineup (target-absent lineup), children as old as age 14 produced greater false positives than adults. That is, children were more likely to select an innocent person from a lineup than adults (see Chapter 5 for a review of general lineup identification issues). In a recent meta-analysis examining identification accuracy across the life-span, Fitzgerald and Price (2015) found that there was an increasing trend for correct identification and correct rejection with children less accurate than adults.

Lineup Procedure and Identification Rates

Pozzulo and Lindsay (1998) examined whether identification rates differed between children and adults as a function of the lineup procedure used. As you may recall from Chapter 5, the sequential lineup has been demonstrated to decrease false-positive responding compared with simultaneous presentation for adults (Lindsay & Wells, 1985), although there has been some debate on the sequential superiority effect (McQuiston-Surrett et al., 2006). Nonetheless, we can examine whether the use of the sequential lineup with children decreases their false-positive responding. Pozzulo and Lindsay (1998) found that with sequential lineup presentation, the gap for false-positive responding between children and adults increased. Thus, the sequential lineup increased false-positive responding with child witnesses, whereas for adults the sequential lineup decreased false-positive responding.

An Identification Procedure for Children In an attempt to develop an identification procedure that decreases children's false-positive responding, Pozzulo and Lindsay (1999) proposed a two-judgment theory of identification accuracy. The researchers postulated that to reach an accurate identification decision, witnesses conduct two judgments: relative and absolute. First, witnesses compare across lineup members and choose the most similar-looking lineup member to the culprit, a relative judgment. Second, witnesses compare the most-similar lineup member to their memory of the culprit and decide if it is in fact the culprit, an absolute judgment. Pozzulo and Lindsay (1999) speculated that children often fail to make an absolute judgment and thereby produce greater false positives than adults.

The researchers explain how a failure to make an absolute judgment would result in greater false positives. They argue that with target-present lineups, a relative judgment is sufficient to lead to a correct identification because it is likely that the culprit looks most like himself or herself compared with the other lineup members. Thus, the culprit is selected. In contrast, with target-absent lineups, solely relying on a relative judgment may lead to an identification of an innocent person because the most similar-looking lineup member is not the culprit—recall that with a target-absent lineup, the culprit is not there. An absolute judgment is necessary with target-absent lineups. If children fail to conduct an absolute judgment, a greater false-positive rate may result.

Based on these notions, Pozzulo and Lindsay (1999) developed an identification procedure for children, known as the **elimination lineup**, that is consistent with the two-judgment theory of identification accuracy. The elimination lineup procedure requests two judgments from the child:

1. All lineup photos are presented to the child, and the child is asked to select the lineup member who looks most like the culprit (relative judgment). Once this decision is made, the remaining photos are removed.

2. The child is asked to compare his or her memory of the culprit with the most similar photo selected in the first stage and to decide if the photo is of the culprit (absolute judgment).

Pozzulo and Lindsay (1999) tested variations of this procedure and the "standard" simultaneous procedure with children and adults. The elimination procedure was found to significantly decrease children's false-positive responding with target-absent lineups compared with the simultaneous procedure. In other words, children's correct rejection rate increased by using the elimination procedure compared with the simultaneous procedure. Moreover, children's false-positive rate (or correct-rejection rate) with the elimination procedure was similar to that of adults when the simultaneous procedure was used.

The elimination procedure continues to be tested with different-aged children and adults while varying the conditions under which an identification needs to be made to determine its robustness and viability for use in "real life" (e.g., Dempsey & Pozzulo, 2008; Pozzulo & Balfour, 2006; Pozzulo et al., 2008; Pozzulo, Dempsey, & Crescini, 2009). For example, in a study by Pozzulo and Balfour (2006), children between the ages of 8 and 13 were tested along with adults when a culprit underwent a change in appearance following the commission of a theft. Simultaneous and elimination lineup procedures were examined under conditions when the culprit was or was not present in the lineup. The researchers found that correct identification rates decreased following a change in appearance regardless of the witness's age and lineup procedure used. In terms of correct-rejection rates, children had an overall lower correct-rejection rate compared with adults. Compared with the simultaneous procedure, the elimination procedure was more effective at increasing correct rejections

Elimination lineup: Lineup procedure for children that first asks them to pick out the person who looks most like the culprit from the photos displayed. Next, children are asked whether the most similar person selected is in fact the culprit when there was no change in the culprit's appearance from the time the crime was committed to the time a lineup was viewed. When a change occurred, however, correct-rejection rates were similar across the two identification procedures for both children and adults.

Social versus Cognitive Factors Responsible for Children's False-Positive Responding   Pozzulo, Dempsey, Bruer, and Sheahan (2010) considered whether children would continue to produce a higher rate of false-positive responding even when the target was familiar to them (e.g., cartoons) compared to adults. The researchers reasoned that if children produce a higher false-positive rate with familiar targets, their responding would reflect a greater influence of social factors (e.g., pressure to make an identification) than cognitive factors (e.g., memory deficit). Familiar cartoons such as *Dora the Explorer* and *Go, Diego, Go!* were used as targets in addition to unfamiliar human faces. As predicted, children correctly identified the familiar targets with virtually 100% accuracy when shown a target-present lineup; however, they produced a significantly lower correct-rejection rate when shown a target-absent lineup compared to adults. Also, children produced a significantly lower correct-rejection rate for human faces compared to adults, as expected. These data suggest that in the target-absent condition, social factors may exert their influence on children more so than memory problems, prompting them to make an erroneous identification.

TESTIFYING IN COURT

Competency inquiry: Questions posed to child witnesses under age 14 to determine whether they are able to communicate the evidence and understand the difference between the truth and a lie, and, in the circumstances of testifying, to see if they feel compelled to tell the truth

Prior to 2006, in Canada (as well as in the United States and some European countries), children under age 14 had to pass a **competency inquiry** before testifying. The notion behind the competency inquiry was that children must demonstrate that they can communicate what they witnessed or experienced. Also, it was felt that it was critical for children to understand the difference between saying the truth and lying, and to feel compelled to tell the truth. It could be argued that the competency inquiry was historically entrenched in the negative views of child witnesses discussed earlier in this chapter.

Bill C-2 came into effect in Canada in the winter of 2006, amending the Canada Evidence Act and the Criminal Code of Canada.

Under the old legislation of the Canada Evidence Act, section 16 stated that witnesses under age 14 must (1) be able to communicate the evidence and (2) understand the difference between the truth and a lie, and, in the circumstances of testifying, feel compelled to tell the truth.

In the first part of the inquiry, children need only demonstrate a general ability to perceive, recall, and communicate rather than demonstrate specific abilities for describing the event/crime in question. Common questions may include the following:

- What grade are you in?
- What is your teacher's name?
- How many siblings do you have?

Children as young as age 2 or 3 may be able to demonstrate a general ability to communicate.

For the second part of the exam, children are questioned regarding their ability to distinguish between the truth and a lie, and must demonstrate an understanding of the meaning of *oath*. Common themes for questioning in this section include the following:

- Defining terms
- Religion and church
- Consequences of lying

The second part of the inquiry may be particularly difficult for young children (and even for some adults).

Under the new Canada Evidence Act, section 16.1, there is a presumption that children have a capacity to testify. Children (defined as persons under the age of 14) are asked simple questions about past events to determine their ability to understand and respond to questions. Children are requested to promise to tell the truth and testify under such a promise. No questions are asked about their understanding of the notion of an *oath* or *truth* (Bala, Lee, Lindsay, & Talwar, 2010).

Courtroom Accommodations

Child witnesses may experience extreme stress and trauma because of having to testify in court while facing the defendant (Goodman et al., 1992). The Canadian justice system has responded to child victims and witnesses by providing a set of alternatives to testifying in court in the presence of the defendant. For example, in 1988, legislation was enacted that allowed children to testify from behind a screen or from another room by way of closed-circuit television (Bala, 1999). These provisions applied to children under the age of 18 who were the complainants in sexual offence cases. Further amendments in 1997 extended these provisions to any child witness for any sexual offence or assault. Bill C-2 further extends these provisions to any offence for which a child (i.e., someone who is under the age of 18) testifies.

A screen used when a child testifies
Mike Theiler/AFP/Newscom

Professor Nicholas Bala has conducted extensive work in the area of child witness testimony. Bala (1999) identified a number of alternatives to in-court testimony that have been used in the Canadian system and are now available to any witness under the age of 18 and to vulnerable witnesses upon application.

1. A shield/screen to separate the child and defendant so that the child does not see the defendant's face. However, the child is visible to the defendant and the rest of the courtroom and may be able to see the defendant's feet.
2. The child is allowed to provide testimony via a closed-circuit television monitor. The child and lawyers are in a separate room from the courtroom and the

child's testimony is televised to the courtroom where the defendant, judge, and jury are present. The defendant can be in touch with his or her lawyer by telephone.

3. The child may have a support person with him or her while providing testimony. The child can decide whom he or she wants, although a person who is a witness in the same case cannot be a support person unless he or she has already provided testimony.

4. A child may be video-recorded while being interviewed about the details of the crime. The video may be admitted into evidence, so that the child does not have to repeat the details in court.

5. Generally, previous statements made by a witness are considered hearsay and are not admissible. However, in sexual abuse cases, judges can apply the rules liberally, and statements made by the child during the initial disclosure of the abuse may be allowed as evidence. For example, a mother may testify about what her child said when disclosing the abuse.

6. The judge may close the courtroom to the public and/or media to protect the privacy of the child. A publication ban prohibiting any information that would identify the complainant or any witness also may be granted to protect the child's identity.

These alternatives also are available in the United States.

In addition, with Bill C-2, children under the age of 18 can no longer be cross-examined personally by the accused (s. 486.2).

CHILD MALTREATMENT

So far, we have highlighted sexual abuse against children; however, there are other forms of maltreatment that a child may experience. Other forms of maltreatment require the same considerations as sexual abuse. The Child Maltreatment Section (CMS) of Health Canada distinguishes four categories of child maltreatment:

Physical abuse: The deliberate application of force to any part of a child's body that results in or may result in a non-accidental injury

Sexual abuse: When an adult or youth uses a child for sexual purposes

Neglect/failure to provide: When a child's caregivers do not provide the requisite attention to the child's emotional, psychological, or physical development

1. **Physical abuse** is defined as the deliberate application of force to any part of a child's body that results or may result in a non-accidental injury. Examples include shaking, choking, biting, kicking, burning, and poisoning. See Box 6.6 for a debate on whether corporal punishment is physical abuse.

2. **Sexual abuse** occurs when an adult or youth uses a child for sexual purposes. Examples include fondling, intercourse, incest, sodomy, exhibitionism, and exploitation through prostitution or the production of pornographic materials.

3. **Neglect/failure to provide** occurs when a child's caregivers do not provide the requisite attention to the child's emotional, psychological, or physical development. Examples include failure to supervise or protect leading to physical harm (such as drunk driving with a child), failure to provide adequate nutrition or clothing, failure to provide medical treatment, and exposing the child to unhygienic or dangerous living conditions.

Box 6.6   Cases in Forensic Psychology

Discipline or Physical Abuse? *R. v. Poulin* (2002)

Seventy-eight-year-old Lucille Poulin was a religious leader in a commune on Prince Edward Island. Poulin was given the responsibility of looking after the children in the commune while their parents worked. She believed children needed discipline to prevent them from engaging in evil acts. Poulin used a wooden paddle when disciplining the children, resulting in assault charges in 2002.

At Poulin's trial, several children testified that she often beat them, at times causing them to pass out. Poulin was found guilty of assaulting five children. The court ruled that Poulin went beyond discipline. She was sentenced to eight months in jail and ordered not to live with or care for children younger than age 14 for three years following her release.

Corporal punishment has been put to the Supreme Court of Canada in a challenge by the Canadian Foundation for Children, Youth, and the Law (*Canadian Foundation for Children, Youth, and the Law v. The Attorney General in Right of Canada*, 2004). The legislation under scrutiny was section 43 of the Canadian Criminal Code, which states, "Every schoolteacher, parent, or person standing in the place of a parent is justified in using force by way of correction toward a pupil or child, as the case may be, who is under his or her care, if the force does not exceed what is reasonable under the circumstances."

The Canadian Foundation for Children, Youth, and the Law argued that section 43 of the Criminal Code violates sections 7 (security of the person), 12 (cruel and unusual punishment), and 15 (equality) of the Canadian Charter of Rights and Freedoms and that it conflicts with Canada's obligations under the United Nations' Convention of the Rights of the Child.

In July 2000, the Ontario Superior Court of Justice upheld the constitutionality of section 43. In January 2002, the decision went to the Ontario Court of Appeal, which upheld the lower court's decision and dismissed the appeal. The appeal then went to the Supreme Court of Canada. In January 2004, the Supreme Court held that section 43 was constitutional. The Supreme Court also ruled the following:

- Corporal punishment is prohibited in schools. Teachers in Canada will still be able to use physical force to remove a student or prevent immediate threats of harm to person or property, but a student can no longer be physically punished.
- Parents are not permitted to spank, slap, or otherwise use any corporal punishment on children younger than age 2 or older than age 12.
- Parents may use physical force on children between the ages of 3 and 12 but may not use an object to hit them.
- Parents are not permitted to strike children between the ages of 3 and 12 on the head or the face, under any circumstances.

Questions

1. What is your position on corporal punishment? Why?

2. Do you think Poulin received an appropriate sentence?

Source: From Province of Prince Edward Island in the Supreme Court-Trial Division, Her Majesty the Queen Against Lucille Poulin, by *R. v. Poulin*. Copyright © 2002.

4. **Emotional maltreatment** is defined as acts or omissions by caregivers that cause or could cause serious behavioural, cognitive, emotional, or mental disorders. Examples include verbal threats, socially isolating a child, intimidation, exploitation, terrorizing, or routinely making unreasonable demands on a child.

Emotional maltreatment: Acts or omissions by caregivers that cause or could cause serious behavioural, cognitive, emotional, or mental disorders

It is likely that children experience multiple forms of maltreatment simultaneously. For example, it is hard to imagine that a child who is neglected is not also emotionally abused.

Government agencies have the authority and responsibility to remove children from their caregivers when they are maltreated or at risk for maltreatment. Also, a child may be removed if a caregiver is unwilling or unable to prevent abuse by a third party. For example, children may be removed from their caregivers' custody because of neglect, physical and sexual abuse, alcohol or other drug use, and mental illness. It is important to recognize that for children to be apprehended, these factors must have negative effects on parenting to the extent that the caregiver cannot adequately parent. The term **in need of protection** is used to describe a child's need to be separated from his or her caregiver because of maltreatment.

All Canadian jurisdictions require the reporting of children suspected to be in need of protection. Legislation across Canada varies the age below which an individual is considered a child. Generally, an individual is no longer considered a child between the ages of 16 and 19. In Ontario, for example, the Child and Family Services Act (i.e., legislation pertaining to children) denotes children as people under 18 years of age.

Beck and Ogloff (1995) surveyed Canadian psychologists and found that more than 98% of the respondents were aware of mandatory reporting laws in their jurisdiction. Although psychologists may be aware of reporting laws, they do not necessarily comply. According to the survey results, psychologists may not report child maltreatment because of insufficient evidence or a belief that child protection agencies cannot help.

When trying to understand how often maltreatment occurs, it is important to clarify the distinction between incidence and prevalence. The CMS defines **incidence** as the "number of new cases in a specific population occurring in a given time period, usually a year." In contrast, the **prevalence** of maltreatment is defined as "the proportion of a population at a specific point in time that was maltreated during childhood."

The Canadian Incidence Study of Reported Child Abuse and Neglect (Trocmé et al., 2010) provides a national estimate of the number of instances of child maltreatment reported to and investigated by child welfare services. Table 6.3 shows the number and incidence of maltreatment-related investigations in 1998, 2003, and 2008.

Neglect (34%), exposure to domestic violence (34%), and physical abuse (20%) were the three primary categories of substantiated maltreatment. Emotional maltreatment accounted for another 9% of cases, while sexual abuse cases represented 3% of all substantiated investigations. See Figure 6.2 for the distribution of child-maltreatment categories.

Table 6.3 Number and Rate of Child Maltreatment Investigations in Canada, 1998 and 2003, and Child Maltreatment Investigations and Risk of Future Maltreatment Investigations, 2008[a]

Child Welfare Investigations					
1998		2003		2008	
Number of investigations	Rate per 1000 children	Number of investigations	Rate per 1000 children	Number of investigations	Rate per 1000 children
135 261	21.47	235 315	38.33	235 842	39.16[b]

[a] Based on a sample of 7633 investigations in 1998; 14 200 investigations in 2003; and 15 980 investigations in 2008.

[b] Difference between 2003 and 2008 incidence rates is not statistically significant (p > .05).

Source: Canadian Incidence Study of Reported Child Abuse and Neglect. Public Health Agency of Canada, 2008. Reproduced with permission from the Minister of Health, 2013.

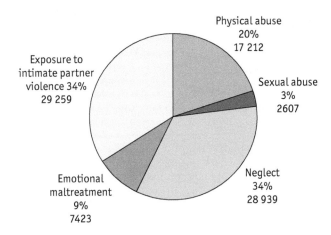

Figure 6.2 Primary Categories of Substantiated Child Maltreatment in Canada, 2008

Source: Canadian Incidence Study of Reported Child Abuse and Neglect. Public Health Agency of Canada, 2008. Reproduced with permission from the Minister of Health, 2013.

Risk Factors Associated with Child Maltreatment

A number of **risk factors**—factors that increase the likelihood for emotional and/or behavioural problems—have been identified for physical and sexual abuse. These can be categorized as child factors, parental factors, and social factors (see Table 6.4).

The risk factors for physical and sexual abuse differ. Physical abuse risk factors are varied and include a parent's past childhood physical abuse as well as the parent's attitude toward pregnancy. In contrast, sexual abuse risk factors tend to revolve around family composition.

Risk factor: A factor that increases the likelihood for emotional and/or behavioural problems

Short-Term and Long-Term Effects of Physical Abuse

Dakil, Cox, Lin, and Flores (2012) examined United States national data from the National Child Abuse and Neglect Dataset, where more than 600 000 children are reported as having been physically abused. The researchers found that domestic violence, parental drug and alcohol use, prior child abuse and neglect, being on public assistance, and child behaviour problems were related to a greater likelihood of substantiated physical abuse compared to the unsubstantiated physical abuse cases. A number of short-term effects of physical abuse have been determined. These include greater perceptual-motor deficits, lower measured intellectual functioning, lower academic achievement, externalizing behaviour such as aggression, and internalizing mental health difficulties such as hopelessness and depression (Ammerman, Cassisi, Hersen, & Van Hasselt, 1986; Conaway & Hansen, 1989; Lamphear, 1985).

Shin, Miller, and Teicher (2012) found that neglect and physical abuse (both individually and in combination) were related to heavy episodic drinking during adolescence and young adulthood. Moreover, additional instances of maltreatment and physical abuse were related to faster increases in heavy episodic drinking during adolescence and greater use during young adulthood. Being physically abused at home

Table 6.4 Risk Factors for Abuse

	Type of Abuse	
	Physical Abuse	*Sexual Abuse*
Child Factors		
	Male	Female
Parental Factors		
	Young maternal age	Living in a family without a biological parent
	Single-parent status	Poor relationship between parents
	History of childhood physical abuse	Presence of a stepfather
	Spousal assault	Poor child–parent relations
	Unplanned pregnancy or negative attitude toward pregnancy	
	History of substance abuse	
	Social isolation or lack of social support	
Social Factors		
	Low socioeconomic status	
	Large family size	

Source: MacMillan, H.L. (2000). Child maltreatment: What we know in the year 2000. *Canadian Journal of Psychiatry,* 45:8, 702–709. p. 704.

can also be associated with being victimized by peers. Lev-Wiesel and Sternberg (2012) found that physical abuse at home and emotional abuse are risk factors for social peer rejection, which in turn is a risk factor for psychological distress.

In a review of studies examining the long-term effects of physical abuse, Malinosky-Rummell and Hansen (1993) reported strong relations between physical abuse and nonfamilial and familial violence. Physically abused persons, especially males, engage in more nonfamilial violence than nonabused persons. About 30% of physically abused or neglected persons abuse their own children (Kaufman & Zigler, 1987; Widom, 1989b). Moreover, being abused as a child predicted inflicting and receiving dating violence in a sample of university students. Also, spouses who were abusive reported higher rates of physical abuse than nonabusive spouses. Thus, experiencing physical abuse appears to increase the likelihood of perpetrating physical abuse.

Short-Term and Long-Term Effects of Sexual Abuse

Kendall-Tackett, Williams, and Finkelhor (1993) examined 45 studies that considered the short-term effects of childhood sexual abuse. Common effects across the studies were behaviour problems, lowered self-esteem, inappropriate sexuality, and symptoms consistent with post-traumatic stress disorder. Research has found that within two years of being abused, children report a number of physical difficulties such as sleep disturbance, eating disorders, stomach problems, and headaches (Adams-Tucker, 1982). After two years have passed, there is a decrease in psychiatric problems compared to within the first year (Ozbaran, et al., 2009).

Putnam (2003) identified three categories of outcomes in adults with a history of childhood sexual abuse: (1) psychiatric disorders, (2) dysfunctional behaviours, and (3) neurobiological dysregulation.

Under psychiatric disorders, major depression in adulthood has been found to be strongly related to sexual abuse in childhood (Paolucci, Genuis, & Violato, 2001). Sexualized behaviour is one of the most closely related dysfunctional behaviours with those who have a history of childhood sexual abuse (Widom & Ames, 1994). In terms of neurobiological dysregulation, magnetic resonance imaging (MRI) studies have found reduced hippocampal volume in adults who experienced sexual abuse as children, similar to that found in war veterans experiencing post-traumatic stress disorder (Stein et al., 1997). Messman-Moore and Long (2003) reported that adults who were sexually abused as children have an increased risk of being sexually abused as adults. Other long-term risks for sexually abused children include depression, self-injurious behaviours, anxiety, and interpersonal distrust (Browne & Finkelhor, 1986).

Pérez-Fuentes et al. (2012) conducted a national study examining child sexual abuse in the United States. Over 34 000 adults 18 years and older were interviewed between 2004 and 2005. Child sexual abuse was found at a prevalence rate of 10.14% (24.8% in men and 75.2% in women). Interestingly, other types of maltreatment (i.e., physical abuse, maltreatment, and neglect) were more likely to have occurred with individuals who had experienced child sexual abuse than those who had not suffered this abuse. Moreover, adults with a history of child sexual abuse were more likely to experience major psychological disorders and suicide attempts. Dube et al. (2005) also found that suicide attempts were twice as likely among both men and women who had reported experiencing child sexual abuse compared with those who had not reported experiencing it. Also, there was an increased risk of alcohol problems, illicit drug use, and family problems when respondents had experienced child sexual abuse.

A survey in the United States found that roughly one in five young people is solicited for sex over the Internet each year (Mitchell, Finkelhor, & Wolak, 2001; see also Box 6.7). Canadian law is catching up to computer technology with the enactment of Bill C-15A in 2002. Now, it is a criminal offence to use the Internet to communicate with a child for the purpose of committing a sexual act (s. 172.1 of the Criminal Code of Canada). This offence carries a maximum five-year prison sentence. This legislation in part satisfies Canada's commitment to a United Nations protocol on the rights of the child that was signed by 105 countries in 2002. An advantage of this protocol is that it sets out consistent law to deal with child abuse issues across countries. Given that the Internet does not have borders, this type of consistency is critical. See the In the Media box to learn more about the media's involvement in the battle against Internet luring.

A Caveat to the Outcomes of Child Maltreatment   Although child maltreatment is always horrific, it is important to note that not all children who experience maltreatment will suffer negative outcomes. Although some children who have undergone maltreatment will experience negative short-term and/or long-term

Box 6.7   Cases in Forensic Psychology

Luring Children over the Internet: *R. v. Symes* (2005)

Advances in computer technology provide a host of benefits to its users. Unfortunately, this technology can also be abused. With the Internet, sexual predators have access to countless children, and they can remain anonymous until they decide to meet a child. Some sexual predators conceal their true ages, and a child may assume that he or she is meeting another child; however, sometimes predators do not conceal their ages, as was the case with Kenneth Symes.

Symes was a 36-year-old former church pastor from Ajax, Ontario. Between April 18 and August 10, 2005, Symes began a series of Internet chats with two girls whom he thought were 12 to 13 years of age. In fact, the "girls" were undercover investigators. The chat exchanges between Symes and the "girls" were sexually explicit and left no doubt that he wanted to have sexual relations with both girls. Symes arranged to meet one of the girls, and when he attended the meeting, police arrested him. Symes pled guilty to two counts of Internet luring and was sentenced to 12 months in prison, which was reduced to 2 months after double credit was given for time served.

Questions

1. Do you think Symes received an appropriate sentence? Why or why not?

2. What sort of penalties should be in place for adults who lure children over the Internet?

Source: *R. v. Symes*, 2005.

effects, others will not. Moreover, some children who have *not* experienced maltreatment will experience negative effects (and, of course, some children who have not undergone maltreatment will not experience negative effects). A number of factors may increase or protect against negative outcomes (see Chapter 12 for a greater discussion on risk and protective factors for children and youth). Thus, it is important to keep in mind that no one factor in childhood can predict outcomes in adulthood with absolute accuracy.

In the Media

To Catch a Predator: Teenage Style

You may have heard of the show *To Catch a Predator*. *Dateline NBC*, a television show based in the United States, got into the business of crime-busting with its series *To Catch a Predator*. It is estimated that one in four children are invited to meet for a sexual encounter. On this reality show, the tables get turned on men who attempt to lure a child for a sexual encounter. Adult men chat online with youngsters, or so they believe, and eventually, these men arrange to meet the child for a sexual encounter. The child, however, is an operative: an adult trained to pretend to be a child while chatting online.

When the male arrives at a prearranged location, he is met with a camera crew and is confronted by the host of the show. These men are shown on air, and the police may be contacted. The men's names and faces are shown to the viewing audience.

A similar version of *To Catch a Predator* was conducted in Canada by the current affairs program *W5*. Although these shows are no longer on the air, three teenagers in British Columbia imitated the format by pretending to be underage girls online to lure potential pedophiles into public places. The teens videotaped the

(continued)

(continued)

interactions and later posted them to YouTube. In one video, two of the teenagers, one dressed as Batman and the other as the Flash, convinced the man they were online chatting with to meet them at a fast-food restaurant and to bring marijuana. The man presumably believed he would be meeting a 15-year-old girl. At the fast-food restaurant, the superheroes screamed out that the man was there with drugs and for a sexual encounter with a young girl. The man quickly left, but the interaction was captured and posted on YouTube. These episodes caught the attention of the RCMP. Although the teens were not charged, they were informed of the dangers of these set-ups. The teens removed the online videos, and the men have not been charged.

But what happens when the predator is part of the criminal justice system? In 2006, Louis Conradt, a 56-year-old Texas prosecutor, reportedly shot himself when police officers tried to arrest him for allegedly attempting to solicit a minor online. The cast and crew of *Dateline NBC* 's

To Catch a Predator were waiting outside his house to film his arrest. Allegedly Conradt attempted to set up a sexual encounter with a 13-year-old boy but failed to show up at the decoy house. A lawsuit against NBC was brought by Conradt's sister alleging that Conradt's civil rights were violated and the show intentionally inflicted emotional distress. Was NBC irresponsible? Should the company be allowed to film these interactions? Should these men's faces be shown? Conradt's sister sued for $100 million in compensatory and punitive damages. The case was settled out of court. *Dateline NBC* has since decided to stop producing *To Catch a Predator*.

Sources: Based on NBC resolves lawsuit over 'To Catch a Predator' suicide. (2008, June 24) Los Angeles Times. Retrieved from http://latimesblogs. latimes.com/showtracker/2008/06/nbc-resolves-la.html; Finlay, P. (2007, March 24). An easy catch. CTV News. Retrieved from http://www.ctv.ca/servlet/ArticleNews/story/CTVNews/20070323/wfive_aneasycatch_070324/200703 24?hub? WFive

SUMMARY

1. The accuracy of children's reporting is highly dependent on how they are asked to report. When children are asked to recall memories using the free-narrative method, the children's recall is as accurate as adults'. A number of procedures and protocols to increase children's accurate responding have been investigated, including statement validity analysis, the step-wise interview, and narrative elaboration. Leading questions and the use of anatomically correct dolls are problematic for accurate reporting.

2. Children report few person descriptors when asked to describe a stranger or culprit. Interior facial items such as freckles and nose shape are more likely to be reported by older children than younger children. However, accurately reporting these features is difficult. The exterior feature of hair is frequently mentioned by both children and adults. Height, weight, and age are unlikely to be reported accurately by children and youth.

3. Children produce comparable correct identification rates with adults' when presented with a target-present lineup. However, children are more likely than adults to select an innocent person with a target-absent lineup. The elimination lineup procedure decreases children's false-positive responding compared with a simultaneous lineup procedure.

4. Historically in Canada (and other countries), children under the age of 14 had to pass a competency inquiry before being allowed to testify. Under the new Bill C-2, children are asked simple questions to demonstrate their ability to communicate. Children testify under a promise to tell the truth. Also as a result of Bill C-2, a number of alternatives to in-court testimony (e.g., screens, a pre-recorded interview, and the presence of a support person) are available for persons under the age of 18.

5. Maltreatment can be categorized into sexual abuse, physical abuse, neglect/failure to provide, and emotional abuse. A number of short-term and long-term effects can result from physical abuse, for example, perceptual-motor deficits, lower measured intellectual functioning, lower academic achievement, externalizing behaviour, internalizing mental health difficulties, and nonfamilial and familial violence. A number of short-term and long-term effects can result from sexual abuse, for example, behaviour problems, lowered self-esteem, inappropriate sexuality, physical symptoms consistent with post-traumatic stress disorder, and continued abuse when an adult.

Discussion Questions

1. In your local community newspaper, you read of a 7-year-old boy who has been physically abused and then abandoned. You wonder what difficulties this boy may experience in the next couple of years and when he becomes an adult. Describe the possible short-term and long-term effects of maltreatment.

2. Why is the use of anatomically correct dolls controversial when assessing child sexual abuse?

Chapter 7

Juries: Fact Finders

Learning Objectives

- Describe how jurors are selected in Canada.

- Distinguish between representativeness and impartiality.

- Describe the effects of pretrial publicity and the available options for dealing with it.

- Outline the stages to reaching a jury verdict.

- Describe the categories of variables that have been examined to predict a verdict.

Kathy Kramer is juror 10. Along with 11 other jurors, she is seated in the jury box, listening to evidence about how the defendant, Melissa Vincent, brutally murdered her roommate in a fit of rage when she found out that her boyfriend and roommate were having an affair. Melissa isn't your "typical" defendant; she is 21 years old and was on an exchange program in Australia, completing her undergraduate degree in psychology, when the crime occurred. She comes from a wealthy family: Both her parents are surgeons. The Crown argues that Melissa left the school library early one night and, as she was nearing her apartment complex, she saw her boyfriend, Mark Carson, leaving the building. Melissa is alleged to have confronted her roommate, Marcy Metcalfe, and when she learned that Mark and Marcy were having a sexual relationship, she became enraged, grabbed a kitchen knife, and stabbed her room-mate, leaving Marcy dead. A phone record shows that Melissa called Mark around the time the victim died. Melissa claims she was just leaving the library when she made this call to ask Mark to meet her at her apartment. According to Melissa, she arrived after Mark was at the apartment and it was Mark who called the police to report the murder. Mark admits to having a relationship with Marcy. He also claims Melissa was extremely jealous of the friendship he had with Marcy. Melissa argues that the apartment complex was located in a "rough" part of town where drug deal-ers and prostitutes hung around. It was not uncommon to hear that apartments were broken into for money or drugs. The murder weapon was never recovered. No one could verify what time Melissa left the library. Mark did not have an alibi, either. Kathy needs to decide on a verdict for this case. What factors should influence her verdict?

In Canada, the courts deal with both civil and criminal cases. Criminal cases are those in which an act was allegedly committed as found in the Criminal Code of Canada. In contrast, civil cases are those that involve a breach of contract or other claims of "harm" (known as *torts*). Civil cases can be heard by jury or judge alone, as can criminal cases. However, the process, jury selection, and decision rules for civil cases are quite different from criminal cases. For example, jury trials for civil cases can have fewer jurors than criminal trials. Six- or eight-member jury trials often occur in civil cases, whereas twelve-member juries are typical in criminal cases. Also, verdicts do not necessarily have to be unanimous in civil trials. This chapter will focus on issues as they relate to criminal cases unless otherwise stated. We will focus on the jury-selection process, how jury research is conducted, and issues related to understanding the rules of law and how well we can predict verdicts.

JURY SELECTION IN CANADA

Before a jury trial can begin, a jury needs to be selected or "seated." The process of jury selection differs by province and territory (and country), although there are a number of commonalities across jurisdictions. Before we discuss jury selection, it is important to consider the types of cases juries will hear.

The Cases Heard by Juries

Television has bombarded us with crime shows such as *Law and Order* and *CSI*. Talk shows, such as *Nancy Grace* and *CNN News*, also highlight the latest developments in various high-profile cases. All this media coverage may distort perceptions of the frequency of trials heard by juries. Only some types of offences can proceed with jury trials. Moreover, in some instances defendants are given an option of a jury trial, but they may opt to be tried by judge alone. Thus, in Canada, relative to the total number of trials that take place, only a few are tried by jury. The remainder of trials are heard and ruled on by judges alone.

There are three types of offences in Canada: (1) summary offences, (2) indictable offences, and (3) hybrid offences.

Summary offences involve a sentence of fewer than 6 months in prison and a fine of less than $2000 (section 787[1] of the Criminal Code). However, for some offences the maximum sentence is 18 months (R.S.C. 1985, C-46, s. 787[1]). Summary offences are tried by judge alone. Moreover, the defendant charged with a summary offence does not have a right to a trial by jury.

Indictable offences fall into three categories:

1. Less serious indictable offences are heard by a judge sitting alone. These are found in section 553 of the Criminal Code and include theft (other than theft of cattle), obtaining money or property by false pretences, and failure to comply with a probation order.

2. Highly serious indictable offences must be tried by judge and jury. These offences include treason, murder, and piracy. However, an exception under section 473

of the Criminal Code indicates that if the attorney general and the accused agree, the trial can proceed without a jury and the judge alone tries the case.

3. For some indictable offences, the accused can choose whether the trial proceeds by judge and jury or judge alone. These are the indictable offences not listed in either section 553 or 469 of the Criminal Code, such as robbery (R.S.C. 1985, C-46, s. 343; 1995, C-34, s. 302), arson (R.S.C. 1985, C-46, s. 433; 1990, C-15, s. 1), and sexual assault with a weapon (R.S.C. 1985, C-46, s. 272; 1995, C-39, s. 145). The defendant has the option to choose (1) to be tried by a provincial or territorial court judge without a jury and without having had a preliminary inquiry, (2) to have a preliminary inquiry and to be tried by a judge without a jury, or (3) to have a preliminary inquiry and to be tried by a judge and a jury. If a defendant does not make a selection, he or she will have a preliminary inquiry and be tried by a judge and a jury.

Hybrid offences are a cross between indictable offences and summary offences. These are offences for which the maximum sentence is five or more years in prison if they proceed by indictment. If the Crown proceeds summarily, the maximum penalty is 6 months, or 18 months in some cases, such as sexual assault. It is up to the Crown attorney to decide whether to proceed with the case as an indictable offence or a summary offence. If the Crown opts for a summary offence, the case is tried by judge alone and the defendant does not have the right to a jury trial.

As you can see, these criteria greatly reduce the number of cases that are tried by jury. Also, it is important to keep in mind that jury trial options vary somewhat across provinces and territories.

Jury Selection

The **Juries Act** is provincial and territorial legislation that outlines the eligibility criteria for jury service and how prospective jurors must be selected. Although legislation varies across jurisdictions, there are a number of commonalities. Differences in eligibility criteria across jurisdictions may include the minimum age to be a juror (e.g., 18 years in Ontario and 19 years in British Columbia) and the professions (e.g., lawyer, police officer) that keep individuals exempt from jury duty.

Prospective jurors (i.e., random community members) receive a **jury summons**—that is, a court order that states a time and place for jury duty. Receiving a jury summons does not guarantee that you will be a juror, though. It simply means that you are expected to show up, typically at the courthouse, prepared to be a juror. If you ignore a summons and do not show up, you may incur a severe legal penalty, such as a fine or jail time.

In Canada, criminal trials have 12-person juries. If you are selected from the juror pool, you will be a juror unless one of the lawyers presents a challenge. Generally, there are two types of challenges lawyers can use to reject a potential juror: (1) peremptory challenge and (2) challenge for cause.

The Crown or defence can use a peremptory challenge to reject jurors who they believe are unlikely to reach a verdict in their favour. When using a peremptory challenge, the lawyer does not need to provide a reason for rejecting the prospective juror.

Juries Act: Provincial and territorial legislation that outlines the eligibility criteria for jury service and how prospective jurors must be selected

Jury summons: A court order that states a time and place to go for jury duty

Both the Crown and defence are allowed a limited number of peremptory challenges. In murder trials, each side has 20 peremptory challenges, whereas for most other crimes each side has 12 peremptory challenges.

In contrast, when using a challenge for cause, the lawyer must give a reason for rejecting the prospective juror. We will discuss challenge for cause later in this chapter.

Keep in mind that Canadian lawyers have very limited information about prospective jurors. This information includes name, address, occupation, and physical demeanour. Also, in many Canadian cases the lawyers are not allowed to ask prospective jurors questions to gain more information about them. Consequently, lawyers have very little information on which to decide whether a juror will reach a verdict in their favour. Although a prospective juror may be challenged and not able to sit for one trial, he or she may be selected for another trial.

Characteristics and Responsibilities of Juries in Canada

The Supreme Court of Canada indicated two fundamental characteristics of juries (*R. v. Sherratt*, 1991):

Representativeness: A jury composition that represents the community where the crime occurred

1. A composition that represents the community in which the crime occurred. This is known as **representativeness**.

Impartiality: A characteristic of jurors who are unbiased

2. A lack of bias on the part of jurors, known as **impartiality**.

Representativeness

For a jury to be considered "representative," it must allow any possible eligible person from the community the opportunity to be part of the jury. Representativeness is achieved through randomness. For example, a community's telephone directory or voter registration is used as a pool from which to randomly draw 100 or so names for potential jury duty. Of course, one could argue that neither of these "pools" is truly representative of the community because there may be people who can serve on a jury but whose names do not appear on these lists. For example, a homeless person may not have a phone but may be eligible to serve on a jury. Also, the Juries Act lists "exemptions" for those who cannot serve on a jury, thus limiting the true representativeness of the jury pool.

In some cases, the Crown or the defence may challenge the composition of the jury, arguing that it does not represent the community on some characteristic. For example, in *R. v. Nepoose* (1991), the defendant was an Aboriginal woman. The jury composition for her trial was successfully challenged for having too few women. See Box 7.1 for a jury-composition challenge of representativeness on the basis of race. Thus, representativeness can apply to both the community as well as the defendant (e.g., jury of a defendant's peers).

In a recent report, retired Supreme Court Justice of Canada Frank Iacobucci noted that Aboriginals are under-represented on juries (Talaga, 2013). Ontario's attorney general appointed Iacobucci in the summer of 2011 to review how Aboriginals on reserves were being selected for possible jury duty. One key issue is that

Was the Jury Racially Balanced? *R. v. Brown* (2005)

In 2001, two white men, Jeffrey Brown and Jeffrey Kindrat, were charged with sexually assaulting a 12-year-old Aboriginal girl. Of approximately 100 potential jurors who showed up for jury duty in Melfort, Saskatchewan, only one was visibly Aboriginal. Not surprisingly, once the jury was composed, all those sitting on the jury were Caucasian.

During the trial, the defendants admitted to picking the girl up, giving her five beers to drink, and then engaging in sexual activity with her outside a truck belonging to a third man, Dean Edmondson. The jury heard the evidence and then deliberated to reach verdicts of not guilty for both Brown and Kindrat.

Were these verdicts a product of a racist jury? The case raised concern about the jury-selection process. The Saskatchewan Justice Department stated that it would contact officials across Canada to determine whether changes to the selection process could be made to make juries more racially balanced. The effect of this case on jury selection has yet to be determined.

Interestingly, in the trial of Edmondson, he was found guilty, also with an all-Caucasian jury. One main difference between the cases was the testimony of the victim. The victim testified more fully against Edmondson; however, she was reluctant to testify against Brown and Kindrat, providing far less information.

In 2005, an appeal from the Crown was allowed by the Saskatchewan Court of Appeal. The acquittals were set aside, and a new trial was ordered for Brown and Kindrat. The appeal was not based on the racial composition of the jury, but rather on the judge's instruction to the jury.

Questions

1. How do you define race?
2. Should a jury be selected based on the "race" of the defendant? Or "race" of the victim?
3. How do you decide on race for multi-racial defendants/ victims?

Sources: Based on *R. v. Brown*, 2005 ONCJ 201, 2005 CarswellOnt 2379, Ontario Court of Justice, 2005.

Aboriginals living on reserves are not part of municipal assessment lists that can be used to identify possible jurors, in particular in Ontario. Thus, an Aboriginal defendant may not see an Aboriginal juror for his or her trial. Iacobucci made 17 recommendations to increase Aboriginal representation on juries, such as using health records databases and allowing those living on reserves to volunteer for jury duty.

Thus far, the government has successfully addressed the first recommendation and established an implementation committee and advisory group to report to the Attorney General. The Juries Review Implementation Committee is responsible for addressing the implementations outlined throughout Iacobucci's report and is composed of First Nation community leaders, elders, and chiefs, alongside criminal policy directors and lawyers. The Aboriginal Justice Advisory Group will provide the Attorney General with advice on Aboriginal justice issues. Ultimately, the goal of the advisory group is to act as an intermediary between the Attorney General and Aboriginal leaders and communities in addressing how the Ontario justice system impacts Aboriginal peoples. The advisory group is composed of multiple First Nations members, as well as law enforcement officials and legal professionals.

In addition, Ontario has also created a new leadership position at the Ministry of the Attorney General, namely, the Assistant Deputy Attorney General (ADAG), Aboriginal Justice. The Assistant Deputy will be responsible for the development of new programs and services to help support Aboriginal people in the justice system.

Impartiality

The juror characteristic of impartiality centres on three issues:

1. For a juror to be impartial, he or she must set aside any pre-existing biases, prejudices, or attitudes and judge the case based solely on the admissible evidence. For example, a juror must ignore that the defendant belongs to an ethnic group against which he or she holds a bias. An impartial juror will not let his or her prejudice cloud the evaluation of the evidence.

2. To be impartial also means that the juror must ignore any information that is not part of the admissible evidence. For example, prior to the start of a trial, a case may have received media attention highlighting facts about the defendant that are biased, irrelevant, or inadmissible.

3. It also is important that the juror have no connection to the defendant so that the juror does not view the evidence subjectively or unduly influence the other jurors. See Box 7.2 for a Canadian case dealing with juror partiality.

Karl Find was tried on 21 counts of sexual assault involving three different complainants all ranging between the ages of 6 and 12 at the time of the crime. Considering the nature of the crime, the defence counsel applied to challenge potential jurors for cause. (*Challenge for cause:* "a request that a prospective juror be dismissed

---

Box 7.2 Cases in Forensic Psychology

A Guilty Juror? *R. v. Guess* (1998)

Peter Gill and five others were tried in Vancouver for two gang-style murders in 1995. Gillian Guess was 1 of the 12 jurors hearing Peter Gill's case. During the trial, Guess and Gill ran into each other outside the courtroom; thereafter, they began to flirt in the courtroom. This flirtation led to a meeting outside the courtroom and escalated into a sexual relationship. Their relationship was ongoing as Guess continued to serve on the jury hearing Gill's case.

The jury, including Guess, found Peter Gill and the other defendants not guilty. When the court became aware of the relationship, both Guess and Gill were charged with obstruction of justice. Guess was found guilty and sentenced to 18 months in jail. She was the first juror in North America to be convicted of attempting to obstruct justice and ended up serving 3 months in prison. Peter Gill had been convicted of obstruction of justice in the past and was sentenced to 5 years and 10 months in prison. Justice Barry Davies of the Supreme Court of British Columbia noted,

"Mr. Gill pursued a deliberate and persistent attack upon one of society's most fundamental democratic institutions" (*R. v. Gill*, 2002, para. 29) by getting involved with Guess.

A new murder trial was ordered for Peter Gill and two other men. The appeal court noted that Guess's impartiality had been compromised and that it was hard to imagine a more remarkable violation of a juror's duty.

Questions

1. Can you be impartial if you have a relationship with the defendant?

2. What is an appropriate penalty for getting involved with the defendant as a juror?

3. Should the defendant be penalized for starting a relationship with a juror?

Sources: Based on *R. v. Guess* 2000 BCCA 547 by Court of Appeal for British Columbia, 1998.

because there is a specific and forceful reason to believe the person cannot be fair, unbiased or capable of serving as a juror"). The defense proposed that potential jurors be asked the following three questions:

1. Do you have strong feelings about the issue of rape and violence on young children?

2. If so, what are those feelings based on?

3. Would those strong feelings concerning the rape and violence on young children prevent you from giving Mr. Find a fair trial based solely on the evidence given during the trial of this case?

At trial, the judge dismissed the proposal stating the request does not concur with previous precedent rulings (see *R. v. Parks*, 1992). However, during the process of empanelling the jury, a potential juror and father of two unexpectedly stated: "I just don't think I could separate myself from my feeling towards them [his children] and separate the case". Upon stating this, the juror was peremptorily challenged and the defence once again renewed their proposal to challenge for cause. Once again, the trial judge dismissed the request and Find was ultimately tried and convicted of 17 of the 21 counts (*R. v. Find*, 2001).

Troy Gilbert Davey was convicted of first-degree murder after slashing a police officer's throat. Typically, the jury panel lists are disclosed to the Crown and defence 10 days before trial. However, in this case the panel lists were provided approximately three weeks before the trial. The defence counsel proceeded to show the lists to the appellant and the appellant's family, as well as the local referring solicitor. The Crown requested personal opinions from police officers from the local police force regarding each of the prospective jury members and their suitability. Police officers were asked to indicate whether they believed the juror would show any partiality to the Crown or the defence. The requests were made under the presupposition that officers would only comment based on prior knowledge about the potential jurors in the community and that they would not use police databases to run background checks. Each police officer was asked to make general comments about the potential juror such as "good," "yes," "ok," or "no," as well as any specific comments regarding the potential juror's relationship and role in the community.

Following his trial, Mr. Davey appealed his conviction and sought a new trial on the grounds that it was a miscarriage of justice for the Crown to compose a collection of opinions from the local police officers and not disclose this information to the defence. The court of appeal allowed fresh evidence for jury vetting, however the appeal was ultimately dismissed. It was concluded that:

1. There was no requirement for the information provided by local police officers to be disclosed.

2. The early release of the jury panel list had no impact on the fairness of the trial.

3. The privacy right of prospective juror was not breached, since the Crown merely asked the local police for opinions, not information contained on any database.

4. There would have been no change in the selected jury members had the comments made by police officers been disclosed (*R. v. Davey*, 2012).

Threats to Impartiality A number of threats to impartiality exist. For example, is it possible to forget the emotionally charged headlines that we read before going to jury duty? Typically, the media attention is negative for the defendant, and that could mean that the defendant does not receive a fair trial. Thus, the concern is that verdicts will be based on emotion and biased media coverage rather than on admissible evidence. Steblay, Besirevic, Fulero, and Jimenez-Lorente (1999) conducted a meta-analysis of 44 studies examining the effects of pretrial publicity. They found a modest positive relationship between exposure to negative pretrial publicity and judgments of guilt. This relation means that as exposure to negative pretrial publicity increases, so do the number of guilty verdicts. Recent research has also confirmed this. Ruva, Dickman, and Mayes (2014) found that when mock jurors were presented with only negative pre-trial publicity, there were more guilty verdicts and higher guilt ratings for the defendant.

In a recent study, Ruva and LeVasseur (2012) conducted a content analysis to examine mock-jury deliberations and whether pretrial publicity influences the content of the deliberations. Jurors who were given information that was anti-defendant (or negative pretrial publicity) were more likely to discuss unclear details in a way that supported the prosecution's case. Unfortunately, despite instructions to ignore the pretrial publicity, jurors discussed the information anyway.

Positive pretrial publicity also seems to have an impact on verdicts. In one study examining negative and positive pretrial publicity, Ruva and McEvoy (2008) had mock jurors read news clips with negative, positive, or unrelated pretrial publicity. Mock jurors watched a murder trial and rendered a verdict along with a number of other ratings. Pretrial publicity, whether positive or negative, influenced the verdict, as well as perceptions of the defendant and attorneys. Positive information biased jurors positively toward the defendant (e.g., fewer guilty verdicts), and negative information biased jurors negatively against the defendant (e.g., more guilty verdicts). It should be noted that positive pretrial publicity is relatively rare in real-life cases.

Using methodology similar to the above study, Ruva, Guenther, and Yarbrough (2011) had mock jurors read news articles that contained negative pretrial publicity, positive pretrial publicity, or unrelated articles that acted as the control condition. After a week, the mock jurors returned and watched a videotaped murder trial. Regardless of the type of pretrial publicity, verdicts were significantly influenced by these news articles. It seems that any pretrial publicity, whether positive or negative, can influence juror decision making.

Keeping Potential Jurors Impartial Before a case goes to trial, a preliminary hearing occurs in which the Crown presents the evidence against the defendant. The judge then determines whether there is sufficient evidence for the case to proceed to trial. In Canada, at the preliminary hearing, the judge typically places a ban on the media's reporting of the evidence before the end of the trial process. If the details of the case can be kept from the public, this decreases the likelihood of potential jurors being exposed to information that may compromise their ability to remain impartial. Moreover, this increases the likelihood of jurors using only the evidence presented during the trial to reach their verdict.

Unfortunately, details do get leaked, especially in high-profile cases involving child victims or violent offences. For example, details about numerous missing women from Vancouver found buried on Robert Pickton's farm in Port Coquitlam made headlines across Canada before Pickton's case was heard (e.g., Saunders & Thompson, 2002). What are the legal options when the defence or Crown fears a partial or biased jury pool?

Some methods for increasing the likelihood of an impartial jury are as follows:

1. The Crown or defence may argue that the trial should be moved to another community because it would be very difficult to obtain an impartial jury from the local community. This option is called a **change of venue** and is found in section 599(1) of the Criminal Code (R.S.C., 1985, C-46, s. 599). The party raising the issue must demonstrate that there is a reasonable likelihood that the local community is biased or prejudiced against the defendant. Factors that may lead to a biased community include extensive pretrial publicity, a heinous crime, and a small community in which many people know the victim and/or the defendant (Granger, 1996).

   Change of venue: Moving a trial to a community other than the one in which the crime occurred

   A change of venue is not granted very often, but when it is, the trial typically stays within the province or territory in which the crime occurred. An example was the trial of Kelly Ellard, a teen charged with the murder of 14-year-old Reena Virk in a suburb of Victoria, B.C. Adrian Brooks, the defence lawyer, successfully argued to move the trial from Victoria to Vancouver. Brooks claimed that the media attention the case received would prohibit Ellard from getting a fair trial in Victoria (Meissner, 2000).

2. An alternative to moving a trial to a new community is to allow sufficient time to pass so that the biasing effect of any pretrial prejudicial information has dissipated by the time the trial takes place. Thus, the judge may call for an **adjournment**, delaying the trial until sometime in the future. A major limitation to adjourning cases is that not only can prospective jurors' memories fade, but witnesses' can as well. Witnesses may forget critical details that they are to testify about. Also, witnesses move or die. Consequently, courts infrequently call for an adjournment.

   Adjournment: Delaying the trial until sometime in the future

3. Another option that may be granted in cases for which bias is suspected among the prospective jury pool is known as a **challenge for cause**. The Crown or defence may argue that, although the prospective jury pool may be partial, if questioned, these prospective jurors could be identified and rejected from serving on the jury. As with the change of venue, the side desiring the judge to allow a challenge for cause must demonstrate that there is reasonable partiality in the community from which the jury pool will be drawn. If the judge grants a challenge for cause, prospective jurors can be probed with a set of predetermined questions approved by the judge. The questions are relatively few (perhaps five or so) and only the prospective jurors' state of mind or thinking can be examined. Lawyers are not allowed to ask prospective jurors about their backgrounds or personalities. See Box 7.3 for two cases where a challenge for cause was granted.

   Challenge for cause: An option to reject biased jurors

Box 7.3   Forensic Psychology in the Spotlight

Cases Allowing a Challenge for Cause

Questions Focused on Racial Bias Ruled Appropriate

In *R. v. McLeod* (2005), two black men of Jamaican origin, Germaine McLeod and Christopher Chung, were charged with murdering a man of Asian descent. The Crown's theory was that all three men were involved in drug trafficking or other illegal activities and that the deceased was killed because he was believed to be a police informant.

The following questions were allowed to be posed to the prospective jurors:

1. Do you believe that black Jamaican men, as a group, are more likely to be violent than other persons generally?

2. Would your ability to judge the evidence in this case without bias, prejudice, or partiality be affected by the fact that the accused persons are black Jamaican men, and the deceased was Asian?

As is the practice in the province of Alberta, where this trial occurred, the trial judge, Judge Slatter, was responsible for posing the questions to the prospective jurors.

Seating a Jury for the Pig Farmer Trial: A Challenge for Cause Granted in Part Because of Intense Pretrial Publicity

Robert Pickton, a pig farmer from Port Coquitlam, B.C., was charged with the first-degree murder of 26 women. The charges were divided into two trials to facilitate the hearing of testimony and evidence. Pickton's first trial focused on six counts of murder. A challenge for cause was declared.

The jury selection occurred in December 2006, with Judge Williams questioning potential jurors. Jury selection started with 600 prospective jurors to find 12 jurors and 2 alternates. Once a trial begins, alternate jurors cannot replace jurors and the alternates are dismissed. In December 2007, the jury found Picton guilty of six counts of second-degree murder. He was sentenced to life in prison with no chance of parole for 25 years. The Crown has decided not to pursue prosecution of the remaining murders. In 2009, Picton made an appeal to the Supreme Court of Canada. On July 30, 2010, Picton's appeal was dismissed and his convictions remained.

Sources: Based on Hunter & Baron, 2006; CBC News, 2007, August 28; Skelton, C. (2010, August 5). Crown drops 20 murder charges against Picton. *Times Colonist.* Retrieved from http://www.timescolonist.com/news/Crown +drops+murder+charges+against+Picton/3362068/story.html.

A challenge for cause changes how the jury is selected. This process is unique to Canada (Granger, 1996). First, two individuals are selected from the jury pool and are sworn to act as triers. A third person is selected as a prospective juror. The lawyers or judge question the prospective juror, while the two triers listen to the answers provided. The triers then discuss the answers with each other to reach a unanimous decision as to whether the prospective juror is impartial.

- If the triers decide that the prospective juror is not impartial, the prospective juror is dismissed, another person is selected to be a prospective juror, and the process begins again.

- If the triers decide that the prospective juror is impartial, then that person becomes the first member of the jury (unless the Crown or defence uses a peremptory challenge) and replaces one of the triers. This first juror acts as a trier for a second juror. Thus, jurors 1 and 2 will act as triers for juror 3, jurors 2 and 3 will act as triers for juror 4, and so on, until 12 jurors are selected.

When trying to evaluate whether a challenge for cause is useful for identifying biased individuals, a number of issues need to be considered:

1. The process may be conducted in open court, where the jury pool can hear the questions the lawyers ask and the responses provided. Moreover, they can hear the answers that lead to a positive or negative decision from the triers. Thus, it is possible for prospective jurors to alter their answers according to whether they want to serve on the jury.

2. Prospective jurors may find it difficult to be honest when answering questions about bias that may put them in an unflattering light, especially if the questioning is conducted in open court.

3. Prospective jurors must be aware of their biases and how their biases may influence their behaviour. Some classic work by Nisbett and Wilson (1977) suggested that individuals are unaware of their biases and how their biases affect their behaviour.

JURY FUNCTIONS

The main legal function of a jury is to apply the law, as provided by the judge, to the admissible evidence in the case and to render a verdict of guilt or innocence. In addition to the main legal function of juries, four other jury functions have been identified:

1. To use the wisdom of 12 (rather than the wisdom of 1) to reach a verdict
2. To act as the conscience of the community
3. To protect against out-of-date laws
4. To increase knowledge about the justice system

Ignoring the Law

While the jury has a responsibility to apply the law as defined by the judge to the admissible evidence and to render a verdict, there are cases in which the jury will ignore that law and the evidence, and render a verdict based on some other criteria. This is known as **jury nullification**. Juries may choose to ignore the law for a number of reasons. For example, they may believe the law is unfair given the circumstances of the case, or the punishment accompanying a conviction is too harsh for the crime. In both these instances, jury nullification may result. Jury nullification typically can occur when the case involves controversial issues, such as abortion and euthanasia (see Box 7.4).

If juries are allowed to ignore the law and vote with their conscience, won't we end up with a biased or random system? **Chaos theory** predicts that when jurors are guided by their emotions and personal biases rather than by the law, chaos in judgments results (Horowitz, Kerr, Park, & Gockel, 2006). Meissner, Brigham, and Pfeifer (2003) examined the influence of a jury nullification instruction in a euthanasia case. Mock jurors were more likely to find the defendant not guilty with a nullification instruction when the jurors had a positive attitude toward euthanasia.

Jury nullification: Occurs when a jury ignores the law and the evidence, rendering a verdict based on some other criteria

Chaos theory: The theory that when jurors are guided by their emotions and personal biases rather than by the law, chaos in judgments results

Box 7.4   Forensic Psychology in the Spotlight

Two Cases of Jury Nullification

Dr. Henry Morgentaler: Baby Killer or Champion of Women's Rights?

Dr. Henry Morgentaler performed his first abortion, secretly, in 1968. He began performing illegal abortions openly in Montreal in 1969, and in 1970 he was arrested for performing an abortion. Intriguingly, the arrest occurred three years before the U.S. Supreme Court landmark case of *Roe v. Wade* (1973), which made abortion a constitutional right for American women.

A Quebec jury of 11 men and 1 woman found Dr. Morgentaler not guilty. The verdict was appealed and overturned in 1974. Dr. Morgentaler was sentenced to prison. When he was released, he continued performing illegal abortions. In two more trials, juries returned not guilty verdicts. In 1975, a significant change to Quebec law occurred in which a jury verdict could no longer be overturned on appeal, known as the Morgentaler Amendment. Furthermore, in 1976, the Quebec government announced it would no longer prosecute abortion cases.

In 1983, while performing abortions in Ontario, Dr. Morgentaler and two colleagues were charged with performing illegal miscarriages. The jury found them not guilty. The Ontario Court of Appeal then reversed this verdict.

Clearly, the voice of the community, via the jury, was incongruent with the law. Change in legislation occurred in 1988 when the Supreme Court of Canada ruled that Canadian women have the right to a safe abortion. More than 100 000 abortions are performed in Canada each year.

Robert Latimer: A Loving Father?

Tracy Latimer lived with her family in Wilkie, Saskatchewan. She had severe cerebral palsy, was quadriplegic, and could communicate only by means of facial expression, laughter, and crying. It was estimated that she had the mental capacity of a 4-month-old baby. Tracy had five to six seizures a day and it was believed that she was in constant pain. She also underwent several surgeries. Another surgery was scheduled for Tracy when she was 12 years old.

Robert Latimer, Tracy's father, felt that this surgery would be a mutilation and could no longer live with seeing his daughter suffer. He decided that he would end his daughter's life. In 1993, he connected a hose to his pickup truck's exhaust pipe, put the hose into the truck's cab, and seated Tracy in the running truck. Tracy died from carbon monoxide inhalation. At first, Latimer claimed that Tracy had passed away in her sleep, but he later confessed to taking Tracy's life. The jury found Robert Latimer guilty of second-degree murder.

Second-degree murder carries a life sentence without eligibility for parole for a minimum of 10 years and up to 25 years. Juries are allowed to make sentencing recommendations in this situation. The jury sent the judge a note asking if they could recommend less than 10 years. The judge explained the mandatory minimum recommendation as outlined in the Criminal Code; however, they could make any recommendation they liked. The jury recommended one year before parole eligibility.

The judge granted a constitutional exemption from the mandatory minimum and sentenced Robert Latimer to one year in prison and one year of probation. In keeping with the law, however, the Court of Appeal upheld the conviction but changed the sentence to life imprisonment with eligibility for parole in ten years. Once again, the law was inconsistent with the community's sentiment, which was expressed by the jury.

Sources: Based on O'Malley & Wood, *R. v. Morgentaler, R. v. Latimer*, By Court of Appeal for British Columbia. 2003, 1988, 2001.

Intriguingly, when jurors were given a standard jury instruction, they reported referring to the legal aspects of the case to make their decisions. However, when they were given a nullification instruction, they reported that they relied on their attitudes toward euthanasia and their perceptions of the defendant's behaviour. Overall, nullification instructions may influence jury decision making, "producing both socially favourable (e.g., sympathetic) and socially unfavorable (e.g., prejudical) verdicts" (Meissner, Brigham, & Pfeifer, 2003, p. 253).

Kerr and colleagues (2008) examined the influence of nullification instructions and emotional biases. The case was a euthanasia case where the victim was either sympathetic or unsympathetic and three different judicial instructions were included (standard vs. nullification vs. nullification-plus). Similar to previous research, those who heard the nullification or nullification-plus instructions were more sensitive to emotionally biasing information compared to when only standard judicial instructions were given. Emotional biases influenced verdicts, providing support for chaos theory.

HOW DO WE STUDY JUROR AND JURY BEHAVIOUR?

Now that we know how juries are selected, and what their characteristics and responsibilities are, we can start understanding and predicting their behaviour. Many researchers in the forensic area have focused their careers on trying to predict verdicts and on the variables that affect verdicts. We will now discuss four methodologies that have been used to gain understanding of juror and jury behaviour.

Post-trial Interviews

In trying to understand why juries reached particular verdicts, perhaps it seems most logical and simple to ask the jurors themselves why they reached the verdicts they did. In Canada, however, actual jurors are not allowed to discuss what occurred in deliberations. All discourse that occurs during the deliberations is confidential. Breaking this confidentiality is a violation of section 649 of the Criminal Code (R.S.C., 1985, C-46, s. 649). A juror who discusses any part of the deliberation process would be committing a summary offence that carries a fine of up to $2000 and/ or imprisonment for up to six months. Although researchers cannot talk to Canadian jurors regarding their deliberations, they can turn to the United States or other countries that do not have this rule.

The main strength of post-trial interviews is high external validity; that is, results come from using real cases and the actual jurors who deliberated. Consequently, results may be more likely to apply to the real world. This methodology, however, also has a number of weaknesses. First, jurors' accounts may not be reliable. For example, jurors may recall details inaccurately, they may forget critical aspects of the deliberation, they may embellish or downplay elements to present themselves more favourably, or they may be unaware of the reasons for their decisions and behaviour. Thus, conclusions may be based on data that are unreliable. Second, a cause-and-effect relationship cannot be established with this type of methodology. At best, researchers can talk about variables that occur together. Alternative hypotheses cannot be ruled out with this methodology.

Archives

Records of trials, such as transcripts and police interviews of witnesses, can be reviewed to uncover relationships among variables. The strength of this methodology is similar to post-trial interviews in that external validity is high. A similar weakness, however, is the inability to establish cause-and-effect relationships. Also, the researcher is restricted to the data available in that the types of questions that can be posed are limited by the information that can be accessed. The researcher is unable to go back and collect more information. Furthermore, the researcher is unaware of how the information was collected and the reliability of that information. For example, police interviews may have been conducted using biased procedures.

Simulation

One of the most common methodologies used to investigate jury issues is simulation. Researchers simulate a trial, or aspects of it, by using a written, audio, or video format. Participants are presented with the trial information, and the researcher can vary and manipulate this trial information. Examples of possible independent variables of interest include the age of the witness or the race of the defendant. Following the presentation of the trial, participants are asked to respond individually (juror research) or in groups (jury research). Typically, jurors and juries will be asked to render a verdict or make other judgments. Verdicts and other participants' responses can be compared to determine whether the independent variable(s) had an effect.

One of the major strengths of this methodology is its high internal validity; that is, researchers can reveal cause-and-effect relationships because they systematically manipulated the independent variables. However, the control the researchers have over the independent variables limits the external validity of this methodology. For example, in simulations, cases are not real and there are no consequences to the verdicts or decisions the jurors render. Furthermore, the participants typically are university students, who may not be representative of real jury pools. These factors limit the generalizability of the results obtained with simulations.

Participants deliberate a mock trial.
Joanna Pozzulo

Field Studies

This methodology involves using actual jurors while they are serving on jury duty, so cooperation from the courts and the jurors is required. Researchers are able to observe variables of interest as they are occurring. For example, they may be interested in how prospective jurors respond to questions posed during the *voir dire* (i.e., preliminary examination of the jurors before they are assigned to the case). Alternatively, researchers may be able to introduce variables that they want to examine. The court may agree to let jurors take notes while the evidence is being presented, for example. Trials in which jurors were allowed to take notes can be compared with trials in which jurors were not allowed to take notes. A comparison of the verdicts can be undertaken across these cases.

The strength of field studies is high external validity. A number of limitations, however, are also present. For example, receiving approval from the courts for conducting the research may be difficult. Even when approval is granted, it is likely that only a small sample of participants will be available, and appropriate comparison groups may be too difficult to identify. Additionally, there are a host of confounding variables that the researcher may not be able to control, such as the gender of lawyers and witnesses.

As you can see, the researcher interested in juror/jury issues has a variety of methodologies to choose from. Each methodology has some strengths and weaknesses. By using all these methodologies, we may be able to gain a more accurate understanding of juror and jury behaviour. Before we start discussing the research as it relates to jurors and juries, there are a number of myths, some of which you may hold, that are not supported by research. See Box 7.5 for a list of myths and what the research actually says.

Box 7.5   Myths and Realities

Jurors and Juries

Myth 1. Jurors can disregard evidence or information when instructed to by the judge.

Fact. Research has demonstrated that instructing jurors to disregard certain information does not motivate them to do so. For example, when inadmissible evidence is introduced, and the judge declares to the jury to disregard the information, jurors' decisions are still impacted by the inadmissible evidence even though they were instructed to disregard it (Steblay, Hosch, Culhane, & McWethy, 2006).

Myth 2. Jurors fully comprehend judicial instructions.

Fact. Many jurors believe that they fully comprehend judicial instructions given by the judge; however, the number of jurors that actually do comprehend the instructions is much lower (Ogloff & Rose, 2005).

Myth 3. Expert witnesses are unnecessary as most information is common sense (e.g., factors that influence eyewitness identification).

Fact. Research utilizing questionnaires has found potential jurors are relatively insensitive to certain factors that are believed to be "common sense" (Houston, Hope, Memon, & Read, 2013).

Myth 4. Jurors are not influenced by their own personal biases in their decision making.

Fact. Certain biases have been shown to differentially influence juror decision making when ideally they should not. For example, personally held racial biases have been shown

to influence both verdict decisions as well as sentence length (Mitchell, Haw, Pfeifer, & Meissner, 2005).

Myth 5. There are no differences between male and female jurors in their decision making.

Fact. Depending on case type, especially those involving child witness/victims, female jurors have been found to be more empathic towards the witness and believe the witness more than male jurors (Bottoms et al., 2014).

Myth 6. Jurors can tell the difference between accurate and inaccurate eyewitnesses.

Fact. Research has shown that jurors have a hard time distinguishing between accurate and inaccurate eyewitnesses (Lindsay, Wells, & O'Connor, 1989).

Myth 7. Jurors believe forensic testing is always 100% accurate in connecting the alleged perpetrator to the crime.

Fact. The potential exists for there to be a mismatch when examining forensic evidence; furthermore, there could be an error in reporting. Both of these scenarios would lead to an inaccurate connection between the alleged perpetrator and the crime (National Research Council, 2009).

Myth 8. A trial participant's personal appearance never influences juror decision making.

Fact. In certain types of cases, a victim's physical attractiveness can be influential in jurors' decisions (Maeder, Yamamoto, & Saliba, 2014).

(continued)

Myth 9. Physical evidence is always present at a crime scene.

Fact. Because of televised crime shows, attorneys now have to explain to jurors that physical evidence is not always available at a crime scene; moreover, they have to explain why physical evidence was not at the crime scene more often than they did before these shows were on the air (Call, Cook, Reitzel, & McDougle, 2013).

Myth 10. Jurors are not influenced by any pre-trial media concerning the case when rendering their verdicts.

Fact. Research has reliably found that when the case is high-profile, and there is a lot of media coverage concerning the defendant and/or case, this information influences their decisions regarding the defendant (Ruva, McEvoy, & Bryant, 2007).

REACHING A VERDICT

Once a jury has been selected, its work begins. Jurors must listen to the admissible evidence and disregard any evidence that the judge does not allow. Once the lawyers deliver their closing arguments, the judge provides the jurors with the law that they must apply to the evidence in order to reach a verdict. The jury then makes its **deliberation**—that is, the jurors discuss the evidence privately among themselves to reach a verdict, which is then provided to the court. We will discuss each stage involved in reaching a jury verdict and the factors that may affect each stage.

Deliberation: When jury members discuss the evidence privately among themselves to reach a verdict that is then provided to the court

Listening to the Evidence

Two innovations have been proposed as aids for jurors while they listen to the evidence: note-taking and asking questions. Advantages and disadvantages have been identified for each aid. We will discuss each aid in turn, including the identified advantages and disadvantages, and the Canadian justice system's position on the aid.

Note-Taking Trials can be lengthy and complex, resulting in missed or forgotten evidence by the time the jury is asked to deliberate. Some have suggested that allowing jurors to take notes may facilitate memory and understanding of the evidence (e.g., Heuer & Penrod, 1994). Moreover, note-takers may be more attentive during the trial than those who do not take notes. Not everyone is in agreement, however, that allowing jurors to take notes is advantageous or even preferable. For example, in the Canadian case of *R. v. Andrade* (1985), a number of disadvantages to juror note-taking were identified:

■ Jurors who take notes may exert influence while in deliberation over those who do not.

■ If disagreements occur about the evidence, jurors will rely on those who took notes to clarify the issue.

A review of the research examining juror note-taking was conducted by Penrod and Heuer (1997). They reached the following conclusions regarding juror note-taking:

- Jurors' notes serve as a memory aid.
- Jurors do not overemphasize the evidence that they have noted at the expense of evidence they have not recorded.
- Notes do not produce a distorted view of the case.
- Note-takers can keep up with the evidence as it is being presented.
- Note-takers do not distract jurors who do not take notes.
- Note-takers do not have an undue influence over those who do not take notes.
- Jurors' notes are an accurate record of the trial.
- Juror note-taking does not favour either the prosecution/Crown or the defence.

As you can see, allowing jurors to take notes does not appear to pose major difficulties. Thorley, Baxter, and Lorek (2015) also concluded that note-taking does not have a significant, negative impact on a juror's memory of the evidence.

At present in Canada, the trial judge in each case decides whether jurors will be allowed to take notes (Ogloff & Rose, 2005).

Asking Questions When watching trials on television, or if you have ever had the opportunity to listen to a trial in court, you may have found yourself wondering about a detail that was mentioned. Would it not help if you could stop the trial and ask a question? The courts have considered the issue of jurors being allowed to ask questions. Heurer and Penrod (1994) reported that typically juries have few questions (usually not more than three), and the questions tend to be concerned with the meaning of key legal terms, such as *reasonable doubt*. In a review of the research examining juror questions, Penrod and Heuer (1997) reached the following conclusions:

- Jury questioning promotes juror understanding of the facts and the issues.
- Juror questions do not clearly help to get to the truth.
- Juror questions do not increase the jurors', judges', or lawyers' satisfaction with the trial and verdict.
- Jurors ask legally appropriate questions.
- If counsel objects, and the objection is sustained, the jury does not draw inappropriate inferences from unanswered questions.
- Jurors do not become advocates.

Thus, the research on allowing jurors to ask questions does not appear to indicate that jurors' questions are particularly harmful or helpful. At present in Canada, jurors may submit their questions in writing to the judge after the lawyers have completed their questioning of the witness. The judge then determines whether the question is permissible. Questions that are permissible then are posed by the judge. Ultimately, allowing jurors to ask questions is up to the judge presiding over the trial.

Does the relatively recent influx of forensic science television programming increase jurors' quest for scientific evidence? Shows such as *CSI: Crime Scene Investigation* and its two spinoffs, *CSI: Miami* and *CSI: NY*, "educate" potential jurors on the latest scientific evidence. Do the shows raise the bar too high? Do they influence the jury pool? See the In the Media box for a discussion of the "*CSI* effect."

Disregarding Inadmissible Evidence

Are jurors able to "forget" what they heard? This question is relevant not only when we consider pretrial publicity, but also when judges request that jurors disregard inadmissible evidence introduced at trial. Often, juries will hear inadmissible evidence when lawyers or witnesses make statements that are not allowed according to legal procedure. Following an inadmissible statement or inadmissible evidence, the judge will instruct the jury to disregard it. The critical component to a fair trial and a just verdict is that the jury uses only admissible statements and evidence. But are jurors able to disregard evidence they have heard?

In the Media

The *CSI* Effect

Do you watch any of the *CSI* shows? If you do, you are not alone. Approximately 60 million people each week watch these programs. The *CSI* shows typically start with a crime, some evidence is collected, high-tech analysis is undertaken, and the crime is solved, all in about 60 minutes. If only real life happened like this. Unfortunately, the more we watch these shows, the more we believe that they demonstrate how our justice system should work, and we may even begin to think that our justice system has failed if it does not mimic what we see on television.

The "*CSI* effect" can be described as the education of jurors whereby they are more likely to convict a suspect if the procedures and techniques from television are used in real life. Their mode of thinking may go something like this, for example: "Why wasn't DNA collected? Is it a match? You can't beat DNA." The *CSI* effect is viewed as the infallibility of forensic science as a function of seeing it on television. This phenomenon has been around for about ten years, since shortly after the first *CSI* installment aired on television.

Are you a product of the *CSI* effect? You need not be a juror to be influenced by these television shows. Universities in the United States report a dramatic increase in forensic science–type undergraduate and graduate programs. A similar pattern can be seen in Canadian universities. For example, the Criminology and Criminal Justice program at Carleton University is one of the largest undergraduate programs at the school. The number of Canadian schools offering forensic psychology courses has also spiked; you may be reading this as part of one of these very courses.

Jurors who have watched these programs may rely on what they have seen on television to evaluate the evidence presented in real-life court. Jeffrey Heinrick (2006) reported on a number of cases where real-life investigation did not live up to the *CSI* shows.

For example, a man from Illinois accused of trying to kill his ex-girlfriend was found not guilty by the jury, reportedly because the police did not test the bloodstained sheets for DNA. After the man was released from jail, he stabbed his ex-girlfriend to death. A jury also found a man from Phoenix not guilty because his bloodstained coat was not tested for DNA. Thanks to the *CSI* effect, jurors now require expensive and sometimes unnecessary DNA tests, gun residue tests, and handwriting analyses, for example. Jurors also may not understand that some lab tests may take months and even years to complete.

Some argue that the *CSI* effect has a negative impact on the justice system, while others argue that it makes

(continued)

(continued)

jurors more informed about what it takes to find someone guilty. Prosecutors argue that it raises the bar unfairly, making the case easier for the defence. What do you think?

A group of Canadian researchers from St. Mary's University, Drs. Smith, Patry, and Stinson (2008) found evidence that crime dramas do indeed influence perceptions of forensic science and, in turn, of what lawyers do in the courtroom. Kim, Barak, and Shelton (2009) found that watching *CSI* shows did not influence jurors' verdicts independently. The *CSI* effect was found to have an indirect influence on conviction in circumstantial cases where it raised expectations about scientific evidence.

In another recent study trying to assess the *CSI* effect, Hayes-Smith and Levett (2011) had individuals who reported for actual jury duty read a trial summary that contained either high, low, or no forensic evidence. These individuals had to render a verdict, rate the evidence, and describe their crime show–watching habits. The researchers found an interaction between amount of forensic evidence and viewing habits. Specifically, individuals who watched crime shows were more inclined to be pro-defence than those who did not watch, but this was the case in only some of the forensic evidence conditions. Consistent with this is the finding by Mancini (2011), who reported that mock jurors who watched a lot of crime show television were more likely to be dissatisfied with

pro-prosecution scientific evidence and needed a higher degree of certainty in finding guilt. Recently, Maeder and Corbett (2015) reported that those who perceive crime television as more realistic rated DNA evidence as more influential compared to those who perceived crime television to be less real. Frequency of watching crime television was also examined, and Maeder and Corbett (2015) reported that those who watched crime television more frequently were more likely to rate the defence's eyewitness as less influential. Moreover, those who perceived crime television to be realistic were more likely to have more positive attitudes towards both DNA evidence as well as eyewitness evidence.

Overall, crime show viewing may influence juror decision making but also may interact with other variables and evidence to exert its influence on verdicts. The jury still seems to be out on whether and how crime shows influence the justice system. With no shortage of crime drama on television, further research is needed in this area.

Sources: Based on Heinrick, J. (Fall, 2006). Everyone's an expert: The CSI effect's negative impact on juries. The Triple Helix. Arizona State University; Smith, S.M., Patry, M., & Stinson, V. (2008). Is the CSI effect real? If it is, what is it? In G. Bourgon, R.K. Hanson, J.D. Pozzulo, K.E. Morton Bourgon, & C.L. Tanasichuk (Eds.), Proceedings of the 2007 North American Correctional & Criminal Justice Psychology Conference (User Report). Ottawa, ON: Public Safety Canada.

Kassin and Sommers (1997) argued that whether jurors will follow a judge's instruction to disregard inadmissible evidence is related to the reason for the instruction rather than to the instruction itself. In their study, mock jurors were presented with a murder trial, and a piece of evidence was manipulated. Jurors in the control condition received only circumstantial and ambiguous evidence. In the experimental conditions, an audiotaped telephone conversation in which the defendant confessed to the murder was included. When this audiotape was admitted into evidence, the defence lawyer objected. The judge either overruled the objection, allowing it into evidence, or sustained the objection and asked jurors to disregard it because it was either illegally obtained or difficult to comprehend. When jurors were asked to disregard the evidence because it was illegally collected, their verdicts were similar to those of the jurors who received the ruling that the tape was admissible, suggesting that they had considered the evidence rather than disregarding it. In contrast, when jurors were instructed to disregard the tape because of comprehension difficulty, they rendered verdicts similar to those of the control jurors who had not heard about the inadmissible evidence, suggesting that they had disregarded it. Thus, Kassin and Sommers concluded that jurors will disregard evidence when they are provided with a logical and legitimate reason for the judge's decision to disregard it.

One other interesting result has been found with the instruction to disregard. Some researchers have found that a judge's instruction to disregard evidence simply makes the evidence more memorable than if no instruction were given, which is known as the *backfire effect* (Paglia & Schuller, 1998). Thus, jurors are more likely to pay attention to inadmissible evidence following a disregard instruction than if no instruction was provided. Similarly, Pickel, Karam, and Warner (2009) found that if the inadmissible evidence was memorable, it was harder for the jury to ignore. In a recent review, Daftary-Kapur, Dumas, and Penrod (2010) reported that at this point it is unclear how to remove the cognitive influences associated with inadmissible evidence.

Overall, the influence of the disregard instruction is not straightforward. Other factors come into play and interact with the effect of the instruction.

Judge's Instructions

A number of studies have examined jurors' abilities to understand the legally dense instructions that the judge charges the jury with prior to its deliberation. The results of these studies generally are not positive. Lieberman and Sales (1997) concluded that jurors do not remember, understand, or accurately apply judges' instructions. Rose, Chopra, and Ogloff (2001) conducted semi-structured interviews of those who served on criminal juries. Rose et al. (2001) concluded that juror comprehension of judicial instructions was very low. Bornstein and Greene (2011) report that it is not uncommon to find levels of juror comprehension of judicial instructions at less than 50% as jurors' comprehension for instructions is generally poor.

Four reforms for judges' instructions have been proposed: (1) rewriting instructions, (2) providing a written copy of the instructions to jurors, (3) providing jurors with pre- and post-evidence instructions, and (4) having lawyers clarify legal instruction during their presentation to the jury. However, these reforms do not necessarily significantly increase comprehension. These four proposed reforms have not been implemented with any consistency within the Canadian justice system.

Jury Decision-Making Models

How do jurors combine the trial evidence to reach a verdict? Moreover, what is the process by which verdicts are reached? Although a number of models of juror/jury decision making have been proposed, they may be categorized as using either a mathematical or an explanation-based approach.

Mathematical Models The common theme with mathematical models is that they view jurors as conducting a set of mental calculations regarding the importance and strength of each piece of evidence (Groscup & Tallon, 2009; Hastie, 1993). A guilty or not guilty verdict is determined by the outcome of the calculations for all the relevant evidence. For example, an eyewitness who identified the defendant may be perceived as strong evidence and be weighed heavily toward a guilty verdict; however, learning that the DNA found at the crime scene does not match the defendant's decreases the likelihood of a guilty verdict. The verdict is a function of the calculation of all the relevant evidence.

A jury listens to evidence.
Image Source/Getty Images

Ellsworth and Mauro (1998) examined the congruency of mental calculations and how jurors perceive their process of reaching a verdict. They found that a mathematical approach was inconsistent with how jurors report that they reach verdicts. Jurors do not appear to provide a value for each piece of evidence presented. Moreover, it may be difficult to partition evidence into discrete pieces that can then be assigned a value. Winter and Greene (2007) discuss how mathematically based models of juror decision making receive little empirical work as research has demonstrated that jurors do not necessarily update their prior beliefs in light of new evidence; moreover, Winter and Greene (2007) conclude by stating that research has shown that jurors' behavior does not conform to principles of probability. Perhaps an explanation-based approach is more consistent with how jurors process the trial evidence.

Explanation Models In contrast to mathematical models, explanation models suggest that evidence is organized into a coherent whole. Pennington and Hastie's (1986) explanation approach is called the *story model.* They proposed that jurors are active at understanding and processing the evidence. Jurors interpret and elaborate on the evidence and make causal connections, and in doing so, they create a story structure. These "stories" are then compared with each verdict option presented by the judge. The verdict option most consistent with the story is the verdict reached.

Of course, jurors listening to the same evidence may construct different stories that are consistent with alternative verdicts. That is to say, individual differences can influence the story-construction process. Jurors bring in their personal experiences, knowledge, beliefs, and attitudes when constructing their stories. Thus, jurors may reach different decisions after hearing the same evidence.

To test the story model, Pennington and Hastie (1986) had 26 participants watch a simulated murder trial and then make individual verdicts at the end of the trial. Following their verdicts, participants were interviewed to determine how they thought about the evidence. The researchers found that participants put the evidence into a story format and different stories were related to different verdicts.

Devine (2012) discusses three criteria for evaluating stories: coverage, coherence, and uniqueness. A lot of evidence is often presented at trial—coverage refers to the extent to which a story can account for all of the evidence. Coherence refers to the logical resilience of the story and comprises three components: (1) consistency, (2) completeness, and (3) plausibility. The story must be consistent such that there is no contradiction within the jurors' story, the story must be complete such that there are no gaps within the story, and the story must be plausible such that it must match the jurors' understanding of how the world works. The uniqueness of the story determines the confidence the juror has in a given story; Devine (2012) states that if only one story structure can account for the evidence, the jurors' confidence in that story is higher than if there are multiple stories that can account for the evidence.

Devine (2012) proposed an integrative, multi-level, decision-making model that incorporates two levels: juror decision making and jury decision making. The decision making on the individual juror level is referred to as the *Director's Cut Model* and proposes that the jurors use the evidence presented at trial to form a narrative. Many factors can affect each jurors' narrative such as case type, juror and defendant characteristics, pre-existing schemas, opening statements, the evidence presented throughout the trial by the prosecution, and the alternative explanations provided by the defense. Jurors then construct their own models of the evidence to test the overall story likelihood. Devine (2012) discusses that at the end of trial, jurors will be in one of four cognitive states: (1) a believer (i.e., favouring the prosecution), (2) a doubter (i.e., favouring the defense), (3) a muller (i.e., trying to choose between two or more plausible stories), or (4) a puzzler (i.e., unable to formulate a story).

The director's cut model precedes what Devine (2012) coins the *Story Sampling Model*, which is the larger jury deliberation model. This is when the jurors share their stories of the information with the other jurors. There are two fundamental premises of the story sampling model. The first is that individual differences relevant to deliberation, including extraversion, gender, socioeconomic status, and need for cognition, will influence who participates and how much each juror says (Devine, 2012). The second is the structure of spoken juror contributions. Deliberation offers a sharing of information or a sampling of the different stories each juror has constructed. Final jury decisions occur from informational influences that arise from the content of discussion, factual assertions, and shared stories, whereas normative influences arise from the perceptions of factions within the jury. Typically, when large factions are observed, they usually succeed with a verdict in that direction (Devine, 2012).

Deliberations

As you may recall, a 12-person jury is necessary for criminal cases in Canada. However, cases can continue with fewer jurors as long as no more than 2 members are excused, possibly for illness or other reasons, during the trial (Granger, 1996).

For example, in the 2003 murder trial of Matti Baranovski in Toronto, an 11-person jury convicted Lee Cochrane and Meir Mariani of manslaughter.

Once all the evidence has been heard and the judge has delivered instructions to the jurors, the jury retires to a secluded room to deliberate. In Canada, the jury is sequestered until the final verdict is reached—then, the jury is dismissed by the judge (Granger, 1996). This means that the jurors are not allowed to talk to anyone outside their 12-person panel, with the exception of the court-appointed officer in the event that they have a request or question.

The expectation from the justice system is that the jury reviews the evidence and determines the most consistent match between the verdict options that were provided by the judge and the admissible evidence. A number of factors can influence a juror's position on the case. A phenomenon known as **polarization** occurs when individuals tend to become more extreme in their initial position following a group discussion (Baron & Bryne, 1991). In contrast, a **leniency bias** also has been found, whereby jurors move toward greater leniency following deliberations (MacCoun & Kerr, 1988). For example, Miller, Maskaly, Green, and Peoples (2011) examined bias toward defendants because of group affiliation. In two studies, mock jurors read that at the time of the crime the defendant was engaged in Christian prayers (study 1), Islamic prayers (study 2), or watching TV (the control condition). In study 1, the crime was associated with fundamentalist Christians (bombing an abortion clinic). Study 2 described a crime stereotypically associated with Muslims (bombing a transportation centre). Pre- and post-deliberation verdicts were provided by the mock jurors. Similar results were found for both studies—specifically, regardless of the stereotypicality of the crime, there was a general leniency effect. Deliberation made jurors less likely to convict Muslim and Christian defendants but not the TV watchers (control group). Religious affiliation of the defendant did not directly influence the verdict.

In another study, Adams, Bryden, and Griffith (2011) examined racial biases against Middle Easterners with mock jurors before and after deliberations. Mock jurors were given a case where the race of the defendant, victim, and eyewitness was manipulated (Caucasian vs. Middle Eastern). The mock jurors provided guilt ratings before and after deliberating. Before deliberation, 61% of the mock jurors found the Caucasian defendants guilty and 52% found the Middle Eastern defendants guilty. After deliberation, however, 33% and 43% of mock jurors found the Caucasian and Middle Eastern defendants guilty, respectively. Deliberation seemed to mediate any biases that may have existed but only when implicit stereotypes were *not* elicited. For example, when the stereotype of Middle Easterners as terrorists was elicited, jurors' decisions were not influenced by deliberation. As you can see, there may be external case factors that can influence whether and how deliberation affects juror decision making.

Polarization: When individuals tend to become more extreme in their initial position following a group discussion

Leniency bias: When jurors move toward greater leniency during deliberations

The Final Verdict

A Canadian jury must reach a unanimous criminal verdict. If it cannot, the jury is said to be a **hung jury** or deadlocked, and a mistrial is declared. Following a hung-jury outcome, the Crown must decide whether it will retry the case.

Hung jury: A jury that cannot reach a unanimous verdict

In contrast to required unanimous verdicts in Canada, the United States has permitted majority votes of eleven to one, ten to two, and nine to three. Similarly, the United Kingdom has allowed juries to render eleven-to-one or ten-to-two majority votes provided that the jury has deliberated for a minimum of two hours. In a meta-analysis examining the effects of jury size, Saks and Marti (1997) found that 6-person juries are less representative of the community, they remember less of the evidence, they return quicker verdicts, and they are more likely to reach a unanimous verdict than 12-person juries. Hastie, Penrod, and Pennington (1983) found that when a jury could retire with a majority vote, they tended to reach a decision faster and did not fully discuss both the evidence and the law, compared with when the jury was required to reach a unanimous verdict.

In general, when a first verdict poll is taken, the final verdict tends to be consistent with the first poll in about 90% of cases (Kalvern & Zeisel, 1966; Sandys & Dillehay, 1995). Devine et al. (2004) examined factors that contribute to a jury's final decision. The study examined 79 juries from actual criminal trials and found that the percentage of jurors who favoured conviction during the first vote strongly correlated to final verdicts. More specifically, if two-thirds or more of the jury members voted to acquit on the first vote, the jury was more likely to acquit. Similarly, if two-thirds or more of the jury members believed the defendant to be guilty on the first vote, juries were more likely to convict. However, seventy-five percent of the juries without a two-thirds majority vote on the first deliberation were likely to convict. Hastie et al. (1983) identified two broad styles that juries tend to adopt when trying to reach a verdict: verdict driven and evidence driven. Verdict-driven juries tend to start the deliberation process by taking an initial verdict poll. In contrast, evidence-driven juries tend to start the deliberation process by discussing the evidence. A verdict poll is not taken until much later during the deliberation. These two styles can influence the outcome of the initial verdict poll (Devine, 2012).

PREDICTING VERDICTS

A great deal of research on juror characteristics has been conducted to determine whether verdicts can be predicted based on these characteristics. We will examine the following six types of variables that have been studied and their relation to the verdict: (1) demographic variables, (2) personality traits, (3) attitudes, (4) defendant characteristics, (5) victim characteristics, and (6) expert testimony.

Demographic Variables

Variables such as the gender, race, socioeconomic status, and education of jurors are demographic variables that have been examined, in part because they are readily available to lawyers but also because they can be used to challenge witnesses. For example, are female jurors more lenient? Are Caucasians more likely to render guilty verdicts?

Eigenberg, McGuffee, Iles, and Garland (2012) surveyed 138 potential jurors to understand whether jurors believed they were dismissed from jury duty as a result of their gender. Results indicated that gender had little impact on jury duty or perceptions about serving on jury duty. Having females on a jury was perceived as fairness in the system and this was true regardless of the respondent's gender.

Juror gender may produce different outcomes in trials depending on the nature of the trial. For example, Hammond, Berry, and Rodriguez (2011) examined the influence of the acceptance of rape myths, sexual attitudes, and belief in a just world (i.e., believing that you receive what you deserve) in a date-rape scenario. Undergraduates read a hypothetical date-rape scenario and completed questionnaires related to rape myths, sexual attitudes, and belief in a just world. Male mock jurors were more likely to endorse rape myths, and as a result they assigned less responsibility to the accused and more responsibility to the accuser compared to female mock jurors. Thus, juror gender *and* beliefs about sexual assault may be relevant in cases involving sexual assault.

In a recent study, Maeder, Dempsey, and Pozzulo (2012) examined the impact of defendant race using Middle Eastern and Caucasian defendants in a mock sexual assault case. In addition, the influence of a female victim wearing a veil when testifying was considered. Intriguingly, mock jurors were more convinced that the defendant was guilty when the victim was wearing a burqa or hijab compared to no veil. Moreover, defendant race did not influence any other ratings asked of the mock jurors (e.g., credibility of the victim, credibility of the defendant).

Racial bias as it relates to jury decision making can be defined as disparate treatment of racial out-groups. In a meta-analysis examining racial bias on verdict and sentencing decisions, Mitchell, Haw, Pfeifer, and Meissner (2005) found a small significant effect of racial bias on jury decisions. Participants were more likely to render guilty verdicts for "other-race" defendants than for defendants of their own race. Also, participants rendered longer sentences for other-race defendants. Is it possible to reduce this effect? Cohn, Bucolo, Pride, and Sommers (2009) found that when a defendant's race was made salient, white juror racial bias toward a black defendant was reduced. Moreover, jurors' prejudicial beliefs were related to the verdict only when the defendant's race was not made salient. Bucolo and Cohn (2010) found similar results such that when race was not made salient, white and black defendants were treated similarly by white mock jurors; however, in conditions where race was made salient, white defendants were found guilty more often than black defendants.

In another study by Bucolo and Cohn (2010), race saliency was examined through racially salient statements made in the defence lawyer's opening and closing statements, considered "playing the race card." Defendant race (black vs. white) and race salience (not salient vs. salient) were manipulated. White undergraduates served as mock jurors. White juror racial bias was reduced when the defence lawyer "played the race card"—that is, made racially salient statements—compared to when no racially salient statements were included. Also, ratings of guilt did not differ between the white and black defendants when race was not made salient. However, high-prejudice participants were more likely than low-prejudice participants to find the black defendant guilty. Overall, "playing the race card" may be a useful strategy for defence lawyers to reduce white jurors' bias toward black defendants.

Other factors also may interact with defendant race. For example, Perez, Hosch, Ponder, and Trejo (1993) found that strength of the evidence may come into play

Racial bias: The disparate treatment of racial out-groups

along with race. When the evidence was weak or ambiguous (not clearly favouring one side), race similarity between defendant and jury led to leniency. When the evidence was strong, race similarity between defendant and jury led to punitiveness. This is known as the **black sheep effect** (Chadee, 1996).

Black sheep effect: When evidence is strong, similarity between defendant and jury leads to punitiveness

Eberhardt, Davies, Purdie-Vaughns, and Johnson (2006) examined racial stereotypes in a death sentence case. The researchers used photos of black defendants and had ethnically diverse university students rate how stereotypically black they looked. They found that in cases where there was a white victim, black defendants who looked more stereotypical were more likely to be sentenced to death than those who looked less stereotypical.

Unfortunately, when using juror demographic variables to predict verdicts, results are less than reliable. Overall, only a small and inconsistent relation exists between juror demographic variables and jury verdicts (e.g., Bonazzoli, 1998).

Personality Traits

The two personality traits that have been commonly measured in connection to jurors are authoritarianism and dogmatism. Individuals high in authoritarianism tend to have right-wing political views and are conservative and rigid thinkers who acquiesce to authority. Similarly, individuals high in dogmatism also tend to be rigid and closed-minded but without the political overtones found with the authoritarianism construct. Are personality traits better for predicting verdicts than demographic variables?

Given the underlying traits associated with dogmatism and authoritarianism, anyone would predict that jurors who score high on these constructs would be more likely to align themselves with the prosecution and, thus, render more guilty verdicts than jurors who score low on these constructs. Devine and Caughlin (2014) conducted a meta-analysis that included juror authoritarianism across 36 samples and found a positive relationship between authoritarianism and guilt judgments such that those who score high on these traits tend to be more inclined to prefer conviction.

Gunnell and Ceci (2010) examined cognitive-experiential self-theory (CEST) in the context of juror decision making. CEST views processing as occurring through two modes, rational and experiential. Rational processing (R-processors) occurs through an analysis of fact and logic. In contrast, experiential processing (E-processors) occurs through emotion and personal experience.

Based on responses to a questionnaire, participants were given a score that would classify them as more of an E-processor or an R-processor. It would be predicted that E-processors are more likely to be influenced by extralegal biases (such as defendant attractiveness) than R-processors. The researchers found that both E- and R-processors convicted attractive defendants at similar rates; however, E-processors were more likely to convict less-attractive defendants. R-processors recommended similar sentences for attractive and less-attractive defendants. In contrast, E-processors provided harsher sentences for less-attractive defendants and more lenient sentences for attractive defendants. Thus, as anticipated, E-processors seemed more susceptible to extralegal factors than R-processors.

Attitudes

Researchers have examined a variety of attitudes linked to specific topics or issues that may be present in cases, such as drunk driving, rape, child sexual abuse, and capital punishment. For example, Spanos, DuBreuil, and Gwynn (1991–1992) examined rape myths (e.g., a woman who wears provocative clothing is interested in having sex) in connection to a date-rape case. University students heard a version of a date-rape case involving expert testimony about rape myths and cross-examination of such, and then deliberated in small groups to reach a verdict. A gender split was observed in which females did not believe the defendant and voted him guilty more often than male mock jurors. However, regardless of the gender of the mock jurors, those with feminist attitudes were more likely to not believe the defendant's testimony.

Devine, Clayton, Dunford, Seying, and Pryce (2001) reported that no group of attitudes or values has received sufficient investigation to reach a definitive conclusion at this point. The one notable exception is attitudes toward capital punishment. For example, Simon, Snow, and Read (2004) reported that mock jurors who were categorized as strong supporters of the death penalty convicted the defendant 44% of the time compared to a 22% conviction rate from those who were opposed to the death penalty. In general, death-qualified jurors are more likely than non-death-qualified jurors to vote for conviction at the end of a trial (Ellsworth & Mauro, 1998).

Overall, attitudes that are case-specific seem to have more predictive power over verdict than more general attitudes.

Defendant Characteristics

A number of studies have examined defendant characteristics and their influence on verdicts. For example, if jurors hear about a defendant's prior criminal record that contains one or more convictions, they are more likely to find the defendant guilty than if they did not have this knowledge (Hans & Doob, 1976).

There also seems to be a small relationship between the attractiveness of the defendant and jury verdict. Izzett and Leginski (1974) provided mock jurors with a picture of either an unattractive defendant or an attractive defendant and found verdict preferences to be more lenient for the attractive defendant and more severe for the unattractive defendant. Patry (2008) examined whether defendant attractiveness and the act of deliberation would have an effect on guilt decision. Indeed, "plain-looking" defendants were more often found to be guilty when mock jurors did not deliberate. However, when mock jurors did deliberate, the attractive defendant was more likely to be found guilty.

Defendant characteristics often are examined in relation to other characteristics, such as victim characteristics. Pozzulo, Dempsey, Maeder, and Allen (2010) examined defendant gender, defendant age (age 25 versus age 40), and victim gender in a sexual assault case of a 12-year-old student by his or her teacher. Male defendants received higher guilt ratings than female defendants, regardless of juror gender. Female jurors found the victim more accurate, truthful, and believable than male jurors did. In contrast, male jurors found the defendant more reliable, credible, truthful, and believable than female jurors did. Moreover, female jurors held the defendant more responsible for the crime than male jurors did, regardless of the defendant's gender. Overall, mock jurors perceived that the younger defendant desired the event more than the older defendant, but only when the victim was a female. A number of variables can interact, including juror gender, to influence jurors' perceptions in cases of a sexual nature.

In three studies conducted by McKimmie, Masters, Masser, Schuller, and Terry (2012), stereotype congruence was examined by considering defendant gender. The researchers reasoned that jurors may pay particular attention to the characteristics of the defendant if the defendant is incongruent with the offender stereotype (i.e., being male). In study 1, mock jurors paid attention to the strength of the evidence presented against the male (stereotypical) defendant but not the female (counter-stereotypical) defendant. Study 2 was consistent with study 1, where mock jurors recalled fewer facts of the case when the defendant was female rather than male. Further consistent support was found in study 3, where mock jurors were found to spend more time looking at the female rather than male defendant.

As you can see, a number of variables can interact and influence verdict.

Victim Characteristics

Characteristics of the victim may become particularly relevant in cases of sexual assault in which a guilty verdict may hinge on the testimony of the alleged victim. In Canada, before the mid-1980s, a woman's prior sexual history was admissible and could be used to infer her credibility and the likelihood that she consented to sexual relations with the defendant. In 1985, rape-shield provisions were legislated, which prevented lawyers from introducing a woman's prior sexual history (R.S.C. 1985, C-46, s. 276).

In the early 1990s, however, some people began to challenge these provisions on the grounds that they prevented defendants from receiving a fair trial (R. v. Gayme, 1991; R. v. Seaboyer, 1991). Defence lawyers argued that it was necessary to admit the accuser's prior sexual history because it would support defendants' claims of an honest but mistaken belief in consent. The rape-shield provisions were amended in 1992, allowing inquiry into a woman's sexual history at the judge's discretion (R.S.C. 1985, C-46, s. 276; 1992, c. 38, s. 2). Only if a woman's sexual history was deemed relevant would the judge allow it to be heard by the jury. Further, the Supreme Court of Canada (R. v. Seaboyer, 1991) recommended that the trial judge provide the jury with cautionary instructions on how this evidence should be used. More specifically, the jurors must be cautioned that a woman's sexual history should be used only in determining a defendant's claim of an "honest but mistaken belief in consent." A woman's sexual history must not be used to demonstrate that the woman is less trustworthy or that she is likely to consent to sexual intercourse. Some have argued that such a distinction is too fine to be made by jurors. How would you interpret a woman's sexual history in a "date-rape" case? (See You Be the Juror box.)

Schuller and Hastings (2002) conducted a study in which the victim's sexual history was varied to include either sexual intercourse, kissing and touching, or no history information in a sexual assault trial. In addition, a judge's instructions limiting the use of the sexual history information was examined. Compared with the

YOU BE THE JUROR

Kerri Williams was in her second year at university. She had met Brian Sugarman in her introductory psychology class. They didn't know each other very well but had a few classes together and knew some of the same people. Kerri thought Brian was cute and told her friends that she'd go out with him if he asked.

Brian had been dating a female from his high school for almost three years. Brian had gone off to university and his girlfriend stayed in town and went to a local community college. Brian's girlfriend decided she no longer wanted a long-distance relationship. She broke up with Brian just before reading break. Brian was upset but decided there were lots of women at university he could go out with instead. He figured it would be his ex-girlfriend's loss. That weekend, a friend of Kerri's and Brian's had a house party to mark the end of reading week. Both Kerri and Brian went to the party.

At the party, Kerri and Brian started chatting and were having a good time together. Both Kerri and Brian had a couple of drinks but neither considered themselves drunk. As the party was breaking up, around 2:00 a.m., Brian asked if Kerri wanted to go back to his room in residence to "hang out." Kerri said, "Sure." While in Brian's room, Brian and Kerri started to get intimate. After a few minutes though, Kerri said she should go home. Brian asked her to stay and continued to kiss Kerri. Kerri repeated that she should go. Kerri and Brian had intercourse and the next morning, Kerri claimed that Brian sexually assaulted her. Brian agreed that they had sex but insisted that it was consensual. Brian claimed that Kerri could have left at any time.

The case went to trial and the judge allowed the defence to question Kerri on her sexual history. Kerri stated that she had, in the past, had intercourse with five other boyfriends; however, she stated that she did not want to have intercourse with Brian that night.

Your Turn . . .

Do you think Brian sexually assaulted Kerri? Would you change your verdict if you did not know about Kerri's sexual history? Do you think an alleged victim's sexual history is relevant? Should the history be admissible in court?

participants who heard no sexual history information, those who heard that the victim and defendant had sexual intercourse in the past were less likely to find the alleged victim credible, more likely to find her blameworthy, and more likely to believe she consented to sexual intercourse. Thus, they were more likely to find the defendant not guilty. The sexual history information did not influence participants' judgments about the defendant's belief in consent, which is contrary to the goal of judges' instructions as intended by the Supreme Court of Canada. It would appear that a judge's instruction to limit the use of the sexual history information is not effective. If a woman's sexual history is admitted into evidence, it is used to assess her credibility.

Cases have continued to challenge the 1992 rape-shield provisions. In *R. v. Darrach* (2000), the defendant, Andrew Darrach, was found guilty of sexually assaulting his former girlfriend. Darrach appealed his conviction, arguing that he did not receive a fair trial because he was unable to present information about his prior sexual history with the accuser. Darrach stated that, given his past relationship with the accused, he thought that the sexual encounter was consensual. During the trial, the judge heard the defence's arguments and ruled that the evidence was inadmissible when Darrach refused to testify or be cross-examined on the claims he was making. In Darrach's appeal, he claimed that the law unfairly required him to testify and denied him access to a full defence. In October 2000, the Supreme Court of Canada upheld Darrach's conviction and upheld the country's rape-shield provisions. The Supreme Court noted that the onus is on the defendant to demonstrate that the accuser's sexual history is relevant before it will be allowed (*R. v. Darrach*, 2000).

Should religious beliefs matter in sexual assault cases? For example, should a female victim be asked to remove her religious veil when providing testimony in a sexual assault case? In a recent case in Ontario, the judge determined that the woman would have to remove her niqab (a full face and body covering that leaves just the eyes exposed) to provide testimony. In December of 2012, the Supreme Court of Canada, under split decision, stated that the appropriateness of wearing a veil during testimony is to be determined on a case-by-case basis. The majority of judges developed the following four questions as part of the assessment to evaluate whether a judge should instruct a woman to remove her niqab when testifying:

1. Would requiring the witness to remove the niqab while testifying interfere with her religious freedom?
2. Would permitting the witness to wear the niqab while testifying create a serious risk to trial fairness?
3. Is there a way to accommodate both rights and avoid the conflict between them?
4. If no accommodation is possible, do the salutary effects of requiring the witness to remove the niqab outweigh the deleterious effects of doing so? (*R. v. NS*, 2012)

Should the onus be on the victim or witness to demonstrate the need to wear such coverings when providing testimony? As a juror, would you be influenced by whether you could see the victim's face? See Box 7.6 to learn more about this possibly precedent-setting case.

Expert Testimony

How well do jurors understand the evidence presented? Sometimes, jurors don't have the background knowledge to understand certain types of evidence, such as DNA. Lawyers may ask that an expert be allowed to testify to explain the evidence. What influence does expert evidence have on jurors' decisions?

A number of findings about expert testimony are available, but no simple conclusion has emerged. For example, Schuller, Terry, and McKimmie (2005) examined whether the expert's gender is used as a cue to evaluate the testimony provided. Along with the gender of the expert, the complexity of the testimony was varied such that the testimony was either more or less complex (e.g., by using technical jargon).

Box 7.6   Forensic Psychology in the Spotlight

When Law Meets Religion

Should Muslim women be allowed to testify wearing a veil that covers their entire face and body except for their eyes? This question is currently before Canadian courts. At this time, no Canadian case law addresses this issue. But as there are approximately 580 000 Muslims living in Canada, the ruling may have implications for Muslim women in future criminal cases.

Currently, a Muslim woman (N.S.) who wears a niqab is the alleged victim in a sexual assault case before a court in Toronto. The woman did not want to remove her veil to testify at her trial. The woman stated that, for religious reasons, she did not want to show her face to "men you are able to marry." The defence argued that showing her face was necessary to assess demeanour so that the defence could tailor its questioning. It also indicated that a visible face is necessary to assess credibility.

In October 2008, Ontario Court Justice Norris Weisman ruled that the Muslim woman would have to show her face when providing testimony in court. In his ruling, Justice Weisman determined that this woman's religious beliefs were "not that strong" and the wearing of the niqab was a "matter of comfort" for her. Justice Weisman also noted that this woman's driver's licence photo shows her face without the veil (as a result, a variety of men, such as police officers and border guards, could ask to see this driver's licence and see the woman's unveiled face).

Alia Hogben, executive director of the Canadian Council of Muslim Women, weighed in on the issue. She accepted the judge's decision, saying that in court "the laws of the country should be acceptable." She also pointed out, however, that when enacting this requirement, "sensitivity [should] be shown" (as quoted in Powell, 2009).

The Muslim woman in question appealed Justice Weisman's ruling. In May 2009, Superior Court Justice Frank Marrocco heard arguments in the case and decided to turn the issue back to Justice Weisman. Justice Marrocco instructed Justice Weisman to undertake another inquiry into why the woman wears the niqab. Justice Weisman ruled on April 24, 2013, that the woman would have to remove the veil that covers her face in order to testify. The judge found that the niqab blocks assessment of her demeanour, limiting effective cross-examination and assessment of her credibility. David Butt, the complainant's lawyer stated that in early 2014, N.S. decided to strike a "compromise" with the courts and testify without her niqab under the condition that the public is excluded from the courtroom. However, in mid 2014, the Crown dropped the sexual assault cases against the alleged attackers.

Sources: Based on Powell, B. (2009, February 2). Order to take off niqab pits law against religion. TheStar.com. Retrieved from http://www.thestar.com/printarticle/580790; Partial court victory for Muslim woman over niqab (2009, May 1). Ctvtoronto.ca. Retrieved from http://montreal.ctv.ca/servlet/an/local/CTVNews/20090501/niqab_ruling_090501?hub=MontrealHome; http://news.nationalpost.com/news/canada/toronto-woman-who-lost-fight-to-wear-niqab-in-court-disillusioned-after-crown-drops-sex-assault-case.

In a civil case that involved an alleged price-fixing arrangement between a crushed-rock supplier and a road construction company, the plaintiff was suing the two companies for damages of $490 000 because of the price-fixing agreement. When the expert testimony was more complex, the jury awarded higher damages to the plaintiff when the expert was male, rather than female. When the expert testimony was less complex, although not significantly so, the jury awarded higher damages when the expert was female, rather than male. Jurors may be affected by gender differently, depending on their ability to process expert testimony.

Expert testimony need not produce a positive effect, however, and jurors may disregard it completely. For example, Sundby (1997) examined the transcripts of 152 jurors who participated in 36 first-degree murder cases in California. Jurors were asked about their perceptions and reactions to three types of witnesses: professional experts, lay experts, and families or friends of the defendant. Of the three types of witnesses, jurors were most likely to view professional experts negatively, believing they had little credibility and hurt the side they were testifying for. Overall, jurors may carefully consider expert testimony.

A study by Klettke, Graesser, and Powell (2010) examined the potential interaction between an expert's credentials, the strength of the evidence, and coherency of the expert's testimony on juror decision making. Mock jurors read a mock summary of a child sexual abuse case that was followed by expert testimony. A number of dependent measures were considered, including guilt of the defendant, effectiveness of the expert testimony, and credibility of the victim. Two key factors influenced all the dependent measures and interacted, namely, evidence strength and coherency of the testimony. Defendants were rated less guilty and the victim rated as less credible when the strength of the evidence *and* coherency were low. The expert's credentials had virtually no impact. Thus, the usefulness of expert testimony can interact with other factors in the case. Moreover, credentials may not be critical to jurors when rendering verdicts.

A Special Case of Expert Testimony on Battered Women's Syndrome A number of studies have examined battered women who kill their abusers and the influence of expert testimony in their trials (Schuller, 1992, 1995; Schuller & Hastings, 1996; Schuller & Rzepa, 2002; Schuller, Smith, & Olson, 1994).

In one study, Freedman and Burke (1996) examined the influence of pre-trial publicity on mock jurors' decision making concerning the Paul Bernardo case. Mock jurors were asked how much they heard about the Paul Bernardo/Karla Homolka case prior to reading a brief description of the case. Half of the mock jurors read a description involving additional rape related charges, while the other half did not; upon completion, mock jurors were asked to rate the degree to which the defendant was guilty or not guilty. Mock jurors were then given a fictitious trial transcript and were again asked to determine whether they thought he was guilty or not guilty. Initial decisions were influenced by how much mock jurors had heard concerning Paul Bernardo such that those who reported hearing more were more likely to think he was guilty compared to those who had heard no information regarding the case. However, once participants read the trial, the gap between those who voted guilty and not guilty diminished; those who had heard about the case prior to the study were just slightly more likely to believe he was guilty compared to those who had not, however, the difference was not significant. Dr. Tara Burke, a Canadian researcher at Ryerson University, has published a number of studies in the area of pre-trial publicity. To learn more about Dr. Burke see Box 7.7.

Terrance, Plumm, and Kehn (2014) examined the influence of expert testimony (concerning battered woman syndrome vs. social/agency testimony vs. no expert) in addition to the timing of expert testimony (before or after defendant's testimony) on jury decision making. While there was no direct influence of expert testimony or timing on jury decision, jurors' individual opinions were influenced. When jurors were exposed to the expert testimony discussing battered woman syndrome and how the defendant acted in self-defence, they were more likely to believe the defendant was not guilty by reason of self-defence. However, similar to the juries' decision making, individual jurors were not influenced by the social agency expert testimony.

Box 7.7

Canadian Researcher Profile: Dr. Tara Burke

Courtesy of Dr. Tara Burke

Dr. Tara Burke started her research career as a graduate student at the University of Toronto. The focus of her dissertation was exploring whether exposure to pretrial publicity changes what jurors discuss during deliberations, how they try to persuade one another throughout the process, and, ultimately, whether this information has any impact on their final verdict. She is a professor at Ryerson University, where she has been for the past 16 years. Much of her research can be summed up by the question of 'how can we prevent wrongful convictions?' Dr. Burke states, "some of our core areas of research include the use (and misuse) of alibi evidence, how suspect characteristics influence decision-makers' assessments of them, and more recently (now that jury trials are becoming less commonplace), how an offer of a plea-bargain may induce an innocent suspect to plead guilty." She also explores the use of technology in court. For example, one of her studies looks at whether 'high-tech' animations, which are becoming increasingly common, have a greater impact on jurors than more mundane forms of evidence (e.g., a transcript of a witness interview).

One of Dr. Burke's favourite studies was conducted with one of her former graduate students, Stéphanie Marion. Dr. Burke states, "we put participants in the position of having to decide whether or not to knowingly corroborate a false alibi. This was a tricky study to run, for many reasons, but it was the first one in the area of alibi research to include a behavioural measure, rather than just asking the standard 'what do you think you would do?' question. That was very interesting and rewarding."

Dr. Burke mentions that what keeps her intrigued with the research is that there are so many unanswered questions when it comes to wrongful convictions. She sees herself continuing in this same vein for many years to come. "The topic of when and why innocent suspects accept a guilty plea is fascinating, and one that I think has a great deal of potential as a research area."

When Dr. Burke isn't in the lab researching, or in the classroom teaching, she sometimes consults on cases, although she cautions that she says "no" far more often than "yes" when asked to consult. This is because "in my experience, one 'side' is usually hoping I will say something that specifically helps them. But, as an expert, our role is to present the research in a way that is understandable, and not to try to convince the jury (or judge) that our view is the 'right' one. Unless, of course, that is what the research itself tells us."

In terms of legislation that Dr. Burke feels need changing, she would like to see more safeguards in place to protect those who are interrogated. She notes, "there is recent evidence suggesting that Canadian law enforcement is moving towards the PEACE model (and away from the Reid Technique) which is very heartening. It is essential, of course, to try to ensure the guilty do not go free, but this shouldn't come at the cost of innocent people being found guilty. This is an age-old issue, but I think we have better tools these days to see some of the obvious places where we can work on making things better."

In her spare time, Dr. Burke enjoys watching Netflix shows about… wrongful convictions, of course.

Female mock jurors who heard expert testimony after the defendant's testimony were more likely to rate the defendant as mentally unstable (Terrance et al., 2014). This may be because female jurors may be better able to relate to the testimony of a battered woman because women may be more likely to be victims of domestic abuse.

Overall, expert testimony and battered women's syndrome can be influential in domestic violence cases. It is important to keep in mind that a number of other case factors can interact with expert testimony and battered women's syndrome to influence a verdict. To learn more about psychological factors related to domestic violence, see Chapter 13.

SUMMARY

1. In Canada, prospective jurors are selected from a set of random names from the community. These prospective jurors receive a jury summons stating the time and place to go for jury duty. If you are randomly selected from this juror pool, you will be a juror unless one of the lawyers presents a challenge.

2. For a jury to be considered representative, it must allow any possible eligible juror from the community the opportunity to be part of the jury. Juror impartiality centres on three issues: (1) being able to set aside any pre-existing biases, prejudices, or attitudes to judge the case solely on admissible evidence; (2) ignoring any information that is not part of the admissible evidence; and (3) not being connected to the defendant in any way.

3. Pretrial publicity threatens juror impartiality. The concern is that verdicts will be based on emotion and biased media coverage rather than on admissible evidence. To reduce or limit the negative effects of pretrial publicity, the judge can order a publication ban until the end of the trial. Other options for dealing with pretrial publicity include a change of venue, an adjournment, or a challenge for cause.

4. Once a jury has been selected, its work begins by listening to the admissible evidence and disregarding any evidence that the judge does not allow. Once the lawyers deliver their closing arguments, the judge provides the jury with the law that it must apply to the evidence to reach a verdict. The jury then deliberates to reach a verdict.

5. Categories that have been examined in predicting verdicts include demographic variables, personality variables, attitudes, defendant characteristics, victim characteristics, and expert testimony.

Discussion Questions

1. Design a study to evaluate the advantages and disadvantages of jury aids (e.g., note-taking, asking questions).

2. To study juror decision making, researchers have used four methodologies. Describe the advantages and disadvantages of each method.

Chapter 8
The Role of Mental Illness in Court

Learning Objectives

- Outline the fitness standard and the changes made to legislation.

- Contrast unfit and fit offenders.

- Explain Canada's insanity standard.

- Describe automatism and examples of cases in which it was used as a defence.

- State the explanations for high rates of mental illness in offender populations.

- Explain the various treatment goals and options for offenders with mental disorders.

Blake Bordeau was adopted by Mr. and Mrs. DeLaroche when he was 2 years old. He had become a ward of the state because his birth mother was a cocaine addict and his father was a drug dealer serving a life sentence for killing one of his drug runners. Mr. and Mrs. DeLaroche were from a small town outside of Vancouver.

Blake started showing some odd behaviour when he was a teenager. He was often found talking to himself, and he seemed to think everyone was against him. He thought that the only way to protect himself was to become a police officer. Blake managed to be hired on as an officer but it quickly became clear that he was not well, and Blake was diagnosed with paranoid schizophrenia. When he was taking his medication, he could function in most of his daily activities; however, Blake did not like how the medication made him feel so he would stop taking his medication without warning.

Mr. and Mrs. DeLaroche had not heard from their son in a month and could not find him. He wasn't in his apartment, and he had been dismissed from the police force. While watching the news, Mr. and Mrs. DeLaroche heard that a local police officer had been murdered outside the police station where Blake had once been employed. Mr. and Mrs. DeLaroche feared that the voices Blake sometimes heard in his head had told Blake to kill. The following day, a news report announced that former police officer Blake Duchane had murdered the officer and was in custody, awaiting a psychological assessment.

Although a number of people convicted of crimes may suffer from mental illness, this chapter will consider mental illness as it relates to the ability to stand trial and to the commission of a crime. In this chapter, we will explore what is meant by the term *fitness to stand trial* within the Canadian criminal justice system. We also will examine the term *mental state at the time of offence* as it pertains to Canadian criminal law and forensic psychology.

PRESUMPTIONS IN CANADA'S LEGAL SYSTEM

Actus reus: A wrongful deed

Mens rea: Criminal intent

The cornerstone of English-Canadian law identifies two elements that must be present for criminal guilt to be established: (1) a wrongful deed, also known as **actus reus**, and (2) criminal intent, also known as **mens rea**. Both of these elements (and the elements of the specific case) must be found beyond a reasonable doubt for a guilty verdict to be reached. Issues of fitness, insanity, automatism, and mental disorders all call into question these two basic elements of criminal law.

Before we start discussing the role of mental illness in the court, examine the myths that surround the topic in Box 8.1. How many myths did you believe?

FITNESS TO STAND TRIAL

It is reasonable to expect that in order for individuals who are charged with the commission of a crime to be tried fairly, they should have some understanding of the charges and proceedings and be able to help in preparing their defence.

Box 8.1 Myths and Realities

Mental Illness and the Court

Myth 1. Those with mental illness commit the most crime.
Fact. Offenders with a mental illness are similar to offenders with no mental illness; research has found that those with and without mental disorders are likely to commit similar crimes (Rice & Harris, 1997a).

Myth 2. All defendants that commit very violent crime use the insanity defence to excuse their behaviour.
Fact. Typically, only around 1% of felony cases will argue the insanity defence (Steadman et al., 1993).

Myth 3. Those with mental illness and who commit violent crime should never be released from prison.
Fact. Some mentally ill offenders would benefit more from psychiatric treatment than incarceration where the treatment for mental illness is scarce. The criminal justice system is ill equipped to address the needs that psychiatric hospitals or mental health courts can offer (e.g., Seltzer, 2005).

Myth 4. Once someone mentally ill has committed a crime, they can never be cured.
Fact. When a mentally ill offender is placed in the right treatment program, recidivism rates can greatly decline; thus, when appropriate help is given, the chance that a mentally ill offender will commit another crime decreases (e.g., Theurer & Lovell, 2008).

Myth 5. If you are mentally ill and kill someone, you should go to jail rather than a mental health facility.
Fact. Depending on the severity of the mental illness, offenders may fare better in a mental health facility, such as a psychiatric institution, to get the help they need with their mental illness (Seltzer, 2005).

A defendant who is deficient in these domains, possibly because of a mental disorder, may be considered unfit to stand trial. Thus, **unfit to stand trial** refers to a defendant's inability to conduct a defence at any stage of the proceedings on account of a mental disorder. For example, a defendant may be found unfit to stand trial if he or she is experiencing an episode of schizophrenia and lacks the ability to understand the situation and tell the lawyer the facts of the case. Also, in a Canadian case, *R. v. Balliram* (2003), it was concluded that an unfit person could not be sentenced. The degree of impairment necessary for an unfit determination has been difficult to pinpoint, however. Once a person is found not criminally responsible on account of mental disorder, this does not constitute an acquittal. Rather, the accused is diverted to a provincial or territorial Review Board composed of approximately five members, usually chaired by a judge and containing at least one member who is entitled under the law of the specific province to practice psychiatry.

Historically, little direction was provided by means of legislation for a finding of unfitness; rather, case law was used to determine the criteria that should be met. Specifically, the case of *R. v. Pritchard* (1836) has been considered the key case for the fitness standard (Lindsay, 1977). Three criteria were delineated in the Prichard case:

- Whether the defendant is mute of malice (i.e., intentionality)
- Whether the defendant can plead to the indictment
- Whether the defendant has sufficient cognitive capacity to understand the trial proceedings

Prior to the enactment of Bill C-30 (1992) and by the mid-1980s, the federal Department of Justice acknowledged a number of problems with the mental disorder provisions of the Criminal Code of Canada (e.g., inconsistencies, omissions, lack of clarity and guidance). Also, there were issues regarding the incompatibility of these provisions with the Canadian Charter of Rights and Freedoms. For example, someone who was declared unfit to stand trial could be confined indefinitely. A number of changes were instituted with the enactment of Bill C-30.

With the enactment of Bill C-30 in 1992, the Criminal Code stated a fitness standard. The fitness standard can be found in section 2 of the Code: A defendant is unfit to stand trial if he or she is

> unable on account of mental disorder to conduct a defence at any stage of the proceedings before a verdict is rendered or to instruct counsel to do so, and, in particular, unable on account of mental disorder to a) understand the nature or object of the proceedings, b) understand the possible consequences of the proceedings, or c) communicate with counsel. (R.S.C., 1985, C-46, s. 2; 1992, c. 20, s. 216, c. 51, s. 32)

This last point about communicating with counsel has been further specified in case law in *R. v. Taylor* (1992). In this case, the Ontario Court of Appeal stated that the test to be applied in terms of "communication with counsel" is with regard to limited cognitive capacity. The court ruled that a defendant need only be able to state the facts relating to the offence that would allow an appropriate defence.

Unfit to stand trial: Refers to an inability to conduct a defence at any stage of the proceedings on account of a person's mental disorder.

Moreover, the defendant need not be able to communicate facts that are in his or her best interests. The court decided that applying the "best interest rule" was too strict a criterion.

One other issue that was altered with Bill C-30 was the length of time a defendant could be held in custody for a fitness evaluation. A five-day limit on court-ordered assessments was legislated, with provisions for extensions, if necessary, to complete the evaluation. The extension, however, is not to exceed 30 days, and the entire length of detention should not exceed 60 days (R.S.C., 1985, C-46, s. 672.15). The evaluation can occur while the defendant is in a detention, outpatient, or in-patient facility. Roesch et al. (1997) found that the average length of time for evaluation was approximately three weeks and that 88% occurred in in-patient facilities (also Zapf & Roesch, 1998). It should be noted that mental health law (i.e., commitment and treatment in psychiatric facilities) is under provincial/territorial jurisdiction. In May 2005, the Standing Senate Committee on Legal and Constitutional Affairs received testimony from mental health organizations as well as psychiatrists, psychologists, police and review board members. Witnesses were noted as having differing opinions regarding (http://www.lop.parl.gc.ca/About/Parliament/LegislativeSummaries/bills_ls.asp?ls=C10&Parl=38&Ses=1):

■ the presentation of a victim impact statement at a court or Review Board hearing;

■ assessments by persons other than medical practitioners (e.g., psychologists in addition to psychiatrists);

■ the dual Review Board/court procedure to grant a stay of proceedings in the case of a permanently unfit accused;

■ the extension of the time for the next review hearing from 12 to 24 months in the case of a serious personal injury offence;

■ and the transfer of physical evidence from courts to Review Boards.

Bill C-10 (An Act To Amend The Criminal Code (Mental Disorder) And To Make Consequential Amendments To Other Acts).

Although the Senate Committee did include the concerns presented above as observations, the bill was reported back to the Senate without amendment.

Raising the Issue of Fitness

The issue of a defendant's fitness may be raised at various points from the time of arrest to the defendant's sentence determination. Examples of instances in which the issue of fitness may be raised include when a plea is entered, when a defendant chooses not to be represented by counsel, and during sentencing (Ogloff, Wallace, & Otto, 1991). The Criminal Code of Canada states that a defendant is assumed to be fit to stand trial unless the court is satisfied on the balance of probabilities that he or she is unfit (R.S.C., 1985, C-46, s. 672.22). The defence or Crown may raise the issue of a defendant's fitness. Also noted in the Code is that the burden of proving unfitness is on the party who raises the issue (R.S.C., 1985, C-46, s. 672.23[2]).

Table 8.1 Number of Accused Given the Legal Status of Unfit, by Jurisdiction (1992–2004)

Jurisdiction	Number of Accused Ruled Unfit
Prince Edward Island	4
Quebec	399
Ontario	1151
Alberta	94
British Columbia	216
Nunavut	2
Yukon	10

Source: From The Review Board Systems in Canada: An Overview of Results from the Mentally Disordered Accused Data Collection Study by J. Latimer & A. Lawrence. Published by Department of Justice Canada, © 2006. Ottawa, ON.

How Many Defendants Are Referred for Fitness Evaluations?

Webster, Menzies, Butler, and Turner (1982) estimated that approximately 5000 fitness evaluations are conducted annually in Canada. In a more recent investigation, Roesch et al. (1997) found that 61% of a sample from a remand facility in British Columbia underwent fitness evaluations. Moreover, 24% were held for assessments of both fitness and criminal responsibility (we will discuss criminal responsibility in more detail later in the chapter). In the United States, Bonnie and Grisso (2000) estimated that somewhere between 2% and 8% of all felony defendants are referred for fitness evaluations—that is, about 25 000 to 38 000 defendants (Hoge et al., 1997). See Table 8.1 for a distribution of the number of accused ruled unfit in seven Canadian jurisdictions during the period 1992–2004. (See also Table 8.2 for the total percentage of cases in which the accused is ruled as unfit or not criminally responsible on account of mental disorder across seven jurisdictions in Canada for the period 1992–2004.)

Table 8.2 Number of Accused Given the Legal Status of NCRMD and Unfit, by Jurisdiction (1992–2004)

Jurisdiction	Number of NCRMD	% of Total Cases That Are NCRMD and Unfit
Prince Edward Island	8	0.1%
Quebec	3378	43.5%
Ontario	2059	37.0%
Alberta	306	4.6%
British Columbia	1036	14.4%
Nunavut	6	0.1%

Source: From The Review Board Systems in Canada: An Overview of Results from the Mentally Disordered Accused Data Collection Study. By J. Latimer & A. Lawrence. Published by Department of Justice Canada, © 2006. Ottawa, ON.

Who Can Assess Fitness?

Traditionally, only medical practitioners have been allowed to conduct court-ordered assessments of such aspects as fitness to stand trial and criminal responsibility (Viljoen et al., 2003). Unlike in the United States and Australia, the Canadian Criminal Justice system continues to take this position. In fact, the Canadian Criminal Code excludes psychologists from conducting court-ordered assessments. The Code specifies that these assessments must be carried out by medical practitioners or any other professional who has been designated by the Attorney General as qualified to conduct an assessment. (R.S.C., 1985, C-46, s. 672.1). It is important to note that the medical practitioners need not have any background in psychiatry or experience with forensic populations. In contrast, Frost, de Camara, and Earl (2006) reported that all but six U.S. states allow psychologists to conduct fitness and criminal responsibility evaluations.

Canadian psychologists can, however, be involved in court-ordered assessments in a variety of ways. For example, psychologists may be asked to conduct psychological testing and to assist with the assessment of defendants who are referred for evaluation. Psychologists submit their results to psychiatrists or other medical practitioners, who then incorporate the results into a report for the court.

Fitness Instruments

A number of screening instruments have been developed to help evaluators quickly screen out defendants who are competent to stand trial. Comprehensive fitness assessments can then be reserved for those defendants who are "screened in." Zapf and Roesch (1998) compared the fitness decisions that were made by using a screening instrument with decisions that were made following a defendant's stay in a psychiatric facility. The researchers found that the two sets of decisions were consistent with each other. They concluded that long stays in mental facilities were unnecessary for most of the fitness decisions. Rather, many fitness decisions could be made quickly by using a screening instrument, which would result in a more cost-effective system.

One screening instrument that has particular relevance for Canadians is the Fitness Interview Test Revised (FIT-R) (Roesch, Zapf, Eaves, & Webster, 1998), which was developed to meet the fitness criteria outlined in the Canadian Criminal Code. The FIT-R is in the form of a semi-structured interview and assesses the three psychological abilities stated in the Code's fitness standard. Each section contains several items that the evaluator probes with the defendant. For example,

- Understand the nature or object of the proceedings
  - Factual knowledge of criminal procedure
    - i   defendant's understanding of the arrest process
    - ii   the nature and severity of the current charges
    - iii   the role of key participants
- Understand the possible consequences of the proceedings
  - Appreciation of personal involvement in and importance of the proceedings
    - i   appreciation of range and nature of possible penalties and defences

- Communicate with counsel
  - Ability to participate in defence
    - i   defendant's ability to communicate facts
    - ii defendant's ability to relate to his or her attorney
    - iii defendant's ability to plan legal strategy

Each response is rated on a 3-point scale, ranging from 0 (indicates no to little impairment) to 2 (indicates severe impairment). Once the interview is complete, the evaluator must make a decision regarding overall fitness. The final decision involves three stages: (1) determining the existence of a mental disorder, (2) determining the defendant's capacity regarding each of the three psychological abilities stated above, and (3) examining the previous information. Although performance on the items contained in each section is considered in determining the section rating, decisions are not made based on a specific cut-off score. Instead, these section ratings constitute a separate judgment based on the severity of impairment and its perceived importance. See Box 8.2 for a look at some other fitness instruments.

Fitness Instruments

Competency Screening Test (CST)

The CST (Lipsitt, Lelos, & McGarry, 1971) has 22 uncompleted sentences that the respondent must finish. For example,

- The lawyer told Bill that . . .
- When I go to court the lawyer will . . .
- Jack felt that the judge . . .

The items measure three constructs: the potential for a constructive relationship between the defendant and his lawyer, the defendant's understanding of the court process, and the ability of the defendant to emotionally cope with the criminal process. Responses are scored by using a 3-point scale (0, 1, 2), depending on the relation between the defendant's response and example responses provided in the scoring manual. A score of 0 would be assigned if the response demonstrated a low level of legal understanding. For example, "The lawyer told Bill that he is guilty" would receive 0 points (Ackerman, 1999). A score of 2 would be assigned if the response demonstrated a high level of legal understanding.

For example, "The lawyer told Bill that he should plead guilty" would receive 2 points (Ackerman, 1999). Scores for each of the items are summed to produce a total CST score. The CST score, in addition to a brief psychiatric interview, is aimed at distinguishing between competent defendants who could proceed to trial and those defendants who should undergo a more complete competency assessment. A score of 20 or below suggests that the defendant should undergo a more comprehensive evaluation.

Competency to Stand Trial Assessment Instrument (CAI)

The CAI (Laboratory of Community Psychiatry, Harvard Medical School, 1973) was designed to accompany the CST in that the CAI is a semi-structured interview and constitutes a comprehensive competency evaluation. The CAI assesses 13 functions corresponding to a defendant's ability to participate in the criminal process on behalf of his or her best interests. Each function is represented in a statement with two or three sample questions that the evaluator may pose to the defendant. For example (Ackerman, 1999),

(continued)

(continued)

Function: Appraisal of available legal defences

Statement: The defendant's awareness of possible legal defences and how consistent they are with the reality of his or her particular circumstances

Question: How do you think you can be defended against these charges?

Following a response, the evaluator can ask follow-up questions to further probe the defendant's response if it is unclear or ambiguous. For each function, responses are rated on a scale from 1 (reflecting a total lack of capacity for function) to 5 (reflecting no impairment—i.e., defendant can function adequately). A score of 6 can be given when there is insufficient information to rate the function. The evaluator examines the scores for each function and then makes an overall determination.

Interdisciplinary Fitness Interview (IFI)

The IFI (Golding, Roesch, & Schreiber, 1984) was developed following an analysis of the CAI. As with the CAI, the IFI is a semi-structured interview measuring three areas of competency: functional memory, appropriate relationship with lawyer, and understanding of the justice system. There are four main sections to the IFI:

Section A: Legal items

Section B: Psychopathological items

Section C: Overall evaluation

Section D: Consensual judgment

Each section has a number of subsections and areas within each subsection that can be assessed. The revision of the IFI (IFI-R) (Golding, 1993) retains the semi-structured interview protocol; however, there are only two sections: Current Clinical Condition and Psycho-Legal Abilities. Each section has a number of subsections. For example, under the heading Current Clinical Condition are the following categories:

- Attention/consciousness
- Delusions
- Hallucinations
- Impaired reasoning and judgment

- Impaired memory
- Mood and affect

The evaluator assesses these major areas of clinical dysfunction. Responses are rated with a scale ranging from 0 (absent or does not bear on defendant's fitness) to 2 (symptom is likely to significantly impair the defendant's fitness).

Under the Psycho-Legal Abilities heading, there are four subsections:

- Capacity to appreciate charges and to disclose pertinent facts, events, and motives
- Courtroom demeanour and capacity to understand the adversarial nature of proceedings
- Quality of relationship with attorney
- Appreciation of and reasoned choice with respect to legal option and consequences

Responses are rated on a scale ranging from 0 (no or minimal capacity) to 2 (substantial capacity). It also has been recommended that when conducting a competency assessment, the defendant's lawyer, previous mental health contacts, and jail personnel are interviewed. In addition, mental health reports, police reports, and prior arrest history should be reviewed (Golding, as cited in Ackerman, 1999).

MacArthur Competence Assessment Tool—Criminal Adjudication (MacCAT-CA)

The MacCAT-CA (Hoge, Bonnie, Poythress, & Monahan, 1992) is a structured interview containing 22 items that assess competencies in three areas:

- Factual understanding of the legal system and the adjudication process
- Reasoning ability
- Understanding of own legal situation and circumstances

These areas are assessed via hypothetical scenarios. Following the presentation of the scenario, the defendant is asked a series of specific questions. The evaluator assigns a score of 0, 1, or 2, based on the scoring criteria. For each area, score ranges are provided for three levels of impairment: none to minimal, mild, or clinically significant.

Distinguishing between Fit and Unfit Defendants

Pirelli, Gottdiener, and Zapf (2011) conducted a meta-analytic review of the research examining competency to stand trial conducted in the U.S. and Canada. A greater proportion of incompetent defendants were diagnosed with a psychotic disorder compared with those who were competent. Both unemployed and unmarried defendants were more likely to be found incompetent compared with those who were employed and married. Competent defendants were more likely to have a current violent criminal charge as opposed to a non-violent charge.

In a previous study, Zapf and Roesch (1998) examined the demographic, mental health, and criminal characteristics that differentiate fit from unfit defendants by using a sample of 180 males undergoing evaluation in a B.C. facility. Using the fit/unfit decision offered to the court by the psychiatrist, the data were divided into these two categories and then compared across criteria.

In examining the demographic variables, only marital status was significant. Fit defendants were significantly more likely to have been married (married, divorced, separated, common law) than unfit defendants. Previous studies have found defendants who are referred for fitness evaluations to be primarily single, unemployed, and living alone (Roesch, Eaves, Sollner, Normandin, & Glackman, 1981; Webster et al., 1982). In a meta-analysis of 30 studies conducted in both Canada and the United States, Nicholson and Kugler (1991) found that fit and unfit defendants differed in age, gender, race, and marital status. Unfit defendants were more likely to be older females belonging to a minority group and to be single. Hubbard, Zapf, and Ronan (2003) examined the *competency* (the term used in the United States for *fitness*) reports of 468 defendants. Differences between competent and incompetent defendants were found in employment status, psychiatric diagnosis, ethnicity, and criminal charges. Incompetent defendants were less likely to maintain employment and had more serious mental illness than competent defendants. Also, more African-American defendants were found incompetent compared with Caucasian defendants. Hubbard et al. (2003) also found that incompetent defendants were more likely to be charged with property and miscellaneous crimes rather than violent crimes compared with competent defendants.

In a recent meta-analysis reviewing the competency-to-stand-trial research, Pirelli, Gottdiener, and Zapf (2011) examined 68 studies published between 1967 and 2008 that compared competent and incompetent defendants on several variables. Defendants with a psychotic disorder were eight times more likely to be found incompetent than defendants without a psychotic disorder. Also, unemployed defendants were twice as likely to be found incompetent than employed defendants. Moreover, defendants with an earlier psychiatric hospitalization were twice as likely to be found incompetent than defendants without a history of hospitalization. It is important to note that not all psychotic defendants are unfit, and the presence of psychosis is not sufficient or equivalent to unfitness (Golding et al., 1984).

How would you rule on the defendant in the You Be the Judge box? Is he fit or unfit?

How Is Fitness Restored?

When a defendant is found unfit to stand trial, the goal of the criminal justice system is to get the defendant fit. The most common form of treatment for fitness is medication. A question facing the justice system concerning this form of treatment is whether a

Jack Chow was a graduate student in psychology working on his PhD. He would often spend his days in the lab conducting file reviews of offenders for his dissertation research. Jack shared the lab with two other students who were also completing their graduate studies. One day, Jack accused his lab mates of tapping into his data set and changing the data. His lab mates didn't know what he was talking about. These accusations escalated when Jack accused them of going into his email account and sending computer viruses to his friends who were contacts in his email list. Jack's lab mates were getting tired of these accusations.

One Friday afternoon, Jack opened his data file and was convinced it had been tampered with. In a rage, Jack threw his chair at one of his lab mates and started punching him. A student walking by quickly called campus security and the police. Jack was charged with assault. On the way to the police station, Jack started yelling that his lab mates had orchestrated his arrest so that they could steal his data and publish his groundbreaking research. Jack was given a court-appointed lawyer. In a preliminary hearing, Jack's lawyer stated Jack had no understanding of what he was being charged with and could not answer any of his questions. Jack kept repeating that he had to get back to his data and didn't have time for these games because he had a Nobel Prize to win. Jack's lawyer claimed Jack was unfit to stand trial and requested an assessment.

Your Turn . . .

Would you grant Jack this assessment? Do you think Jack is showing signs of unfitness? What are some of your concerns regarding Jack's behaviour?

defendant has the right to refuse medication. The courts will take into account the individual's capacity to comprehend and appreciate the consequences of his or her actions and public safety. Defendants sometimes may argue for not taking medication because of the serious side effects. A treatment order may be imposed by the court (R.S.C., 1985, C-46, s. 672.58); however, the courts also must grapple with having a heavily medicated defendant and whether this serves justice. See Box 8.3 for a look at a case involving a defendant with a mental illness, who fought against taking medication.

What Happens after a Finding of Unfitness?

The proceedings against a defendant who is found unfit to stand trial are halted until competency is restored. In the United States, almost all jurisdictions limit the time a defendant may be "held" as unfit. In the landmark case of *Jackson v. Indiana* (1972), the United States Supreme Court stated that a defendant should not be held for more than a reasonable period of time to determine whether there is a likelihood of the person gaining competency (fitness). Of course, what constitutes a reasonable period of time is open to interpretation.

Box 8.3   Cases in Forensic Psychology

Mentally Ill but Competent to Make Treatment Decisions?
Starson v. Swayze, (1999)

Scott Starson (a.k.a. Scott Jeffery Schutzman) has a special skill in physics. Without having formal training, he works with the top physics researchers in the world. In 1991, he co-authored an article with a physics professor from Stanford University. In addition to his physics ability, Starson also has a long history of battling a mental disorder. He has been diagnosed as having bipolar affective disorder. Starson has been admitted to several mental health facilities over the years.

In 1998, Starson was charged with uttering two death threats to tenants in his apartment complex. He was found not criminally responsible on account of mental disorder. In January 1999, the Ontario Review Board ordered that he be detained at the Centre for Addiction and Mental Health (CAMH) in Toronto. Dr. Ian Swayze and Dr. Paul Posner, both psychiatrists at CAMH, proposed to treat Starson with mood stabilizers and antipsychotic, anti-anxiety, and anti-Parkinsonian medication. Starson refused pharmaceutical intervention and appealed the Ontario Review Board's decision in provincial court. He argued that "he would not be able to do his work while on the proposed medication, not because of the side effects, but because of the very effects that the drugs are intended to achieve.... Starson said that after periods of treatment with such medications, it would always take him some time to 'work his way up the academic ladder'" (*Starson v. Swayze*, 1999, para. 55).

In November 1999, the Ontario Superior Court of Justice overturned the Ontario Review Board's decision, stating that it was unreasonable. Justice Anne Molloy stated that the board's conclusion that Starson was in denial of his mental illness was an error and that it was wrong for the board to accept unsubstantiated claims that Starson suffered delusions that others were out to harm him. Starson's doctors appealed the decision to the Ontario Court of Appeal. The appeal court ruled that Starson was

capable of making treatment decisions and could appreciate the possible consequences of refusing treatment. The doctors appealed to the Supreme Court of Canada. In June 2003, the Supreme Court upheld the lower court's decision that Starson had the capacity to refuse medical treatment. Intriguingly, refusing treatment is allowable under Ontario law; however, some other provinces and some other countries do not permit refusal of treatment (Gray & O'Reilly, 2009).

In 2005, Mr. Starson nearly died when claiming that his nonexistent son would be tortured if he (Mr. Starson) were to eat or drink anything. Following the incident, his mother became the substitute decision maker and allowed for Mr. Starson to begin treatment with neuroleptic medication (Haldol) following the Consent and Capacity Board ruling that deemed Mr. Starson as incapable of making a treatment decision. In April of 2008, Mr. Starson appealed the aforementioned ruling and although treatment was temporarily suspended, his condition deteriorated and he was once again involuntarily hospitalized. His subsequent appeal to the Ontario Superior Court was declined and the court upheld the finding of incapacity.

Questions

1. Is it more "just" to keep someone incarcerated indefinitely or to force treatment?

2. Are there any ethical concerns with forcing someone to take medication?

3. At what point should a doctor's opinion override a patient's decision not to take medication?

Sources: Based on *Starson v. Swayze*, 1999; *Starson v. Swayze*, 2003; Fighting for the right to refuse treatment: Part 2 (2005), *The Ottawa Citizen*; Dull. M.W. (2009). *Starson v Swayze*, 2003–2008: Appreciating the judicial consequences. *Health Law Journal*, 17, 51–79.

For unfit defendants in Canada, the judge may order that the defendant be detained in a hospital or that the defendant be conditionally discharged. The defendant is reassessed for fitness within 45 days. In the event that the defendant becomes fit, he or she returns to court and the proceedings resume (R.S.C., 1985, C-46, s. 672.28). If the defendant remains unfit after 90 days, he or she is referred to a

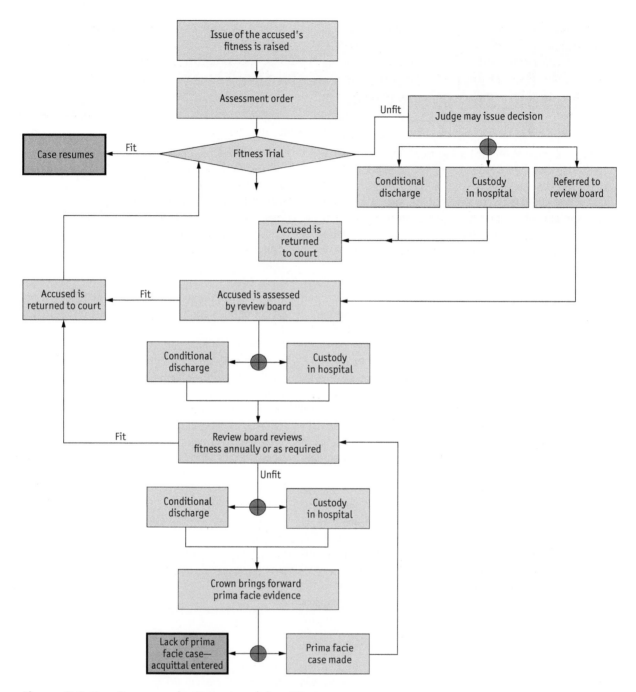

Figure 8.1 Key Processes in Cases Involving Fitness

*Although both the court and review board have the authority to detain a person found not criminally responsible on account of mental disorder in hospital, the accused may refuse treatment while detained.

**In accordance with the decision of the Supreme Court of Canada in *R. v. Swain* in 1991, the Crown may not "raise the issue of the defendant's mental capacity before the Crown proved that the crime had been committed or until the accused had put their mental capacity into issue."

review board for assessment and disposition (R.S.C., 1985, C-46, s. 672.47). Cases of defendants who continue to be unfit are reviewed on an annual basis by the review board. In these cases, the Crown must prove that there is sufficient evidence to bring the case to trial (referred to as making a **prima facie case**) every two years and at any time the defendant requests the proceeding. For youth found unfit, the court must review the case every year instead of every two years, according to section 141(10) of the Youth Criminal Justice Act. If the court determines that sufficient evidence is no longer available to prosecute the case, the case is dropped and the defendant is found not guilty (R.S.C., 1985, C-46, s. 672.33).

Even though a defendant may be restored to fitness, it is possible that he or she will become unfit once again during the trial proceedings. If unfitness occurs again, the proceedings stop until the defendant becomes fit. If a defendant becomes fit while in custody (e.g., detained in a mental health facility) and there is reason to believe that he or she may become unfit if released, the defendant will be required to remain in the facility until the trial is complete (R.S.C., 1985, C-46, s. 672.29). Also, it is possible for a defendant to become unfit while waiting to be sentenced (Manson, 2006).

What if a defendant is unlikely to become fit (e.g., possibly because of permanent brain damage)? Until recently, an absolute discharge could not be issued to defendants unlikely to become fit. However, in *R. v. Demers* (2004), the Supreme Court of Canada ruled that the inability of the courts or review boards to issue an absolute discharge to defendants who are unlikely to become fit and who pose no significant threat to society was in violation of the liberties guaranteed under section 7 of the Charter of Rights and Freedoms. This infringement was addressed by an amendment to the Criminal Code with the passing of Bill C-10, which occurred in January 2006. A court now has the authority to stay the proceedings for a defendant who is unlikely to become fit if any the following are true:

- The accused is unlikely ever to become fit.
- The accused does not pose a significant threat to the safety of the public.
- A stay of proceedings is in the interests of the proper administration of justice.

Bill C-10 still does not provide review boards with the ability to absolutely discharge an accused who is found unfit; only the courts have this power. A review board, however, can recommend to a court that an inquiry be undertaken to determine if a stay of proceedings is in the interests of the proper administration of justice. If a stay is not ordered, the accused remains under the disposition determined by the review board.

See Figure 8.1 for key processes in cases involving fitness.

MENTAL STATE AT TIME OF OFFENCE

Insanity has been defined as not being of sound mind, and being mentally deranged and irrational (Sykes, 1982). In a legal context, insanity removes the responsibility for performing a particular act because of uncontrollable impulses or delusions, such as hearing voices. There have been two primary British cases that have shaped the

Prima facie case: Case in which the Crown prosecutor must prove there is sufficient evidence to bring the case to trial

Insanity: Impairment of mental or emotional functioning that affects perceptions, beliefs, and motivations at the time of the offence

current standard of insanity in Canada (as cited in Moran, 1985). The first was that of James Hadfield, who in 1800 attempted to assassinate King George III. Hadfield had suffered a brain injury while fighting against the French. His lawyer successfully argued that he was out of touch with reality and therefore met the insanity standard of the time. Following this case, the Criminal Lunatics Act (1800) was established, and it stated the insanity standard of the day.

The second case influencing Canada's current insanity standard was that of Daniel McNaughton in 1843 (R. v. McNaughton, 1843). Daniel McNaughton was born and raised in Glasgow, Scotland. Eventually he found his way to London in July 1842. While in London, he purchased two pistols that he carried in his waistcoat. On Friday, January 20, 1843, he shadowed Edward Drummond, one of Prime Minister Robert Peel's secretaries, who was returning home from Drummond's Bank. McNaughton approached Drummond from behind, took a pistol out of his pocket, and shot Drummond in the back. Drummond then turned to see who shot him and pointed at McNaughton. McNaughton reached for his other pistol and at that point was tackled by James Silver, a constable. McNaughton was handcuffed and his weapons were removed. Drummond died five days later.

There is some debate as to McNaughton's reason for shooting and whether Drummond or Peel was the intended target.

McNaughton was charged with murder, and the judge interpreted his plea as "not guilty." McNaughton was found not guilty because of his mental status: insanity. He would serve out his life in a mental institute (see Dalby, 2006, for the full details of the story).

Five critical elements emerged from the McNaughton verdict, with three specific to the insanity defences of today:

1. A defendant must be found to be suffering from a defect of reason/disease of the mind.

2. A defendant must not know the nature and quality of the act he or she is performing.

3. A defendant must not know that what he or she is doing is wrong.

The elements in the McNaughton standard emerged in legislation in parts of the United States, England, and Canada. Little would change for the insanity standard in Canada for many years.

In the mid-1970s, a review of the policies for offenders with mental disorders was undertaken by the Law Reform Commission of Canada. Forty-four recommendations on law and policy were provided (Law Reform Commission of Canada, 1976). In response to this review, the Department of Justice commissioned the Mental Disorder Project in the early 1980s. This review found that the mental disorder legislation in the Criminal Code was in conflict with the Charter of Rights and Freedoms. The ruling from the Supreme Court of Canada in R. v. Swain (1991) was consistent with the review and foreshadowed the changes to the Criminal Code. For example, in R. v. Swain (1991), the Supreme Court determined that defendants who were found not guilty by reason of insanity could not be automatically detained until their level of dangerousness was decided or an appropriate disposition was determined. Finding a defendant guilty before either of these things was done would be in conflict with the Charter. Moreover, the court also decided that the defendant could raise the issue of his or her mental capacity at any point in the trial, but the Crown could not do so until it had proved the crime against the defendant or until the defendant raised his or her mental capacity.

In 1992, Bill C-30 was enacted and the following changes were made to the justice system:

- The term *not guilty by reason of insanity* was changed to *not criminally responsible on account of mental disorder* (NCRMD).

- The wording of the standard was altered and stated in section 16 of the Criminal Code of Canada: "No person is criminally responsible for an act committed or an omission made while suffering from a mental disorder that rendered the person incapable of appreciating the nature and quality of the act or omission or of knowing that it was wrong."

- **Review boards** were created. These legal bodies were mandated to oversee the care and disposition of defendants found unfit and/or not criminally responsible on account of a mental disorder. Review boards were required to review each unfit and NCRMD case every year.

Review boards: Legal bodies mandated to oversee the care and disposition of defendants found unfit and/or not criminally responsible on account of a mental disorder

Another change occurred in 1999. In *Winko v. British Columbia*, the Supreme Court of Canada stated that a defendant who is NCRMD should be detained only if he or she poses a criminal threat to the public; otherwise, the defendant should receive an absolute discharge. Another review on justice and human rights was undertaken in 2002 concerning mental disorder provisions in the Criminal Code. Another review was conducted in 2007 to allow for further data collection on mental health issues and the Criminal Code. See Box 8.4 for a description of a case in which the defendant was found NCRMD.

Box 8.4 Forensic Psychology in the Spotlight

Sportscaster Shot Dead by Patient with a Mental Illness

Brian Smith, a former hockey player, was a sportscaster for CJOH, an Ottawa television station. On August 1, 1995, after his evening sportscast, Smith left the station and walked out to the parking lot, where he was shot in the head. A day later, Smith died in the hospital. In the reports of Smith's death, many questioned the reason for his murder. Why would someone kill him? Jeffrey Arenburg, the confessed killer, said that he was angry with the media and wanted to harm a media personality. Arenburg said he went to the CJOH parking lot and shot the first media personality he recognized, Brian Smith.

Before Arenburg was tried for Smith's murder, he was assessed for fitness to stand trial. The jury found Arenburg fit and he was charged with first-degree murder. The defence raised the issue of Arenburg's sanity and argued for an NCRMD verdict. Indeed, in May 1997, Arenburg was found NCRMD for first-degree murder. He was sent to a maximum-security psychiatric facility, the Ontario Mental Health Centre in Penetanguishene, for an indefinite period of time. Less than ten years after the shooting, Arenburg wanted to be released. He had a mandatory review before the Ontario Review Board in May 2003, at which time his

(continued)

(continued)

lawyer argued for a conditional discharge. Arenburg was granted a conditional discharge and was required to live with his brother in Barrie, Ontario. In the fall of 2003, Arenburg was free to attend classes at Georgian College during the day, having to return to live with his brother in the evening. He graduated in June 2005.

In November 2006, the Ontario Review Board granted Arenburg an absolute discharge. The board heard that Arenburg no longer poses a significant risk to the community and no longer suffers from the symptoms of paranoid schizophrenia.

This case drew a great deal of attention to current legislation regarding the Mental Health Act. Arenburg had a history of mental illness. For example, in 1990, he went to a Nova Scotia courthouse demanding to be seen by a judge. When taken to the local hospital, he said that he heard his thoughts being broadcast by television and radio. He was diagnosed with paranoid psychosis and released. In 1991, he was brought to the Royal Ottawa Hospital because he had threatened a radio station. Once again, Arenburg stated that he was hearing voices. Arenburg was committed to the hospital. However, he appealed his commitment to the psychiatric review board. The board did not find Arenburg mentally ill or at risk to hurt others. However, it did find that Arenburg was not competent to refuse treatment. Arenburg discharged himself against doctor's advice. Arenburg was able to refuse treatment for two years following Smith's shooting. In response to an inquest into Smith's death, it was recommended that there should be more public protection against people with mental illnesses. Both the Mental Health Act and the Health Care Consent Act in Ontario were reviewed, and in 2000, Bill 68, also known as Brian's Law, was passed.

Brian's Law led to the implementation of community treatment orders, which are requirements for people with mental illnesses who are living in the community to report to a mental health caregiver on a regular basis. Also, as a condition of being released from a mental health facility to the community, those who have a mental illness may be forced to take prescribed medication. If they refuse medication, they can be re-institutionalized. Also under the new legislation, the word *imminent* was removed from the Mental Health Act. This change means that there no longer must be an immediate danger for someone to be confined to a psychiatric facility (R.S.O., 1990, s. 33.1). Other provinces, including British Columbia, Manitoba, and Saskatchewan, have similar legislation.

In November 2007, Arenburg was arrested after punching a U.S customs officer in the head while attempting to enter Buffalo, New York. Officials denied his entry due to previous convictions. Following the assault, Arenburg was sentenced to 2 years in jail and was subsequently released in September of 2009. In November 2014, after running away from his hometown of Bridgewater, Nova Scotia, Arenburg returned to Ottawa where he resided in a shelter awaiting his Canada Pension Plan Disability cheque. In an interview with the Fifth Estate, Arenburh claimed that he was no longer mentally ill and admitted to being off his prescribed medication.

Sources: *R. v. Arenburg*, 1997; Warmington, 2007; Willing, 2009; Brian Smith's killer jailed after border guard attacked, Ottawa Citizen (2007); Hurley, M., Dimmock, G., (2014), Brian Smith's Killer, Jeffrey Arenburg, returns to Ottawa. *The Ottawa Citizen*.

Raising the Issue of Insanity

Studies have found that few defendants use the insanity defence. For example, in the United States, one study found that less than 1% of all felony cases will argue an insanity defence (Steadman et al., 1993). Moreover, the success rate of such a defence is variable. It has been reported that approximately 25% of defendants who argue an insanity defence succeed (Steadman et al., 1993; Valdes, 2005). See Table 8.2 for a distribution of NCRMD and unfit cases in Canada.

Insanity defences typically occur when opposing sides (prosecution and defence) agree to such a verdict (Melton, Petrila, Poythress, & Slobogin, 1997). It is not common to have opposing experts testify on this issue in jury trials. Ogloff, Schweighofer, Turnbull, and Whittemore (1992) reported that defendants found NCRMD are likely to have major psychiatric disorders, such as schizophrenia, and many past mental health problems that resulted in hospitalization or prior rulings of unfitness. When comparing males and females found NCRMD, both genders were found to have similar violent offences and both were just as likely to be aggressive toward other patients (Nicholls, Brink, Greaves, Lussier, & Verdun-Jones, 2009).

Within the Canadian criminal justice system, a defendant is considered not to suffer from a mental disorder unless the issue of insanity is raised by the defence. In Canada, there are only two situations in which the Crown may raise the issue of insanity:

1. Following a guilty verdict, the Crown could argue that the defendant was NCRMD. This situation may occur if the Crown believes that the defendant requires psychiatric treatment and a mental facility is best suited for the defendant's needs.

2. If the defence states that the defendant has a mental illness, the Crown can then argue it.

The party that raises the issue must prove it beyond a balance of the probabilities (R.S.C., 1985, C-46, s. 16).

Assessing Insanity

Just as with fitness to stand trial, an insanity defence requires a psychiatric assessment. Richard Rogers developed the first standardized assessment scales for criminal responsibility: the Rogers Criminal Responsibility Assessment Scales (R-CRAS) (Rogers, 1984).

The R-CRAS is the only instrument of its kind. It has five scales:

1. Patient reliability
2. Organicity
3. Psychopathology
4. Cognitive control
5. Behavioural control

Each scale has 30 items, which are given a score from 0 to 6, with higher values representing greater severity (Rogers & Sewell, 1999). It is important to note that the R-CRAS was developed to standardize evaluations and ensure particular areas are evaluated, rather than produce a cut-off score to indicate criminal responsibility (Rogers & Ewing, 1992). The clinician is to take all the information into account and use it as the basis for a decision regarding the defendant's mental status and criminal responsibility.

What Happens to a Defendant Found NCRMD?

Three dispositions can be made following a finding of NCRMD. If the defendant is not a threat to society or poses low risk for reoffending, the court or review board can order an **absolute discharge**. That is, the defendant is released into the community without

Absolute discharge: The defendant is released into the community without restrictions to his or her behaviour

Conditional discharge: A defendant is released; however, release carries certain conditions (e.g., not to possess firearms) that the defendant must meet. Failure to meet the conditions imposed with a conditional discharge may result in the defendant being incarcerated or sent to a psychiatric facility

restrictions on his or her behaviour. A second disposition option is to order a discharge with conditions, known as a **conditional discharge**. In this case, the defendant is released but must meet certain conditions, such as not possessing firearms. Failure to meet the conditions imposed with a conditional discharge may result in the defendant being incarcerated or sent to a psychiatric facility. Lastly, the court or review board may order that the defendant be sent to a psychiatric facility (R.S.C., 1985, C-46, s. 672.54).

It is important to note that a defendant who is sent to a psychiatric facility need not comply with treatment. It is only when the defendant's mental health has deteriorated to a point that he or she is no longer competent to make treatment decisions that steps may be taken to force treatment on the defendant (R.S.C., 1985, C-46, s. 672.54). In such instances, the provincial and territorial mental health policies would be followed.

In Canada, dispositions may be made by the court or referred to a provincial or territorial review board. Dispositions that are made by the court also are reviewed by a review board within 90 days and can be changed at any point. An exception to this rule occurs if the court makes an absolute discharge (R.S.C., 1985, C-46, s. 672.81). This decision does not go before a review board. In addition, review boards review the defendant's disposition every year. There is a great deal of information that review boards will take into account, including

- charge information
- trial transcript
- criminal history
- risk assessment
- clinical history, such as previous admissions to hospital
- psychological testing
- hospital's recommendation

As you read earlier, historically, defendants who were found insane would spend the remainder of their lives in an insane asylum. More recently, it was not uncommon for "insane" defendants to be given indeterminate sentences, only to be released when they were deemed sane. Moreover, insane defendants often would serve more time in a mental institute than their prison sentence would have been following a standard guilty verdict. Bill C-30 introduced **capping**, which refers to the maximum period of time a person with a mental illness can be affected by his or her disposition. For example, the disposition period for a defendant with a mental illness who committed a violent offence is ten years, the same length of time as the prison term. Once the cap is reached, the defendant may be released without restrictions. However, if the defendant is still perceived to be dangerous, he or she could be involuntarily committed to a secure hospital. Moreover, if the defendant was declared a mentally disordered dangerous/violent offender, this designation could increase the cap.

Capping: Notion introduced through Bill C-30 where there is a maximum period of time a person with a mental illness could be affected by his or her disposition

When deciding on a disposition, the court and review board must choose the option that is least limiting to the defendant. Four main criteria are considered when deciding a disposition:

- public safety
- mental state of the defendant

- reintegration of the defendant into society
- other needs of the defendant

See Figure 8.2 for key processes in cases involving NCRMD defences.

A recent study by Crocker, Braithwaite, Côté, Nicholls, and Seto (2011) examined factors related to review board decisions on whether to detain or release individuals found NCRMD. The study involved cases between October

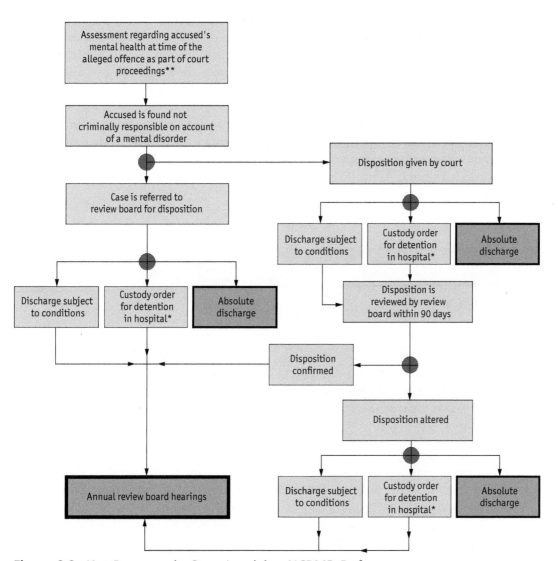

Figure 8.2 Key Processes in Cases Involving NCRMD Defences

*Although both the court and review board have the authority to detain a person found NCRMD in hospital, the accused may refuse treatment while detained.

**In accordance with the decision of the Supreme Court of Canada in *R. v. Swain* (1991), the Crown may not "raise the issue of the defendant's mental capacity before the Crown proved that the crime had been committed or until the accused had put their mental capacity into issue."

2004 and August 2006 from a forensic psychiatric hospital and two civil psychiatric hospitals designed to care for individuals found NCRMD. Examining the cases of 96 males, the researchers found that dynamic risk factors (i.e., factors that are changeable) rather than static factors (i.e., factors that cannot be changed, such as an individual's criminal history) were related to the decision to detain or release the individual. The researchers concluded that dynamic factors seem appropriate for review boards to consider given the objective behind an NCRMD decision.

Early in 2013, the prime minister's office introduced Bill C-54, which would make changes to how those defendants found not criminally responsible are dealt with. This bill is directed at those who committed a serious offence and have a high likelihood of reoffending and toward acts that are so heinous that the public could be at risk. If this bill passes as it currently is proposed, these high-risk offenders would not be granted a conditional or absolute discharge, and only a court could lift the high-risk designation. As of June 18, 2013, Bill C-54 was undergoing the second reading by the Senate and hence the bill has not yet become law. See Box 8.5 for an example of a defendant who may or may not fall under this new bill if it is legislated. Some argue that the bill does not go far enough, whereas others argue that it contradicts the available research. What do you think? See the section later in this chapter on mentally ill offenders.

Box 8.5   Forensic Psychology in the Spotlight

Police Officer Run Over by Snowplow

At 5 a.m. on January 12, 2011, in the middle of winter in Toronto, Richard Kachkar jumped into a running snowplow. Kachkar had run out of the Good Shepherd homeless shelter without any shoes or socks on and stolen the snowplow. After two hours of running into cars and injuring drivers, Kachkar ran over Sergeant Ryan Russell, who was later pronounced dead in hospital. The police officer was trying to stop Kachkar and the runaway snowplow. Kachkar was charged with first-degree murder. At issue for the criminal case was not whether Kachkar killed Russell. He did. At issue was Kachkar's mental state at the time of the offence.

In a trial by jury, a verdict of not criminally responsible on account of mental disorder was reached. The Crown decided not to appeal the verdict. Both the Crown and Kachkar's lawyer jointly recommended that Kachkar be held at Ontario Shores Centre for Mental Health Sciences in Whitby, Ontario. A five-member review board will decide whether Kachkar will remain in custody or be released into the community. If it is determined that Kachkar should be held at the mental health facility, his case will be reviewed yearly and he will be released only when he is deemed not to be a risk to the public. According to Kachkar's lawyer, Kachkar is very remorseful. Also, Kachkar has stated that he is sick, and he has been started on antipsychotic medication to help with his symptoms. On April 29, 2013, the Ontario Review Board agreed that Kachkar would be sent to the mental health facility in Whitby. He will be allowed escorted walks on the hospital grounds and in the community at the hospital's discretion. The review board also stated that police would have to be notified if Kachkar is going into the community.

Sources: Based on http://www.thestar.com/news/crime/2013/04/26/richard_kachkar_snowplow_killer_is_free_of_psychotic_symptoms_but_needs_protection_hearing_told.html; http://www.thestar.com/news/insight/2013/04/29/richard_kachkar_how_a_cop_killer_was_found_not_criminally_responsible.html; http://news.nationalpost.com/tag/richard-kachkar/ Retrieved May 9, 2013.

AUTOMATISM

If you don't have control over your behaviour, should you be held responsible for your actions? Consider the case of Kenneth Parks (*R. v. Parks*, 1992). He got up in the middle of the night, got dressed, got into his car, and drove to where his parents-in-law lived. He went into their home, got a kitchen knife, stabbed his mother-in-law to death and almost killed his father-in-law. He then drove to the police station and turned himself in. He was charged and tried for murder and attempted murder. Parks's defence was that he was sleepwalking, a form of automatism. **Automatism** refers to unconscious, involuntary behaviour; that is, the person committing the act is not aware of what he or she is doing. Parks was acquitted on both charges. See Box 8.6 for an example of automatism involving a Canadian socialite.

Automatism: Unconscious, involuntary behaviour such that the person committing the act is not aware of what he or she is doing

The Criminal Code of Canada does not specifically address automatism as a defence; rather, judges have had to rely on their own judgment and case law when such defences are raised. In *R. v. Stone* (1999) (see Box 8.7), the Supreme Court of Canada stated that there were two forms of automatism: noninsane and insane. Noninsane automatism refers to involuntary behaviour that occurs because of an external factor. The verdict in such cases is "not guilty." Insane automatism refers to an involuntary action that occurs because of a mental disorder. In these cases, a finding of NCRMD would be entered and the legislation for NCRMD would be applied.

In *R. v. Stone* (1999) the Supreme Court outlined a two-stage process for addressing defences of automatism. First, the trial judge must decide whether there is sufficient evidence that a jury could find that the defendant's behaviour was involuntary. The following factors are considered:

- Psychiatric assessments
- Severity of triggering event
- History of automatic behaviour

Box 8.6   Forensic Psychology in the Spotlight

A Gas Company, a Tire Company, and a Case of Automatism

Dorothy and Earl Joudrie were teen sweethearts. They married in 1957, and although they had only $25 at the time, they managed to amass quite a fortune. They had a 650-square-metre home, a vacation home in Hawaii, and were millionaires. Earl had become the chair of both Gulf Canada Resources Limited and the Canadian Tire Corporation, to name just two of his many accomplishments. In 1989, the couple separated. In 1994, Earl petitioned for a divorce but Dorothy contested the petition.

It was January 21, 1995, when Dorothy Joudrie took a handgun and shot Earl Joudrie six times. The motivation for the shooting was unclear. Abuse early in the marriage? Loss of marital status? Or some other reason? Dorothy had no memory of the shooting. At her trial for attempted murder, three psychiatrists told the court that Dorothy was in a dissociative state at the time of the shooting. One psychiatrist for the Crown, Dr. Arboleda-Florez, stated that Dorothy was in an automatistic state. There are two types of automatism: sane and insane. Dorothy's state was determined to be insane automatism (more about this distinction in the main text). The jury of 11 women and 1 man reached the same conclusion, returning an NCRMD decision. Dorothy Joudrie was ordered to undergo a psychiatric assessment. Dorothy spent five months in a psychiatric facility after the verdict and then was given an absolute discharge. The Joudries were divorced in 1995.

Source: Based on British Journal of Social Psychology by Charlan Nemeth and John Rogers, 1996.

Box 8.7   Cases in Forensic Psychology

Can Insults Lead to Automatism? *R v. Stone* (1999)

There was no question that Bert Stone stabbed his wife 47 times (*R. v. Stone*, 1999). He was holding a hunting knife and his wife was dead in her seat. His defence was that his behaviour was not under his control. Stone argued that when he stabbed her, he was in an automatistic state that was triggered by his wife's insults. After Stone stabbed his wife, he got rid of the body, cleaned up, left a note for his stepdaughter, and then checked into a hotel. Later, he sold his car and flew to Mexico. It was there that he woke up one morning to a feeling of having his throat cut. While trying to remember this bad dream, he remembered stabbing his wife two times. After about six weeks, Stone returned to Canada and gave himself up to police. He was charged with murder. Stone was found guilty and sentenced to seven years in prison.

Questions

1. Do you think you could forget that you killed someone? If you forget, how do you remember to "clean up"?
2. What is an appropriate sentence for forgetting?

Source: Based on *R. v. Stone*, *[1999]* 2 S.C.R. 290, http://scc-csc.lexum.com/scc-csc/scc-csc/en/item/1705/index.do. Supreme Court of Canada.

Second, the trial judge determines if the condition is a mental disorder (insane) or non-mental-disorder (noninsane) automatism.

If the judge decides that the condition is the result of an external factor, the defence can argue noninsane automatism. The judge and/or jury will need to decide whether the defendant acted involuntarily. If so, the defendant will be found not guilty. If the judge decides that the condition is the result of a mental disorder, the defence can argue insane automatism, and the case proceeds as an NCRMD case. The NCRMD standard as outlined in section 16 of the Canadian Criminal Code must be met. A successful defence in this situation would result in an NCRMD verdict.

Canadian courts have recognized defences of noninsane automatism in the following circumstances:

- A physical blow (e.g., a blow to the head)
- Physical ailments, such as stroke
- Hypoglycemia (e.g., low blood sugar)
- Carbon monoxide poisoning
- Sleepwalking
- Involuntary intoxication
- Psychological blow from an extraordinary external event that might reasonably be expected to cause a dissociative state in an average, normal person

It is important to note that everyday life stresses that may lead to a dissociative state would not be sufficient for a defence of automatism. Dissociative states from psychological factors, such as grief and mourning or anxiety, are more consistent with diseases of the mind and may be applicable for the insanity defence.

How Do NCRMD and Automatism Differ?

The main difference between defences of NCRMD and automatism lies in their verdict outcomes. An NCRMD verdict may result in the defendant being sent to a mental health facility. In contrast, a successful (noninsane) automatism verdict means that the defendant is not guilty and is then released without conditions. Insane automatism verdicts result in an NCRMD ruling. The defendants in these cases are subject to the same dispositions as those with a successful NCRMD defence.

Intoxication as a Defence

One evening, Mr. Daviault brought a 40-ounce bottle of brandy over to Ms. X's home at her request (*R. v. Daviault*, 1994). X was 65 years old and partially paralyzed. She was confined to a wheelchair. X had a half glass of brandy and fell asleep in her wheelchair. During the middle of the night, she awoke to go to the bathroom, at which point Daviault sexually assaulted her and left the apartment. X noticed that the bottle of brandy was empty. Daviault had drunk the remainder of the bottle; he was an alcoholic. During the trial proceedings, Daviault stated that he had had seven or eight bottles of beer earlier that day. Although he remembered having a glass of brandy when he arrived at X's, he did not remember what happened afterward and that he awoke naked in X's bed. He denied sexually assaulting her.

A pharmacologist testified for the defence and stated that "an individual with this level of alcohol in his blood might suffer an episode of 'L'amnesie-automatisme,' also known as a blackout. In such a state the individual loses contact with reality and the brain is temporarily dissociated from normal functioning. The individual has no awareness of his actions when he is in such a state and will likely have no memory of them the next day" (*R. v. Daviault*, 1994, para. 73).

The judge found that the defendant committed the offence but, because of the level of intoxication, found that he did not have the intent to commit the act. Daviault was found not guilty. On appeal, the court reversed the judge's decision, entering a guilty verdict for Daviault. The appeal court stated that self-induced intoxication resulting in a state similar to automatism is not available as a defence for a general intent offence—that is, an offence that requires only an intention to commit the act. Moreover, in 1995 Bill C-72 was passed, which stated that intoxication was not recognized as a defence for violent crimes.

Royal Ottawa Mental Health Centre
The Royal Ottawa Mental Health Centre

As you can see, automatism is not a straightforward defence. It is a challenge to prove and may result in variable verdicts. Until legislation can clarify this defence, there will remain ambiguity in the use and success of this defence.

DEFENDANTS WITH MENTAL DISORDERS

If a defendant does not receive an unfit finding or an NCRMD verdict, this does not necessarily mean that he or she does not have mental health difficulties. In a Canadian study examining males from the Edmonton Remand Centre, Bland, Newman, Dyck, and Orn (1990) found that 92% of the sample had a lifetime prevalence of psychiatric disorders (see Table 8.3). More recently, Brink, Doherty, and Boer (2001) examined the prevalence of mental disorders in federally incarcerated offender and found 43.1% of the sample had a lifetime prevalence of a DSM-IV Axis I diagnosis when substance abuse disorders were not included. To give you a comparison, in 2002 (in Canada) approximately 10% of the general population reported mental health problems (Pearson, Janz, & Ali, 2013). Between 2006 and 2007, 10% of incarcerated offenders were found to have a mental disorder at the time of admission (Public Safety Canada Portfolio Corrections Statistics Committee, 2007). Lafortune (2010) found that that during 2002–2007, 61% of the 671 offenders sent to a short-term correctional facility in Canada were given at least one mental disorder diagnosis. Males were found to suffer from psychotic disorders, anxiety disorders, and drug dependency. Females were found to suffer from anxiety, personality disorders, and substance abuse–related disorders.

A substantial number of offenders in the United States also have mental health needs. For example, 25% of offenders incarcerated in Colorado suffer from mental

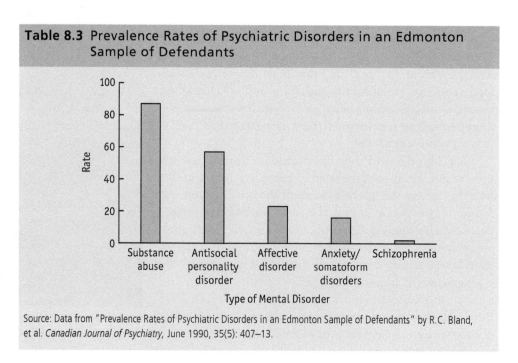

Table 8.3 Prevalence Rates of Psychiatric Disorders in an Edmonton Sample of Defendants

Source: Data from "Prevalence Rates of Psychiatric Disorders in an Edmonton Sample of Defendants" by R.C. Bland, et al. *Canadian Journal of Psychiatry,* June 1990, 35(5): 407–13.

illness (O'Keefe & Schnell, 2007). Also, it is important to note that mentally ill offenders are likely to have more than one mental health issue. It is estimated that approximately 75% of mentally ill offenders (in the United States) have dual diagnoses (Chandler, Peters, Field, & Juliano-Bult, 2004). Elsayed, Al-Zahrani, and Rashad (2010) examined characteristics of 100 mentally ill offenders in Saudi Arabia. Thirteen percent of the sample were diagnosed with schizophrenia, 56% of the sample had substance-related issues, and 10% were diagnosed with antisocial personality disorder. More than half of the cases (58%) had experienced contact with a psychiatric health care facility prior to the offence, with 9% having contact within the previous 12 weeks.

Recently, the issue of what to do with mentally ill offenders has been in the Canadian media. See the In the Media box for a discussion of what to do with offenders who have mental illnesses but do not meet criteria for unfitness or NCRMD.

In the Media

What to Do with Mentally Ill Offenders?

What happens to offenders who do not meet the criteria to be considered unfit or NCRMD? Currently, inmates who are mentally ill are segregated from other offenders. Segregation is used if inmates are suicidal or at risk of seriously injuring themselves. However, the Correctional Service of Canada has taken steps to change this. Howard Sapers, Canada's federal prison ombudsman, stated that "the practice of confining mentally ill offenders to prolonged periods of isolation in austere conditions with limited meaningful social interaction must end" (as quoted in Quan, 2010). Sapers also noted that the Correctional Service of Canada has hired outside experts to examine the practice of segregating mentally ill offenders. Sapers would like to see alternatives to segregation for those who are mentally ill.

Offenders who experience acute mental illness are sent to one of five regional psychiatric hospitals in Canada. Unfortunately, there are virtually no options if an offender does not meet hospital admission criteria but suffers mental illness. Sapers has suggested the development of intermediate-care units that would be located within the prison to offer offenders a therapeutic setting.

The Correctional Service of Canada (CSC) investigated this option and has now implemented a computerized mental health screening at intake.

Intriguingly, Vic Toews, then Minister of Public Safety, stated, "Although we've taken significant steps to improve services for the mentally ill in our corrections system, prisons should not be relied on to provide treatment for mental illness" (quoted in Quan, 2010).

Interest in these issues follows an investigation report in 2008 regarding the death of Ashley Smith, who died from self-asphyxiation while in custody in an Ontario prison. The report found that Smith, who was 19 years old at the time of her death, did not receive proper mental health services and was placed in solitary confinement for the entire time she was in custody (11.5 months). The report noted that the prison staff did not adequately respond to her needs, which often resulted in medical emergencies. The Smith family filed a lawsuit against CSC for negligence—it was settled out of court in May 2011. An inquest into Ashley's suicide began in 2011 but was subsequently dismissed after several challenges around the scope of the inquest. Video evidence of Ashley being dehumanized and degraded while in prison was released to the media. A second inquest began in early 2013 that includes the video evidence.

Sources: Based on Quan, D. (2010, March 25). Stop isolating mentally ill inmates: Ombudsman. Canwest News Service. Retrieved from http://www.globalmontreal.com/health/Stop+isolaing+mentally+inmates+Ombudsman/2726481/story.html?hub=WFive; http://www.cbc.ca/news/canada/story/2012/11/23/can-ashley-smith-inquest-.html; http://www.cbc.ca/news/canada/story/2012/10/31/ashley-smith-inquest-scope.html.

Why Are There Such High Rates of Mental Illness in Offender Populations?

A variety of explanations have been postulated to understand the high rates of mental illness in offender populations in Canada (Bland et al., 1990):

1. Individuals with a mental illness are likely to be arrested at a disproportionately high rate compared with those who do not have a mental illness.

2. Individuals with a mental illness are less adept at committing crime and therefore more likely to get caught.

3. Individuals with a mental illness are more likely to plead guilty, possibly because of an inability to access good representation or to understand the consequences of their plea.

In 2004, the Canadian Mental Health Association suggested that individuals with mental health issues are likely to be detected and arrested for nuisance offences such as trespassing and disorderly conduct, and are more likely to be remanded into custody for these minor offences.

It is possible that all these explanations are appropriate. Moreover, there may be alternative explanations to the high rates of mental illness in offender populations that have yet to be articulated. Further research is needed to explain this phenomenon.

Dealing with Offenders Who Are Mentally Ill

Police have great latitude in how they deal with offenders in the community who are mentally ill. Provincial and territorial mental health legislation grants police two options for handling these offenders. If an individual has a mental disorder and poses a threat to him- or herself or to others, the police may bring the individual to a hospital or a mental health facility for assessment and possible treatment. As an alternative, the police may charge and arrest the individual. In this scenario, mental health services may be obtained through the criminal justice system. Thus, the mental health system and the criminal justice system are both available to police, providing two alternative routes for dealing with people with a mental illness. Some have argued that people with mental illnesses are more likely to be processed through the justice system because of the difficulty of obtaining services for them through the mental health system (Teplin, 1984).

Bias against Mentally Ill Offenders

As part of a Canadian national study examining mental health problems in federally incarcerated offenders, Porporino and Motiuk (1995) compared 36 male offenders meeting criteria for a mental disorder (e.g., mania or schizophrenia) with 36 male offenders not meeting these criteria. The two groups were similar on a number of variables, including age, type of crime committed, and history of criminal activity. The researchers were interested in the conditional release patterns for both groups.

Specifically, they wanted to know whether offenders with a mental illness were treated differently.

Offenders can receive a conditional release from a federal facility in Canada in two ways: parole or mandatory supervision. Parole is determined by a parole board and is dependent on eligibility criteria. Ultimately, the National Parole Board has discretionary power in whether parole is granted. In contrast, mandatory supervision occurs after serving two-thirds of a sentence.

Porporino and Mortiuk found that a similar proportion of offenders from both groups (67% of those with a mental disorder versus 75% of those without one) received conditional releases. However, the reason for granting a conditional release differed across the two groups. Offenders with mental disorders were more likely to be conditionally released as a result of mandatory supervision, whereas offenders who did not have a mental disorder were more likely to be conditionally released because of parole.

Moreover, the researchers found that the offenders with mental disorders were more likely to have their release suspended (e.g., for not abiding by their supervision order) compared with other offenders. The offenders without mental disorders were likely to be re-admitted for committing a new offence. In one study, individuals with mental illness, according to police records, were twice as likely to be at risk for coming back into contact with the criminal justice system compared with other offenders (Hartford, Heslop, Stitt, & Hoch, 2005). Thus, offenders with mental disorders may be treated cautiously by the criminal justice system because of a presumption that they are a greater risk for committing more crime. Is this presumption correct?

Baillargeon et al. (2009) examined the relationship between parole revocations (including new offences) and mental disorders of 8149 offenders for a time period of 12 months after the offenders' release from incarceration. Those with only a psychiatric disorder were less likely to violate their parole and commit a new offence compared to those with a combination of a major psychiatric disorder and a substance abuse disorder. As you can see, a number of factors can be related to rates of re-arrest, not just mental illness.

Are People with Mental Illnesses Violent?

A commonly held belief is that people who have a mental illness are violent predators. Does the research support this view? Two epidemiological surveys were conducted to examine the relationship between violence and mental disorders. In a Canadian study conducted in Edmonton, violence referred to physical acts, such as fist fighting and using weapons (Bland & Orn, 1986). Mental disorders included antisocial personality disorder, major depression, and alcohol/drug dependence. Approximately 55% of respondents who met criteria for a psychiatric diagnosis committed violent acts. In contrast, only about 16% of respondents who did not meet criteria for a psychiatric diagnosis engaged in violent behaviour. When respondents met criteria for two diagnoses—for example, alcoholism and antisocial personality disorder and/or depression—80 to 93% of these respondents committed violent acts. Similar results were found in a sample from the United States (Swanson, Holzer, Ganju, & Jono, 1990). Over 50% of the U.S. respondents who met criteria for a psychiatric disorder committed violent acts. In both studies, substance abuse increased the risk of engaging in violence.

Baillargeon, Binswanger, Penn, Williams, and Murray (2009) defined violence as homicide, kidnapping, sexual assault, robbery assault, and terrorism. Approximately 23% of offenders with no psychiatric disorder committed violent acts whereas 28% of offenders diagnosed with any psychiatric disorder engaged in violent behaviour.

Examining a European sample, Fazel and Grann (2006) reviewed cases of patients who had been discharged from hospitals in Sweden over a 12-year period. Persons who had been admitted were classified into two groups based on whether they had schizophrenia or other psychosis. Fazel and Grann found that patients with severe mental illness were more likely to have a violence conviction when compared with the general population. When comparing the schizophrenic group with the other psychosis group, those diagnosed with schizophrenia were more likely to have committed a violent crime than those diagnosed with other psychoses. A peak in criminal behaviour was reflected in the 15–24-year-old age group and a decline in criminal behaviour was observed in offenders who were 40 and older.

In a 38-year follow-up study, Fazel, Wolf, Palm, and Lichtenstein (2014) examined the relationship between schizophrenia and adverse outcomes in 24 947 patients diagnosed with schizophrenia, as well as a matched sample from the population and unaffected siblings. Within five years of the initial diagnosis, 10.7% of men and 2.7% of women committed a violent offence; odds of conviction for a violent offence were higher in patients with schizophrenia and related disorders than the general population (Fazel et al., 2014). However, drug use disorders and previous criminality prior to the diagnosis were among the three risk factors predictive of adverse outcomes; moreover, these same factors raised the risk of adverse outcomes in the general population as well. This research indicates that while psychiatric diagnoses such as schizophrenia may influence the likelihood of committing a violent offence, prior violence and substance abuse also seem to effect the likelihood of future violence.

Overall, the notion that people with mental illness are more violent may not be a completely accurate view. However, see Box 8.8 for an example of an extremely violent crime committed by a mentally ill individual.

Types of Offences Committed by People with Mental Illnesses

Rice and Harris (1990) compared three groups of offenders: a group of males found NCRMD, a random group of convicted offenders who were sent for pretrial psychiatric evaluations, and a group of convicted offenders who were matched on the offence committed. The researchers found that NCRMD defendants were more likely to have committed murder or attempted murder than the other groups. Overall, however, offenders with mental disorders committed a variety of crimes, such as fraud, shoplifting, and murder. In other words, mentally disordered offenders were similar to other offenders and not distinguishable based solely on offence type (Rice & Harris, 1997b).

A Violent Crime Committed by a Mentally Ill Man

On July 30, 2008, 22-year-old Tim McLean boarded a Greyhound bus in Edmonton on his way home to Winnipeg. McLean put his headphones on and fell asleep in one of the bus seats. A man named Vincent Li sat beside him. While McLean was asleep, Li started stabbing him with a hunting knife. He then beheaded and cannibalized McLean. Who could commit such a horrific, violent act? Li was a 40-year-old who had immigrated to Canada from China in 2001. He had worked at a number of jobs—for example, he had worked as a contractor, a newspaper deliverer, and a fast-food employee. Li had no previous criminal record. Li was charged with second-degree murder and his trial started on March 3, 2009, with Li pleading not criminally responsible on account of mental disorder.

According to a psychiatrist who testified, Li was a schizophrenic who heard a voice telling him to kill. Li was found to suffer hallucinations even though he was on medication. Li was found NCRMD and was sent to a high-security mental health facility for a year. After that time, he will be re-assessed. As of 2015, Li has been moved to a Level 5 group home, allowing him more freedom.

McLean's mother, Carol de Delley has created the deDelley Foundation for Life to change criminal law. In 2014, the foundation and bank account associated with it were closed. She wants people who voluntarily take someone else's life to lose their freedom for the rest of their lives, regardless of whether they are declared not criminally responsible.

Recently, the Canadian government has announced it will introduce legislation that will make it more difficult for offenders found NCRMD to be released from custody.

Between 2000 and 2005, Crocker, Seto, Nicholls, and Cote (2013) found that of the 165 NCRMD cases examined (including convictions of homicide, attempted murder, and sexual offence) 18.1% of offenders received a conditional release whereas nearly half (49.1%) of individuals received an absolute discharge.

Sources: Based on McIntyre, M. (2009, March 5). Victim's family incensed as beheading killer avoids jail time. National Post. Retrieved from http://www.nationalpost.com/related/topics/story.html?id=1356797; Suspect in bus killing delivered newspapers, worked at McDonald's: employer (2008, August 1). CBC News. Retrieved from http://www.cbc.ca/canada/story/2008/08/01/stabbing-victim.html http://www.cbc.ca/news/canada/story/2012/11/22/pol-mentally-ill-killers-nicholson-moore.html.

Recidivism Rates and People with Mental Illnesses

To determine whether offenders with mental disorders are more likely to reoffend, Charette and colleagues (2015) examined recidivism rates among NCRMD defendants across British Columbia, Ontario, and Quebec. Criminal history, psychiatric diagnosis, and nature of the index offence were controlled for when examining rates of recidivism. Charette et al. (2015) found that after three years, the recidivism rate was 17% following index verdict, 20% following conditional discharge, and 22% following absolute discharge. When examining provincial differences, recidivism rates for British Columbia and Ontario were roughly the same, while Quebec's rate was roughly double that in the other two provinces. The recidivism rates found in the study were lower than that of the general population of offenders as well as that of the inmate population treated for mental disorder (e.g., Johnson & Grant, 2000; Villeneuve & Quinsey, 1995).

A meta-analysis examining the recidivism of more than 23 000 mentally disordered offenders was conducted by Bonta, Blais, and Wilson (2014). The average recidivism follow-up time (until someone followed up to see whether the offender had re-offended) was 4.9 years. Bonta et al. (2014) found that having a mental disorder was not predictive of recidivism. The researchers also suggested that while there are cases when a crime is committed while the perpetrator is in a psychotic state, the fact of having psychosis is not a useful predictor of recidivism. A group of researchers (Phillips et al., 2005) investigated the ability of personal demographic, criminal history, and clinical variables to predict reoffending in mentally disordered offenders in the United Kingdom. Both general and violent reoffending were considered. The best predicting factors were age on admission, number of days hospitalized, and number of previous offences. The strongest predictor was number of previous offences. A mental disorder diagnosis was *not* predictive of reoffending. Moreover, none of the factors could distinguish between general offenders and violent offenders. Castillo and Alarid (2011) found that offenders with an alcohol problem were more likely to recidivate earlier and be re-arrested for a violent offence than offenders without an alcohol problem.

Treatment of Offenders with Mental Disorders

The goals for treatment of offenders with mental disorders vary greatly and are somewhat dependent on whether the offender is dealt with through the mental health system or the criminal justice system. Some of the treatment goals identified for offenders with mental disorders include symptom reduction, decreased length of stay in the facility, and no need to be re-admitted to hospital (Test, 1992). Of course, reducing the risk of recidivism has garnered much attention as a treatment goal among those in the criminal justice system (Lipsey, 1992).

There are a number of types of facilities at which mentally disordered offenders can receive treatment, including psychiatric institutions, general hospitals, and assisted housing units, but there appears to be little agreement on which type of treatment is most appropriate for offenders with mental disorders (Quinsey & Maguire, 1983). However, for those who experience active psychotic symptoms, such as delusions, hallucinations, suspicion, and noncompliance with medication, there are two key treatment options: antipsychotic drugs and behaviour therapy (Breslin, 1992). Medication can help to control psychotic symptoms, while behaviour therapy can help to ensure that patients take the medication consistently. The critical aspects of behaviour therapy appear to be in providing positive social and material reward for appropriate behaviour, while decreasing or eliminating attention for symptomatic behaviour (Beck, Menditto, Baldwin, Angelone, & Maddox, 1991; Paul & Lentz, 1977).

The availability of facilities and different treatment programs vary across the country. Moreover, the willingness of an offender to engage in a particular program will vary. Even if an offender is motivated to receive treatment, an appropriate program may not be available at a particular facility. Thus, there are difficulties in matching programs to offenders' needs and willingness to participate.

A group of researchers (Morgan et al., 2012) used meta-analysis to review 26 empirical studies and found that intervening with mentally ill offenders reduced the offenders' distress and improved their ability to deal with their problems, in turn improving behavioural outcomes. If the interventions were geared to meet the psychological as well as the behavioural issues of the mentally ill offenders, significant reductions in mental illness and recidivism were found.

One overarching treatment goal of many offender programs is to reintegrate the offender into society. The mental health and criminal justice system has developed options with this goal in mind. For example, a **community treatment order** allows the offender who has a mental illness to live in the community, with the stipulation that he or she will agree to treatment or detention in the event that his or her condition deteriorates. Another option for the courts dealing with offenders with mental illnesses who are facing minor charges is **diversion**—that is, diverting the offenders directly into a treatment program rather than having them go through the court process. Generally, only defendants who are willing to participate in treatment will be diverted.

Treatment can be critical for offenders who have certain mental disorders, such as schizophrenia.

The former Mental Health Centre Penetanguishene Oak Ridge Division (now Waypoint Centre for Mental Health Care)
WayPoint Centre

A NEW COURT FOR THE MENTALLY ILL: THE MENTAL HEALTH COURTS

A new court is in town, designed for those in need of fitness examinations and criminal responsibility assessments, guilty pleas, and sentencing hearings. These courts, known as mental health courts, have been emerging across Canada since the mid-1990s (Bloom & Schneider, 2007). These courts attempt to redirect those with mental health needs back into the mental health care system rather than the criminal justice system. Mental health courts have four main objectives (Schneider, Bloom, & Heerema, 2007):

1. To divert accused who have been charged with minor to moderately serious criminal offences and offer them an alternative
2. To facilitate evaluation of a defendant's fitness to stand trial
3. To ensure treatment for a defendant's mental disorders
4. To decrease the cycle that mentally disordered offenders experience by becoming repeat offenders

In general, mental health courts offer a rehabilitative reaction to behaviour that would otherwise have been dealt with through the criminal justice system. Alternatives to serving a sentence in prison for less serious offences, such as theft, shoplifting, property damage, and minor assaults, are available. One goal for these courts is to ensure that defendants and offenders receive the proper assessments and treatments. The courts make referrals to medical experts, as well as case workers who help to develop a "release plan" (e.g., provide clothes, find housing, and select treatment options) once the accused is in the community. Mental health courts can be

Community treatment order: Sentence that allows the mentally ill offender to live in the community, with the stipulation that the person will agree to treatment or detention in the event that his or her condition deteriorates

Diversion: A decision not to prosecute, but rather have an offender undergo an educational or community-service program. Also an option for the courts dealing with offenders with mental illnesses who are facing minor charges. The court can divert the offender directly into a treatment program rather than have him or her go through the court process

found in a number of communities across Canada, including those in Saskatchewan, Ontario, and Newfoundland and Labrador.

Perceptions of Mental Health Courts

A recent Canadian survey of over 400 members of the general public and over 100 members from professional groups assessed perceptions of mental health courts (McDougall et al., 2012). The majority of participants from both groups reported positive attitudes toward the courts. For example, approximately 80% of the general public and 70% of the professional group members reported supporting government funding for a mental health court in their community, with 58% and 57%, respectively, agreeing to such a court even if it would mean a tax increase. Positive attitudes toward mental health courts were predicted by a number of factors that were somewhat similar but varied in degree for both groups. Being older, having prior exposure to mental health coursework, displaying psychological openness, having positive help-seeking attitudes, and having positive attitudes toward mental illness generally were factors predictive of positive attitudes toward the courts. Educating participants about the effectiveness of mental health courts increased positive perceptions about such courts, suggesting that positive perceptions can be enhanced through education.

Are Mental Health Courts Effective?

At the outset, it must be noted that little research has been conducted to evaluate mental health courts, but what we do know is that there is great variability across different courts. For example, courts may differ on how defendants are referred, the criteria for a defendant's eligibility, and the quality and quantity of services available. It also appears that defendants going through mental health courts are more likely to be connected to services than those not going through a mental health court (Schneider et al., 2007). Offenders who have gone through the mental health system also report more satisfaction with the process and perceptions of higher levels of fairness, lower levels of coercion, and increased confidence with the administration of justice (Poythress, Petrila, McGaha, & Macaulay, 2004). In a recent meta-analysis, Sarteschi, Vaughn, and Kim (2011) found a medium effect size for improving mental health outcomes, such as increasing access to mental health services, reducing recidivism, and decreasing the length of incarceration. Overall, the data so far encourages support for mental health courts. Burns, Hiday, and Ray (2013) found further support for the positive effect of mental health courts—approximately 80% of their sample had a lower recidivism rate in the two years after treatment when compared with the two years prior to treatment.

Campbell, Canales, Wei, Totten, Macaulay, and Wershler (2015) examined the impact of mental health courts on mental health recovery, criminogenic needs, and recidivism in 196 offenders. Compared to offenders who did not start or complete the treatment program as mandated by the health court, those who completed the program had a reduction in both recidivism risk and criminogenic needs. Although not statistically significant, offenders who completed the program tended to re-offend at lower rates than partial completers and those who never began the program.

Similarly, Campbell et al. (2015) found that offenders who completed the program had better recovery compared with those who only partially completed the program. Dr. Mary Ann Campbell has conducted research into mental health courts and their efficacy. To learn more about Dr. Campbell and her work, read Box 8.9.

Courtesy of Dr. Mary Ann Campbell

Dr. Mary Ann Campbell started her research career as an undergraduate student at Dalhousie University in Halifax, Nova Scotia. She then went to Lakehead University for her MA and returned to Dalhousie to complete her Ph.D. Her dissertation research focused on the assessment of recidivism risk with an incarcerated sample of young offenders. Currently, Dr. Campbell is a professor at the University of New Brunswick. Since 2006, she has been the Director of the Centre for Criminal Justice Studies, an organization dedicated to research, policy development, and professional training in areas related to criminal behaviour and the criminal justice system.

Dr. Campbell has conducted research on topics related to the study of criminal behaviour in youth and adults, forensic risk assessment, and treatment/program evaluation in forensic-related contexts. Dr. Campbell's interest in criminal justice topics began as a teenager, listening to her father tell stories about his work as a probation officer and later as a court administrator of a family court that also heard cases involving youth. Dr. Campbell states, "I recognized early the need for quality support and services for justice-involved youth". She believes it is critical to include the study of adults involved in the justice system as well. She notes the very rewarding experience of being able to advance best practices with regard to criminal justice systems and services. This major theme underlies her research.

Dr. Campbell states, "My favorite study is Campbell, French and Gendreau (2009) because it demonstrated to me the value of meta-analysis as a means of condensing and understanding large research literatures to address a specific question or series of questions. This study examined the predictive validity of various psychological measures and risk assessment tools for estimating the risk of future violence. It also examined potential moderators of these effects. This study has had significant impact on best practices in violent risk assessment by providing guidance to clinicians and policy-makers on considerations for the selection of assessment instruments for this type of work. Research that has real-world impact on best practices are always winners in my book! This paper also gave me the opportunity to work collaboratively with the esteemed Order of Canada recipient, Dr. Paul Gendreau."

As a licensed clinical psychologist, Dr. Campbell conducts mental health and risk assessments for adult and youth courts. She also consults with social services and mental health agencies regarding treatment and risk management strategies for justice-involved persons. She has received many media requests to discuss psychological and criminal justice issues related to particular cases featured in the news. For example, Dr. Campbell was once asked to discuss sexual offending dynamics on CBC Radio's *The Current* for their segment on the serial murder and sexual crimes committed by Colonel Russell Williams.

Dr. Campbell would like to see modifications to the legislation pertaining to the Review Board processes for justice involved persons found unfit to stand trial or not criminally responsible. Dr. Campbell has remarked that the changes

(continued)

(continued)

made to this legislation is inconsistent with evidence-based practice for offender rehabilitation and mental health recovery. She also would like to see modifications to the definition of criminal harassment to be more inclusive of bullying behaviour. She has stated, "however, significant thought needs to be given to the definition of criminal bullying thresholds first. As we recently learned in Nova Scotia, rushed legislation intended to help the courts address bullying won't stand up in court for very long."

On the training of future researchers interested in forensic psychology, Dr. Campbell believes students should be given relevant course work and practical field experience. She states, "It is one thing to learn about theory and research from a textbook and through course work, and an entirely other thing to see this knowledge mobilized into action in the field. By having exposure to both, students learn about the gaps between theory and practice".

When Dr. Campbell isn't researching criminal justice issues, she enjoys researching her family's genealogy. She has discovered a missing distant uncle who had disappeared when he set off looking to be part of the gold rush!

More recently, Ennis, McLeod, Watt, Campbell, and Adams-Quackenbush (2016) examined gender differences in mental illness and crime. Women had higher rates of mood personality disorders, whereas men had higher rates of psychotic disorders. When examining psychiatric disorders, Ennis et al. (2016) found that being admitted to a mental health court were higher for offenders with a psychotic disorder; mood disorders also raised the likelihood of admittance. Crime type was also examined and Ennis et al. found that men admitted to a mental health court committed more violent offences than women; however, neither gender nor offence type predicted whether a person would be admitted to a mental health court. Women were more likely to be admitted as their number of violent offences increased; however, the admission for men remained stable regardless of the number of violent offences committed.

SUMMARY

1. A defendant is found to be unfit if he or she is unable, because of a mental disorder, to understand the nature of the proceedings, to understand the consequences of the proceedings, or to communicate with counsel. In 1992, Bill C-30 legislated the length of time a defendant could be held in custody for a fitness evaluation.

2. Compared with fit defendants, unfit defendants are more likely to be unemployed and living alone, and are less likely to have ever been married. They also tend to be older females belonging to a minority group and are single, and they are more likely to have met criteria for a psychotic disorder. Defendants who are found fit are about as likely to have been diagnosed with a psychotic disorder as not. Also, unfit defendants are less likely to have problems with substance abuse than fit defendants.

3. The term used for Canada's insanity standard is *not criminally responsible on account of mental disorder* (NCRMD). The defendant is not criminally responsible

for an act that was committed (or omitted) while he or she was suffering from a mental disorder to the extent that he or she could not appreciate the nature or quality of the act or of knowing that it was wrong.

4. Automatism is defined as unconscious, involuntary behaviour. Canadian courts have recognized factors such as a physical blow, carbon monoxide poisoning, and sleepwalking as defences for automatism.

5. A number of explanations have been suggested for the high rates of mental illness in offender populations. For example, individuals with a mental illness may be less adept at committing crime and, therefore, more likely to get caught.

6. Treatment goals for offenders with mental disorders vary greatly. Some goals are symptom reduction, decreased length of stay in the facility, no need to be re-admitted to hospital, and reduced recidivism.

Discussion Questions

1. As part of your summer internship program at the courthouse, the judge has asked you to review the cases heard over the past year and identify the ones in which noninsane automatism was used as a defence. Describe some factors that can lead to automatism that may come up in the cases you will review.

2. You have been hired by the police department to help police quickly identify those who may need psychiatric services—that is, those who should not be processed through the criminal justice system. Develop a brief checklist for police to use when they come in contact with disorderly individuals so that the police can take the most appropriate action.

Chapter 9
Sentencing and Parole in Canada

Learning Objectives

- Describe the structure of the Canadian court system.

- List the primary purposes and principles of sentencing.

- Describe the various sentencing options available in Canada.

- Define the term *sentencing disparity* and explain how it can be studied.

- List the principles that form the basis for effective correctional interventions.

- Describe some of the myths associated with parole decision making.

Philip Jefferson was just found guilty of robbery with the use of a firearm. Judge Cane, who presided over the case, has made the difficult decision to incarcerate Philip for 7 years. When reading out his sentencing decision, Judge Cane stated that the crime Philip committed was a very serious one, requiring a minimum sentence of 5 years in prison. His reason for handing down a slightly stiffer penalty, he said, was that Philip exhibited very little remorse for the crime during his trial and did not seem to understand the psychological harm he had inflicted on his victim. In determining what an appropriate sanction was, Judge Cane said his first goal was to hand down a sentence that was harsh enough to teach Philip the lesson that crime doesn't pay. He hoped that spending serious time in prison would give Philip the time he needed to reflect on his life and the wrong direction it was heading. He also indicated that Philip needed time in prison to take advantage of the treatment programs that would be offered, particularly programs that might help Philip learn to manage his anger problems and his impulsivity. During the sentencing hearing, Judge Cane also said that he hoped his sentence would send a clear message to the community that violent crimes like the sort Philip committed are not tolerated by the Canadian criminal justice system.

Throughout this chapter, we will discuss sentencing and parole in Canada by focusing on some of the issues raised in the opening vignette. We will first describe the structure of the Canadian court system. We will then discuss the sentencing process, focusing specifically on the purposes and principles of sentencing and the various options available to Canadian judges like Judge Cane when sentencing adult offenders.

Our attention will then turn to one of the major problems that can result from this process and one of the solutions that have been proposed to solve this problem in some parts of the world. Specifically, we will focus on sentencing disparity, which can result from the high degree of discretion Canadian judges have when deciding on appropriate sentences, and sentencing guidelines, which are meant to limit this discretion to some extent. We will finish our discussion of sentencing by reviewing research that examines whether the goals of sentencing are achieved. To conclude the chapter, we will describe the parole process in Canada. In this section, we will focus our attention on the types of parole that are available in Canada, how parole decisions are made, and whether the decisions rendered by the Parole Board of Canada tend to be correct ones.

THE STRUCTURE OF THE CANADIAN COURT SYSTEM

The Canadian court system is one component of the larger Canadian criminal justice system that also includes policing agencies and correctional institutions. Some of the major roles of courts in Canada include hearing evidence presented at trial, determining the guilt and innocence of defendants, and rendering sentencing decisions across a wide range of criminal and civil cases. In this chapter, we will focus on the sentencing aspect of the Canadian court system. However, before we do that, we will first briefly discuss the structure of our court system.

As illustrated in Figure 9.1, the court system in Canada is relatively complex in that it is made up of numerous types of courts that are separated by *jurisdiction* and

Outline of Canada's Court System

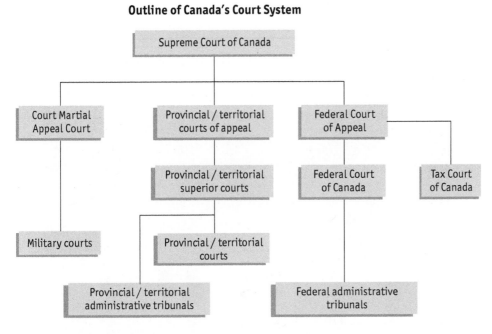

Figure 9.1 The Canadian Court System

Source: Department of Justice Canada (DOJ), 2015. Canada's system of justice, 2015. Retrieved from http://canada.justice.gc.ca/eng/csjsjc/just/img/courten.pdf. Reproduced with the permission of the Department of Justice Canada, 2016.

levels of legal superiority (Horner, 2007). In terms of jurisdiction, courts in Canada can be split into provincial, federal, and military courts (military courts, which deal with offences committed by members of the Canadian Armed Forces under the National Defence Act, will not be discussed here). Provincial courts in Canada have jurisdiction over most criminal and civil matters, whereas federal courts focus exclusively on matters specified in federal legislation (e.g., cases involving Crown corporations, such as Canada Post). In terms of levels, Canadian courts can be conceptualized as forming a four-tier hierarchy of legal superiority. Courts at higher levels of the hierarchy possess more legal authority than courts at lower levels. By this we mean that Canadian courts are essentially bound by the rulings of courts positioned above them in the hierarchy (Horner, 2007).

The bottom layer of Figure 9.1 represents administrative tribunals. These tribunals resemble courts in a variety of ways, but they are not officially part of the Canadian court system (DOJ, 2015; Horner, 2007). Administrative tribunals are responsible for resolving disputes in Canada over a wide range of administrative issues in both provincial and federal jurisdictions. One example of a provincial/territorial administrative tribunal is the Liquor Licensing Board. An example at the federal level is the Parole Board of Canada, which will be discussed at the end of this chapter. Decisions made by tribunals can be reviewed in court to ensure that the decisions are consistent with the law (DOJ, 2015).

The next layer in Figure 9.1, which relates to the lowest level of the four-tier hierarchy mentioned previously, consists of provincial and territorial courts. These courts are sometimes referred to as "inferior" courts and they can be found in all provinces and territories with the exception of Nunavut (Nunavut has its own Nunavut Court of Justice, which deals with all cases that inferior and superior courts would hear in other jurisdictions; DOJ, 2015). The range of cases heard in these courts is broad and can include criminal offences (e.g., traffic violations) and civil issues (e.g., small claims) (DOJ, 2015). Provincial and territorial courts can also hear appeals from

The Supreme Court of
Canada in Ottawa
AioK/Shutterstock

administrative tribunals. A number of courts at this level specialize in particular areas (Horner, 2007). For example, some inferior courts act as drug treatment courts.

The next level up in the provincial/territorial court system consists of provincial and territorial "superior" courts. One of the primary roles of these courts is to act as the court of first appeal for inferior courts (DOJ, 2015). In addition, these courts try the most serious criminal and civil cases—cases that often involve juries (Horner, 2007). As with inferior courts, provincial and territorial superior courts often specialize in a particular area (e.g., family law) (Horner, 2007). In the federal jurisdiction, the court at this level is referred to as the Federal Court of Canada. This court primarily serves to review administrative decisions made by federal administrative tribunals. A specialized court in the federal system, the Tax Court of Canada, deals with tax disputes between the federal government and Canadian taxpayers (DOJ, 2015).

Above these courts in the hierarchy can be found the provincial and territorial courts of appeal and the Federal Court of Appeal. The function of these courts is to review decisions rendered by the superior-level courts. Unlike superior-level courts, appellate courts do not normally conduct trials or hear evidence from witnesses (Horner, 2007).

Finally, at the top of the court hierarchy in Canada is the **Supreme Court of Canada** (SCC), which was created in 1875 (SCC, 2016a). The SCC is the final court of appeal in Canada. However, before the SCC will hear an appeal, the case must typically have been appealed in the relevant courts lower in the hierarchy—and even then, people still have limited rights to appeal to the SCC (Horner, 2007). The SCC also provides guidance to the federal government on law-related matters (e.g., interpretation of the Canadian Constitution). The SCC consists of eight judges plus the chief justice (currently Beverley McLachlin; SCC, 2016b). These judges are all appointed by the federal government.

Supreme Court of Canada: Created in 1875, the Supreme Court of Canada consists of eight judges plus the chief justice, who are all appointed by the federal government. The Supreme Court is the final court of appeal in Canada, and lower Canadian courts are bound by its rulings. The Supreme Court also provides guidance to the federal government on law-related matters, such as the interpretation of the Canadian Constitution

Aboriginal Courts

Although Figure 9.1 captures the basic structure of Canada's court system, it is important to highlight specific problems facing Aboriginal offenders in Canada and to examine how these problems have had an impact on our court system. The most important issue that needs to be discussed here is the disproportionate involvement of Aboriginals in the Canadian criminal justice system, or the **Aboriginal overrepresentation** problem. Despite attempts to reduce this problem, Aboriginal offenders are still greatly overrepresented in our criminal justice system (Jeffries & Stenning, 2014). For example, according to recent statistics, Aboriginal people make up about 3% of the general population in Canada. However, Aboriginal offenders make up approximately 18% of the federal inmate population (Correctional Service Canada; CSC, 2013) and 18% of the provincial/territorial inmate population (Perreault, 2009).

Much effort has gone into understanding the causes of Aboriginal overrepresentation (e.g., Jeffries & Bond, 2012) and several factors have been highlighted as potential contributors. For example, it appears that Aboriginal people may commit more crimes than non-Aboriginal people (Brzozowski, Taylor-Butts, & Johnson, 2006; Ruddell, Lithopoulus, & Jones, 2014) and that the crimes they commit may be more

Aboriginal overrepresentation: The discrepancy between the relatively low proportion of Aboriginal people in the general Canadian population and the relatively high proportion of Aboriginal people involved in the criminal justice system

likely to result in sentences of incarceration (Quann & Trevethan, 2000). Aboriginal people also appear to be processed by the criminal justice system in a different way than non-Aboriginal people, which could result in their overrepresentation (Rudin, 2006). For instance, access to adequate legal representation appears to be more problematic for Aboriginal people involved in the criminal justice system (Aboriginal Justice Inquiry of Manitoba, 2009). Finally, certain criminal justice policies appear to have a differential (i.e., more adverse) effect on Aboriginal offenders due to the fact that they are, on average, more economically disadvantaged than non-Aboriginal people (Weinrath, 2007). Consider the common practice of fining offenders. Given their lack of financial resources (Perusse, 2008), it should come as no surprise that Aboriginal people are more likely than non-Aboriginal people to be serving time in prison for fine defaults (Mann, 2013).

Rather than focusing on why Aboriginal offenders are overrepresented in the criminal justice system, we will focus on some of the things being done in Canada to try to reduce this problem. Of particular importance is legislation that has been passed by the federal government to deal with this issue and court rulings that have provided guidance on how this legislation should be interpreted. Bill C-41, which was passed by Parliament in 1996, is particularly important, especially Section 718.2. This section of the bill deals with the use of incarceration and states that "all available sanctions other than imprisonment should be considered for all offenders, *with particular attention to the circumstances of Aboriginal offenders* [emphasis added]" (R.S.C., 1985, s. 718.2[e]). As discussed by Roberts and Melchers (2003), that section of Bill C-41 has been interpreted by the Supreme Court of Canada in *R. v. Gladue* (1999) as an attempt to "ameliorate the serious problem of overrepresentation of Aboriginal people in prisons" (para. 93). More recent Supreme Court cases, such as *R. v. Ipeelee* (2012), have reiterated this interpretation.

Essentially, the Supreme Court was telling judges in Canada that they had to pay special attention to the circumstances of Aboriginal offenders when making sentencing decisions. Canadian judges reacted to this ruling with concern that they didn't have the time or the expertise to do this. In response to these concerns, special courts have been developed that specialize in cases involving Aboriginal offenders (Aboriginal Legal Services of Toronto, 2001). Judges in these Aboriginal courts have access to resources that in theory, at least, should allow them to provide more appropriate sentences to Aboriginal offenders. For example, Gladue reports can be requested, which provide the judge with an analysis of factors in the offender's background that *may* serve to mitigate or reduce the culpability of the offender. Gladue factors can include, but are not limited to, issues related to substance abuse; poverty; exposure to abuse; lack of employment; loss of identity, culture, or ancestral knowledge; and attendance at a residential school (Law Courts Education Society of British Columbia, 2009).

Restorative justice: An approach for dealing with a crime that emphasizes repairing the harm caused by it. Based on the philosophy that when victims, offenders, and community members meet voluntarily to decide how to achieve this, transformation can result

Consideration of Gladue factors will *sometimes* result in the application of a **restorative justice** approach to sentencing in order to heal those affected by the criminal act, instead of using prison as a deterrent (Law Courts Education Society of British Columbia, 2009). Although this sentencing option is not exclusively available to Aboriginal offenders in Canada, it is an option that is particularly consistent with the Aboriginal culture. According to Brown et al. (2016), "a major tenet of restorative justice is that it puts the emphasis on the wrong done to a person as well as the wrong done to the community" (pp. 115–116). The goal is typically for the victim of a crime, the offender, and members of the community to voluntarily meet in an attempt to restore the imbalance that was caused by the crime. The primary objectives are to prevent further damage from occurring (community safety), to ensure that the offender is made responsible for the crime and "repays" the victim and/or the community (accountability), and to provide the offender with whatever he or she needs to become a law-abiding citizen in the future (skills development).

Unfortunately, Aboriginal courts appear to be having little impact on the over-representation problem (Rudin, 2008). This might reflect the fact that these courts aren't dealing with the full range of issues that cause Aboriginal people to become involved in the criminal justice system in the first place (Rudin, 2006). In addition, some scholars have argued that more recent legislation (e.g., Bill C-10, or *The Safe Streets and Communities Act*) may work in opposition to *Gladue*. This bill "gets tough on crime" by increasing sentence length, making it more difficult for judges to have discretion when sentencing (Rudin, 2013).

Other recent findings, such as those described in Box 9.1, suggest that alternative ways of dealing with the Aboriginal overrepresentation problem in Canada are also failing.

SENTENCING IN CANADA

Probably the most visible and controversial component of the court system in Canada is the sentencing process, which is defined as "the judicial determination of a legal sanction upon a person convicted of an offence" (Canadian Centre for Justice Statistics, 1997). According to Roberts (1991), the sentencing process is highly visible because, unlike the majority of decisions made in the criminal justice system, sentencing decisions are made in the open and presented before the court. The sentencing process is highly controversial because of the great number of problems that can potentially result from the sentencing process, such as issues with sentencing disparity and sentencing effectiveness (Roberts, 1991), both of which will be discussed in this chapter. As a result of its high visibility and controversy, the sentencing process in Canada has been the subject of extensive research.

The Purposes of Sentencing

To understand the sentencing process in Canada, we must begin by discussing the reasons why we sentence offenders. Perhaps the most obvious goal of sentencing is to change the behaviour of both convicted offenders and potential offenders who reside in the community. More specifically, offenders are sentenced to reduce the probability that they, and the rest of the community, will violate the law in the future (referred to as **specific deterrence** and **general deterrence**, respectively). One of the reasons that sentencing attracts so much attention from forensic psychologists is that psychologists are interested in understanding human behaviour and how that behaviour can be changed (Roberts, 1991). The area of sentencing provides fertile ground for psychologists to explore these issues.

Specific deterrence: Sentencing to reduce the probability that an offender will reoffend in the future

General deterrence: Sentencing to reduce the probability that members of the general public will offend in the future

Box 9.1 Forensic Psychology in the Spotlight

Do Aboriginal Healing Lodges Reduce Aboriginal Overrepresentation?

Canada's attempt to deal with the Aboriginal overrepresentation problem in prisons goes beyond the establishment of Aboriginal courts, which have arguably had little impact. Another major initiative was the adoption of the Corrections and Conditional Release Act (CCRA) in 1992. A particularly important section of this act related to the problem of Aboriginal overrepresentation is Section 81. This section was intended to enable Aboriginal communities to deliver culturally appropriate programs to Aboriginal offenders by transferring offenders housed in Correctional Service Canada (CSC) facilities to Aboriginal healing lodges (Office of the Correctional Investigator, 2012). These correctional facilities incorporate Aboriginal traditions in delivering services to offenders. It was hoped that this approach to correctional programming would decrease an individual's involvement in future criminal activity, thus helping to reduce Aboriginal overrepresentation in the criminal justice system.

The impact of this section was recently reviewed in a report produced by the Office of the Correctional Investigator. The report, published in 2012, argued that Section 81 has not been implemented by CSC in the way it was intended and thus has had little impact on Aboriginal overrepresentation. For example, the report concluded that very few Section 81 agreements have ever been signed between the Aboriginal community and CSC, despite the obvious need for bed spaces in Aboriginal healing lodges. Indeed, the report stated that as of March 2012, "there were only 68 Section 81 bed spaces [available] in Canada and no Section 81 agreements in British Columbia, Ontario, and Atlantic Canada or in the North" (p. 3). In addition, until September 2011, "there were no Section 81 Healing Lodge spaces available for Aboriginal women" (p. 3). If these numbers are accurate, Section 81 is going to do little to effectively combat Aboriginal overrepresentation in federal correctional facilities.

Potential reasons for these findings were also provided within the report. Some reasons relate to policy decisions around the types of offenders who can be transferred to Section 81 healing lodges. For example, these transfers are typically restricted to minimum-security offenders, which effectively rules out the large majority of Aboriginal offenders (approximately 90%) who do not fall into this low-risk group (that being said, the report also suggested that Aboriginal healing lodges could easily reach capacity by housing only low-risk Aboriginal offenders).

Other potential reasons relate to funding models, which have been argued to be problematic for Section 81 healing lodges, especially when they are underused. For example, in addition to Section 81 healing lodges, CSC runs several lodges as minimum-security facilities. In contrast to these CSC facilities, the report suggested that Section 81 healing lodges are not guaranteed continuous funding and the amount of funding they receive is far less. If true, this obviously has implications for the sorts of services that can be provided to offenders in Section 81 healing lodges, but it also has implications for staffing. For instance, according to the report, salaries appear to vary drastically between CSC-run facilities and Section 81 healing lodges, with staff in CSC facilities sometimes making $25 000 to $30 000 more per year than staff in Section 81 healing lodges (making it difficult to attract high-quality staff).

Other potential reasons why Section 81 healing lodges are not having their intended effect have little to do with CSC. For example, the report suggested that, like many other communities, "many Aboriginal communities are not prepared to have offenders released to their community or to take on the responsibility of managing offenders" (p. 22). Fear of victimization is an obvious concern, especially for those in close proximity to correctional facilities. In addition, the location of Section 81 healing lodges could potentially be problematic and restrict the sorts of offenders who can be transferred to them. Most lodges are in remote areas, for example, making it difficult to provide appropriate care for offenders who could in theory be transferred, but have specialized medical and/or mental health needs that would be difficult to treat.

Many tools are currently available to help manage the chronic Aboriginal overrepresentation problem, including Aboriginal courts and the CCRA, but these tools need to be used as they were intended in order to have their desired effect. Such efforts also need to be combined with a greater attempt to understand the effects of other factors that likely bring Aboriginal people into contact with the law. Obvious examples include high levels of poverty, high rates of substance abuse, and the impact of residential school experiences.

Sources: Office of the Correctional Investigator. (2012). Spirit matters: Aboriginal people and the Corrections and Conditional Release Act. Retrieved September 12, 2016 from http://www.oci-bec.gc.ca/cnt/rpt/pdf/oth-aut/oth-aut20121022-eng.pdf

As made clear in the Criminal Code of Canada, judges also sentence offenders for many other reasons. For example, as stated in section 718 of the Criminal Code, the fundamental purpose of sentencing is to contribute to respect for the law and the maintenance of a just, peaceful, and safe society by imposing sanctions on individuals who commit crimes. This is accomplished by having the following sentencing goals (in addition to specific and general deterrence):

- To denounce unlawful conduct
- To separate offenders from society
- To assist in rehabilitating offenders
- To provide **reparations** for harm done to victims or the community
- To promote a sense of responsibility in offenders

Reparations: A sentence where the offender has to make a monetary payment to the victim or the community. See *restitution* on page 271

At present, it is not clear if one of these sentencing goals is any more dominant than another in Canada. The following facts, however, are clear:

1. Judges often consider more than one goal when handing down a sentence. For example, an offender may be sentenced to prison to reduce the probability that he or she will commit another crime and to separate that offender from society.

2. These goals can, at times, be incompatible with one another. For example, handing down a long prison sentence will separate an offender from society. However, as will be discussed later in this chapter, long sentences may not be an effective way of rehabilitating an offender.

3. Judges across Canada likely hand down sentences for different reasons, even when dealing with offenders and offences that are similar. For example, under similar circumstances, one judge may hand down a sentence that he or she feels promotes a sense of responsibility in the offender, while another judge may hand down a sentence primarily intended to deter the general public from violating the law. The reliance on different objectives is understandable, but it can result in problems such as sentencing disparity, which we will discuss.

The Principles of Sentencing

Just as there are numerous reasons for imposing sanctions on offenders, there are also numerous sentencing principles in Canada that are meant to guide a judge's sentencing decisions. Again, these are laid out explicitly in the Criminal Code. The **fundamental principle of sentencing**, as defined in section 718.1 of the Criminal Code, is that a sentence must be proportionate to the gravity of the offence and the degree of responsibility of the offender. Thus, when handing down a sentence in Canada, judges should consider the seriousness of the specific offence in addition to any other factor that might relate to the offender's degree of responsibility, such as the offender's age at the time of the offence.

Fundamental principle of sentencing: The belief that sentences should be proportionate to the gravity of the offence and the degree of responsibility of the offender

Beyond this fundamental principle, the Criminal Code consists of other sentencing principles. For example, when handing down sentences judges should take into account the following principles:

- A sentence should be adjusted to account for any relevant aggravating or mitigating circumstances relating to the offence or the offender. For example, if the offender has committed previous crimes, this should be considered.

- Sentences should be similar for similar offenders committing similar offences under similar circumstances.

- Where consecutive sentences are imposed, the combined sentence should not be unduly harsh.

- An offender should not be deprived of liberty (e.g., imprisoned) if less restrictive sanctions are appropriate under the circumstances.

- If reasonable, sanctions other than imprisonment should be considered for all offenders.

Just because the Criminal Code directs judges to consider these principles when making their sentencing decision, this doesn't mean that the desired effect is always achieved. For example, despite the fact that an offender's criminal record should play an important role in sentencing (with repeat offenders receiving harsher penalties), recent research suggests that Canadian judges do not always take this factor into account when handing down sentences (e.g., Plecas, Cohen, Mahaffy, & Burk, 2013).

Sentencing Options in Canada

In addition to the purposes and principles of sentencing, Canada's Criminal Code also describes the various sentencing options available for particular offences and the maximum (and minimum) penalties that can be handed down. However, while the Criminal Code provides a general framework for making sentencing decisions, judges still have a great deal of discretion. For example, while it may be possible to sentence criminals to a prison term for the crime(s) they are convicted of, it is highly likely that some other, less severe sentencing option will be used instead. Indeed, in her recent analysis of the types of sentences handed down in adult criminal court in 2013 and 2014, Maxwell (2015) found that severe prison sentences were not the norm. Instead, she found that probation (being released into the community with conditions imposed) was the most common type of sentence imposed, accounting for over 40% of all sanctions. When custodial sentences (i.e., to a secure facility) were used, the sentence length tended to be very short (e.g., the median sentence length in 2013–2014 was 30 days; Maxwell, 2015).

Depending on the circumstances of the offence being considered and the characteristics of the offender, judges in Canada have many sentencing options available to them. The following are just some of the options that you might see being used in Canada (John Howard Society, 1999):

- *Absolute or conditional discharge.* If it is in the best interest of the offender and the community, a judge in Canada can use discharges. If an offender is given an

absolute discharge, then that person is found guilty but will not be convicted and will have no criminal record. An offender who is given a **conditional discharge** is essentially on probation and will have to follow certain rules in the community for a specified period of time. If the probation period is completed successfully, the discharge will become absolute and the individual's criminal record will be clean, but if the offender breaches the conditions he or she could be sanctioned.

- *Restitution*. **Restitution** is a payment made by an offender to the victim to cover expenses resulting from a crime, such as monetary loss resulting from property damage or expenses incurred owing to injuries.

- *Fines and community service*. A **fine** requires that the offender pay money to the court. The judge sets the amount of the fine, the way the fine is to be paid, and the time by which the fine must be paid. In some cases, the offender will be able to pay off the fine by performing **community service**. If an offender does not pay a fine, he or she can serve a term of imprisonment.

- *Conditional sentence*. A **conditional sentence** is a prison sentence served in the community. It requires the offender to follow a set of rules for a specific period of time. If the offender abides by these rules, the prison sentence is suspended, but if the offender breaks these rules, he or she may be required to serve the remainder of the sentence in prison.

- *Imprisonment*. **Imprisonment** is the most serious consequence that can be handed out to offenders in Canada. Prison sentences vary depending on the seriousness of the offence. Offenders sentenced to prison terms of less than two years serve their sentences in provincial or territorial prisons. Sentences of two or more years are served in federal penitentiaries. In Canada, there has been a push towards using alternatives to prison sentences if other less restrictive sanctions can accomplish the goals of sentencing. While this has led to other sentencing options being considered by Canadian judges, such as probation and fines, we have yet to see the widespread use of creative (some would say bizarre) sentencing options that are becoming increasingly popular among American judges. Some of the more unusual sentences that have been relied on recently in the United States are described in Box 9.2.

Factors That Affect Sentencing Decisions

As indicated, the Criminal Code highlights various factors that should be taken into account when judges decide on sentences in Canada. These include the seriousness of the offence, the offender's degree of responsibility, various aggravating and mitigating factors, the harshness of the sentence, and so forth. According to Roberts (1991), some researchers suggest that these legally relevant factors can explain most of the variation that occurs in sentencing decisions across judges or for the same judge over time (e.g., Andrews, Robblee, & Saunders, 1984). This clearly is as it should be. However, other researchers argue that many judges appear to rely on extra-legal factors (i.e., factors that have little to do with the crime) when making their sentencing decisions, which is cause for concern.

Absolute discharge: The release of an offender into the community with no conditions put in place

Conditional discharge: The release of an offender into the community with conditions put in place

Restitution: A sentence where the offender has to make a monetary payment to the victim or the community

Fine: A sentence where the offender has to make a monetary payment to the courts

Community service: A sentence that involves the offender performing a duty in the community, often as a way of paying off a fine

Conditional sentence: A sentence served in the community

Imprisonment: A sentence served in prison

Box 9.2   Forensic Psychology in the Spotlight

Creative Sentencing Options

As in Canada, there appears to be a movement by some judges in the United States to rely on alternatives to imprisonment when sentencing offenders, especially for crimes that are relatively minor. As we will discuss in the section on sentencing effectiveness, this generally seems to be a wise move, and one that is likely to save taxpayer dollars, improve the probability of rehabilitation, and reduce the overcrowding problem in prisons. However, some American judges are being *extremely* creative in their sentencing decisions, as indicated in these recent examples reported in the media. It will be interesting to see if Canadian judges follow suit in the future.

- Three men who were involved in a prostitution ring were sentenced to spend time in chicken suits in Painesville, Ohio. The men were ordered to put on the chicken suits and to stand outside the courthouse with signs reading "No Chicken Ranch in Painesville," which refers to the brothel in the movie *The Best Little Whorehouse in Texas*.

- Also in Ohio, this time in Coshocton, two men were given the choice of a jail sentence or being forced to dress as women and walk around the town square after being convicted of throwing bottles at a woman's car. They were also fined $250 each.

- An Illinois judge in Champaign County sentenced a man to listen to 20 hours of classical music as a punishment for playing his hip-hop music excessively loudly from his car. If he did, his fine would be reduced from $135 to $35. After about 15 minutes of the classical music, the man decided to pay the high fine instead.

- Offenders convicted in the courtroom of Judge Frances Gallegos in Santa Fe, New Mexico, of domestic violence or fighting have been sentenced to new age anger management classes, held in the lobby of the courtroom, which is transformed with candles, mirrors, and aromatherapy.

- When a 13-year-old girl and her 11-year-old friend purchased a pair of scissors and chopped off chunks of a toddler's hair in a McDonald's restaurant in Utah, the 13-year-old was ordered to serve 30 days detention, pay damages to the victim, and serve nearly 300 hours of community service. However, the girl's mother accepted the judge's offer to reduce the number of community service hours if she agreed to cut her daughter's hair in the courtroom, which she did.

For example, an important Canadian study conducted by Hogarth (1971) found that "only about 9% of the variation in sentencing could be explained by objectively defined facts, while more than 50% of such variation could be accounted for simply by knowing certain pieces of information about the judge himself" (p. 382). Likewise, in a more recent American study, Ulmer (1997) found that a variety of extra-legal factors influence sentencing even when relevant factors, such as crime seriousness and prior criminal history, are held constant. Some of these factors included the gender and race of the defendant. In the United States, these factors still appear to play a large role in sentencing decisions. In a recent examination of gender disparities in federal criminal cases, for instance, Starr (2012) found that "Conditional on arrest offense, criminal history, and other pre-charge observables, men receive 63% longer sentences on average than women do. Women are also significantly likelier to avoid charges and convictions, and twice as likely to avoid incarceration if convicted" (p. 154).

Clearly, there are many factors that judges need to consider when making sentencing decisions. Review the case of Steve Patterson in the You Be the Judge box and determine what factors you would consider when handing down a sentence.

YOU BE THE JUDGE

Steve Patterson, a young man of 26, has pleaded guilty to robbery. Late one night, Steve entered a local grocery store. Pointing a plastic replica gun at the cashier, Steve demanded that he hand him all the money from the cash register. Steve ran out of the store with over $1000 in cash. The police picked him up later that night.

This is the first time Steve has ever been charged with a crime. For the last four years, he had been working as a forklift driver, but he was recently laid off from the company because it went bankrupt. Steve tells the court he robbed the store to buy food for his wife and newborn child. He pleads with the judge to spare him from prison and states that his wife and child depend on him.

Your Turn . . .

If you were the judge presiding over this case, what sort of sentence do you feel Steve should receive? What factors would you consider when determining an appropriate sentence and why? How might a reliance on these factors potentially lead to sentencing disparity (e.g., you handing down a sentence that might differ from the sentence handed down by another judge hearing a very similar case)?

Sentencing Disparity

One of the reasons that it is important to appreciate the various factors that affect sentencing decisions is so that we can understand **sentencing disparity**. Sentencing disparity refers to variations in the severity of sentences handed down by different judges when presiding over similar cases committed by similar offenders, or by the same judge when presiding over similar cases across time (McFatter, 1986). Because sentencing disparity can lead to serious injustices, it is commonly viewed as a major problem within our criminal justice system (e.g., Roberts, 1991; Roberts & Bebbington, 2013).

Sources of Unwarranted Sentencing Disparity The real problem occurs when disparities in sentencing happen because of a reliance on extra-legal factors. In this case, we can refer to the disparity as **unwarranted sentencing disparity** (Roberts, 1991). Unwarranted sentencing disparity can result from many factors, and researchers have attempted to classify these factors into groups. For example, McFatter (1986) discussed two major sources of unwarranted sentencing disparity: **systematic disparity** and **unsystematic disparity**. Systematic disparity represents *consistent* disagreement among judges about sentencing, such as how lenient they feel sentences should be. Sources of systematic disparity can include differences between judges in terms of their personality, philosophy, experience, and so on. Conversely, unsystematic disparity results from a given judge's *inconsistency* across time in judging the same type of offender or crime. This type of disparity can also arise from a number of sources, including fluctuations in mood, focusing on irrelevant stimuli, or the way in which the facts of the case are interpreted by the judge on any particular day (McFatter, 1986).

Sentencing disparity: Variations in sentencing severity for similar crimes committed under similar circumstances

Unwarranted sentencing disparity: Variations in sentencing severity for similar crimes committed under similar circumstances that result from reliance by the judge on legally irrelevant factors

Systematic disparity: Consistent disagreement among judges about sentencing decisions because of factors such as how lenient judges think sentences should be

Unsystematic disparity: Inconsistencies in a judge's sentencing decisions over time when judging the same type of offender or crime because of factors such as the judge's mood

Studying Sentencing Disparity In an attempt to understand (and reduce) sentencing disparity, researchers typically use one of two procedures to study it—laboratory-based simulation studies or the examination of official sentencing statistics in an attempt to uncover variations in judicial sentencing decisions. Of the two procedures, simulation studies appear to be more common so we will focus our discussion on this procedure.

In a simulation study, researchers present mock judges, or real judges, with details of a case (or cases) and examine if and how sentencing decisions assigned to those cases by the judges vary. Because the details of a given case are typically held constant, any variation that is found across judges (or for the same judge over time) can presumably be attributed to a reliance on legally irrelevant factors (e.g., a judge's personality, philosophy, training, and so on). The experiment conducted by Palys and Divorski (1986), while somewhat dated, provides a classic example of such a study.

These researchers provided 206 Canadian provincial court judges with five criminal cases. For each case, judges were given a description of the incident, the circumstances leading up to and surrounding the incident, the offender's reaction in court, the impact of the incident upon the victim, and a detailed presentence report on the offender. The cases that were used included (1) assault causing bodily harm; (2) impaired driving; (3) break and enter of a dwelling house; (4) armed robbery, indecent assault, and possession of a weapon (involving two offenders: offender 1 was an Aboriginal offender with a deprived background but no adult criminal record, and offender 2 was a Caucasian offender who was married and employed but had an adult criminal record); and (5) theft over $200. The task for the judges was to impose a sentence for each offender, indicate which case facts they felt were relevant, and list the objective they were trying to achieve when handing down the sentence. The judges also completed a demographic questionnaire to capture their characteristics (e.g., length of time as a judge) and their sentencing environment (e.g., type of community served).

The results of this study showed clear evidence of sentencing disparity. Indeed, as illustrated in Table 9.1, while the degree of disparity varied from case to case, it was sometimes quite extreme. For example, in the case of the armed robbery offence (offender 2), the minimum sentence involved a suspended sentence and the most severe involved a 13-year prison term. When examining the extent to which the information collected from judges could be used to explain the variation in sentencing severity, all three sets of variables (legal objectives, case facts, and demographic information) had some predictive power. However, differential weighting of legal objectives was the most important predictor of sentence severity, followed by the importance placed on various case facts, and the demographic characteristics and sentencing contexts associated with the judges.

While similar results have been reported in other Canadian studies of sentencing disparity (e.g., Doob & Beaulieu, 1992), is it possible that sentencing reforms introduced in Canada since the time of these published studies have significantly reduced sentencing disparity? We turn our attention to this issue next.

Reducing Sentencing Disparity Regardless of how sentencing disparity is studied, the conclusion is often that a reasonably high degree of disparity exists across sentences handed down by different judges considering similar crimes and across

Table 9.1 Sentencing Decisions across Five Simulated Cases

| Case | Sentencing Range | | Types of Sentences | | |
	Least Severe	Most Severe	No Incarceration	Provincial Jail	Federal Prison
Assault causing bodily harm	$500 fine plus 6 months' probation	5 years in prison	4%	92%	4%
Impaired driving	$300 fine	2 years in prison	31%	68%	1%
Break and enter	Suspended sentence plus probation	1 year in jail with temporary absence parole recommended plus program	77%	23%	0%
Armed robbery offender 1	8 months in jail	13 years in prison	0%	6%	94%
Armed robbery offender 2	Suspended sentence	13 years in prison	1%	24%	75%
Theft over $200	$1000 fine and probation	3 years in prison	21%	72%	7%

sentences handed down by the same judge when considering similar crimes on different occasions. As discussed above, a number of sources can account for this disparity, but ultimately, sentencing disparity exists because the law in Canada allows judges a great deal of discretion when making sentencing decisions.

A common approach that is used in many jurisdictions to deal with this issue is to develop and impose **sentencing guidelines**. These guidelines attempt to provide a more consistent, structured, and often restrictive method for arriving at sentencing decisions, which should reduce sentencing disparity. In the United States, for example, federal sentencing guidelines exist that are designed to limit disparity by imposing restrictions on the sentences that judges can hand down when dealing with individuals who have committed similar crimes and have a similar criminal history (Mustard, 2001). These guidelines require judges to make certain decisions (based on offence severity and offender's prior criminal history) unless they have reasons for departing from the guidelines. Research examining the impact of such guidelines is mixed. Some studies in the United States have found that sentencing guidelines have little impact on sentencing disparity (e.g., Cohen & Tonry, 1983), whereas other research has shown a more positive effect (e.g., Kramer & Lubitz, 1985; Moore & Miethe, 1986).

Despite the fact that sentencing guidelines have been extensively studied in Canada, and have been previously recommended (e.g., Daubney, 1988), the government in this country has been reluctant to adopt the same sorts of formal guidelines

Sentencing guidelines: Guidelines that are intended to reduce the degree of discretion that judges have when handing down sentences

that are used in other parts of the world to reduce sentencing disparity. (However, see Box 9.3 for other ways that sentencing uniformity may be encouraged.) Indeed, while various sentencing reforms have taken place in Canada (e.g., Bill C-41), the general goal with these reforms has been to make sentencing more severe rather than more rational (e.g., through the introduction of mandatory minimum terms of imprisonment for certain types of crimes; Roberts, 2012). According to a number of leading sentencing scholars, the driving force behind these reforms has been political rather than an attempt to develop evidence-based sentencing policies that might effectively reduce issues such as sentencing disparity (Doob, 2011; Roberts, 2012; Roberts & Bebbington, 2013).

Are the Goals of Sentencing Achieved?

Recall from the beginning of this chapter that judges can consider many different goals when handing down a sentence. As a result, the question of whether the goals of sentencing are achieved is a difficult one to answer because, to a large extent, the answer depends on what goal we are most concerned with. For some goals, the answer to this question is often "yes." For example, if a judge sentences an offender to a term in prison, he or she can be reasonably confident that the offender will be separated from society for a certain period of time. However, with respect to some other goals, the answer is less clear-cut. In particular, there is an ongoing debate as to whether current sentencing practices in Canada achieve the goals of deterring people from committing crimes and whether they assist in the rehabilitation of offenders. Canadian forensic psychologists have played, and continue to play, a crucial role in this debate. See Motiuk and Serin (2001) for an excellent overview of the contributions made by these psychologists.

Recent research suggests that "get-tough" strategies for offenders, such as incarceration, may not reduce the chance of reoffending.
Spirit of America/Shutterstock

Box 9.3   Cases in Forensic Psychology

Using Starting Point Sentences to Increase Sentencing Uniformity: *R. v. Arcand* (2010)

At the time Jordan Arcand sexually assaulted his relative, Arcand was 18 years old. The relative had taken Arcand into her home out of kindness, and one night while they were talking and drinking on a bed in her basement, she passed out. When the relative awoke, she found Arcand having intercourse with her. The woman had not made any advances toward Arcand before she passed out and when she woke up she immediately pushed Arcand off her.

The trial judge found that Arcand knew what he did was wrong and that he did not have consent from his relative to have intercourse with her. The Crown proposed a sentence of 3 to 4 years' imprisonment for the crime, but the judge agreed with the recommendation by the defence and sentenced Arcand to an intermittent sentence of 90 days, plus 3 years of probation (an intermittent sentence is one that is served in chunks of time, such as on weekends, rather than all at once).

The leniency of the sentence raised concerns and the case was appealed to Alberta's Court of Appeal. On analysis, the lenient sentence was attributed at least in part to the personal views of the sentencing judge, particularly his views about the seriousness of the sexual assault that Arcand had committed. These views seemed to be heavily influenced by the trial judge's apparent acceptance of various rape myths.

For example, at one point the trial judge commented, "I have no doubt that you're guilty of the offence, but the circumstances are such that I really have difficulty considering it a major sexual assault, although technically it is" (*R. v. Arcand*, 2010, para. 255). At another point, the trial judge stated, "I think temptation just got to you, and you were weak. You were drunk. And this girl was by your side.... I mean, it's not the ordinary scenario for a sexual assault" (para. 267).

The court of appeal took issue with these statements. For example, they suggested that the judge's view "wrongly stereotypes both men and women. It implies that a woman has an obligation not to 'tempt' a man or she assumes the risk of being sexually assaulted. It also implies that a man is unable to control himself in the presence of an unconscious woman" (para. 268). The court went on to argue that these views seem to rest on "the notion that non-consensual sexual intercourse is only a 'real' major sexual assault if the complainant has been violated by a stranger who has, for example, broken into her home or pulled her off the street" (para. 269).

On the basis of such arguments, the Court of Appeal concluded that the sentence handed down by the trial judge was inappropriately lenient and that the judge had incorrectly treated several factors as mitigating factors. Because of his characterization of the offence, the court of appeal also argued that the trial judge had ignored previous court judgments, which suggested that an appropriate "starting-point" sentence for major sexual assaults was a term of 3 years in prison.

Starting-point sentences are those that courts of appeal have determined to be appropriate for particular crime categories, such as major sexual assaults. As a way of ensuring fairness (e.g., by decreasing sentencing disparity), these sentences are to be used by trial judges as starting points, which can be revised (up or down) once the judge takes into account relevant aggravating and mitigating factors.

In the Arcand trial, the absence of any explicit justification for deviating from the established starting point (or even relying on a starting-point sentence) was deemed an error by the court of appeal. More specifically, it was argued that "the sentencing judge simply set the starting point ... aside.... By taking this approach, the sentencing judge downplayed ... the gravity of the offence and the offender's degree of responsibility for it" (para. 279). The court of appeal ruled that the appropriate sentence for Arcand, after taking into account aggravating and mitigating factors, was imprisonment for 2 years less a day plus 2 years of probation.

By relying on starting-point sentences in this fashion, courts of appeal may have devised a method (in the absence of legislated guidelines) of accomplishing some degree of uniformity in sentencing while still allowing judges discretion in making sentencing decisions.

Questions

1. Are starting-point sentences a good method for reducing unwarranted sentencing disparity, in your opinion?

2. Should the federal government establish more formal sentencing guidelines that judges must adhere to?

3. What would be some of the advantages and disadvantages of formal guidelines?

Source: *R. v. Arcand*, 2010, ABCA 363.

Box 9.4   Forensic Psychology in the Spotlight

The Death Penalty in Canada: What Does the Public Think?

At 12:02 a.m. on December 11, 1962, in Toronto, Arthur Lucas and Robert Turpin were the last people to be executed in Canada. Although the death penalty in Canada was formally abolished in 1976 for offences under the Criminal Code, and in 1999 for military offences under the National Defence Act, there are very good reasons that it is still important to discuss this issue.

One reason is that the Canadian public appears to support the death penalty under certain conditions. For example, in a recent public opinion poll of 1514 Canadians, 63% of respondents supported the reinstatement of the death penalty for murder (Angus Reid, 2013). Canadians in Manitoba and Saskatchewan (75%), and Alberta (73%), were particularly supportive of capital punishment, as were Canadians who supported the Conservative Party in the 2011 elections (78%).

Another reason it's important to consider the issue of capital punishment in Canada is that some of the reasons Canadians give for supporting it are based on potentially faulty logic. For example, the number one reason given for supporting the death penalty in the 2013 survey (53%) was that it would serve to act as a deterrent for potential murderers (Angus Reid, 2013). While such a view is understandable, research highlights a number of potential problems with this argument.

For example, the deterrence argument assumes that offenders think about the punishment before acting, which does not appear to be the case for many offenders (Benaquisto, 2000). In fact, a very large number of murders are committed in the heat of passion, or under the influence of alcohol and other drugs, with the offenders paying very little attention to the consequences of their crimes. In addition, if the death penalty does act as a crime deterrent, we would have expected to see an increase in the Canadian murder rate since abolition. However, the murder rate in Canada has generally declined since 1975, around the time when the death penalty was abolished (Mahoney, 2011).

A great deal of research has focused specifically on the effectiveness of "get-tough" strategies, which include a range of punishment-based sentencing options such as incarceration, house arrest, curfews, electronic monitoring, and so on (Cullen & Gendreau, 2000; Gendreau et al., 2001; Klenowski, Bell, & Dodson, 2010; Renzema & Mayo-Wilson, 2005). It has long been assumed that experiencing one of these sanctions would change the antisocial behaviour of offenders and reduce the likelihood that they will reoffend. However, as is the case with the most serious of sanctions, the death penalty, recent research does not support this hypothesis (e.g., Gendreau et al., 2001). See Box 9.4 for a discussion of this issue as it relates to the death penalty.

In a review, Gendreau et al. (2001) examined the rehabilitative and deterrent effect of prison sentences and various community-based sanctions, including arrests, boot camps, drug testing, electronic monitoring, fines, restitution, scared straight programs, and supervision programs. These researchers used the technique of meta-analysis to summarize findings from research studies that examined the impact of these specific sanctions. Based on the results from this study, it was concluded that there is very little evidence that punishment-based sanctions lead to substantial decreases in recidivism rates (compared with regular probation). Indeed, most of the sanctions that were examined resulted in moderate increases in recidivism. Only two sanctions (fines and restitution) resulted in decreases in recidivism, but the decreases were very small. In addition, Gendreau et al.'s study found that sanctions consisting of incarceration had little impact on recidivism. In fact, longer periods of incarceration led to slightly higher rates of recidivism across the studies that were examined. In addition, those offenders who were sent to prison for brief periods of time exhibited higher rates of recidivism compared with offenders who received a community-based sanction.

What Works in Offender Treatment?

So, given these results, does this mean that nothing can be done to deter or rehabilitate offenders? Historically, some researchers have taken the view that nothing will work with offenders (Martinson, 1974), but new research suggests that this is not the case. In fact, Canadian researchers have led the way in establishing principles of effective correctional intervention, and a growing body of research is beginning to show the value of these principles (Andrews & Bonta, 2010). Although quite a large number of principles are emerging as potentially important (Andrews, 2001), we will focus on three that appear to be particularly valuable in determining which correctional interventions will be effective (Andrews & Bonta, 2010).

The first of these principles is known as the **need principle**. It states that effective intervention will target criminogenic needs rather than non-criminogenic needs (i.e., factors that are known to contribute to reoffending; Andrews & Bonta, 2010). Some of the better known criminogenic needs highlighted by Andrews and Bonta include antisocial attitudes, antisocial personality factors (e.g., impulsivity), interactions with antisocial peers, and substance abuse.

The second principle is known as the **risk principle**. It states that effective interventions will focus on those offenders who are at high risk of reoffending (Andrews & Bonta, 2010). Not only are low-risk offenders unlikely to reoffend, but also their chances of reoffending may actually increase if exposed to an intervention (Andrews & Dowden, 2006) because of the fact that they will be brought into contact with people who hold antisocial attitudes. The exact level of treatment intensity that is required to manage high-risk offenders is debatable, but some recent reviews (e.g., Andrews & Bonta, 2010) estimate that it should be in the range of 100 hours for high-risk juveniles and 300 hours for high-risk adults.

The third principle is known as the **responsivity principle**. It states that effective interventions will match the general learning styles and abilities of the offender being targeted, as well as more specific factors such as the offender's personality, gender, and ethnicity (Andrews & Bonta, 2010). When referencing the "general learning styles and abilities of the offender," Andrews and Bonta are really suggesting that structured, cognitive-behavioural interventions are likely to be most useful with offenders.

The often-cited meta-analytic study conducted by Andrews et al. (1990) was one of the first attempts to determine whether interventions consisting of these core principles with a wide range of juvenile and adult offenders do in fact lead to reductions in recidivism. These researchers examined 80 program evaluation studies and coded the interventions in each study as appropriate, inappropriate, or unspecified. Interventions were defined as appropriate if they included the three principles of effective intervention described above (most of these programs involved the use of behavioural and social-learning principles, which included techniques such as behavioural modelling, rehearsal, role-playing, and reinforcement). Interventions were coded as

Need principle: Principle that correctional interventions should target known criminogenic needs (i.e., factors that relate to reoffending)

Risk principle: Principle that correctional interventions should target offenders who are at high risk to reoffend

Responsivity principle: Principle that correctional interventions should match the general learning style of offenders

inappropriate if they were inconsistent with these principles (many of these programs were based on get-tough or psychodynamic strategies). Interventions were coded as unspecified if they could not be categorized as appropriate or inappropriate because of a lack of information. The hypothesis was that offenders exposed to appropriate interventions would exhibit lower rates of recidivism compared with offenders exposed to inappropriate interventions.

This is exactly what was found. Offenders taking part in appropriate programs exhibited a decrease in recidivism, whereas offenders taking part in inappropriate programs exhibited an increase in recidivism. Offenders taking part in unspecified programs exhibited a decrease in recidivism, though less of a decrease compared with offenders in appropriate programs. Since this study, this same general pattern of results has been found on numerous occasions for various offending groups in both community and residential settings who have committed various types of crimes (see Andrews & Bonta, 2010, for a review).

In conclusion, then, it does appear that something can be done to deter and rehabilitate offenders. By focusing on an understanding of the "psychology of human conduct" (Andrews & Bonta, 2010), interventions can be developed that significantly reduce the chance that offenders will go on to commit further crimes. Certainly, this does not suggest that all new sentencing options will be effective, since many of these new options will not be consistent with the principles of effective correctional programming. However, a number of options have been developed—many in Canada—that do correspond with these principles. Early indications suggest that they hold promise for achieving some of the goals of sentencing that we discussed at the beginning of this chapter (Motiuk & Serin, 2001).

PAROLE IN CANADA

Parole: The release of offenders from prison into the community before their sentence term is complete

Ever since August 11, 1899, when Parliament enacted the Ticket of Leave Act, **parole** has played an important part in the history of criminal justice in Canada. Sir Wilfrid Laurier, the prime minister at the time, recognized the value of actively reintegrating certain offenders into society as soon as possible to enhance their chances of rehabilitation (Parole Board of Canada [PBC], 2016a). Since the time of Laurier, many things about parole have changed, but the essence of parole remains the same. Notably, parole still involves (1) the conditional release of offenders into a community so they can serve the remainder of their sentences outside an institution, (2) an attempt to rehabilitate offenders so they can become productive contributors to society, (3) a high degree of community supervision to ensure the parolee is abiding by certain rules, and (4) a clause that, if the conditions of parole are not complied with, an offender's parole can be revoked and he or she can be sent back to prison.

Types of Parole

Parole Board of Canada: The organization in Canada responsible for making parole decisions

In addition to making pardoning decisions, the **Parole Board of Canada** (PBC) can grant various types of parole to offenders. These include temporary absence, day parole, full parole, and statutory release.

Kelly Ellard Denied Day Parole

In 1997, a 14-year-old female approached a group of teens (mostly female) gathered outside who were drinking and smoking pot. The teenager was viciously assaulted by the group, including being burned by a lit cigarette, punched, and kicked. After the beating, the victim attempted to flee across a bridge, but two individuals in the larger group, Kelly Ellard (a female) and Warren Glowatski, followed her. Accounts of what happened at that point differ, but it is believed that Ellard and Glowatski continued to beat up the victim and ultimately drowned her by holding her head under water.

Glowatski was convicted of second-degree murder in 1999 and received a sentence of life in prison with no chance of parole for 7 years. In 2010, he was released on full parole. Ellard was originally convicted of second-degree murder in 2000 for the 1997 killing, but due to technical issues in that trial, the conviction was overturned. A second trial, occurring in 2004, resulted in a deadlocked jury and a mistrial. A third trial, which took place in 2005, resulted in a conviction for second-degree

murder and a life sentence for Ellard with no chance of parole for at least 7 years.

In 2016, Ellard applied for day parole. Before a two-person parole panel, Ellard accepted responsibility for the murder, reportedly revealed additional details about the crime, and indicated that she needed additional help for a substance abuse problem. However, the Board questioned Ellard's sincerity, suggesting she wasn't speaking from the heart, but rather "from what is most strategic and beneficial to you". Ellard application for parole was also not supported by her parole officer, which presumably played a part in the board's decision. The parole officer discouraged the board from granting parole because of Ellard's substance abuse problems and "deflection of blame for her actions."

Ellard will be eligible to apply for day parole again after a period of one year.

Sources: Burgmann, 2016; Proctor, 2016; The Canadian Press, 2016.

Temporary Absence A **temporary absence** is "usually the first type of release an offender will be granted" (PBC, 2016b). Offenders may be granted unescorted or escorted temporary absences (unescorted absences would typically follow successful escorted absences) so that they can take part in activities such as substance-abuse programs, family violence counselling, and technical training courses.

> **Temporary absence:** A form of parole that allows the offender to enter the community on a temporary basis (e.g., for the purpose of attending correctional programs)

Day Parole Day parole allows offenders to participate in activities within the community, such as treatment programs. Offenders on day parole must typically return to their institution or halfway house at the end of the day (PBC, 2016b). Performance on day parole is considered when the PBC reviews an offender's application for full parole. See the In the Media Box where we discuss the case of Kelly Ellard, who was convicted for the murder of a female teenager in 2005. Ellard recently applied for day parole, but her application was denied by the PBC.

> **Day parole:** A form of parole that allows the offender to enter the community for up to one day (e.g., for the purpose of holding down a job)

Full Parole Full parole allows offenders to serve the remainder of their sentence in the community. Before an offender is granted full parole, a thorough assessment is done to predict the likelihood of reoffending, as described below (PBC, 2016b). Consideration is also given to what conditions should be implemented to address the chance of risk. To be granted full parole, offenders must usually have been granted (and must have successfully completed) unescorted temporary absences and day parole. The offender is closely supervised while on full parole.

> **Full parole:** A form of parole that allows the offender to serve the remainder of his or her sentence under supervision in the community

Statutory release: The release of offenders from prison after they have served two-thirds of their sentence

Statutory Release Most federal inmates must be released with supervision, by law, after serving two-thirds of their sentence. This is known as **statutory release** (PBC, 2016b). (Offenders serving life, however, are not eligible for statutory release.) As with full parole, an assessment is carried out to predict the likelihood of reoffending and consideration is given as to what conditions should be implemented to address the chance of risk.

In each of the above cases, Correctional Service Canada is responsible for supervising offenders on parole, usually with the assistance from community agencies such as the John Howard Society. If an offender does not abide by his or her parole conditions, he or she may be returned to prison. Common parole conditions given by the PBC include things like having the offender report to his or her parole officers on a regular basis, remaining within the country, obeying the law, informing the authorities of changes in address or employment, not possessing any weapons, and so forth. Other parole conditions may be specific to the crime that the offender was convicted for (e.g., convicted child molesters may be required to avoid contact with children).

See Box 9.5 for other information about parole in Canada.

Parole Decision Making

So, how are parole decisions made? In Canada, an offender must usually serve the first third of his or her sentence or the first seven years, whichever is less, before being eligible for full parole. Most parole decisions are made after a formal hearing with the offender. When making their decisions, parole board members carefully review the risk that an offender might present to society if he or she is released. A large number of factors are available to be considered when carrying out this risk assessment (PBC, 2016d), including the following:

- Statistical measures of an offender's risk to reoffend
- The offender's criminal history
- Social problems experienced by the offender, such as drug use and family violence
- Information about the offender's relationships and employment history
- Psychological or psychiatric reports
- The offender's institutional behaviour
- Opinions from other professionals, such as police officers
- Information from victims
- Information that indicates evidence of change and insight into the offender's own behaviour
- Benefits derived from treatment that may reduce the risk posed by the offender
- Performance on earlier releases
- Any other information indicating whether release would pose a risk to society
- The feasibility of the offender's release plans

282 Chapter 9

Box 9.5   Myths and Realities

Parole in Canada

The general public has many misconceptions when it comes to issues of parole, and the PBC continually strives to correct them. The following list provides some of the myths people adhere to, along with the correct information provided by the PBC.

Myth 1. Parole reduces the sentence imposed by the courts.
Fact. Parole does not reduce the sentence imposed by the courts; it affects only the way in which a sentence will be served. Parole allows offenders to serve their sentences in the community under strict conditions and the supervision of a parole officer. If offenders abide by these conditions, they will remain in the community until their sentence is completed in full, or for life in the case of offenders serving life or indeterminate sentences.

Myth 2. Parole is automatically granted when an inmate becomes eligible for parole consideration.
Fact. Parole is not automatically granted when inmates become eligible. In fact, the PBC denies full parole to approximately six out of ten offenders at their first parole review date.

Myth 3. The PBC grants parole to offenders who express remorse for the offences they have committed.
Fact. Whether offenders express remorse is only one of the factors the PBC considers. Of greater importance is whether offenders understand the factors that contributed to their criminal behaviour, the progress they made while incarcerated, and the feasibility of their plans upon release.

Myth 4. Most of the offenders released on parole are convicted of new crimes.
Fact. Most offenders released on parole successfully complete their sentences without committing new offences or breaching the conditions of their parole.

Myth 5. Victims do not have a role in the parole process, and their views are not taken into account.
Fact. Victims and their families have a significant role in the parole process. They have the opportunity to present a statement directly to the PBC about any concerns they have for their safety or the safety of the community. In addition, victims may remain in contact with the PBC while the offender is under sentence. Moreover, the PBC allows victims, as well as other members of the public, to observe parole hearings and to request copies of written decisions.

Source: Based on PBC, © 2013.

Despite the fact that PBC members are instructed to consider all these factors, research in Canada indicates that they may not actually consider them when making release decisions. For example, recent research conducted by Dr. Ralph Serin, who is profiled in Box 9.6, used hypothetical offender vignettes to examine the release decisions made by 31 parole board members from Canada and New Zealand (Gobeil & Serin, 2009). The vignettes summarized the cases of different types of offenders (e.g., a male violent offender, a woman offender, a male Aboriginal offender), while keeping the length of the vignettes constant and incorporating very similar information into each vignette (e.g., risk assessments, correctional staff recommendations, and other information). After reading each vignette, the parole board member was asked to make a release decision or access additional information in one of six areas that is mandated for consideration by parole boards: risk-assessment information, mental health information, victim information, program information, release plan

Canadian Researcher Profile: Dr. Ralph Serin

Courtesy of Ralph Serin

Dr. Ralph Serin began his career with Correctional Service Canada (CSC) at Kingston Penitentiary as a psychology intern in the summer of 1975. After 27 years, following an exciting career as a psychologist with CSC and as the director of operations and programs research, he joined the forensic program at Carleton University.

Most of Dr. Serin's early corrections research examined unique offender groups (violent offenders, sexual offenders, and criminal psychopaths) and their relevance to both risk assessment and correctional programming. However, upon arriving at Carleton in 2003, and finding very few parolees available to participate in research, Dr. Serin turned his attention to correctional decision making, particularly parole decision making.

This new interest in parole decision making was greatly enhanced when Dr. Serin received funding from the Canadian Foundation for Innovation to build a new research laboratory at Carleton. The construction of the Criminal Justice Decision Making Laboratory improved the space for his graduate students and allowed for expanded research

collaborations. Soon after the construction of his lab, Dr. Serin and his students were working collaboratively with the Parole Board of Canada (PBC) to review and refine the board's approach to parole decision making.

Over an eight-year period, Dr. Serin and his students completed various studies, all aimed at developing and validating a framework, or best practice model, for making parole decisions. This research has taken place in Canada and is now being replicated in various parole sites in the United States. One of Dr. Serin's previous graduate students, Dr. Renée Gobeil, has been instrumental to the success of this program of research and Dr. Serin continues to work closely with her today. This research is now expanding to examine parole agency fidelity, parole board member competency, and parole efficacy.

This research ultimately led to Dr. Serin's appointment as an advisor to the National Institute of Corrections and the National Parole Resource Center in the United States. Encouragingly, this work has also now been implemented as a PBC policy. This means that all parole decisions in Canada must incorporate this framework; it has also been incorporated into the training curriculum for new parole officers in CSC. In 2015, Dr. Serin received the President's Award from the Association of Paroling Authorities International for significant contributions to the field of parole.

With parole currently enjoying a kind of renaissance, Dr. Serin's evidence-based approach to parole decision making has led international parole boards to seek assistance and training from his Criminal Justice Decision Making Laboratory. By implementing the framework and other research measures developed by Dr. Serin and his colleagues, parole boards around the world will be able to make more informed and transparent decisions, which will ultimately enhance public safety while ensuring that offenders are treated fairly.

information, and criminal history information. Once parole board members decided not to access any additional information, or after all information had been accessed, they were forced to make a release decision.

The results of Gobeil and Serin's (2009) study revealed several interesting things. For example, release decisions were found to vary as a function of offender type. More specifically, "the release rate was considerably higher for the woman offender and sex offender vignettes than for the other vignettes, [whereas] the release rate was notably lower for the Aboriginal offender and domestic violence offender vignettes" (p. 100). Interestingly, these differences were not related to potentially important participant characteristics (e.g., the age, gender, experience, or professional background of the parole board member). Also of importance was the finding that variability existed in the amount and type of information accessed by the parole board members. For example, information related to risk assessment and release plan was commonly accessed, but not mental health or victim information. This finding is potentially problematic because parole board members are required to consider these sources of information when making release decisions.

These sorts of findings led Dr. Serin and his colleagues to develop an empirically based framework for making parole decisions, which has now been adopted by the PBC. The tool does not highlight any factors that the PBC are not already mandated to review when making parole decisions. Instead, it provides a structured procedure for considering the potentially overwhelming range of factors that do need to be assessed when making release decisions and facilitates a final decision that should, in theory, be equitable, transparent, and defensible (Gobeil & Serin, 2010). In essence, the framework lists key domains that are relevant to release decisions (e.g., the offender's release plan); describes issues that should be taken into account when considering the domains (e.g., does the offender have protective factors in place in case of lapses, such as prosocial friends?); and provides a simple scoring mechanism for determining how the factors should be treated in the overall assessment of risk (e.g., should the offender's release plans be considered aggravating (decreasing) the likelihood of release; mitigating (increasing) the likelihood of release; or having no impact?). Research thus far demonstrates that parole recommendations produced when using Serin's framework result in lower rates of decision errors than traditional (i.e., unstructured) parole decision making (Gobeil, Scott, Serin, & Griffith, 2007). This appears to be the case across a range of situations, including release decisions for female offenders (e.g., Yesberg, Scanlan, & Polaschek, 2014) and Aboriginal offenders (Serin, Gobeil, Lloyd, Chadwick, Wardrop, & Hanby, 2016).

The Effectiveness of Parole Decisions in Canada

The PBC provides updates on the success of their parolees on an annual basis. Many of the statistics published by the PBC compare the success rates of offenders granted day and full parole (i.e., release based on discretionary decision making) to those offenders granted statutory release. Recall that, by law, most federal inmates must be released with supervision after serving two-thirds of their sentence. If the PBC is making effective decisions, we would expect to see higher rates of success for offenders on day and full parole, compared with those who have been granted statutory release. Despite the fact that unfortunate release decisions are sometimes made, available statistics confirm exactly this.

For example, as indicated in the most recent *Performance Monitoring Report* published by the PBC (2014), federal offenders who are granted parole based on discretionary decision making are more likely to complete their supervision period in the community compared with offenders released as a result of statute-based systems.

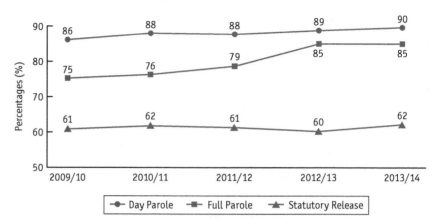

Figure 9.2 Success Rates for Federal Offenders on Conditional Release

Source: PBC, 2014. http://www.pbc-clcc.gc.ca/rprts/pmr/pmr_2013_2014/index-eng.pdf, Figure 32, p. 48.

Of course, this is not to say that offenders granted day or full parole never breach the conditions of their paroles or commit further crimes—just that this tends to be the exception rather than the rule.

In support of these claims, Figure 9.2 provides data relating to the success rates of offenders across different types of parole. This graph clearly indicates that, during the period 2009–2014, offenders who were granted day or full parole were more successful compared to those granted statutory release; however, even in the case of statutory release, the majority of offenders are successful. During the period between 2012 and 2014, offenders let out on full parole were nearly as successful as offenders released on day parole.

Importantly, Figures 9.3 and 9.4 indicate that most of the failures experienced by offenders on parole (and statutory release) are due to breach of conditions rather

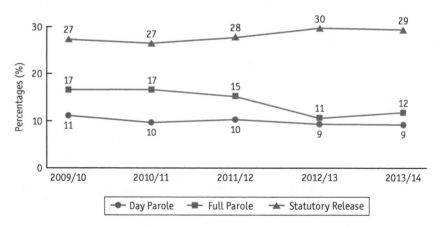

Figure 9.3 Breach of Condition Rates for Federal Offenders on Conditional Release

Source: PBC, 2014. http://www.pbc-clcc.gc.ca/rprts/pmr/pmr_2013_2014/index-eng.pdf, Figure 33, p. 49.

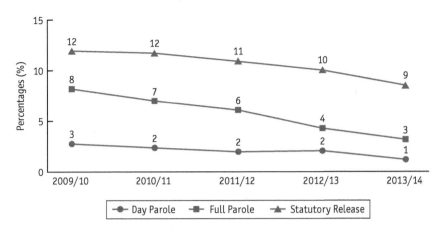

Figure 9.4 Offence Rates for Federal Offenders on Conditional Release

Source: PBC, 2012. 2014. http://www.pbc-clcc.gc.ca/rprts/pmr/pmr_2013_2014/index-eng.pdf, Figure 34, p. 49.

than the commission of new offences (PBC, 2014). Indeed, relatively few offenders go on to commit additional crimes upon their release, and very few commit new violent offences (PBC, 2014).

SUMMARY

1. The Canadian court system is one component of the larger Canadian criminal justice system that also includes policing agencies and correctional institutions. The court system in Canada is made up of numerous types of courts that are separated by jurisdiction and levels of legal superiority. Courts that are designed to deal specifically with Aboriginal offenders are also part of this system.

2. Sentences are supposed to serve a number of purposes in Canada. Deterring people from committing crimes and offender rehabilitation are two of the primary purposes. Sentencing in Canada is also guided by numerous principles, such as the fundamental sentencing principle, which states that a sentence must be proportionate to the gravity of the offence and the degree of responsibility of the offender. Such principles are meant to provide judges with guidance when handing down sentences.

3. Judges have many sentencing options at their disposal. These range from discharges, fines, community service, and reparation, to very serious options such as imprisonment. New sentencing options have also been recently proposed, such as the conditional sentence, in which an offender can serve his or her prison time in the community.

4. One of the major problems with sentencing in Canada is unwarranted sentencing disparity, which refers to differences in the severity of sentences handed down by different judges (or the same judge on different occasions) because of a

reliance on extra-legal factors. These factors can include the judge's personality, philosophy, experience, and so on. Researchers often examine official sentencing statistics to study sentencing disparity, although the use of laboratory-based simulation studies is a more common strategy.

5. Research examining the impact of punishment-based sentences suggests they are not effective for reducing recidivism. In contrast, correctional interventions based on core correctional principles show more promise. These principles include the need principle (effective interventions target criminogenic needs), the risk principle (effective interventions target high-risk offenders), and the responsivity principle (effective interventions match the general learning style, and the particular characteristics, of the offender).

6. The PBC makes parole decisions in Canada. Contrary to popular belief, parole is not automatically granted to offenders as soon as they become eligible. Offender remorse plays only a small part in parole decisions. Most offenders let out on parole do not go on to commit more crimes, and victims do have a significant say in the parole process.

Discussion Questions

1. In your opinion, should offenders who are convicted of serious crimes, such as sexual assault, ever become eligible for parole? Why or why not?

2. Your neighbour thinks Canada is getting soft on crime by providing community "rehabilitation" programs. He thinks the only way to really rehabilitate offenders is to lock them up in cells with nothing to do but think about the crimes they've committed. Do you think your neighbour is right? Explain.

Chapter 10
Risk Assessment

Learning Objectives

- Define the components of risk assessment.

- List what role risk assessments play in Canada.

- Describe the types of correct and incorrect risk predictions.

- Differentiate among static, stable, and acute dynamic risk factors.

- Describe unstructured clinical judgment, actuarial prediction, and structured professional judgment.

- Address some of the important differences amongst unique sub-populations of offenders.

Joanne Marshall has served two years of a three-year sentence for aggravated assault. The assault occurred late one evening after Joanne had returned home from drinking with her friends. She got into a heated argument with her boyfriend, grabbed a knife from the kitchen, and stabbed him in his shoulder. An institutional psychologist completed a risk assessment and is supporting her application for parole. Joanne is going to appear before the three-member parole board to discuss the offence she committed, her plans if released, and what intervention programs she has participated in. The parole board members will need to also consider what level of risk Joanne poses for reoffending, including whether or not she will engage in another violent act. They will also attempt to determine whether she has developed more appropriate ways of dealing with interpersonal conflict.

Every day, individuals make judgments about the likelihood of events. Predictions are made about being admitted into law school, recovering from depression, or committing a criminal act after release from prison. Our legal system frequently requires decisions about the likelihood of future criminal acts that can significantly influence the lives of individuals. With the possibility that offenders could spend years or even the remainder of their lives in confinement, decisions by psychologists can have a significant impact. Predicting future violence has been described as "one of the most complex and controversial issues in behavioral science and law" (Borum, 1996, p. 945).

Although it is clear that significant advances have taken place since the 1990s, risk assessment and prediction remains imperfect. Bonta (2002) concluded that "risk assessment is a double-edged sword. It can be used to justify the application of severe sanctions or to moderate extreme penalties. . . . However, the identification of the violent recidivist is not infallible. We are not at the point where we can achieve a level of prediction free of error" (p. 375). Nonetheless, the systematic assessment of risk provides judicial decision makers, such as judges and the National Parole Board, with much-needed information to help them make challenging decisions.

The goal of this chapter is to explore the major issues associated with risk prediction in a forensic context. In particular, the focus will be on understanding the task of assessing risk and predicting violence.

WHAT IS RISK ASSESSMENT?

In the past two decades, we have seen a change in the way risk is viewed. Prior to the 1990s, risk was seen as a dichotomy—the individual was either dangerous or not dangerous. Nowadays, risk is regarded as a range—the individual can vary in the degree to which he or she is considered dangerous (Steadman, 2000). In other words, this shift has added a dimension of probability to the assessment of whether a person will commit violence. The focus on probability reflects two considerations. First, it highlights the idea that probabilities may change across time. Second, it recognizes that risk level reflects an interaction among a person's characteristics, background, and possible future situations that will affect whether the person engages in violent behaviour.

The process of risk assessment includes both a "prediction" and "management" component (Hart, 1998). The prediction component describes the probability that an individual will commit future criminal or violent acts. The focus of this component is

ScienceCartoonsPlus.com

on identifying the risk factors that are related to this likelihood of future violence. The management component describes the development of interventions to manage or reduce the likelihood of future violence. The focus of this component is on identifying what treatment(s) might reduce the individual's level of risk or what conditions need to be implemented to manage the individual's risk. As described by Hart (1998), "the critical function of risk assessments is violence *prevention*, not violence *prediction*" (p. 123).

RISK ASSESSMENTS: WHEN ARE THEY CONDUCTED?

Risk assessments are routinely conducted in civil and criminal contexts. Civil contexts refer to the private rights of individuals and the legal proceedings connected with such rights. Criminal contexts refer to situations in which an individual has been charged with a crime. Common to both contexts is a need for information that would enable legal judgments to be made concerning the probability of individuals committing some kind of act that would disrupt the peace and order of the state or individuals within the state.

Civil Setting

A number of civil contexts require risk assessment:

- *Civil commitment* requires an individual to be hospitalized involuntarily if he or she has a mental illness and poses a danger to him- or herself or others. A mental health professional, usually a psychiatrist or psychologist, would need to know the probability of violence associated with various mental illness symptoms and disorders and be able to identify whether the circumstances associated with individual patients would affect the likelihood that they would harm others or themselves. In Canada, only a psychiatrist can civilly commit someone to a hospital.

- Assessment of risk in *child protection* contexts involves the laws that are in place to protect children from abuse. The risk of physical abuse, sexual abuse, or neglect is considered when a government protection agency, such as the Children's Aid Society, decides whether to temporarily remove a child from his or her home or to terminate parental rights. To provide assistance to protection agencies, professionals need to be familiar with the risk factors that predict childhood maltreatment.

- *Immigration* laws prohibit the admission of individuals into Canada if there are reasonable grounds for believing they will engage in acts of violence or if they pose a risk to the social, cultural, or economic functioning of Canadian society.

- *School* and *labour regulations* also include provisions to prevent any kind of act that would endanger others.

- Mental health professionals are expected to consider the likelihood that their patients will act in a violent manner and to intervene to prevent such behaviour. This responsibility is called *duty to warn*. The Canadian Psychological Association's Code of Ethics for Psychologists includes a guide to help psychologists decide the most ethical action for any potential dilemma.

Criminal Settings

The assessment of risk occurs at nearly every major decision point in the criminal justice and forensic psychiatric systems, including pretrial, sentencing, and release. A person can be denied bail if there is a substantial likelihood that he or she will commit another criminal offence. In the case of adolescent offenders, the judge can decide to apply adult criminal sanctions depending on the age, type of offence, and risk level posed by the youth. Risk also plays a role in decisions about whether a youth should be sent to secure custody. For example, adolescent offenders should be committed to secure custody only if they are considered high risk; if not, they should be placed in open custody or serve a probation term in the community.

An important issue in risk assessment in criminal settings is the disclosure of information about potential risk. This disclosure must be considered in light of the solicitor–client privilege that is fundamental to criminal proceedings. For lawyers to adequately represent their clients, they must be able to freely discuss the case with the clients.

This privilege is also extended to experts retained by lawyers. A case in Canada has clarified when solicitor–client privilege and doctor–patient confidentiality must be set aside for the protection of members of the public. *Smith v. Jones* (1999) involved a psychiatrist who was hired to aid a defence lawyer in preparing a case. The client was a man accused of aggravated sexual assault on a prostitute. The accused told the psychiatrist of his plans to kidnap, sexually assault, and kill prostitutes. The psychiatrist told the defence lawyer about his concerns that the accused was likely to commit future violent offences unless he received treatment. When the psychiatrist found out that the defence lawyer was not going to address his concerns at the sentencing hearing (the accused pled guilty to the charge of aggravated assault), he filed an affidavit providing his opinion about the level of risk posed by the accused. The trial judge ruled that because of concerns about public safety, the psychiatrist was duty-bound to disclose to the police and the Crown counsel the information he obtained. The case was appealed to the Supreme Court that ruled that in cases where there is "clear, serious, and imminent danger," public safety outweighs solicitor–client privilege (*Smith v. Jones*, 1999, para. 87).

Although risk assessment is a routine component of many sentencing decisions, it is a critical component of certain kinds of sentencing decisions. For example, after 1947, when habitual criminal legislation was introduced, offenders could be sentenced to an indefinite period of incarceration. In 1977, dangerous offender legislation was enacted that requires mental health professionals to provide an assessment of risk for violence. Changes to the legislation in 1997 made indefinite incarceration the only option if an offender is found to be a dangerous offender (see Chapter 9 for more information about dangerous offenders). At the same time, a new category of dangerous persons was created, referred to as long-term offenders. To be declared a long-term offender, a person must pose a substantial risk for violently reoffending. Thus, risk assessment is also a core component of this legislation.

Risk assessment is also required for decisions concerning release from correctional and forensic psychiatric institutions, such as parole. If a person is sentenced to prison in Canada, he or she can apply to the National Parole Board to get early release.

Parole board members use a variety of sources of information (including risk assessments provided by institutional psychologists) to decide the likelihood that the offender will commit another offence if released. Although most offenders get released on statutory release (after serving two-thirds of their sentences), statutory release can be denied if the offender is likely to commit further violent offences. Finally, a patient who has been found not criminally responsible on account of a mental disorder (see Chapter 8) can be released from a secure forensic psychiatric facility only if a risk assessment is completed.

Clearly, risk assessment plays an integral role in legal decision making, in both civil and criminal settings, allowing informed decisions that weigh the likelihood that an individual will engage in a dangerous or criminal act in the future. In the sections that follow, we will look at the predictive accuracy of these assessments, as well as the factors that actually predict antisocial outcome.

TYPES OF PREDICTION OUTCOMES

Predicting future events will result in one of four possible outcomes. Two of these outcomes are correct, and two are incorrect. The definitions provided below are stated in terms of predicting violent acts but could be used for any specific outcome (see also Table 10.1):

- A **true positive** represents a correct prediction and occurs when a person who is predicted to be violent engages in violence.

- A **true negative** is also a correct prediction and occurs when a person who is predicted not to be violent does not act violently.

- A **false positive** represents an incorrect prediction and occurs when a person is predicted to be violent but is not.

- A **false negative** is also an incorrect prediction and occurs when a person is predicted to be nonviolent but acts violently.

The last two types of errors are dependent on each other. Minimizing the number of false positive errors results in an increase in the number of false negative errors. The implication of these errors varies depending on the decisions associated with them, and in many cases the stakes are high. A false positive error has implications for

True positive: A correct prediction that occurs when a person who is predicted to engage in some type of behaviour (e.g., a violent act) does so

True negative: A correct prediction that occurs when a person who is predicted not to engage in some type of behaviour (e.g., a violent act) does not

False positive: An incorrect prediction that occurs when a person is predicted to engage in some type of behaviour (e.g., a violent act) but does not

False negative: An incorrect prediction that occurs when a person is predicted not to engage in some type of behaviour (e.g., a violent act) but does

Table 10.1 Predictions: Decisions versus Outcomes

Decision	Outcome	
	Does not reoffend	**Reoffends**
Predicted not to reoffend	True negative (correct prediction)	False negative (incorrect prediction)
Predict to reoffend	False positive (incorrect prediction)	True positive (correct prediction)

A gun-free sign at a high school
Sascha Burkard/Fotolia

the individual being assessed (such as denial of freedom), whereas a false negative error has implications for society and the potential victim (such as another child victimized by a sexual offender). In some cases, it is perhaps tolerable to have a high rate of false positives if the consequences of such an error are not severe. For example, if the consequence of being falsely labelled as potentially violent is being supervised more closely while released on parole, the consequence may be acceptable. However, if the consequence of being falsely labelled as potentially violent contributes to a juror's decision to decide in favour of the death penalty, then this price is too high to pay. As in many legal settings, the consequences for the individual must be weighed in relation to the consequences for society at large.

The Base Rate Problem

Base rate: Represents the percentage of people within a given population who commit a criminal or violent act

A problem with attempting to predict violence is determining base rates. The **base rate** represents the percentage of people within a given population who commit a criminal or violent act. It is difficult to make accurate predictions when the base rates are too high or too low. A problem that emerges when attempting to predict events that have a low base rate is that many false positives will occur. For example, the past decade has seen several high-profile school shootings. However, although these events generate much media coverage, they occur infrequently. Any attempt to predict which individual youths might engage in a school shooting would result in many youths being wrongly classified as potential shooters.

The base rate can vary dramatically depending on the group being studied, what is being predicted, and the length of the follow-up period over which the individual is monitored. For example, the base rate of sexual violence tends to be relatively low, even over extended follow-up periods, whereas the base rate for violating the conditions of a conditional release is very high. The base rate problem is not such a concern if predictions of violence are limited to groups with a high base rate of violence, such as incarcerated offenders. The general rule is that it is easier to predict frequent events than infrequent events.

A HISTORY OF RISK ASSESSMENT

Before 1966, relatively little attention was paid to how well professionals could assess risk of violence. In the 1960s, civil rights concerns provided the rare opportunity to study the accuracy of mental health professionals in predicting violence. In the case of *Baxstrom v. Herald* (1966), the U.S. Supreme Court ruled that the plaintiff Johnnie Baxstrom had been detained beyond his sentence expiry and ordered him released into the community. As a result of this case, more than 300 mentally ill offenders from the Dannemora State Hospital for the Criminally Insane and another state hospital were released into the community or transferred to less secure institutions. Steadman and Cocozza (1974) followed 98 of these patients who were released into the community but had been considered by mental health professionals as too dangerous to be released. Only 20 of these patients were arrested over a four-year period, and of these, only 7 committed a violent offence.

In a larger study, Thornberry and Jacoby (1979) followed 400 forensic patients released into the community because of a similar civil rights case in Pennsylvania (*Dixon v. Attorney General of the Commonwealth of Pennsylvania*, 1971). During an average three-year follow-up period, 60 patients were either arrested or rehospitalized for a violent incident.

The two studies we have just described are known as the Baxstrom and Dixon studies. These cases and similar ones call into question the ability of mental health professionals to make accurate predictions of violence. Two key findings emerged from the research. First, the base rate for violence was relatively low. For example, in the Baxstrom study, 7 out of 98 (roughly 7%) violently reoffended, as did 60 out of 400 (15%) in the Dixon study. Second, the false positive rate was very high. In the Baxstrom and Dixon studies, the false positive rates were 86% and 85%, respectively. These findings indicate that in the past many mentally disordered forensic patients were needlessly kept in restrictive institutions based on erroneous judgments of violence risk.

Ennis and Litwack (1974) characterized clinical expertise in violence risk assessment as similar to "flipping coins in the courtroom" and argued that clinical testimony should be barred from the courtroom. Other researchers have gone even further, concluding that "no expertise to predict dangerous behavior exists and . . . the attempt to apply this supposed knowledge to predict who will be dangerous results in a complete failure" (Cocozza & Steadman, 1978, p. 274).

This pessimism continued into the 1980s. John Monahan, a leading U.S. researcher, summarized the literature in 1981 and concluded that "psychiatrists and psychologists are accurate in no more than one out of three predictions of violent behavior over a several-year period among institutionalized populations that had both committed violence in the past (and thus had a high base rate for it) and who were diagnosed as mentally ill" (Monahan, 1981, p. 47).

Notwithstanding the above conclusion, both Canadian and U.S. courts have ruled that predictions of violence risk do not violate the basic tenets of fundamental justice, nor are they unconstitutional. In *Barefoot v. Estelle* (1983), the U.S. Supreme Court determined the constitutionality of a Texas death-penalty appeal decision. Thomas Barefoot burned down a bar and shot and killed a police officer. Barefoot was convicted of capital murder and, at the sentencing phase of the trial, testimony was presented from two psychiatrists (one being Dr. James Grigson, whom we will discuss later in the chapter) about the threat of future dangerousness posed by Thomas Barefoot. Both psychiatrists testified, based on a hypothetical fact situation, that the individual described would be a threat to society. The judge sentenced Barefoot to death. The U.S. Supreme Court rejected the defendant's challenge that psychiatrists were unable to make sufficient accurate predictions of violence and ruled that the use of hypothetical questions to establish future dangerousness was admissible. The court concluded that mental health professionals' predictions were "not always wrong . . . only most of the time" (p. 901).

Canadian courts have also supported the role of mental health professionals in the prediction of violent behaviour (R. Moore v. the Queen, 1984). For example, in a dangerous offender case, the issue of whether psychiatric testimony should be admitted as evidence was evaluated. The court concluded, "The test for admissibility is relevance, not infallibility . . . psychiatric evidence is clearly relevant to the issue whether a person is likely to behave in a certain way" (R. v. Lyons, 1987, para. 97).

METHODOLOGICAL ISSUES

Risk assessment assumes that risk can be measured. Measurement, in turn, assumes that an instrument exists for the measurement of risk. What would be the ideal way to evaluate an instrument designed to measure risk? The way to proceed would be to assess a large number of offenders and then, regardless of their risk level, release them into the community. The offenders would then be tracked to see if they commit another criminal act. This way, the risk instrument could be evaluated to determine if it could accurately predict future criminal acts. However, although this is an ideal scenario from a research perspective, it is not ethically feasible to release high-risk individuals into the community. In reality, the sample available for evaluating a risk-assessment instrument is limited to those with a relatively low risk of reoffending. This constrains the kinds of conclusions that can be drawn when risk assessment is evaluated in the real world.

Monahan and Steadman (1994) identified three main weaknesses of research on the prediction of violence. The first issue concerns the limited number of risk factors being studied. Violent behaviour is due to a complex interaction between individual dispositions and situational factors. In other words, people engage in violence for many different reasons. Thus, many risk factors are likely involved, including the person's background, social situation, and biological and psychological features. Many studies have focused on only a limited number of risk factors. Assessment of risk may be improved by measuring more of the reasons why people engage in violence. Yang and Mulvey (2012) recommended researchers pay more attention to understanding how an individual's subjective state leads an individual to commit violence.

The second issue concerns how the criterion variable (the variable you are trying to measure) is measured. Researchers have often used official criminal records as their criterion measure. However, many crimes may never be reported to police. Thus, many false positives may be undiscovered true positives. Even violent crimes may go undiscovered and many violent *sexual* crimes are recorded as simply *violent* in nature. In short, use of official records underestimates violence. When official records are combined with interviews with patients or offenders and with collateral reports (information from people or agencies who know the patient or offender), the rate of violence increases. The MacArthur Violence Risk Assessment Study (Steadman et al., 1998) illustrates the effect of using different measures. Using official agency records, the base rate for violence was 4.5%, but when patient and collateral reports were added, the base rate increased to 27.5%, a rate of violence six times higher than the original base rate.

Finally, how the criterion variable is defined is a concern. In some studies, researchers will classify their participants as having either engaged in violence or not. Monahan and Steadman (1994) recommended that researchers expand this coding to include the severity of violence (threatened violence versus severe violence), types of violence (spousal violence versus sexual violence), targets of violence (family versus stranger), location (institutions versus community), and motivation (reactive [unplanned violence in response to a provocation] versus instrumental [violence used as an instrument in the pursuit of some goal]). It is likely that some risk factors will be associated with certain forms of violence; for example, a history of sexual offences may predict future sexual offences but not future bank robberies.

JUDGMENT ERROR AND BIASES

How do psychologists make decisions when conducting risk assessments? Researchers have identified the typical errors and biases in clinical decision making (Elbogen, 2002). The shortcuts people use to help to make decisions are called *heuristics* (Tversky & Kahneman, 1981). Some of these heuristics lead to inaccurate decisions. Clinicians may make several types of decision errors by including traits they intuitively believe to be important or assume to be associated with the risk but that actually are not (Odeh, Zeiss, & Huss, 2006). Chapman and Chapman (1967) defined an **illusory correlation** as the belief that a correlation exists between two events that in reality are either not correlated or are correlated to a much lesser degree than believed. For example, a clinician might assume a strong correlation between a diagnosis of mental disorder and high risk for violent behaviour. Although some forms of mental disorder are related to an increased risk, a relationship has not been consistently found (Monahan & Steadman, 1994). For example, Bonta, Law, and Hanson (1998) reported that offenders without a mental disorder were more likely to recidivate than those with a mental disorder. Whereas Bonta, Blais, and Wilson (2014) found no significant difference in recidivism between the mentally disordered group and the non-mentally disordered group. Clinicians also tend to ignore base rates of violence (Monahan, 1981), where clinicians working in prisons or forensic psychiatric facilities may not be aware of how often individuals with specific characteristics act violently. For example, the base rate for recidivism in homicide offenders is extremely low, however, given the nature of their crime, they might be perceived as high risk. Other investigators (Borum, Otto, & Golding, 1993) have noted the tendency to rely on highly salient or unique cues, such as bizarre delusions.

In general, people tend to be overconfident in their judgments (see Kahneman & Tversky, 1982). Clinicians who are very confident in their risk assessments will be more likely to recommend and implement intervention strategies. However, while

Illusory correlation: Belief that a correlation exists between two events that in reality are either not correlated or correlated to a much lesser degree

people can be very confident in their risk assessments, they may not be accurate. Desmarais, Nicholls, Read, and Brink (2010) investigated the association between clinicians' confidence and accuracy of predicting short-term in-patient violence. Clinicians completed a structured professional judgment measure designed to assess the likelihood of violent behaviour (e.g., verbal and physical aggression, self-harm) and indicated on a five-point scale their level of confidence. Most clinicians were highly confident; however, the association between confidence and accuracy was minimal. This pattern of findings suggested clinicians tended to have an overconfidence bias.

APPROACHES TO THE ASSESSMENT OF RISK

What are the existing methods of risk assessment? Three methods of risk assessment are most commonly described. **Unstructured clinical judgment** is characterized by a substantial amount of professional discretion and lack of guidelines. There are no predefined rules about what risk factors should be considered, what sources of information should be used, or how the risk factors should be combined to make a decision about risk. Thus, risk factors considered vary across clinicians and vary across cases (Grove & Meehl, 1996; Grove, Zald, Lebow, Snitz, & Nelson, 2000). Grove and Meehl (1996) described this type of risk assessment as relying on an "informal, 'in the head,' subjective, impressionistic, subjective conclusion, reached (somehow) by a human clinical judge" (p. 294). See Box 10.1 for an example of a professional using this type of risk assessment.

In contrast, mechanical prediction involves predefined rules about what risk factors to consider, how information should be collected, and how information should be combined to make a risk decision. Thus, risk factors do not vary as a function of the clinician and the same risk factors are considered for each case. A common type of mechanical prediction is called **actuarial prediction**. With actuarial prediction, the risk factors used have been selected and combined based on their empirical or statistical association with a specific outcome (Grove & Meehl, 1996; Grove et al., 2000). In other words, a study has been done in which a number of risk factors have been measured, a sample of offenders have been followed for a specific period, and only those risk factors that were actually related to reoffending in this sample are selected (for an example of an actuarial scale, see the Violence Risk Appraisal Guide described later in this chapter).

A debate in the literature exists concerning the comparative accuracy of unstructured clinical versus actuarial prediction. In a review of 20 studies, Paul Meehl (1954) concluded that actuarial prediction was equal to or better than unstructured clinical judgment in all cases. A similar conclusion was reached almost 50 years later, when Meehl and his colleagues (Grove et al., 2000) conducted a meta-analysis of prediction studies for human health and behaviour (including criminal behaviour). In sum, the weight of the evidence clearly favours actuarial assessments of risk (Ægisdóttir et al., 2006; Mossman, 1994), even with samples of offenders with mental disorders (Bonta, Law, & Hanson, 1998; Phillips et al., 2005) and sex offenders (Hanson & Morton-Bourgon, 2009). A criticism of many actuarial assessments has been their sole reliance on static risk factors, which do not permit measuring changes in risk over time or provide information relevant for intervention (Wong & Gordon, 2006).

Unstructured clinical judgment: Decisions characterized by a substantial amount of professional discretion and lack of guidelines

Actuarial prediction: Decisions are based on risk factors that are selected and combined based on their empirical or statistical association with a specific outcome

Box 10.1   Forensic Psychology in the Spotlight

Dr. Death: A Legendary (Notorious) Forensic Psychiatrist

Dr. James Grigson was a Dallas psychiatrist who earned the nicknames "Dr. Death" and "the Hanging Shrink" because of his effectiveness at testifying for the prosecution in death-penalty cases. For nearly three decades, Dr. Grigson testified in death-penalty cases in Texas.

Death-penalty trials are divided into two phases. First, the defendant's guilt is decided. Next, if the defendant is guilty of a serious crime, the same judge and jury decide whether to impose life in prison or to sentence the defendant to die. For example, under the Texas Penal Code, one of the issues the jurors must decide on is "whether there is a probability that the defendant would commit criminal acts of violence that would constitute a continuing threat to society." Psychiatrists and psychologists are often hired to testify about the likelihood of future violence.

Dr. Grigson's testimony was very effective. He often diagnosed defendants as being sociopaths and stated with 100% certainty that they would kill again. For example, in *Estelle v. Smith* (1981), Dr. Grigson testified on the basis of a brief examination that the defendant Smith was a "very severe sociopath," who, if given the opportunity, would commit another criminal act. The diagnosis of *sociopath* appears to have been based on the sole fact that Smith "lacked remorse."

Dr. Grigson has been proven wrong. In the case of Randall Dale Adams (documentarian Errol Morris made a movie about Adams's story in 1988, called *The Thin Blue Line*, which helped to get the case reopened), Dr. Grigson testified that Randall Adams was a "very extreme" sociopath and would continue to be a threat to society even if kept locked in prison. Dr. Grigson based his assessment on a 15-minute interview in which he asked about Adams's family background, had Adams complete a few items from a neuropsychological test designed to measure visual-motor functioning (Bender Gestalt Test), and asked Adams the meaning of two proverbs: "A rolling stone gathers no moss" and "A bird in the hand is worth two in a bush." Randall Adams was sentenced to death. However, after he spent 12 years on death row, his conviction was overturned and he was released (another inmate confessed to the murder Adams had been charged for). It has been 13 years since Randall Adams was released. He is now married, employed, and living a non-violent life. Dr. Grigson was wrong in this case—and potentially in how many others?

In 1995, Dr. Grigson was expelled from the American Psychiatric Association (APA) for ethical violations. He was disqualified for claiming he could predict with 100% certainty that a defendant would commit another violent act (and, on at least one occasion, testifying that the defendant had a "1000%" chance of committing another violent act). The APA was also concerned that Dr. Grigson often testified in court based on hypothetical situations and diagnosed an individual without even examining the defendant. Dr. Grigson often diagnosed defendants as sociopaths on the basis of his own clinical opinion and not on any structured assessment procedures.

Dr. Grigson was also involved in the death-penalty case of Canadian Joseph Stanley Faulder, who was convicted and sentenced to death for the robbery and murder of Inez Phillips. Dr. Grigson testified that Stanley Faulder was an "extremely severe sociopath," that there was no cure, and that he would certainly kill again. We will never assess the accuracy of Dr. Grigson's predictions, since on June 17, 1999, after spending 22 years on death row, Stanley Faulder was executed. When Dr. Grigson died in 2004 at the age of 72, he had testified in 167 trials. How many of these defendants fell victim to Dr. Grigson and his misguided attempt to protect society is unknown.

Sources: Based on The Washington Times. (Dec 20, 2003) Texas 'Dr. Death' retires after 167 capital case trials. Retrieved from http://www.washingtontimes.com/news/2003/dec/20/20031220-113219-5189r/?page=all; Gross, A. (2004). Dangerous predictions: The case of Randall Dale Adams. The Forensic Examiner, 13(4). Retrieved from http://www.biomedsearch.com/article/Dangerous-predictions-case-Randall-Dale/125957151.html; Amnesty International. (undated). USA: Adding insult to injury: The case of Joseph Stanley Faulder. Retrieved from http://www.amnesty.org/en/library/asset/AMR51/086/1998/en/c619ed89-d9a2-11dd-af2b-b1f6023af0c5/amr510861998en.html.

Structured professional judgment: Decisions are guided by a predetermined list of risk factors that have been selected from the research and professional literature. Judgment of risk level is based on the evaluator's professional judgment

Arising from the limitations associated with unstructured clinical judgment and concern that the actuarial method did not allow for individualized risk appraisal or for consideration of the impact of situational factors to modify risk level, a new approach to risk assessment has emerged—**structured professional judgment** (SPJ) (Borum, 1996; Webster, Douglas, Eaves, & Hart, 1997). According to this method, the professional (the term *professional* is used to acknowledge that it is not only clinicians who make evaluations of risk but a diverse group, including law enforcement officers, probation officers, and social workers) is guided by a predetermined list of risk factors that have been selected from the research and professional literature. The professional considers the presence and severity of each risk factor, but the final judgment of risk level is based on the evaluator's professional judgment. The reliability and predictive utility of these risk summary judgments are only beginning to be assessed.

Skeem and Monahan (2011) described violence-risk-assessment approaches as having four components. Not all risk approaches include all these components. These components include "(a) identifying empirically valid risk factors, (b) determining a method for measuring (or 'scoring') these risk factors, (c) establishing a procedure for combining scores on the risk factors, and (d) producing an estimate of violence risk" (p. 39). Table 10.2 provides a summary of which risk-assessment approaches include these components. Some structured professional judgment measures, such as the Level of Service/Case Management Inventory, include all components, whereas others, such as the HCR-20, do not.

Dr. R. Karl Hanson, the Canadian researcher profiled in Box 10.2, has done extensive research on the predictive validity of actuarial risk-assessment measures.

Types of Risk Factors

The risk assessments used by clinicians and researchers use various risk factors to predict antisocial and violent behaviour. A risk factor is a measurable feature of an individual that predicts the behaviour of interest, such as violence. Traditionally, risk factors were divided into two main types: static and dynamic.

Table 10.2 Components Used across Risk-Assessment Approaches

Components	Unstructured Clinical Judgment	Actuarial	Structured Professional Judgment
Identify risk factors	No	Yes	Yes
Measure risk factors	No	Yes	Yes
Combine risk factors	No	Yes	Varies
Produce risk estimate	No	Yes	Varies

Source: Based on Skeem and Monahan, 2011. © 2011.

Box 10.2

Canadian Researcher Profile: Dr. R. Karl Hanson

Courtesy of Dr. R. Karl Hanson

Dr. Karl Hanson's research has focused on the assessment and treatment of serious offenders, particularly sexual offenders. Originally trained as a clinical psychologist at the University of Waterloo (under Donald Meichenbaum), Dr. Hanson's early experience working in conventional mental health settings convinced him that much of what we label as psychopathology was intimately connected with how we have been treated by others. Individuals presenting with intense personal suffering often recounted harrowing stories of abuse, maltreatment, and victimization. Dr. Hanson quickly realized that "what happens to us matters." He strongly believes if we are going to alleviate the burden of victimization, we need to understand why we do things that leave others with lasting psychic scars.

When Dr. Hanson was forming his research agenda, the issue of sexual abuse was just entering public discourse in Canada. Whereas textbooks in the 1970s identified incestuous abuse as very rare (one in a million), surveys studies

in the early 1980s found that it was actually common: rates of sexual victimization of girls during childhood were more like 1 in 10 or even 1 in 4. So, why was it so common? And what can we do about it? Dr. Hanson's answers to these questions were deeply influenced by sexual offender researchers, such as Vernon Quinsey and William Marshall, was well as leaders in correctional rehabilitation, including Donald Andrews, Jim Bonta, and Paul Gendreau. Jim Bonta's influence, in particular, was important (and unavoidable) given that Jim was his boss during the more than 20 years they both worked as researchers for the Government of Canada (Solicitor General/Public Safety Canada).

Dr. Hanson's most significant contributions have been in sexual offender risk assessment. His work has helped evaluators focus on risk relevant factors and combine these factors into an overall evaluation of risk. His STATIC suite of risk scales (e.g., Static-99R, Static-2002R) are by far the most commonly used sexual offender risk tools in the world. He has also helped shaped the research methods used in the field by teaching and providing accessible examples of useful statistics (e.g., meta-analysis, survival analysis) that had previously been rarely taught in psychology courses.

Dr. Hanson is heartened by the substantial progress in the field of forensic and correctional psychology during the past 30 years. Whereas his clinical supervisors in the 1980s warned him that working with offenders was beyond the scope of reputable clinical practice ("nothing we can do for antisocial personality disorder"), there is now strong evidence that psychologists can identify and address the risk relevant propensities of individuals prone to crime and violence. "With the current generation building on what we have learned, and many highly talented individuals entering the field, I am confident that we can help more people stop hurting others".

Static risk factors are factors that do not fluctuate over time and are not changed by treatment. Age at first arrest is an example of a static risk factor, since no amount of time or treatment will change this risk factor. Static risk factors have also been called *historical risk factors*. **Dynamic risk factors** fluctuate over time and are amenable to change. An antisocial attitude is an example of a dynamic risk factor, since it is possible that treatment could modify this variable. Dynamic risk factors have also been called *criminogenic needs* (see Chapter 9 for a discussion).

Static risk factor: Risk factors that do not fluctuate over time and are not amenable to change (e.g., criminal history)

Dynamic risk factor: Risk factors that fluctuate over time and are amenable to change (e.g., antisocial attitude)

More recently, correctional researchers have begun to conceptualize risk factors as a continuous construct (Douglas & Skeem, 2005; Grann, Belfrage, & Tengström, 2000; Zamble & Quinsey, 1997). At one end of the continuum are the static risk factors described above. At the other end are acute dynamic risk factors. These risk factors change rapidly within days, hours, or minutes and often occur just prior to an offence. Factors at this end of the continuum include variables such as negative mood and level of intoxication. In the middle of the continuum are stable dynamic risk factors. These risk factors change but only over long periods of time, such as months or years, and are variables that should be targeted for treatment. These factors include criminal attitudes, coping ability, and impulse control.

Recent research has found that dynamic risk factors are related to the imminence of engaging in violent behaviour. Quinsey, Jones, Book, and Barr (2006) had staff make monthly ratings of dynamic risk factors in a large sample of forensic psychiatric patients. Changes in dynamic risk factors were related to the occurrence of violent behaviours. Jones, Brown, and Zamble (2010) compared the predictive accuracy of risk ratings by researchers and parole officers in released offenders across three different time intervals (i.e., one, three, and six months). Both parole officers and researchers were moderately accurate, but it was the combination of time-dependent dynamic factors with static factors that showed the strongest predictive accuracy.

IMPORTANT RISK FACTORS

Historical risk factors: Risk factors that refer to events that have been experienced in the past (e.g., age at first arrest). Also known as *static risk factors*

Static risk factors: Risk factors that do not fluctuate over time and are not changed by treatment (e.g., age at first arrest). Also known as *historical risk factors*

Dispositional risk factors: Risk factors that reflect the individual's traits, tendencies, or styles (e.g., negative attitudes)

Clinical risk factors: Types and symptoms of mental disorders (e.g., substance abuse)

Contextual risk factors: Risk factors that refer to aspects of the current environment (e.g., access to victims or weapons). Sometimes called *situational risk factors*

Situational risk factors: Risk factors that refer to aspects of the current environment (e.g., access to victims or weapons). Sometimes called *contextual risk factors*

Since the late 1980s, a great deal of research has investigated what factors are associated with future violence. These can be classified into historical, dispositional, clinical, and contextual risk factors. **Historical risk factors** (sometimes called **static risk factors**) are events experienced in the past and include general social history and specific criminal history variables, such as employment problems and a history of violence. **Dispositional risk factors** are those that reflect the person's traits, tendencies, or style and include demographic, attitudinal, and personality variables, such as gender, age, criminal attitudes, and psychopathy. **Clinical risk factors** are the symptoms of mental disorders that can contribute to violence, such as substance abuse or major psychoses. **Contextual risk factors** (sometimes referred to as **situational risk factors**) are aspects of the individual's current environment that can elevate the risk, such as access to victims or weapons, lack of social supports, and perceived stress.

Some of these factors are likely relevant to risk assessment only, while others are relevant to both risk assessment and risk management. These factors vary in terms of how much they are subject to change. For example, some are fixed (e.g., gender), some cannot be undone (e.g., age of onset of criminal behaviour), and some may be resistant to change (e.g., psychopathy), whereas others (e.g., social support or negative attitudes) may be subject to intervention or may vary across time.

Several meta-analytic reviews have examined the predictors of general and violent recidivism in adult offenders, sexual offenders, and patients with mental disorders (Bonta et al., 1998; Gendreau, Little, & Goggin, 1996; Hanson & Morton-Bourgon, 2005). Two key findings have emerged. First, factors that predict general recidivism also predict violent or sexual recidivism. Second, predictors of recidivism in offenders with mental disorders overlap considerably with predictors found among offenders who do not have a mental disorder.

More recently, attempts have been made to determine if there are unique risk factors for various sub-populations including women offenders, aboriginal offenders, and terrorists. See Box 10.3 for a description of risk factors regarding violent extremism.

Dispositional Factors

Demographics Researchers in the 1970s identified young age as a risk factor for violence (Steadman & Cocozza, 1974): The younger the person is at the time of his or her first offence, the greater the likelihood that the person will engage in criminal behaviour and violence. Dozens of studies have firmly established age of first offence as a risk factor for both general and violent recidivism in both offenders with mental disorders (Bonta et al., 1998) and offenders without mental disorders (Gendreau et al., 1996). Offenders who are arrested prior to age 14 tend to have more serious and more extensive criminal careers than those who are first arrested after age 14 (DeLisi, 2006; Piquero & Chung, 2001). Males are at higher risk than females for general offending (Cottle, Lee, & Heilbrun, 2001; Gendreau et al., 1996). Notably, males engage in more serious violent acts, such as sexual assaults, homicides, and assaults causing bodily harm (Odgers & Moretti, 2002). Some studies using self-report measures have found that females engage in similar or even higher rates of less serious violence (Nichols, Graber, Brooks-Gunn, & Botvin, 2006; Steadman et al., 1994).

Psychologist conducting a risk-assessment interview with a young offender
Lisa F. Young/Shutterstock

Personality Characteristics Two personality characteristics have been extensively examined: impulsiveness and psychopathy. Not being able to regulate behaviour in response to impulses or thoughts increases the likelihood of engaging in crime and violence (Webster & Jackson, 1997). Lifestyle impulsivity (being impulsive in most areas of life) distinguishes recidivistic rapists from non-recidivistic rapists (Prentky, Knight, Lee, & Cerce, 1995).

Psychopathy is a personality disorder defined as a callous and unemotional interpersonal style characterized by grandiosity, manipulation, lack of remorse, impulsivity, and irresponsibility (see Chapter 11 for more information on psychopaths and the Hare Psychopathy Checklist–Revised [PCL-R], the most widely used measure of psychopathy). Given these features, it is not surprising that psychopathic individuals engage in diverse and chronic criminal behaviours. A recent meta-analysis found that psychopathy is moderately related to general and violent recidivism (Leistico, Salekin, DeCoster, & Rogers, 2008) and moderately related to violence in a prison setting (Guy, Edens, Anthony, & Douglas, 2005). Psychopathy predicts reoffending across different countries, such as Canada, the United States, the United Kingdom,

Box 10.3   Forensic Psychology in the Spotlight

Predicting Terrorism: Are There Unique Risk Factors?

Although there have been tremendous advances in predicting general violence, the attempt to develop risk-assessment instruments for terrorism is still in its infancy. Whether or not the same risk factors identified for general violence are also valid risk factors for terrorism remains unknown. In a review of the literature, Monahan (2012) identified the following risk factors for politically motivated violence:

- *Age:* The average age of violent terrorists is between 20 and 29.

- *Gender:* Most terrorists are male; however, there is gender variation across terrorist groups. For example, few al-Qaeda terrorists are female, but about half of Chechen and Kurd terrorists are female. Female terrorists are often able to get closer to targets than male terrorists can (Berko, Erez, & Globokar, 2010).

- *Marital status:* Most terrorists are single. This is especially true of suicide terrorists (Merari, 2010).

- *Social class:* Terrorists are not primarily from lower social classes, but rather are representative of the local population they come from. One study found that suicide terrorists are more highly educated compared to the population they come from (Merari, 2010).

- *Prior crime:* Many terrorists do not have a record of past violent criminal behaviour (Merari, 2010). Whether or not past violent terrorism predicts future terrorism is unknown since so few terrorists have been released. According to Bergen, Tiedemann, and Lebovich (2011) only 6% of released Guantanamo detainees committed or were suspected of committing terrorism.

- *Suicidality:* Although only a small number of terrorists commit suicide terrorism, these individuals differ substantially from people who commit suicide in the general population (Merari, 2010; Townsend, 2007).

- *Major mental illness:* There are very low rates of major mental illness such as bipolar disorder or schizophrenia in terrorists.

- *Substance abuse:* Although terrorist organizations often engage in drug trafficking to help finance their illegal activities, substance abuse in terrorists is very rare (Merari, 2010).

- *Psychopathy:* The rate of psychopathy among terrorists appears to be relatively low (Borum, 2011; Merari, 2010). Most psychopaths show little commitment to ideology and would be unlikely to sacrifice themselves for others.

However, many individuals who commit general violence are young, male, and single; this leaves no risk factors that may uniquely contribute to risk amongst violent extremists. As Monahan (2012) stated, "Terrorists in general tend not to be impoverished or mentally ill or substance abusers or psychopaths or otherwise criminals; suicidal terrorists tend not to be clinically suicidal" (p. 179). In other words, violent extremists do not tend to have the same risk factors as the general offender population. Indeed, it has been indicated that commonly used risk factors are equally present as not present among those who have committed acts of terrorism (e.g., educated versus non-educated; de Mesquita, 2005). Recently, researchers have begun to identify risk factors that might uniquely apply to this sub-population. Malik, Sandholzer, Khan, and Akbar (2015) surveyed Pakistani security officials in order to establish risk factors related to terrorism, and identified 13 critical factors falling within five categories:

1. Social wellbeing (e.g., inequality, non-availability of basic facilities, and a gathered population)

2. Economic indicators (e.g., unemployment and a higher consumer price index)

3. Governance (e.g., dishonest leadership, unjust or unfair accountability system, corruption, improper political process development, underprivileged state of sovereignty, and non-inclusiveness of public wishes in policy making)

4. Law enforcement (e.g., poor judicial system and poor state of national forces)

5. Armed conflict (e.g., unobserved presence of non-combatant foreigners)

Furthermore, sympathies and justifications for violent extremism have been noted amongst those who are politically influential and amongst those who have experienced acts of discrimination (Bhui, Warfa, & Jones, 2014; Victoroff, Adelman, & Matthews, 2012).

While research is beginning to emerge on risk factors that might contribute to acts of terror, there are still considerable gaps in the literature that must be addressed before we are accurately able to predict risk for violent extremism. It is important to understand the underlying factors that contribute to acts of terror in order to accurately predict their likelihood. As stated by Borum (2015), ". . . a robust empirical foundation does not yet exist for understanding the risk of terrorism or involvement in violent extremist activity" (p. 1).

Belgium, Germany, the Netherlands, New Zealand, and Sweden (Hare, 2003), in both male and female offenders (Richards, Casey, & Lucente, 2003), offenders with mental disorders (Nicholls, Ogloff, & Douglas, 2004; Steadman et al., 2000; Strand, Belfrage, Fransson, & Levander, 1999), male adolescent offenders (Corrado, Vincent, Hart, & Cohen, 2004; Forth, Hart, & Hare, 1990; Gretton, Hare, & Catchpole, 2004; Murrie, Cornell, Kaplan, McConville, & Levy-Elkon, 2004), and sexual offenders (Barbaree, Seto, Langton, & Peacock, 2001; Rice & Harris, 1997a). However, psychopathy may be weakly related or unrelated to violent reoffending in adolescent females (Odgers, Repucci, & Moretti, 2005; Schmidt, McKinnon, Chattha, & Brownlee, 2006; Vincent, Odgers, McCormick, & Corrado, 2008).

Several studies have found that the combination of psychopathy and deviant sexual arousal predicts sexual recidivism (Hildebrand, de Ruiter, & de Vogel, 2004; Olver & Wong, 2006; Rice & Harris, 1997a). Deviant sexual arousal is defined as evidence that the sexual offender shows a relative preference for inappropriate stimuli, such as children or violent nonconsensual sex. For example, Rice and Harris (1997a) found that about 70% of sexual offenders with psychopathic features and evidence of deviant sexual arousal committed a new sexual offence, compared with about 40% of the other offender groups.

Historical Factors

Past Behaviour The most accurate predictor of future behaviour is past behaviour. Past violent behaviour was first identified as a predictor in the 1960s and 1970s (see Cocozza, Melick, & Steadman, 1978) and has consistently been associated with future violence in diverse samples, including adolescents and adults, correctional offenders, mentally disordered offenders, and civil psychiatric patients (Farrington, 1991; McNiel, Sandberg, & Binder, 1988; Phillips et al., 2005). Interestingly, it is not only past violent behaviour that predicts violence, but also past nonviolent behaviour (Harris, Rice, & Quinsey, 1993; Lipsey & Derzon, 1998). For example, offenders who have a history of break and enter offences are at an increased risk for future violence.

Age of Onset As noted earlier, individuals who start their antisocial behaviour at an earlier age are more chronic and serious offenders (Farrington, 1991; Tolan & Thomas, 1995). For example, Farrington (1991) found that 50% of the boys in his study who committed a violent offence prior to age 16 were convicted of a violent offence in early adulthood. In another longitudinal study, Elliott (1994) reported that 50% of male youth who committed their first violent acts prior to age 11 continued their violent behaviour into adulthood, compared with 30% whose first violence was between the ages of 11 and 13, and only 10% of those whose first violent act occurred during adolescence. Age of onset is not as strong a predictor for female offenders (Piquero & Chung, 2001).

Childhood History of Maltreatment Having a history of childhood physical abuse or neglect is associated with increased risk for violence (Smith & Thornberry, 1995; Zingraff, Leiter, Johnsen, & Myers, 1994). In a large-scale study of childhood abuse, Widom (1989a) reported that victims of sexual abuse were no more likely than those who were not sexually abused to commit delinquent or violent offences. Those who were victims of physical abuse or neglect were much more likely to commit criminal acts as compared with those who were not abused. Being abused in childhood predicts initiation into delinquency, but continued abuse predicts chronic offending (Lemmon, 2006). Physical abuse in adolescence is also directly related to adolescent offending and may be related to some types of offending in adulthood as well (Fagan, 2005; Smith, Ireland, & Thornberry, 2005).

Clinical Factors

Substance Use Drug and alcohol use has been associated with criminal behaviour and violence. However, the drug–violence link is complex because of both direct effects (e.g., the pharmacological effects of the drugs) and indirect effects (e.g., the use of violence to obtain drugs; Hoaken & Stewart, 2003). The obvious link between drugs and crime is that the use, possession, and sale of illegal drugs are crimes. In some cases, the individual commits offences to support a drug habit (Klassen & O'Connor, 1994). For example, Chaiken and Chaiken (1983) found that severe drug users commit 15 times as many robberies and 20 times as many burglaries as non-drug-using offenders. The drug that has been most associated with crime is heroin (Inciardi, 1986). A large study of 653 opiate users in Edmonton, Montreal, Quebec City, Toronto, and Vancouver concluded that individuals with greater heroin and crack use are at the greatest risk of committing property crimes (Manzoni, Brochu, Fischer, & Rehm, 2006). Not all classes of drugs are related to the same degree with criminal behaviour and violence, and in some cases the strength of the association depends on the amount of the drug used (Hoaken & Stewart, 2003).

Dowden and Brown (2002) conducted a meta-analysis of 45 studies to examine the association between substance abuse and recidivism. Alcohol and drug use problems were moderately related to general recidivism. Zanis et al. (2003) followed a sample of 569 offenders with a prior history of substance abuse or dependence for two years after release from prison on parole. Factors relating to a new conviction included the number of prior convictions, younger age, parole without treatment, and cocaine dependence.

Drug abusers also come in contact with antisocial people, thus leading to violent confrontations. Laboratory research (Taylor & Sears, 1988) has found that aggression displayed by intoxicated individuals is a joint function of the pharmacological effects of alcohol intoxication (disinhibition effects), expectancies, and the situation (what is happening in the environment). Neuropsychological deficits (i.e., executive functioning) also play a role in the effects of alcohol on aggression (Giancola, Parrott, & Roth, 2006).

In one of the largest surveys done, Swanson (1994) interviewed 7000 individuals in two U.S. cities (Durham and Los Angeles), asking about the presence of substance abuse, psychiatric disorders, and violent behaviour. Based on data from the previous year, less than 3% of men and women with no psychiatric diagnosis committed violence. However, for those with a diagnosis of substance abuse, the rates of violence for men and women were 22% and 17%, respectively. More recently, Morley, Lynskey, Moran, Borschmann, and Winstock (2015) conducted a study exploring polysubstance abuse and mental health in relation to high risk behaviours in a large sample from the UK, Australia, and the United States. Individuals with a diagnosis of anxiety were more likely to use cannabis and medications. Violent behaviour was associated with the use of all drugs (i.e., cannabis, ecstasy, cocaine, stimulants, nitrous, ketamine, benzodiazepines, and opioid painkillers). Sexual risk taking was also predicted by the use of all drugs, including ecstasy and cocaine use. Overall, while a mental illness diagnosis predicted minor drug use, high-risk behaviours were predicted by more serious polysubstance abuse (Morley et al., 2015).

Mental Disorder Much controversy exists over the connection between major mental disorder and violence. The general public believes that these two items are linked (Pescosolido, Monahan, Link, Stueve, & Kikuzawa, 1999). Although most people with mental disorders are not violent, a diagnosis of affective disorders and schizophrenia has been linked to higher rates of violence (Swanson, 1994). Hillbrand (1995) reported that in a sample of forensic psychiatric patients, those with a history of suicide attempts and engaging in self-harm behaviours were more likely to engage in verbal and physical aggression than other patients.

In a meta-analysis of 204 studies, Douglas, Guy, and Hart (2009) concluded that psychosis was associated with between a 49% and 68% increase in the odds of violence. However, the strength of the psychosis–violence link depended on several factors, including study design (settings, comparison group), measurement (types of symptoms), and timing of the symptoms and the violence.

Contextual Factors

Lack of Social Support This risk factor refers to the absence of strong support systems to help individuals in their day-to-day lives. Henggeler, Schoenwald, Borduin, Rowland, and Cunningham (1998) described four kinds of support: (1) *instrumental*, "to provide the necessities of life"; (2) *emotional*, "to give strength to"; (3) *appraisal*, "to give aid or courage to"; and (4) *information*, "by providing new facts." Assessing the kinds and levels of support a person has and what types of support must be created will help to evaluate that person's level of risk. Klassen and O'Connor (1989) found that the current relationship an offender with a mental disorder has with his or her parents and siblings is related to violence.

Access to Weapons or Victims If the offender is released into an environment that permits easy access to weapons or victims, the potential for another violent act increases. An offender who moves into a skid-row rooming house that houses many other antisocial individuals and provides easy access to drugs may start associating with antisocial people or using drugs (Monahan & Steadman, 1994). If the offender has engaged in violence with other associates or under the influence of substances, releasing the offender to live in the same circumstances that led to past violence may induce future violence. In addition, if offenders who have assaulted their spouses and refused treatment for domestic violence return to live with their spouses, they have a much higher likelihood of violence than those who do not have easy access to a past victim.

Risk Assessment

Risk assessment can be associated with some misinformed beliefs. Below is a list of these myths, accompanied by facts that challenge them.

Myth 1. Commonly used risk assessment tools are applicable across all offender populations.
Fact. While most of the commonly used risk assessment tools do predict across offender populations (e.g., general, female, and Aboriginal), they predict with less accuracy. Much more research is needed to understand why these tools perform less accurately and, further, to determine if it is appropriate to apply these tools to the various sub-populations.

Myth 2. Risk statements provide objective information on an offender's risk to reoffend.
Fact. While the most common language used to describe an offender's risk is a ranking of *low, moderate,* or *high,* these seemingly clear explanations can mean various things in different contexts. Although many professional prefer this ranking, often the true outcome of the risk assessment (i.e., the correct interpretation of a given score) is lost when described so simply. Furthermore, the definitions of these categories are not the same across settings.

Myth 3. There is clear consensus amongst researchers as to which type of risk assessment should be utilized.
Fact. There is a strong debate amongst researchers and clinicians as to which type of risk assessment should be used. Typically, the sides are advocates for actuarial risk assessment and advocates for structured professional judgement. Those advocating for the use of actuarial risk tools do so for their objective, mechanical nature. Those advocating for structure professional judgement believe that actuarial tools do not leave room for important, clinically relevant factors that are not necessarily considered criminogenic needs. While research indicates that there is no large difference between the predictive accuracies of either tool, the debate continues.

Myth 4. Unstructured professional judgement is no longer used by clinicians to assess risk.
Fact. Despite the robust findings that unstructured professional judgement should *not* be relied upon (i.e., poor predictive accuracy), some clinicians or professionals still conduct risk assessments utilizing this method.

Risk-Assessment Instruments

Many of the factors affecting risk assessment that we've discussed above serve as the basis for various kinds of risk-assessment instruments. Some instruments have been developed to predict specific kinds of risk, while others utilize particular strategies outlined above, such as actuarial or structured clinical assessments. An example of an actuarial risk assessment and a structured professional judgment will be described. See Box 10.4 for a description of some of the misconceptions associated with risk assessment.

The Static-99 (Hanson & Thornton, 1999) is a 10-item actuarial scale designed to predict sexual recidivism. All items on this scale are static in nature. Scores on the Static-99 can range from 0 to 12, with scores being associated with four risk categories: low, moderate-low, moderate-high, and high. Items on the Static-99 include the following:

- Young age at time of release
- Ever lived with intimate partner
- Any prior nonsexual violent convictions
- Any index nonsexual violent convictions
- Number of prior sex offences

- Number of prior sentences
- Any male victims
- Any unrelated victims
- Any stranger victims
- Any noncontact sex offences

The HCR-20 (Webster et al., 1997) was designed to predict violent behaviour in correctional and forensic psychiatric samples. The HCR-20 uses the structured professional judgment approach to risk assessment developed by a group of researchers in British Columbia. In this approach, the evaluator conducts a systematic risk assessment and refers to a list of risk factors, each having specific coding criteria and a demonstrated relationship with violent recidivism based on the existing professional and empirical literature. The HCR-20 stands for the list of 20 items organized into three main scales that align risk factors into past (historical), present (clinical), and future (risk management):

Historical (primarily static in nature):

- Past violence
- Age at first violent offence
- Relationship instability
- Employment instability
- Relationship problems
- Substance-use problems
- Major mental disorder
- Psychopathy
- Early maladjustment
- Personality disorder
- Prior supervision failure

Clinical (reflect current, dynamic risk factors):

- Lack of insight
- Negative attitudes
- Active mental disorder symptoms
- Impulsivity
- Treatability

Risk management (future community or institutional adjustment of the individual):

- Feasibility of plans
- Exposure to destabilizers
- Level of personal support
- Stress
- Likelihood of treatment compliance

Campbell, French, and Gendreau (2009) conducted a meta-analysis comparing the predictive effectiveness of several risk assessment measures (HCR-20, LSI/LSI-R, HCR-20, PCL-R, VRAG) for institutional violence and violence recidivism. All the risk measures were equally predictive of violent offending (effect sizes ranged from .24 to .27), whereas the HCR-20 (effect size = .31) and the LSI-R (Andrews & Bonta, 1995; effect size = .24) were the most predictive of institutional violence. In a more recent meta-analysis, Yang, Wong, and Coid (2010) found similar results, concluding that each risk assessment tool was a good predictor of violence, with no given tool producing superior predictive accuracy to the rest.

CURRENT ISSUES

Where Is the Theory?

Much of the focus in risk-assessment research has been on perfecting the prediction of violence. This focus is especially true for actuarial methods of risk assessment in which risk factors are selected based on their statistical relation to a specific outcome. There is less attention paid to *why* these risk factors are linked to violence. Understanding the causes of violence will aid in the development of prevention and intervention programs.

Recently, Silver (2006) recommended that researchers use criminological theories to help guide "the next generation of empirical research in the area of mental disorder and violence" (p. 686). One example of a criminological theory is the Coping-Relapse Model of Criminal Recidivism. Figure 10.1 illustrates the recidivism process and how each level interacts as outlined by Zamble and Quinsey (1997). According to the model, the first event is some type of environmental trigger. What will be

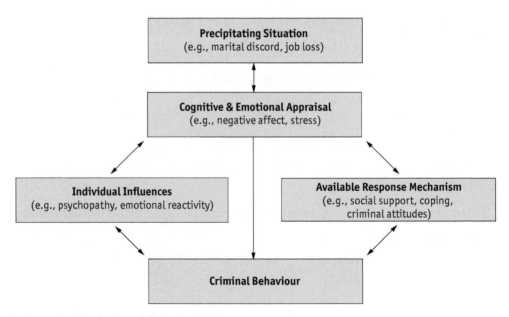

Figure 10.1 The Recidivism Process

considered a trigger varies across individuals and can range from stressful life events, such as losing a job, having relationship problems, and financial difficulties, to more mundane daily events, such as being stuck in a traffic jam. Once the event has occurred, the individual will invoke both an emotional and cognitive appraisal of the event. If this appraisal process results in the experience of negative emotions (e.g., anger, hostility, fear) or elevated levels of stress, the individual will attempt to deal with these unpleasant feelings. If the individual does not possess adequate coping mechanisms, a worsening cycle of negative emotions and maladaptive cognitions occurs, eventually resulting in criminal behaviour. The model also posits that how an individual perceives and responds to an environmental trigger is dependent on two factors: individual and response mechanisms.

Individual influences include factors such as criminal history and enduring personality traits (e.g., psychopathy, emotional reactivity). These factors influence how an individual will perceive an event and the likelihood that he or she will engage in criminal conduct, both of which are relatively stable. For example, research has found that psychopathic individuals are impulsive and more likely to interpret ambiguous events as hostile (Serin, 1991). These factors increase the likelihood of engaging in criminal behaviour.

Available response mechanisms also influence how an individual will perceive a situation, which, in turn, will mediate that person's response. These factors are considered more dynamic in nature and, thus, are important targets for intervention. Examples of these factors include coping ability, substance use, criminal attitudes and associates, and social supports. Imagine an individual who loses his job. He becomes angry and upset, and reverts to drinking to deal with these negative feelings. His drinking angers his intimate partner, who becomes less and less supportive of him. These factors increase the likelihood that he will resume his criminal behaviour.

Unique Sub-populations of Offenders

Most of the risk-assessment measures have been developed and validated with Caucasian male offenders. How well these measures generalize to women or other ethnic groups is an empirical question. If the causes and explanations for female and male criminality, or Caucasian and Aboriginal criminality are similar, then risk-assessment measures developed with male offenders likely can be used with female and Aboriginal offenders. However, if there are important differences in criminality across these various groups, then it may be inappropriate to apply measures developed with Caucasian male offenders to females and Aboriginal offenders.

What about Female Offenders? There are a number of gender differences in criminality. First, women engage in much less criminal behaviour than men. In 2005, about 21% of people accused of a criminal offence were female (Kong & AuCoin, 2008). Women represented 6.8% of admissions to federal custody in 2011–2012 (Public Safety Canada, 2012). In addition, women are arrested for different crimes than men. The only crime women commit more often than men is prostitution. When women engage in violence, they are more likely than men to target family members. Second, women reoffend at a lower rate than men. In 2011–2012, the percentage of successful full paroles and statutory releases for women was higher than for men (83% versus 78% for full parole and 73% versus 61% for statutory release; Public Safety Canada, 2012). Third, childhood victimization is more prevalent in women offenders than men offenders. For example, 50% of incarcerated female offenders reported childhood sexual abuse and 70% experienced childhood physical abuse (Shaw, 1994). Finally, female offenders are more likely than male offenders to have a serious mental disorder, such as schizophrenia, bipolar disorder, depression, and anxiety disorders (Correctional Service Canada, 1989; Warren et al., 2002). See the In the Media box about the case of Ashley Smith, a female offender whose serious mental health problems were not adequately treated during incarceration.

Gender-specific risk factors may exist; however, the research to date has found more similarities than differences in both adolescents and adults (Andrews & Bonta, 2006; Blanchette & Brown, 2006; Simourd & Andrews, 1994). Blanchette and Brown (2006) provided a review of static and dynamic risk factors in female offenders. They concluded that many of the static risk factors associated with recidivism in men, such as criminal history and age, are also predictors with women. Similar dynamic risk factors for women and men include substance abuse, antisocial attitudes, and antisocial associates. Evidence also suggests that women have further risk factors, such as a history of self-injury or attempted suicide, and self-esteem problems. Overall, additional research is needed to understand the static and dynamic risk factors for recidivism in women offenders. Further research is also needed to fully understand protective factors that may improve women's success in the community upon release from prison. For example, Benda (2005) found that being married was a protective factor for men but a risk factor for women.

How well do the risk-assessment instruments predict reoffending in female offenders? One risk-assessment scale that has been well researched with female offenders is the LSI-R. In a recent meta-analysis, Smith, Cullen, and Latessa (2009) reported that the LSI-R predicted general recidivism as well for women as for men (effect sizes of 0.27 and 0.26 for men and women, respectively). In addition, Andrews and colleagues (2012) found that both the LS/CMI eight risk domains and the total risk/needs score were equally predictive of general recidivism in an aggregate sample of female and male offenders. In this study, the substance abuse risk domain was more strongly associated with recidivism in female offenders as compared to male offenders.

What about Aboriginal Offenders? The overrepresentation of Aboriginal peoples in the Canadian criminal justice system has highlighted the need to better understand this sub-population of offenders. Aboriginal peoples make up approximately 4% of the general population across Canada (Statistics Canada, 2013). However, they account for approximately 22% of the total offender population (Public Safety Canada, 2015). This overrepresentation is especially prominent in the prairies and northern territories. Perreault (2009) reported that 11% of the population in the province of Saskatchewan identifies as Aboriginal, but 81% of all sentenced offenders are Aboriginal. Federally, Aboriginal offenders account for approximately 25% of the incarcerated offender population and approximately 17% of the community supervision population (Public Safety Canada, 2015). Overall, the proportion of offenders in custody was approximately 11% greater for Aboriginal

Ashley Smith: A Preventable Death?

It is challenging for individuals with serious mental health problems to receive the intensive treatment they need in prison. The tragic case of Ashley Smith illustrates this point. Ashley Smith was a 19-year-old offender who was in segregation at Grand Valley Institution for Women. She was on suicide watch, having been assessed by a psychologist as being at high risk to commit suicide. Ashley had an extensive history of engaging in self-harm, and on October 19, 2007, she tied a cloth around her neck. Correctional officers saw her with the ligature around her neck but did not intervene right away and she died. The correctional officers claimed that they had been told by their supervisors not to intervene unless Ashley Smith stopped breathing.

The Smith family launched an $11 million wrongful death lawsuit against CSC that was settled out of court in 2011. On December 19, 2013 a coroner's inquest ruled that Ashley Smith's death was a homicide and made 104 recommendations on how to better support female offenders. The following timeline summarizes some of the major issues related to this case:

- 1998–1999: Ashley Smith, age 10, started having problems at school in Grade 5 with being disruptive and talking excessively.

- 2001–2002: At age 13, her escalating disruptive problems in school resulted in several suspensions and, in February 2002, with her being moved to an alternative school. She also started having more serious conflicts with her parents.

- March 2002: At age 14, she was charged with numerous public disturbance offences and was sentenced to one-year probation. She was enrolled in the Intensive Supervision Program for high-risk youth.

- April 2002: At age 15, she was sent to New Brunswick Youth Centre for breach of probation, assaults, causing a disturbance, and trespassing. A psychiatric assessment concluded she had a learning disorder, attention deficit hyperactivity disorder, borderline personality disorder, and narcissistic personality traits.

- 2003–2006: Ashley Smith was incarcerated in two youth custody facilities, where she continued to engage in chronic disruptive and noncompliant behaviour, including self-harm and suicide attempts (approximately 800 incidents were recorded over this time period). She was released into the community to live with her parents numerous times, but each time she breached the conditions of her release. She was also placed in foster care/group homes, but these placements failed owing to Ashley's disruptive and aggressive behaviours. At the youth centres, Ashley spent much of the time in therapeutic quiet (segregation) as a result of her disruptive and aggressive behaviour. She was also charged with several criminal offences, including assaulting correctional officers.

- October 31, 2006: Ashley Smith, age 18, was transferred to an adult federal institution to serve her sentence.

- 2006–2007: During her 11.5 months of federal incarceration, she was transferred 17 times between federal institutions. These transfers interfered with any attempts by mental health professionals to develop a comprehensive treatment program for her.

Sources: Based on The Ashley Smith Report (2008). Office of the Ombudsman & Child and Youth Advocate, New Brunswick. Sapers, H. (2008). A preventable death. Correctional Investigator of Canada. © 2008.

offenders (i.e., 73%) than non-Aboriginal offenders (i.e., 62%; Public Safety Canada, 2015). Furthermore, Aboriginal women make up 41% of sentenced women across jurisdictions (Sinha, 2012). These problematic figures fuel the need for research identifying the potential causes of Aboriginal overrepresentation in our criminal justice system.

An important starting place is to explore whether commonly used risk factors are applicable to the Aboriginal offender population. Meta-analytic results suggest that the majority of the risk factors discussed previously predict general and violent

Are the Tools Valid? *Ewert v. Canada (2015)*

On September 18, 2015, a Federal Court in Vancouver, BC released a decision in the case of *Ewert v. Canada (Correctional Service of Canada)* which allowed for action against the Correctional Service of Canada's use of risk assessments. Jeffery Ewert is a 53-year-old Métis federal offender currently serving two life sentences for second degree murder and attempted murder. Over the past 30 years, Ewert has served time in federal institutions for various offences.

In 2006 and 2007, Ewert sued the Correctional Service of Canada on the grounds that they were utilizing culturally biased risk assessments with Aboriginal offenders, and he stated that this practice damaged his rehabilitation process. Although the trial was not successful, Ewert's case re-entered the court in 2015 where the judge ruled that the Correctional Service of Canada was indeed in violation of section seven of the *Canadian Charter of Rights and Freedoms* (i.e., right to life, liberty, and security of the person) and was not complying with section four of the *Corrections and Conditional Release Act* (i.e., "correctional policies, programs and practices respect gender, ethnic, cultural and linguistic differences and are responsive to the special needs of women, Aboriginal peoples, persons requiring mental health care and other groups"). This final ruling indicated that the Correctional Service of Canada must cease the use of risk assessments (i.e., the PCL-R, V-RAG, SORAG, Static-99, and VRS-SO) with Aboriginal offenders until proper validation and empirical findings regarding the cultural bias were conducted and made available. The judge ordered that a Remedies Hearing was to take place in order to determine how the Correctional Service of Canada should utilize risk assessments with Aboriginal offenders in the future; this included the use of research to validate the existing tools.

This case is an important landmark in the area of risk assessment as it highlights the importance of validating risk tools with various offender sub-groups. On August 3, 2016 the Federal Court of Appeal overturned the decision. Justice Eleanor Dawson ruled that the evidence presented during the original trial was not sufficient to conclude that the assessments were inaccurate or unreliable with Aboriginal offenders.

Questions

1. Will simply validating the existing tools inform researchers and other professionals about *why* they are less accurate predictors amongst Aboriginal populations?

2. What additional research do you think should be conducted on risk assessment measures with Aboriginal offenders?

Source: *Ewert v. Canada*, 2015; *Canada v. Ewert*, 2016.

recidivism amongst Aboriginal offenders (Gutierrez, Wilson, Rugge, & Bonta, 2013). However, Gutierrez and colleagues (2013) highlight that the most predictive factors for Aboriginal offenders were not necessarily the best predictors amongst non-Aboriginal offenders. Given this discrepancy, it has been proposed that *culturally-relevant* risk factors pertaining to Aboriginal offenders may provide more accurate estimations of risk (Wilson & Gutierrez, 2014). However, to date, a empirical exploration of *culturally-relevant* risk factors has not been conducted.

Despite the lack of research regarding risk factors and Aboriginal offender populations, some research has been conducted on Aboriginal offenders and commonly used risk assessment tools. Wilson and Gutierrez (2014) conducted a meta-analysis exploring the use of the LSI in Aboriginal and non-Aboriginal samples. Similar to the findings regarding risk factors, the LSI (e.g., total score and sub-scales) moderately predicted general recidivism for Aboriginal offenders. However, when compared to the accuracies amongst the non-Aboriginal samples, the LSI was less predictive for Aboriginal offenders. Similarly, the predictive accuracy of the Static-99R and the Static-2002R for Aboriginal offenders has also been explored using meta-analysis (Babchishin, Blais, & Helmus, 2012). While results for the Static-2002R were similar to those findings already reported (i.e., less predictive with Aboriginal offenders versus non-Aboriginal offenders), the Static-99R was found to have comparable effect sizes across both populations (Babchishin et al., 2012). While the research has generally found that some commonly used risk assessment tools predict less accurately for Aboriginal offenders, the reason for this remains unknown. See Box 10.5 for two recent court rulings about the use of actuarial risk measures with Aboriginal offenders.

The above research indicates that some risk-assessment instruments developed and validated with Caucasian male offenders may also be used with women and Aboriginal populations. However, it is not appropriate to assume that this will always be the case, and a considerable amount of research still needs to be conducted.

What about Protective Factors?

Various historical, dispositional, clinical, and contextual risk factors have been shown to have predictive utility. **Protective factors** are factors that mitigate or reduce the likelihood of antisocial acts or violence in high-risk offenders (Borum, 1996). Understanding the positive attributes could help to explain why some individuals with many risk factors do not become violent. For example, a youth may have antisocial parents at home (a risk factor) but also be strongly attached to school (a protective factor). Like risk factors, protective factors vary across time, and the impact they have depends on the situation. Most of the research on protective factors has been conducted with children and youth. The following factors have been identified as protective factors: prosocial involvement, strong social supports, positive social orientation (e.g., school, work), strong attachments (as long as attachment is not to an antisocial other), and intelligence (Caldwell, Silverman, Lefforge, & Silver, 2004; Caprara, Barbaranelli, & Pastorelli, 2001; Hoge, Andrews, & Leschied, 1996; Lipsey & Derzon, 1998). More research on protective factors in adult offenders is beginning. A variable identified as a potential protective factor for high-risk offenders is employment stability, whereas strong family connections appears to be a protective factor for lower-risk male offenders (DeMatteo, Heilbrun, & Marczyk, 2005). Two separate studies have identified the following protective factors for adult male sex offenders: professional support, social network, structured group activities, goal-directed living, and a hopeful or persistent attitude to desistance (ceasing antisocial behaviour) (Blacker, Beech, Wilcox, & Boer, 2011; Lofthouse et al., 2011). See the You Be the Forensic Psychologist box to try to identify risk and protective factors for an offender applying for parole.

Protective factors: Factors that mitigate or reduce the likelihood of a negative outcome (e.g., delinquency, aggression)

Risk Assessment: Risky Business?

Risk assessments have limitations that forensic evaluators and decision makers need to be aware of (Glazebrook, 2010). Most actuarial risk-assessment measures provide probability statements about reoffending based on group data. However, currently there is no method of determining what the specific risk level is for an individual (see Hart, Michie, & Cooke, 2007, for a review). In contrast to actuarial measures, structured

YOU BE THE FORENSIC PSYCHOLOGIST

Jason Booth is a 23-year-old first-time federal offender currently serving a three-year sentence at a medium-security federal penitentiary for possession of property obtained by crime over $5000, carrying a concealed weapon, and failure to comply with a probation order. He pled guilty to all these charges. He has served one year of his sentence and has applied for full parole.

When Jason was arrested, he was driving a stolen car and had a handgun, and because he was on probation for a previous conviction at the time, his possession of both of these items constituted a breach of probation. He had been released from custody for his previous charge only two weeks prior to committing these offences.

Official records indicate that the courts have sentenced Jason 10 times (7 times in youth court and 3 times in adult court) for a total of 17 convictions (10 in youth court and 7 in adult court) for assault, assault with a weapon, carrying a concealed weapon, criminal harassment, obstructing a peace officer, breaking and entering, theft under $1000, theft under $5000, failure to attend court, unlawfully at large, and failure to comply with a probation order.

Jason has violated probation several times and has engaged in violence in institutions (e.g., spitting in a correctional officer's face, stabbing another inmate with a pen). He has also engaged in violence in the community (e.g., assaulting his girlfriend, threatening to kill a bouncer at a bar).

At his parole hearing, Jason explained that he committed the current offences because he had just been released from prison and would not be receiving any social assistance for two weeks. He seemed to feel that the only way to obtain money was to steal a car. He was unable to generate any prosocial alternatives by which he could have obtained assistance. In addition, Jason minimized his criminal history and the harm he has done to his victims. For example, he stated that one of his past victims, a woman whom he had criminally harassed and threatened to kill, was "a spoiled brat who deserved what she got." Most of Jason's friends are criminals.

In the psychological report, Jason was described as hostile, arrogant, manipulative, impulsive, and remorseless. Jason denies any current problems with drugs or alcohol. Neither drugs nor alcohol have been involved in his current or past offences.

Jason was reportedly diagnosed with attention deficit hyperactivity disorder when he was 9 years old. He was never interested in school and was expelled numerous times. He completed Grade 9 but was absent for most of Grade 10. He dropped out of school when he was 16 years old. Jason's employment history consists of several short-term jobs, with the longest job lasting for one year. He has few employment skills and tends to get into altercations with his boss and other employees. He was fired from his last job for stealing merchandise from the company's warehouse. During his current incarceration, he has refused educational and vocational training.

Jason's biological father, who reportedly has been incarcerated himself, left Jason's mother when Jason was 3 years old. Jason was raised by his biological mother and an alcohol-abusing stepfather. His stepfather reportedly threw Jason out of the house when he was 13 years old because of his stealing and other disruptive behaviours.

Jason was subsequently placed in a series of foster and group homes. He was often moved from home to home because of his aggressive and disruptive behaviour.

There is evidence that Jason has assaulted former intimate partners. Past reports indicate Jason can be jealous and overly controlling, having unreasonable expectations in relationships with women. He reportedly has two children of his own but does not maintain contact with either of them. At his parole hearing, Jason said that when he is released he and his ex-common-law spouse, a partner he assaulted in the past, plan to resume their relationship.

Jason plans to live with his mother when he is released. His mother is very supportive of Jason and has agreed to try to help him adjust as much as possible. He typically lives on social assistance or obtains money from criminal behaviours when in the community.

There is no evidence that Jason has ever successfully completed either institutional or community programming. He is typically uncooperative with attempts at assessment and treatment. However, he has recently expressed an interest in treatment programs.

Your Turn . . .

You are the forensic psychologist assessing Jason. What risk factors for future reoffending are present? Are there any protective factors present? How likely is Jason to commit another nonviolent or violent crime if he is released? Which risk-assessment instrument would you use to help determine Jason's risk for future crime and violence?

professional judgment measures typically ask evaluators to state the level of risk in terms of low, moderate, or high. However, researchers have found that forensic evaluators do not agree on what is meant by low, moderate, or high risk (Hilton, Carter, Harris, & Sharpe, 2008; Mills & Kroner, 2006). Measures developed in one country or in one population may not generalize to another country or population (Austin, 2006). For example, Boccaccini, Murrie, Caperton, and Hawes (2009) reported that the Static-99 was not as predictive of sexual reoffending in a sample of sex offenders in the United States as compared with the published norms from Canada and the United Kingdom for this measure. Risk-assessment measures need to be validated in the community on which they will be used. Recently, some concerns have also been raised about the field reliability of risk-assessment measures (Murrie, Boccaccini, Johnson, & Janke, 2008). Finally, clinicians who are writing risk-assessment reports or providing evidence to decision makers (e.g., an expert testifying in court) must ensure they use terminology that can be understood by the decision makers (e.g., juries, judges, lawyers, probation officers).

Are Psychologists and Decision Makers Using the Scientific Research?

Despite the considerable strides that have been made in refining methods of violence prediction, many practitioners are not using these instruments. This gap in integrating science and clinical practice represents a significant challenge to this area. A survey by

Boothby and Clements (2000) asked 820 correctional psychologists what tests they used in their assessments. The most commonly used test was the Minnesota Multiphasic Personality Inventory (MMPI), which was used by 87% of the psychologists. Only 11% of the respondents mentioned using the Hare PCL-R, and less than 1% mentioned using the VRAG or the LSI-R. However, a recent survey by Viljoen, McLachlan, and Vincent (2010) found the use of risk-assessment tools to be much more common. In a sample of 199 forensic clinicians, 75% always or almost always used a risk-assessment tool when assessing an adult offender's risk for violent reoffending. The assessment tools most often used were the Psychopathy Checklists, the HCR-20, the MMPI-II, the WASI-III (measure of intelligence), the Static-99, and the VRAG. Wilson, Crocker, Nicholls, Charette, and Seto (2015) reported on the use of the HCR-20 and the VRAG in review board hearings for individuals found not criminally responsible on account of a mental disorder. Similar to previous findings, these tools were typically used for the purposes of these hearings, however less than half of the risk factors included in both measures were included in the decision-making process (e.g., expert reports). While both tools have been found to be accurate assessments of risk, not utilizing the entire tool calls this validity into question. The results reported by Wilson and colleagues (2015) highlight the considerable gap between research and practice.

What impact do psychologists' recommendations have on forensic decision making? Past research has found that judicial decision making relies heavily on recommendations made by mental health professionals (Konecni & Ebbesen, 1984). In Canada, decisions to release forensic patients are strongly related to recommendations by clinicians (Quinsey & Ambtman, 1979), and reports by clinicians about treatment gains made by sex offenders strongly influence decisions about granting parole (Quinsey, Khanna, & Malcolm, 1998). Another related question is whether decision makers are relying on results of the newly developed actuarial risk instruments. Hilton and Simmons (2001) studied the influence of VRAG scores and clinical judgments on decisions made to transfer offenders with mental disorders in a maximum-security facility to less secure institutions. Review board decisions were not related to scores on the VRAG but to senior clinicians' testimony at the review board hearing. Patients who caused few institutional problems, who were compliant with medication, who were more physically attractive, and who had less serious criminal histories were more likely to be recommended by the clinician for transfer. Clinicians make more accurate decisions when they are given a statement that summarizes an individual's risk along with case information (i.e., "64% of people in Mr. Smith's risk category reoffended violently within ten years after release") (Hilton, Harris, Rawson, & Beach, 2005). Clinicians also are able to make accurate decisions when they are provided with the information that relates to risk.

Why Do Some Individuals Stop Committing Crimes?

Much of the research discussed in this chapter focuses on the risk factors related to engaging in crime and violence. However, if we want to prevent or reduce crime, knowledge about the factors relating to desistance from crime is probably equally important (Farrington, 2007). **Desistance** occurs when an individual who has engaged

Desistance: The process of ceasing to engage in criminal behaviour

in criminal activities stops committing crime. Research even reveals that a majority of offenders show large declines in their criminal activity in early adulthood (Blumstein & Cohen, 1987; Piquero et al., 2001). As many as 70% of offenders show significant declines in crime (and only a small percentage of offenders maintain criminal activity well into adulthood; Piquero et al., 2001). Yet, the reasons why offenders give up crime are poorly understood. Some research shows that the factors that relate to the onset of a criminal career do not necessarily explain desistance from crime (Stouthamer-Loeber, Wei, Loeber, & Masten, 2004). The desistance process occurs over time and may be related to such factors as "good" work or "good" marriages (Maume, Ousey, & Beaver, 2005; Sampson & Laub, 2005; Uggen, 1999). Although marriage is a protective factor, researchers have found that offenders with longer criminal histories are less likely to marry, and if they do they tend to marry criminal others (van Schellen, Poortman, & Nieuwbeerta, 2012). Age is strongly related to criminal behaviour, and the age-related decline in criminal offending is connected to the maturation process (Menard & Huizinga, 1989). LeBlanc (1993) defined *maturation* as the "development of self- and social control" (p. 65). Shover and Thompson (1992) suggested that as people age, they become less interested in a criminal lifestyle and are more able to understand and fear the consequences of engaging in crime. Recently, Serin and Lloyd (2009) developed a model that proposes the transition between criminal offending and desistance is influenced by several intrapersonal moderators, such as crime expectancies (what benefits do they see from not engaging in crime), beliefs about their ability to change (how hard will it be to change), and attributions for engaging in crime. See Box 10.6 for excerpts from a study that examines why high-risk offenders stop offending.

Box 10.6   Forensic Psychology in the Spotlight

Why Do High-Risk Violent Offenders Stop Offending?

In a study titled "Against All Odds: A Qualitative Follow-up of High-Risk Violent Offenders Who Were Not Reconvicted," Haggard, Gumpert, and Grann (2001) explored what factors were related to why repeat violent offenders stopped reoffending. To be eligible to participate in the study, the offender had to score high on the historical subscale of the HCR-20, to have been convicted of at least two violent crimes, and not to have been convicted for any crime for at least ten years. From a sample of 401 violent offenders, only six individuals were eligible to participate. Of these six, only four consented to be interviewed. The participants reported that the following factors are related to desistance. For each factor, a quotation from one of the participants is provided.

■ *Insight triggered by negative events connected to their criminal lifestyle.* "It grows within during a long time,

the insight, but you have to reach a point where it feels wrong. . . . To me, it was mostly due to the last time, when I was admitted to the forensic psychiatric hospital. The whole thing was crazy, and then I realized how off track I was—when you strike down a person with an axe because of a trivial thing . . . then you start wondering. I did anyway." (p. 1055)

■ *Social avoidance.* "I have a terrible temper and I can become violent, very violent. . . . You have to avoid different situations, you have to think about it all the time so that you don't put yourself in situations you can't handle." (p. 1057)

■ *Orientation to the family.* "After I served my sentence, I became more committed to my children. To help them not to make the same mistake I did." (p. 1057)

SUMMARY

1. An assessment of risk requires two components: (1) an analysis of the likelihood of future criminal or violent acts, and (2) the development of strategies to manage or reduce the risk level.

2. Risk assessments are routinely conducted in the civil and criminal contexts. Risk assessments in civil contexts include civil commitments, child protection, immigration, and duty to warn. In criminal settings, the assessment of risk occurs at pretrial, sentencing, and release stages.

3. There are different types of errors when attempting to make predictions. Each of these errors has different consequences. False-positive errors affect the offender, whereas false-negative errors affect society and the victim.

4. Risk factors vary in terms of how fixed or changeable they are. Static factors either do not change or are highly resistant to change. Dynamic factors are changeable and are often targeted for intervention.

5. Various approaches have been developed to assess violence prediction. These include unstructured clinical judgment, actuarial prediction, and structured professional judgment. There are advantages and disadvantages to each approach.

6. Major risk factors can be classified into historical, dispositional, clinical, and contextual factors. Historical risk factors include general social history and specific criminal history variables, such as employment problems and past history of violence. Dispositional factors include demographic, attitudinal, and personality variables, such as gender, age, negative attitudes, and psychopathy. Clinical factors refer to those things that contribute to violence, such as substance abuse or major psychoses. Contextual factors refer to aspects of the individual's situation that can elevate the risk, such as access to victims or weapons, lack of social supports, or perceived stress.

7. Commonly used risk factors and risk assessment tools cannot simply be applied to sub-populations of offenders that differ from the development sample. Generally, these risk factors and risk assessments are less reliable when applied to these sub-populations. More research is needed to fully understand why they are less reliable and if they are applicable. More research is also needed to explore the possibility of unique risk factors (e.g., gender specific and culturally-relevant risk factors).

Discussion Questions

1. You have decided to take a summer job working at Correctional Service Canada. You are asked to help devise a study to evaluate the accuracy of a new instrument designed to predict hostage-taking by federal offenders. How would you approach this task?

2. A school board wants to know how to identify the next potential school shooter and has contacted you for your expertise. Describe what you know about problems with trying to identify low-base-rate violent acts.

Chapter 11
Psychopaths

Learning Objectives

- Define psychopathy.
- Outline the different assessment methods developed to measure psychopathy.
- Describe the association between psychopathy and violence.
- Describe the effectiveness of treatment programs for adult and adolescent psychopaths.
- Identify the concerns associated with labelling a youth as a psychopath.
- Explain the two main theories of psychopathy.

Jason Roach is a 19-year-old working in a convenience store. He dropped out of college and spends most of his time partying, and getting drunk and stoned. He decides that he does not want to spend the rest of his life working in a convenience store—a job he describes as "menial." One of his 16-year-old friends, Shawn, has been complaining about his parents and has started talking about wanting to "get rid of them." Jason offers to help, stating that if he helps he wants half of the insurance money. Jason convinces another 17-year-old friend with a car to help them with their murderous plan. Jason knows that they will need to have an alibi, so on the night of the murder they go to the nearby town to a strip club. Jason gets into an altercation with the bouncer to ensure the bouncer will remember them. Around midnight, armed with a baseball bat and a tire iron, they enter Shawn's house and beat his parents and his 14-year-old sister. While the beatings are taking place, Jason pours gasoline downstairs. As the offenders leave, Jason sets the house on fire. Two people die, and one is severely injured. Jason and his two friends are all charged and convicted of first-degree murder. At his trial, Jason describes himself as the "puppet master," appears proud of his ability to manipulate his younger friends, and shows no remorse for his actions.

Psychopaths have been called *intraspecies predators* (Hare, 1993). They seek vulnerable victims to use for their own benefit. Sometimes they get what they want by charming their victims, while at other times they use violence and intimidation to achieve their goals. Lacking a conscience and feelings for others, they satisfy their own selfish needs by preying on others. **Psychopathy** is a personality disorder defined by a

Psychopathy: A personality disorder defined by a collection of interpersonal, affective, and behavioural characteristics, including manipulation, lack of remorse or empathy, impulsivity, and antisocial behaviours

collection of interpersonal, affective, and behavioural characteristics. Psychopaths are dominant, selfish, manipulative individuals who engage in impulsive and antisocial acts and who feel no remorse or shame for behaviour that often has a negative impact on others. Jason in the above vignette displays many psychopathic traits.

Descriptions of psychopathy exist in most cultures. Murphy (1976) found that the Inuit in Alaska use the term *kulangeta* to described an individual who "repeatedly lies and cheats and steals things and does not go hunting and, when the other men are out of the village, takes sexual advantage of many women—someone who does not pay attention to reprimands and who is always being brought to the elders for punishment" (p. 1026). When Murphy asked an Inuit elder what the group would typically do with a *kunlangeta*, he replied, "Somebody would have pushed him off the ice when nobody else was looking" (p. 1026).

In this chapter, we focus on methods for the assessment of psychopathy, how prevalent psychopathy is, its overlap with other psychiatric disorders, the relationship between psychopathy and violence, and the effectiveness of treating psychopathy.

ASSESSMENT OF PSYCHOPATHY

Hervey Cleckley (1976), a psychiatrist in Georgia, provided one of the most comprehensive clinical descriptions of the psychopath in his book *The Mask of Sanity*. Cleckley (1976) described 16 features, ranging from positive features (e.g., good intelligence, social charm, and absence of delusions and anxiety), emotional-interpersonal features (e.g., lack of remorse, untruthfulness, unresponsiveness in interpersonal relations), and behavioural problems (e.g., inadequately motivated antisocial behaviour, unreliability, failure to follow any life plan).

Currently, the most popular method of assessing psychopathy in adults is the **Hare Psychopathy Checklist–Revised** (PCL-R) (Hare, 1991, 2003). This assessment instrument was developed by Robert Hare at the University of British Columbia and is now being used around the world. The development of the PCL-R was strongly influenced by the work of Hervey Cleckley. The PCL-R is a 20-item rating scale that uses a semi-structured interview and a review of file information to assess interpersonal (e.g., grandiosity, manipulativeness), affective (e.g., lack of remorse, shallow emotions), and behavioural (e.g., impulsivity, antisocial acts) features of psychopathy. Each item is scored on a 3-point scale: 2 indicates that the item definitely applies to the individual; 1 indicates that it applies to some extent; and 0 indicates that the symptom definitely does not apply. The items are summed to obtain a total score ranging from 0 to 40.

Initial factor analyses of the PCL-R indicated that it consisted of two correlated factors (Hare et al., 1990). Factor 1 reflects the combination of interpersonal and affective traits, whereas factor 2 is a combination of unstable and socially deviant traits. Researchers have examined the differential correlates of these two factors and found that factor 1 is more strongly related to instrumental violence, emotional-processing deficits, dropping out of treatment, and poor treatment response (Hare, Clark, Grant, & Thornton, 2000; Olver, Stockdale, & Wormith, 2011; Patrick, Bradley, & Lang, 1993; Seto & Barbaree, 1999; Woodworth & Porter, 2002), whereas factor 2 is strongly related to reoffending, substance abuse, lack of education, and poor family background (Hare, 2003; Leistico, Salekin, DeCoster, & Rogers, 2008; Porter, Birt, &

Hare Psychopathy Checklist–Revised: The most popular method of assessing psychopathy in adults

Boer, 2001; Rutherford, Alterman, Cacciola, & McKay, 1997). Some researchers have argued for a three-factor model of psychopathy (Cooke & Michie, 2001). These three factors are (1) arrogant and deceitful interpersonal style, (2) deficient affective experience, and (3) impulsive and irresponsible behavioural style. This factor structure splits the original factor 1 into two factors and removes some of the antisocial items from factor 2. The most recent factor analysis of the PCL-R includes these three factors plus a fourth factor called *antisocial* that includes the antisocial items (Neumann, Hare, & Newman, 2007).

A considerable amount of research supports the use of the PCL-R in a range of samples, including male and female offenders, forensic psychiatric patients, sexual offenders, and substance abusers (Hare, 2003). Dr. Hare has been studying psychopaths for more than 40 years and is profiled in Box 11.1.

Box 11.1

Canadian Researcher Profile: Dr. Robert Hare

Courtesy of Robert Hare

Dr. Robert Hare is one of the world's leading authorities on psychopathy. Currently, he is a professor (emeritus) in the Department of Psychology at the University of British Columbia and President of Darkstone Research Group, Ltd. Dr. Hare has a BA and MA from the University of Alberta and a PhD from the University of Western Ontario.

Dr. Hare's more than 40-year career studying psychopathy began when he encountered a manipulative inmate while working as a prison psychologist between his MA and PhD studies. Hervey Cleckley's book *The Mask of Sanity* played a pivotal role in his thinking about the clinical nature of psychopathy. Dr. Hare's early research focused on the use of theories, concepts, and procedures from learning, motivation, and psychophysiology in the laboratory study of psychopathy, with emphasis on information-processing and emotional correlates. However, a recurrent issue was the lack of a reliable, valid, and generally acceptable method for assessing the disorder. In the late 1970s, he and his students and colleagues began development of what was to become the Hare Psychopathy Checklist–Revised (PCL-R). The PCL-R is recognized worldwide as the leading instrument for the assessment of the psychopathy construct, both for scientific research and for practical applications in mental health and criminal justice.

Dr. Hare consistently acknowledges and praises the important contributions of his students to the theory and research on psychopathy, and he is pleased that many have established themselves as major figures in the field. He describes the collaborative efforts with his former students as invigorating and fruitful, with major advances being made in the assessment of psychopathy, its neurobiological nature, and its implications for the mental health and criminal justice systems. Currently, he is involved in a number of international research projects on assessment and treatment issues, risk for recidivism and violence, and functional neuroimaging. Although Dr. Hare has most often studied psychopaths in prison, he has recently begun to study them in a very different sphere—the corporate world.

(continued)

(continued)

He lectures widely about psychopathy and has consulted with law enforcement, including the FBI, the RCMP, and Her Majesty's Prison Service. He has been recognized worldwide for his research on psychopathy, receiving the Silver Medal of the Queen Sophia Center in Spain; the Canadian Psychological Association Award for Distinguished Contributions to the International Advancement of Psychology; the Isaac Ray Award from the American Psychiatric Association—the American Academy of Psychiatry and Law Award for Outstanding Contributions to Forensic Psychiatry and Psychiatric Jurisprudence; the B. Jaye Anno Award for Excellence in Communication from the National Commission on Correctional Health Care; the Canadian Psychological Association D. O. Hebb Award for Distinguished Contributions to Psychology as a Science; the Canadian Psychological Association Distinguished Scientist Award for Applications of Psychology; the Order of Canada; the Queen Elizabeth II Diamond Jubilee Medal; Docteur Honoris Causa, Université de Mons, Belgium; Don Andrews Career Contribution Award, Canadian Psychological Association, June, 2014; Canadian Psychological Association Gold Medal for Distinguished and Enduring Lifetime Contributions to Canadian Psychology; and 2016 Bruno Klopfer Award for Outstanding, long-term professional contribution to the field of personality assessment, Society for Personality Assessment. He was the first recipient of the R. D. Hare Lifetime Achievement Award by the Society for the Scientific Study of Psychopathy.

Dr. Hare believes future forensic psychology researchers and clinicians should ensure that they are familiar with the important advances being made in cognitive/affective neuroscience and their implications for forensic psychology. The courses he most enjoyed teaching at the undergraduate level were Brain and Behaviour (third year) and Forensic Psychology (fourth year).

Dr. Hare enjoys listening to jazz and blues and is an erstwhile sailor. He credits his wife, Averil, whom he met in the back row of a course in abnormal psychology at the University of Alberta, with much of his success. In spite of a demanding professional career of her own, she found the time and energy to actively support and encourage his work. To this day, she remains his best friend and closest confidant. Their only child, Cheryl, died in 2005 after a long battle with multiple sclerosis and leukemia. Her courage and dignity in the face of adversity has had a profound influence on their appreciation of the power of the human spirit.

Another way of assessing for psychopathic traits is via self-report questionnaires. Using self-report measures has a number of advantages. First, they are able to measure those attitudes and emotions that are not easily observed by others (e.g., feelings of low self-esteem). Second, they are easy to administer (they can be administered on the web for research), quick to score, and relatively inexpensive. Third, it is not necessary to worry about inter-rater reliability since only the individual is completing the score. Finally, although there are concerns about psychopaths lying on self-report measures (see next paragraph), some questionnaires include measures of response styles to detect faking good or faking bad.

There are also a number of challenges with using self-report measures to assess for psychopathy (Lilienfeld & Fowler, 2006). First, as noted, psychopaths often lie. Some psychopaths are "master manipulators" and will say whatever will be in their best interests. For example, they may malinger and claim they have a mental disorder to avoid facing more serious sanctions. Second, psychopaths may not have sufficient insight to accurately assess their traits. For example, psychopaths may not consider themselves as arrogant, dominant, or opinionated, whereas others might. Third, it will likely be difficult for psychopaths to report on specific emotions if they have not experienced these emotions. For example, if asked if they feel remorse for the suffering they have caused others, they may mistake this feeling with the regret they feel for the consequences of getting caught.

Two of the most widely used self-report scales are the **Psychopathic Personality Inventory–Revised** (PPI-R; Lilienfeld & Widows, 2005) and the

Psychopathic Personality Inventory–Revised: A self-report measure of psychopathic traits

Self-Report Psychopathy Scale (SRP; Paulhus, Neumann, & Hare, 2016). The PPI-R is a 154-item inventory designed to measure psychopathic traits in offender and community samples. It consists of eight content scales and two validity scales (to check for carelessness and positive or negative response styles), and it measures two factors (fearless dominance and self-centred impulsivity). The SRP is a 64-item self-report measure designed to assess psychopathic traits in community samples. It consists of four factors: erratic lifestyle (e.g., "I'm a rebellious person"), callous affect (e.g., "I am more tough-minded than other people"), interpersonal manipulation (e.g., "I think I could 'beat' a lie detector"), and criminal tendencies (e.g., "I have been arrested by the police"). There is also a short form of the SRP (Paulhus et al., 2016) that consist of 28 items that is often used when conducting online surveys. Recently, Patrick, Fowles, and Krueger (2009) have developed the triarchic model of psychopathy, which includes three main components: boldness, meanness, and disinhibition. See Box 11.2 for research using self-report psychopathy scales in university students.

Self-Report Psychopathy Scale: A self-report measure of psychopathic traits

---

Box 11.2   Forensic Psychology in the Spotlight

Subclinical Psychopaths: University Samples

Psychopathic traits are dimensional, meaning that people vary on the number and severity of psychopathic features exhibited. Although most research has been conducted with offenders or forensic psychiatric patients, an increasing amount of research has examined people outside institutional settings. Much of this research has used self-report psychopathy measures. Four studies that investigated a range of different behaviours in university students are described here.

Detecting Vulnerable Victims (Wheeler, Book, & Costello, 2009)
Method: University students were unknowingly videotaped walking down a hallway and were classified as being vulnerable or not based on their self-report of experienced victimization. Male university students were asked to pretend to be a mugger and rated the videotapes on vulnerability.

Results: Students with higher SRP scores were more accurate at detecting victim vulnerability.

Faking Remorse (Book et al., 2015)
Method: This was a two-part study. First male students who scored high on the PPI-R were invited into the lab. They were videotaped describing a time when they did something that they should have felt remorseful for but did not. In the second part of the study, other undergraduates watched these videotapes and rated them for how genuine they sounded.

Results: The higher the story tellers scored on factor 1 traits, the more genuine their fake stories were rated by others.

Defrauding a Lottery (Paulhus, Williams, & Nathanson, 2002)
Method: A student participating in a study had a chance of winning $100. After the study was completed, all study participants were sent an email in which the experimenter stated that he lost the information about who was supposed to receive the five $100 prizes. Participants were asked to email the experimenter to let him know it they had previously been a winner.

Results: Students scoring higher on the SRP were more likely to try to defraud the experimenter and claim they were the "true" winner.

Cheating on Exams (Nathanson, Paulhus, & Williams, 2006)
Method: The experimenters obtained computerized multiple-choice exam answers and seating plans from the instructors of several large introductory psychology classes. The experimenters wanted to determine which personality traits were related to cheating.

Results: Four percent of students were identified as cheating pairs, in which one student copied the answers from an adjacent student. Psychopathic traits, as measured by the SRP, were the strongest predictors of cheating.

PSYCHOPATHY AND ANTISOCIAL PERSONALITY DISORDER

Antisocial personality disorder: A personality disorder characterized by a history of behaviour in which the rights of others are violated

Sociopathy: A label used to describe a person whose psychopathic traits are assumed to be due to environmental factors

Antisocial personality disorder (APD; American Psychiatric Association [APA], 2013) refers to a personality disorder in which there "is a pervasive pattern of disregard for, and violation of, the rights of others that begins in childhood or early adolescence and continues into adulthood" (p. 659). There are 7 adult symptoms that including engaging in criminal behaviours, being a risk taker, failing to be truthful, and having little guilt for one's actions.

Additional confusion surrounds the diagnosis of APD and its relationship to both psychopathy and **sociopathy**. The three terms are sometimes used interchangeably, whereas a general consensus among most researchers is that the constructs of APD, psychopathy, and sociopathy are related but distinct (Hare & Neumann, 2008). The term *sociopath* was coined in 1930 by Partridge to describe those people who had problems with or refused to adapt to society. Lykken (2006) proposed that sociopaths manifest similar traits as psychopaths but develop these traits as a result of poor parenting and other environmental factors, whereas psychopaths are genetically predisposed to a temperament that makes them difficult to socialize. The term *sociopath* is rarely used in the empirical literature, and no assessment instruments have been developed to identify this construct. However, some prosecution experts still use the term *sociopath* in capital hearings in the United States (Edens & Cox, 2012) and the term is also sometimes used by the media or in films.

Although psychopathy and APD share some features, APD places more emphasis on antisocial behaviours than the PCL-R. The prevalence of APD is very high in prisons, with up to 80% of adult offenders being diagnosed with this disorder (Hare, Forth, & Strachan, 1992; Motiuk & Porporino, 1991). Using a cut-off of 30 on the PCL-R, 10% to 25% of adult offenders can be classified as psychopaths (Hare, 2003). An asymmetrical relation exists between these two disorders: Nearly all psychopathic offenders meet the diagnostic criteria for APD, but most offenders diagnosed with APD are not psychopaths. APD symptoms are most strongly related to the behavioural features of psychopathy and not to the interpersonal or affective features. Figure 11.1 illustrates the overlap between psychopathy and APD.

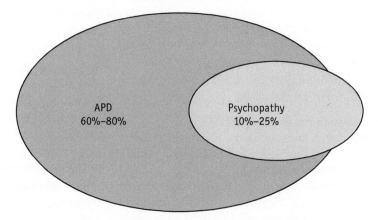

Figure 11.1 Antisocial Personality Disorder and Psychopathy: Construct Overlap

FORENSIC USE OF PSYCHOPATHY

Several studies have surveyed the use of expert testimony regarding the assessment of psychopathy, sociopathy, or APD in criminal and civil court proceedings. Zinger and Forth (1998) reviewed cases in which an expert testified about psychopathy, sociopathy, or APD, whereas in studies by DeMatteo and Edens (2006) and Walsh and Walsh (2006) only cases in which the PCL-R was used by the expert were included. More recently, Viljoen, MacDougall, Gagnon, and Douglas (2010) reviewed 111 American and Canadian youth offender cases. These researchers found that psychopathy has played a role in a diverse range of criminal cases, with the majority of testimony regarding psychopathy being associated with an increased severity of disposition. In Canada, psychopathy and associated constructs were used in making sentencing decisions: to support a case's transfer from youth to adult court, to contribute to dangerous offender hearings, to help to determine parole eligibility, and to assess mental state at time of offence hearings (Zinger & Forth, 1998). In the United States, the PCL-R was also used in sexual violent predator evaluations and death-penalty sentencing and in civil cases for child custody decisions. For example, in death-penalty hearings in the United States and dangerous offender proceedings in Canada, a diagnosis of psychopathy, sociopathy, and APD is an aggravating factor for the death penalty (in the United States), and is considered to be associated with a higher risk of violent recidivism and a lack of treatment responsivity in dangerous offender hearings. With respect to the insanity defence, a diagnosis of psychopathy does fulfill the disease of the mind requirement, but it has never fulfilled the second requirement of not appreciating the nature or quality of the act or knowing that it is wrong.

Are mental health professionals hired by the prosecution or the defence influenced by who hires them? Murrie et al. (2009) have used the term **adversarial allegiance** to describe the tendency for forensic experts to be biased toward those who hire them. Researchers have found that PCL-R scores provided by prosecution experts are higher compared to those provided by defence experts (Blais & Forth, 2014; Edens, Cox, Smith, DeMatteo, & Sörman, 2015; Lloyd, Clark, & Forth, 2010; Murrie et al., 2009; Murrie, Boccaccini, Caperton, & Rufino, 2012). For example, DeMatteo and colleagues (2014) reported defense experts had scores on average 7 points lower than prosecution experts. Recently, Murrie, Boccaccini, Guarnera, and Rufino (2013) asked a sample of forensic psychologists and psychiatrists to complete the PCL-R on offenders from case information. The interesting component of this study was that the researchers deceived the mental health professionals, telling some they were consulting for the prosecution and some for the defence. Similar to what has been found in actual court cases, there was evidence for an adversarial allegiance, with "prosecution" professionals giving higher PCL-R scores compared to "defence" professionals. Hare (2016) suggests that these scoring differences might be related to a lack of training, improper use of the PCL-R, or that some experts might be a 'hired gun' (an expert who adapts their assessment to the side who hires them). There is some evidence that those raters who have attended a workshop on how to administer and score the PCL-R are more reliable than those who have not (Boccaccini, Murrie, Rufino, & Gardner, 2014). Given the serious consequences to individuals assessed as being psychopathic, it is imperative that clinical users of the PCL-R ensure they are adequately trained on this measure.

Adversarial allegiance: The tendency for forensic experts to be biased toward the side (defence or prosecution) that hired them

There has been some concern about the use of risk assessment measures with Aboriginal offenders (see Chapter 10 for discussion of this topic). In Canada, about 18% of male adult offenders are of Aboriginal descent, whereas they represent only 3% of the Canadian population (Correctional Service of Canada, 2013). A recent study examined the factor structure and predictive accuracy of the PCL-R in a sample of Aboriginal and non-Aboriginal male offenders (Olver, Neumann, Wong, & Hare, 2013). A similar 4-factor model was found for both ethnic groups and PCL-R was moderately predictive of reoffending in both ethnic groups. Aboriginal offenders scored about 3 points higher on the PCL-R compared to the non-Aboriginal offenders.

PSYCHOPATHY AND VIOLENCE

The characteristics that define psychopathy are compatible with a criminal lifestyle and a lack of concern for societal norms. Characteristics that ordinarily help to inhibit aggression and violence, such as empathy, close emotional bonds, and internal inhibitions, are lacking or relatively ineffective in psychopaths. Psychopathy is significant because of its association with criminal behaviour in general and violence in particular. Although psychopaths make up a relatively small proportion of the population, their involvement in serious repetitive crime and violence is out of proportion to their numbers. As stated by Hart (1998), "The two are so intimately connected that a full understanding of violence is impossible without consideration of the role played by psychopathy" (p. 367).

Psychopaths are high-density (prolific), versatile offenders. The crimes of psychopaths run the gamut from minor theft and fraud to "cold-blooded" murder. Compared to nonpsychopathic offenders, they start their criminal career at a younger age and persist longer, engage in more violent offences, commit a greater variety of violent offences, engage in more violence within institutions, and, as seen in Chapter 10, are more likely to be violent after release (Hare, 2003). The one type of offence that psychopaths do not commit more often is homicide.

The nature of psychopaths' violence also differs from other types: "Psychopathic violence is more likely to be predatory in nature, motivated by readily identifiable goals, and carried out in a callous, calculated manner without the emotional context that usually characterizes the violence of other offenders" (Hare, 2003, p. 136). Several studies have found that offenders who engage in instrumental violence (premeditated violence to obtain some goal) score significantly higher on measures of psychopathy than offenders engaging in reactive violence (impulsive, unplanned violence that occurs in response to a provocation; Cornell et al., 1996; Walsh, Swogger, & Kosson, 2009). (Chapter 14 discusses instrumental and reactive violence in more detail.) One study by Williamson, Hare, and Wong (1987) found that when nonpsychopaths commit violence, they are likely to target people they know and their violent behaviour is likely to occur in the context of strong emotional arousal. In contrast, psychopaths are more likely to target strangers and be motivated by revenge or material gain. In a recent meta-analysis of 53 studies examining the association between psychopathy and types of violence in youth and adults, Blais, Solodukhin, and Forth (2014) found that psychopathy was related to both reactive and

Box 11.3   Myths and Realities

Psychopathy

Psychopathy is associated with several myths. Here is a list of these misconceptions, accompanied by facts that challenge these false beliefs.

Myth 1. Psychopaths are born, not made.
Fact. Although there is a strong genetic contribution, the environment you grow up in and the experiences you have can influence how psychopathic traits are manifested.

Myth 2. Once a psychopath, always a psychopath.
Fact. Although there is moderate to strong stability in psychopathic traits across developmental periods, the most change is seen during adolescence.

Myth 3. All psychopaths are violent.
Fact. Although many psychopaths will engage in violence or threats of violence to get what they want, some psychopaths are never violent. They use charm, deceit, and manipulation to get what they want.

Myth 4. You either are or are not a psychopath.
Fact. Psychopathy is not an all-or-nothing construct. People vary in the degree to which they possess psychopathic traits.

Myth 5. There are no female psychopaths.
Fact. Although psychopathy is slightly more common in men, women also display psychopathic traits.

Myth 6. Psychopathy and APD are different labels for the same construct.
Fact. Although these constructs overlap, they are distinct. Psychopathy focuses more on the interpersonal and affective traits, whereas APD focuses more on the behavioural and antisocial traits.

Myth 7. Psychopaths are all intelligent.
Fact. A strong association has not been found between psychopathic traits and intelligence. Both smart psychopaths and not-so-smart psychopaths exist.

Myth 8. Psychopaths are untreatable.
Fact. Although psychopaths may be challenging to treat, there is evidence that, especially in youth, they are amenable to treatment.

Myth 9. Psychopathic traits cannot be measured via self-report instruments.
Fact. Although you need to be cautious with using self-report scales, there is evidence that self-report scales can measure the range of psychopathic traits.

Myth 10. Psychopaths do not know the difference between right and wrong.
Fact. Psychopaths know the difference between what is morally right and wrong, but they do not care.

Source: Based on Berg, Smith, Watts, Ammirati, Green, and Lilienfeld, 2013.

instrumental violence. The interpersonal features (facet 1) were most strongly related to the use of instrumental violence and factor 2 (social deviance) was most strongly related to the use of reactive violence.

Psychopaths' use of instrumental motives extends to homicide. Woodworth and Porter (2002) investigated the association between psychopathy and the nature of homicides committed by 135 Canadian offenders. Using PCL-R scores to divide the offenders into the three groups described above—nonpsychopaths (PCL-R scores of less than 20), medium scorers (PCL-R scores between 20 and 30), and psychopaths (PCL-R scores of 30 or greater)—the percentage of homicides that were primarily instrumental (planned and motivated by an external goal) were 28%, 67%, and 93%, respectively. The researchers concluded that psychopaths engage in "cold-blooded" homicides much more often than nonpsychopaths.

In 1985, Ted Bundy (a notorious serial killer) in an interview stated he could "tell a victim by the way she walked down the street, the tilt of her head, the manner in which she carried herself" (Holmes & Holmes, 2009, p. 221). To test Bundy's claim,

Book, Costello, and Camilleri (2013) showed incarcerated offenders 10-second video clips of undergraduates walking down a hallway. Some of the walkers had been sexually or violently victimized in the past, whereas others had not. Offenders were asked to provide a rating of vulnerability to victimization and to describe the reasons for their ratings. Offenders scoring higher on PCL-R factor 1 scores were more accurate at detecting victim vulnerability and reported using gait cues to rationalize their vulnerability ratings.

Box 11.3 describes some of the misconceptions associated with psychopathy.

Recent evidence for psychopaths' ability to manipulate the criminal justice system comes from a study by Porter, ten Brinke, and Wilson (2009). Psychopathic offenders (both sexual and nonsexual offenders) were given early release from prison more often than nonpsychopathic offenders. However, when followed up on, the psychopathic offenders were less successful than the nonpsychopathic offenders. It is critical that people making decisions about release be familiar with psychopathy and the psychopath's abilities to engage in impression management (i.e., telling people what they want to hear).

PSYCHOPATHS IN THE COMMUNITY

Much of the research in community samples has used self-report scales or the Hare Psychopathy Checklist: Screening Version (PCL:SV; Hart, Cox, & Hare, 1995). This 12-item version takes less time to administer and places less emphasis on criminal behaviour for scoring than the PCL-R. In the general population, psychopathy is rare. Coid, Yang, Ullrich, Roberts, and Hare (2009) assessed 301 male and 319 females in the community and found that only 0.6% of the sample had scores of 13 or greater on the PCL:SV (only one person scored above the cut-off score of 18), with 71% of the sample having no psychopathic traits (i.e., scoring 0 on the PCL:SV). In another community sample in the United States (Neumann & Hare, 2008), about 75% of the sample had scores of 2 or less and only 1.2% had scores in the "potential psychopathic" range (i.e., scores of 13 or greater on the PCL:SV). Regardless of sample, females consistently score lower than males on the PCL:SV and other psychopathy measures (Dolan & Völlm, 2009).

Not all psychopaths are violent, nor do they all end up in prison. As Hare (1993) noted, "[We] are far more likely to lose our life savings to an oily tongued swindler than our lives to a steely-eyed killer" (p. 6). Paul Babiak (2000), an organizational psychologist, consulted with six companies undergoing dramatic organizational change, such as merging and downsizing. In each of these companies, Babiak found employees with many psychopathic features to be at the root of some of the company problems. These employees were skilled at getting information on other employees, spreading unwarranted vicious rumours about others, and causing dissension among employees. What they were not doing was pulling their own weight on the job. They were particularly good at manipulating the key players in the organization (employees who can provide them with information or upper management) and blaming others for their failures (see Babiak, 1995 for a case study of the corporate psychopath).

Babiak, Neumann, and Hare (2010) assessed psychopathic traits in 203 corporate professionals. The average PCL-R score was 3.6; however, eight professionals (or 4.9%) scored above the 30-point cut-off for a diagnosis of psychopathy. The professionals with psychopathic traits were less likely to be team players, had poorer management skills, and had poorer performance appraisals than professionals with few psychopathic traits. However, the more psychopathic professionals were more creative, engaged in more strategic thinking, and had stronger communication skills than the less psychopathic professionals. Boddy (2014) conducted an online survey with 304 senior white-collar employees in Britain and asked them to assess their past and current managers for psychopathic traits. Respondents who had a psychopathic manager reported more conflict (e.g., more arguments, having people yell at them), counterproductive work behaviours (e.g., wasting materials, failing to follow instructions), and negative emotions (e.g., anxiety, depression, anger). Boddy (2014, p. 114) concluded that psychopathic managers cause "a toxic work environment as evidenced by a culture of conflict and bullying."

What type of leadership style do psychopathic supervisors use? Mathieu, Neumann, Babiak, and Hare (2015) asked 491 civic employees and 116 bank employees to rate their supervisors on the B-Scan (a corporate psychopathy measure) and a leadership questionnaire. Supervisors who scored higher on psychopathic traits were more likely to use a Lassez-Faire leadership style (provide little guidance, leader is unconcerned about employees) and less likely to use a positive leadership style.

The largest study to ever measure psychopathic traits examined sex differences across the globe. Neumann, Schmitt, Carter, Embley, and Hare (2012) used a short form of the SRP to measure psychopathic traits in 33 016 people (females, 19 183; males, 13 833) across 11 major world regions. Across the world, males scored higher than females, with lifestyle traits (e.g., impulsivity, risk-taking) being most prevalent and antisocial traits (e.g., arrest history, violence) being least prevalent. However, there were variations in psychopathic traits suggesting that cultural factors likely play an important role in how psychopathic traits are expressed.

One area of research that has been vastly neglected is research with victims of psychopaths. To date, there is only one published study exploring the experiences of victims of psychopaths. Through interviews with 20 female victims, Kirkman (2005) aimed to identify the behavioural and personality characteristics of nonincarcerated psychopathic males who may or may not have abused their partners. Eight characteristics of male psychopaths in heterosexual relationships were extracted from the interviews: (1) talking victim into victimization, (2) lying, (3) economic abuse, (4) emotional abuse/psychological torture, (5) multiple infidelities, (6) isolation and coercion, (7) assault, and (8) mistreatment of children. Future research using a larger, more diverse sample of victims needs to be conducted. See the In the Media box for how psychopaths are portrayed in the media.

PSYCHOPATHY AND SEXUAL VIOLENCE

Psychopathy and sexual violence have been the focus of much research. As noted above, psychopathy is associated with violent offences. However, it is not as strongly associated with sexual offences. At the same time, offenders with many psychopathic

Mean on the Screen: Media's Portrayal of Psychopaths

When you think of the term *psychopath* who comes to mind? If you think of psychopaths in movies, the first character that most people think of is Hannibal Lector. This character was introduced in Thomas Harris's book *Red Dragon*, which was published in 1981. In 1988, the sequel was turned into the popular movie *The Silence of the Lambs*, with actor Anthony Hopkins playing Hannibal Lector. Lector is a psychiatrist who happens also to be a cannibalistic serial killer incarcerated in a secure forensic psychiatric institution. A trainee FBI agent is sent to interview Lector in hopes that he will help her capture another serial killer. The film revolves around Lector's manipulation of this agent and his escape. Although Lector has many psychopathic traits, most psychopaths are not serial killers, nor are they as intelligent or as successfully manipulative as Lector.

What about psychopaths on television shows? In recent years, the most popular psychopathic television character has been Dexter Morgan. The *Dexter* series follows the day-to-day life of Dexter, a blood-spatter analyst who also happens to be a serial killer. However, Dexter is a serial killer with some morals, since he targets killers who have escaped justice. In reality, most serial killers target vulnerable victims, such as children, sex-trade workers, runaways, or the homeless, not other violent criminals.

Both Hannibal Lector and Dexter Morgan experienced serious trauma in their early childhood. At age 8, Lector's parents were killed in an explosion and his sister was murdered and cannibalized in front of him. Lector was put in an orphanage and started having deviant violent fantasies focused on avenging his sister's death.

Dexter witnessed the murder of his mother at age 3 and was adopted by Harry, a police officer. Harry recognized Dexter's "psychopathic traits" and taught him to channel his passion for killing to murder other killers. Harry also realized that Dexter had no emotions and taught Dexter to fake emotions.

Is experiencing a traumatic event in childhood related to the development of psychopathy? Although some psychopaths do experience trauma, many do not, which suggests that trauma is not a necessary precursor for psychopathy. Also, although these fictional psychopaths may have some characteristics associated with psychopathy, they are definitely not "typical" psychopaths. Leistedt and Linkowski (2015) examined how psychopathic characters were portrayed in 126 films between 1915 and 2010. Most films failed to depict the range of psychopathic traits seen in actual psychopaths but, over time, psychopathic portrayals in films have become more realistic. For some more realistic protrayals, the authors suggest the character Anton Chigurh in the 2007 film *No Country for Old Men* and Gordon Gekko in the 1987 film *Wall Street*.

Anthony Hopkins, actor
"El silencio de los corderos"
©Beitia Archives
DIGITAL PRESS PHOTO

Beitia Archives Digital Press Photos/Newscom

SHOWTIME/Album/Newscom

traits who also show deviant sexual arousal are much more likely to engage in sexual reoffending than other offenders (Hawes, Boccaccini, & Murrie, 2013). Brown and Forth (1997) reported that in a sample of 60 rapists, their PCL-R score was associated with their number of prior offences but not the number of prior sexual offences. In a larger sample of sexual offenders, Porter, Fairweather, et al. (2000) found that psychopaths engaged in significantly more violent offences than nonpsychopaths (7.3 versus 3.0, respectively) but engaged in fewer sexual offences (2.9 versus 5.9, respectively). One potential explanation for this finding is the high rate of sexual offending found in child molesters, who tend not to have many psychopathic traits.

In general, offenders who commit **sexual homicides** (homicides that have a sexual component or in which sexual arousal occurs) are the most psychopathic, followed by mixed sexual offenders (those who sexually assault both children and adults), followed by rapists, with the lowest psychopathy scores found among child molesters (Brown & Forth, 1997; Firestone, Bradford, Greenberg, & Larose, 1998; Porter, Fairweather, et al., 2000; Quinsey, Rice, & Harris, 1995).

Sexual homicide: Homicides that have a sexual component

Other studies have evaluated the motivations of psychopaths when committing sexual crimes. Brown and Forth (1997) examined specific motivations for psychopathic and nonpsychopathic rapists. The Massachusetts Treatment Center Rapist Typology (MTC: R3; Knight & Prentky, 1990) identifies different types of rapists based on motivation and level of social competence. Brown and Forth reported that 81% of psychopathic rapists were opportunistic or vindictive, as compared with 56% of the nonpsychopathic rapists. Nonpsychopaths were more likely to report feelings of anxiety or alienation in the 24-hour period leading up to the rape, whereas psychopaths reported positive emotions. Porter, Woodworth, Earle, Drugge, and Boer (2003) investigated the relation between psychopathy and severity of violence in a sample of 38 sexual homicide offenders. Level of sadistic violence (evidence for overkill and that the offender obtained enjoyment from hurting the victim) was related to the PCL-R total scores and with the interpersonal and affective features of psychopathy.

In a study of 100 male German forensic patients (all sexual offenders), Mokros, Osterheider, Hucker, and Nitschke (2010) studied the association between psychopathy and **sexual sadism**. Sexual sadists are those people who are sexually aroused by fantasies, urges, or acts of inflicting pain, suffering, or humiliation on another human (APA, 2000). PCL-R total scores, affective deficits facets, and antisocial facets were all related to sexual sadism.

Sexual sadism: People who are sexually aroused by fantasies, urges, or acts of inflicting pain, suffering, or humiliation on another person

PSYCHOPATHY AND TREATMENT

Are psychopathic adults responsive to treatment? Most clinicians and researchers are pessimistic, although some (e.g., Salekin, 2002) are more optimistic. As Hare (1998) stated, "Unlike most other offenders, they suffer little personal distress, see little wrong with their attitudes and behavior, and seek treatment only when it is in their best interests to do so (such as when seeking probation or parole)" (p. 202).

The best-known study of treatment outcome in psychopaths was a retrospective study by Rice, Harris, and Cormier (1992). These researchers investigated the effects of an intensive therapeutic treatment program on violent psychopathic and nonpsychopathic forensic psychiatric patients. Using a matched group design, forensic patients who spent two years in the treatment program (treated group) were paired with forensic patients who were assessed but not admitted to the program (untreated group). Using file information, all patients were scored on the PCL-R and were divided into psychopaths (scores of 25 or greater) and nonpsychopaths (scores of less than 25). Patients were followed for an average of ten years after release. The violent recidivism rate was 39% for untreated nonpsychopaths, 22% for treated nonpsychopaths, 55% for untreated psychopaths, and 77% for treated psychopaths. Treatment was associated with a reduction in violent recidivism among nonpsychopaths but an increase in violent recidivism among psychopaths. Some clinicians have concluded from the above study that we should not bother to treat psychopaths, since treatment will only make them worse: "This was the wrong program for serious psychopathic offenders" (Quinsey, Harris, Rice, & Cormier, 1998, p. 88).

Caution is required in interpreting the results of studies such as that carried out by Rice et al. (1992). Although at first glance such research implies that psychopaths are untreatable, an alternative but perhaps equally plausible account is that the treatments for psychopaths that have been tried so far have not worked (Hare et al., 2000; Richards et al., 2003; Seto & Barbaree, 1999). Reasons why a treatment may not work include the use of an inappropriate treatment and problems in implementing the treatment, such as inadequate training of those administering it or lack of support from management.

A more promising treatment outcome study has been reported by Olver and Wong (2006). These researchers found that although psychopathic sex offenders who dropped out of treatment were more likely to violently reoffend, those psychopathic sex offenders who stayed in treatment showed positive treatment gains and were less likely to violently reoffend. More recently, Olver, Lewis, and Wong (2013) reported that in a sample of high-risk forensic psychiatric patients with relatively high PCL-R scores (scores >25), treatment was effective at reducing violent reoffending. We hope that in the future, with better understanding of what causes psychopathy, treatment programs can be developed to target potentially changeable factors linked to why psychopaths engage in crime and violence (see Box 11.4).

Box 11.4   Cases in Forensic Psychology

Predatory Psychopath Prompts Change in Legislation: Section 754—The "Faint Hope Clause"

On August 22, 1997, a jury in Surrey, B.C., took just 15 minutes to reject Clifford Olson's bid for early parole. Olson was serving a life sentence for the murders of 11 children in 1980 and 1981. Clifford Olson is notorious, not only for being one of Canada's most prolific serial killers, but also for the deal he made with the police, what he called his "cash for corpses" deal. Olson negotiated a payment of $10 000 for each body he uncovered for the RCMP. The money did not go to Olson but to a trust for Olson's wife. In total, $100 000 was paid to this trust fund.

According to section 745 of the Criminal Code of Canada, first-degree and second-degree murderers can apply for a judicial hearing to request an earlier parole eligibility date after serving 15 years. This provision has been

(continued)

(continued)

called the *faint hope clause* and was introduced in 1976, when the death penalty was abolished and replaced by mandatory life sentences for first-degree and second-degree murder. The parole ineligibility period for first-degree murder was 25 years; for second-degree murder, it was 10 years, although the judge has the power to increase this period to up to 25 years. The underlying motivation for this clause was to provide murderers with an incentive to behave in prison, making prisons safer for correctional officers, and to motivate murderers to participate in rehabilitation.

Dr. Stanley Semrau, a forensic psychiatrist, was hired by the Crown prosecution to evaluate Olson for this judicial review hearing. Dr. Semrau assessed Olson on the Hare Psychopathy Checklist–Revised and gave him a score of 38 out of 40. At the judicial review hearing, he stated, "It's certainly the highest score I have ever given anyone" (Semrau & Gale, 2002, p. 273). Dr. Semrau also concluded that Olson was "completely untreatable" (Semrau & Gale, 2002, p. 286) and was more dangerous now than he was when arrested in 1981, since he currently saw himself as "the ultimate serial killer" (Semrau & Gale, 2002, p. 272).

In Dr. Semrau and Judy Gale's book, *Murderous Minds on Trial*, they devoted a chapter to describing the evaluation Dr. Semrau conducted on Olson. In this chapter, he stated, "I saw almost nothing that wasn't a perfect fit with the psychopath's cold, guilt-free use of others for his own ends, and chronically antisocial and deviant lifestyle" (Semrau & Gale, 2002, p. 289).

Partly in response to Olson's use of the faint hope clause, changes were made to section 745 of the Criminal Code. On March 23, 2011, these changes came into force. Bill C-48, Protecting Canadians by Ending Sentence Discounts for Multiple Murders Act, allows judges to give consecutive life sentences to people convicted of multiple murders. Multiple (including serial) murderers are now ineligible for a section 745 review.

Olson spent his time in maximum-security prison in protective custody to safeguard him from other offenders. He was allowed out of his cell for one hour a day to participate in solitary exercise, to work alone as a cleaner, or to attend meetings. Shortly prior to his death, Olson was in the news bragging about receiving old age pension cheques from the government. After spending nearly 30 of his 70 years in prison, he was receiving $1169.47 a month in pension. The government is now looking into denying pensions to violent offenders serving life sentences. Olson died on September 30, 2011, from cancer at age 71.

Questions

1. Should multiple murderers be eligible for early release from prison?

2. Do you think psychopaths are amenable to treatment? What types of treatment might be most effective with psychopaths?

3. How likely are psychopaths to commit another violent crime once released?

PSYCHOPATHY IN YOUTH

Research is increasingly focused on identifying the emergence of psychopathic traits in youth. The assumption is that psychopathy does not suddenly appear in adulthood but instead gradually develops from various environmental and biological antecedents. In line with this viewpoint, several measures have been developed to identify psychopathic traits early in development. Two assessment instruments have been adapted from the PCL-R: one for use with children and the other for adolescents. The **Antisocial Process Screening Device** (APSD) (Frick & Hare, 2001) is designed for assessing the precursors of psychopathic traits in children. The child is assigned a rating on various questions by parents or teachers. A self-report version of this scale also has been developed for use with adolescents. Frick, Bodin, and Barry (2000) found that the APSD has a three-dimensional structure consisting of a callous-unemotional factor, an impulsivity factor, and a narcissism factor. The **Hare Psychopathy Checklist: Youth Version** (PCL:YV) (Forth, Kosson, & Hare, 2003) is a rating scale designed to measure psychopathic traits and behaviours in male and female adolescents between the ages of 12 and 18.

Antisocial Process Screening Device: Observer rating scale to assess psychopathic traits in children

Hare Psychopathy Checklist: Youth Version: Scale designed to measure psychopathic traits in adolescents

Reservations have been raised concerning the appropriateness of applying the construct of psychopathy to children and adolescents (Edens, Skeem, Cruise, & Cauffman, 2001; Seagrave & Grisso, 2002). One concern has been the use of the label *psychopath*, a label that has many negative connotations for the public and for mental health and criminal justice professionals. As stated by Murrie et al. (2004), "The use of the label 'psychopath' has ominous connotations that may adversely influence treatment decisions, social service plans, and juvenile justice determinations" (p. 64). Studies examining the effects of the *psychopathy* label in adults and juveniles are described in Box 11.5.

Box 11.5   Forensic Psychology in the Spotlight

Psychopathy Label: The Potential for Stigma

If an individual is called a *psychopath* in court, are judges and juries likely to be more punitive toward him or her? The results from mock juror decision-making trials have been mixed. Two studies examined the effect of the *psychopath* label in a death-penalty trial: one in which the defendant was an adult (Edens, Colwell, Deforges, & Fernandez, 2005) and one in which the defendant was a juvenile (Edens, Guy, & Fernandez, 2003). In both studies, undergraduates were presented with written descriptions of a defendant in a murder case. All aspects about the case presented to the students were the same except that the authors manipulated the diagnosis or personality traits

of the defendant. In the Edens et al. (2005) study, the defendant was described as a psychopath, as psychotic, or as having no mental disorder. As can be seen in Figure 11.2, mock jurors were more likely to support the death penalty for the psychopathic defendant than for the psychotic or nondisordered defendant.

Edens et al. (2003), in a study that examined the influence of psychopathic traits, presented undergraduates with one of two versions of a modified newspaper clipping about a 16-year-old facing the death penalty. In one version, the juvenile defendant was described as having psychopathic traits; he was "the kind of teenager who did not

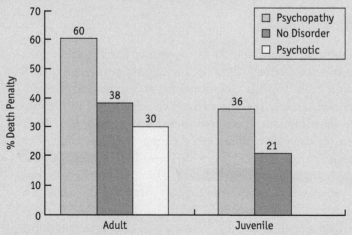

Figure 11.2 Death-Penalty Verdicts Based on Mental Disorder of Offender and Age of Offender

Data from Edens et al. (2003) and (2005)

(continued)

(continued)

feel remorse for his behavior or guilt when he got into trouble . . . a pathological liar who manipulated people . . . arrogant" (p. 22). In contrast, the nonpsychopathic traits version described the youth as "the kind of teenager who felt remorseful and guilty when he got into trouble . . . a trustworthy adolescent who never conned people . . . modest and humble" (p. 22).

In this study, the mock jurors presented with the psychopathic traits version were more likely to support the death penalty and to be less supportive of the defendant receiving intervention in prison. As can be seen in Figure 11.2, mock jurors also were less likely to support the death penalty for juveniles than for adults. Recently Edens, Davis, Fernandez Smith, and Guy (2013) found that Texas undergraduates were more likely to support capital punishment if the defendant was described as being psychopathic. The one trait that was most strongly associated with capital punishment was a lack of remorse.

Blais and Forth (2013) also studied the potential influence of a diagnosis (psychopath versus conduct disorder/antisocial personality disorder versus no diagnosis), age (15 versus 30), and sex (male versus female) on mock undergraduate jurors in Canada. Defendants described as psychopaths were rated as less credible compared to other defendants. Defendants described as diagnosed with conduct disorder/antisocial personality disorder and psychopathy were more likely to be found guilty and were rated as a higher risk for future violence and recidivism. Contrary to what was predicted, neither age nor sex of the defendant influenced mock jurors' ratings. The results from this study and others (Murrie, Boccaccini, McCoy, & Cornell, 2007) demonstrate the evidence for a general labelling effect, not one specific to psychopathy.

Psychopathy in adults is associated with violence, is assumed to be a stable trait, and is resistant to intervention attempts. Whether psychopathic traits in youth are stable has recently been studied. For example, a study using the APSD indicated fairly high stability across a four-year period (Frick, Kimonis, Dandreaux, & Farell, 2003). There have been several longitudinal studies assessing psychopathic traits in youth and reassessing for psychopathy in adulthood. Lynam, Caspi, Moffitt, Loeber, and Stouthamer-Loeber (2007) reported there was a moderate degree of stability in psychopathic traits from age 13 to age 24. In the study with the longest length of time between assessments, Bergstrøm, Forth, and Farrington (2016) examined the stability of psychopathic traits from childhood to age 48 and found moderate level stability. These authors note that the developmental period that demonstrated the largest change was during adolescence. Another concern that has been raised is whether "scores on measures of psychopathy arguably may be inflated by general characteristics of adolescence" (Edens et al., 2001, p. 59). Arguing against this last point are the few studies measuring psychopathic traits in community youth that have found the scores on psychopathy measures to be very low (Forth et al., 2003; Sevecke, Pukrop, Kosson, & Krischer, 2009).

Research has provided some support for extending the construct of psychopathy to youth. For example, boys who score high on the callous/unemotional dimension of the APSD have more police contacts, have more conduct problems, and are more likely to have a parent with APD than are children who score low on this dimension. Research using the PCL:YV has found that adolescents with many psychopathic traits become involved in criminal behaviours at an earlier age, engage in more violence in institutions and in the community, and are at a higher risk of reoffending once released as compared with other adolescents (Corrado et al., 2004;

Forth et al., 2003; Kosson, Cyterski, Steuerwald, Neumann, & Walker-Matthews, 2002; Murrie et al., 2004). In contrast, however, more recent research has questioned the utility of the PCL:YV to predict violence in adolescent female offenders (Odgers, Reppucci, & Moretti, 2005; Schmidt et al., 2006).

One aspect of psychopathy in youth that may differ from its adult counterpart is that youth with psychopathic traits may be more responsive to interventions (da Silva, Rijo, & Salekin, 2013; Salekin, Rogers, & Machin, 2001). Caldwell, Skeem, Salekin, and Van Rybroek (2006) compared the treatment outcome of two groups of incarcerated youth, both with very high PCL:YV scores. Youth who were given intensive treatment at a juvenile treatment centre were compared with youth who were given treatment at a juvenile correctional centre. Youth who were released from the correctional centre violently reoffended at twice the rate in a two-year follow-up as compared with the youth receiving the intensive treatment at the treatment centre. These findings and others suggest that with the appropriate intensive treatment, youth with many psychopathic traits are amenable to treatment (Caldwell, McCormick, Umstead, & Van Rybroek, 2007; Salekin, Lester, & Sellers, 2012).

Recently, researchers have begun to study whether there are effective interventions for children who exhibit callous-unemotional (CU) traits. Dadds and his colleagues (2012) have suggested that children with CU traits may fail to attend to the eyes of their parents and that this leads to problems with the development of empathy and conscience. In a study of children between the ages of 4 and 8 years, Dadds, Allen, McGregor, Woolgar, Viding, and Scott (2014) observed mothers interacting with their children and measured eye contact and affection. Children with high levels of CU traits were more likely to reject affection from their mothers and have low levels of eye contact. Future research will need to determine if interventions designed to target child–parent relationships enhances empathy and emotional responsiveness in children with high levels of CU traits.

PSYCHOPATHY: NATURE VERSUS NURTURE?

The nature versus nurture debate focuses on the relative importance of a person's innate characteristics (nature) as compared with his or her personal experiences (nurture). Growing evidence suggests a strong genetic contribution to psychopathy.

In all research designed to tease apart the role of genes (nature) and environment (nurture) in the development of psychological traits, investigators try to hold constant the effect of either genes or environment. Typically, this involves comparing individuals who have similar genes but who are raised in different environments. Variations on this basic idea can take several forms. Identical twins (who have identical genes) can be compared when raised apart from each other. This method holds genetic influences constant while allowing the environment to vary. In this kind of study, the twins are usually compared with randomly paired individuals. Also, fraternal twins (who share half their genes) raised together can be compared with identical twins (who share all their genes) raised together. Finally, biological siblings (who share half their genes) raised together can be compared with adoptive siblings (who share no genes but who are raised in the same environment).

To date, the only type of studies that have been done to measure the heritability of psychopathic traits are studies comparing identical and fraternal twins. Several twin studies have been done and all have yielded similar findings in children, adolescents, and adults. In a study of adult male twins, Blonigen, Carlson, Krueger, and Patrick (2006) had each pair of identical and fraternal twins complete the Psychopathic Personality Inventory (PPI) (Lilienfeld & Andrews, 1996). Identical twins were much more similar in their PPI scores than fraternal twins. Genetic influences accounted for between 29% and 59% of the variance for each of the different PPI subscales. In an adolescent twin study in Sweden, Larsson, Andershed, and Lichtenstein (2006) also found a strong genetic influence using the Youth Psychopathic Inventory (Andershed, Gustafson, Kerr, & Håkan, 2002). In a recent study of 604 fourteen to fifteen-year-old twins in the United States, Tuvblad, Bezdjian, Raine, and Baker (2014) reported that genetic influences explained 69% of the variance in psychopathy scores. Finally, in a sample of 7-year-old twin pairs in the United Kingdom, Viding, Blair, Moffitt, and Plomin (2005) found that callous-unemotional traits were moderately to highly heritable. These studies point to the importance of genetic factors, but environmental factors, such as adverse family background, may influence how these innate traits are expressed.

Does Family Matter?

The best research method to determine whether family experiences are related to the development of psychopathy is to do a prospective longitudinal study. Such research would study a group of young children and follow them through childhood, adolescence, and into adulthood, measuring family background variables and psychopathic traits. The strength of this type of study is that it allows researchers to avoid retrospective bias (the tendency to reconstruct past events so that they are consistent with an individual's current beliefs) and to establish causal order. Unfortunately, there are very few prospective longitudinal studies that specifically investigate the development of psychopathy. Several studies (Gao, Raine, Chan, Venables, & Mednick, 2010; Kimonis, Cross, Howard, & Donoghue, 2013) using retrospective designs (assessing callous/unemotional traits in youth or psychopathy in adults and asking them about their childhood experiences) have found that psychopathic individuals report lower levels of parental care (i.e., warmth, attachment).

The Cambridge Study in Delinquent Development is a 40-year prospective study of antisocial behaviour of 411 boys from London, England who have been followed up from age 8 to age 48. At age 48, the men were assessed using the PCL:SV (Hart et al., 1995). Farrington (2006) reported that of those men scoring 10 or more, 97% had been convicted of an offence and 48.5% of these men were chronic offenders (i.e., convicted more than ten times). Measuring family background variables between ages 8 and 10, the best predictors of adult psychopathy were having a criminal father or mother, being a son whose father was uninvolved with him, having a low family income, coming from a disrupted family, and experiencing physical neglect.

In another longitudinal study, Weiler and Widom (1996) used court records to identify over 900 children who had been abused or neglected prior to age 11 and compared them with a control group matched on age, race, gender, elementary school class, and place of residence. Children were followed up after 20 years and assessed on a modified PCL-R. Children who had been abused had slightly higher modified PCL-R scores as compared with the control sample.

Likely no single variable or combination of family background variables is responsible for the development of psychopathy. Current research is consistent with the view that there are multiple developmental pathways to the development of psychopathy, some of which involve family background and others in which psychopathy emerges irrespective of family background.

PSYCHOPATHY AND LAW ENFORCEMENT

According to O'Toole (2007), "psychopathy can be described as one of law enforcement's greatest challenges" (p. 305). Psychopaths engage in high rates of crime, including violent offences. Thus, law enforcement personnel will often come into contact with psychopaths. In some cases, the contact can lead to lethal consequences. For example, Pinizzotto and Davis (1992) conducted a study of the characteristics of killers of police officers. Almost half of these killers had personality and behaviour features consistent with psychopathy. O'Toole (2007) described the potential crime scene characteristics manifested by a psychopathic violent offender. For example, impulsivity (a feature of psychopathy) can be manifested at a crime scene by injury pattern to the victim, choice of weapon, and time and location of crime. Some psychopaths are charming and manipulative and will be more likely to use a con to minimize the threat they pose when approaching a victim. For example, a prolific serial killer convinced sex-trade workers that he was not a threat by having children's toys visible in his car and a photograph of his young son on the dashboard.

Another challenge for law enforcement personnel is to develop effective methods for interrogating psychopathic suspects. For example, when interrogating a suspected psychopathic serial killer, trying to get the suspect to confess by saying such things as "Think about the family of the victims" or "You will feel better if you tell us about it" will likely be counterproductive. Instead, appealing to the psychopath's sense of grandiosity and need for status might be more productive. Quayle (2008), a police officer in the United Kingdom, suggested that psychopathic suspects are likely to engage in the following types of behaviours during an interrogation:

- Try to outwit the interrogator (they may consider the interrogation a "game" to win)
- Enjoy being the focus of attention (they may act like they are holding a press conference)
- Attempt to control the interrogation (they may attempt to "turn the tables" and become the interrogator)
- Will not be fooled by bluffs (they are adept at conning others and may see through interrogators' attempts to obtain a confession)
- Attempt to shock (they may speak in a matter-of-fact manner about how they have treated other people)

Quayle (2008) offered several suggestions for interviewing a psychopathic suspect, including the following:

- Ensure case familiarity (interrogators should be extremely familiar with the evidence to counteract the psychopath's evasiveness and deceitfulness)
- Convey experience and confidence (interrogators need to be able to control the interview and create an atmosphere of authority)
- Show liking or admiration (psychopaths respond to thinking that interrogators want to learn from them; this apparent desire to learn encourages psychopaths to keep talking)
- Avoid criticism (psychopaths may become hostile and stop the interview)
- Avoid conveying emotions (interrogators should avoid conveying their own emotions about the offence or lack of progress in the case)

Christopher Porco was a 21-year-old student at the University of Rochester in New York who was convicted of first-degree murder for the axe murder of his father and of attempted murder of his mother. According to Perri (2011), Christopher Porco had many psychopathic traits that the investigators failed to take into account during their interrogation. Initially, the investigators appealed to Porco's feelings of remorse and empathy to encourage him to confess. When this strategy failed, they become more confrontational, which resulted in Porco demanding to see a lawyer. Although Porco continues to deny being responsible, the police believe Porco wanted to kill his parents in order to stop his parents from disclosing to authorities the numerous frauds he had been involved in.

WHAT MAKES THEM TICK? COGNITIVE AND AFFECTIVE MODELS OF PSYCHOPATHY

A number of theories have been proposed to help forensic psychologists understand the development of psychopathy. Two of the most prominent theories of psychopathy place emphasis on either cognitive or affective processes. Newman, Brinkley, Lorenz, Hiatt, and MacCoon (2007) have proposed that psychopaths have a **response modulation deficit**. According to this theory, psychopaths fail to use contextual cues that are peripheral to a dominant response set to modulate their behaviour. In other words, if psychopaths are engaging in specific rewarded behaviour, they will not pay attention to other information that might inhibit their behaviour. This theory has been used to explain why psychopaths fail to learn to avoid punishment (i.e., have poor passive avoidance).

The other theory proposes that psychopaths have a deficit in the experience of certain critical emotions that guide prosocial behaviour and inhibit deviance (Blair, 2006; Hare, 2007; Patrick, 2007). Hervey Cleckley (1976) was the first person to theorize that psychopaths have a deep-rooted emotional deficit that involves the disconnection between cognitive-linguistic processing and emotional experience. In one of the first

Response Modulation Deficit Theory: A theory that suggests that psychopaths fail to use contextual cues that are peripheral to a dominant response set to modulate their behaviour

Tim Cordell, www.cartoonstock.com

YOU BE THE RESEARCHER

You have just finished reading Hervey Cleckley's book *The Mask of Sanity*. According to Cleckley, psychopaths are fundamentally deficient in the capacity for emotional experience. This lack of emotional response enables psychopaths to manipulate and exploit others without feeling any remorse for their actions. In Cleckley's view, the psychopath's characteristic "mask of sanity" results in the psychopath attempting to simulate emotional reactions to obtain what he or she wants. You are intrigued by Cleckley's ideas about the psychopath's core deficit in emotional experience and reactions.

Your Turn . . .

Develop a study to test whether psychopaths have a core emotional deficit. First, decide what sample you will study and how you will measure psychopathic traits. Second, select what stimuli or task will you use; that is, how will you try to elicit emotions? Finally, decide how you will measure emotions; that is, will you ask them how they are feeling? Will you measure their physiological responses? Will you code their facial expressions?

experimental studies to measure this deficit, Williamson, Harpur, and Hare (1991) administered a lexical-decision task to psychopathic and nonpsychopathic offenders. In this task, emotional and neutral words and nonwords (e.g., *cancer, tree* versus *cercan, eter*) were presented briefly on a screen and participants indicated as quickly as possible whether what was on the screen was a word. When the word was emotional, nonpsychopaths were able to do this task faster than if the word was neutral. However, psychopaths failed to show the normal, faster reaction time to emotional words. In addition, the study found that psychopaths' brain-wave activity did not differentiate between emotional and neutral words.

Researchers have used measured affective processing in a range of different paradigms. For example, Blair, Budhani, Colledge, and Scott (2005) asked children to identify the emotions in neutral words spoken with intonations conveying happiness, disgust, anger, sadness, and fear. Boys with many psychopathic traits were impaired at recognizing fearful vocal affect. In adults, Patrick, Bradley, and Lang (1993) compared startle reflexes of psychopathic and nonpsychopathic sexual offenders to slides of positive (e.g., puppies, babies, eroticism), neutral (e.g., table, glass), and negative (e.g., baby with tumour, injured kitten, homicide scene) stimuli. The startle-elicited blinks of nonpsychopathic offenders were smaller when watching positive slides, moderate when watching neutral slides, and enhanced when watching negative slides. In contrast, the psychopathic offenders' startle-elicited blink did not differ in magnitude across the different types of slides. Read the scenario in the You Be the Researcher box and develop your own study to determine if psychopaths have an affective deficit.

These findings of emotional deficits in psychopaths have led some researchers to propose an amygdala dysfunction theory (Blair, 2006, 2008). The amygdala is a small almond-shaped structure located in the medial temporal lobes. The amygdala is part of the limbic centre, which regulates the expression of emotion and emotional memory. It is linked to many other brain regions responsible for memory, control of the autonomic nervous system, aggression, decision making, approach and avoidance behaviour, and defence reactions. Other researchers have proposed that other brain areas are implicated and have suggested a paralimbic model to explain the emotional deficits seen in psychopaths. Recently, Newman, Curtin, Bertsch, and Baskin-Sommers (2010) argued that the emotional deficits seen in psychopaths can be explained by an attention deficit and are not due to an amygdala-mediated deficit.

Psychopathy is a complex disorder but one that causes a substantial amount of damage to society. Research over the past 30 years has led to many advances in researchers' knowledge about psychopathy's measurement, its associations with aggression, its genetic and environmental origins, and its treatment. Within the next few years, new research will provide further insights into how to prevent the development of this devastating disorder.

SUMMARY

1. Psychopathy is a personality disorder defined by a cluster of interpersonal, affective, and behavioural features. Psychopathy, sociopathy, and antisocial personality disorder are overlapping but distinct constructs.

2. The Hare Psychopathy Checklist–Revised (PCL-R) is the most popular tool used to measure psychopathic traits in adults. The Hare Psychopathy Checklist: Youth Version is an adaptation of the PCL-R for use with adolescents. Several self-report measures have been developed to assess psychopathic traits in community samples.

3. Psychopaths begin their criminal career earlier, persist longer, and are more violent and versatile than other offenders. They commit both reactive and instrumental violence. Most of the murders committed by psychopaths are instrumental.

4. Psychopaths are difficult to treat. They are not motivated to change their behaviour, and providing the wrong type of treatment can result in high rates of violent reoffending. However, some recent research has obtained more promising treatment outcome effects, especially with adolescent offenders with many psychopathic features.

5. Research is increasingly focused on identifying the emergence of psychopathic traits in youth, and assessment instruments have been developed to measure psychopathic traits in children and adolescents with some success. Concerns have been raised about the potential problems with labelling youth as psychopaths. These concerns have focused on (1) the issue of labelling a youth as a psychopath, (2) the stability of psychopathic traits from late childhood to early adulthood, and (3) the possibility that characteristics of psychopathy are common features of normally developing youth.

6. Two of the most prominent theories of psychopathy place emphasis on either cognitive or affective processes. Newman and his colleagues have proposed that psychopaths have a response modulation deficit. According to this theory, psychopaths fail to use contextual cues that are peripheral to a dominant response set to modulate their behaviour. The other theory proposes that psychopaths have a deficit in the experience of certain critical emotions that guide prosocial behaviour and inhibit deviance. This latter theory has been related to an amygdala dysfunction.

Discussion Questions

1. Your friend has recently met a man via an online dating site. She has been dating him for a few months but is starting to feel uneasy about the stories he has been telling her. She knows you have been studying forensic psychology and asks you about psychopathy. Describe what you know about psychopathy and what red flags your friend might want to watch for.

2. You have been hired by the police department to consult on a serial killing case. You suspect the serial killer might be a psychopath. Describe to the homicide investigators the key features of psychopathy, the potential crime scene characteristics of psychopathic serial killers, and any suggestions you have for the interrogation of this suspect.

Chapter 12

Assessment and Treatment of Young Offenders

Learning Objectives

■ Describe the history of young offender legislation.

■ Identify the psychiatric diagnoses, and their trajectories, relevant to young offenders.

■ Differentiate between the theories of antisocial behaviour.

■ List the risk and protective factors associated with externalizing disorders in youth.

■ Distinguish among primary, secondary, and tertiary interventions for children, youth, and young offenders.

Sixteen-year-old Amir had been dating 14-year-old Sheena for two years. They lived in the same neighbourhood and were inseparable. For teenagers in love, Amir and Sheena had quite a volatile relationship, and they often had screaming matches in which objects were thrown. Following these arguments, the young couple would break up but not for long. Amir would often send Sheena emails and texts letting her know how sorry he was because the fights typically revolved around Amir's jealousy over Sheena's male friends. Amir would claim that Sheena flirted with other boys who hung out at the local fast-food restaurant where she would go get a snack after school. In their last fight, Amir punched Sheena in the face so that no one else would find her attractive. This violence was the final blow for Sheena: She ended her relationship with Amir for good. Unfortunately, Amir wanted Sheena back and felt that if he could not be with her, no one could. Later that night, Amir showed up at Sheena's house with a gun he had bought from a gang member he knew. Amir demanded that Sheena come down to see him. When Sheena's parents would not let Amir see Sheena, he started shooting. Sheena's father was killed and her mother was wounded. Amir left in a panic. Sheena had hidden in the bathroom and called 911. Amir was arrested a block away from Sheena's home.

Did Amir have behavioural problems growing up? Did he have difficulties at school and in other relationships? Should teens be given adult sentences for violent crimes? In this chapter, we will focus on young offenders. We will consider the assessment and treatment of this group, along with the types of crimes they commit. We also will provide a discussion regarding the legal sanctions available to police and the justice system when dealing with this group.

Adolescents (i.e., older than age 12 and younger than age 18, generally) who come into contact with the criminal justice system pose several challenges to the adult-based system. Legislation has changed over the years in an attempt to address the special needs of adolescents. Moreover, it is critical to consider the developmental paths to youthful offending in order to prevent and rehabilitate. A number of treatment options have been developed for young offenders. Anyone younger than age 12 who engages in criminal acts is processed through family and social service agencies, usually under provincial or territorial legislation.

HISTORICAL OVERVIEW

Youth who committed criminal acts in Canada during the seventeenth, eighteenth, and nineteenth centuries were treated as adult offenders. The criminal justice system made no accommodations or considerations for how youth were charged, sentenced, or incarcerated. They were kept in the same facilities as adults while awaiting their trials, received the same penalties as adults, and served their sentences with adults. Even in cases involving the death penalty, youth were dealt with in a similar manner to adults.

Canada enacted the Juvenile Delinquents Act (JDA) in 1908, partly in response to the justice system's past disregard for the special population of youthful offenders. The JDA applied to children and youth between the ages of 7 and 16 (age 18 in some jurisdictions). Terminology was used to reflect a difference between youth and adults. For example, youth were called *delinquents* rather than *offenders* and were considered to commit acts of delinquency, such as truancy, rather than criminal offences. A separate court system for youth was established, and it was suggested that court proceedings be as informal as possible in that delinquents were seen as misguided children in need of guidance and support. When possible, parents were encouraged to be part of the judicial process. In serious cases, the JDA made it possible for delinquents to be transferred to adult court. Punishments for delinquents were to be consistent with how a parent would discipline a child. For example, delinquents could be sentenced to an industrial school where they learned skills or a trade for future employment. Other dispositions for delinquents included adjournment without penalty, fines, probation, and foster care. Table 12.1 highlights the key changes to the Canadian criminal justice system under the JDA.

Many saw the JDA as a positive step toward youth justice. However, the JDA was not without critics. For example, the services to be provided to delinquents as outlined in the JDA were not always available. Also, given the informality of youth court, some youth were denied their rights, such as the right to counsel and the right

Table 12.1 The Juvenile Delinquents Act's Key Changes to Canadian Criminal Justice

1. A separate court system for youth was established.

2. A minimum age (7 years old) was set at which a child could be charged with a criminal offence.

3. Judges had sentencing discretion and sentencing options increased (e.g., foster care, fines, and institutionalization).

4. Parents were encouraged to be part of the judicial process.

to appeal, and judges could impose open-ended sentences. Furthermore, the broad definition of delinquency included acts that were not illegal for adults.

The JDA was in effect until 1984, when it was replaced with the Young Offenders Act (YOA). The YOA represented a shift in how youth who broke the law were perceived. Youth were to be held responsible for their actions. However, the YOA acknowledged that youth were different from adults, having a different level of cognitive development, for example. The differences between youths and adults were to be recognized through the level of accountability and the consequences of the behaviour committed. The YOA also recognized the need to protect the public from young offenders. Lastly, the YOA recognized that youths should be afforded all the rights stated in the Canadian Charter of Rights and Freedoms (R.S.C., 1985, c. Y-1, s. 3).

Changes in the YOA included the age of criminal responsibility. Under the YOA, youth had to be at least 12 years old (and up to 18 years old) to be processed through the justice system. Children younger than age 12 would be dealt with through child and family services. Some of the changes brought forward with the JDA remained with the YOA. For example, youth courts continued under the YOA. As with the JDA, for serious indictable offences, such as murder, youth could be transferred to adult courts, provided they were at least 14 years of age (R.S.C., 1985, c. Y-1, s. 16).

The YOA allowed for youth cases to be diverted. Diversion is a decision not to prosecute the young offender but rather have him or her undergo an educational or community service program. However, for diversion to be possible, the young offender would have to plead guilty (R.S.C., 1985, c. Y-1, s. 4). Other dispositions available for young offenders included absolute discharge (i.e., the young offender received no sentence other than a guilty verdict), fine, compensation for loss or damaged property, restitution to the victim, prohibition order (i.e., no weapons), community service, probation, and custody. Two types of custody are available: open (placing the youth in a community residential facility, group home, child-care facility, or wilderness camp) or secure (incarcerating the youth in a prison facility; R.S.C., 1985, c. Y-1, s. 20).

A number of amendments have been made to the YOA. For example, Bill C-106 section 16 (1986) required the youth court to consider whether the Crown or defence would like to make an application to transfer the case to adult court. This amendment was introduced to address the problem of defendants making guilty pleas to avoid transfers. Bill C-37 changed section 16 once again in 1995. With this amendment, 16- and 17-year-olds charged with murder, manslaughter, or aggravated sexual assault would go to adult court. On application, these cases could stay in youth court, if the youth court felt the objectives of rehabilitation and public protection could be reconciled. Also under Bill C-37, sentences for youth changed. For first-degree murder, a ten-year maximum, with a six-year maximum to be served incarcerated, was available. For second-degree murder, a seven-year maximum, with a four-year maximum to be served incarcerated, was available. Table 12.2 highlights the key changes to the Canadian criminal justice system under the YOA.

Overall, the YOA attempted to make youth more accountable for their behaviour, while supporting rehabilitation through treatment programs and providing alternatives to incarceration for less serious crimes. One of the major criticisms of the YOA was that serious, violent offences carried relatively short ("light") sentences. Other criticisms included disagreement over raising the minimum age of responsibility from age 7

Table 12.2 The Young Offenders Act's Key Changes to Canadian Criminal Justice

1. Youth are to be held accountable for their actions, however, not to the full extent that adults are.
2. The public has the right to be protected from young offenders.
3. Young offenders have legal rights and freedoms, including those described in the Canadian Charter of Rights and Freedoms.
4. Children have to be at least 12 years of age to be charged with a criminal offence.

to age 12. Also, the YOA allowed for discrepancies in the factors leading to transfer to adult court that suggested an arbitrariness in how cases were handled.

On April 1, 2003, the Youth Criminal Justice Act (YCJA) replaced the YOA. The three main objectives of the YCJA are the following:

1. To prevent youth crime
2. To provide meaningful consequences and encourage responsibility of behaviour
3. To improve rehabilitation and reintegration of youth into the community

With the YCJA, there is a movement to keep young offenders out of the court and out of custody. There is an onus on police to consider community outlets and less serious alternatives for youth before bringing them to the attention of youth court (Youth Criminal Justice Act, 2002, s. 7). These alternatives are called **extrajudicial** measures and include giving a warning or making a referral for treatment (with the consent of the youth; Youth Criminal Justice Act, 2002, s. 10). Note that police now need to keep records when they impose extrajudicial measures to help identify patterns of reoffending (Youth Criminal Justice Act, 2002, s. 115). A new custodial sentence also became available under the YCJA known as the Intensive Rehabilitative Custody and Supervision order (IRCS). This sentence was designed to deal with very serious cases where a mental health issue exists.

Extrajudicial: Term applied to measures taken to keep young offenders out of court and out of custody (e.g., giving a warning or making a referral for treatment)

Naming Youth

Under the current YCJA, the name of the youth cannot be reported to the public but, rather, can be released only under special circumstances. For instance, defendants between the ages of 14 and 17 who are convicted of serious, violent offences, such as murder and aggravated sexual assault, may have their names published and communicated to the public (Bill C-10, clauses 185 and 189). Moreover, if the youth is considered dangerous, his or her photo may be published. An exception to releasing a youth's name and photo also can be made if the youth has not yet been apprehended.

In 2012, the Safe Streets and Communities Act was passed which made further changes to the YCJA. This act focused on the way in which serious violent or repeated offenders are dealt with. Changes included the definition of serious violent offences and violent offences (Section 167, 1-3) and the inclusion of additional sentencing principles.

In a recent case that involved the murder of 14-year-old Stefanie Rengel of Toronto on January 1, 2008, the YCJA's "privacy clause" was put to the test. Within a few hours of the murder, the names of the victim and the two youths charged (David

Box 12.1 Cases in Forensic Psychology

Teen Love, Not So Innocent? The Stefanie Rengel Murder (2008)

Fifteen-year-old Melissa Todorovic and 17-year-old David Bagshaw were two teens in love who had a mutual obsession with and jealousy of each other. They began dating in March 2007. Bagshaw texted Todorovic over 3300 times in four months. Todorovic monitored Bagshaw's Facebook and MSN chats. She also seemed to be jealous of any former relationships that Bagshaw had had. She seemed fixated on one particular former girlfriend, Stefanie Rengel. Rengel was 14 years old and had some of the same friends Bagshaw had. Rengel and Bagshaw's relationship was not sexual, and they had broken up after a few weeks. Neither of these things mattered to Todorovic, however: She wanted Rengel dead. Todorovic demanded that Bagshaw kill Rengel. Todorovic taunted Bagshaw and said she would have sex with someone else if he didn't do what she wanted.

On January 1, 2008, Bagshaw took a kitchen knife to Rengel's home. Several phone calls occurred between Bagshaw and Todorovic on his way to Rengel's. Bagshaw then called Rengel and said he wanted her to come outside so they could talk. After Rengel went outside to talk to Bagshaw, he used the kitchen knife to stab Rengel six times. He then ran off, leaving Rengel to die in a snowbank. Later that evening, Bagshaw went to Todorovic's home to tell her he had killed Rengel. Bagshaw and Todorovic then had sex, which was Bagshaw's reward for killing his old girlfriend. Bagshaw was arrested at his home that evening.

Bagshaw pleaded guilty to the murder of Rengel and was sentenced as an adult, receiving life in prison with no chance of parole for ten years.

In a separate trial from Bagshaw's, Todorovic pleaded not guilty but was found guilty of first-degree murder. She was sentenced as an adult to life in prison, with no chance of parole for seven years, which is the maximum sentence allowed for a defendant who is under the age of 16. Todorovic was a few days shy of her sixteenth birthday when the murder occurred. Todorovic appealed to stay in the Roy McMurtry Youth Centre in Brampton, Ontario, rather than be sent to an adult facility when she turned 20 (at 20 years old, she was older than the other inmates). The judge denied the appeal and ruled that Todorovic was to move to an adult facility to complete her sentence.

Questions

1. Should both murderers be treated comparably? Why or why not?

2. Would you change the age at which a teen can be sentenced as an adult? Why or why not?

Sources: Based on: Rengel killer sentenced to life (2009, September 28). CBC News. Retrieved from http://www.cbc.ca/canada/toronto/story/2009/09/28/rengel-killer-sentencing265.html; Stefanie Rengel case statement of facts (2009, April 9). CityNews. Retrieved from http://www.citytv.com/toronto/citynews/news/local/article/10094—stefanie-rengel-case; http://www.huffingtonpost.ca/2011/12/22/melissa-todorovic-teen-murderer_n_1166461.html.

Bagshaw and Melissa Todorovic) were posted on the social network site Facebook. It should be noted that names of victims from youth crime also have their identities protected from publication until consent is provided. Although police and Facebook website staffers removed the prohibited information to comply with the privacy clause, the information was reposted shortly thereafter. It can be quite difficult to police the posts of individual users. See Box 12.1 to learn more about the Rengel case.

Sentencing options have increased under the YCJA. Judges are able to provide a reprimand (i.e., lecture or warning to the youth), an intensive support and supervision order, an attendance order (i.e., youth must attend a specific program), a deferred custody and supervision order (i.e., youth can serve their sentence in the community as long as imposed conditions are met), and an intensive rehabilitative custody and supervision order (i.e., youth in custody receive intensive services and supervision) (Youth Criminal Justice Act, 2002, s. 42).

A youth vandalizing a wall in the community
Stewart Cohen/Blend Images/Getty Images

In terms of transferring youth to adult court, the YCJA has made a number of changes from the process outlined in the YOA. Under the YCJA, the transfer process is eliminated. Instead, youth court determines whether the youthful defendant is guilty, and if so, the judge can impose an adult sentence with youth as young as 14 years old (this age can be set at 15 or 16 years of age). Onus is on the Crown to prove the appropriateness of an adult sentence if the Crown decides to seek one (Youth Criminal Justice Act, 2002, s. 64, s. 72

An adult sentence cannot be applied unless the Crown notifies the youth court that it will be seeking an adult sentence (Youth Criminal Justice Act, 2002, s. 61). A key issue in determining sentencing is that the sentence must be proportionate to the seriousness of the offence (Youth Criminal Justice Act, 2002, s. 38(2)(c)).

The YCJA has made a serious attempt at improving the interests of victims. Under the YCJA, victims are to be informed of the court proceedings and given an opportunity to participate. Victims also have the right to access youth court records. Moreover, victims can participate in community-based dispositions (Youth Criminal Justice Act, 2002, s. 3). Table 12.3 highlights the key changes to the Canadian criminal justice system under the YCJA. See the In the Media box to learn how the YCJA is perceived overseas.

Before we try to gain a better understanding of young offenders, see Box 12.2 for a list of myths and the reality.

Table 12.3 The Youth Criminal Justice Act's Key Changes to the Canadian Criminal Justice System

1. Less serious and less violent offences should be kept out of the formal court process.
2. The number of extrajudicial measures is increased.
3. There is a greater focus on prevention and reintegration into the community.
4. Transfers to adult court are removed; instead, youth court judges can impose adult sentences.
5. The interests and needs of victims are recognized.

In the Media
Canada's Youth Crime Legislation

Canada's Youth Criminal Justice Act is getting approval from overseas. Two British researchers, Enver Solomon and Rob Allen (2009), reported that the YCJA is successful at reducing the crime rate and imprisoning fewer youth. They hailed YCJA as one of the most progressive pieces of youth legislation in the Western world. The researchers found that a high incarceration rate in England and Wales is expensive and may actually lead to more adult incarceration.

According to Stats Canada, we have seen a 14% decrease in total custody (including pretrial detention) from 2012–2013 to 2013–2014 (http://www.statcan.gc.ca/pub/85-002-x/2015001/article/14164/tbl/tbl04-eng.htm). A 14% decrease has also been found for total community supervision and 14% decrease for total correctional services from the same years (http://www.statcan.gc.ca/pub/85-002-x/2015001/article/14164/tbl/tbl04-eng.htm).

Box 12.2   Myths and Realities

Young Offenders

Myth 1. Youth violence in on the rise.
Fact. Since the YCJA was implemented in 2004, youth violence has remained stable or decreased. For example, the Uniform Crime Reporting Survey (2015) conducted by Statistics Canada has indicated that police-reported youth violent crime (i.e., the number of youth accused of a crime) has decreased by 27% from 2004 to 2014. Following this downward trend, the youth Crime Severity Index (youth CSI) has shown a 10% decrease in the rate of police-report violent crime from 2013 to 2014 (Boyce, 2015). Declines in violent crime also has been found for the most serious offences. The youth homicide rate hit an all-time low since 1984, with a 38% decrease from 2013 to 2014 (Boyce, 2015). Finally, the majority of court cases (71%) completed for youth in 2013–2014 involved non-violent offences (Alam, 2015).

Myth 2. Female youth only commit relational violence.
Fact. There exists a stereotype that female youth only commit relational violence (e.g., verbal aggression, social exclusion; Hamby, Finkelhor, & Turner, 2013). However, research shows that *both* male and female youth have been found to be perpetrators of relational violence or aggression (e.g., verbal aggression, social exclusion) with negligible differences between the two groups (Archer, 2004). Female youth have also been reported to engage in various forms of overt violence. For example, although female youth accounted for only 23% of youth court cases in 2011/2012, they accounted for approximately 36% of common assault cases (Public Safety Canada, 2014). Moreover, at-risk female youth often report engaging in higher rates of physical or overt forms of violence (e.g., fist-fights, using a weapon, shooting at someone; Odgers et al., 2007; Sector-Turner, Garwick, Sieving, & Seppelt, 2014), sometimes more frequently than verbal violence (Sector-Turner et al., 2014), suggesting that females do engage in physically violent behavior.

Myth 3. The majority of crime is committed by youth.
Fact. The majority of crime committed in Canada is committed by adults. Only a small amount of crime is committed by youth in Canada. For example, in 2010, youth accounted for only 13% of overall Criminal Code violations (excluding traffic) (National Crime Prevention Centre, 2012). Furthermore, the police-reported Youth Crime Severity Index, which measures both the volume and severity of youth crime, decreased by approximately 40% from 2004 to 2014 (Boyce, 2015).

Myth 4. We need to get tough with our young offenders in order to reduce juvenile crime.
Fact. "Get-Tough" approaches to crime have consistently been found to be unsuccessful in reducing recidivism among offender populations. For example, reforms emphasizing youth incarceration in the United States have been found to be ineffective in reducing youth crime rates (Stahlkopf, Males, & Macallair, 2010). Alternative approaches to dealing with youth crime have been found to be more effective in reducing rates of recidivism when compared to incarceration (Lipsey, 2009).

Myth 5. Young offenders who commit violent crime should be given adult sentences because they know what they are doing.
Fact. Research has found that adolescents may not, in fact, always 'know what they are doing' when it comes to engaging in risky or delinquent behaviors. When compared to adults, youth lack the same cognitive and psychosocial maturity as adults, which can impair their decision-making abilities (Steinberg, 2009). Additionally, during adolescence our brain is still developing, particularly in the frontal lobe systems where important cognitive functions take place (e.g., understanding, decision making, and reasoning; Steinberg, 2009). The lack of maturation during adolescence can lead to a number of poor outcomes. For example, youth are more likely than adults to engage in thrill-seeking or risky behaviors, lack the capacity to perceive risk and vulnerability in the same way as adults (Steinberg, 2007), are more impulsive, more easily influenced by peers, and less able to consider long-term consequences of their behavior (Steinberg, 2009).

YOUTH CRIME RATES

Generally, the total number of crimes committed by youth has been decreasing for the past few years. This pattern also can be seen for violent offences. See Table 12.4 for a distribution of young offender cases by major crime category.

Probation remained the most common sentence provided to youth in youth court in 2013–2014. When youth are sentenced to probation, they are given a probation officer or other designated officer that they must check in with, along with any number of other conditions imposed by the court (e.g., curfew). Fifty-eight percent of youth found guilty in court were given probation, either as a stand-alone sentence or in combination with another sentence (Alam, 2015).

Table 12.4 Type of Offence, Median Length of Cases as a Function of Reporting Year

Type of Offence[1]	2012/2013		2013/2014		Percent Change in Number of Cases 2012–2013 to 2013–2014 (%)	Difference in Median Length of Cases 2012/2013 to 2013/2014 (Days)
	Number[2]	Median Length of Case (Days)[3]	Number[2]	Median Length of Case (Days)[3]		
Violent offences	**12 792**	**161**	**11 720**	**166**	**−8**	**5**
Homicide	31	448	33	611	6	163
Attempted murder	21	316	20	248	−5	−68
Robbery	2336	184	1904	201	−18	17
Sexual assault	696	252	750	256	8	4
Other sexual offences[4]	635	232	667	240	5	8
Major assault[5]	2715	168	2396	164	−12	−4
Common assault	3878	127	3613	134	−7	7
Uttering threats	2029	134	1867	143	−8	9
Criminal harassment	186	163	192	174	3	11
Other crimes against persons	265	203	278	184	5	−19
Property offences	**15 723**	**113**	**13 370**	**120**	**−15**	**7**
Theft[6]	5476	100	4658	102	−15	2
Break and enter	3606	137	3100	141	−14	4
Fraud	474	131	465	115	−2	−16
Mischief	2948	108	2489	113	−16	5
Possess stolen property	2779	111	2294	120	−17	9
Other property crimes	440	138	364	155	−17	17
Administration of justice offences	**4893**	**84**	**4290**	**82**	**−12**	**−2**
Fail to appear	281	71	246	69	−12	−2

(continued)

Table 12.4 *(continued)*

Type of Offence[1]	2012/2013 Number[2]	2012/2013 Median Length of Case (Days)[3]	2013/2014 Number[2]	2013/2014 Median Length of Case (Days)[3]	Percent Change in Number of Cases 2012–2013 to 2013–2014 (%)	Difference in Median Length of Cases 2012/2013 to 2013/2014 (Days)
Breach of probation	128	52	117	83	−9	31
Unlawfully at large	306	8	258	7	−16	−1
Fail to comply with order	3230	91	2875	91	−11	0
Other administration of justice offences	948	92	794	92	−16	0
Other Criminal Code offences	**2424**	**148**	**2160**	**146**	**−11**	**−2**
Weapons offences	1555	155	1451	147	−7	−8
Prostitution	6	249	11	174	83	−75
Disturb the peace	132	102	86	103	−35	1
Residual Criminal Code	731	141	612	153	−16	12
Criminal Code (excluding traffic)	**35 832**	**127**	**31 540**	**130**	**−12**	**3**
Criminal Code traffic offences	**828**	**113**	**646**	**120**	**−22**	**7**
Impaired driving	424	79	318	116	−25	37
Other Criminal Code traffic offences	404	129	328	122	−19	−7
Total Criminal Code offences	**36 660**	**126**	**32 186**	**130**	**−12**	**4**
Other federal statute offences	**8781**	**64**	**7715**	**69**	**−12**	**5**
Drug possession	1844	92	1568	92	−15	0
Other drug offences[7]	718	141	662	141	−8	0
Youth Criminal Justice Act	4542	37	3841	42	−15	5
Residual federal statutes	1677	103	1644	99	−2	−4
Total offences	**45 441**	**114**	**39 901**	**120**	**−12**	**6**

[1]Cases that involve more than one charge are counted according to the most serious offence rule.

[2]A case is one or more charges against an accused person or company that were processed by the courts at the same time and received a final disposition.

[3]Case lengths are calculated based on the number of days it takes to complete a case, from first appearance to final decision.

[4]Includes, for example, sexual interference, invitation to sexual touching, child pornography, luring a child via a computer, and sexual exploitation.

[5]Includes, for example, assault with a weapon (level 2) and aggravated assault (level 3).

[6]Includes, for example, theft over and under $5000 as well as taking a motor vehicle without consent.

[7]Includes drug trafficking, exportation and importation, and production.

Source: Statistics Canada, Canadian Centre for Justice Statistics, Integrated Criminal Court Survey, 2013–2014 http://www.statcan.gc.ca/pub/85-002-x/2012001/article/11645/tbl/tbl03-eng.html.

YOU BE THE POLICE OFFICER

Jimmy Jones is the neighbourhood "bad boy." He and his mom have lived in one of the government-subsidized housing units since Jimmy was 4 years old. Now he is 14. Jimmy is well known at school and in his neighbourhood. As a young boy, Jimmy would take toys from other children and often would become aggressive if he didn't get his way. His schoolteachers called Mrs. Jones on a weekly basis because they could not manage Jimmy's aggression and tantrums. Jimmy bullied other kids and was cruel to his pet dog.

Jimmy's problems just seemed to keep escalating. As he got older, he started hanging around with some older teenaged boys known to belong to a local street gang. Jimmy liked how the gang boys always had money. He soon began selling drugs for the gang leader. At first, Jimmy was selling drugs at the high schools in the neighbourhood. The high schools were visited by police officers who were trying to work with the drug dealers to change their ways. The police knew Jimmy well.

One night, Jimmy's gang leader said he needed Jimmy to do him a favour. A rival gang had set up shop in an abandoned warehouse and was trying to get in on the drug dealing. Jimmy was asked to set fire to the warehouse to burn it down. Jimmy knew that if he could do this successfully he would be rewarded financially and would move up in the gang hierarchy. He agreed to set the fire. Although Jimmy did not want to hurt anyone, some of the rival gang members were in the warehouse when he started the fire, and three rival gang members received serious burns. Police were informed that Jimmy set the fire.

Your Turn . . .

You are a police officer dealing with Jimmy's case. How should you handle it? Should you keep Jimmy out of the criminal justice system? Should Jimmy be dealt with using extrajudicial measures? If so, which ones?

In 2013–2014, 15% of guilty youth were sentenced to custody, which is a decrease for this type of sentence (Alam, 2015).

> More specifically, the proportion of guilty youth court cases being sentenced to custody fell from 22% in 2003/2004 to 15% in 2013–2014. In 2003 deferred custody was introduced under the YCJA. Seen as an alternative to custody, deferred custody orders allow a young person who would otherwise be sentenced to custody to serve their sentence in the community under a set of strict conditions. If these conditions are violated, the young person may be sent to custody to serve the remainder of their sentence. (Alam, 2015, p. 9)

Under the YCJA, a two-year maximum sentence can be given to youth. Similar to previous years, the median length of probation sentences was 360 days (Alam, 2015). Examine the You Be the Police Officer box below to consider how you would deal with a youth engaged in unlawful behaviour.

As in previous years, the most common decision in youth court cases was one of guilt. However, over the past 10 years the proportion of cases resulting in a guilty outcome has decreased. For example, 56% of youth court cases rendered a guilty verdict in 2013/2014, which was the lowest proportion of guilty verdicts since the 1990's when Statistics Canada began to collect this information (Alam, 2015). Approximately 4 in 10 completed youth court cases resulted in a stay or withdrawal, and a small number of cases (2%) resulted in an acquittal (Alam, 2015).

ASSESSMENT OF YOUNG OFFENDERS

Assessing Those under Age 12

Often a clinician will obtain two levels of consent before assessing a child or adolescent. Because children and adolescents are not legally capable of providing consent, consent will be sought from parents or guardians. Following parental consent, assent or agreement to conduct the assessment will also be sought from the child or the adolescent. Although court-ordered assessments do not necessarily require consent or assent, clinicians often will seek it before commencing the assessment.

Broadly, children's and youth's emotional and behavioural difficulties can be categorized as internalizing or externalizing problems (Rutter, 1990). **Internalizing problems** are emotional difficulties such as anxiety, depression, and obsessions. **Externalizing problems** are behavioural difficulties such as delinquency, fighting, bullying, lying, and destructive behaviour. Externalizing problems have been considered more difficult to treat and more likely to have long-term persistence (Ebata, Peterson, & Conger, 1990; Peterson, Bates, Dodge, Lansford, & Pettit, 2015; Robins, 1986). Externalizing disorders have been known to be quite stable, though symptoms are often low in childhood, peak during adolescence, then begin to decrease into adulthood (Leve, Kim, & Pears, 2005; Peterson et al., 2015). Males are more likely to have externalizing difficulties than females (Bongers, Koot, van der Ende, & Verhulst, 2004; Broidy et al., 2003). It should be noted that internalizing problems that should also be assessed and treated might co-occur with externalizing difficulties.

To assess externalizing problems, multiple informants are necessary to obtain an accurate assessment because there is often variability in reporting across different types of respondents (e.g., child or youth, parent, or teacher; Graves, Blake, & Kim, 2012; Korsch & Petermann, 2014; Salbach-Andrae, Klinkowiski, Lenz & Lehmkuhl, 2009; Salbach-Andrae, Lenz, & Lehmkuhl, 2009). The inclusion of multiple informants allows for a more complete and comprehensive picture of the externalizing problem. As a result, parents, teachers, and peers may be interviewed or asked to rate the child or adolescent. Also, it is important that behaviour be viewed within a developmental context. For example, rebelling against rules set by parents may be normative for adolescents but worrisome if younger children are oppositional and continually refuse to comply with parents' requests. The duration, severity, and frequency of troublesome behaviours should be measured.

Three childhood psychiatric diagnoses occur with some frequency in young offenders: **attention deficit/hyperactivity disorder** (AD/HD), **oppositional defiant disorder** (ODD), and **conduct disorder** (CD). AD/HD is described in the *DSM-5* as

Internalizing problems: Emotional difficulties such as anxiety, depression, and obsessions experienced by a youth

Externalizing problems: Behavioural difficulties such as delinquency, fighting, bullying, lying, or destructive behaviour experienced by a youth

Attention deficit/hyperactivity disorder: A disorder in a youth characterized by a persistent pattern of inattention and hyperactivity or impulsivity

Oppositional defiant disorder: A disorder in a youth characterized by a persistent pattern of negativistic, hostile, and defiant behaviours

Conduct disorder: A disorder characterized by a persistent pattern of behaviour in which a youth violates the rights of others or age-appropriate societal norms or rules

"a persistent pattern of inattention and/or hyperactivity-impulsivity that interferes with functioning or development, as characterized by (1) inattention and/or (2) hyperactivity and impulsivity" (APA, 2013, p. 59). To qualify for an AD/HD diagnosis, a number of symptoms must be present, according to the criteria listed in the *DSM-5*. When making an AD/HD diagnosis, it is important to consider the age of the child. In young children, many of the symptoms of AD/HD are part of normal development and behaviour and may not lead to criminal activity later on. However, there may be some hyperactive-impulsive or inattentive symptoms before the age of 7 that cause impairment. Many children with AD/HD also receive diagnoses of ODD or CD (Harvey, Breaux & Lugo-Candelas, 2016; Nock, Kazdin, Hiripi, & Kessler, 2007; Waschbusch, 2002).

ODD is described in the *DSM-5* as "a pattern of angry/irritable mood, argumentative/defiant behavior, or vindictiveness lasting at least 6 months as evidenced by at least four symptoms from any of the [listed] categories, and exhibited during interaction with at least one individual who is not a sibling" (APA, 2013, p. 462). Approximately 40% of children with ODD develop CD (Loeber, Keenan, Lahey, Green, & Thomas, 1993). If a child with ODD qualifies for a CD diagnosis, an ODD diagnosis is not used. Conduct disorder is defined as "a repetitive and persistent pattern of behavior in which the basic rights of others or major age-appropriate societal norms or rules are violated, as manifested by the presence of at least three of the . . . 15 criteria in the past 12 months . . . , with at least one criterion present in the past 6 months" (APA, 2013, p. 469). Approximately 30–50% of children meeting criteria for CD go on to receive diagnoses of antisocial personality disorder in adulthood (Kendall et al., 2009; Burke, Waldman & Lahey, 2010). In fact, the presence of conduct disorder in childhood is predictive of Antisocial Personality Disorder symptoms later in life (Rowe, Costello, Angold, Copeland, & Maughan, 2010). Thus, CD often is the precursor to antisocial personality disorder. ODD and CD are not diagnosed if the individual is over 18 (the individual may meet criteria for antisocial personality disorder).

Assessing the Adolescent

Once an adolescent's antisocial behaviour receives the attention of the courts, a court-ordered assessment may be issued. In such cases, the adolescent does not need to provide consent/assent. The issue for the courts is to determine what level of risk the young person poses for reoffending. In other words, will having this young offender in the community pose a risk for others? Does the young offender have the potential to change in a positive manner? Young offenders are assessed so that resources can be used effectively and the risk to the community is reduced.

The instruments used to assess a young offender's risk generally include a "checklist," where items are scored on a scale, the points are summed, and a cut-off value is set for either detaining or releasing the young offender. Risk-assessment instruments collect information about a set of factors, both static (i.e., factors that cannot change, such as age of first arrest) and dynamic (i.e., factors that can change, such as antisocial attitudes). Interviews with the young offender as well as case files and histories may be used to complete a risk assessment. A total risk score is then obtained. Generally, the notion is that the more relevant risk factors that are present, the more likely it is that the youth will reoffend. Any number of professionals (front-line staff in institutions, probation staff, credentialed professionals) may be responsible for conducting the risk assessment.

The task of identifying risk factors for young offenders who will reoffend is different than for adults (Mulvey, 2005). For example, history of behaviour often is considered in the risk assessment of adult offenders. This information may be limited and ambiguous for young offenders. Young offenders simply do not have the years behind them that can be examined. Child and adolescent behaviour may be more influenced by context than enduring character. Children and adolescents may display behaviour that is adaptive to the environment they are in rather than a behaviour that demonstrates their character across all situations (Masten & Coatsworth, 1998). A child who is disruptive in one school may not be disruptive in another—so interpreting a behaviour problem may be inaccurate. Children and adolescents experience more developmental and character changes than adults. It is a challenge to separate developmental issues from persistent personality and character for the prediction of future offending. Some researchers argue further that risk assessment may differ between adolescent boys and girls (Odgers, Moretti, & Reppucci, 2005).

Box 12.3 provides a list of risk-assessment tools used with young offenders in Canada.

Rates of Behaviour Disorders in Youth

Disruptive or behavioral disorders (e.g., CD, ODD, AD/HD) are some of the most common types of disorders found in children or youth (Frick & Nigg, 2012; Roberts, Ramsay Roberts, & Xing, 2007) and have been reported to affect tens of millions of youth worldwide (Polanczyk, Salum, Sagaya, Caye, & Rhode, 2015). Worldwide prevalence rates for mental disorders in children and youth suggest a prevalence rate of 5.7% for any disruptive disorder (i.e., 3.6% for ODD, 2.1% for CD), and approximately 3.4% for AD/HD (Polanczyk, et al., 2015).

Similar prevalence rates have been found in other studies. For example, Roberts and colleagues (2007) examined the prevalence of disruptive disorders and AD/HD in youth aged 11 to 17 years old in a metropolitan area in the United States. They found that disruptive disorders were one of the most prevalent disorders in youth, with an estimated 6.4% prevalence rate for a disruptive disorder and 2.1% prevalence rate for AD/HD in their sample.

Researchers also have found that behavioural and/or defiant disorders are likely to co-occur. For example, Yoshimasu and colleagues (2012) examined the comorbidity of AD/HD and CD and found that of a sample of 343 participants diagnosed with AD/HD, 22.5% also were diagnosed with a defiant disorder (CD or ODD). Other researchers have estimated that 20% to 50% of children with AD/HD also have symptoms consistent with CD or ODD (Offord, Lipman, & Duku, 2001).

Box 12.3   Forensic Psychology in the Spotlight

Risk-Assessment Tools Used with Young Offenders in Canada

Adolescent Chemical Dependency Inventory (ACDI)—Corrections Version II

This instrument is designed for 12- to 17-year-olds to screen for substance (alcohol and other drugs) use and abuse, overall adjustment, and issues for troubled youth. Young offenders respond to 105 items that constitute five scales: (1) truthfulness, (2) alcohol, (3) drugs, (4) adjustment, and (5) distress.

HCR-20

The HCR-20 takes its name from the three scales it assesses—historical, clinical, and risk management—and from the number of items. It examines risk and violence broadly, including risk factors from the past, present, and future. The scale consists of ten historical factors, five clinical items that reflect current factors related to violence, and five risk-management items that focus attention on situational post-assessment factors that may aggravate or mitigate risk.

Offender Risk Assessment and Management System (ORAMS)

ORAMS is a set of tools developed by Manitoba Corrections to assess the different risks offenders pose. Two scales can be used with young offenders: Inmate Security Assessment and Primary Risk Assessment.

1. **Inmate Security Assessment (ISA)—Young Offenders**

   The objective of the ISA is to obtain information to assess a young offender's threat to him- or herself and others in an institution. Dangerous behaviour includes suicide attempts, assaults on other inmates or staff, and escape risk. This scale is completed once an offender has been admitted into an institution for security reasons and also assists decisions relating to institutional placement or transfer.

2. **Primary Risk Assessment (PRA)—Young Offenders**

   This scale is a modified version of the Youthful Offender—Level of Service Inventory (YO-LSI). It is used to predict a young offender's risk to reoffend in any type of offence (as opposed to specific types of offences, such as sexual assault). This information is then used to determine the degree and type of

supervision needed and to assist in the formulation of a case plan.

Structured Assessment of Violence Risk in Youth (SAVRY) (Borum, Bartel, & Forth, 2002)

The SAVRY is used to make assessments and recommendations about the nature and degree of risk that a youth may pose for future violence. Twenty-four risk factors and six protective factors are considered.

Youth Level of Service/Case Management Inventory (YLS/CMI) (Hoge & Andrews, 2002)

This standardized instrument includes a 42-item checklist for use by professional workers in assessing risk of future violence, need for correctional programs to reduce future violence, and responsivity factors that have an impact on case plan goals. A detailed survey of youth risk and needs factors is produced that can be used to create a case plan. The instrument contains seven sections: (1) assessment of risk and need; (2) summary of risk/need factors; (3) assessment of other needs/special considerations; (4) assessment of the client's general risk/need level; (5) contact level; (6) case management plan; and (7) case management review. An updated version of this assessment tool (YLS/CMI 2.0) was released in 2010, which includes an expanded age range (12–18) and is gender and culturally informed. Some additional items that address responsivity factors specific to females (e.g., pregnancy/motherhood) have been included.

Youthful Offender—Level of Service Inventory (YO-LSI)

The YO-LSI is a risk/needs assessment instrument used to classify and assess a young offender's overall risk level and to identify and target areas of criminogenic need. The YO-LSI consists of 82 static and dynamic predictors of criminal risk/needs that are grouped into the following seven categories: (1) criminal history, (2) substance abuse, (3) educational/employment problems, (4) family problems, (5) peer relation problems, (6) accommodation problems, and (7) psychological factors.

Source: Based on Hannah-Moffat, K., & Maurutto, P. (2003). Youth risk/need assessment: An overview of issues and practices. Ottawa, ON: Department of Justice Canada, Research and Statistics Division.

Trajectories of Young Offenders

When examining the aggressive histories of young offenders, two categories emerge. Young offenders may be categorized as those who started with social transgressions and behavioural problems in very early childhood (child-onset, life-course persistent) or those whose problem behaviours emerged in the teen years (adolescent-onset, adolescent limited; Moffitt, 1993). Thus, two developmental pathways to youthful antisocial behaviour have been suggested: childhood onset versus adolescent onset.

Age of onset is a critical factor in the trajectory to adult offending. A number of researchers have found that early onset of antisocial behaviour is related to more serious and persistent antisocial behaviour later in life (Fergusson & Woodward, 2000; Loeber & Farrington, 2000). Those with a childhood onset also may have a number of other difficulties, such as AD/HD, learning disabilities, and academic difficulties (Hinshaw, Lahey, & Hart, 1993). The childhood-onset trajectory is a less frequent occurrence than adolescent onset, with about 3% to 5% of the general population showing a childhood-onset trajectory (Moffitt, 1993). It is important to remember, however, that most young children with behavioural difficulties do not go on to become adult offenders (or even young offenders for that matter).

The adolescent-onset pattern occurs in about 70% of the general population (Moffitt, 1993). When examining the prevalence of adolescent-onset in offender samples (i.e., in a sample of participants who had a conviction), Kratzer and Hodgins (1999) found that 9.9% of males (3.5% of females) fell into the adolescent-onset category. Many young people engage in social transgressions during their adolescence, but adolescents who engage in only a few antisocial acts do not qualify for a CD diagnosis. Although it is more common for adolescent-onset youth to desist their antisocial behaviour in their early adulthood than for those with a childhood onset, some of these adolescent-onset youth continue to engage in antisocial acts in adulthood (Moffitt, Caspi, Harrington, & Milne, 2002).

In a study by Broidy and colleagues (2003) six different groups of boys across three countries were followed from early childhood (i.e., 5- to 7-years-old) to adolescence. They found that the majority of participants who engaged in physical aggression during childhood desisted over time. However, with each of the six groups, they found that a small number of children (less than 10% of the entire sample) who engaged in high levels of aggression continued to engage in chronic aggressive behavior with relative stability into adolescence. Furthermore, they found that high rates of physical aggression identified in childhood was a predictor of both physical and nonphysical delinquency during adolescence.

THEORIES TO EXPLAIN ANTISOCIAL BEHAVIOUR

Biological Theories

To explain why some youth engage in antisocial acts, researchers have examined the relation between frontal lobe functioning and antisocial behaviour. The frontal lobe is responsible for the planning and inhibiting of behaviour. Moffit and Henry (1989) have found that conduct-disordered youth have less frontal lobe inhibition of behaviour. Thus, the likelihood that these youth will act impulsively is increased, making it more likely that they will make poor behavioural choices.

Physiologically, conduct-disordered youth have been found to have slower heart rates than youth who do not engage in antisocial behaviour (Wadsworth, 1976). Genetic studies have found a relation between paternal antisocial behaviour and child offspring antisocial behaviour (Burt, 2009; Burt & Klump, 2012; Frick et al., 1992). Moreover, adoption and twin studies also find a biological link to youthful offending. That is, children who have an antisocial biological father are more likely to engage in antisocial behaviour, even when raised apart from the biological father (Cadoret & Cain, 1980; Jaffee, Moffitt, Caspi, & Taylor, 2003; Jarey & Stewart, 1985). More recent studies have found similar results suggesting that genetics influence antisocial behavior. Burt & Klump (2012) found a genetic link between aggressive antisocial behavior in children and self-reported antisocial behavior in their parents. Similarly, researchers in London examined over 2200 sets of twins as part of the Environmental Risk (E-Risk) Longitudinal Twin Study of 5- to 12-year-olds. They found that genetic factors played a greater role in pervasive antisocial behaviors (i.e., behaviors that occur across settings) for boys than girls. Furthermore, they found genetic factors played a role in early-onset of antisocial behaviors (Wertz et al., 2016). The heritability of antisocial behaviors has also been found in meta-analytic reviews of twin and adoptions studies (e.g., Burt, 2009). Overall, there is likely an interaction between biology, physiology, genetics, and behavior.

Cognitive Theories

Kenneth Dodge and his colleagues proposed a model of conduct-disordered behaviour that focuses on the thought processes that occur in social interactions (Crick & Dodge, 1994; Dodge, 2000). Thought processes start when individuals pay attention to and interpret social and emotional cues in their environment. The next step in the model is to consider alternative responses to the cues. Finally, a response is chosen and performed. Conduct-disordered youth demonstrate cognitive deficits and distortions (Fontaine, Burks, & Dodge, 2002). These youth often attend to fewer cues and misattribute hostile intent to ambiguous situations. Moreover, conduct-disordered youth demonstrate limited problem-solving skills, producing few solutions to problems, and these solutions are usually aggressive in nature. Cognitive deficits are likely to be present in early childhood and may contribute to child-onset conduct disorder (Coy, Speltz, DeKlyen, & Jones, 2001).

Dodge and his colleagues also have distinguished between two types of aggressive behaviour: reactive aggression and proactive aggression (Dodge, 1991; Schwartz et al., 1998). Reactive aggression is described as an emotionally aggressive response to a perceived threat or frustration. In contrast, proactive aggression is aggression directed at achieving a goal or receiving positive reinforcers. Referring to Dodge's model, deficiencies in the process occur at different points for reactive and proactive aggression. Reactively aggressive youth are likely to demonstrate deficiencies early in the cognitive process, such as focusing on only a few social cues and misattributing hostile intent to ambiguous situations. In contrast, proactive aggressive youth are likely to have deficiencies in generating alternative responses and often choose an aggressive response. Furthermore, reactive and proactive aggressors tend to have different trajectories. Reactive aggressors tend to have an earlier onset of problems than proactive aggressors (Dodge, Lochman, Harnish, Bates, & Pettit, 1997; Fite, Raine, Stouthamer-Loeber, Loeber, & Pardini, 2010).

One longitudinal study examined the differential trajectories of male youth (16-years-old) identified as proactive or reactive aggressors into early adulthood (26-years-old; Fite et al., 2010). They found that proactive aggression was uniquely related to antisocial behavior, binge drinking, antisocial personality traits (e.g., callous affect), violence, and delinquent behavior. This was not found in youth categorized as reactive aggressive, suggesting proactive aggression may be associated with long-term (i.e., life-course persistent) offending (Fite et al., 2010). Reactive aggression, on the other hand, was related to substance use (e.g., use of hard drugs) and anxiety in adulthood.

Social Theories

Bandura's (1965) **social learning theory** suggests that children learn their behaviour from observing others. Children are more likely to imitate behaviour that receives positive reinforcement than behaviour that receives negative reinforcement or punishment. As children are developing, numerous models are available to imitate, including parents, siblings, peers, and media figures. Studies have found that children who are highly aggressive and engage in antisocial behaviour often have witnessed parents, siblings, or grandparents engage in aggression and antisocial behaviour (Farrington, 1995; Waschbusch, 2002; Wolfe, Crooks, Lee, McIntyre-Smith, & Jaffe, 2003). In this pattern of intergenerational aggression, one aggressive generation produces the next aggressive generation (Glueck & Glueck, 1968; Huesmann, Eron, Lefkowitz, & Walder, 1984; van de Weijer, Bijleveld & Blokland, 2014). For example, van de Weijer and colleagues (2014) examined the pattern of intergenerational aggression by conducting a multigenerational study examining the paternal transmission (i.e., father to son) of violent offending. They found that participants were at an increased risk for engaging in violent behavior if their father was violent during their childhood and/or adolescence. Similarly, Raudino, Fergusson, Woodward, & Horwood (2013) found that conduct problems in children were moderately related to conduct problems in parents.

Van Weijer et al. (2014) also found that although the pattern of intergenerational violence was found when fathers were convicted of a violent offence during childhood/adolescence, the same pattern of increased risk was not found if the father was convicted before birth, suggesting that exposure (social learning theory) plays an important role (vs. genetics). They also note that as we move from generation to generation, the younger generations appear to be engaging in violent offending earlier than the older generations.

Watching extremely violent television and movies in which actors are rewarded for their aggression also increases children's likelihood of acting aggressively (Anderson et al., 2010; Bushman & Anderson, 2001). In addition, playing aggressive video games has been found to increase players' aggressive cognitions and behaviors, which, in turn, may increase the likelihood of children and youth acting aggressively in real life (Anderson & Dill, 2000; Bartlett, Branch, Rodenheffer, & Harris, 2009). Moreover, some data find a link from violent video exposure and aggressive

Social learning theory: A theory of human behaviour based on learning from watching others in the social environment and reinforcement contingencies

behaviour to brain processes believed to be associated with desensitization to real-world violence (Anderson et al., 2010; Barthlow, Bushman, & Sestir, 2006; Engelhardt, Bartholow, Kerr, & Bushman, 2011).

However, some researchers have found violent video games to be unrelated to aggressive behavior (Ferguson & Rueda, 2010; Markey, Markey, & French, 2015). It is possible that previous findings from laboratory studies linking violent video games to aggressive behavior should not be directly applied to the "real world" (Markey et al., 2015). This may be due to the "mundane" operationalization of aggression in laboratory studies (e.g., giving too much hot sauce to another person; Markey, et al., 2015, p. 290) that cannot be generalized to real world violent behavior. For example, Markey and colleagues (2015) found that violent video games were not a contributing factor to violent crimes (e.g., assaults, homicides) in the real world.

RISK FACTORS

A number of individual and social factors place children at increased risk for developmental psychopathology, such as emotional and behavioural problems (Coie, Lochman, Terry, & Hyman, 1992; Fitzpatrick, 1997; Jessor, Turbin, & Costa, 1998; Rutter, 1988, 1990; Wasserman & Saracini, 2001; Werner & Smith, 1992). It is important to remember that it is not just one risk factor but rather multiple risk factors that can lead to negative child outcomes (Rutter, 1979).

Individual Risk Factors

A variety of genetic or biological factors have been linked to behavioural problems. Even before a child is born, factors can operate to increase the likelihood for later behavioural difficulties. For example, a parent's own history of AD/HD or behavioural difficulties are known risk factors for their offspring, especially for sons (Cohen, Adler, Kaplan, Pelcovitz, & Mandel, 2002; National Crime Prevention Council, 1995, 1997). In a longitudinal study, Bernat, Oakes, Pettingell, and Resnick (2012) found that 12% of participants who were 14 years old and 8% of participants who were 18 to 20 years old had engaged in violence within the past 12 months. Risk factors for violence at age 14 was increased by a diagnosis of AD/HD, lack of engagement in school, low grades, and peer delinquency. A lower risk of violence for those age 18 to 20 was found for those who had low peer delinquency at age 13.

A pregnant woman's use of drugs and alcohol can place the fetus at risk for later behavioural problems (Cohen et al., 2002). Once the child is born, diet and exposure to high levels of lead are risk factors for externalizing disorders (Cohen et al., 2002; National Crime Prevention Council, 1995, 1997).

A child's temperament also can be a risk factor. For example, children who are difficult to soothe or who have a negative disposition can be at risk for later behavioural difficulties (Farrington, 1995). It also has been found that impulsive children are at risk for behavioural problems (Farrington, 1995).

Interestingly, Khurana and Gavazzi (2011) examined 2931 male teens who had been in conflict with the law across five midwestern state counties in the United States. Both African-American and European-American youth in the study were just as likely to be "teen dads." However, the risk factors for engaging in criminal behaviour differed for teen dads across these two "racial" groups. African-American teen dads had a greater number of prior offences, associated with more delinquent peers, had more traumatic backgrounds, engaged in risky sexual behaviour, and had greater educational risk factors compared to European-American males. European-American teen dads, on the other hand, were more likely to engage in substance use.

Familial Risk Factors

Parents play a critical role in the development of their children. Children of parents who are neglectful (Shaw, Keenan, & Vondra, 1994) or children who do not attach securely to their parents are at risk for later behavioural problems (Fagot & Kavanagh, 1990). Divorce and familial conflict are risk factors for children (Amato & Keith, 1991; Cummings, Davies, & Campbell, 2000). Parenting style also can be problematic. For example, inconsistent and overly strict parents who apply harsh discipline pose a risk to the child (Dekovic, 1999). In addition, not properly supervising a child presents a risk factor to the child for later behavioural problems (Dekovic, 1999; Farrington, 1995; Hoge, Andrews, & Leschied, 1996; National Crime Prevention Council, 1995, 1997; Patterson, Reid, & Dishion, 1998; Rutter, 1990).

It has been suggested that parents who drink heavily are less likely to respond appropriately to their children's behaviour, thus increasing the likelihood of future negative behaviour (Lahey, Waldman, & McBurnett, 1999). Also, heavy drinking has been implicated in inept monitoring of children and less parental involvement, both being familial risk factors (Lahey et al., 1999).

Consequences of child abuse may be psychological, physical, behavioural, academic, sexual, interpersonal, self-perceptual, or spiritual (Health Canada, 2003). Boys, in particular, may respond to abuse by acting aggressively and later engaging in spousal abuse (Fergusson & Lynskey, 1997; Health Canada, 2003; Loos & Alexander, 1997). Cohen et al. (2002) found that physical abuse experienced during adolescence increases the risk for developing lifetime mental health difficulties and behavioural problems.

Numerous other family variables have been reported as risk factors, including low socioeconomic status, large family size, and parental mental health problems (Frick, 1994; Patterson et al., 1998; Waschbusch, 2002).

School and Social Risk Factors

Having trouble reading and having a lower intelligence are both risk factors for antisocial behaviour (Elkins, Iacono, Doyle, & McGue, 1997; Rutter, 1990). The school environment also provides an opportunity for peer influences on behaviour. Young children who play with aggressive peers at an early age are at risk for externalizing behaviour (Fergusson & Horwood, 1998; Laird, Jordan, Dodge, Petit, & Bates, 2001). Children with early CD symptoms who do not end up with CD tend to associate with less delinquent peers compared with children who later qualify for a CD diagnosis (Fergusson & Horwood, 1996). As children get older, they may get involved in gangs. See Box 12.4 for a discussion of youth gangs.

Box 12.4   Forensic Psychology in the Spotlight

Running Around with the Wrong Crowd: A Look at Gangs

The National Crime Prevention Centre (NCPC) of Public Safety Canada is the federal organization responsible for providing direction on how to deal with the problem of youth gangs in Canada. There are three key elements to a youth gang:

1. The individuals involved must identify themselves as a group (e.g., they may have a group name and group colours).

2. Other people see the members as a distinct group.

3. Group members commit "delinquent" acts, often imposing on the rights of others in the community.

Although anyone can be a gang member, gangs are often composed of individuals from lower socioeconomic backgrounds who belong to a minority ethnic group. In Canada, the largest proportion of youth gang members are African-Canadian at 25%, then First Nations at 21%, and Caucasian at 18%. An overwhelming proportion of gang members are male (approximately 94%). However, the trend of female Aboriginal gang membership in western Canada is increasing. In addition, it is not uncommon for gang members to have a pre-existing substance-abuse problem and to have engaged in violent young offending prior to joining the gang. The motivation to join a gang often involves a desire to attain prestige, status, protection, and an opportunity to make money.

A Canadian police survey conducted in 2002 (Astwood Strategy Corporation, 2003) estimated that there are approximately 434 youth gangs in Canada with a total membership slightly over 7000. The top three provinces with absolute number of gangs and gang membership (not taking population into account) are Ontario, Saskatchewan, and British Columbia. Table 12.5 illustrates youth gang numbers and membership as a function of province/territory.

Table 12.5 Youth Gang Numbers in Canada

Province	Number of Youth Gangs	Number of Gang Members	Youth Gang Members per 1000
British Columbia	102	1027	0.26
Alberta	42	668	0.22
Saskatchewan	28	1315	1.34
Manitoba	15	171	0.15
Ontario	216	3320	0.29
Quebec*	25	533	0.07
Nova Scotia	6	37	0.04
Prince Edward Island	0	0	0
Newfoundland and Labrador	0	0	0
Yukon	0	0	0
Northwest Territories	0	0	0
Nunavut	0	0	0

*Data were obtained from only four police agencies and should be interpreted cautiously; figures may not be representative of the province.

Source: Astwood Strategy Corporation (Dec., 2003). Results of the 2002 Canadian Police Survey on Gangs. Minister of Public Safety and Emergency Preparedness. Cat. No. PS4-4/2002 ISBN 0-662-68124-X, http://www.astwood.ca/assets/gangs_e.pdf. Reprinted by permission of Astwood Strategy Corporation.

Erickson and Butters (2006) examined the relationship between gangs, guns, and drugs in Toronto and Montreal. A total of 904 male high school students, school dropouts, and young offenders were interviewed. The researchers found that as gang presence in schools increased, so did the number of guns and amount of drugs. Almost 19% of the boys studied who were aged 14 to 17 in Toronto and 15% in Montreal brought a gun to school. Dropouts who sell drugs are more likely to be engaged in gun violence than dropouts who do not sell drugs.

Social disapproval and being rejected are likely to occur with aggressive children and adolescents (Coie, Belding, & Underwood, 1988; Ebata et al., 1990; Rutter, 1990), and these rejected, aggressive children are at risk for behavioural problems (Parker & Asher, 1987; Rudolph & Asher, 2000).

McDaniel (2012) looked at risk and protective factors (see below) for gang-affiliated youth. Survey data were collected from 4131 youth in Grades 7, 9, 11, and 12 from "high-risk" urban public schools in the United States. Approximately 7% of the youth belonged to a gang. Being part of a gang was positively related to engaging in delinquent behaviour and using alcohol and drugs frequently. Parental supervision and coping skills were negatively related to gang membership.

Overall, gang youth are more likely to reoffend than non-gang youth (e.g., Chu, Daffern, Thomas, & Lim, 2012). Chu, Daffern, Thomas, and Lim (2011) examined the risk-assessment and treatment needs of gang youth and non-gang youth. Both groups scored similarly on the Structured Assessment of Violence Risk in Youth (SAVRY) and the Youth Level of Service/Case Management Inventory (YLS/CMI), with the only exception occurring for peer delinquency.

PROTECTIVE FACTORS

Although children may experience a similar environment and adversity, children's responses and outcomes vary, with some children prevailing and prospering, and others having a number of difficulties and negative outcomes. The child who has multiple risk factors but who can overcome them and prevail has been termed resilient. Resilience has been described as the ability to overcome stress and adversity (Winfield, 1994).

It has been suggested that resilient children may have protective factors that allow them to persevere in the face of adversity. The notion of protection and protective factors was introduced in the early 1980s (Garmezy, 1985). Garmezy (1991) identified a number of areas in which protectiveness can be present: genetic variables, personality dispositions, supportive family environments, and community supports. There is some debate over the definition of protective factors and how protective factors work. Many agree, however, that protective factors help to improve or sustain some part of an individual's life (Fougere & Daffern, 2011; Leadbeater, Kuperminc, Blatt, & Hertzog, 1999). Rutter (1990) identified four ways that protective factors are effective:

1. Protective factors reduce negative outcomes by changing the risk level of the child's exposure to a risk factor.

2. They change the negative chain reaction following exposure to risk.

Resilient: Characteristic of a child who has multiple risk factors but who does not develop problem behaviours or negative symptoms

3. They help to develop and maintain self-esteem and self-efficacy.

4. They provide opportunities to children that they would not otherwise have.

Protective factors can be grouped into three categories: (1) individual, (2) familial, and (3) social/external factors (Grossman et al., 1992).

Individual Protective Factors

Protective factors that reside within the individual, known as resilient temperaments (Hoge, 1999), include exceptional social skills, child competencies, confident perceptions, values, attitudes, and beliefs within the child (Vance, 2001).

Work from twin studies has suggested that social support may have a heritable component that is influenced by personality. For example, likeable children may respond to good role models in a positive manner, thus promoting a positive and continuing relationship.

Intriguingly, Salekin, Lee, Schrum Dillard, and Kubak (2010) found that "motivation to change" was a protective factor for general and violent reoffending in a sample of 140 male and female adolescents at a detention centre in the United States.

In a sample of adolescents from the United Kingdom, protective factors from reoffending included being older when first arrested, offending less overall, and having fewer psychopathological problems (Rennie & Dolan, 2010).

Familial Protective Factors

Protective familial factors are those positive aspects of the child's parents/guardians and home environment. For example, a child who has a positive and supportive relationship with an adult may display less negative behaviour. Thus, a good parent/adult–child relationship is a protective factor for the child who is growing up in an underprivileged community.

Social/External Protective Factors

Peer groups can have a strong effect on child outcomes (Vance, 2001). Associating with deviant peers is a risk factor for antisocial behaviour. The converse is a protective factor. That is, associating with prosocial children is a protective factor against antisocial behavior and is related to desistance in juvenile offending (Herrenkohl, Tajima, Whitney, & Huang, 2005; van Domburgh, Looeber, Bezemer, Stallings, & Stouthammer-Loeber, 2009).

Just as there are risk factors leading to increased negative outcomes, there are also protective factors that may reduce negative outcomes in the presence of risk factors (Grossman et al., 1992; Lösel & Farrington, 2012; Masten, Best, & Garmezy, 1990). Protective factors may counteract risk (Loeber & Farrington, 1998b; Lösel & Farrington, 2012; Rutter, 1988). Further research is necessary to understand the role protective factors play in positive outcomes.

PREVENTION, INTERVENTION, AND TREATMENT OF YOUNG OFFENDING

Prevention, intervention, and treatment of young offending can be conceptualized as occurring at three levels: primary, secondary, and tertiary (DeMatteo & Marczyk, 2005; Flannery & Williams, 1999; Mulvey, Arthur, & Reppucci, 1993). **Primary intervention strategies** are strategies that are implemented prior to any violence occurring, with the goal of decreasing the likelihood that violence will occur later on. **Secondary intervention strategies** are strategies that attempt to reduce the frequency of violence. **Tertiary intervention strategies** are strategies that attempt to prevent violence from reoccurring.

Primary Intervention Strategies

At the primary level of intervention, the goal is to identify groups (of children) that have numerous risk factors for engaging in antisocial behaviour later on. The belief is that if the needs of these children are addressed early, before violence has occurred, then the likelihood that they will go on to become young offenders is reduced. Because "groups" (rather than specific individuals) are targeted, often these intervention strategies occur at broad levels such as in the family, at school, and in the community (Mulvey et al., 1993). The following strategies are examples of primary intervention approaches.

Family-Oriented Strategies Targeting the family may be an effective means of preventing young offending, given that family poses a number of risk factors (Kumpfer & Alvarado, 2003). According to Mulvey et al. (1993), family-based intervention efforts can generally be classified as either parent-focused or family-supportive. **Parent-focused interventions** are interventions directed at assisting parents to recognize warning signs for later youth violence and/or training parents to effectively manage any behavioural problems that arise. **Family-supportive interventions** are interventions that connect at-risk families to various support services (e.g., child care, counselling, medical assistance) that may be available in their community.

An example of a family-oriented strategy is a popular parent-education program known as the Incredible Years Parenting Program (IYP), a 12-week training program that starts with building a strong emotional bond between parent(s) and child, and then teaches parents how to set behavioural expectations for their children, to monitor children's behaviour, to reinforce positive behaviour, to provide consequences for inappropriate behaviour, and to develop and use effective communication skills (Webster-Stratton, 1992, 2001; Webster-Stratton & Reid, 2010). Videos are used to demonstrate parenting techniques and enhance parent learning. Since its initial development, teacher-focused and child-focused programs have also been developed (Webster-Stratton, 2001).

Although parent-focused approaches have shown some success in the shorter term, the most common research finding is that parents of high-risk children tend to discontinue the training at rates that may exceed 50% (Mulvey et al., 1993).

Primary intervention strategies: Strategies that are implemented prior to any violence occurring, with the goal of decreasing the likelihood that violence will occur later on

Secondary intervention strategies: Strategies that attempt to reduce the frequency of violence

Tertiary intervention strategies: Strategies that attempt to prevent violence from reoccurring

Parent-focused interventions: Interventions directed at assisting parents to recognize warning signs for later youth violence and/or training parents to effectively manage any behavioural problems that arise

Family-supportive interventions: Interventions that connect at-risk families to various support services

However, long-term evaluations of the IYP have found benefits for completers. For example, children with severe conduct and behavioral problems whose parent's completed the program were found to have fewer conduct problems (e.g., delinquency, substance abuse) than anticipated 8- to 12-years later (Weber-Stratton, Rinaldi, & Reid, 2011). Despite promising results with completers, with such high attrition rates, particularly among families with the greatest need for these services, it is unlikely that parent-focused approaches are a reliable mechanism for preventing youth violence. Parenting programs usually are not "stand alone" and are part of more comprehensive programs that may involve a child component, school component, and/or community program.

School-Oriented Strategies Given the amount of time children spend in school and the number of difficulties that can arise there, school is a common environment for primary prevention strategies. School-based prevention programs include preschool programs (e.g., Project Head Start, which incorporates the Incredible Years Parenting Program); social skills training for children, which may include cognitive behavioural-therapy; and broad-based social interventions, which are designed to alter the school environment (Loeber & Farrington, 1998a; Mulvey et al., 1993).

Project Head Start is designed for children from low socioeconomic backgrounds. A number of social services are provided to these children and families (e.g., nutrition, structured activities, academic tutoring, medical services) to reduce disadvantages that may interfere with learning. Preschool programs can produce some positive outcomes in the short term (e.g., cognitive improvement; Cooper & Lanza, 2014), and many target factors that have been found to be associated with antisocial behavior in adolescence (Zigler, Taussig, & Black, 1992); however the positive effects at reducing antisocial behaviour over the long term are questionable (Loeber & Farrington, 1998a; Mulvey et al., 1993) as few of the studies examining the efficacy of these programs look at the impact on later antisocial behavior (May, Osmond, & Billick, 2014; Zigler, et al., 1992).

The Chicago Child-Parent Center (CPC) program, however, is one preschool program that has been found to impact later delinquency. Specifically, a 15-year follow-up study found that children who participated in the CPC program during early childhood had lower rates of juvenile delinquency (i.e., general and violent arrests) than a comparison sample.

It is not uncommon to recommend a social skills program to children showing some early signs of interpersonal and behavioural difficulties. Social skills training may involve a structured program with a limited number of sessions (e.g., 12), teaching alternative methods for conflict resolution, adjusting social perceptions (recall that a cognitive theory approach suggests that aggressive children may interpret ambiguous situations aggressively [e.g., Lochman, Whidby, & Fitzgerald, 2000]), managing anger, and developing empathy. Cognitive-behavioural therapy usually is a component of social skills programs. The cognitive-behavioural component focuses on children's thought processes and social interactions. Concrete strategies for handling interpersonal conflict are outlined, which children practise through role-playing and modelling with others in the class. Program evaluations have suggested that social skills training with cognitive-behavioural therapy can be beneficial in the short term, although long-term follow-up suggests that the effects on reducing antisocial behaviour may be small (e.g., Denham & Almeida, 1987). Larger effects may be obtained if social skills programs are combined with others, such as parent education (Webster-Stratton & Hammond, 1997).

Social process intervention is another school-based approach that alters the school environment (Gauce, Comer, & Schwartz, 1987; Mulvey et al., 1993). Changes include increasing the connection among students with learning problems, assisting the transition from elementary school to high school, improving the perception of safety in school, and providing students with experiences in the community (Mulvey et al., 1993). Although these efforts may improve academic success, their influence on reducing the likelihood of young offending is unclear.

Community-Wide Strategies Community approaches include providing structured community activities for children and increasing a community's cohesion. Few community-based programs exist for children younger than age 12 who are at risk for future young offending. One such program, developed in Canada in 1985, is known as the SNAP (Stop Now And Plan) Under 12 Outreach Project (ORP). Dr. Leena Augimeri was central to the development and refinement of SNAP. To learn more about Dr. Augimeri see Box 12.5.

The ORP is a standardized 12-week outpatient program with five key components:

1. The SNAP Children's Club—a structured group that teaches children a cognitive-behavioural self-control and problem-solving technique called SNAP (Stop Now And Plan) (Earlscourt Child and Family Centre, 2001a)

2. A concurrent SNAP parenting group that teaches parents effective child management strategies (Earlscourt Child and Family Centre, 2001b)

3. One-on-one family counselling based on SNAP parenting (Levene, 1998)

4. Individual befriending for children who are not connected with positive structured activities in their community and require additional support

5. Academic tutoring to assist children who are not performing at an age-appropriate grade level

A recent study examined the effectiveness of SNAP when compared to a standard behavioral health service (Burke & Loeber, 2014). Participants' in this study included 252 boys identified as high-risk for antisocial behavior. Participants were randomly assigned to the SNAP or standard program, and outcome measures were collected at baseline, and 3, 9, and 15 months after baseline. Results indicated a significant reduction in aggressive and externalizing behaviors for those in the SNAP group compared to the standard group (Burke & Loeber, 2014). A decrease in symptoms related to conduct disorder, oppositional defiant disorder, and attention-deficit hyperactivity disorder were also found. Furthermore, participation in the SNAP program appeared to be extremely effective for those youth identified as having more severe behavioral problems at intake. Finally, children in the SNAP group had less contact with the criminal justice system (i.e., fewer charges) when compared to the

Box 12.5

Canadian Researcher Profile: Dr. Leena Augimeri

Courtesy of Dr. Leena Augimeri

Dr. Leena Augimeri's passion for understanding developmental issues as they relate to antisocial behaviour began during her adolescence and continued into her undergraduate studies at the University of Toronto. This passion inspired her to pursue a Masters and PhD in this same area of study and has led to a very rewarding career working with children with serious disruptive behaviour problems and their families. In her current role, Dr. Augimeri serves as the Director of Scientific and Program Development and Centre for Children Committing Offences at Child Development Institute in Toronto, Ontario. Some of her areas of interest include: (1) child delinquency and aggression; (2) risk, promotive, and protective factors and their impact on children, families, and communities; (3) the development of evidence-based, gender-sensitive

programming for children and youth with serious disruptive behaviour problems (i.e., SNAP Boys, SNAP Girls, and SNAP Youth Justice); (4) structured professional judgment risk/need assessment tools that predict antisocial behaviour and inform treatment planning; and (5) implementation science.

When asked how she first became interested in this area of research, Dr. Augimeri explains, "Growing up in a number of communities in and around Toronto, I was exposed to a variety of diverse experiences that shaped my interests and ultimately defined who I am as a person and professional. I was always interested in how different families functioned, and how risk, protective, and promotive factors influenced the lives of others including my own family members and peers. In particular, growing up with three brothers and their extended network of friends made me question what it was about certain kids who thrived and succeeded versus those who struggled, got in trouble with the law, and/or ended up with serious addictions or mental health issues. These experiences led me to pursue a career in children's mental health, crime and deviance, and sociology, which eventually led me to the doors of a wonderful children's mental health centre, Child Development Institute (CDI). Starting as a program researcher, one of my early accomplishments with CDI was the co-development of the SNAP® (Stop Now And Plan) program, a program designed specifically for young children in conflict with the law. This experience began my professional journey, where I was exposed to the importance of the scientist-practitioner framework that connects research and clinical practice. A few years later, I was given the opportunity to manage the SNAP program, which further honed my research, clinical, and program development skills. Today, my work focuses on leading the SNAP National Expansion, which aims to bring SNAP to communities across Canada (in addition to the United States and Europe) to help create massive social change using an innovative venture philanthropy model. It has been an incredible 30 year journey of learning, developing, and working alongside amazing researchers and clinicians to help impact the lives of at-risk children, youth, and their families. The journey continues..."

(continued)

(continued)

Though she has already contributed 30 years of her career to the SNAP program's research, development, and implementation, Dr. Augimeri is as passionate as ever. "Knowing that my colleagues and I are contributing to the scientific evidence on important topics like what works, what doesn't, and what active treatment ingredients are necessary for a successful, measurable, and replicable intervention model is so rewarding," says Dr. Augimeri. "Our ultimate goal is to help improve the life chances of at-risk children and their families by increasing our knowledge of who these kids are, what is impacting their lives, and how we can effectively intervene to address their individual risks and needs to help create happier, healthier children and families and safer communities. We firmly believe that all children have tremendous potential if given the right opportunities and supports, especially if we can catch them early and provide them with effective evidence-based programming. Our children deserve that."

A key part of Dr. Augimeri's research is ensuring that it reaches the hands of those who can ignite change. Dr. Augimeri has consulted on the Ontario Ministry of Education's Expert Panel on Safe and Inclusive Schools, the Ontario Ministry of Children and Youth Services' Youth Justice forums, and the Study Group on Very Young Offenders (U.S. Office of Juvenile Justice and Delinquency Prevention), to name a few. She typically consults on cases where young children with disruptive behaviour problems engage in very serious criminal offences, or where a child's problematic behaviour has had dire consequences on their own well-being and the well-being of others. Three cases that have resonated with Dr. Augimeri and influenced her work are: (1) the murder of James Bulger, a two-year-old boy from Kirkby, England who was abducted and killed by two ten-year-old boys, Robert Thompson and Jon Venables, on February 12, 1993; (2) the Columbine High School shootings, where two senior students, Eric Harris and Dylan Klebold, murdered twelve students and a teacher on April 20, 1999; and (3) Myles Neuts, a ten-year-old boy from Chatham, Ontario who tragically died as the result of a "bullying incident gone wrong" on February 6, 1998. "These cases have left such an impression on me for different reasons," says Dr. Augimeri. "They have influenced my work in a variety of ways, from launching the first police-community referral protocol in Canada, to creating a tool to predict future offending in young children, to developing effective early intervention programs for young children in conflict with the law. With measures such as these, we hope to improve the life chances of at-risk children and their families. To quote Martin Luther King Jr., 'Our lives begin to end the day we become silent about the things that matter.'"

Outside of work, Dr. Augimeri shares a wonderful life with her husband Enzo, their two daughters, Melissa and Jessie, and their dog, Ruffles. She leaves us with a quote from Dr. Seuss she shares with her daughters and students, alike: "To the world you may be one person, but to one person you may be the world."

standard group. Overall, SNAP appears to be an effective program to help reduce aggressive and behavioral difficulties in high-risk children (Burke & Loeber, 2014).

Secondary Intervention Strategies

Secondary intervention strategies are directed at young offenders who have either had contact with the police or criminal justice system or have demonstrated behavioural problems at school. The goal of these strategies is to provide social and clinical services so that young offenders do not go on to commit serious violence. Many of the same approaches used in primary intervention strategies are used here. One of the main differences is the target (i.e., which children are involved in the program) rather than the content of the intervention. Common secondary intervention strategies include diversion programs, alternative and vocational education, family therapy, and skills training (see Mulvey et al., 1993).

Diversion programs "divert" youth offenders from the youth justice system into community- or school-based treatment programs. The belief is that the justice system may cause more harm than good in reducing offending. Intervention and treatment in the community may be more successful at reducing the likelihood that the young offender will escalate his or her offending. Alternative and vocational education programs offer the option of mainstream schooling. Family therapy and skills-training programs incorporate the youth and family. Diversion and certain school-, family-, and community-based interventions have shown some success at reducing antisocial behaviour in youth (e.g., Davidson & Redner, 1988; Kazdin, 1996).

One particular secondary intervention program that has undergone considerable evaluation is Multisystemic Therapy (MST). MST examines a child across the contexts or "systems" in which he or she lives: family, peers, school, neighbourhood, and community (Henggeler & Borduin, 1990; Henggeler, Melton, & Smith, 1992; Henggeler, Schoenwald, & Pickrel, 1995; Henggeler, Schoenwald, Borduin, Rowland, & Cunningham, 1998). MST has been implemented in 11 different countries, including various parts of Canada and the United States (Henggeler, 2010). To evaluate its effectiveness, a four-year randomized study was conducted across four Ontario communities: London, Mississauga, Simcoe County, and Ottawa (Leschied & Cunningham, 2002). Approximately 200 families received MST from 1997 to 2001. During the same period, another 200 families (acting as the comparison group) were asked to access the services that were available through their local youth justice and social service organizations. These services included probation and specialized programs. All families underwent psychological testing at the start of the study and then again at the end. The psychological testing included measures to assess family functioning, caregiver depression, the youth's social skills, procriminal attitudes, and behavioural problems. Based on this assessment, the youth and families in the MST group were provided services and had access to a case manager 24 hours a day, 7 days a week. Areas that may be targeted in MST treatment include family communication, parent management, and cognitive-behavioural issues. All youth were followed for three years after the end of treatment (until 2004). Overall, MST was not found to be more effective than the typical services available in Ontario. For example, after the three-year follow-up, 68% of the participants in the MST group had at least one conviction, compared with 67% of those in the comparison group. The average number of days to reconviction for the MST group was about 283, compared with 310 for the control group (this difference was not statistically significant). It is important to note, however, that MST may have benefited youth and their families on factors that were not measured. Interestingly, some studies evaluating MST in the United States have found it more effective than incarceration, individual counselling, and probation (Henggeler et al., 1992, 1995). Perhaps the quantity and quality of programs available in various parts of the United States differ from those in Canada—accounting for some of the differing results between the two countries.

More recently, the use of the short term efficacy of MST was examined with a sample of 94 youth aged 12- to 17-years-old in Scarborough, Ontario (McIntosh, 2015). They found that adolescents who completed the MST program were less likely to be arrested for an offence compared to non-completers. Furthermore, youth who completed the program saw increased benefits compared to non-completers, such that they were more likely to be employed, attending school, engaging with prosocial peers/activities, and living at home (McIntosh, 2015).

A recent meta-analysis examining the effectiveness of MST found that it has a small effect on juvenile delinquency and other problem behaviours (e.g., substance use; van der Stouwe, Asscher, Stams, Deković, & van der Laan, 2014). However, there were a number of factors that moderated the effect (e.g., treatment quality, duration of program, etc.), such that MST programs appeared to be the most effective in the United States, and more effective with younger adolescents (i.e., age 15-years-old or younger) and Caucasian participants.

Tertiary Intervention Strategies

Tertiary intervention strategies are aimed at youth who have engaged in criminal acts and who may have already been processed through formal court proceedings (Flannery & Williams, 1999). As such, these intervention efforts are actually more "treatment" than prevention, and the recipients are often chronic and serious young offenders. The goal of tertiary intervention strategies is to minimize the impact of existing risk factors and foster the development of protective factors, which may reduce the likelihood that the at-risk adolescent will engage in future offending.

Tertiary intervention strategies include in-patient treatment (i.e., institutional, residential) and community-based treatment (Mulvey et al., 1993). The approach can be one of retribution or rehabilitation. Those who favour retribution believe that young offenders should be held accountable for their actions, punished accordingly, and separated from society. Treatment for these young offenders should be provided in an institutional setting (e.g., youth detention centre). By contrast, those who favour rehabilitation believe that treatment based in the community is a more effective way to reduce the likelihood of reoffending. One meta-analysis reported that shorter stays (rather than longer stays) in institutional settings and greater involvement with community services are more effective for violent young offenders (Wooldredge, 1988).

Grunwald, Lockwood, Harris, and Mennis (2010) examined the influence of neighbourhoods on the likelihood that young offenders would reoffend. The researchers examine 7061 young offenders committed to community-based programs in Philadelphia, Pennsylvania. Not all offences are the same, however, and neighbourhood-level factors were found to reduce only drug offence reoffending, not violent offending or property-related offences.

A relatively new program, known as "The Grow Academy," is a residential program developed in Wisconsin as an alternative to incarceration (http://doc.wi.gov/families-visitors/juvenile-services/the-grow-academy). In this 120-day program, youth work towards their high school diploma in an agricultural-based curriculum. At the Grow Academy, youth learn a number of skills, such as organic vegetable farming, nutrition and cooking skills, financial literacy, and they participate in horticulture therapy, among others. Cognitive behavioural treatments and a focus on community involvement are also components of this program, which was developed as a way to reduce recidivism.

SUMMARY

1. The Juvenile Delinquents Act (JDA) in 1908 was the first piece of legislation in Canada to address youthful offenders. In 1984, the Young Offender's Act (YOA) replaced the JDA with several notable changes to youth justice. Although the YOA underwent several amendments, it was eventually replaced in 2003 with the Youth Criminal Justice Act (YCJA).

2. Three common disorders are diagnosed in youthful offenders: attention deficit hyperactivity disorder (AD/HD), oppositional defiant disorder (ODD), and conduct disorder (CD). Young children diagnosed with conduct disorder are at greatest risk for youthful and adult criminal offending.

3. Biological theories focus on genetic and physiological differences between young offenders and those who do not behave antisocially. Cognitive theories propose a model of antisocial behaviour that focuses on thought processes occurring in social interactions. Social theories are based in social learning theory, which proposes that children learn behaviour from observing others and through reinforcement contingencies.

4. Risk factors increase the likelihood of behavioural (and emotional) disorders in children and youth. Protective factors provide a buffer against the risk factors children and youth may experience.

5. Primary intervention strategies are implemented prior to any violence occurring, with the goal of decreasing the likelihood that violence will occur later on. Secondary intervention strategies attempt to reduce the frequency of violence. Tertiary intervention strategies attempt to prevent violence from reoccurring.

Discussion Questions

1. Fifteen-year-old Andrew Smith is appearing before Judge Brown in youth court for the third time in two years. Andrew's current offences are robbery and possession of a handgun. Given the objectives of the Youth Criminal Justice Act, discuss the sentencing options available to Judge Brown. Consider which option is most appropriate in this case. Why?

2. In your opinion, what factors should the courts consider when determining whether a young offender should be given an adult sentence?

Chapter 13
Intimate Partner Violence

Learning Objectives

- Differentiate between the different forms of abuse, and outline the prevalence of intimate partner violence.

- Outline how social learning and evolutionary psychology theories have been used to understand and explain intimate partner violence.

- Explain why some women remain in, or return to, abusive relationships.

- Describe the various types of male batterers.

- Outline the effectiveness of intimate partner violence offender treatment.

- Define stalking and identify the various types of stalkers.

Garner Ogondo is serving a federal sentence for criminal harassment, threatening, and assault causing bodily harm. His abusive behaviour started when his wife, Shayanne, was pregnant with their first child. He engaged in verbally abusive behaviour, calling her names and threatening to use violence against her. After the baby was born, the verbal abuse escalated and he started physically abusing his wife (i.e., slapping her, shoving her into walls, punching her). After the birth of their second child, he became very controlling and refused to allow his wife to have contact with her family or friends unless he was present. After a particularly brutal beating, she left him and took the children to her sister's home and told Garner she wanted a divorce. For three weeks, Garner phoned her and on several occasions showed up at the home demanding to see her and the children. The police were called and Garner was charged with criminal harassment. One evening Garner broke into the house, threatened to kill his brother-in-law, and repeatedly punched his wife. He was arrested and charged with threatening and assault causing bodily harm. He was sentenced to four years in prison and has been attending the high-risk intimate partner violence treatment program for the past two months. The program consists of individual and group therapy. One therapist thinks Garner is making considerable progress in treatment, whereas the other therapist is less optimistic. In group therapy, Garner is evasive when challenged, has been vindictive toward other group members, and is continually testing boundaries. The therapist who has been concerned with Garner's attitudes and behaviour thinks that he is not genuinely interested in changing.

Violence occurring within the family has a major impact on victims, witnesses, and society. Violence and its aftermath are also a major focus of forensic psychology, with psychologists involved in developing assessment and intervention programs for victims and offenders. Reading the opening vignette raises a number of questions. How common is this sort of behaviour? Why would someone hurt a person he or she claims to love? After being caught, does the violence stop? What can be done to prevent the development of attitudes supportive of abuse? Are treatment programs effective at reducing risk for future violence? We shall address these and other questions in this chapter.

Domestic violence: Any violence occurring between family members

The term **domestic violence** refers to any violence occurring between family members. Domestic violence typically occurs in private settings. Although not necessarily condoned, historically it was tolerated and was not subject to effective legal sanctions. Reasons for this were varied, but religious and cultural attitudes generally positioned women and children in deferential roles within families. In Canada, little attention was paid to domestic violence prior to the 1980s. It was the women's liberation movement and the growth of feminism that gave women the courage to speak out against such violence. Since that time, domestic violence has become a major focus of research and legal action.

Intimate partner violence: Any violence occurring between intimate partners who are living together or separated. Also known as *spousal violence*

Spousal violence: Any violence occurring between intimate partners who are living together or separated. Also known as *intimate partner violence*

In this chapter, we will focus on violence occurring between intimate partners who are living together or separated (called **intimate partner violence** or **spousal violence**). Abuse and aggression within intimate relationships has a long history and is, unfortunately, still common. We will review the different types of abuse experienced and the prevalence of intimate partner violence. We will present theories that attempt to explain why some people engage in violence against their partners. Research examining the different types of abusive men will be provided. In addition, some of the major approaches to treatment will be presented and research on their effectiveness will be reviewed. Finally, research examining the prevalence of stalking and types of stalkers will be summarized. The most common type of stalker is someone who engages in stalking after an intimate relationship breakup.

TYPES OF VIOLENCE AND MEASUREMENT

Violence against partners is varied in terms of types and severity and includes physical (e.g., hitting, punching, stabbing, burning), sexual, financial (e.g., restricting access to personal funds, stealing from the victim, refusing to allow the victim to work), and emotional abuse (e.g., verbal attacks, degradation, threats about hurting family members or pets, isolation from family members, unwarranted accusations about infidelity). This latter form of violence, emotional abuse, although often less visible to others, is common and is often viewed by victims as being as damaging as physical violence (Williams, South Richardson, Hammock, & Janit, 2012).

The scale most commonly used to measure intimate partner assault has been the Conflict Tactics Scale (CTS; Straus, 1979) or its most recent update, the revised Conflict Tactics Scale (CTS2; Straus, Hamby, Boney-McCoy, & Sugarman, 1996). The CTS2 scale consists of 39 items divided into five scales (Table 13.1). Respondents are asked how frequently they have engaged in the behaviour and how often they have experienced these acts. The CTS scales have been used in hundreds of studies to

Table 13.1 CTS2 Scales, What Each Scale Measures, and Example Items

Scale Name	Measurement	Example Item
Negotiation scale	Constructive problem solving	Suggesting a compromise during an argument
Psychological scale	Verbal/indirect aggression	Swearing, threatening to hit
Physical assault scale	Physical aggression	Slapping, hitting
Sexual coercion scale	Sexual aggression	Forcing partner to have sex
Injury scale	Consequences of aggression	Visits to a doctor because of partner's aggression

Source: Straus, M.A., Hamby, S.L., Boney-McCoy, S., & Sugarman, D.B. (1996). The revised Conflict Tactics Scales (CTS2): Development and preliminary psychometric data. *Journal of Family Issues, 17*, 283–316.

assess the prevalence of intimate partner violence. Despite ongoing research, some myths about intimate partner violence are still prevalent. Some of these myths are outlined in Box 13.1.

Archer (2002) conducted a meta-analysis of 48 studies by using the CTS scales and found that females are more likely to engage in minor physical aggression, such as slapping, kicking, or hitting with an object, whereas men are more likely to beat up or choke their partners. For couples in treatment for intimate partner violence, men engage in much higher rates of minor and severe physical violence compared with men from student and community samples. Within community and university student samples, males and females commit equal amounts of violence. Comparing self- and partner-reports, respondents report fewer violent acts than their partners, and men are more likely to under-report than women. A common form of emotional abuse is

A victim of intimate partner violence
Artem Furman/Fotolia

Box 13.1 Myths and Realities

Intimate Partner Violence

Intimate partner violence is associated with many myths. Here is a list of these myths accompanied by facts that challenge these false beliefs.

Myth 1. Intimate partner violence is not a common problem.
Fact. Because of the private nature of intimate partner violence and the shame and embarrassment that inhibits many victims from talking about the issue, it is impossible to determine exactly how many people are subject to violence. In Canada, about one in eight women are abused by their partners. You likely know someone who has been assaulted by his or her partner or who is currently in an abusive relationship. The highest rates of intimate violence are experienced by women between the ages of 15 and 25.

Myth 2. Only heterosexual women get battered. Men are not victims, and women never batter.
Fact. Such myths ignore and deny the realities of violent relationships. Men can be and are victims of intimate partner violence. Women can be and are batterers. Men and women in same-sex relationships also can and do experience and perpetrate intimate partner violence.

Myth 3. When a woman leaves a violent relationship, she is safe.
Fact. The most dangerous time for a battered spouse is after separation. Of all spousal homicides, 75% occur after separation. At this time, the abusive partner may feel they are losing control, which may cause an escalation of abuse in an attempt to regain control.

Myth 4. Alcohol and/or drugs cause people to act aggressively.
Fact. Although alcohol and drug abuse is often present in incidents of spousal abuse, it is not the alcohol or drug that *causes* the violence. People will, however, often use this excuse to rationalize their behaviour by saying, "I wasn't myself" or "I hit you because I was drunk." Blaming alcohol or drugs takes the responsibility away from the abusive person and can prevent that person from thinking they need to change.

Myth 5. When a woman gets hit by her partner, she must have provoked him in some way.
Fact. No one deserves to be hit. Whether or not there was provocation, violence in relationships is always wrong. It never solves problems, although it often silences the victim.

Myth 6. Maybe things will get better.
Fact. Once violence begins in a relationship, it usually gets worse without some kind of intervention. Waiting and hoping the abusive partner will change is not a good strategy. Partners in an abusive relationship need help and support to break out of the abusive pattern.

---

verbal aggression. Stockdale, Tackett, and Coyne (2013) reviewed 20 studies in a meta-analysis on the sex differences of verbal aggression in intimate relationships. They found that women used verbal aggression significantly more often than men ($d = -0.25$).

Although commonly used, the CTS or CTS2 is often criticized for a number of reasons (Dobash, Dobash, Wilson, & Daly, 1992; Sillito, 2012):

1. The CTS/CTS2 do not include all potential violent acts. However, if a scale is to have practical utility, it cannot be excessively long or clinicians and researchers will not use it.

2. The CTS/CTS2 does not take into account the different contexts or consequences of the same act for men and women. For example, treating a punch by a woman and a man as equivalent ignores the difference in the injury that might be inflicted (Nazroo, 1995). Surveys have consistently shown that women are more likely than men are to suffer both physical and psychological consequences from

intimate violence (Saunders, 2002). In the most recent Statistics Canada survey (Burczycka, 2016), 40% of women respondents versus 24% of men reported being injured in the most recent violent episode.

3. The CTS/CTS2 does not assess motive for violence, and therefore initiating and responding with violence are treated equally. For example, consider the case of a couple arguing. If he threatens to punch her, and she pushes him away from her, both acts would be included on the CTS/CTS2.

Recently, Straus (2012) has responded to these criticisms, concluding that the criticisms are mostly concerned with theoretical disagreements and seem to neglect evidence that women also exhibit violence in relationships. He argues that researchers should be concerned with reducing all violence and not just violence perpetrated by men. Box 13.2 provides more details about the prevalence and severity of mutual violence, as well as sex-specific and same-sex patterns of violence.

Box 13.2   Forensic Psychology in the Spotlight

Husband Battering and Same-Sex Battering Does Exist

Intimate partner violence is certainly not exclusively initiated by heterosexual men. Researchers reviewing the literature on heterosexual women as perpetrators of intimate violence (Carney, Buttell, & Dutton, 2007) and researchers interested in same-sex relationship violence (Stiles-Shields & Carroll, 2015) are beginning to ask questions and shed light on partner abuse beyond the heterosexual male perpetrator.

■   Is intimate partner violence invariably male-initiated?

The answer is no. It appears that women engage in the same amount of violence as men, and some studies found that women engaged in more minor violence then men (Archer, 2002; Stockdale et al., 2013). Williams and Frieze (2005) analyzed the different violence patterns of 3519 couples and found that the most common type of violence was mutual mild violence, followed by mutual severe violence. Thus, the long-assumed gender gap likely does not exist. As Carney et al. (2007) concluded, "Female [partner] violence is common, [and] occurs at the same rate as male [partner] violence" (p. 113).

■   Is there a gender bias in police responses to intimate partner violence?

The limited research indicates the answer is yes. Brown (2004) studied differences in arrest rates in cases of injury and no-injury assaults. When the female partner was injured, the male was charged in 91% of the cases; however, when the male was injured, the female was charged

60% of the time. When no injury occurred, the female was charged in 13% of cases as compared with 52% of the time for males.

■   Is there intimate partner violence in same-sex relationships?

The answer is yes. In fact, in Canada, the General Social Survey of 2014 showed that Canadians identifying as gay, lesbian, or bisexual were twice as likely than heterosexual Canadians to experience intimate partner violence in the previous 5 years (Burczycka, 2016). Particularly concerning was the fact that lesbian and bisexual women were nearly four times more likely to be intimate partner victims compared to heterosexual women.

■   Are the patterns of intimate partner violence the same in gay and lesbian couples?

The answer is no. Some risk factors for same-sex intimate partner abuse are substance and alcohol abuse, mental health issues, and HIV-positive status (Stiles-Shields & Carroll, 2015). However, gay men and lesbian women have unique patterns of partner violence. Gay men incur many types of intimate partner violence (e.g., emotional, physical) and are often both perpetrators and victims. A major pattern observed in lesbian intimate partner violence is the tendency to become socially isolated as a couple. More social isolation seems to predict more physical abuse.

Intimate Partners: A Risky Relationship

In the 1993 Statistics Canada Violence Against Women Survey, 51% of women reported at least one incident of physical or sexual violence since the age of 16 (Johnson, 1996). The most recent Canadian survey, the General Social Survey (GSS), on intimate partner assault was conducted by Statistics Canada in 2014 (Burczycka, 2016). This survey used a modified CTS to measure psychological, physical, and sexual violence in intimate relationships. A large sample (33 127) of men and women aged 15 and older from all provinces were asked eleven questions about their experiences with various forms of intimate partner violence, ranging from threats to sexual assault, in the last 12 months and the past 5 years. In the year preceding the survey, about 1% of men and women experienced physical and/or sexual assault, which was down from 2% in the GSS report from 2009 (Brennan, 2011). About 4% of male and female respondents each reported having experienced physical and/or sexual assault between 2009 and 2014. Rates of intimate partner violence seem to be declining over the past decade with 4% of Canadians now reporting physical and/or sexual abuse in the past 5 years compared to 7% of Canadians reporting such abuse in 2004 and 6% in 2009. Violence was more common in previous partners than in current relationships, and rates of violence across age were similar except for lower rates in older couples (55 years and older). Canadians who identified as gay, lesbian, or bisexual were twice as likely to report violence and, particularly, lesbian or bisexual women were four times more likely to report violence as compared to heterosexual women. Table 13.2 presents the percentage of Canadians experiencing different types of violence in the five years between 2009 and 2014. The results indicate that both men and women experience violence, although women report experiencing more severe forms of violence (34% of women versus 16% of men report being beaten, choked, sexually assaulted, or threatened by a partner with a knife or gun). For every ten cases of intimate partner violence, three people reported being injured, with women more likely to get injured (40%) as compared to men (24%). Respondents were asked whether the violence was reported to police. Less than one in five cases of abuse were reported to the police (19%) and violence against women was more likely to be reported to the police compared to violence against men. The most common reason for reporting to the police was to stop the violence from happening again. The most common reason for not reporting to the police was the victim felt it was a personal

Table 13.2 Types of Relationship Violence (Percent) Experienced over the Past Five Years Between 2009 and 2014

Type of Violence	2009	2014
Threatened to hit, threw something	18.0	17.0
Pushed, grabbed, shoved, slapped	34.7	34.8
Kicked, bit, hit, hit with something	24.5	23.7
Sexually assaulted, beaten, choked, threatened with gun or knife	22.1	24.5

Source: "Family Violence in Canada: A Statistical Profile", © Minister of Industry, 2016. January 2016, Catalogue no. 85-002-X ISSN 1209-6393.

matter to try to resolve. The most recent GSS added a question about childhood experiences of physical and/or sexual abuse. Almost half (48%) of intimate violence victims also reported having experienced childhood physical and/or sexual abuse.

The first self-report survey of residents in Canada's territories was done in 2009 (Perreault & Mahoney, 2012). A sample of 1094 residents were asked about their experiences with intimate partner violence. In the 12 months prior to the survey, 4% reported experiencing violence, and 10% of men and women reported experiencing intimate partner violence in the past five years. Similar to the results from the provinces, younger residents and Aboriginal people had higher rates of intimate partner violence than older residents or non-Aboriginals. Injury rates were relatively high with 42% of victims reported being injured; police-reporting rates were also higher than in the provinces with 51% of victims having police contact. One possible explanation for the higher police contact is that there is a higher concentration of police per population in the territories as compared to the provinces.

Prevalence of Intimate Partner Violence in Aboriginal Populations   The GSS in Canada showed that Aboriginal respondents (9%) reported more than two times the amount of intimate partner violence compared to non-Aboriginal respondents (4%) over the past 5 years (Burczycka, 2016). Aboriginal women were particularly more likely to be victimized compared to non-Aboriginal women. Additional questions on the most recent GSS asked respondents about their childhood experiences with abuse. Aboriginal respondents reported more experiences with abuse as children and witnessing abuse perpetrated by an authority figure during childhood compared to non-Aboriginal respondents. Interestingly, Akers and Kaukinen (2009) found that Aboriginal women are more likely to contact the police in cases involving intimate partner violence compared to non-Aboriginal, non-minority women. Despite relying on law enforcement more, Aboriginal women seem to still have a higher incidence of intimate partner violence. Further research into the effectiveness of law enforcement in helping Aboriginal women stay free from intimate partner violence needs to be conducted.

The Prevalence of Dating Violence in University Students   The International Dating Violence Study (Chan, Strauss, Brownridge, Tiwari, & Leung, 2008) examined the prevalence of dating violence in 15 927 university students across 22 countries. The CTS2 scale was administered, asking students whether they had engaged in any physical and sexual violence with their dating partner and whether they had experienced any physical and sexual violence by their dating partners. Students responded to items about any assaults, including violence ranging from minor (e.g., having something that could hurt them thrown at them, being slapped, having their arm twisted) to serious (e.g., being choked, being beaten up, being threatened by a knife or a gun). Rates of perpetration and victimization of sexual coercion, from minor acts (e.g., was made to have sex without a condom, partner insisted on sex when they did not want to) to more severe acts (e.g., was forced to have oral or anal sex, had sex because of partner threats), were measured. Table 13.3 presents the perpetration and victimization results across male and female students in Canada. Female students were less likely to be perpetrators of serious assaults and sexual coercion as compared with

Table 13.3 Rates of Violence as Reported by Canadian University Students

Measure	Women (%)	Men (%)
Perpetration of any assault	23.6	25.1
Victim of any assault	19.5	28.3
Perpetration of serious assault	3.0	15.5
Victim of serious assault	3.7	15.3
Perpetration of sexual coercion	20.7	32.4
Victim of sexual coercion	28.6	27.9

Source: Chan, K.L., Strauss, M.R., Brownridge, D.A., Tiwari, A., & Leung, W.C. (2008). Prevalence of dating partner violence and suicidal ideation among male and female university students worldwide. *Journal of Midwifery & Women's Health*, 53, 529–537.

male students. The median rates across all the countries of having physically assaulted their partners was 29.8% for any assaults, 5.8% for serious assaults, and 21.5% for any sexual coercive acts. Canadian dating physical violence rates were in the lower half of countries surveyed; about one in five Canadian university students reported having experienced physical assault by their dating partner in the last 12 months. However, Canada had higher rates of sexual coercion as compared with many other countries. These findings suggest that dating violence is a real and substantial problem. Moreover, if university students are engaging in dating violence, this violence will likely continue in future intimate relationships. One variable that is strongly linked to dating violence in university students is substance use. Both alcohol use (e.g., frequent drinking, problem drinking, or heavy episodic drinking) and drug use increases the risk of perpetrating dating violence (Shorey, Stuart, & Cornelius, 2011).

THEORIES OF INTIMATE VIOLENCE

Some researchers believe that a patriarchal society contributes to men's relationship abuse of women (e.g., Dobash & Dobash, 1979; Ellis, 1989; Straus, 1977). The theory of patriarchy was first described in the 1970s and is often associated with sociology and feminism. **Patriarchy** refers to a broad set of cultural beliefs and values that support the male dominance of women. As stated by Dobash and Dobash (1979), "the seeds of wife beating lie in the subordination of females and in their subjection to male authority and control" (p. 33). To study the association between patriarchy and spousal abuse, Yllo and Straus (1990) compared the rates of spousal abuse across American states with the degree to which each state was characterized by patriarchal structure. States with male-dominant norms had much higher rates of spousal assault than those with more egalitarian norms. Although patriarchal perspectives likely contribute to the perpetuation of men's use of intimate partner violence against women, a more encompassing theory of partner abuse is required to explain why it exists in society at so many levels (e.g., male-initiated, female-initiated, same-sex) and is often maintained generation after generation.

Patriarchy: Broad set of cultural beliefs and values that support the male dominance of women

Social Learning Theory

Social learning theory, developed by Bandura (1973) to explain aggression generally, has been used by Dutton (1995) to explain intimate partner violence specifically. There are three main components to social learning theory: origins of aggression, instigators of aggression, and regulators of aggression. One way people acquire new behaviours is via **observational learning**. Bandura (1973) described three major sources for observational learning: family of origin, the subculture the person lives in, and televised violence. Studies of the family background of male batterers have found they are much more likely to have witnessed parental violence than nonviolent men (Kalmuss, 1984; Straus, Gelles, & Steinmetz, 1980). Not all behaviour that is observed, however, will be practised. Social learning theory posits that for a person to acquire a behaviour, it must have functional value for him or her. Behaviour that is rewarded increases in likelihood of occurrence, and behaviour that is punished decreases in likelihood of occurrence.

> **Observational learning:** Learning behaviours by watching others perform these behaviours

The next requirement is that even acquired behaviours are manifested only if an appropriate event in the environment acts as a stimulus for the behaviour. These events are called **instigators**. Dutton (1995) described two types of instigators in partner assault: aversive instigators and incentive instigators. Aversive instigators produce emotional arousal, and how a person labels that emotional arousal will influence how he or she responds. Studies with male batterers have found that they tend to label many different emotional states as anger (Gondolf [1985] labelled this the *male-emotional funnel system*). Incentive instigators are perceived rewards for engaging in aggression. When people believe they can satisfy their needs by using aggression, they may decide to be violent.

> **Instigators:** In social learning theory, these are events in the environment that act as a stimulus for acquired behaviours

Social learning theory assumes that behaviour is regulated by its consequences. Two types of **regulators** include external punishment and self-punishment. An example of external punishment would be if the person was arrested for engaging in violence. An example of self-punishment would be if the person felt remorse for engaging in violence. If the consequences outweigh the rewards for engaging in the behaviour and if alternatives are provided to cope with instigators, the likelihood of violence should diminish.

> **Regulators:** In social learning theory, these are consequences of behaviours

Another helpful way to conceptualize the interaction among factors related to violence within intimate relationships is in terms of the nested ecological model first proposed by Dutton (1995). This model focuses on the relationship among the multiple levels that influence intimate violence, including cultural beliefs and attitudes, social institutions and laws, relationship qualities, and psychological and biological factors unique to the individual. Dutton's model is useful because it recognizes the importance of various levels of explanation and acknowledges the significance of the interactions that can occur among levels. See Box 13.3 for more information on Dr. Donald Dutton.

Evolutionary Psychology Theory

Another theory that seeks to understand why intimate partner violence exists and in what specific contexts it is manifested is evolutionary psychology theory. **Evolutionary psychology** takes the evolutionary history of a species into account when trying

> **Evolutionary psychology:** The scientific study of psychology that takes the evolutionary history of a species into account when understanding a psychological trait and what led to its origination, development, and maintenance

Box 13.3

Canadian Researcher Profile: Dr. Donald Dutton

Courtesy of Don Dutton

The research of Dr. Donald Dutton is an amazing blend of basic and applied research. He has contributed greatly to the understanding of why men engage in intimate violence while showing how to apply this knowledge to real-world situations. Dr. Dutton completed his degrees at the University of Toronto, focusing on social psychology. Currently, he is a professor of psychology at the University of British Columbia, where he conducts research on intimate partner violence, spousal homicide, and other forms of extreme violence, such as genocide.

In a review of his more than 30 years of research on intimate violence, Dutton (2008) described how he became interested in the topic:

> I started by riding on police patrol and asking the police what part of their job they felt the least equipped to handle. The answer was "domestic disturbances." I developed a police training manual and was then asked to assist with police intervention. (p. 1)

Dr. Dutton recognized early on in his career that to protect victims from future violence, a treatment program was needed. He and his colleagues developed a court-mandated cognitive-behavioural treatment (CBT) program in the early 1980s. This program and subsequent CBT programs have been found to be the most effective type of treatment for reducing future spousal assaults.

In response to a question about what keeps him interested in research, Dr. Dutton replied, "Curiosity." He is intrigued with the question of why someone would kill someone they love or how "ordinary men" become cruel and sadistic in war situations. He uses a range of methodologies in his research, from laboratory studies to field studies, and more recently, to forensic ethology. Forensic ethology is a perspective that examines the details of real-world events to understand the motivation of individual perpetrators.

Dr. Dutton's favourite research topic is also the title of his book, *The Abusive Personality*, which was first published in 2003. In it, he describes abusive personalities as constellations of traits that lead people to become easily threatened and jealous, and to mask these feelings with anger and control behaviours. In the second edition of his book, published in 2007, Dr. Dutton extended the concept to explain women's use of violence in intimate relationships. He encourages students interested in intimate violence to become familiar with the considerable amount of research conducted on the psychology of intimate violence. He is frustrated by the focus of policymakers and treatment providers on attempting to explain intimate violence by male dominance and society's acceptance of violence. He believes that the causes of intimate violence are complex, that both men and women engage in this form of violence, and that a multifaceted treatment approach is needed.

Dr. Dutton was called to testify at one of the most high-profile criminal trials in U.S. history—the O.J. Simpson murder trial. His expertise in the areas of spousal violence and homicide was particularly relevant to the case.

Dr. Dutton enjoys teaching forensic psychology, social psychology, and a graduate course titled Nested Ecology of Violence. He recently published a book, *The Psychology of Genocide, Massacres, and Extreme Violence* (2007), which he dedicated to his dog. When asked why, Dr. Dutton stated, "Dogs are inherently nicer than humans"—a statement many dog-lovers would agree with.

to understand a specific psychological trait and involves a recognition of selective pressures facing ancestral humans that would have led to the traits' origination, development, and maintenance over time. For example, human history was likely rife with periods of famine. This presents a **selective pressure**—an environmental circumstance that provides an opportunity for new genes to develop that give a survival and/or reproductive advantage for those who have those genes. Ancestral humans that evolved a trait that enabled a strong preference for energy-rich foods such as sweet and fatty foods would have overcome the selective pressure of famine relatively more than those who did not because their diet would include more energy-rich foods. These people would have survived famines more on average, enabling them to have more surviving children that would carry that same trait into future generations. Therefore, psychological traits likely exist today because they carried some advantage in our ancestors.

Selective pressure: In evolutionary psychology, an environmental circumstance that presents an opportunity for new genes to develop that give a survival and/or reproductive advantage to the individual that has those genes

Buss and Duntley (2011) argue that some selective pressures facing humans in intimate partner relationships are (1) losing access to resources from the relationship (e.g., sexual access) and (2) events that threaten access to those resources (e.g., another person flirting with your partner). As a result of these selective pressures, the opportunity for strategies that fight to maintain access to relationship resources and from preventing events that threaten access to those resources may have developed over human evolutionary history. Intimate partner violence may be one of these strategies. For example, emotional abuse may be an evolved tactic that makes the partner think they cannot possibly be loved by anyone else, effectively discouraging the partner from leaving them in hopes of finding someone else. Physical abuse may be a more direct way of preventing a partner from leaving the relationship, and threats of physical violence may be a tactic to prevent the partner from flirting or showing sexual interest in other potential partners. The ultimate goal of using intimate partner violence from this perspective is to maintain exclusive access to the partner for sexual and social resources. Many other selective pressures exist in relationships as well (e.g., cooperation, trust, mutual care for children), so it would not be expected that all relationships should have intimate partner violence.

A benefit in taking an evolutionary perspective is in making precise predictions for what contexts might bring about intimate partner violence. Some contexts that may precipitate intimate partner violence are when there is sexual infidelity (perceived or actual), flirting outside the relationship, love triangles, when the perceived attractiveness or desirability of the two partners are not similar, and in families involving stepchildren. Finally, evolutionary psychology provides a grounded theory from which to understand other intimate partner relationship facts such as why stalking is so prevalent and why women tend to stay in abusive relationships.

WHY DO BATTERED WOMEN STAY?

One of the more perplexing questions is, "If a woman is in an abusive relationship, why doesn't she just leave?" Although intimate violence is no longer sanctioned by society, negative myths and stereotypes concerning battered women still prevail. These myths include that a battered woman has a masochistic desire to be beaten, that she is emotionally disturbed, that the violence cannot be as bad as she claims, and that the woman is partially to blame for her victimization (Ewing & Aubrey, 1987; Harrison & Esqueda, 1999; Walker, 1979).

The extent to which people believe such myths varies (Ewing & Aubrey, 1987; Greene, Raitz, & Lindblad, 1989). To examine myths about battered women, Ewing and Aubrey (1987) gave community samples a hypothetical scenario about a couple having ongoing marital problems, including a description of an incident in which the husband assaulted his wife (the husband accused his wife of cheating on him and then grabbed her and threw her to the floor). The percentage of males and females agreeing with each statement are shown in parentheses:

- The female victim "bears at least some responsibility." (Males = 47%; Females = 30%)
- The battered woman could simply leave her battering husband. (Males = 57%; Females = 71%)
- The battered woman who stays is "somewhat masochistic." (Males = 24%; Females = 50%)
- The woman can prevent battering by seeking counselling. (Males = 86%; Females = 81%)
- Battering is an isolated event. (Males = 40%; Females = 27%)
- The woman can rely on the police to protect her. (Males = 18%; Females = 15%)

Researchers have asked victims of intimate partner violence why they stay in abusive relationships, and for those who returned after separating, why they did so. The decision to stay with, to leave, or to return to an abusive partner is complex, especially because the violence experienced is often not constant. Walker (1979) proposed that there is a three-phase cycle of abuse that occurs. First, there is a tension-building phase occurring prior to the assault with increasing conflict and stress between partners. Second, there is the acting-out phase when the batterer engages in intimate partner violence. Third, there is the honeymoon phase, when the batterer apologizes and often promises not to engage in future violence. According to Walker, the cycle repeats itself with the honeymoon phase sometimes disappearing. Figure 13.1 illustrates the cycle of violence phases. Critiques of the cycle of abuse claim that not all abuse is as predictable as the cycle of abuse model suggests and that many abusers do not cycle through the different stages. Another reason why some women may remain in abusive relationships is learned helplessness (Walker, 1979). Learned helplessness was originally described by Seligman and colleagues (Abramson, Seligman, & Teasdale, 1978), who investigated the reaction of punished dogs to their environment. They found that dogs who could not avoid an electric shock essentially "gave up," a finding that has parallels with how humans deal with unavoidable aversive stimuli. Walker (1979) applied this theory of learned helplessness to abused women to help explain their passivity in response to repeated abuse and their lack of effort to leave the abusive situation. This theory has been critiqued because some women may be passive on purpose in order to placate their abusers. In addition, many women do make active attempts to leave their abusive partners.

According to the Violence Against Women Survey (Johnson, 1996), 42% of women left their abusive partners for a short while or permanently. The primary reasons given for leaving were related to experiencing an increase in the severity of

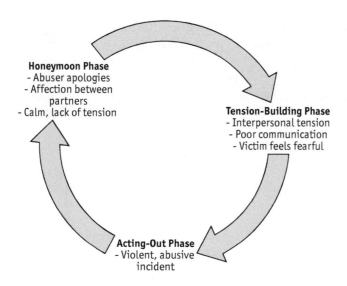

Figure 13.1 Lenore Walker's Cycle of Violence

Source: Based on Walker, 1979.

the violence (e.g., if they feared for their lives or were physically injured), having children witness the violence, and reporting the abuse to the police. However, 70% of women who left their abusive partners returned home at least once. The most common reasons for returning were

■ for the sake of the children (31%)

■ to give the relationship another chance (24%)

■ the partner promised to change (17%)

■ lack of money or a place to go (9%)

This study and others point to the environmental, social, and psychological barriers that exist for victims. For a woman to leave, environmental barriers need to be overcome, including access to money, a place to go, and support from the criminal justice system. In addition, many women return because they do not want their children to suffer (35%). Psychological barriers also exist. Some victims reported that they felt safer remaining in the relationship than leaving, because they knew what the abuser was doing (22%).

Kim and Gray (2008) examined which variables were associated with a woman's decision to stay or leave after being physically abused by her partner. A sample of 452 women was interviewed one week after being physically abused. The decision to leave was influenced by how much the women were financially dependent on the perpetrator and the level of fear (lower fear = more likely to leave), self-esteem (higher self-esteem = more likely to leave), and locus of control (more internal locus of control = more likely to leave). For those who do manage to leave and stay away, are there changes in the quality of life they experience? Alsaker, Moen, and Kristoffersen (2008) found that at a one-year follow-up after leaving an abusive relationship, women were significantly better in measures of vitality, mental health, and social domains

Box 13.4 Cases in Forensic Psychology

Battered Woman Syndrome: Should It Be Admissible in Court? *R. v. Lavallee* (1990)

Angélique Lyn Lavallee, age 22, was the common-law wife of Kevin Rust. They were together for about four years and their relationship was marked by frequent arguments and violence. Lyn Lavallee was physically abused by Kevin Rust and between 1983 and 1986 made several trips to the hospital for injuries she had received.

On the evening of August 30, 1986, the couple hosted a party. Lyn and Kevin were seen arguing at the party, and at one point Kevin chased Lyn outside the house and punched her. In the early hours of August 31, Lyn hid in the closet of the bedroom. Kevin came in, pulled her out of the closet, and hit her twice. He then gave her a gun and told her "wait till everybody leaves, you'll get it then" and "either you kill me or I'll get you." One shot was fired that went through the window screen. As he turned to leave, Lyn shot him. The bullet hit Kevin in the back of the head and he was killed instantly. Guests downstairs at the time said that they had heard sounds of yelling, pushing, and thumping from upstairs prior to the gunshots. A neighbour reported hearing sounds like someone was being beaten up between the two gunshots.

Once the police arrived Lyn admitted to shooting Kevin and stated, "I hope he lives. I really love him." Lyn was charged with second-degree murder. At her trial a psychiatrist, Dr. Shane, testified that Kevin had terrorized Lyn and had left her feeling vulnerable, worthless, and trapped in the relationship, unable to escape. Dr. Shane testified that Lyn felt her life was in danger and that the shooting was a desperate act to save herself. He reported that Lyn would lie to friends and doctors about how she had received her injuries. Dr. Shane also testified that Lyn described numerous times that she was beaten by Kevin, and that after the beating Kevin would beg for forgiveness, give her flowers, and temporarily be nice to her. Dr. Shane testified that this cycle described by Lyn conformed to the cycle of violence described by Dr. Lenore Walker. The jury acquitted Lyn, believing she had acted in self-defence. The Crown appealed to the Manitoba Court of Appeal, which ordered a new trial. The case was then appealed to the Supreme Court of Canada, where Madam Justice Bertha Wilson delivered the unanimous judgment. The Supreme Court disagreed with the Manitoba Court of Appeal and restored the acquittal, thereby recognizing battered wife syndrome as a defence to murder (currently the term used is *battered woman syndrome*).

In this case, Madam Justice Wilson felt that self-defence did apply and that the testimony of Dr. Shane helped the jury understand the effects of being battered. Madam Justice Wilson stated that "given the relational context in which the violence occurs, the mental state of an accused at the vital moment she pulls the trigger cannot be understood except in terms of the cumulative effect of months or years of brutality (which) … led to feelings of escalating terror on the part of the appellant." She stated that expert evidence was needed to explain to the jury "that it may in fact be possible for a battered spouse to accurately predict the onset of violence before the first blow is struck, even if the outsider to the relationship cannot." Madam Justice Wilson also felt that expert evidence could help to explain why a battered wife did not simply leave and how a repeatedly battered woman might experience learned helplessness.

The decision to acquit Lyn Lavalle does not give battered women a licence to kill their batterers. However, this case illustrates the importance of psychological research in understanding the behaviour of battered women.

Questions

1. Some clinicians caution that not all women who are battered develop battered woman syndrome and are concerned that a claim of self-defence might not be open to those who do not conform to this syndrome. Do you think evidence of battered woman syndrome should be admitted as expert evidence?

2. Do you think a claim of self-defence can be used if a battered woman kills her abuser while he is sleeping or if she attempts to hire a hit man?

3. Battered woman syndrome has been applied only to women. Do you think men can also develop a similar syndrome?

compared to when they first left the relationship. These women, however, still scored below average scores for the average woman. Future research should help clarify the long-term environmental and psychological factors involved with women wanting to and actually leaving abusive relationships.

Box 13.4 describes the first Canadian case in which battered woman syndrome was used to help explain why a battered woman might use lethal violence.

Recently, researchers have begun to study the link between family violence and animal maltreatment. One study found that 41% of men arrested for intimate partner violence have committed at least one act of animal abuse compared to only 1.5% of the men from the general population (Febres et al., 2014). Growing evidence suggests that one reason women delay leaving is out of concern for the welfare of their animals (Ascione, 1998; Faver & Strand, 2003; Flynn, 2000). Box 13.5 expands on this relationship. Although a link between maltreatment of animals and intimate violence may appear insignificant in relation to other factors, it underscores the complexity of the variables associated with remaining in a violent relationship.

Box 13.5   Forensic Psychology in the Spotlight

Woman's Best Friend: Pet Abuse and Intimate Violence

Only recently have researchers started to investigate the link between animal maltreatment and violence against women (Ascione, 1998; Ascione et al., 2007; Faver & Strand, 2003). In a study of women in intimate violence shelters, Ascione (1998) reported that 72% said their partners had either threatened to harm or actually had harmed their pets. Moreover, 54% reported that their pets had actually been injured or killed by their abusive partners. Compared with women who said they had not experienced intimate violence, Ascione et al. (2007) found that women in intimate violence shelters were 11 times more likely to indicate that their partners had hurt or killed their pets. Faver and Strand (2003) questioned 50 abused women who owned pets and found that 49% reported their partners had threatened their pets and 46% indicated that their partners had actually harmed their pets. Although there is a clear link between animal abuse and intimate partner violence, only 45% of intimate violence shelters in the United States ask victims about animal abuse (Krienert, Walsh, Matthews, & McConkey, 2012). Furthermore, when animal abuse is present and severe, women are often hesitant to bring their pets to a veterinarian for fear of having to explain the injuries (Tiplady, Walsh, & Phillips, 2012).

Flynn (2000) asked a series of questions about the women's experiences with their pets:

1. In dealing with the abuse, how important has your pet been as a source of emotional support?
2. Has your partner ever threatened to harm your pet, actually harmed your pet, or killed your pet?
3. Where is your pet now?
4. Did concern about your pet's safety keep you from seeking shelter sooner?

Flynn divided the sample of 42 battered women into a pet-abuse group (n = 20) and the no-pet-abuse group (n = 22). Ninety percent of the women in the pet-abuse group considered their pet a source of emotional support, compared with 47% of the no-pet-abuse group. About half of the pets in both groups were left with the abusive partner. In light of the partner's history of pet abuse, it is not surprising that 65% of the women in the pet-abuse group worried about the safety of their pets, whereas only 15% of the women in the no-pet-abuse group were concerned. Eight women actually delayed leaving their abusive partners out of concern for their pets' safety, with five of these women reporting that they delayed leaving for more than two months. Flynn concluded that "efforts to prevent and end such violence must not only recognize the interconnections, but grant legitimacy to all victims, human and animal" (p. 176).

A HETEROGENEOUS POPULATION: TYPOLOGIES OF MALE BATTERERS

An increasing body of empirical research demonstrates that not all batterers are alike. Categories of male batterers have been developed to help understand the causes of intimate violence. Holtzworth-Munroe and Stuart (1994) divided male batterers into three types based on severity of violence, generality of violence, and personality disorder characteristics: family-only, dysphoric/borderline, and generally violent/antisocial.

The **family-only batterer**

Family-only batterer: A male spousal batterer who is typically not violent outside the home, does not show much psychopathology, and does not possess negative attitudes supportive of violence

- of all types of batterers, engages in the least amount of violence
- typically is neither violent outside the home nor engages in other criminal behaviours
- does not show much psychopathology, and if a personality disorder is present, it would most likely be passive-dependent personality
- does not report negative attitudes supportive of violence and has moderate impulse-control problems
- typically displays no disturbance in attachment to his partner
- is the most common type, with 50% of batterers being this type

The **dysphoric/borderline batterer**

Dysphoric/borderline batterer: A male spousal batterer who exhibits some violence outside the family, is depressed, has borderline personality traits, and has problems with jealousy

- engages in moderate to severe violence
- exhibits some extra-familial violence and criminal behaviour
- of all types of batterers displays the most depression and borderline personality traits and has problems with jealousy
- has moderate problems with impulsivity and alcohol and drug use
- has an attachment style that would be best described as preoccupied
- makes up 25% of batterers

The **generally violent/antisocial batterer**

Generally violent/antisocial batterer: A male spousal batterer who is violent outside the home, engages in other criminal acts, has drug and alcohol problems, has impulse-control problems, and possesses violence-supportive beliefs

- engages in moderate to severe violence
- of all types of batterers, engages in the most violence outside of the home and in criminal behaviour
- has antisocial and narcissistic personality features
- likely has drug and alcohol problems
- has high levels of impulse-control problems and many violence-supportive beliefs
- shows a dismissive attachment style
- makes up 25% of batterers

Several studies have provided support for this typology both in offender and community samples of male batterers (Tweed & Dutton, 1998; Waltz, Babcock, Jacobson, & Gottman, 2000). See the You Be the Researcher box on page 392 for a profile of an intimate violence victim who knew her abuser.

Some research has looked at typologies for female batterers as well. Babcock, Miller, and Siard (2003) identified two groups of abusive female batterers based on the amount of violence they exhibited. The first group was the Partner-Only (PO) group, believed to use reactive violence primarily out of fear and self-defence. The second group was the Generally Violent (GV) group. GV women demonstrated more instrumental violence, reported more traumatic symptoms, and experienced more physical abuse from their mothers compared to PO women. The different characteristics and experiences of these female batterers suggest a different underlying tendency for intimate partner violence among women. Thus, types of intimate partner abusers seem to exist beyond heterosexual male batterers and future research may help clarify the characteristics of individuals who tend to batter (independent of gender) and those who tend to be victimized (independent of gender).

CRIMINAL JUSTICE RESPONSE

For centuries, wife battering was seen as a private family matter and police were reluctant to become involved (Dobash & Dobash, 1979). When called to a domestic violence scene, police would attempt to calm the people involved and, once order was restored, they would leave (Jaffe, Hastings, Reitzel, & Austin, 1993). Since the 1980s, however, mandatory charging policies have been in effect in Canada and in most jurisdictions in the United States. **Mandatory charging policies** give police the authority to lay charges against a suspect when there are reasonable and probable grounds to believe that an assault has occurred. Prior to mandatory charging, women were required to bring charges against their partners. Women were often hesitant to do this for fear of further violence; as a result, charges were usually not laid.

Mandatory charging policies: Policies that give police the authority to lay charges against a suspect where there are reasonable and probable grounds to believe a domestic assault has occurred

The first experimental study to examine the specific deterrence effect of arrest on spousal violence was conducted by Sherman and Berk (1984) in Minneapolis. This study involved the random assignment of 314 partner assault calls to three police responses: separation (order for suspect to leave premises for at least eight hours), mediation (provide advice to victim), or arrest. A six-month follow-up of the men was conducted by using both police reports and victim reports. The recidivism rates for the arrested men were much lower (13% and 19% from police reports and victim reports, respectively) than those of men in the separation (26% and 28%) or mediation (18% and 37%) groups. Attempts to replicate this finding have met with mixed results. Tolman and Weisz (1995) also found a deterrent effect for arrest, whereas Hirschell, Hutchinson, and Dean (1990) did not. In an attempt to replicate their findings, Sherman, Schmidt, and Rogan (1992) randomly assigned police calls of intimate partner violence to nonarrest or arrest. Using police and victim reports, lower rates of recidivism were reported in the short term (30 days after police contact) for both arrest and nonarrest groups. However, in the long-term follow-up (seven to nine months after police contact) the arrest group had slightly higher rates of recidivism than the nonarrest group. The authors found that arrest did not work for those offenders who were unemployed. In other words, arrest worked as a deterrent only for those men who had something to lose.

Do mandatory arrest policies increase the probability of partner abusers being arrested? Arrest rates for intimate partner violence have increased dramatically since

On March 11, 1982, Jane Hurshman-Corkum shot and killed her husband, Billy Stafford, when he had passed out after drinking all evening. Stafford was killed by a single shot to his head. For five years, Hurshman-Corkum had experienced regular beatings by her husband. Stafford had shot at her, held a knife to her throat, raped her, and forced her to engage in bizarre sexual acts. Stafford also directed his violence toward his son, Darren.

Stafford was known and feared in the Bangs Falls area of Nova Scotia by both community members and the RCMP. He had a violent temper, was unpredictable, and would physically attack others. He was often drunk and would regularly get into fights at bars.

Stafford's two previous partners left after being abused by him. Hurshman-Corkum described feeling totally trapped with nowhere and no one to turn to. Stafford had threatened to track her down and kill her, her sons, and her family if she ever tried to leave him.

On that fateful day, Stafford had said that he planned to set fire to his neighbour's trailer and to "deal" with Hurshman-Corkum's 16-year-old son, Allen, who was temporarily living with them. Hurshman-Corkum finally decided that she had had enough and killed Stafford.

Hurshman-Corkum was charged with first-degree murder. At her first trial, her lawyer argued that she had acted in self-defence. The jury agreed, and she was found not guilty. The courtroom applauded when the verdict was announced. The Crown appealed, and 15 months later, on the advice of her lawyer, Hurshman-Corkum pleaded guilty to the charge of manslaughter. She was sentenced to six months in jail and two years' probation.

After her release from jail, Hurshman-Corkum became a vocal advocate for battered women. She lobbied for the establishment of transition houses for battered women and became a symbol of hope and resistance in the fight against intimate partner violence.

Hurshman-Corkum never got over the trauma of the abuse. She was often depressed and was embarrassed by her kleptomania (an uncontrollable urge to steal that led to several shoplifting convictions). On February 22, 1992, she was found dead in her car in Halifax. The autopsy report ruled that Hurshman-Corkum died from a point-blank bullet wound to her chest that was consistent with suicide.

Your Turn ...

What type of male batterer was Stafford? Why do you think Hurshman-Corkum did not leave Stafford? What triggered her to commit homicide?

mandatory arrest policies were implemented (Simon, Ellwanger, & Haggerty, 2010). For example, in the 1970s and 1980s, arrest rates in Canada and the United States ranged from 7% to 15%, whereas more recent rates of 30% to 75% have been reported. However, one unanticipated outcome of these policies has been an increase in dual arrests (Hirschell & Buzawa, 2002). If the police are unable to determine the identity of the primary aggressor, and if there are minor injuries to both parties, then the police will charge both the man and the woman.

Another consequence of the increase in the number of arrests for partner assault has been the dramatic increase in the number of men who are court-mandated to attend treatment. Since most batterers are not motivated to attend treatment programs, having judges impose a treatment order forces men to obtain treatment. If the man fails to attend treatment, then the judge can impose a prison term. The use of court-mandated treatment is based on the belief that it is possible to treat male batterers. However, the effectiveness of treatment for batterers is still very much in question.

Does Treatment of Male Batterers Work?

A number of procedures have been developed to treat male batterers. The two most common forms of intervention are feminist psychoeducational group therapy (also referred to as the Duluth model, since the treatment was designed at the Duluth Domestic Abuse Intervention Project in Minnesota) and cognitive-behavioural group therapy. According to the Duluth model (Pence & Paymar, 1993), the primary cause of intimate partner violence is patriarchal ideology. Group therapy in this model focuses on challenging the man's perceived right to control his partner. The atmosphere in treatment often has a blaming, punitive orientation, which can result in very high drop-out rate (up to 75%).

The Duluth model has been criticized on several grounds. First, the entire focus is on violence done by men to women. This restricted gendered approach limits its usefulness for dealing with women's use of violence (which is common) against men, and women-to-women and men-to-men violence within same-sex relationships. Second, violence is viewed as one-sided and not as an interaction between people. Much

Couples therapy for domestic violence couples
Wavebreakmedia/Shutterstock

of violence in relationships is mutual. For the treatment to be effective, it cannot be only the man in these relationships who needs to change. Third, the focus of the Duluth model is on shaming the man and therapists fail to establish a therapeutic bond with their clients. Finally, there is a limited focus on changing the man's attitudes about power and control in relationships. The cause of intimate partner violence is multi-determined, and focusing solely on power and control is not sufficient to effect change. In a review of the effectiveness of the Duluth model, Dutton and Corvo (2006) concluded this model has "negligible success in reducing or eliminating violence among perpetrators" (p. 462).

The other, more common, treatment program is cognitive-behavioural therapy (CBT), which subscribes to the beliefs that violence is a learned behaviour and that use of violence is reinforcing for the offender because he or she obtains victim compliance and reduces feelings of tension (Sonkin, Martin, & Walker, 1985). CBT focuses on the costs of engaging in violence. Alternatives to violence such as anger-management and communication-skills training, are taught. Some CBT programs also address perpetrators' attitudes about control and dominance. The rationale for using group therapy is to help to break through the barriers of denial and minimization. The Correctional Service of Canada has developed a family violence program that is described in more detail in Box 13.6.

Box 13.6   Forensic Psychology in the Spotlight

The Correctional Service of Canada's Family Violence Prevention Programs

The Correctional Service of Canada's (CSC) National Family Violence Prevention Programs are primarily focused on male offenders who have been abusive in their intimate relationships with female partners or ex-partners. These programs include a moderate-intensity program for offenders with less extensive histories of partner abuse, a high-intensity program for higher-risk offenders, a high-intensity program for higher-risk Aboriginal offenders, a maintenance program for offenders who have completed the programs, and a treatment primer designed to enhance motivation of potential participants.

Philosophy
The programs are based on a social learning model that conceptualizes violence against women as a learned pattern of behaviour that can be modified. These programs teach offenders to understand the dynamics of their abusive relationships by using cognitive-behavioural techniques. These techniques allow them to identify their abusive behaviours and replace them with alternative skills

and behaviours that help them form positive nonabusive relationships.

The High Intensity Family Violence Prevention Program (HIFVPP, established in 2001) provides intervention to federal offenders who are assessed as high risk to be violent in their intimate relationships. This program is offered only in institutions. It consists of about seventy-five 2.5-hour group sessions, delivered over a period of about 15 weeks. There are also eight to ten individual counselling sessions scheduled with each participant's primary counsellor. The program is delivered by a team made up of a psychologist and a qualified program officer.

The Moderate Intensity Family Violence Prevention Program (MIFVPP, established in 2001) is intended to help offenders who are at a moderate risk to engage in future violence in their intimate relationships. This program is offered in the community and institutions. It consists of twenty-four 2.5-hour group sessions, delivered over a period of between 5 and 13 weeks. There are also three

(continued)

individual counselling sessions. The program is delivered by two training program facilitators.

The Aboriginal High Intensity Family Violence Prevention Program is similar to the HIFVPP, but the process and method of delivery reflect the teachings, traditions, and cultural values of Aboriginal people. The program was approved by Aboriginal Elders, and Elders are involved in the delivery of the program; they provide counselling and conduct ceremonies. This program was established in 2004.

To promote change, the programs focus on a number of treatment targets including motivation to change, education on intimate partner violence, attitudes, managing emotions, building relationship skills, and relapse prevention and coping strategies.

Effectiveness

Stewart, Gabora, Kropp, and Lee (2005) conducted a preliminary evaluation of the high and moderate family violence prevention programs. A sample of 572 male offenders were assessed prior to and after completing the program. Moderate to strong treatment effects were found: offenders who completed treatment showed lower levels of jealousy, fewer negative attitudes about relationships, better recognition of relapse prevention skills, and more respect and empathy for their partners. Feedback from parole officers who supervised program completers reported positive attitudes and behaviours while under supervision. Participants also reported that they felt the program was useful and they were able to use the skills they learned. A six-month follow-up study was conducted comparing 160 offenders who completed the treatment program (high and moderate intensity program) and 86 offenders who dropped out of treatment or who did not participate in the treatment. Figure 13.2 presents the six-month recidivism for another arrest for spousal assault, any violent offence, or any infractions across treated and untreated groups. Treated offenders were less likely to engage in spousal assault or violent reoffending as compared with the untreated group. There was no group difference in rates of any infractions. Whether these treatment gains will continue after a longer period needs to be determined. In addition, recidivism was based on official statistics and not on self-reports from the offender or the offender's intimate partner. However, the preliminary results are promising, suggesting that the treatment programs are targeting the criminogenic needs of male batterers. One important issue to target is motivation for treatment. In a recent evaluation of the MIFVPP, Conners, Mills, and Gray (2012) found that incarcerated male batterers who were more motivated learned the skills faster and were more engaged with treatment than less motivated offenders.

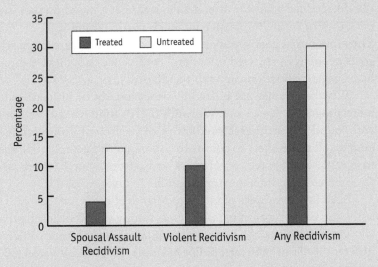

Figure 13.2 Recidivism Rates for Treated and Untreated Groups

Source: http://sgdatabase.unwomen.org/uploads/Canada%20-%20Treatment%20Outcome%20for%20Canadian%20Federally%20Sentenced%20Offenders%202005.pdf. Reprinted by permission of Lynn Stewart.

Babcock, Green, and Robie (2004) conducted a meta-analysis of 22 studies to evaluate the efficacy of treatment for male batterers. Studies were included only if the outcome was measured by either police reports or partner reports of violence (i.e., studies using only batterer self-report were not included). Studies were also divided into three types of treatment: the Duluth model, CBT, and other (e.g., couples therapy). There were no differences in efficacy among the three treatment types in terms of recidivism rates. Based on partner reports, the effect size for quasi-experimental studies was $d = 0.34$, and for experimental studies, it was $d = 0.09$. The authors concluded that "regardless of reporting method, study design, and type of treatment, the effect on recidivism rates remains in the small range" (p. 1044). Based on experimental studies and the use of partner reports, these results mean there is a 5% increase in success rate because of treatment. Although a small effect statistically, the 5% decrease in violence because of treatment has undoubtedly been meaningful for those who no longer face partner abuse.

Recent research, however, is more optimistic about the promise of intimate partner violence treatment. Bennett, Stoops, Call, and Flett (2007) found that even when controlling for differences in the history of violence, personality, demographic variables, and motivation, men who completed treatment were less than half as likely to be re-arrested for intimate partner violence than those who did not finish the intervention program. Bowen and Gilchrist (2006) identified participant characteristics that predict program attrition, including youthful age, having served a previous prison sentence, and self-reporting a low level of partner violence. The researchers recommended using these static factors to tailor intimate partner violence treatment and prevent program attrition so that participants can benefit from treatment. In another study, Lee, Uken, and Sebold (2007) recommended the inclusion of more self-determined goals for offenders in treatment, based on their study of 88 male perpetrators of intimate partner violence participating in court-mandated treatment. They found that goal specificity and the facilitator's agreement with the participant's goals positively predicted offenders' confidence to achieve their goals, which in turn had a negative relationship with recidivism.

Which variables are related to dropping out of intimate partner violence treatment programs? Jewell and Wormith (2010) conducted a meta-analysis of 30 studies and found the strongest predictors of treatment completion were employment (employed more likely to complete compared to unemployed), age (older more likely to complete compared to younger), and referral source (court-mandated more likely to complete than non-court-mandated).

Specific subsamples of intimate partner abusers may respond to treatment differently, including types of batterers (e.g., family-only, borderline/dysphoric, and generally violent/antisocial), batterers with substance-abuse problems, and batterers at different levels of motivation. For example, Huss and Ralston (2008) found that family-only batterers attended more treatment sessions that the other types. Generally, violent/antisocial batterers were the most likely to drop out of treatment, reoffend sooner, and reoffend more often compared to the other types. Saunders (2001) asserted, "The best intervention outcomes for men who batter may be obtained when the type of offender is matched to the type of treatment" (p. 237). Failure to match a batterer to treatment services may lead to a batterer completing a program that does not meet his or her specific treatment needs. Cavanaugh and Gelles (2005) pointed out that a victim could thus be led to have a "false sense of security, with the belief that she is now safer when, in fact, she is not" (p. 162). According to Gondolf and Fisher (1988), the variable most predictive of whether a woman will return to a violent partner after a shelter stay is if the batterer has sought treatment.

Future research should examine the treatment of violent women and mutually violent relationships as well. A preliminary study by Wray, Hoyt, and Gerstle (2013) found that intimate partner violence and 1-year follow-up conviction rates were the lowest for couples when both partners attended the treatment sessions compared to when one or neither partner did. In addition, subjective ratings about the treatment program were mostly positive suggesting that participants may find joint treatment enjoyable and useful. Recognizing the complex nature of relationships and involving both partners in treatment may be an optimistic step forward in overcoming repeat instances of intimate partner violence.

STALKING: DEFINITION, PREVALENCE, AND TYPOLOGIES

Interest in stalking has increased dramatically over the past decade. Often, it has been the cases of celebrity stalking that have caught the attention of the media. However, celebrities aren't the only people who get stalked. Stalking can occur when an abusive relationship ends. Stalking is a form of violence that is known in Canadian criminal law as criminal harassment. According to section 264 of the Criminal Code of Canada, **criminal harassment** can involve repeatedly following, communicating with, watching, and/or threatening a person either directly or through someone a person knows. The person being stalked must fear for his or her own safety or the safety of someone they know for the police to charge someone.

Criminal harassment: Crime that involves repeatedly following, communicating with, watching, or threatening a person directly or indirectly

The prevalence of stalking can be measured via official statistics or by victimization studies. In 2008, there were 18 347 charges of criminal harassment in Canada. The largest victimization study to be done in Canada was conducted by Statistics Canada in 2014 (Ibrahim, 2016). As part of the GSS, a sample of 33 127 men and women were asked, "In the past five years, have you been the subject of repeated and unwanted attention that caused you to fear for your safety or the safety of someone known to you?" Participants were asked about receiving repeated unwanted phone calls; being followed; having someone wait outside their home, school, or workplace; and receiving unwanted gifts or letters. Women were more likely to be victims of stalking than men. As compared with men (4%), more than twice the amount of women (7%) reported being stalked over the past five years in a way that caused them to fear for their safety. Women between the ages of 15 and 24 have the highest rates of being stalked (AuCoin, 2005). Prevalence of stalking is more common in university students than the general public. Studies measuring stalking in students have found rates of between 9% and 30% for university females and between 11% and 17% for university males (Bjerregaard, 2002; Fremouw, Westrup, & Pennypacker, 1997). The prevalence rates vary depending on the definition of stalking used and the time period (e.g., last 12 months versus ever).

Most stalking victims know their stalkers. In a meta-analysis of 175 studies of stalking, Spitzberg and Cupach (2007) reported that 79% of stalking victims knew their stalkers. The most common type of relationship was romantic (49%)—that is, the stalking occurred after a romantic relationship between the stalker and the stalking victim had ended. In a Canadian national survey examining cases of criminal harassment reported to the police, most of the victims were female (76%; Milligan, 2011). This survey also found that women are more likely to be criminally harassed by former partners and men more likely to be harassed by acquaintances. Some researchers have suggested that more males are actually stalked by ex-intimates than some surveys indicate (Kropp, Hart, & Lyon, 2002). However, these men do not report that they have been stalked since the behaviour does not cause them to fear for their safety.

If you are a victim of criminal harassment, one of the most important questions to ask is, "What is the likelihood of being a victim of a violent act?" A meta-analysis has attempted to differentiate stalkers who represent a significant risk of violence from those who pose less of a risk (Rosenfeld, 2004). Rosenfeld analyzed 10 studies that included 1055 stalking offenders. Violence occurred in 38.6% of the cases. The following variables were significantly related to violence:

- *Clinical variables.* Substance-abuse disorder, personality disorder, and the absence of a psychotic disorder predicted violence.
- *Case-related variables.* A former intimate relationship between offender and victim and threats toward the victim predicted violence.

Stalking offenders who are at the greatest risk for continuing stalking behaviour after release from prison are those who have both a personality disorder and a history of substance abuse (Rosenfeld, 2004).

Imagine being in constant fear of what might happen to you. Stalking victims suffer intense stress, anxiety, sleep problems, and depression, as well as disruptions in social functioning and work. Overall, victims of stalking experience a decrease in the quality of their lives (Davis & Frieze, 2000; Fisher, Cullen, & Turner, 2002; Spitzberg & Cupach, 2007). McFarlane, Campbell, and Watson (2002) examined the prevalence and type of stalking behaviours 12 months prior to an attempted or actual murder or assault by an ex-partner. This study consisted of 821 women, 174 who had survived an attempt on their lives by their intimate partners (attempted femicides), 263 who had been killed by their intimate partners (actual femicides), and 384 who had been physically abused or threatened with physical harm but no attempt on their lives had been made (controls). Stalking was more common in the attempted/actual femicide group (68%) than in the controls (51%). Women who were spied on or followed were twice as likely to become attempted or actual homicide victims. In addition, in cases involving threats of harm to children, if the woman did not go back to having a relationship with the stalker, the likelihood of attempted or actual homicide increased by nine times. This study suggests that certain types of stalking behaviours are associated with increased risk of lethal violence, and stalking victims and police need to be aware of these risk factors.

Stalking victims often change their behaviours to try to protect themselves. Victims most often avoided certain places or people, followed by getting an unlisted phone number or call display, and about a third of the victims would not leave their homes alone (AuCoin, 2005). Only 37% of the stalking victims contacted the police, and charges were laid against the stalker in 23% of the cases (the most common charge was criminal harassment). In 11% of cases, victims received restraining orders in an attempt to stop their stalkers from contacting them. Of those victims who secured a restraining order against their stalkers, just under half (49%) of these orders were violated—that is, the stalker contacted the victim.

Categories of stalkers have been developed to help to understand the causes of stalking. Several different typologies of stalkers have been proposed. Kropp, Hart, and Lyon (2002) formulated a typology that classifies stalkers into four categories based on their relationships with their victims.

The **ex-intimate stalker**

- is the most common type
- engages in stalking after an intimate relationship breaks up
- is an individual who is disgruntled or estranged, and unable to let go of his or her partner
- has a history of domestic violence in intimate relationships

Ex-intimate stalker: A stalker who engages in stalking after an intimate relationship breaks up

The **love-obsessional stalker**

- is a rare type
- is an individual who has never had an intimate relationship with the victim but has been an acquaintance or co-worker
- has intense emotional feelings for the victim
- does not have symptoms of depression or psychosis

Love-obsessional stalker: A stalker who has intense emotional feelings for the victim but who has never had an intimate relationship with the victim

The **delusional stalker**

- is a rare type
- is an individual who has never had any relationship with the victim but believes that a relationship exists
- sometimes targets a celebrity, media figure, or politician
- is often diagnosed with delusional disorders, schizophrenia, or bipolar disorder

Delusional stalker: A stalker who suffers from delusions and wrongly believes he or she has a relationship with the victim

The **grudge stalker**

- is a rare type
- is an individual who knows the victim but has not had an intimate relationship with the victim
- is an angry individual seeking revenge for a perceived injustice

Grudge stalker: A stalker who knows and is angry at the victim for some perceived injustice

Because of their high profile, politicians are more vulnerable to being stalked than the general population. In a recent survey of 424 Canadian federal and provincial politicians, Adams, Hazelwood, Pitre, Bedard, and Landry (2009) reported that 30% of participants had experienced harassment. The most common communication was telephone calls or emails, the most common theme was threats, and a small portion (about 8%) were declarations of love. Of those politicians harassed, 60% were

Dangerous Fixations: Celebrity Stalkers

Although most stalking takes place in the context of ex-partners or prior acquaintances, it is the stalking of celebrities that catches the attention of the media. The stalking of celebrities prompted several countries to introduce criminal code offences. In 1990, California was the first state to introduce anti-stalking laws in the aftermath of the Rebecca Schaeffer murder. In 1993, Canada introduced the new offence of criminal harassment. Three high-profile cases of celebrity stalkers are described below.

Rebecca Schaeffer

Born in 1967, Rebecca Schaeffer was the only child of a clinical psychologist and a writer. She lived in Los Angeles and starred in the TV series *My Sister Sam*. In 1986, John Bardo (born in 1970), who was working as a fast-food cook living in Tuscon, Arizona, developed an obsession with Schaeffer and started sending her letters. She responded to these fan letters and sent him a response signed "with love Rebecca." In 1987, he travelled to Burbank Studios with a teddy bear and a bouquet of roses and demanded to see Schaeffer. The security guards refused to allow him entrance. Bardo sent hundreds of letters to Schaeffer and his bedroom was decorated with dozens of photos of her. At the age of 21, Bardo saw Schaeffer in the movie *Scenes from the Class Struggle in Beverly Hills* in which Schaeffer was shown in a sex scene with a male actor. Bardo was extremely upset and asked his older brother to buy him a gun. Bardo sent his older sister a letter, which stated that if he could not have Rebecca no one could. In July 1989, he travelled to Hollywood and hired a private investigator to find out where Schaeffer lived. On the morning of July 18, 1989, he rang her doorbell. When she answered the door, he told her he was her biggest fan. She asked him to leave. He returned an hour later and shot her twice, killing her. Bardo was convicted of capital murder and was sentenced to life without eligibility of parole. He is currently serving his sentence at a maximum-security prison in California. On July 27, 2007, Bardo was stabbed 11 times by another inmate but survived.

David Letterman

Margaret Ray (born 1958) developed an obsession with David Letterman in the mid-1980s after the breakup of her marriage. Ray was diagnosed with schizophrenia. She was first arrested in 1988 when she stole Letterman's Porsche and was caught driving it with her 3-year-old son in the stolen car. She told the police that she was Letterman's wife and the child was Letterman's son. Over the next few years, Ray repeatedly showed up at Letterman's house, leaving letters, books, and cookies. She was charged with trespassing eight times. In the early 1990s, she served a ten-month prison sentence for harassing Letterman. After her release, she shifted her obsession to astronaut Story Musgrave. In 1998, Ray committed suicide by kneeling in front of a train. Both Letterman and Musgrave expressed sympathy upon her death.

Jodie Foster

In 1976, John Hinckley (born 1955) watched the movie *Taxi* in which Jodie Foster played a child prostitute. Hinckley became obsessed with Foster. When Foster went to Yale University, Hinckley followed her there, called her, and left messages and poems in her mailbox. These attempts failed to get Foster to notice him. Hinckley then planned to get her attention by assassinating the president of United States. He spent a couple of months trailing President Jimmy Carter but was stopped at the Nashville airport for carrying handguns in his luggage. He was fined and released. On March 30, 1981, he fired six shots at President Ronald Reagan, injuring him and three others. Just prior to the shooting, he sent a letter to Foster stating,

> As you well know by now I love you very much. Over the past seven months I've left you dozens of poems, letters and love messages in the faint hope that you could develop an interest in me. Although we talked on the phone a couple of times I never had the nerve to simply approach you and introduce myself. . . . The reason I'm going ahead with this attempt now is because I cannot wait any longer to impress you.

Hinckley was found not guilty by reason of insanity and was sent to a secure forensic psychiatric hospital. In 1999, he was allowed supervised visits to his parents' house. However, in 2004, these visits were halted because he smuggled materials about Foster back into the hospital. In 2009, he was allowed to visit his mother for nine days at a time.

Sources: Based on Bruni, 1998; "The Hinckley Trial," n.d.; "John W. Hinckley Jr.," n.d.; "Killer of Actress," 2007; Wilkins, 2003.

personally approached, with 24% having some form of physical contact with their stalker and 6% being physically assaulted. Another group that has higher rates of being stalked are doctors. In a recent study of 1190 Canadian physicians, Abrams and Robinson (2011) found that 14.9% reported having been stalked by their patients. Psychiatrists had the highest prevalence of being stalked (26%). Both male and female patients engaged in stalking, but their motives differed. Male patients stalked as a result of delusional ideas and being upset over treatment outcomes, whereas female patients stalked because of delusional ideas and being in love with their physician. Another group that experiences stalking more often than the general public is university faculty members. In a nationwide survey of 4811 faculty members in United States, Morgan and Kavanaugh (2011) found that 25.4% had experienced stalking, with English, psychology, and nursing faculty members being the most frequent victims. The most common stalking behaviour was unwanted calls or emails, waiting outside a faculty member's office, and inappropriate class behaviour. Student stalkers were classified into three groups based on perceived motivations. Most faculty believed the student stalker had a psychological disorder (46%). The next most common reported motive was that the student was attracted to them and wanted a romantic relationship (36%). The last group consisted of students who were dissatisfied by a grade or mark they received or by something the faculty member said in class (14%). Given the prevalence of stalking behaviour at university, faculty members need to be provided with guidance on how to prevent stalking from occurring, and if stalking does occur, how to respond. See the In the Media box for a description of some high-profile celebrity stalking cases.

Although stalking may be viewed as entertaining when we see it happening to celebrities, the reality is that it happens to many people and may present serious and real dangers for those involved. Further research examining this interesting phenomenon, its causes, and the factors that predict its occurrence, will help us understand these behaviours and promote implementation of strategies for managing its influence on people's lives.

SUMMARY

1. The prevalence rates of intimate partner violence are difficult to estimate accurately since the violence often occurs in private. Intimate partner violence can be classified into the following types: physical abuse, sexual abuse, financial abuse, and emotional abuse.

2. Abused women remain in, or return to, abusive relationships for a number of reasons. Environmental, socialization, and psychological barriers exist that make it difficult for abused women to leave these relationships.

3. Social learning theory has been used to explain intimate partner violence. There are three main components to social learning theory: origins of aggression, instigators of aggression, and regulators of aggression. One way people acquire new

behaviours is via observational learning. Instigators are events in the environment that act as stimuli for the behaviour, and behaviour is regulated by the prospect of its consequences. Behaviours that are rewarded increase in frequency, and behaviours that are punished decrease in frequency.

4. Holtzworth-Munroe and Stuart (1994) divided male batterers into three types based on severity of violence, generality of violence, and personality disorder characteristics: family only, dysphoric/borderline, and generally violent/antisocial.

5. Treatment for intimate partner violent offenders involves modifying attitudes that condone violence, enhancing conflict-resolution skills, learning to manage emotions, and developing relapse-prevention plans. The effectiveness of treatment programs for male batterers varies, with some cognitive-behavioural treatment programs showing promising results.

6. Research on stalking has found (a) most stalkers know their victims; (b) males are more likely to be stalkers and females are more likely to be victims; (c) spying, following, and making threats of violence are related to an increased risk for lethal violence; and (d) the most common type of stalker is the ex-intimate stalker.

Discussion Questions

1. What are the barriers to some battered women leaving an abusive relationship? What could be done at both an individual and a societal level to help battered men and women?

2. Compare and contrast social learning theory and evolutionary psychology theory in how they explain intimate partner violence. What kind of evidence about intimate partner violence would support or dispute each theory? Design a research study that would test each theory.

Chapter 14
Sexual Offenders

Learning Objectives

- Describe the prevalence of sexual offences.

- Outline the effects of sexual assault on victims.

- List the different typologies of rapists and child molesters.

- Describe the unique characteristics of adolescent, female, and Aboriginal sexual offenders.

- Outline treatment targets for sexual offenders.

- Describe the effectiveness of treatment for sexual offenders.

Trevor Cook was 26 years old when the police finally caught up with him. For years, he had terrorized women in the city where he lived. Throughout his teenage years, Trevor was known as a womanizer and a con man who was always trying to make a quick buck. The first of Trevor's crimes could be traced back to when he was 16 years old. He had just started dating a 17-year-old girl and they were sexually active. One night, his girlfriend wasn't feeling well and denied his sexual advances. Upset at being rejected, Trevor pushed her onto the bed and held her down and raped her. Similar incidents occurred with several other girlfriends, and Trevor's behaviour toward women quickly became more parasitic and aggressive. He regularly stole money from his girlfriends, and in addition to frequently cheating on them, he was emotionally and verbally abusive.

By the time he was in his early 20s, Trevor's behaviour had escalated to the point where he was committing sexual assaults against women he met at bars. He would spot a young woman he thought was attractive and follow her home. The first few times Trevor attacked a woman, he put on a ski mask, fondled the woman, and ran away. However, that didn't satisfy him for long and, when he was 23 years old, Trevor raped and beat one of the women he followed home in a back alley outside of her house. He would commit several more rapes that year, with each rape being more vicious than the previous one. Trevor's crimes ended when one of his victims finally got away before he could attack her. This woman had ripped Trevor's ski mask off and gotten a good look at his face. The description she gave to the police ultimately led to his arrest. The police had been searching for Trevor for more than five years. By the time he was arrested at the age of 26, the police had identified 12 women that had been raped by Trevor. It is possible that Trevor victimized more women, but these individuals have yet to approach the police.

Violence of the sort displayed by Trevor in the opening vignette has a major impact on victims and society. For example, the victims of such crimes can be scarred for life and the family members of these victims sometimes fare no better. Some victims may even be so upset that they avoid reporting their experiences to the police. In addition, the media often focuses on sexual crimes and, as a consequence, sexual violence is on the minds of the Canadian public. How common is sexual violence? Are there common features of different types of sexual offenders? Are there unique characteristics among female, adolescent, and Aboriginal sexual offenders? What are the major approaches to treating sexual offenders and how effective are they?

Sexual violence and its aftermath is also a major focus of forensic psychology. For example, many forensic psychologists are involved in developing theories to explain why people become sexual offenders. They conduct research to understand the nature of sexual violence and develop procedures to assess and programs to rehabilitate sexual offenders. This chapter discusses the prevalence sexual violence, its causes, and interventions.

NATURE AND EXTENT OF SEXUAL VIOLENCE

Sexual violence is on par with homicide in terms of how perpetrators are vilified by society. In 2014, just over 20 735 sexual assaults against adults were reported to the police in Canada (Boyce, 2015). The rate per 100 000 population was 58, a 3% decrease from the rate per 100 000 in 2013 (Boyce, 2015). Sexual assaults in which the victim was unable to provide consent to sexual activity as a result of drugs, intoxication, or having been manipulated or forced in ways other than physically accounted for 9% of the sexual assaults reported by Canadians in 2014 (Perreault, 2015). Of the remaining percentage of sexual assaults reported, sexual touching accounted for 71% and forced sexual activity accounted for 20%. During the same year, there were 4452 sexual assaults against children (Boyce, 2015). The rate per 100 000 population was 13, a 6% increase from the rate per 100 000 in 2013 (Boyce, 2015). The rate of sexual assaults among the Aboriginal population was more than double that of non-Aboriginals, where the rate per 1000 population was 115 among Aboriginals and 35 among non-Aboriginals (Perreault, 2015). In 56% of incidences involving sexual assault, the victim previously knew their attacker (Perreault, 2015). It is important to note that official statistics do not provide an accurate measure of the true incidence of this type of crime, since the majority of victims do not report the crime to the police. For example, a study using data from the General Social Survey found that in 2014, 95% of adult sexual assault victims did not report the assault to the police (Perreault, 2015). Adult victims do not report sexual offences for the following reasons: victims often don't feel that the matter is important enough, they fear revenge by the offender, they believe the police would not be able to find the offender, they do not want to get the offender in trouble, they fear they would bring shame or dishonor to their family, they feel the matter is too personal and do not want others to know, or they simply do not want to involve the police and deal with the hassle of the court process (Perreault, 2015). Child victims often do not report being sexually abused for the following reasons: they are fearful about what will happen to them or to their parents, they don't think they will be believed, they believe they are in some way to blame for the abuse, or they were not aware that was happening was unacceptable (Alaggia, 2005; Schaeffer, Levanthal, & Asnes, 2011).

Sexual assault affects a large percentage of the population. High victimization rates are reported among children and youth (roughly 1 in 20 in the United States; Finkelhor, Turner, Shattuck, & Hamby, 2013) and adult women (roughly 1 in 5 women will experience rape or attempted rape in their lifetime; MacDonald, 2000). In a review of community samples, Gorey and Leslie (1997) calculated the prevalence of childhood sexual abuse as 17% for females and 8% for males. One type of victimization experience that has been ignored by many researchers is male rape by female perpetrators (Fisher & Pina, 2013). In a study of university students, Larimer, Lydum, Anderson, and Turner (1999) found that 20.7% of men and 27.5% of women reported being the recipient of unwanted sexual contact (i.e., being pressured, given drugs or alcohol, or physically forced).

Given the large number of victims, it is not surprising that sexual offenders admit to having many victims. For example, Abel, Becker, Mittelman, and Cunningham-Rathner (1987) investigated the number of victims reported by 127 rapists, 224 female-victim child molesters, and 153 male-victim child molesters. High victim rates were reported, with rapists having on average 7 victims, female-victim child molesters having 20 victims, and male-victim child molesters averaging 150 victims. Sexual offenders also appear to under-report the number of individuals they have victimized. Although adult sexual offenders report an average of two victims at the time of their arrest, they have been found to report an average of 184 victims once incarcerated and placed in treatment (Ahlmeyer, Heil, McKee, & English, 2000). Child molesters tend to report having an average of 88 victims once in treatment (Underwood, Patch, Cappelletty, & Wolfe, 1999). Similarly, rapists have been found to report six times as many victims as had been recorded in official records when guaranteed that their responses would be kept anonymous (Weinrott & Saylor, 1991). In studies of community samples (e.g., university students) in which the respondent was assured there would be no negative consequences of reporting, 10% to 20% of men admitted to sexually assaulting women or children (Hanson & Scott, 1995; Lisak & Roth, 1988).

DEFINITION OF SEXUAL ASSAULT

In Canada, the definition of sexual assault has undergone substantial change over the past three decades. Prior to 1983, a number of different offences were lumped together under the label of *rape*. According to the Criminal Code of Canada at that time, "a male person commits rape when he has sexual intercourse with a female person who is not his wife . . . without her consent" (section 143). In response to criticism, and to make the definition more inclusive of diverse sexual relationships and more representative of the nature of sexual assault, rape was reclassified. *Sexual assault* became defined as any nonconsensual sexual act by either a male or female person to either a male or female person, regardless of the relationship between the people involved. Sexual assault, like physical assault, was divided into three levels based on severity issues. Each level comes with different maximum penalties: simple sexual assault (maximum sentence: 10 years), sexual assault with a weapon or causing bodily harm (maximum sentence: 14 years), and aggravated sexual assault (maximum sentence: life imprisonment).

CONSEQUENCES FOR VICTIMS

Sexual aggression has serious psychological and physical consequences for victims. For example, child victims of sexual abuse develop a wide range of short- and long-term problems (see Chapter 6 for a description of these). Adult victims of rape also report high levels of stress and fear that often disrupts social, sexual, and occupational functioning, while also generating high levels of anxiety and depression (Hanson, 1990). Physically, Koss (1993) reports that up to 30% of rape victims contract sexually transmitted diseases, and pregnancy results in about 5% of cases. Psychologically, a wide range of negative consequences have been reported, as will be discussed.

Rape trauma syndrome: A group of symptoms or behaviours that are frequent after-effects of having been raped

In 1974, Burgess and Holmstrom first proposed the term **rape trauma syndrome** to describe the psychological after-effects of rape. Burgess and Holmstrom interviewed 92 women who had been raped. The first interview took place within 30 minutes of the women's arriving at the hospital and the second interview took place one month later. The effects of rape identified by the researchers were divided into two phases: an acute crisis phase and a long-term reactions phase.

According to Burgess and Holmstrom (1974), the acute crisis phase lasts for a few days to several weeks and the symptoms are often quite severe. These symptoms can include very high levels of fear, anxiety, and depression. Victims of rape also often ask questions about why the rape happened to them, and they commonly engage in self-blame (Janoff-Bulman, 1979), which is perhaps unsurprising given the common myth that rape victims sometimes "ask for it" by the way they dress or act (see Box 14.1 for a discussion of other sexual assault myths). Heightened levels of distrust and self-doubt are also common reactions.

The second phase is more protracted, lasting anywhere from a few months to several years. A quarter of women who have been raped do not significantly recover, even after several years (Resick, 1993). Long-term reactions include the development of phobias, such as a fear of being left alone or a fear of leaving the house. Another long-term reaction is the development of sexual problems and depression. Often, victims make dramatic changes in their lifestyles. Researchers have also identified chronic physical health symptoms (e.g., back pain, muscle tension, headaches, sleep problems) that develop as a result of rape (Campbell, Sefl, & Ahrens, 2003). Over the past two decades, rape trauma syndrome has been the focus of ample debate (Keogh, 2007; McGowan & Helms, 2003). Specifically, there has been controversy over the admissibility of rape trauma syndrome as evidence in court, and whether it can be used to establish the credibility of rape complainants.

The psychological consequences of rape victimization also include post-traumatic stress disorder (PTSD). The *DSM-5* (American Psychiatric Association, 2013) defines PTSD as a trauma- and stress-related disorder that may develop as a result of exposure to death, serious injury, or sexual violence, whether actual or threatened. The four symptom clusters of PTSD include an avoidance of stimuli, reoccurring distressing memories, a negatively altered cognition and mood, and an altered state of arousal and reactivity.

Box 14.1 Myths and Realities

Sexual Assault

Sexual assault myths are stereotypic ideas that people have about sexual assault (Burt, 1980). Sexual assault myths appear to be accepted across many levels of society (Gylys & McNamara, 1996; Kershner, 1996; Szymanski, Devlin, Chrisler, & Vyse, 1993), though men appear to be more accepting of rape myths than women (Bohner et al., 1998). The following list of some of the many myths associated with sexual assault or rape includes facts that challenge these false beliefs.

Myth 1. Sexual assault is not a common problem.
Fact. One in every four women and one in every six men have experienced some type of sexual assault. You likely know someone who has been sexually assaulted.

Myth 2. Sexual assault is most often committed by strangers.
Fact. Women face the greatest risk of sexual assault from men they know, not from strangers. About half of all sexual assaults occur in dating relationships. In about 60% of cases, victims of sexual assault knew the attacker.

Myth 3. Women who are sexually assaulted "ask for it" by the way they dress or act.
Fact. Victims of sexual assault range across the age span (from infants to elderly), and sexual assaults can occur in almost any situation. No woman "deserves" to be sexually assaulted, regardless of what she wears, where she goes, or how she acts. Blaming sexual assault on how a victim behaves would be like blaming a mugging on a person for carrying a wallet. Unfortunately, even individuals in positions of power are accepting of this myth. For example, in January of 2011, a Toronto police officer told female students at York University that they could prevent sexual assault simply by not "dressing like sluts." More recently, in September of 2014, a Canadian federal judge suggested that a rape victim allowed the sex to happen because she "couldn't keep her knees together."

Myth 4. Avoid being alone in dark, deserted places, such as parks or parking lots, and this will protect you from being sexually assaulted.
Fact. Most sexual assaults occur in a private home and many in the victim's home.

Myth 5. Women lie about sexual assault.
Fact. False accusations happen but are very rare. Sexual assault is a vastly under-reported crime, and most sexual assaults are not reported to the police.

Rothbaum, Foa, Riggs, Murdock, and Walsh (1992) assessed the PTSD symptoms in 95 female rape victims over a nine-month follow-up period. One month after the rape, 65% of victims were diagnosed with PTSD and, at nine months, 47% were classified as having PTSD. Some victims continue to experience PTSD symptoms years after the rape. In one study, 16.5% of rape victims had PTSD 15 years after the rape (Kilpatrick, Saunders, Veronen, Best, & Von, 1987). Fortunately, effective treatment programs have been developed to help rape victims overcome the emotional suffering caused by this trauma (Foa & Rothbaum, 1998; Iverson, King, Cunningham, & Resick, 2015).

CLASSIFICATION OF SEXUAL OFFENDERS

Sexual offenders are usually divided into categories based on the type of sexually deviant behaviour they exhibit, the relationship between victim and offender, and the age of the victim. **Voyeurs** obtain sexual gratification by observing unsuspecting people, usually strangers, who are naked, in the process of undressing, or engaging in

Voyeur: Someone who obtains sexual gratification by observing unsuspecting people, usually strangers, who are naked, in the process of undressing, or engaging in sexual activity

Exhibitionist: Someone who obtains sexual gratification by exposing his or her genitals to strangers

Rapist: Person who sexually assaults victims over 16 years of age

Pedophile: Person whose primary sexual orientation is toward children

Child molester: Someone who has actually sexually molested a child

Intra-familial child molester: Someone who sexually abuses his or her own biological children or children for whom he or she assumes a parental role, such as a stepfather or live-in boyfriend. Also known as *incest offenders*

Incest offender: Someone who sexually abuses his or her own biological children or children for whom he or she assumes a parental role, such as a stepfather or live-in boyfriend. Also known as *intra-familial child molesters*

Extra-familial child molester: Someone who sexually abuses children not related to him or her

sexual activity. **Exhibitionists** obtain sexual gratification by exposing their genitals to strangers. These two types of sexual offenders are sometimes referred to as hands-off or no-contact sexual offenders.

Rapists are offenders who sexually assault victims aged 16 years or older. The term pedophilia means "love of children", and a **pedophile** is an adult whose primary sexual orientation is toward children. The term **child molester/sexual offender against children** refers to individuals who have actually sexually molested a child. Although the general public often uses the terms pedophile and child molester interchangeably, they are not synonyms. Many pedophiles would not be classified as child molesters, as they have never actually offended against a child. Child molesters can fall into two categories: intra-familial and extra-familial. **Intra-familial child molesters** (also called **incest offenders**) are those who sexually abuse their own biological children or children for whom they assume a parental role, such as a stepfather or live-in boyfriend. **Extra-familial child molesters** sexually abuse children outside the family.

Rapist Typologies

As highlighted in Box 14.2, it is important to understand that rapists are not part of a homogeneous group and do not all engage in sexual assault for the same reasons. Several different rapist typologies have been proposed. During the 1990s, an ambitious project was undertaken at the Massachusetts Treatment Center to develop and empirically validate a typology for rapists. The resulting classification system, the

---

Box 14.2   Forensic Psychology in the Spotlight

Is Resisting a Sexual Attack a Good Idea?

One question often posed by women is, "If attacked, should I fight back or not?" Responses to this answer are common and websites abound where advice is given to women so that they can prevent themselves from being victimized. Unfortunately, the answer to the question is complicated, for reasons discussed below. For example, based on the typologies described on pages 409 and 410, the answer to the question will likely depend on the type of rapist under consideration.

Research with incarcerated rapists indicates that they search for vulnerable victims in certain areas and attack women who they believe cannot or will not resist the attack (Stevens, 1994). That being said, many women do resist their attackers, and research has shown that, compared with the use of nonresistance strategies, such as pleading with the offender, crying, or reasoning, victims who use forceful measures to resist their attacker (either verbal or physical) are more likely to avoid being raped (Ullman & Knight, 1993; Zoucha-Jensen, & Coyne, 1993).

However, the association between victim injury and resistance is inconclusive at present. For example, Zoucha-Jensen and Coyne (1993) found no association between victim resistance and injury. In contrast, Ullman and Knight (1993) found that if the offender had a weapon, which is probably more common with certain types of rapists, women who resisted the rape suffered more physical injury than those who did not resist.

In a review of universities' sexual assault prevention programs, Gidycz and Dardis (2014) found promising evidence that self-defence training empowers women to be confident in their ability to resist sexual assault and subsequently reduces their likelihood of victimization. In addition to self-defence skills, research suggests that prevention programs are more effective when they are oriented towards a single gender (Orchowski, Gidycz, & Murphy, 2010).

Revised Rapist Typology, Version 3 (MTC:R3; Knight & Prentky, 1990), consists of five primary subtypes of rapists based on motivational differences:

1. The opportunistic type commits sexual assault that is generally impulsive, void of sexual fantasies, controlled primarily by situational or contextual factors, and void of gratuitous violence. These offenders often engage in other criminal behaviours. For example, a rapist who breaks into a home with the intention of stealing but who rapes the female occupant could be classified as opportunistic.

2. The pervasively angry type has a high level of anger that is directed toward both men and women. These offenders tend to be impulsive, use unnecessary force, cause serious victim injury, and be void of sexual fantasies.

3. The sexual type is distinguished from the other types in that these offenders' crimes are primarily motivated by sexual preoccupation or sexual fantasies.

4. The sadistic type is differentiated from the sexual type in that there must be a sadistic element to the offence.

5. The fifth type is labelled vindictive. In contrast to the pervasively angry type, the vindictive rapist's anger is focused solely on women. These offenders are not impulsive, nor are they preoccupied by sexual fantasies. The goal of this type of rapist is to demean and degrade the victim.

The opportunistic, sexual, and vindictive subtypes are further subdivided based on their level of social competence. The sadistic type is also further subdivided into overt or muted sadists based on the presence or absence of gratuitous violence (Knight & Prentky, 1990). Research using the MTC:R3 has found that these types differ on prevalence of psychopathy (Barbaree, Seto, Serin, Amos, & Preston, 1994; Brown & Forth, 1997), rates of sexual recidivism (Knight, Prentky, & Cerce, 1994), and treatment needs (Knight, 1999). Knight and Guay (2006) described a restructuring of the MTC:R3 in which the muted sadistic type of sexual offender is dropped, since the existence of this type of sexual offender has not been supported by research.

Another typology that uses motivations to classify rapists was proposed by Groth (1979). Groth suggested that rapists can be divided into three main types: anger rapists, power rapists, and sadistic rapists.

The features of the **anger rapist** include

- the use of more force than necessary to obtain compliance and engagement in a variety of sexual acts to degrade the victim

- high levels of anger directed solely toward women

- not being motivated primarily by sexual gratification

Anger rapist: A rapist, as defined by Groth, who uses more force than necessary to obtain compliance from the victim and who engages in a variety of sexual acts to degrade the victim

Most of these rapes are precipitated by conflict or perceived humiliation by some significant woman, such as the offender's wife, mother, or boss. Approximately 50% of rapists fit this type.

The features of the **power rapist** include

- the intention to assert dominance and control over the victim

- variation in the amount of force used depending on the degree of submission shown by the victim

Power rapist: A rapist, as defined by Groth, who seeks to establish dominance and control over the victim

- not being motivated primarily by sexual gratification
- frequent rape fantasies

About 40% of rapists fit into this category.
The features of the **sadistic rapist** include

- obtaining sexual gratification by hurting the victim
- high levels of victim injury, including torture and sometimes death
- frequent violent sexual fantasies

Approximately 5% of rapists fit this type.

There is considerable overlap between the MTC:R3 and Groth typologies. Both typologies describe a sadistic rapist. The vindictive rapist is similar to the anger rapist and the pervasively angry rapist shares some of the features of the power rapist.

Child Molester Typologies

With respect to child molesters, the most widely used typology is Groth's typology of the fixated and regressed child molester (Groth, Hobson, & Gary, 1982). Groth developed his typology based on research with incarcerated child molesters.

Fixated child molesters tend to have the following features:

- Their primary sexual orientation is toward children, and they have little or no sexual contact with adults.
- Their sexual interest in children begins in adolescence and is persistent.
- Male children are their primary targets.
- Precipitating stress is not evident.
- Their offences are planned.
- They are emotionally immature, have poor social skills, and are usually single.
- They usually have no history of alcohol or drug abuse.
- They often feel no remorse or distress over their behaviour.

Regressed child molesters usually have the following characteristics:

- Their primary sexual orientation is toward adults.
- Their sexual interest in children begins in adulthood and is episodic.
- Female children are their primary targets.
- Precipitating stress and feelings of inadequacy are usually present.
- Their offences are more impulsive.
- They are often married and are having marital problems.
- Many of their offences are related to alcohol use.
- They are more likely to report feeling remorse for their behaviour.

Box 14.3 describes how the death of an 11-year-old boy in Ontario by a convicted sadistic child molester prompted the creation of a sex offender registry.

Sadistic rapist: A rapist, as defined by Groth, who obtains sexual gratification by hurting the victim

Fixated child molester: A child molester, as defined by Groth, who has a long-standing, exclusive sexual preference for children

Regressed child molester: A child molester, as defined by Groth, whose primary sexual orientation is toward adults, but whose sexual interests revert to children after a stressful event or because of feelings of inadequacy

Box 14.3   Forensic Psychology in the Spotlight

National Sex Offender Registry: Is It Helping the Police to Locate Sex Offenders?

On December 15, 2004, the Canadian government created the National Sex Offender Registry in order to provide police forces with rapid access to information about convicted sexual offenders. The goal of the registry is to help police when investigating sexual crimes to identify sexual offenders living near the crime scene. For example, if a child is abducted, the police will want to know if there are any child molesters living or visiting near where the abduction occurred. The RCMP administers the registry and local police forces are responsible for entering information into the national database.

What information does the registry contain?

The act was amended in 2007 to include military personnel convicted of sexual offences and in 2010 to include vehicle information and to register Canadians who are convicted of sexual offences in other countries. The registry includes addresses, telephone numbers, offence history, aliases, identifying marks (e.g., tattoos, scars), vehicle information, employment information, and a photo of the offender.

What prompted the development of sexual offender registries?

The Canadian government was originally prompted to develop the registry by the June 18, 1988, murder in Ontario of 11-year-old Christopher Stevenson by paroled child molester Joseph Fredericks. Fredericks abducted Christopher from a shopping mall, brought him to his apartment, and sexually assaulted him for 36 hours before slitting his throat and dumping the body. The police were at the mall within minutes of the abduction but were not able to find Christopher. Had the police known there was a high-risk child molester living in the neighbourhood, perhaps they could have saved Christopher. A coroner's inquest recommended that police have access to an electronic database that indicates the residence of all high-risk convicted sexual offenders. On April 23, 2001, the Ontario government proclaimed Christopher's Law and was the first province in Canada to establish a sex offender registry.

In United States, the first sex offender registry was established in 1994 in response to the rape and murder of 7-year-old Megan Kanka in New Jersey. A convicted sex offender, Jesse Timmendequas, moved into the house across from Megan. Timmendequas lured Megan into his house by offering to show her a puppy. He raped and strangled her and left her body in a nearby park.

Who has access to the registry?

In Canada, the public does not have access to information in provincial or federal sex offender registries. In 2014, however, as part of Bill C-26's Tougher Penalties for Sexual Offenders Act, the Conservative government recommended Canada's sexual offender registry be made publically available. Despite this proposition, the sexual offender registry in Canada remains available only to law enforcement officials.

Alternatively, it is possible for the public to obtain information about registered sex offenders (called *community notification*) in most American states. Websites in the U.S. allow anyone to check to see if there are registered sex offenders living near them. Information on the website includes names, aliases, home addresses, identifying marks (e.g., tattoos), vehicle information, brief description of prior sex offences (victim age and sex), and photos. For example, there are 4318 registered sex offenders on the New Jersey Sex Offender Registry.

Do public sexual offender registries make communities safer?

The answer is no. Rather than making communities safer, public sexual offender registries appear to instill a false sense of security. There has been no noticeable decline in the frequency of sexual offending in areas where sexual offender registries have been made available to the public. Public sexual offender registries also reinforce the stereotype that most sexual offenders prey on strangers and are likely to reoffend. In reality, we know that sexual offenders are more likely to victimize people they know (Perreault, 2015) and are typically at a low likelihood of reoffending upon release (Hanson et al., 2002). Public sexual offender registries are also thought to further marginalize those who have committed sex offences, making it more challenging to reintegrate back into society successfully.

ADOLESCENT SEXUAL OFFENDERS

Prior to the 1980s, sexually aggressive behaviour by adolescents was not deemed serious and was discounted by some as normal experimentation. However, crime reports and victimization surveys indicate that about 20% of rapes and between 30% and 50% of child sexual abuse is committed by adolescents (Davis & Leitenberg, 1987). In 2013, 645 adolescents were tried in youth court for sexual assault in Canada (Alam, 2015). Of those tried for sexual assault, 98% were male, and the majority were between 12 and 15 years of age among both males (64%) and females (93%).

Like their adult counterparts, adolescent sexual offenders consistently report having been victims of sexual abuse themselves. The prevalence rate for sexual abuse committed against adolescent sexual offenders ranges from about 40% to 80% (Friedrich & Luecke, 1988; Ryan, Miyoshi, Metzner, Krugman, & Fryer, 1996). However, although early sexual victimization and later sexual offending are related, the majority of sexually abused children do not go on to become adolescent or adult sexual offenders, and prior history of childhood sexual victimization is not related to sexual recidivism in samples of adult sexual offenders (Hanson & Bussière, 1998) or samples of adolescent sexual offenders (Worling & Curwen, 2000). Clearly, being the victim of sexual abuse is only one factor that affects later sexual offending. Rasmussen, Burton, and Christopherson (1992) suggested that in addition to sexual abuse, other factors such as social inadequacy, lack of intimacy, and impulsiveness also play a role. In a meta-analysis of 59 studies, Seto and Lalumière (2010) compared adolescent sex offenders to other adolescent offenders. Adolescent sex offenders were similar to other adolescent offenders on the majority of risk factors, but adolescent sex offenders were more likely to have a history of sexual abuse, exposure to sex or pornography, and atypical sexual interests.

Many youth have grown up playing video and computer games. Box 14.4 describes a recent research study examining the link between playing violent video games and negative attitudes toward women.

FEMALE SEXUAL OFFENDERS

Research on female sexual offenders is limited. This relative lack of attention is probably because only 2% to 5% of incarcerated sex offenders are female. However, some researchers have suggested that sexual abuse of children by women is more prevalent than previously believed. The rate of sexual reoffending is substantially lower in female sex offenders (1.5% over 6-year follow-up; Cortoni, Hanson, & Coache, 2010) compared to male sex offenders (13.5% over 5.5 years; Hanson & Morton-Bourgeon, 2005). Female sex offenders also appear to receive shorter sentences on average than male sex offenders (Embry & Lyons, 2012).

The rates of sexual abuse by females vary dramatically, depending on the definition used. For example, should a female be classified as a sexual abuser if she knew that her husband was sexually abusing their child and did nothing to stop the abuse? Does a mother sleeping with her child constitute sexual abuse in the absence of sexual touching? What if the child is a teenager who becomes sexually aroused by sleeping with his mother? Most people would agree that it is sexual abuse for a 20-year-old

Box 14.4 Forensic Psychology in the Spotlight

Sexual Objectification in Video Games and Sexual Assault Myths: Is There a Link?

You and many of your friends likely grew up playing video or computer games. Some of these games may have had a violent theme and others may have sexually objectified women. At the extreme are computer games such as Rapeplay, where the goal of the game is to rape women. This game has been banned internationally, but there are other games that allow players to imitate sexual and violent acts against women. Dietz (1998) coded how women were portrayed in video games and found that when female characters were present, in 21% of the games violence was depicted against women, and in 28% of the games women were portrayed as sex objects. Is there an association between playing these violent video/computer games and negative attitudes toward women? One of the challenges in doing this type of research is causality, or determining which came first. It is possible that people who have negative attitudes toward women are more likely to play violent video/computer games, rather than the violent video/computer games creating these negative attitudes. Another challenge is ethical concerns. Should we ask students who do not play violent computer games to participate in research where they are asked to play them?

In a recent study, Beck, Boys, Rose, and Beck (2012) examined the relationship between short-term exposure to a violent video game and the acceptance of rape myths in university students:

Sample: 141 male and female undergraduates

Measure: Illinois Rape Myth Acceptance Scale (Payne, Lonsway, & Fitzgerald, 1999) is a 20-item self-report scale designed to assess rape-myth acceptance. It includes such items as "A lot of women lead a man on and then they cry rape."

Design: Solomon four-group design was used with participants randomly assigned to one of four groups.

Treatment 1: pretest, watched violent video game, post-test

Treatment 2: watched violent video game, post-test (no pretest)

Control 1: pretest, watched nonviolent video game, post-test

Control 2: watched nonviolent video game, post-test

Treatment video: Participants saw a video game being played in which a researcher directed the character, Niko, to go to a strip club and receive a private lap dance. Niko then picked up a sex-trade worker, had sex with her, paid her, and shot her as she walked away from the car. Niko took back his money. Niko was able to outwit the police in a car chase and avoid capture.

Control video: Participants saw a video game of a nonviolent baseball game.

Results: Watching a video game that depicted sexual objectification of women and violence against women was related to increased rape-myth attitudes in male undergraduates but not female undergraduates.

Additional research is needed to obtain a better understanding of the influence of video/computer games on people's attitudes. Computer games are becoming more and more realistic, with players using the motion of their bodies to control characters. What influence these more interactive violent video/computer games might have on people's attitudes remains to be studied.

to have sexual contact with an 8-year-old boy, but not if the boy is 16. But what if the boy is 14? If the 14-year-old boy initiates the sexual act and views it positively, should this be classified as sexual abuse?

Retrospective surveys of university students have found that a large percentage of perpetrators are females. For example, Fritz, Stoll, and Wagner (1981) reported that of the 5% of college men who were molested as children, 60% were molested by females, most being older female adolescents. In a large survey of 2972 university students that used broad criteria for sexual abuse, Risin and Koss (1987) reported that 7.3% were abused. They found that almost half of the perpetrators were female (43%), and of these, almost half were female adolescent babysitters. Similar to other studies, about half of the male respondents reported that they participated in the sexual acts voluntarily and did not feel victimized. In contrast to these studies, fewer female perpetrators have been reported by other researchers (Finkelhor, 1984; Reinhart, 1987). For example, Finkelhor (1984) found that only 6% of university women and 16% of university men who reported childhood sexual abuse indicated that the offender was a woman.

Some researchers have speculated that the rate of sexual abuse by females is underestimated. Some reasons include the following (Banning, 1989; Groth, 1979):

- Women are able to mask their sexually abusive behaviours through caregiving activities and thus are more difficult to recognize.

- Women sexual offenders are more likely to target their own children, who are less likely to disclose the abuse.

- Boys are more frequent targets than girls, and boys are less likely to disclose abuse.

Research designed to determine the characteristics of female sexual offenders has generally been plagued with very small sample sizes. Whether the findings will generalize to larger samples of female sexual offenders remains to be investigated. Keeping this limitation in mind, Atkinson (1996) suggested there are four types of female sexual offenders:

1. *Teacher/lover*. These offenders initiate sexual abuse of a male adolescent whom they relate to as a peer. The offender is often in a position of authority or power. It is unknown how common this type of female sex offender is because the victim rarely reports the abuse to authorities. This type has not likely experienced childhood sexual abuse, although substance-use problems are common. These offenders often are not aware that their behaviour is inappropriate. Teacher/lovers often describe themselves as being "in love" with the victim. Victims often report they participated voluntarily and do not feel victimized.

2. *Male-coerced*. These offenders are coerced or forced into sexual abuse by an abusive male. Often the victim is the female offender's own daughter. These offenders are unassertive, are dependent on men, and are relatively passive partners in the abuse.

3. *Male-accompanied*. These offenders also engage in sexual abuse with a male partner. However, they are more willing participants than the male-coerced type. Victims are both inside and outside the family.

4. *Predisposed*. This offender initiates the sexual abuse alone. She has often experienced severe and persistent childhood sexual abuse and has been a victim of intimate violence. This type often reports having deviant sexual fantasies, the offences are more violent and bizarre, and they typically involve younger children. Victims are often their own children, and they also frequently physically abuse and neglect the victim.

See the case of Paul Bernardo and Karla Homolka profiled in the In the Media box for an example of a male-accompanied female sex offender.

A Seemingly Normal Couple: The Facade of Paul Bernardo and Karla Homolka

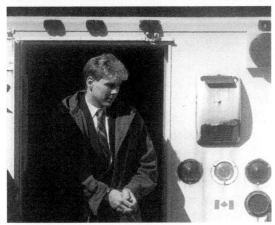

Keith Beaty/Toronto Star/ZUMAPRESS/Newscom

On the surface, Paul Bernardo and Karla Homolka appeared to be a normal married couple. They were married in 1991 in a lavish ceremony at Niagara-on-the-Lake and went to Hawaii for their honeymoon. Karla Homolka worked as a vet technician, and Paul Bernardo appeared to many to be a well-educated, well-adjusted, and congenial young man. However, in reality Paul Bernardo was a sadistic rapist. He and Karla Homolka sexually assaulted and murdered three young teenagers, including Homolka's younger sister. Details of some of the major events in Bernardo and Homolka's criminal history are presented below.

- May 4, 1987: Bernardo rapes a young woman in Scarborough, Ontario. The rapist is dubbed by the media "the Scarborough rapist." It is estimated that Bernardo raped over 30 women before he was arrested in 1993.

- October 17, 1987: Homolka, 17, meets Bernardo, 23, at a restaurant in Scarborough.

- November 20, 1990: Bernardo provides hair, saliva, and blood samples to the Scarborough rapist investigation. Several people had called police saying Paul Bernardo looked like the Scarborough rapist composite. Investigators who interview Bernardo do not believe he fits the profile of a sadistic serial rapist. The samples are sent to the Centre for Forensic Science for DNA testing.

- December 23, 1990: Bernardo asks Homolka to help him sexually assault her younger sister, Tammy. He claims that since Homolka was not a virgin when they met, he wants to have sex with her younger sister. Homolka steals an inhalant anaesthetic from her vet job. Tammy is given alcohol laced with sleeping pills. Homolka holds a cloth soaked with anaesthetic over Tammy's face. Homolka and Bernardo videotape themselves sexually assaulting Tammy in the basement while her parents and older sister sleep upstairs. Tammy chokes on her vomit and dies. The death is ruled accidental.

- June 7, 1991: Homolka invites a 15-year-old girl (Jane Doe) home, where she plies her with alcohol laced with sleeping pills. Homolko and Bernardo videotape themselves sexually assaulting the unconscious girl.

- June 14, 1991: Bernardo kidnaps 14-year-old Leslie Mahaffy. Homolka and Bernardo sexually assault and murder her at their house. They videotape the sexual assaults.

- June 29, 1991: Leslie Mahaffy's dismembered body is found encased in concrete in Gibson Lake.

- June 29, 1991: Bernardo and Homolka are married.

- August 10, 1991: Bernardo and Homolka drug and sexually assault Jane Doe again.

- April 16, 1992: Bernardo and Homolka kidnap, torture, and murder Kristen French at their house. They videotape the sexual assault. They leave her naked body in a ditch.

- December 27, 1992: Bernardo beats Homolka, who leaves and files charges against him. Homolka describes to the police being repeatedly physically, sexually, and emotionally abused by Bernardo.

- February 1, 1993: Bernardo's DNA is found to be a match for three sexual assaults.

- February 17, 1993: Bernardo is arrested for the sexual assaults and two murders.

- May 6, 1993: Bernardo's lawyer, Ken Murray, goes to Bernardo's house and retrieves hidden videotapes of the sexual assaults. He keeps these for 16 months.

(continued)

(continued)

- May 14, 1993: The Crown offers Homolka a plea bargain in exchange for her testifying against Bernardo.

- July 6, 1993: Homolka pleads guilty to two counts of manslaughter, receiving a 12-year-sentence.

- September 12, 1994: Ken Murray quits as Bernardo's lawyer. He hands the videotapes over to the new lawyer, who gives them to the police on September 22.

- September 1, 1995: Bernardo is found guilty of two counts of first-degree murder and is sentenced to life.

- November 3, 1995: Bernardo is declared a dangerous offender for the sexual assaults and given an indeterminate sentence.

- March 15, 1996: The inquiry by Justice Gilligan into the plea bargain offered Karla Homolka concludes that if the videotapes had been available there would have been no plea bargain, but that given the circumstances the plea bargain was appropriate.

- June 1996: An inquiry by Justice Campbell into the police investigation concludes it was hampered by a lack of communication between police forces and that four rapes and two murders would have been prevented if Bernardo's DNA had been tested sooner.

- January 23, 1997: Ken Murray is charged with obstruction of justice and possession of child pornography for failing to give the videotapes to police.

- June 13, 2000: Ken Murray is acquitted.

- December 2001: The videotapes depicting torture and sexual assaults are destroyed.

- July 4, 2005: Homolka is released after serving her 12-year sentence.

- December 17, 2007: Homolka, her husband, and their 2-year-old son move to the Caribbean.

- June 3, 2015: News Sources announce Paul Bernardo applied for day parole in Toronto. He is eligible to apply for full parole February 17, 2018.

- November 13, 2015: Paul Bernardo self-published an ebook on Amazon titled "A MAD World Order", a fictional novel about Russia and Al-Qaeda planning an attack on the United States. News of this book caused a public uproar and boycott of Amazon. This ebook was subsequently removed from Amazon and is no longer available for purchase.

- April 19, 2016: Karla Homolka reported to be living in Châteauguay, Quebec, under the new name Leanne Teale.

- Paul Bernardo continues to serve his sentence without day parole at Millhaven Institution.

Sources: Campbell, 1996; "Key Events in the Bernardo/Homolka Case," 2010; Delean, 2016.

ABORIGINAL SEX OFFENDERS

There is a surprising lack of research on Aboriginal sexual offenders, despite the fact that 40% of the Aboriginal offender population in Canada has committed a sexual offence (Correctional Service of Canada, 2013). Compared to non-Aboriginal sexual offenders, Aboriginal sexual offenders have been found to score higher on a number of risk factors. For example, Aboriginal sexual offenders appear to have lengthier criminal and substance abuse histories, lower education, and higher rates of unemployment than their non-Aboriginal counterparts (Ellerby & MacPherson, 2002; Olver & Wong, 2006).

A study conducted by the Correctional Service of Canada (CSC) found that the majority of Aboriginal sexual offenders fell between the ages of 19 and 40 (CSC, 2013). When committing the sexual offence, approximately 89% of Aboriginal sexual offenders were under the influence of alcohol (CSC, 2013). Aboriginal sexual offenders are significantly less likely to have male victims (CSC, 2013; Ellerby & MacPherson, 2002; Rojas & Gretton, 2007) than their non-Aboriginal counterparts. Aboriginal sexual offenders also appear to be less likely to victimize young children

(CSC, 2013; Ellerby & MacPherson, 2002). The majority of victims appear to be part of the Aboriginal community and known to the offender, where less than 16% of victims are non-Aboriginal and less than 15% of victims were strangers (CSC, 2013). More research is needed to develop a full profile of Aboriginal sexual offenders.

THEORIES OF SEXUAL AGGRESSION

It is important that we understand why child molestation and rape occurs, and a number of theories have been proposed to account for these forms of antisocial behaviour. One of the most popular and widely cited theories is Finkelhor's precondition model (1984) of child molestation. Finkelhor's theory of child molesting proposes that four preconditions must be met for the sexual abuse to occur:

1. The offender must be motivated to sexually abuse. Motivation is due to three factors: (1) emotional congruence, which is the offender's desire for the child to satisfy an emotional need, (2) sexual attraction to the child, and (3) blockage of emotional outlets for the offender to meet his sexual and emotional needs.

2. The next precondition relates to the offender's lack of internal inhibitions. For example, alcohol and impulse-control problems can weaken the offender's ability to restrain the behaviours that lead to abuse.

3. The offender must overcome external inhibitors for the abuse to occur. For example, the offender might need to create opportunities to be alone with the child.

4. The offender must overcome the child's resistance. Offenders will reward the child with attention or bribes to encourage the child to cooperate. Alternatively, some offenders will use the threat of harm to intimidate the child.

Marshall and Barbaree (1990) proposed an integrated model of sexual aggression that includes biological factors, childhood experiences, sociocultural influences, and situational events. They argued that males normally learn to inhibit sexually aggressive behaviour via a socialization process that promotes the development of strong, positive attachments. The authors suggested that sexual offenders fail to acquire effective inhibitory control because they experienced childhood abuse (emotional, physical, or sexual abuse) or because they were raised in extremely dysfunctional families (e.g., harsh and inconsistent punishment, lack of supervision, hostility). They also acknowledged the importance of the structure of society that reinforces the use of aggression and the acceptance of negative attitudes toward women.

A number of theorists have also applied evolutionary theory to sexual offending (Quinsey & Lalumière, 1995; Thornhill & Palmer, 2000). Evolutionary theories focus on how behaviour is the product of our ancestral history and how features that are related to reproductive success become more frequent. Quinsey (B) provided a clear example of a mating strategy that would not be very successful. "Consider a man in an ancestral environment who preferred trees as sexual partners. We can surmise that this man is very unlikely to be among our ancestors if his tree preference was caused by genes, because these genes would decrease in frequency over generations" (p. 2). Quinsey and others view rape as a consequence of a mating strategy that

Canadian Researcher Profile: Dr. Martin Lalumière

Courtesy of Martin Lalumiére

Dr. Lalumière earned his PhD in psychology at Queen's University and is now a professor of clinical psychology at the University of Ottawa. His research is about sexual offending, the paraphilias, and differences between men and women in their sexual responses.

As an undergraduate at the Université de Montréal, he became fascinated by forensic psychology after joining a research laboratory headed by Dr. Christopher Earls. At the time, Dr. Earls was studying the development of paraphilic (atypical) sexual arousal and testing a Pavlovian conditioning model of sexual preferences. Later at Queen's University, Dr. Lalumière studied sexual aggression with Dr. Vernon Quinsey and started a program of research that has led to over 115 publications. That work is ongoing and he has also conducted research on hypersexuality, psychopathy, birth order, and risk-taking. Dr. Lalumière will always be grateful to Drs. Earls and Quinsey for their mentorship and for giving him the chance to explore this field of science.

His favourite course is The Psychology of Crime, which he has taught in some form at the graduate and undergraduate level since 1999. His favourite study in the area of

sex offending is probably a recent two-part investigation conducted with his longtime colleagues Dr. Michael Seto and the late Dr. Grant Harris. They examined whether the unique pattern of sexual arousal shown by men charged with sexual assault against women is sadism (a strong sexual attraction to violence and injury) or biastophilia (a strong sexual attraction to nonconsensual sex).

They developed new sexual stories that factorially varied in three ways: (1) the presence or absence of sex and nudity, (2) the presence or absence of violence and injury inflicted by the male character, and (3) the presence or absence of active consent shown by the female character. They then presented these stories to men who had committed sexual assault against a woman (incarcerated rapists), men with histories of violent consensual sexual activity (sadists), and men who had no record of sex offences and no reported interest in violence or nonconsensual sex (community men). Through examination of genital responses, rapists could be best discriminated from community men by the presence of nonconsent in the stories, and sadists could be best discriminated from community men by the presence of violence and injury in the stories. This study suggested that biastophilia is a distinct paraphilia, and that rapists are more biastophilic than sadistic. Some rapists, then, may be particularly sexually motivated by expressions of nonconsent on the part of their victims. Dr. Lalumière thinks more research is required before they can be certain of these conclusions.

Dr. Lalumière believes the Canadian criminal justice system, like all complex systems, is slow to respond to research findings but eventually does. He thinks that forensic research is a good way to make a real difference in the lives of offenders and in reducing the number of future victims.

Forensic research is a challenging but also very rewarding and interesting endeavour. Because of the nature of the research, Dr. Lalumière believes it is important not to work all the time and to have a balanced and healthy lifestyle; thus, he spends quite a bit of time fly-fishing, hiking, and spending time with his friends and family.

was selected for because it resulted in a reproductive advantage for males (Lalumière, Harris, Quinsey, & Rice, 2005). Evolutionary theories of sexual aggression have been criticized both for having a limited scope and lacking explanatory depth (see Ward & Siegert, 2002, for a detailed criticism). See Box 14.5 for a profile of sexual offender researcher Dr. Martin Lalumiére.

ASSESSMENT AND TREATMENT OF SEXUAL OFFENDERS

Researchers assess sexual offenders to help to determine future risk for reoffending, identify treatment needs, and evaluate whether the treatment has had the desired effect. The focus of this section will be on the assessment of treatment needs and the effectiveness of treatment programs.

Most treatment programs are designed to address the following: denial, minimizations and cognitive distortions, victim empathy, modification of deviant sexual interest, enhanced social skills, substance-abuse problems, and the development of relapse-prevention plans (Marshall, 1999).

Denial, Minimizations, and Cognitive Distortions

As is clearly illustrated in the You Be the Forensic Psychologist box, sex offenders often deny (i.e., they claim they didn't do what they are accused of or that the victim consented) or fail to take full responsibility for their sexual offending (Barbaree, 1991). In fact, approximately 70% of sexual offenders deny or minimize having ever committed a sexual crime (Jung & Daniels, 2012). Often, blame is shifted to someone else, including the victim or some external factor. For example, sex offenders will often say, "The victim wanted to have sex with me" or "I was drunk and didn't know what I was doing." Assessments of denial and acceptance of responsibility are most often done through self-report questionnaires, such as the Clarke Sex History Questionnaire (Langevin, Handy, Paitich, & Russon, 1985), or by a comparison of police and victim reports with what the offenders admit in interviews. While most research has not found a link between denial and sexual recidivism, some researchers provide evidence that denial is related to sexual recidivism among low-risk sexual offenders and incest offenders (Harkins, Beech, & Goodwill, 2010; Nunes, Firestone, Wexler, Jensen, & Bradford, 2007). Thus, denial may have more of an impact on recidivism outcomes among sexual offenders with fewer risk factors, particularly those designated as low-risk to reoffend.

Cognitive distortions are deviant cognitions, values, and beliefs that the sexual offender uses to justify deviant behaviours. For example, a child molester might state, "Having sex with a child in a loving relationship is a good way to teach a child about sex," or an incest offender might claim, "It was better for her to have her first sexual experience with me since I love her, rather than with some teenager who would just want to use her." Both these child molesters are reporting cognitive distortions that are self-serving and inhibit them from taking full responsibility for their offences. In a recent meta-analysis on 45 samples, Helmus, Hanson, Babchishin, and Mann (2013) report that cognitive distortions or attitudes supportive of sexual offending are more predictive of recidivism among child molesters than among rapists.

Some treatment programs refuse to accept deniers because a person who refuses to admit to having committed a sexual offence cannot fully participate in the treatment, since the focus is on sexual offending. In treatment, offenders are asked to disclose in detail what happened before, during, and after the sexual abuse. The therapist has access to the police and victim reports in order to challenge an offender who is denying or minimizing aspects of the event. Other group members are encouraged to also challenge what the offender discloses.

Cognitive distortions: Deviant cognitions, values, or beliefs that are used to justify or minimize deviant behaviours

You have just been hired as a psychologist at a forensic psychiatric hospital. Larry Wilkins is a child molester who has been at the hospital for some time. He has just been assigned to your caseload, and you are now responsible for developing a treatment plan for Larry and working with him to address his serious offending problem.

Most of Larry's victims have been very young girls. When you talk to Larry, he doesn't seem to see anything wrong with the fact that he regularly engages in sexual interactions with these girls. Usually, the encounters involve just touching the girls, he says, and not much else. In fact, he thinks he has been a good influence on many of the girls and says that they rarely resist his advances.

He says that occasionally the girls make the first move and they are usually very affectionate toward him. He assures you that he never actually hurts the girls and says he does just the opposite. He frequently buys them presents, takes them on nice outings, and always says nice things to them.

Larry also says he is aware of research that indicates sexual relations between men and children may be healthy for kids because it provides them with a sense of belonging and shows them that they are loved. Before being caught by the police, he actually belonged to an organization that promotes sexual relations between adults and kids and he assures you that many men think the same way he does. He has heard them say so at meetings.

Your Turn . . .

As the psychologist working with Larry, what are some of the issues you would need to deal with? How would you proceed with your assessment of Larry and his treatment?

Empathy

Although some sex offenders have a general deficit in empathy (e.g., psychopathic sex offenders), most have a specific deficit in empathy toward their victims (Marshall, Barbaree, & Fernandez, 1995). Empathy is the ability to perceive others' perspectives and to recognize and respond in a compassionate way to the feelings of others. Cognitive distortions can cause empathy problems in sexual offenders. Because they minimize the amount of harm they have done, they do not think the victim has suffered, and therefore they do not empathize with the victim. Measures of empathy have focused on self-report scales, such as the Rape Empathy Scale (Deitz, Blackwell, Daley, & Bentley, 1982), and interviews.

Empathy training typically focuses on getting the offender to understand the impact of the abuse on the victim and the pain caused, and to develop feelings such as remorse. Offenders read survivor accounts of rape and child abuse and compare these accounts with how their victim likely felt. Videos of victims describing the emotional damage they have suffered and the long-term problems they experience are often used. Some therapy programs use role-playing, with the offender taking the part of the victim. Finally, although controversial, some programs may have sexual offenders meet with adult survivors of rape or child sexual abuse. Only those sexual offenders who are demonstrating empathy are permitted to take part in these meetings.

Social Skills

Sexual offenders lack a variety of social skills, including self-confidence in interpersonal relations, capacity for intimacy, assertiveness, and dealing with anger (Bumby & Hansen, 1997; Marshall, Anderson, & Champagne, 1997; Marshall et al., 1995). Self-report questionnaires, interviews, and responses to scenarios have all been developed to assess social-skill deficits (see Marshall, 1999, for a review). Treatment programs for sexual offenders vary in terms of which social-skill deficits are targeted. Some programs focus on anger and communication skills (Pithers, Martin, & Cumming, 1989), whereas others target relationship skills, anger control, and self-esteem (Marshall et al., 1997).

Substance Abuse

Substance-abuse problems are common in nonsexual offenders and sexual offenders (Kraanen & Emmelkamp, 2011). It is likely that some sexual offenders use alcohol to facilitate offending by reducing their inhibitions. Self-report measures are often used to assess problems with alcohol and drugs.

Sexual offenders with substance-abuse problems are often referred to substance-abuse programs. These programs are usually based on the relapse-prevention model developed by Marlatt and his colleagues, which is described in more detail on page 423 (Marlatt & Gordon, 1985).

Deviant Sexual Interests

Deviant sexual interests motivate some sexual offenders. However, many other salient motives also play a role, including power and control over others, anger toward others, and desire for emotional intimacy. One of the most popular methods to assess deviant sexual interests is the use of **penile phallometry**. Penile phallometry involves placing a measurement device around the penis to measure changes in sexual arousal. To measure deviant sexual interests in child molesters, photos of naked male and female children and adults are presented, as well as rapists' recorded descriptions of nondeviant and deviant sexual behaviour. Phallometric assessments have been used to differentiate extra-familial child molesters from nonoffenders. However, most intra-familial child molesters do not differ in their phallometric responses from nonoffenders (see Marshall, 1999, for review). Research with rapists is mixed and seems to be dependent on the methodology used. Some studies have found differences between rapists and nonrapists (Harris, Lalumière, Seto, & Chaplin, 2012), whereas others have not (Marshall & Fernandez, 2003). The largest group differences between rapists and non-rapists are identified when participants are presented with vignettes involving the presence or absence of consent. Specifically, rapists appear to respond more favorably to situations involving non-consensual sex than non-rapists (Harris et al., 2012).

Penile phallometry: A measurement device placed around the penis to measure changes in sexual arousal

Many techniques have been developed to train offenders to eliminate deviant thoughts and interests and to increase the frequency of appropriate sexual thoughts and interests. For example, in **aversion therapy**, the offender is sometimes given an aversive substance to smell (e.g., ammonia) whenever he has a deviant sexual fantasy. The underlying goal is to reduce the attractiveness of these deviant fantasies by pairing them with a negative event.

Another approach is called *masturbatory satiation*. In this treatment, the offender is told to masturbate to ejaculation to a nondeviant fantasy. After ejaculation, he is told to switch to a deviant fantasy, thus pairing the inability to become aroused to this deviant fantasy. The effectiveness of these techniques to change deviant sexual interests has been questioned by several researchers (Quinsey & Earls, 1990).

When combined with psychotherapy, pharmacological interventions appear to be effective at suppressing deviant sexual desires (e.g., Thibaut, De La Barra, Gordon, Cosyns, & Bradford, 2010). Drugs used in the past acted to suppress all sexual interests and compliance was a serious problem (Baratta, Javelot, Morali, Halleguen, & Weiner, 2012; Meston & Frohlich, 2000). The use of selective serotonin-reuptake inhibitors (SSRIs) has shown to be most effective for sexual offenders with paraphilia (Adi, Ashcroft, Browne, Beech, Fry-Smith, & Hyde, 2002) and those presenting with exhibitionism, compulsive masturbation, and pedophilia (Garcia & Thibaut, 2011).

Relapse Prevention

Sexual offenders need to identify their offence cycle (e.g., emotional states and stress factors that put them at risk, grooming strategies) and develop ways to avoid these problems or to deal with them.

Programs with a **relapse prevention** (RP) component usually consist of two main parts. First, offenders are asked to list emotional and situational risk factors that lead to either fantasizing about sexual abuse or actually committing the abuse. For example, for a rapist, perhaps feelings of anger toward women would be a risk factor; for a child molester, perhaps feeling lonely and sitting on a bench, watching children in a playground would be a risk factor. Second, offenders need to develop plans to deal more appropriately with their problems (e.g., meeting their emotional needs in a prosocial way) and ways to avoid or cope with high-risk situations. Box 14.6 describes in more detail how the relapse prevention model has been applied with sexual offenders.

EFFECTIVENESS OF TREATMENT FOR SEXUAL OFFENDERS

If we are going to treat sexual offenders, it is important to know whether the treatment actually works. There is a lack of consensus about whether sex offender treatment is effective. Some researchers argue that treatment does not work (Quinsey, Harris, Rice, & Lalumière, 1993), whereas others are more optimistic (Marshall, Eccles, & Barbaree, 1991).

Box 14.6   Forensic Psychology in the Spotlight

Relapse Prevention with Sexual Offenders

Relapse prevention (RP) is a self-control program designed to teach sexual offenders to recognize risky situations that could lead to reoffending and to learn coping and avoidance strategies to deal with those situations. The RP model was initially developed for the treatment of addictive behaviours, such as smoking, alcohol abuse, and overeating (Marlatt & Gordon, 1985). Sexual offenders are asked to develop a personalized sexual offence cycle that identifies their pre-offence thoughts, feelings, and behaviours. At each step of the cycle, the offender generates options or alternative behaviours that interrupt the offence cycle. RP is not considered a cure, but it helps the sexual offender manage the urge to offend sexually. RP is a way of teaching sexual offenders to think and look ahead to prevent committing another sexual offence. For RP to be successful, the sexual offender must be motivated to stop offending.

The following are some relevant terms (used in Figure 14.1) associated with relapse prevention:

- *Lapse:* Any occurrence of fantasizing about sexual offending or engaging in behaviours in the offence cycle

- *Relapse:* Occurrence of a sexual offence
- *High-risk situation:* Any situation that increases the likelihood of a lapse or a relapse
- *Apparently irrelevant decisions:* Conscious or unconscious decisions made by offenders that put them in high-risk situations
- *Coping response:* Development of avoidance strategies to sidestep high-risk situations and escape plans if the high-risk situation cannot be avoided
- *Abstinence violation effect:* Refers to how the offender reacts to a lapse. Both cognitive reactions (e.g., lack of willpower) and emotional states (e.g., feeling guilty) are considered. If the offender views the lapse as an irreversible failure, then this can promote a relapse. Alternatively, if the lapse is seen as a reasonable mistake in a learning process, the offender can become more confident in his ability to avoid or handle future lapses.

Figure 14.1 presents the sequences of events that may lead to a relapse in a child molester.

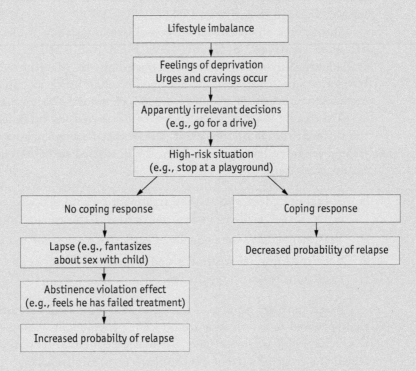

Figure 14.1 Sequence of Events Leading to Relapse in a Child Molester

What we do know is that incarceration does not appear to be a deterrent for sexual or other offenders. Nunes et al. (2007) reported that there was no association between incarceration and sexual recidivism rates in a sample of 627 Canadian adult male sexual offenders. Certainly, incarceration may be an effective method for handling high-risk sexual offenders, however, community alternatives may be a more effective and less expensive option for the majority of sexual offenders.

Numerous problems face researchers wanting to evaluate the effectiveness of sexual offender treatment programs. The main problem is that it is unethical to carry out the ideal controlled study. The optimal design would randomly assign motivated sexual offenders (i.e., offenders all wanting treatment) to either treatment or no treatment. Then, both treated and untreated sexual offenders would be released at the same time, they would be followed up for several years, and rates of reoffending would be measured. Most treatment outcome studies have not used this design (see Marques, 1999, for one of the few studies to use random assignment). It is unlikely that many sexual offenders would agree to participate in this ideal study since untreated sexual offenders are held in custody longer than treated offenders.

Another challenge for researchers has been the relatively low base rates of sexual recidivism, even in untreated offenders (Barbaree, 1997). On average, only 15% of sex offenders are detected committing a new sexual offence after five years and 20% after ten years (Hanson & Bussière, 1998; Hanson & Thornton, 2000). Thus, for researchers to detect any differences between treatment groups, they need to wait many years. As a way of trying to deal with this problem, some researchers have begun to use unofficial data, such as child protection agency files or self-reports, to detect reoffending (see Marshall & Barbaree, 1988).

Despite the challenges described above, a number of meta-analyses of sexual offender treatment programs have been published (e.g., Alexander, 1999; Gallagher, Wilson, Hirschfield, Coggeshall, & MacKenzie, 1999; Hall, 1995; Hanson et al., 2002; Lösel & Schmucker, 2005). For example, in one well-cited meta-analytic study, Hanson et al. (2002) examined 42 separate studies with a total of 5078 treated sex offenders and 4376 untreated sex offenders. Averaged across the different types of treatment, the sexual recidivism rate was 12.3% for the treated sex offenders and 16.8% for the untreated sexual offenders. The following results were found:

- Sexual offenders who refused treatment or who dropped out of treatment had higher sexual recidivism rates compared with those who completed the treatment.
- Treatment effects were equally effective for adolescent and adult sex offenders.
- Both institutional treatment and community treatment were associated with reductions in sexual recidivism.

Based on their findings, Hanson et al. (2002) concluded that "the treatments that appeared most effective were recent programs providing some form of cognitive-behavioral treatment, and, for adolescent sex offenders, systemic treatment aimed at a range of current life problems (e.g., family, school, peers)" (p. 187). This finding has received continued support from more recent research (e.g., Woodrow

& Bright, 2011). In contrast, the treatment approach that Lösel and Schmucker (2005) reported to be the most effective was surgical castration. However, this form of treatment has been considered by some to be unethical. In addition, the sexual offenders willing to participate in this form of intervention are a very select group and highly motivated.

Not all sexual offenders stay in treatment. In a meta-analysis of treatment attrition, Olver, Stockdale, and Wormith (2011) found that 27.6% of sexual offenders drop out of treatment. The following variables were related to treatment attrition: number of prior offences, psychopathy, denial, negative treatment attitudes, and level of motivation. Sexual offenders with these features may need additional support in order to encourage them to remain in treatment.

Nor are sexual offenders all the same. Different types of sexual offenders are linked to higher reoffending rates. Treatment providers need to do a comprehensive assessment in order to match the risk level of the sex offender to the most effective treatment. Sexual offenders also need to be provided with support in the community to maximize the likelihood they will able to cope successfully. Further research on sexual offenders and their victims is essential if we want to prevent sexual assaults from occurring in the future.

SUMMARY

1. Sexual offences affect a large percentage of the population. However, it is difficult to get a true incidence of this type of crime since most victims do not report being sexually assaulted to the police. Victims do not report sexual offences to the police for a variety of reasons.

2. Rapists are offenders who sexually assault adults, and child molesters are offenders who sexually assault children. Sexual aggression has serious psychological and physical consequences for victims and their friends, intimate partners, and family. The psychological consequences of rape victimization include anxiety, depression, and post-traumatic stress disorder.

3. Typologies of both rapists and child molesters have been proposed that focus on the motives for sexual abuse. Rapists have been classified into the following five primary types based on research by Knight and Prentky (1990): (1) opportunistic, (2) pervasively angry, (3) sexual, (4) sadistic, and (5) vindictive. Groth (1979) proposed a different rapist typology, consisting of the following three types: (1) angry, (2) power, and (3) sadistic. Groth et al. (1982) proposed that child molesters be classified into two main types: (1) regressed and (2) fixated.

4. Treatment for sexual offenders involves recognizing denial, minimizations, and cognitive distortions; gaining victim empathy; modifying deviant sexual interest; enhancing social skills; dealing with substance-abuse problems; and developing relapse-prevention plans.

5. Meta-analyses of sexual offender treatment programs have found the following: (1) sexual offenders who complete treatment have lower rates of sexual recidivism than dropouts or treatment refusers, (2) treatment is effective for both adolescent and adult sexual offenders, (3) both institutional and community treatment programs are associated with reductions in sexual recidivism, and (4) cognitive-behavioural treatments are more effective than other forms of treatment.

Discussion Questions

1. You are interested in doing a study on the association between childhood sexual abuse and sexual offending later in life. Describe the methodology you would use and what variables you would measure.

2. Sexual assault myths are still prominent in our society. What do you think could be done to ensure future generations do not accept these myths as reality?

Chapter 15
Homicidal Offenders

Learning Objectives

- Describe the characteristics of homicide in Canada.
- Differentiate between instrumental and reactive homicide.
- Describe the various categories of maternal filicide.
- Differentiate between serial, mass, and spree murders.
- Describe the theories used to explain homicidal behaviour.
- Describe the effectiveness of treatment for violent offenders.

For years, Stephen James terrorized women in the city where he lived before the police could stop him. He grew up as a troubled child from a broken home and was known around town because of his aggressive outbursts. Stephen committed his first violent crime when he was just 16 years old. This was when he sexually assaulted a young girl who had rejected his sexual advances. According to the police officer who investigated the case, the assault was very aggressive and the girl spent a week in hospital recovering from her injuries. By the time he was in his early 20s, Stephen's behaviour had escalated to the point where he was regularly committing assaults against women and his aggression toward them seemed to grow with each offence. At the age of 25, Stephen committed his first homicide in reaction to a woman who physically resisted him when he tried to rape her. Later, Stephen would say that the feeling of power he experienced while carrying out that murder is what led him to commit other murders over the next ten years. Luckily, Stephen's last victim managed to escape before she was killed and the description she gave to the police ultimately led to Stephen's apprehension.

Fortunately, serial murders of the sort displayed by Stephen in the opening vignette are very rare, and even the more typical "one-off" homicides that we hear about in the news are not that common in Canada. But regardless of how often homicides occur, these crimes deserve our attention. Homicide represents the ultimate violent act. Indeed, of all the crimes that have been described in this textbook, homicide is perhaps the most devastating, for the victims obviously, but also for their families, friends, and society more generally.

Homicide is also a major area of study within the field of forensic psychology. For many years, forensic psychologists have been trying to understand how people can kill one another and why this lethal form of violence has emerged in our society. Forensic psychologists are also interested in understanding the various forms of homicidal violence that exist, ranging from homicides that occur between husband and wife in the "heat of passion" to homicides committed by young children, new mothers, serial killers, and mass murderers. Forensic psychologists are also involved in the development of treatment programs to rehabilitate violent offenders, including those that have committed homicide, and they sometimes attempt to evaluate the effectiveness of these programs. This chapter discusses some of the research that has been conducted to understand homicidal offenders and how to effectively manage their violence.

NATURE AND EXTENT OF HOMICIDAL VIOLENCE

Canadian criminal law recognizes four different types of homicide: first-degree murder, second-degree murder, manslaughter, and infanticide (the killing of a baby by its mother). Different penalties are imposed for each type, with a maximum of 5 years of imprisonment for infanticide and life in prison (25 years with no chance of parole) for the other three. In considering different kinds of homicide, it should be noted that some forms of killing in Canada are exempt from penalties, such as killing during war or killing in self defence.

In Canada, first-degree murder includes all murder that is planned and deliberate. It also includes the murder of a law enforcement officer or correctional staff member, or a murder occurring during the commission of another violent offence (e.g., sexual assault), regardless of whether the murder was unplanned or deliberate. All murder that is not considered first-degree murder is classified as second-degree murder.

Manslaughter is unintentional murder that occurs during the "heat of passion" or because of criminal negligence. If a man returns home unexpectedly from a business trip to find his wife in bed with her lover, and during the ensuing altercation he grabs a rifle and shoots and kills the lover, that man could be charged with manslaughter; the crime occurred in the "heat of passion." On the other hand, if a drunk driver accidentally kills an individual who was crossing the street, this driver has not committed a crime in the "heat of passion;" instead, the driver could be charged with manslaughter due to criminal negligence.

Despite what many members of the public might think, homicide is actually a relatively rare offence in Canada, representing less than 1% of all violent crimes (Statistics Canada, 2015). As illustrated in Figure 15.1, Canada's homicide rate has been declining since the early 1990s and is currently at its lowest rate since the 1960s (Miladinovic & Mulligan, 2015). Attempted homicide has also gradually decreased over the same time period and is at its lowest rate since the mid-1970s.

Additional interesting details related to homicide in Canada, described by Miladinovic & Mulligan (2015), include the following:

■ In 2014, Newfoundland and Labrador reported the lowest homicide rate of all the provinces and Manitoba reported the highest homicide rate. In terms of

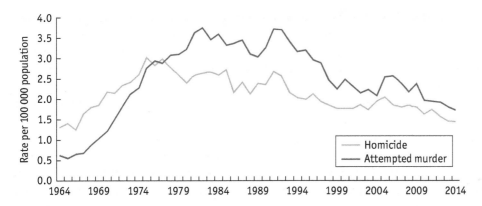

Figure 15.1 Rates (per 100 000 population) of homicide and attempted homicide in Canada between 1964 and 2014.

Source: Statistics Canada, Homicide Survey and Uniform Crime Reporting Survey by Statistics of Canada © 2015. Reproduced and distributed on an "as is" basis with the permission of Statistics Canada.

metropolitan areas, Thunder Bay reported the highest homicide rate in Canada, followed by Winnipeg. The territories report significantly higher homicide rates than the provinces.

■ Consistent with previous years, most solved homicides in 2014 were committed by someone known to the victim (83%), including an acquaintance (37%), a family member (34%), or some other individual (e.g., an ex-spouse).

■ Youth commit relatively few homicides. In 2014, 25 homicides were committed by youth (out of 516). The rate of homicides committed by youth in 2014 is the lowest since 1969.

■ In 2014, nearly a quarter of all homicide victims (23%) were Aboriginal and the Aboriginal homicide rate was 6 times higher than the non-Aboriginal homicide rate. Of people accused of homicide in 2014, 32% were Aboriginal people.

BIMODAL CLASSIFICATION OF HOMICIDE

In their attempt to understand the nature of homicidal behaviour, researchers have developed methods for classifying homicides. One particular classification system that has become very popular characterizes homicidal aggression in a bimodal manner. Following Fesbach (1964), Kingsbury, Lambert, and Hendrickse (1997) proposed a bimodal classification scheme for the study of homicide in humans, in which homicides are classified as **reactive (affective) aggression** or **instrumental (predatory) aggression**. Reactive homicide is defined as impulsive, unplanned, immediate, driven by negative emotions, and occurring in response to some perceived provocation. Instrumental homicide is defined as proactive rather than reactive, and is a premeditated, calculated behaviour, motivated by some goal. This goal could be to obtain money, power, control, or even the gratification of sadistic fantasies (Meloy, 1997).

Reactive homicide occurs more often among relatives, and instrumental homicide among strangers (Daly & Wilson, 1982). In a large-scale study, Miethe and Drass (1999) coded 34 329 single-victim, single-offender homicides in the United States

Reactive (affective) aggression: Aggression that is impulsive, unplanned, immediate, driven by negative emotions, and occurring in response to some perceived provocation

Instrumental (predatory) aggression: Aggression that is premeditated, calculated, and motivated by some goal (e.g., to obtain money)

between 1990 and 1994. They classified 80% as reactive and 20% as instrumental. In this study, the victim–offender relationship was divided into three categories: strangers, acquaintances, and family members/intimates. Most of the homicides involved acquaintances (55%), with most of these being classified as reactive (80%). Family members and intimate partners accounted for 28% of the cases, with nearly all these homicides being classified as reactive (93%). Finally, in 17% of the cases, the victim was a stranger, with 52% being classified as reactive.

In a Canadian study, Woodworth and Porter (2002) used a continuum of violence—from purely reactive through reactive-instrumental and instrumental-reactive to purely instrumental—to code homicides committed by 125 adult male offenders. In this sample, 12.8% of homicides were coded as purely reactive, 23.2% as reactive-instrumental, 20% as instrumental-reactive, and 36% as purely instrumental (8% of the sample could not be coded). Interestingly, Woodworth and Porter found that there was a relationship between the instrumentality of the homicide and the degree to which the offender exhibited features of psychopathy. Specifically, offenders who scored higher on the PCL-R were more likely to commit instrumental (vs. reactive) homicides compared to offenders who scored lower on the PCL-R. That being said, more recent meta-analytic research suggests that the relationship between psychopathy and violence is more complicated (Blais, Solodukhin, & Forth, 2014). Blais and her colleagues found significant relationships between psychopathy and both types of violence; interpersonal features of psychopathy were associated with instrumental violence, social deviance features of psychopathy were associated with reactive violence, and lifestyle features of psychopathy were associated with both types of violence.

TYPES OF HOMICIDE

Without taking into consideration serial killings and mass murders, which will be discussed in more detail later in the chapter, there are still many different types of homicide committed in Canada. Many of these forms of homicide are distinguished from one another based on the relationship between the offender and his or her victim. We describe several different types of homicide that forensic psychologists have carefully studied.

Filicide: When Parents Kill

Filicide: The killing of children by their biological parents or step-parents; includes neonaticide (killing a baby within 24 hours of birth) and infanticide (killing a baby within the first year of life)

The term **filicide** refers to the killing of children by their biological parents or step-parents and includes neonaticide (killing a baby within 24 hours of birth) and infanticide (killing a baby within the first year of life). The killing of a child by a parent is difficult to understand and attitudes toward parents killing their children vary across cultures and time. For example, in ancient Rome, a father had a right to kill his children (Finkel, Burke, & Chavez, 2000). A few cultures have also sanctioned the gender-based killing of children. Notably, in China and India, female children are more likely to be killed than male children because of the greater value these societies place on male children (Myers, 2012). In the past, certain Inuit societies also killed infants that had birth defects or killed one infant when twins were born (Garber, 1947).

Between 2003 and 2013, 319 children and youth (aged 0 to 17 years) were victims of familial homicide (Statistics Canada, 2015). Children (0 to 11 years) were more at risk of familial homicide than youth (12 to 17 years) during this time period, but children under the age of 1 were most at risk of familial homicide. Sadly, since 2003, 22% of infant victims were killed the day they were born. In terms of cause of death, the most common method of familial homicide in cases involving children and youth between 2003 and 2013 was strangulation, suffocation, or drowning (27%) (Statistics Canada, 2015). These methods are much rarer when children and youth are murdered by non-family members (7%). In non-familial homicides of children and youth, stabbing is the most common method of death (34%), but this is rarer in cases of familial homicides of children and youth (16%).

Why would family members kill children and youth? There appear to be many motivating factors in these tragic deaths, but the motivation varies to some extent based on the age of the victim. For example, for young victims (<6 years), frustration on the part of the accused accounts for the majority of homicides committed between 2003 and 2013, although concealment of the child appears to be another important factor for victims that are <1 years old (Statistics Canada, 2015). In contrast, frustration only accounted for 28% of homicides for victims between the ages of 12 and 17 during this time period. Other factors that play a more important role for victims in this age range (compared to younger victims) include an argument or quarrel between the accused and the victim, and revenge (Statistics Canada, 2015).

Historically, there has been disagreement in the literature with respect to offender characteristics in cases of filicide. For example, some studies have suggested that fathers are more likely than mothers to be the perpetrator of filicides (Ogrodnik, 2008), whereas other research has indicated the opposite (Dalley, 2008). Similarly, some studies have found that stepfathers and stepmothers are more likely to kill a child than biological fathers and mothers (Harris, Hilton, Rice, & Eke, 2007), whereas other studies have failed to replicate this finding (Temrin, Nordlund, Rying, & Tullberg, 2011).

Mothers Who Kill Despite the fact that fathers are clearly capable of murdering their own children, and perhaps even more likely in Canada (Dawson, 2015), the focus of most research (and certainly most news stories) has been on mothers. Why would a mother kill her child (or children)? There appear to be several potential reasons. A number of studies have classified maternal filicides (Cheung, 1986; Resnick, 1970). Stanton and Simpson (2002) reviewed these and other studies of child murder and concluded that there are three broad types of maternal filicides: (1) neonaticides, (2) those committed by battering mothers, and (3) those committed by mothers with mental illnesses.

According to Stanton and Simpson (2002), the neonaticide group (those who kill their children within 24 hours of birth) are typically young, unmarried women with no prior history of mental illness, who are not suicidal, and who have concealed their pregnancies, fearing rejection or disapproval from their families. Battering mothers have killed their children impulsively in response to the behaviour of the child. These mothers have the highest rates of social and family stress, including marital stress and financial problems. The group with mental disorders tends to be older and married.

They are likely to have killed older children, to have multiple victims, and to be diagnosed with a psychosis or depression. They are also the group that is most likely to attempt suicide after the murder. Some researchers have used the term *altruistic filicide* (Resnick, 1969) to describe mothers who kill out of love. In these cases, the murder is in response to the mother's delusional beliefs that the child's death will somehow protect the child.

Infanticide and Mental Illness Does childbirth trigger mental illness? One common assumption underlying the offence of infanticide is that women who kill their infants are suffering from a mental illness related to childbirth. Three types of mental illness have been identified during the postpartum period: postpartum blues, postpartum depression, and postpartum psychosis.

The most common type of mental illness that can occur in the postpartum period is postpartum blues (experienced by up to 85% of women), which includes crying, irritability, and anxiety, beginning within a few days of childbirth and lasting from a few hours to days but rarely continuing past day 12 (Affonso & Domino, 1984; O'Hara, 1995). Postpartum depression (experienced by 7% to 19% of women) occurs within the first few weeks or months after birth and usually lasts for several months (O'Hara, 1995). The symptoms are identical to clinical depression and include depressed mood, loss of appetite, concentration and sleep problems, and suicidal thoughts. The most severe and rare type of mental illness that has been associated with childbirth is postpartum psychosis (occurring in 1 or 2 of every 1000 births). Postpartum psychosis usually involves delusions, hallucinations, and suicidal or homicidal thoughts within the first three months after childbirth (Millis & Kornblith, 1992).

Postpartum psychosis has received a lot of attention (from both researchers and the media) because of its potential role in maternal infanticides. Indeed, several tragic cases of infanticide have highlighted the devastating, potentially lethal effects of postpartum psychosis. Perhaps the best known case is that of Andrea Yates, the Houston mother who drowned her five children in the family's bathtub (McLellan, 2006). Andrea Yates had been diagnosed with postpartum depression and postpartum psychosis. According to her defence lawyers, Yates was delusional when she murdered her children, believing that she had to murder them to save them from Satan (Diamond, 2008). The prosecution agreed that Andrea Yates had a mental illness, but argued that she knew what she was doing and knew that killing her children was wrong. In March 2002, a jury rejected Andrea Yates's insanity plea and found her guilty of capital murder (Yardley, 2002). Yates was originally sentenced to life in prison. However, in 2005, the Texas Court of Appeal reversed Yates's convictions because of false testimony given by a psychiatrist testifying for the prosecution. A new trial ended on July 26, 2006, when Yates was found not guilty by reason of insanity and committed to a state mental hospital ("Andrea Yates Case", 2006).

In the Media box describes two additional cases of filicide that have taken place in Canada. Both cases involved a mother killing her children. In the case involving Suzanne Killinger-Johnson, mental illness appears to have played a significant role in the death of her infant child. This contrasts with the more recent case of Sonia Blanchette. In this case, despite the horrifying nature of the murders she committed and her own self-inflicted death, mental illness did not appear to play a role.

Mothers Who Kill

When children are killed by their parents, fathers are often responsible for the deaths. Despite this, more attention seems to be paid to mothers who kill their children, presumably because the public has a particularly difficult time comprehending how mothers, who are often assumed to be particularly nurturing, can murder their own children. Probably for the same reason, mental illness is often assumed to be at the root of maternal filicides; what else could explain such horrific crimes? But while mental illness does appear to play a role in some cases, this is not always true. The following two cases demonstrate this point.

Suzanne Killinger-Johnson

Suzanne Killinger-Johnson was a physician with a psychotherapy practice in Toronto. She had a history of depression while in medical school at the University of Western Ontario. She had a successful marriage, a flourishing career, and supportive family and friends. In February 2000, she gave birth to a son named Cuyler. Sometime after the birth, Killinger-Johnson started to become more and more obsessive about caring for Cuyler. By the spring, she started to see a therapist and was taking medication for depression. In July, she stopped taking her antidepressants because she was worried about the effects of the medicine in her breast milk. Subsequently, she avoided her friends and missed her therapy appointments. Her husband, family, and friends attempted to help her. However, at 6:30 a.m. on August 11, while her father had left her alone for a few minutes, she took her son, drove to a nearby subway station, and with Cuyler in her arms jumped in front of a train. Cuyler died instantly and his mother died eight days later on August 19, 2000. Suzanne's depression was assumed to be a contributing factor in the death of her and her infant son.

Sonia Blanchette

Unlike the case of Killinger-Johnson, mental illness did not appear to play a significant role in the case involving Sonia Blanchette. Blanchette was accused of strangling and drowning her three children in her apartment in Drummondville, Quebec in December of 2012. Her children at the time were aged 2, 4, and 5. Blanchette had lost custody of her three children to her ex-husband the previous year and was only supposed to have supervised visits with them. At the time, she was facing legal trouble in a

Sonia Blanchette was accused of strangling and drowning her three kids, but starved herself to death in jail before her trial began.
Ryan Remiorz/Canadian Press Images

separate case where she was accused of kidnapping her youngest child. Appearing before court to face charges of murdering her three children, Blanchette's court-appointed lawyer asked that she be evaluated to determine if she was fit to stand trial; a request the Crown did not object to. The evaluation indicated that she was fit to stand trial and did not suffer from any mental illness. However, before Blanchette's trial for the murder of her children could even begin, Blanchette died. While in jail awaiting her trial, Blanchette made the decision to starve herself to death, which she achieved with the help of right-to-die advocates in Quebec. Ironically, her being found mentally competent by the courts allowed her to refuse treatments under Quebec law; treatments, such as force feedings, that would have prevented her death. Eventually, Blanchette was moved from the jail where she was being held before her trial into a palliative care facility. She ultimately died the same day she was scheduled to appear in court to set a trial date for the murder charges.

Sources: Based on Banerjee, 2012; CBC, 2015; "Mother Who Killed Son," 2000; Perreaux, 2015.

Familicide: The killing of a spouse and children

Fathers Who Kill Despite the fact that fathers and mothers both commit filicides, **familicide**, which occurs when a spouse *and* children are killed, is almost always committed by a man. The homicide is often accompanied by a history of spousal and child abuse prior to the offence. Wilson, Daly, and Daniele (1995) examined 109 Canadian and British cases of familicide and also found that in about half of the cases the killer committed suicide. Those who killed their spouse and their own children (i.e., genetic offspring) had a greater likelihood of committing suicide than those who killed their spouse and their stepchildren.

Wilson et al. (1995) described two types of familicide murderers: the despondent non-hostile killer and the hostile accusatory killer. The despondent non-hostile killer is depressed and worried about an impending disaster for himself or his family. He kills his family and then commits suicide. Past acts of violence toward children and spouse are not characteristic of this type of killer. The hostile accusatory killer, however, expresses hostility toward his wife, often related to alleged infidelities or her intentions to terminate the relationship. A past history of violent acts is common for this type of killer.

Youth Who Kill

In 2014, 25 youths between the ages of 12 and 17 were accused of homicide in Canada, which represents a decline compared to 2013 (16 fewer than in 2013) and is well below the 10-year youth homicide average of 59 (Boyce, 2015). In fact, the 2014 youth homicide rate of 1.07 per 100 000 youth is the lowest rate recorded since 1984 (Boyce, 2015). Unfortunately, a different picture emerges for attempted homicide. In 2013, 38 youth were accused of attempted murder. This number rose to 51 youth in 2014, representing a 37% increase (Boyce, 2015). Despite this increase, the 2014 rate of attempted homicide among youth in Canada (2.18 per 100 000 youth) is still below the 10-year average (2.25 per 100 000 youth).

According to Perreault (2012), in contrast to homicides committed by adults, when youth commit homicides, they often have at least one accomplice. For example, of the 46 youths who committed murder in Canada in 2011, Perrault reports that 57% of them had an accomplice, compared to only 31% of adult homicide offenders. However, like adults who commit murders, youth who kill are often acquainted with their victims, either intimately (e.g., the victims are their parents) or as criminal associates (Perreault, 2012). Box 15.1 describes the case of Jasmine Richardson, who, with the help of her boyfriend, killed her parents and 8-year-old brother.

Although the number of homicides committed by youth represents only a small portion of the total number of homicides committed in Canada, homicide by youth, such as the murders committed by Richardson and Steinke, holds a particular fascination in the mind of the public. What motivates youth to kill? What factors underlie homicide by youth?

To shed light on these issues, Corder, Ball, Haizlip, Rollins, and Beaumont (1976) compared three groups of youths: ten youths charged with killing parents, ten youths charged with killing relatives or acquaintances, and ten youths charged with killing strangers. Youth charged with parricide (killing parents) were more likely to have been physically abused, to have witnessed spousal abuse, and to report amnesia for

The Youngest Convicted Multiple Murderer in Canada: The Case of Jasmine Richardson

On April 23, 2006, in Medicine Hat, Alberta, the parents and brother of Jasmine Richardson were found dead in their home. Just over a year later, in July 2007, Richardson was convicted of the triple murder. Her boyfriend, Jeremy Steinke, was similarly convicted in November 2008.

Richardson's parents were both found covered in blood with multiple stab wounds and Richardson's 8-year-old brother, Jacob, had his throat cut. The motivation behind the crimes, it seems, was that Richardson's parents were attempting to prevent her from seeing the 23-year-old Steinke. Richardson was in grade 7 at the time.

Steinke was an unemployed high school dropout who was heavily involved in goth culture. In fact, he claimed to be a 300-year-old werewolf and was known to wear a vial of blood around his neck. Richardson also had a fascination with goth culture.

During the trial, questions were raised about the role that Jasmine played in the murder of her family. While Steinke appeared to have carried out the killings, it was argued that Richardson persuaded Steinke to commit the murders, told Steinke how to gain access to her house, and willingly fled with Steinke after the murders to a town in Saskatchewan. Emails between the pair also appeared to corroborate Richardson's involvement in the crimes, as did a picture found in Jasmine's locker. The picture depicted four stick figures. The smiling figure in the middle was throwing gasoline on the other three and setting them ablaze before running to "Jeremy's truck."

During the trial, references were made to Oliver Stone's movie *Natural Born Killers*, starring Woody Harrelson (Mickey) and Juliette Lewis (Mallory) as a pair of spree killers. In the movie, the spree starts with the killing of Mallory's abusive parents. Both Richardson and Steinke had watched the film and Steinke apparently loved it.

The jury in the Richardson trial took four hours to deliberate before coming back with a guilty verdict on three counts of first-degree murder. Under Canadian law, because Richardson was 12 at the time of the killings, she could not receive an adult sentence. Instead, in November 2007, she was sentenced to the maximum 10 years that she could receive, making her the youngest person in Canada to ever receive a conviction for multiple murders. Part of Richardson's sentence was spent in a psychiatric facility and the remainder was under conditional supervision in the community. While still serving the remainder of her sentence, Richardson is currently pursuing studies at a university in Alberta.

In December 2008, Steinke received a harsher penalty than Richardson of three life sentences for his involvement in the crimes. These are being served concurrently. He will be eligible for parole after serving 25 years.

Questions

1. Should children as young as 12 be sentenced as adults in Canada for the sorts of crimes that Jasmine Richardson was involved in, or should they be sentenced as children? Why?

2. If you disagree with the sentence that Richardson received, what would an appropriate sentence be for her involvement in the crimes committed against her family? Why is this sentence appropriate?

3. What do you think the likelihood is of young killers like Richardson being rehabilitated? What specific challenges might these individuals face as they try to reintegrate back into society?

Sources: Based on "Medicine Hat girl guilty of first-degree murder", published by CBC/Radio-Canada.

the murders, compared with the other youth who committed murder. More recently, Darby, Allan, Kashani, Hartke, and Reid (1998) examined the association between family abuse and suicide attempts in a sample of 112 adolescents convicted of homicide. Abused youth were younger, more often Caucasian, and more likely to have attempted suicide prior to the homicide than non-abused youth.

Cornell, Benedek, and Benedek (1987) developed a typology of juvenile homicide offenders based on the circumstances of the offence. The types of homicide were labelled *psychotic* (youth who had symptoms of severe mental illness at the time of the murder), *conflict* (youth who were engaged in an argument or conflict with the victim when the killing occurred), and *crime* (youth who killed during the commission of another crime, such as robbery or sexual assault). When the classification system was applied to 72 juveniles charged with murder, 7% were assigned to the psychotic subgroup, 42% to the conflict subgroup, and 51% to the crime subgroup. Differences across these homicide subgroups in family background, criminal history, and psychopathology have been reported (Greco & Cornell, 1992).

Woodworth, Agar, and Coupland (2013) recently examined the motivations underlying youth homicides in Canada. Their sample included 105 youth homicide offenders (13 girls and 92 boys) who were referred for court-ordered or court-related assessments. They found that nearly half (46.2%) of all homicides in their sample were committed while the youth was committing another crime. For example, 38.6% of the homicides in their sample involved theft of money, property, or substances, and 8.9% involved sexual assault. Woodworth and his colleagues also applied the previously described instrumental-reactive classification scheme to the homicides and found that 36.7% of the crimes could be classified as purely instrumental, 33.7% as instrumental-reactive, 6.1% as reactive-instrumental, and 23.5% as purely reactive. Thus, more than three quarters of youth homicides in the sample involved some level of instrumentality, which is slightly less than the rate of instrumentality found in adult homicides (85%) (Woodworth & Porter, 2002). In Woodworth et al.'s (2013) study, family members were less likely to be victims in instrumental homicides and more likely to be victims in reactive homicides. Acquaintances and strangers, on the other hand, were more likely to be targeted by youth for instrumental reasons.

Spousal Killers

Femicide is the general term applied to the killing of women, and *uxoricide* is the more specific term denoting the killing of a wife by her husband. **Androcide** refers to the killing of men, and *mariticide* is the term denoting the killing of a husband by his wife.

Uxoricide appears to be much more common than mariticide. Indeed, while the intimate-partner crime rate has declined over time in a fashion that is similar to homicide more generally, this particular pattern of offending (i.e., a disproportionate rate of uxoricides) has remained stable over time (Perreault, 2012; Sinha, 2012).

Given this pattern of offending, attempts have been made to understand why husbands kill their wives. For example, Crawford and Gartner (1992) found that the most common motive for uxoricide (in 43% of cases they examined) was the perpetrators' anger over either estrangement from their partners or sexual jealousy about perceived infidelity. More recent research supports these findings. Sinha (2012) found that the two primary motivations underlying intimate-partner homicides that were committed between 2000 and 2010 in Canada were escalations of arguments/quarrels and jealousy. However, jealousy was a motive more often in cases where the

Femicide: The killing of women
Androcide: The killing of men

female intimate partner was killed (24% of cases) compared to when the male partner was the victim (10% of cases).

Other research has focused on risk factors in cases of uxoricide. For example, comparing police records from Canada, Australia, and the United States, Wilson and Daly (1993) found that recent or imminent departure by the eventual victim was associated with a husband killing his wife (but not with a wife killing her husband). A study of risk factors for femicide in abusive relationships by Campbell, Webster, and Koziol-McLain (2003) found the following factors increased the risk for homicide: the offender having access to a gun, previous threats having been made with a weapon, estrangement, and the victim having left for another partner.

Offence characteristics have also been examined. For example, unlike wives who kill their husbands, husbands often use close contact methods when killing their partners (e.g., beating or strangling; Dobash, Dobash, Cavanagh, & Lewis, 2004), and uxoricides are often characterized by a use of excessive force, or overkill (i.e., more violence than is required to cause death; Crawford & Gartner, 1992). Another common finding concerning uxoricides is the high incidence of perpetrator suicide following the murder (Crawford & Gartner, 1992). This finding is especially interesting considering that wives rarely commit suicide after killing their husbands (Rosenbaum, 1990), and that male offenders rarely commit suicide after killing acquaintances or strangers (Stack, 1997).

Although arguably fewer studies exist on the topic of mariticide, researchers have also attempted to understand this form of homicide. This is important because, despite the lower rate of mariticide, when a man is killed by a woman, the perpetrator is often the man's wife. Research has identified many differences between uxoricide and mariticide, some of which have been discussed above, but most of the attention in the literature centres on the issue of motive. Whereas men most often kill their wives due to anger or jealousy, research suggests that wives often kill their husbands out of fear for themselves or their children (Johnson & Hotton, 2003). Supporting this is recent Canadian research, which suggested that when a wife kills her husband, the husband is often the one who used or threatened violence first (Sinha, 2012). A lot of research now exists on battered women and the role that abuse plays in cases of mariticide (see Chapter 13). Currently in Canada, under certain circumstances the courts allow abuse to be used as a defence in such cases (see *R. v. Lavallee*, 1990).

Sexual Homicide

Unlike most of the homicides we've previously discussed, some murders are sexually motivated and often committed against strangers (Chan, Heide, & Myers, 2013). Various definitions of **sexual homicide** exist, but perhaps the most commonly cited definition was proposed by Ressler, Burgess, and Douglas (1988). In their seminal work, *Sexual Homicide: Patterns and Motives*, they suggested that for a homicide to be considered a sexual homicide, one of the following sexual indicators must be present: "victim attire or lack of attire [i.e., the victim was found undressed]; exposure of the sexual parts of the victim's body; sexual positioning of the victim's body; insertion of foreign objects into the victim's body cavities;

Sexual homicide: Killing that involves a sexual component

Some homicides, especially sexual homicides where the offender and victim are strangers, can be difficult for the police to solve.
Couperfield/Shutterstock

evidence of sexual intercourse (oral, vaginal, anal); and evidence of substitute sexual activity, interest, or sadistic fantasy" (p. xiii).

Relatively little research exists on the topic of sexual homicide, presumably because these crimes rarely occur (Beauregard & Martineau, 2013) and they can be difficult for the police to solve, especially when no relationship exists between the murderer and his victim (Proulx, Beauregard, Cusson, & Nicole, 2007). Research that does exist has attempted to identify the characteristics of the offender who commits these types of homicides, the typical victim characteristics, and the methods used by the offenders to target, kill, and dispose of their victims (e.g., Beauregard & Proulx, 2002; Carter & Hollin, 2010; Chan, Myers, & Heide, 2012).

Over the last decade or so, attention has been paid to this type of homicide in Canada. Much of this research has been conducted by Dr. Eric Beauregard (e.g., Beauregard & Proulx, 2002; Beauregard & Field, 2008; Beauregard & Martineau, 2013), who is profiled in Box 15.2. In one excellent study, Beauregard and Martineau (2013) present a detailed descriptive analysis of a large sample of sexual homicides (350 cases) that were committed in Canada from 1948 to 2010. Beauregard and Martineau examined offender and victim characteristics, victim targeting and access, and the modus operandi (MO) used by offenders to commit their crimes.

Box 15.2

Canadian Researcher Profile: Dr. Eric Beauregard

Courtesy of Eric Beauregard

Eric Beauregard is a Professor in the School of Criminology at Simon Fraser University in Burnaby, B.C. Dr. Beauregard completed his B.Sc., M.Sc., and Ph.D. in the School of Criminology at the University of Montreal. It was during his last year as an undergraduate student that he met the person who would become his mentor and supervisor for his M.Sc. and Ph.D., Dr. Jean Proulx. Originally interested in psychopaths, Dr. Beauregard was offered the opportunity to travel through the province of Quebec to interview all incarcerated sexual murderers for his M.Sc. He has always been fascinated by criminals, more specifically by the "the worst of the worst"; those posing the greatest challenge to the police. Over several months, he visited all the penitentiaries and interviewed more than 60 sexual murderers, which provided him with invaluable experience interviewing inmates. Moreover, this face-to-face interaction with murderers allowed him to go beyond what he was reading in textbooks and better understand criminal behaviour. Soon after starting his Ph.D., Dr. Beauregard was offered a job at Correctional Service of Canada (CSC), where he was responsible for the assessment of the deviant sexual preferences of sex offenders. During his six years at CSC, he evaluated and interviewed more than 1200 sex offenders.

Although still interested in sexual homicide when he began his Ph.D., Dr. Beauregard also became very interested in a new investigative tool that was emerging at the time: geographic profiling. Influenced by the work of Kim Rossmo, one of the pioneers of geographic profiling,

Dr. Beauregard designed his Ph.D. project to investigate the hunting patterns of serial sex offenders. Because of his unique access to sex offenders, Dr. Beauregard was able to interview serial sex offenders again for his project. Dr. Beauregard was very interested by the offenders' decision making so he used this opportunity to ask the sex offenders the rationales behind their different actions. He was able to convince 92 serial sex offenders, who had committed a total of 361 sexual crimes, to participate in his project. As of 2016, more than 20 studies have been published from this database in collaboration with different researchers.

Just prior to completing his Ph.D. in May 2005, Dr. Beauregard was hired as an Assistant Professor in the Department of Criminology at the University of South Florida in Tampa. After spending two years in Florida, Dr. Beauregard joined Simon Fraser University in 2007 where his research agenda really took off. Although most of his research has focused on sex offenders, Dr. Beauregard has made sure to use different lenses to investigate this population. In addition to examining different aspects of the crime-commission process of sex offenders, Dr. Beauregard has conducted studies on the interrogation of sex offenders, their decision making, spatial and hunting patterns, as well as on criminal and geographic profiling. More recently, he has started a large research project on sexual homicide in collaboration with the RCMP, which includes detailed police information on 350 sexual homicide cases in Canada. In addition to examining the offender and victim characteristics associated with these sexual homicide cases, this project has examined the offenders' ability to evade police detection, as well as their spatial behaviour when committing murder (and how their spatial behaviour correlates with other offending behaviours). One of his future objectives is to be able to design a risk assessment tool to predict sex offenders who are most at risk of killing when recidivating.

In addition to his research, Dr. Beauregard teaches courses on sex offenders, criminal profiling, psychology in policing, and advanced theories at the graduate level. He has been involved as an expert witness in cases of sexual homicide in the U.S. and has provided training to the Behavioral Science Unit of the Gendarmerie National in France. When he is not working, Dr. Beauregard enjoys running, hiking, and swimming.

As illustrated in Table 15.1, the average age of the offender in Beauregard and Martineau's (2013) sample was 28.4 years, the majority of offenders were white, most offenders were single at the time of the crimes, and the offenders had a diverse criminal history. The victims in their sample were 27.2 years old on average, mostly female, mostly white, and often engaged in a high risk lifestyle (e.g., abusing alcohol and drugs, being homeless, working as a prostitute, etc.). In the majority of cases examined by Beauregard and Martineau, the offender made contact with the victim, killed the victim, and disposed of the victim's body outdoors, although the victim's residence was also a common contact point, killing site, and body recovery scene. In terms of the offender's MO, they usually used a con to approach the victim (i.e., feigning an emergency), they would frequently beat the victim or strangle them, they would frequently use a weapon of some type in the offence, and they would often exhibit behaviours such as overkill (i.e., exhibiting more violence than was necessary to kill the victim) and theft (i.e., taking items from the victim). A wide range of sexual acts were also committed in the crimes, with the two most common being vaginal and anal penetration.

Table 15.1 Characteristics of Sexual Homicides in Canada

Offender Characteristics	Percent
Average Age	28.4
Race	
White	66.0
Aboriginal	28.8
Other	4.4
Black	0.4
Asian	0.4
Marital Status	
Single	57.2
Married	27.6
Separated/Divorced	15.2
Criminal Convictions	
Property	7.3
Violent	1.7
Sexual	0.4
Victim Characteristics	
Average Age	27.2
Gender	
Female	89.7
Race	
White	62.8
Aboriginal	33.1

Table 15.1 *(continued)*

Asian	2.0
Other	1.2
Black	0.9
Abuses Alcohol	38.0
Abuses Drugs	25.7
Homeless	11.1
Prostitution	17.7
Contact Site	
Outside	30.0
Victim's Residence	21.4
Killing Site	
Outside	36.3
Victim's Residence	21.4
Body Recovery Site	
Outside	61.4
Victim's Residence	20.3
Modus operandi	
Approach	
Con	40.6
Blitz	12.3
Surprise	7.1
Type of Violence	
Beating	47.1
Strangulation	41.7
Stabbing	22.3
Use of a Weapon	60.6
Other Behaviours	
Overkill	43.1
Theft	37.7
Foreign Objects Inserted into Victim	11.4
Post-mortem Sexual Activity	10.6
Sexual Behaviours	
Vaginal Intercourse	46.3
Anal Intercourse	16.3
Fondling	9.1
Fellatio	8.6
Inanimate Object Penetration	8.0

Source: Beauregard and Martineau (2013): Adapted from Tables 1, 2, 3, 4, and 5.
Note: This table only presents a portion of the results reported by Beauregard and Martineau (2013).

MULTIPLE MURDERERS

Most murderers kill a single individual. However, others kill multiple individuals. People who commit multiple murders are generally categorized into one of three types: serial murderers, mass murderers, and spree murderers. Despite the fact that there is disagreement over how to define these different types of multiple murderers, the classification criteria that are typically used relate to the number of victims killed, the number of events during which the killings took place, the number of locations involved in the crime series, and whether a "cooling-off" period is present between the crime events (Holmes & DeBurger, 1988).

Serial murder occurs when an individual has killed two or more victims, in separate events, at separate locations, with a cooling-off period between the murders (i.e., an inactive time interval between the murders). **Mass murder** occurs when an individual has killed multiple victims in one event at one location. Given that the murders take place at one time in a single location, a cooling-off period is not relevant. Finally, for a series of murders to be considered a **spree murder**, the offender must usually have killed two or more victims in one continuous "event" at two or more locations, with no cooling-off period between the murders.

While serial murderers and mass murderers have received significant attention from researchers in the field of forensic psychology, spree murderers have not. Given this, we will focus our attention here on research that has examined serial and mass murder.

Serial Murder

Despite how we just defined serial murder, there is still a considerable amount of disagreement regarding the definition of serial murder. For example, people have debated the number of victims that should be required before an offender is classified as a serial murderer (Morton & Hilts, 2008). Another definitional issue that is often debated is the matter of motive—specifically, whether serial killers must be driven by internal motivations. For example, should contract killers, who are clearly motivated by external factors (i.e., money), be considered serial killers? These and other definitional issues need to be explored further. However, for our purposes, the definition of serial murder provided above will suffice.

Characteristics of Serial Murderers Although they belong to a heterogeneous group, many serial killers appear to have certain characteristics in common (Aamodt, 2015). These include the following:

- Most serial murderers are male. For example, in a review of 2743 American serial murderers who have committed crimes since 1900, Aamodt (2015) reported that 92.5% were male and 7.5% were female.

- A slight majority of serial murderers in the U.S. are white. Aamodt (2015) reported that 51.7% of serial murderers who committed crimes since 1900 were white and 40.6% African-American.

- The most common motive for serial homicides committed in the U.S. appears to be enjoyment (i.e., thrill, lust, power). For example, out of the 3688 serial killers

---

Serial murder: The killing of a minimum of two people over time. The time interval between the murders varies and has been called a cooling-off period. Subsequent murders occur at different times, have no apparent connection to the initial murder, and are usually committed in different locations

Mass murder: The killing of multiple victims at a single location during one event with no cooling-off period

Spree murder: The killing of two or more victims in one continuous event at two or more locations, with no cooling-off period between the murders

Box 15.3   Myths and Realities

Serial Killers

Myth 1. There is a typical "type" of serial killer.
Fact. While there are some common characteristics associated with serial killers, such as being male, there are also many differences. Research shows that serial killers can differ by gender, age, ethnicity, nationality, intelligence, childhood experiences, victim preferences, motivation to kill, etc.

Myth 2. Serial killers are psychopathic.
Fact. Some research does suggest that most serial killers are psychopathic. However, serial killers who have been assessed for psychopathy using the PCL-R do not always meet the diagnostic criteria for psychopathy. So, simply because one kills numerous people does not mean that the offender is necessarily a psychopath.

Myth 3. Most serial killers are super-intelligent and because of this they rarely get caught.
Fact. Unlike the famous Hannibal Lecter in *Silence of the Lambs*, research on U.S. serial killers suggests that they tend to be of average intelligence, and while some serial killers do evade the police, many get caught for their crimes. Advances in both investigative and forensic techniques are helping the police detect and apprehend offenders who commit serial homicides.

Myth 4. Serial killers travel far distances to commit their crimes, often picking up victims along their travels.
Fact. Movies often present serial killers as travelers who target unsuspecting victims as the offender roams the highways. However, like most serial offenders, serial killers tend to travel relatively short distances to commit their crimes (although travelling serial killers do exist). This allows techniques like geographic profiling (see Chapter 3) to be used in serial homicide cases to assist the police with their investigations.

---

examined by Aamodt (2015) where motive could be determined, 40.1% of serial killers appeared to be driven by enjoyment. Other common motives included financial gain (28.28%) and anger (15.10%).

- Victims of serial murderers are usually females (53.49%), white (67.33%), and relatively young (modal victim age of 19 years) (Aamodt, 2015).

- Shooting is the most common method of death in serial murders committed in the U.S. since 1900. For example, in an analysis of 8832 deaths, Aamodt (2015) reported that the victim died by a gun shot in 41.73% of cases. Other common modes of death included strangulation (23.21%) and stabbing (15.22%).

Other facts about serial murderers are discussed in Box 15.3.

Female Serial Murderers Like female offenders in general, female serial murderers have not been the focus of much research. One reason for this is because serial killing by females is extremely rare. Many female serial killers appear to be either "black widows," those who kill for financial gain, or "angels of death," nurses who kill their patients. For example, Dorothea Puente was charged with nine murders of her tenants and, in 1993, convicted of three of the murders. The murders were supposedly done in order for Puente to collect the tenants' social security cheques. Puente claims that the seven people whose bodies were found in her yard had all died of natural causes and that she is innocent (Vronsky, 2007).

Table 15.2 Differences between Male and Female Serial Murderers

Point of Comparison	Male Serial Murderers	Female Serial Murderers
Prior criminal history	Males tend to have a prior criminal history.	Females tend not to have a prior criminal history.
Accomplice	Only about 25% of males have an accomplice.	About 50% of females have an accomplice.
Murder method[1]	Males are more likely to use a firearm or to strangle or stab their victims.	Females are much more likely to use poison.
Murder motive[2]	Males are more likely to kill for sexual gratification or control.	Females are more likely to kill for money.
Victim type[3]	Males are more likely to kill strangers.	Females are much more likely to kill family members.
Geographic type	Males tend to be more geographically mobile.	Females are more likely to be place specific (i.e., to carry out all killings in one location).

[1]Hickey (2006) reported that 35% of female serial murderers killed by using poison, as compared with only 5% of male serial murderers.

[2]Hickey (2006) reported that in 74% of female serial murders, money played a role, as compared with only 26% of male serial murders. In contrast, he reported that sexual gratification played a role in 55% of male serial murders, as compared with only 10% of female serial murders.

[3]Hickey (2006) found that 50% of female serial murderers had killed at least one family member, as compared with 1% of males.

Source: Based on Hickey, 2006. © 2006.

Aileen Wuornos was a female serial murderer who did not fit into the category of black widow or angel of death (although she did steal cash, belongings, and some of the victims' cars). In 1989 and 1990, she killed seven men she had agreed to have sex with. Initially, Wuornos claimed that she had killed each of them in self-defence because they had become violent with her, but she later recanted this and suggested her motivation was robbery. Wuornos was executed in Florida in 2002 and her story was told in the Hollywood movie *Monster*, which starred Charlize Theron as Wuornos.

Table 15.2 summarizes the differences between male and female serial murders. Compared with male serial murderers, female serial murderers are more likely to have no prior criminal record, have an accomplice, use poison, kill for money, and kill a family member or someone they know (Hickey, 2006).

Typologies of Serial Murderers A number of classification systems have been developed to classify serial murderers. One typology that focuses on crime scenes and offenders is the organized-disorganized model proposed by the FBI in the 1980s. This typology was described in Chapter 3.

In 1998, Holmes and Holmes proposed another typology. They used 110 case files of serial murderers to develop a classification system based on victim characteristics and on the method and location of the murder. They proposed four major types of serial murders: (1) **visionary**, (2) **mission-oriented**, (3) **hedonistic**, and

Visionary serial murderer: A murderer who kills in response to voices or visions telling him or her to kill

Mission-oriented serial murderer: A murderer who targets individuals from a group that he or she considers to be "undesirable"

Hedonistic serial murderer: A murderer who is motivated by self-gratification. This type of killer is divided into three subtypes: lust, thrill, and comfort

(4) **power/control oriented**. The visionary serial murderer kills in response to voices or visions telling him or her to kill. This type of serial murderer would most likely be diagnosed as delusional or psychotic. The mission-oriented serial murderer believes there is a group of undesirable people who should be eliminated, such as homeless people, sex-trade workers, or a specific minority group. Hedonistic serial murderers are motivated by self-gratification. These killers have been divided into three subtypes based on the motivation for killing: **lust murderer**, **thrill murderer**, or **comfort murderer**. The lust serial murderer is motivated by sexual gratification and becomes stimulated and excited by the process of killing. The thrill murderer derives excitement from seeing his or her victims experience terror or pain. The comfort serial murderer is motivated by material or financial gain. The power/control serial murderer is not motivated by sexual gratification but by wanting to have absolute dominance over the victim. According to Holmes and Holmes, each of these different killers commits their crimes in a particular way.

The above typology is compelling, but it has been criticized for the following reasons. First, there is considerable overlap among categories. For example, lust, thrill, and power/control murders are all characterized by a controlled crime scene, a focus on process (i.e., an enjoyment of the act of killing), and a selection of specific victims. Second, and perhaps more importantly, the typology's developers failed to test it empirically. Canter and Wentink (2004) tested whether the crime characteristics supposedly displayed by each type of killer would tend to co-occur in 100 U.S. serial murderers. The researchers failed to find support for the proposed typology. One reason for the lack of support for this typology is that murderers' motives may change over the course of their killings.

Keppel and Walter (1999) proposed a classification system for serial sexual murderers. More specifically, they applied the motivational rapist typology proposed by Groth, Burgess, and Holmstrom (1977) to classify sexual murder. They proposed two types of sexual murders that reflect the theme of power (power-assertive and power-reassurance) and two types reflecting the theme of anger (anger-retaliation and anger-excitation). The authors described how these types differ with regard to crime scene behaviours (and the offenders' background characteristics). For example, it is believed that the power-reassurance type of killer commits a planned rape that escalates to an unplanned murder of the victim. In contrast, the rapes and murders of anger-excitation killers are both planned. Using prison files from the Michigan Department of Corrections, Keppel and Walter classified 2475 sexual homicides as follows: 38% power-assertive, 34% anger-retaliation, 21% power-reassurance, and 7% anger-excitation.

Like the typology proposed by Holmes and Holmes (1998), Keppel and Walter's (1999) classification system has only recently been tested empirically. Just as Canter and Wentink (2004) tested the classification system proposed by Holmes and Holmes, Bennell, Bloomfield, Emeno, and Musolino (2013) tested Keppel and Walter's system. Using a sample of serial homicides committed by U.S. serial killers, the researchers found very little evidence to support the types of serial sexual murders and murderers that Keppel and Walter proposed. Indeed, no distinct clustering of behaviours or characteristics could be found in the analyses conducted by Bennell et al. (2013) corresponding to the underlying themes of power-assertive, power-reassurance, anger-retaliation, or anger-excitation.

Power/control serial murderer: A murderer who is motivated not by sexual gratification but by wanting to have absolute dominance over the victim

Lust serial murderer: A murderer who is motivated by sexual gratification

Thrill serial murderer: A murderer who is motivated by the excitement associated with the act of killing

Comfort serial murderer: A murderer who is motivated by material or financial gain

Mass Murderers

As discussed, **mass murder** is often defined as the killing of four or more victims at a single location during one event with no cooling-off period. Well-known school shootings in the United States, such as those at Columbine High School and, more recently, Virginia Tech and Sandy Hook Elementary School, are examples of mass murder, as are school shootings in Canada, such as those that have taken place at Centennial Secondary School in Brampton, Ontario, and the more recent shooting at Dawson College in Montreal, Quebec. Canada's deadliest mass murder, the massacre at École Polytechnique, is described in Box 15.4.

Box 15.4   Forensic Psychology in the Spotlight

Canada's Deadliest Mass Murder

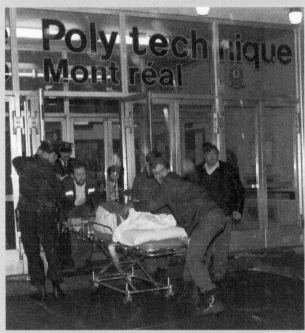

Shaney Komulainen/The Canadian Press

On December 6, 1989, 25-year-old Marc Lépine walked into a classroom at the Montreal engineering school École Polytechnique, fired a shot into the ceiling, and said, "Separate. The girls on the left and the guys on the right." He told the men to leave. He then stated, "I am fighting feminism." One of the nine women left behind responded, "I am not a feminist." All nine of the women were shot (six died and three were injured). Lépine then moved to

other parts of the school, where he shot and killed others. In total, 14 women were killed, and 10 women and 4 men were injured that day at École Polytechnique. The killing ended when Lépine committed suicide.

What prompted Lépine to commit this massacre, and why did he target women? According to media reports, Lépine's father had little respect for women and was verbally and physically abusive toward both his wife and their two children (Lépine and his sister). Lépine's parents separated when he was 7 years old and divorced when he was 12. He graduated from high school and attended CEGEP but dropped out during his last term. In 1986, he applied to study engineering at École Polytechnique and was offered admission conditional on completing two courses at CEGEP. Lépine has been described as quiet and shy, as showing little emotion, and as having problems with accepting authority. He had no history of alcohol or drug problems or prior criminal behaviour. Lépine was apparently uncomfortable around women and expressed his dislike of career women and women who held jobs in traditionally male occupations, such as the police force and the military. He applied to the military but was not accepted.

Lépine applied for a firearm's acquisition in September and received his permit in October 1989. On November 21, 1989, he purchased a Ruger Mini-14 semi-automatic rifle, which he used in the shootings. A suicide note found on Lépine's body stated, "The feminists have always enraged me. They want to keep the advantages of women (e.g., cheaper insurance, extended maternity leave preceded by a preventative leave, etc.) while seizing for themselves those of men."

(continued)

In the classic mass murder, an individual goes to a public place and kills strangers at that location. In contrast, in a family mass murder, four or more family members are killed, usually by another family member. Mass murders can also occur when the murderer intends to kill a specific person but, in doing so, kills others, as illustrated by the case of Joseph-Albert Guay. Guay placed a bomb on a Canadian Pacific Airlines flight between Quebec City and Baie-Comeau on September 9, 1949, to kill his wife, Rita. In the ensuing explosion over Sault-au-Cochon, not only was his wife killed, but 22 others were also killed.

As discussed by Fox and Levin (2012), mass murderers are not all motivated by the same reasons, but the outcome is always the same: the deaths of many innocent people. Mass murderers are often depressed, angry, frustrated individuals who believe they have not succeeded in life. They are often described as socially isolated and lacking in interpersonal skills. In some cases, the murder is triggered by what they perceive as a serious loss or a social injustice. In most cases, these offenders select targets who represent whom they hate or blame for their problems. They often feel rejected by others and come to regard homicide as a justified act of revenge. Most mass murderers plan their crimes and obtain semi-automatic guns in order to maximize the number of deaths. In other words, they do not "just snap," but in fact display warning signs that, if recognized by others, may help to prevent tragedies. In addition, mass murderers often plan to commit suicide or be killed by law enforcement officers.

THEORIES OF HOMICIDAL AGGRESSION

Many theories have been proposed to explain the emergence of specific forms of aggression. For example, a motivational model of sexual homicide was proposed by Burgess, Hartman, Ressler, Douglas, and McCormack (1986) to explain why people commit such crimes, and Hickey's (2006) trauma-control model of serial homicide is also a popular theory. However, most of our thinking about homicidal aggression is guided by general theories of aggression. Although many general theories of aggression exist (see Anderson & Bushman, 2002), we will focus on just three theories that have been particularly influential in the field of forensic psychology: social learning theory, evolutionary theory, and the general aggression model.

According to social learning theorists (e.g., Akers, 1973; Akers & Jennings, 2016), aggressive behaviour is learned the same way non-aggressive behaviour is, through a process of reinforcement. Specifically, the likelihood of engaging in aggressive behaviour is thought to increase as a function of how rewarding aggressive behaviour has been in an individual's past. Rewards for aggressive behaviour are often experienced directly, such as when an individual beats up a schoolmate and experiences an increase in status among his or her friends (as "tough" or "cool"). However, social learning theorists also place a great deal of emphasis on rewards that are not experienced directly, but vicariously, as a result of observing others. Social learning theory highlights several major sources that can influence behaviour in this indirect fashion, including the family circle, the peer group, and the mass media (e.g., Akers, Krohn, Lanza-Kaduce, & Radosevich, 1979; Decker, 1986). Aggressive behaviour can be common in each of these settings and research has confirmed that observing aggressive behaviour being reinforced in each context can increase the likelihood that the observer will model that aggressive behaviour (e.g., Anderson et al., 2003; Greitmeyer & Mügge, 2014; Pratt & Cullen, 2000).

As is the case with sexual offences, evolutionary theories of homicide are also popular. The focus in evolutionary theories is on how crime can be thought of as adaptive behaviour, developed as a means for people to survive (and pass on genes) in their ancestral environment (Daly & Wilson, 1988). In an ancestral environment characterized by recurring challenges or conflicts, such as finding mates, securing shelter, and/or establishing status, certain physiological, psychological, and behavioural characteristics became associated with reproductive success. From an evolutionary perspective, homicide emerged as one approach to best competitors who were competing for limited resources, and modern humans have simply inherited this strategy from their successful ancestors (Buss & Shackelford, 1997). Notwithstanding criticisms made against this theory (e.g., Sussman, Cheverud, & Bartlett, 1994), a growing body of research is exploring these ideas and showing how they can be used to account for different forms (and rates) of homicide (e.g., Daly & Wilson, 1988; Friedman, Cavney, & Resnick, 2012; Shackleford, Buss, & Peters, 2000).

The General Aggression Model (GAM) is one of the more recent theories of aggression (Anderson & Bushman, 2002). As its name implies, the GAM is a general theory of human aggression in that it integrates a number of domain-specific theories to explain the emergence of all types of aggression. Despite the fact that the model has generally been tested to determine if it can explain aggression between strangers, more recent attempts have been made to extend its application to other forms of aggression, such as intimate partner violence, intergroup violence, and even suicide (DeWall, Anderson, & Bushman, 2011). The model is complex and a full discussion of it is beyond the scope of this text. However, we will discuss its main components, which are highlighted in Figure 15.2.

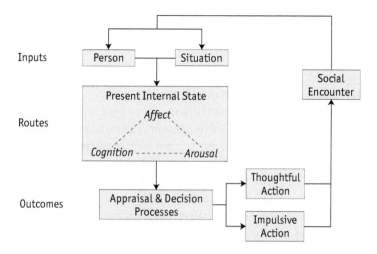

Figure 15.2 The General Aggression Model

Source: Human Aggression by Craig A. Anderson and Brad J. Bushman. Reproduced with permission of Annual Review of Psychology Vol. 53: 27-51 Copyright © 2002 by Annual Reviews, http://www.annualreviews.org.

The first component is referred to as inputs, which are biological, environmental, psychological, and social factors that influence aggression in a specific social encounter. Inputs are categorized into person factors (e.g., traits, attitudes, genetic predispositions) and situation factors (e.g., incentives, provocation, frustration). According to the GAM, inputs influence behaviour via the internal states that they create within an individual. Specifically, input variables are thought to influence cognitions (e.g., hostile thoughts), emotions (e.g., anger), and arousal, and these three routes are also thought to influence one another (e.g., hostile thoughts can lead to increases in anger). These internal states in turn influence behavioural outcomes through a variety of appraisal and decision processes. Some of the outcomes reflect relatively automatic, impulsive actions, whereas other actions are heavily controlled and thoughtful in nature. These outcomes influence the social encounter, which has an impact on the inputs in the next social encounter. Research supports many of the links proposed in the GAM (e.g., see Anderson & Bushman, 2002), and the model appears useful, not only for understanding human aggression, but also for developing interventions to reduce aggression. Try your hand at applying the GAM to the offender described in the You Be the Forensic Psychologist box.

TREATMENT OF HOMICIDAL OFFENDERS

The treatment of homicidal offenders has not received the same degree of attention as the treatment of sexual offenders (Serin, Gobeil, & Preston, 2009). While this may be unsurprising in the case of serial murderers, given the very long sentences these offenders will likely receive and their low potential for rehabilitation or reintegration into society, it is more surprising for other types of homicide offenders. Indeed, given the serious consequences of their actions, it is surprising that so little attention has been given to the development and evaluation of treatment programs for homicidal offenders relative to sexual offenders.

YOU BE THE FORENSIC PSYCHOLOGIST

Bob is a 45-year-old white male who is currently serving time in prison for a murder he committed 5 years ago. In his counselling sessions, Bob and his psychologist often talk about the crime that he committed and, more generally, about his tendency to deal with his problems in an aggressive manner. In trying to explain his violent outbursts, Bob admits that he tends to get "hot under the collar", especially around guys who "don't know when to keep their mouths shut." He often feels that other men look down on him and make fun of him. Most of Bob's outbursts occur when he's been drinking, but he claims that the fights he gets in are never his fault; he's just "trying to have a few drinks to relax after hard shifts at work." It's obvious to the psychologist that Bob has low self-esteem. When pushed about this issue Bob says this is why the comments made by others get him really upset. Bob blames his self-esteem problems (and his anger) on his wife, who left him for a much younger guy, and his father, who was always very aggressive towards him as a young boy. Both his wife and his father often made him "feel like a piece of crap" and he gets reminded of this every time someone puts him down.

Your Turn ...

As an experimental forensic psychologist who is interested in understanding the causes of homicidal behaviour, and aggression more generally, how might you explain Bob's aggressive behaviour? Using the General Aggression Model proposed by Anderson and Bushman (2002), describe some relevant inputs, internal states, and behavioural outcomes that might explain Bob's behaviour.

Like the various forms of sexual offending described in Chapter 14, nonsexual violent offending has a multitude of interacting causes and these causes inform treatment programs for violent offenders. While there is no such thing as a "typical" treatment program for violent offenders, many treatment programs are designed to target some or all of the following factors: anger (and emotions) management, self-regulation (i.e., self-control), problem solving, interpersonal skills, and social attitudes (e.g., beliefs supporting violence; Polaschek & Collie, 2004).

Given these factors, it makes sense that some of the intervention programs used for sexual offenders (e.g., relapse prevention programs) are sometimes also used to treat nonsexual violent offenders. However, a wide variety of other programs are also used to intervene with violent offenders (see Jolliffe & Farrington, 2007; Polaschek & Collie, 2004). When it comes to the effectiveness of these treatment programs, there are few well-controlled evaluations (Polaschek & Collie, 2004). That being said, there have been some attempts recently to fill this gap using meta-analysis techniques.

For example, the meta-analysis by Jolliffe and Farrington (2007) was designed to evaluate treatment effectiveness for violent (male) offenders specifically (the study was not restricted to homicide offenders, but it excluded domestic and sexual offenders). These researchers included eight studies in which treated and untreated violent offenders were compared and they calculated an effect size to determine the impact of treatment. In each of these studies, violent reoffending (in addition to general reoffending) was used as the outcome measure of interest.

In this study, positive effect sizes indicated lower rates of reoffending in the treated group and negative effect sizes indicated higher rates of reoffending in the treated group. Jolliffe and Farrington (2007) found the average effect to be about 0.13 when comparing the reoffending rates of violent offenders who did, or did not, participate in treatment. Thus, their results indicate that the treatment programs that they examined were effective to some extent, though the effect certainly wasn't very large.

Jolliffe and Farrington (2007) also found that not all violent offender treatment programs were equally effective. Whether a treatment program resulted in reductions in violent reoffending depended partially on what the treatment program targeted. For example, on the one hand, treatment programs that targeted anger control were associated with an average effect size of 0.14. On the other hand, treatment programs that provided empathy training were associated with an average effect size of −0.05 (i.e., reoffending actually increased).

Beyond the content of the intervention, other factors that had an impact on the effectiveness of treatment included features of the study (e.g., providing longer treatment sessions increased effectiveness), the delivery of the intervention (e.g., having the intervention delivered by correctional staff versus a rehabilitation professional increased effectiveness), and the methodology of the study (e.g., restricting the samples to only offenders who completed the treatment increased effectiveness).

SUMMARY

1. Homicide occurs relatively infrequently in Canada and is at the lowest rate since the 1960s. Certain trends are present in Canadian homicide statistics: homicide rates currently vary across Canada, with some of the highest rates being reported in Manitoba and some of the lowest rates being reported in Newfoundland and Labrador; most homicides are committed by offenders who know the victim, including acquaintances and family members; youth commit relatively few homicides relative to adults, and the youth homicide rate is currently the lowest it has been for decades; Aboriginals are disproportionately represented, both as homicide victims and homicide offenders.

2. Reactive homicide is defined as impulsive, unplanned, immediate, driven by negative emotions, and occurring in response to some perceived provocation. Instrumental homicide is defined as proactive rather than reactive and is a premeditated, calculated behaviour, motivated by some goal.

3. Maternal filicides involve mothers killing their children. There are three broad types of maternal filicides. Neonaticide involves the murder of children within 24 hours of birth. Battering mothers kill their children impulsively in response to the behaviour of the child. Mothers with certain mental illnesses may also be more likely to kill their children, particularly women who suffer from postpartum

psychosis, which involves delusions, hallucinations, and suicidal or homicidal thoughts within the first three months after childbirth.

4. Different types of multiple murderers can be identified. Serial killers murder three or more victims, in three or more separate events, at two or more separate locations, with a cooling-off period between the murders. Mass murderers kill four or more victims in one event at one location. Given that the murders take place at one time in a single location, a cooling-off period is not relevant. Spree killers murder two or more victims, in one continuous event, at two or more locations, with no cooling-off period between the murders.

5. While theories have been proposed to explain specific forms of aggression (e.g., serial homicide), most of our thinking about homicidal aggression is guided by general theories of aggression. Social learning theories suggest that aggressive behaviour is learned in the same way non-aggressive behaviour is learned, by being reinforced (or seeing others being reinforced) for such behaviour. Evolutionary theories view homicide as adaptive behaviour, inherited from our ancestors, which develops as an approach to best competitors when competing for limited resources. The General Aggression Model suggests that aggression occurs when factors in the immediate social situation trigger cognitions and emotions that increase aggressive behavioural responses.

6. Compared with studies that have examined the effectiveness of sexual offender treatment programs, less research has been conducted to examine the effectiveness of treatment programs for other violent offenders, such as individuals who commit homicide. However, recent meta-analytic studies suggest that existing programs may have a small but significant impact on these offenders, such that they are less likely to reoffend violently after taking part in treatment.

Discussion Questions

1. Homicide offenders have been classified into instrumental and reactive types. Can you think of homicide offenders who don't fit neatly into either of these two types? What other sorts of motivations might be important to consider when trying to fully capture the nature of homicidal behaviour?

2. Male serial killers appear to far outnumber their female counterparts. Why is this so? What factors can you think of to explain why female serial killers are so rare?

Glossary

Aboriginal overrepresentation The discrepancy between the relatively low proportion of Aboriginal people in the general Canadian population and the relatively high proportion of Aboriginal people involved in the criminal justice system

Absolute discharge The defendant is released into the community without restrictions to his or her behaviour

Absolute judgment Witness compares each lineup member to his or her memory of the perpetrator to decide whether the lineup member is the perpetrator

Actuarial prediction Decisions are based on risk factors that are selected and combined based on their empirical or statistical association with a specific outcome

Actus reus A wrongful deed

Adjournment Delaying the trial until sometime in the future

Adversarial allegiance The tendency for forensic experts to be biased toward the side (defence or prosecution) that hired them

Anatomically detailed dolls A doll, sometimes like a rag doll, that is consistent with the male or female anatomy

Androcide The killing of men

Anger rapist A rapist, as defined by Groth, who uses more force than necessary to obtain compliance from the victim and who engages in a variety of sexual acts to degrade the victim

Antisocial personality disorder A personality disorder characterized by a history of behaviour in which the rights of others are violated

Antisocial process screening device Observer rating scale to assess psychopathic traits in children

Assessment centre A facility in which the behaviour of police applicants can be observed in a number of situations by multiple observers

Attention deficit/hyperactivity disorder A disorder in a youth characterized by a persistent pattern of inattention and hyperactivity or impulsivity

Automatism Unconscious, involuntary behaviour such that the person committing the act is not aware of what he or she is doing

Aversion therapy The pairing of an aversive stimuli with a deviant fantasy for the purpose of reducing the attractiveness of these deviant fantasies

Base rate Represents the percentage of people within a given population who commit a criminal or violent act

Biased lineup A lineup that "suggests" whom the police suspect and thereby whom the witness should identify

Black sheep effect When evidence is strong, similarity between defendant and jury leads to punitiveness

Capping Notion introduced through Bill C-30 where there is a maximum period of time a person with a mental illness could be affected by his or her disposition

Challenge for cause An option to reject biased jurors

Change of venue Moving a trial to a community other than the one in which the crime occurred

Chaos theory The theory that when jurors are guided by their emotions and personal biases rather than by the law, chaos in judgments results

Child molester Someone who has actually sexually molested a child

Classic trait model A model of personality that assumes the primary determinants of behaviour are stable, internal traits

Clinical forensic psychologists Psychologists who are broadly concerned with the assessment and treatment of mental health issues as they pertain to the law or legal system

Clinical risk factors Types and symptoms of mental disorders (e.g., substance abuse)

Coerced-compliant false confession A confession that results from a desire to escape a coercive interrogation environment or gain a benefit promised by the police

Coerced-internalized false confession A confession that results from suggestive interrogation techniques, whereby the confessor actually comes to believe he or she committed the crime

Cognitive ability tests Procedure for measuring verbal, mathematical, memory, and reasoning abilities

Cognitive distortions Deviant cognitions, values, or beliefs that are used to justify or minimize deviant behaviours

Cognitive interview Interview procedure for use with eyewitnesses based on principles of memory storage and retrieval

Comfort serial murderer A murderer who is motivated by material or financial gain

Community service A sentence that involves the offender performing a duty in the community, often as a way of paying off a fine

Community treatment order Sentence that allows the mentally ill offender to live in the community, with the stipulation that the person will agree to treatment or detention in the event that his or her condition deteriorates

Comparison Question Test A type of polygraph test that includes irrelevant questions that are unrelated to the crime, relevant questions concerning the crime being investigated, and comparison questions concerning the person's honesty and past history prior to the event being investigated

Competency inquiry Questions posed to child witnesses under age 14 to determine whether they are able to communicate the evidence and understand the difference between the truth and a lie, and, in the circumstances of testifying, to see if they feel compelled to tell the truth

Compliance A tendency to go along with demands made by people perceived to be in authority, even though the person may not agree with them

Concealed Information Test A type of polygraph test designed to determine if the person knows details about a crime

Conditional discharge A defendant is released; however, release carries certain conditions (e.g., not to possess firearms) that the defendant must meet. Failure to meet the conditions imposed with a conditional discharge may result in the defendant being incarcerated or sent to a psychiatric facility

Conditional sentence A sentence served in the community

Conduct disorder A disorder characterized by a persistent pattern of behaviour in which a youth violates the rights of others or age-appropriate societal norms or rules

Confabulation The reporting of events that never actually occurred

Contextual risk factors Risk factors that refer to aspects of the current environment (e.g., access to victims or weapons). Sometimes called *situational risk factors*

Countermeasures As applied to polygraph research, techniques used to try to conceal guilt

Criminal harassment Crime that involves repeatedly following, communicating with, watching, or threatening a person directly or indirectly

Criminal profiling An investigative technique for identifying the major personality and behavioural characteristics of an individual based upon an analysis of the crimes he or she has committed

Criterion-based content analysis Analysis that uses criteria to distinguish truthful from false statements made by children

Cross-race effect Phenomenon of witnesses remembering own-race faces with greater accuracy than faces from other races. Also known as the *other-race effect* and the *own-race bias*

Cue-utilization hypothesis Proposed by Easterbrook (1959) to explain why a witness may focus on the weapon rather than other details. The hypothesis suggests that when emotional arousal increases, attentional capacity decreases

Daubert criteria An American standard for accepting expert testimony, which states that scientific evidence is valid if the research on which it is based has been peer reviewed, is testable, has a recognized rate of error, and adheres to professional standards

Day parole A form of parole that allows the offender to enter the community for up to one day (e.g., for the purpose of holding down a job)

Deception detection Detecting when someone is being deceptive

Deductive criminal profiling Profiling the background characteristics of an unknown offender based on evidence left at the crime scenes by that particular offender

Defensiveness Conscious denial or extreme minimization of physical or psychological symptoms

Deliberation When jury members discuss the evidence privately among themselves to reach a verdict that is then provided to the court

Delusional stalker A stalker who suffers from delusions and wrongly believes he or she has a relationship with the victim

Desistance The process of ceasing to engage in criminal behaviour

Direct question recall Witnesses are asked a series of specific questions about the crime or the perpetrator

Dispositional risk factors Risk factors that reflect the individual's traits, tendencies, or styles (e.g., negative attitudes)

Disputed confession A confession that is later disputed at trial

Distractors Lineup members who are known to be innocent of the crime in question. Also known as *foils*

Diversion A decision not to prosecute, but rather have an offender undergo an educational or community-service program. Also an option for the courts dealing with offenders with mental illnesses who are facing minor charges. The court can divert the offender directly into a treatment program rather than have him or her go through the court process

Domestic violence Any violence occurring between family members

Dynamic risk factor Risk factors that fluctuate over time and are amenable to change (e.g., antisocial attitude)

Dysphoric/borderline batterer A male spousal batterer who exhibits some violence outside the family, is depressed, has borderline personality traits, and has problems with jealousy

Elimination lineup Lineup procedure for children that first asks them to pick out the person who looks most like the culprit from the photos displayed. Next, children are asked whether the most similar person selected is in fact the culprit

Emotional maltreatment Acts or omissions by caregivers that cause or could cause serious behavioural, cognitive, emotional, or mental disorders

Enhanced cognitive interview Interview procedure that includes various principles of social dynamics in addition to the memory retrieval principles used in the original cognitive interview

Estimator variables Variables that are present at the time of the crime and that cannot be changed

Event-related brain potentials Brain activity measured by placing electrodes on the scalp and by recording electrical patterns related to presentation of a stimulus

Evolutionary psychology: The scientific study of psychology that takes the evolutionary history of a species into account when understanding a psychological trait and what led to its origination, development, and maintenance

Exhibitionist Someone who obtains sexual gratification by exposing his or her genitals to strangers

Ex-intimate stalker A stalker who engages in stalking after an intimate relationship breaks up

Experimental forensic psychologists Psychologists who are broadly concerned with the study of human behaviour as it relates to the law or legal system

Expert witness A witness who provides the court with information (often an opinion on a particular matter) that assists the court in understanding an issue of relevance to a case

Externalizing problems Behavioural difficulties such as delinquency, fighting, bullying, lying, or destructive behaviour experienced by a youth

Extra-familial child molester Someone who sexually abuses children not related to him or her

Extrajudicial Term applied to measures taken to keep young offenders out of court and out of custody (e.g., giving a warning or making a referral for treatment)

Fabricating Making false claims

Factitious disorder A disorder in which the person's physical and psychological symptoms are intentionally produced and are adopted for no external rewards

Fair lineup A lineup where the suspect does not stand out from the other lineup members

False confession A confession that is either intentionally fabricated or is not based on actual knowledge of the facts that form its content

False memory syndrome Term to describe clients' false beliefs that they were sexually abused as children, despite having no memories of this abuse until they enter therapy to deal with some other psychological problem, such as depression or substance abuse

False negative An incorrect prediction that occurs when a person is predicted not to engage in some type of behaviour (e.g., a violent act) but does

False positive An incorrect prediction that occurs when a person is predicted to engage in some type of behaviour (e.g., a violent act) but does not

Familicide The killing of a spouse and children

Family-only batterer A male spousal batterer who is typically not violent outside the home, does not show much psychopathology, and does not possess negative attitudes supportive of violence

Family-supportive interventions Interventions that connect at-risk families to various support services

Femicide The killing of women

Filicide The killing of children by their biological parents or step-parents; includes neonaticide (killing a baby within 24 hours of birth) and infanticide (killing a baby within the first year of life)

Fine A sentence where the offender has to make a monetary payment to the courts

Fixated child molester A child molester, as defined by Groth, who has a long-standing, exclusive sexual preference for children

Foils Lineup members who are known to be innocent of the crime in question. Also known as *distractors*

Forensic psychiatry A field of medicine that deals with all aspects of human behaviour as it relates to the law or legal system

Forensic psychology A field of psychology that deals with all aspects of human behaviour as it relates to the law or legal system

Free narrative Witnesses are asked to either write or orally state all they remember about the event without the officer (or experimenter) asking questions. Also known as *open-ended recall*

Full parole A form of parole that allows the offender to serve the remainder of his or her sentence under supervision in the community

Fundamental principle of sentencing The belief that sentences should be proportionate to the gravity of the offence and the degree of responsibility of the offender

General deterrence Sentencing to reduce the probability that members of the general public will offend in the future

Generally violent/antisocial batterer A male spousal batterer who is violent outside the home, engages in other criminal acts, has drug and alcohol problems, has impulse-control problems, and possesses violence-supportive beliefs

Geographic profiling An investigative technique that uses crime scene locations to predict the most likely area where an offender resides

Geographic profiling systems Computer systems that use mathematical models of offender spatial behaviour to make predictions about where unknown serial offenders are likely to reside

Ground truth As applied to polygraph research, the knowledge of whether the person is actually guilty or innocent

Grudge stalker A stalker who knows and is angry at the victim for some perceived injustice

Hare Psychopathy Checklist–Revised The most popular method of assessing psychopathy in adults

Hare Psychopathy Checklist: Youth Version Scale designed to measure psychopathic traits in adolescents

Hedonistic serial murderer A murderer who is motivated by self-gratification. This type of killer is divided into three subtypes: lust, thrill, and comfort

Historic child sexual abuse Allegations of child abuse having occurred several years, often decades, prior to when they are being prosecuted

Historical risk factors Risk factors that refers to events that have been experienced in the past (e.g., age at first arrest). Also known as *static risk factors*

Hung jury A jury that cannot reach a unanimous verdict

Illusory correlation Belief that a correlation exists between two events that in reality are either not correlated or correlated to a much lesser degree

Impartiality A characteristic of jurors who are unbiased

Imprisonment A sentence served in prison

In need of protection A term used to describe a child's need to be separated from his or her caregiver because of maltreatment

Incest offender Someon who sexually abuse his or her own biological children or children for whom he or she assumes a parental role, such as a stepfather or live-in boyfriend. Also known as *intra-familial child molesters*

Incidence Number of new child-maltreatment cases in a specific population occurring in a given time period, usually a year

Inductive criminal profiling Profiling the background characteristics of an unknown offender based on what we know about other solved cases

Insanity Impairment of mental or emotional functioning that affects perceptions, beliefs, and motivations at the time of the offence

Instigators In social learning theory, these are events in the environment that act as a stimulus for acquired behaviours

Instrumental (predatory) aggression Aggression that is premeditated, calculated, and motivated by some goal (e.g., to obtain money)

Internalization The acceptance of guilt for an act, even if the person did not actually commit the act

Internalizing problems Emotional difficulties such as anxiety, depression, and obsessions experienced by a youth

Intimate partner violence Any violence occurring between intimate partners who are living together or separated. Also known as *spousal violence*

Intra-familial child molester Someone who sexually abuse his or her own biological children or children for whom he or she assumes a parental role, such as a stepfather or live-in boyfriend. Also known as *incest offenders*

Investigator bias Bias that can result when police officers enter an interrogation setting already believing that the suspect is guilty

Inwald Personality Inventory An assessment instrument used to identify police applicants who are suitable for police work by measuring their personality attributes and behaviour patterns

Job analysis A procedure for identifying the knowledge, skills, and abilities that make a good police officer

Juries Act Provincial and territorial legislation that outlines the eligibility criteria for jury service and how prospective jurors must be selected

Jury nullification Occurs when a jury ignores the law and the evidence, rendering a verdict based on some other criteria

Jury summons A court order that states a time and place to go for jury duty

Known-groups design As applied to malingering research, involves comparing genuine patients and malingerers attempting to fake the disorder the patients have

Leniency bias When jurors move toward greater leniency during deliberations

Lineup A set of people presented to the witness who must state whether the perpetrator is present and, if so, which person it is

Linkage blindness An inability on the part of the police to link geographically dispersed serial crimes committed by the same offender because of a lack of information sharing among police agencies

Love-obsessional stalker A stalker who has intense emotional feelings for the victim but who has never had an intimate relationship with the victim

Lust serial murderer A murderer who is motivated by sexual gratification

Malingering Intentionally faking psychological or physical symptoms for some type of external gain

Mandatory charging policies Policies that give police the authority to lay charges against a suspect where there are reasonable and probable grounds to believe a domestic assault has occurred

Mass murder The killing of multiple victims at a single location during one event with no cooling-off period

Maximization techniques Scare tactics used by police interrogators that are designed to intimidate a suspect believed to be guilty

Memory conformity When what one witness reports influences what another witness reports

Memory impairment hypothesis Explanation for the misinformation effect where the original memory is replaced with the new, incorrect, information

Mens rea Criminal intent

Minimization techniques Soft sell tactics used by police interrogators that are designed to lull the suspect into a false sense of security

Minnesota Multiphasic Personality Inventory An assessment instrument for identifying people with psychopathological problems

Misinformation acceptance hypothesis Explanation for the misinformation effect where the incorrect information is provided because the witness guesses what the officer or experimenter wants the response to be

Misinformation effect Phenomenon where a witness who is presented with inaccurate information after an event will incorporate that misinformation into a subsequent recall task. Also known as the *post-event information effect*

Mission-oriented serial murderer A murderer who targets individuals from a group that he or she considers to be "undesirable"

Mohan criteria A Canadian standard for accepting expert testimony, which states that expert testimony will be admissible in court if the testimony is relevant, is necessary for assisting the trier of fact, does not violate any exclusionary rules, and is provided by a qualified expert

Munchausen syndrome by proxy A rare factitious disorder in which a person intentionally produces an illness in his or her child

Narrative elaboration An interview procedure whereby children learn to organize their story into relevant categories: participants, settings, actions, conversation/affective states, and consequences

Need principle Principle that correctional interventions should target known criminogenic needs (i.e., factors that relate to reoffending)

Neglect/failure to provide When a child's caregivers do not provide the requisite attention to the child's emotional, psychological, or physical development

Observational learning Learning behaviours by watching others perform these behaviours

Occupational stressors In policing, stressors relating to the job itself

Open-ended recall Witnesses are asked to either write or orally state all they remember about the event without the officer (or experimenter) asking questions. Also known as a *free narrative*

Oppositional defiant disorder A disorder in a youth characterized by a persistent pattern of negativistic, hostile, and defiant behaviours

Organizational stressors In policing, stressors relating to organizational issues

Organized-disorganized model A profiling model used by the FBI that assumes the crime scenes and backgrounds of serial offenders can be categorized as *organized* or *disorganized*

Other-race effect Phenomenon of witnesses remembering own-race faces with greater accuracy than faces from other races. Also known as the *cross-race effect* and the *own-race bias*

Own-race bias Phenomenon of witnesses remembering own-race faces with greater accuracy than faces from other races. Also known as the *cross-race effect* and the *other-race effect*

Parent-focused interventions Interventions directed at assisting parents to recognize warning signs for later youth violence and/or training parents to effectively manage any behavioural problems that arise

Parole The release of offenders from prison into the community before their sentence term is complete

Parole Board of Canada The organization in Canada responsible for making parole decisions

Patriarchy Broad set of cultural beliefs and values that support the male dominance of women

Pedophile Person whose primary sexual orientation is toward children

Penile phallometry A measurement device placed around the penis to measure changes in sexual arousal

Perpetrator The guilty person who committed the crime

Physical abuse The deliberate application of force to any part of a child's body that results in or may result in a non-accidental injury

Polarization When individuals tend to become more extreme in their initial position following a group discussion

Police discretion The freedom that a police officer often has for deciding what should be done in any given situation

Police interrogation A process whereby the police interview a suspect for the purpose of gathering evidence and obtaining a confession

Police selection procedures A set of procedures used by the police to either screen out undesirable candidates or select in desirable candidates

Polygraph A device for recording an individual's autonomic nervous system responses

Polygraph disclosure tests Polygraph tests that are used to uncover information about an offender's past behaviour

Post-event information effect Phenomenon where a witness who is presented with inaccurate information after an event will incorporate that misinformation into a subsequent recall task. Also known as the *misinformation effect*

Power/control serial murder A murderer who is motivated not by sexual gratification but by wanting to have absolute dominance over the victim

Power rapist A rapist, as defined by Groth, who seeks to establish dominance and control over the victim

Predictive validity The extent to which scores on a test (e.g., a cognitive abilities test) predict scores on some other measure (e.g., supervisor ratings of police performance)

Prevalence In the study of child abuse, the proportion of a population at a specific point in time that was maltreated during childhood

Prima facie case Case in which the Crown prosecutor must prove there is sufficient evidence to bring the case to trial

Primary intervention strategies Strategies that are implemented prior to any violence occurring, with the goal of decreasing the likelihood that violence will occur later on

Protective factors Factors that mitigate or reduce the likelihood of a negative outcome (e.g., delinquency, aggression)

Psychological debriefing A psychologically oriented intervention delivered to police officers following exposure to an event that resulted in psychological distress and an impairment of normal functioning

Psychology and the law The use of psychology to examine the operation of the legal system

Psychology in the law The use of psychology in the legal system as that system operates

Psychology of the law The use of psychology to examine the law itself

Psychopathic Personality Inventory–Revised A self-report measure of psychopathic traits

Psychopathy A personality disorder defined by a collection of interpersonal, affective, and behavioural characteristics, including manipulation, lack of remorse or empathy, impulsivity, and antisocial behaviours

Racial bias The disparate treatment of racial out-groups

Rape trauma syndrome A group of symptoms or behaviours that are frequent after-effects of having been raped

Rapist Person who sexually assaults victims over 16 years of age

Reactive (affective) aggression Aggression that is impulsive, unplanned, immediate, driven by negative emotions, and occurring in response to some perceived provocation

Recall memory Reporting details of a previously witnessed event or person

Recognition memory Determining whether a previously seen item or person is the same as what is currently being viewed

Regressed child molester A child molester, as defined by Groth, whose primary sexual orientation is toward adults, but whose sexual interests revert to children after a stressful event or because of feelings of inadequacy

Regulators In social learning theory, these are consequences of behaviours

Reid model A nine-step model of interrogation used frequently in North America to extract confessions from suspects

Relapse prevention A method of treatment designed to prevent the occurrence of an undesired behaviour (e.g., sexual assault)

Relative judgment Witness compares lineup members to one another and the person who looks most like the perpetrator is identified

Reparations A sentence where the offender has to make a monetary payment to the victim or the community; see restitution

Representativeness A jury composition that represents the community where the crime occurred

Resilient Characteristic of a child who has multiple risk factors but who does not develop problem behaviours or negative symptoms

Resiliency training Training delivered to police officers to improve their ability to effectively adapt to stress and adversity

Response Modulation Deficit Theory A theory that suggests that psychopaths fail to use contextual cues that are peripheral to a dominant response set to modulate their behaviour

Responsivity principle Principle that correctional interventions should match the general learning style of offenders

Restitution A sentence where the offender has to make a monetary payment to the victim or the community

Restorative justice An approach for dealing with a crime that emphasizes repairing the harm caused by it. Based on the philosophy that when victims, offenders, and community members meet voluntarily to decide how to achieve this, transformation can result

Retracted confessions A confession that the confessor later declares to be false

Review boards Legal bodies mandated to oversee the care and disposition of defendants found unfit and/or not criminally responsible on account of a mental disorder

Risk factor A factor that increases the likelihood for emotional and/or behavioural problems

Risk principle Principle that correctional interventions should target offenders who are at high risk to reoffend

Sadistic rapist A rapist, as defined by Groth, who obtains sexual gratification by hurting the victim

Secondary intervention strategies Strategies that attempt to reduce the frequency of violence

Selection interview In recruiting police officers, an interview used by the police to determine the extent to which an applicant possesses the knowledge, skills, and abilities deemed important for the job

Selective pressure In evolutionary psychology, an environmental circumstance that presents an opportunity for new genes to develop that give a survival and/or reproductive advantage to the individual that has those genes

Self-Report Psychopathy Scale A self-report measure of psychopathic traits

Sentencing disparity Variations in sentencing severity for similar crimes committed under similar circumstances

Sentencing guidelines Guidelines that are intended to reduce the degree of discretion that judges have when handing down sentences

Sequential lineup Alternative lineup procedure where the lineup members are presented serially to the witness, and the witness must make a decision as to whether the lineup member is the perpetrator before seeing another member. Also, a witness cannot ask to see previously seen photos and is unaware of the number of photos to be shown

Serial murder The killing of a minimum of two people over time. The time interval between the murders varies and has been called a *cooling-off period*. Subsequent murders occur at different times, have no apparent connection to the initial murder, and are usually committed in different locations

Sexual abuse When an adult or youth uses a child for sexual purposes

Sexual homicide Homicides that have a sexual component

Sexual sadism People who are sexually aroused by fantasies, urges, or acts of inflicting pain, suffering, or humiliation on another person

Showup Identification procedure that shows one person to the witness: the suspect

Simulation design As applied to malingering research, people are told to pretend they have specific symptoms or a disorder

Simultaneous lineup A common lineup procedure that presents all lineup members at one time to the witness

Situational risk factors Risk factors that refer to aspects of the current environment (e.g., access to victims or weapons). Sometimes called *contextual risk factors*

Situational test A simulation of a real-world policing task

Social learning theory A theory of human behaviour based on learning from watching others in the social environment and reinforcement contingencies

Sociopathy A label used to describe a person whose psychopathic traits are assumed to be due to environmental factors

Source misattribution hypothesis Explanation for the misinformation effect where the witness has two memories, the original and the misinformation; however, the witness cannot remember where each memory originated or the source of each

Specific deterrence Sentencing to reduce the probability that an offender will reoffend in the future

Spousal violence Any violence occurring between intimate partners who are living together or separated. Also known as *intimate partner violence*

Spree murder The killing of two or more victims in one continuous event at two or more locations, with no cooling-off period between the murders

Statement validity analysis A comprehensive protocol to distinguish truthful or false statements made by children containing three parts: (1) a structured interview of the child witness, (2) a systematic analysis of the verbal content of the child's statements (criterion-based content analysis), and (3) the application of the statement validity checklist

Static risk factors Risk factors that do not fluctuate over time and are not changed by treatment (e.g., age at first arrest). Also known as *historical risk factors*

Statutory release The release of offenders from prison after they have served two-thirds of their sentence

Step-wise interview Interview protocol with a series of "steps" designed to start the interview with the least leading and directive type of questioning, and then proceed to more specific forms of questioning, as necessary

Structured professional judgment Decisions are guided by a predetermined list of risk factors that have been selected from the research and professional literature. Judgment of risk level is based on the evaluator's professional judgment

Supreme Court of Canada Created in 1875, the Supreme Court of Canada consists of eight judges plus the chief justice, who are all appointed by the federal government. The Supreme Court is the final court of appeal in Canada, and lower Canadian courts are bound by its rulings. The Supreme Court also provides guidance to the federal government on law-related matters, such as the interpretation of the Canadian Constitution

Suspect A person the police "suspect" committed the crime, who may be guilty or innocent of the crime in question

System variables Variables that can be manipulated to increase (or decrease) eyewitness accuracy

Systematic disparity Consistent disagreement among judges about sentencing decisions because of factors such as how lenient judges think sentences should be

Target-absent lineup A lineup that does not contain the perpetrator but rather an innocent suspect

Target-present lineup A lineup that contains the perpetrator

Temporary absence A form of parole that allows the offender to enter the community on a temporary basis (e.g., for the purpose of attending correctional programs)

Tertiary intervention strategies Strategies that attempt to prevent violence from reoccurring

Thrill serial murderer A murderer who is motivated by the excitement associated with the act of killing

True negative A correct prediction that occurs when a person who is predicted not to engage in some type of behaviour (e.g., a violent act) does not

True positive A correct prediction that occurs when a person who is predicted to engage in some type of behaviour (e.g., a violent act) does so

Truth-bias The tendency of people to judge more messages as truthful than deceptive

Unfit to stand trial Refers to an inability to conduct a defence at any stage of the proceedings on account of a person's mental disorder

Unstructured clinical judgment Decisions characterized by a substantial amount of professional discretion and lack of guidelines

Unsystematic disparity Inconsistencies in a judge's sentencing decisions over time when judging the same type of offender or crime because of factors such as the judge's mood

Unwarranted sentencing disparity Variations in sentencing severity for similar crimes committed under similar circumstances that result from reliance by the judge on legally irrelevant factors

ViCLAS The Violent Crime Linkage Analysis System, which was developed by the RCMP to collect and analyze information on serious crimes from across Canada

Visionary serial murderer A murderer who kills in response to voices or visions telling him or her to kill

Voluntary false confession A false confession that is provided without any elicitation from the police

Voyeurs Someone who obtain sexual gratification by observing unsuspecting people, usually strangers, who are naked, in the process of undressing, or engaging in sexual activity

Walk-by Identification procedure that occurs in a naturalistic environment. The police take the witness to a public location where the suspect is likely to be. Once the suspect is in view, the witness is asked whether he or she sees the perpetrator

Weapon focus Term used to describe the phenomenon of a witness's attention being focused on the perpetrator's weapon rather than on the perpetrator

References

Aamodt, M.G. (2004). *Research in law enforcement selection*. Boca Raton, FL: Brown Walker Press.

Aamodt, M.G. (2015). *Serial killer statistics*. Retrieved April 4, 2016 from http://maamodt.asp.radford.edu/serial killer information center/project description.htm.

Aamodt, M.G., & Custer, H. (2006). Who can best catch a liar? A meta-analysis of individual differences in detecting deception. *The Forensic Examiner, 15*, 6–11.

Aamodt, M.G., & Stalnaker, N.A. (2006). *Police officer suicide: Frequency and officer profiles*. Retrieved from PoliceOne.com website www.policeone.com/health-fitness/articles/137133-Police-Officer-Suicide-Frequency-and-officer-profiles/.

Abdollahi, M.K. (2002). Understanding police stress research. *Journal of Forensic Psychology Practice, 2*, 1–24.

Abel, G.G., Becker, J.V., Mittelman, M., & Cunningham-Rathner, J. (1987). Self-reported sex crimes of nonincarcerated paraphiliacs. *Journal of Interpersonal Violence, 2*, 3–25.

Abootalebi, V., Moradi, M.H., & Khalilzadeh, M.A. (2006). A comparison of methods for ERP assessment in a P300-based GKT. *International Journal of Psychophysiology, 62*, 309–320.

Aboriginal Justice Inquiry of Manitoba. (2009). *Report of the Aboriginal Justice Inquiry of Manitoba*. Retrieved from www.ajic.mb.ca/volume.html.

Aboriginal Legal Services of Toronto. (2001). *Gladue (Aboriginal persons) court. Ontario Court of Justice—Old City Hall. Fact sheet*. Retrieved from www.aboriginallegal.ca/docs/apc_factsheet.htm.

Abrams, K., & Robinson, G.E. (2011). Stalking by patients: Doctors' experiences in a Canadian urban area. *The Journal of Nervous and Mental Disease, 199*, 738–743.

Abramson, L.Y., Seligman, M.E.P., & Teasdale, J.D. (1978). Learned helplessness in humans: Critique and reformulation. *Journal of Abnormal Psychology, 87*(1), 49–74.

Ackerman, M.J. (1999). *Forensic psychological assessment*. New York, NY: John Wiley & Sons.

Adams, L.T., Bryden, M.W., & Griffith, J.D. (2011). Middle Eastern racial bias and the impact of jury deliberation. *American Journal of Forensic Psychology, 29*(3), 41–59. Retrieved from http://search.proquest.com/docview/901195467?accountid=9894.

Adams, S.H., & Harpster, T. (2008, June). 911 homicide calls and statement analysis: Is the caller the killer? *FBI Law Enforcement Bulletin, 77*(6), 22–31.

Adams, S.M., Hazelwood, T.E., Pitre, N.L., Bedard, T.E., & Landry, S.E. (2009). Harassment of members of parliament and the legislative assemblies in Canada by individuals believed to be mentally disordered. *The Journal of Forensic Psychiatry & Psychology, 20*, 801–814.

Adams-Tucker, C. (1982). Proximate effects of sexual abuse in childhood: A report on 28 children. *American Journal of Psychiatry, 139*, 1252–1256.

Adi, Y., Ashcroft, D., Browne, K., Beech, A., Fry-Smith, A., & Hyde, C. (2002). Clinical effectiveness and cost-consequences of selective serotonin reuptake inhibitors in the treatment of sex offenders. *Health Technological Assessment, 6*(28), 1–66.

Ægisdóttir, S., White, M.J., Spengler, P.M., Maugherman, A.S., Anderson, L.A., Cook, R.S., Nichols, C.N., Lampropoulous, G.K., Walker, B.S., Cohen, G., & Rush, J.D. (2006) The meta-analysis of clinical judgment project: Fifty-six years of accumulated research on clinical versus statistical prediction. *The Counseling Psychologist, 34*(3), 341–382.

Affonso, D.D., & Domino, G. (1984). Postpartum depression: A review. *Birth: Issues in Perinatal Care and Education, 11*, 231–235.

Aglionby, J. (2006). Thai police hold maid for JonBenet murder. *Guardian.co.uk*. Retrieved from www.guardian.co.uk/world/2006/aug/17/usa.johnaglionby.

Agricola, B.H. (2009). The psychology of pretrial identification procedures: The showup is showing out and undermining the criminal justice system. *Law & Psychology Review, 33*, 125–137.

Ahlmeyer, S., Heil, P., McKee, B., & English, K. (2000). The impact of polygraph on admissions of victims and offenses of adult sex offenders. *Sexual Abuse: A Journal of Research and Treatment, 12*(2), 123–138.

Ainsworth, P.B. (1993). *Psychological testing and police applicant selection: Difficulties and dilemmas*. Paper presented to the European Conference on Law and Psychology, Oxford, England.

Aitken, C.C.G., Connolly, T., Gammerman, A., Zhang, G., Bailey, D., Gordon, R., & Oldfield, R. (1996). Statistical modelling in specific case analysis. *Science & Justice, 36*, 245–256.

Akers, C., & Kaukinen, C. (2009). The police reporting behavior of intimate partner violence victims. *Journal of Family Violence, 24*, 159–171.

Akers, R.L., & Jennings, W.G. (2016). Social learning theory. In A.R. Piquero (Ed.), *The handbook of criminological theory* (pp. 230–240). Oxford, UK: John Wiley and Sons, Inc.

Akers, R.L. (1973). *Deviant behavior: A social learning approach*. Belmont, CA: Wadsworth.

Akers, R.L., Krohn, M.D., Lanza-Kaduce, L., & Radosevich, M. (1979). Social learning and deviant behavior: A specific test of a general theory. *American Sociological Review, 44*, 636–655.

Alaggia, R. (2005). Disclosing the trauma of child sexual abuse: A gender analysis. *Journal of Loss & Trauma, 10*, 453–470.

Alam, S. (2015). Youth court statistics in Canada 2013–2014. Canadian Centre for Justice Statistics. Retrieved from Statistics Canada website at http://www.statcan.gc.ca/pub/85-002-x/2015001/article/14224-eng.pdf.

Alamenciak, T. (2013). *Sammy Yatim 'wasn't stable,' says witness on street care*. Retrieved March 4, 2016 from http://www.thestar.com/news/gta/2013/07/31/streetcar_witness_says_crazedlooking_sammy_yatim_wasnt_a_real_threat.html.

Aldridge, N. (1998). Strengths and limitations of forensic child sexual abuse interviews with anatomical dolls: An empirical review. *Journal of Psychopathology and Behavioral Assessment, 20*, 1–41.

Alexander, D.A., Innes, G., Irving, B.L., Sinclair, S.D., & Walker, L.G. (1991). *Health, stress and policing: A study in Grampian policing*. London, England: The Police Foundation.

Alexander, M.A. (1999). Sexual offender treatment efficacy revisited. *Sexual Abuse: Journal of Research and Treatment, 11*, 101–116.

Alison, L.J., Bennell, C., Mokros, A., & Ormerod, D. (2002). The personality paradox in offender profiling: A theoretical review of the processes involved in deriving background characteristics from crime scene actions. *Psychology, Public Policy, and Law, 8*, 115–135.

Alison, L.J., Smith, M., & Morgan, K. (2003). Interpreting the accuracy of offender profiles. *Psychology, Crime and Law, 9*, 185–195.

Alison, L.J., Smith, M., Eastman, O., & Rainbow, L. (2003). Toulmin's philosophy of argument and its relevance to offender profiling. *Psychology, Crime and Law, 9*, 173–183.

Almond, L., Alison, L., & Porter, L. (2007). An evaluation and comparison of claims made in behavioural investigative advice reports compiled by the National Policing Improvements Agency in the United Kingdom. *Journal of Investigative Psychology & Offender Profiling, 4*, 71–83.

Alsaker, K., Moen, B.E., & Kristoffersen, K. (2008). Health-related quality of life among abused women one year after leaving a violent partner. *Social Indicators Research, 86*, 497–509.

Amato, P.R., & Keith, B. (1991). Parental divorce and the well being of children: A meta-analysis. *Psychological Bulletin, 110*, 26–46.

American Academy of Forensic Sciences. (2016). *Types of forensic scientists: Disciplines of the AAFS*. Retrieved March 3, 2016 from http://www.aafs.org/students/choosing-a-career/types-of-forensic-scientists-disciplines-of-aafs/.

American Psychiatric Association (APA). (2000). *Diagnostic and statistical manual of mental disorders* (4th ed., text rev.). Washington, DC: Author.

American Psychiatric Association. (2013). *Diagnostic and statistical manual of mental disorders* (5th ed.). Arlington, VA: American Psychiatric Publishing.

American Psychological Association (APA). (1962). *Brief for American Psychological Association Amicus Curiae*. Retrieved March 3, 2016 from http://www.apa.org/about/offices/ogc/amicus/jenkins.pdf.

American Psychological Association (APA). (2016). *Jenkins v. United States*. Retrieved March 3, 2016 from http://www.apa.org/about/offices/ogc/amicus/jenkins.aspx.

Ammerman, R.T., Cassisi, J.E., Hersen M., & Van Hasselt, V.B. (1986). Consequences of physical abuse and neglect in children. *Clinical Psychology Review, 6*, 291–310.

Amnesty International. (n.d.). Document—USA: Adding insult to injury: The case of Joseph Stanley Faulder. Retrieved from www.amnesty.org/en/library/asset/AMR51/086/1998/en/c619ed89-d9a2-11dd-af2b-b1f6023af0c5/amr510861998en.html.

Andersen, J.P., Papazoglou, K., Nyman, M., Koskelainen, M., & Gustafsberg, H. (2015). Fostering resilience among the police. *Journal of Law Enforcement, 5*.

Anderson, C.A., & Bushman, B.J. (2002). Human aggression. *Annual Review of Psychology, 53*, 27–51.

Anderson, C.A., & Dill, F.E. (2000). Video games and aggressive thoughts, feelings, and behavior in the laboratory and in life. *Journal of Personality and Social Psychology, 78*, 772–790.

Anderson, C.A., Shibuya, A., Ihori, N., Swing, E.L., Bushman, B.J., Sakamoto, A., Rothstein, H.R., & Saleem, M. (2010). Violent video game effects on aggression, empathy, and prosocial behavior in Eastern and Western countries: A meta-analytic review. *Psychological Bulletin, 136*, 151–173.

Anderson, D.E., DePaulo, B.M., Ansfield, M.E., Tickle, J.J., & Green, E. (1999). Beliefs about cues to deception: Mindless stereo- types or untapped wisdom? *Journal of Nonverbal Behaviour, 23*, 67–89.

Anderson, M., Gillig, P.M., Sitaker, M., McCloskey, K., Malloy, K., & Grigsby, N. (2003). "Why doesn't she just leave?": A descriptive study of victim reported impediments to her safety. *Journal of Family Violence, 18*, 151–155.

Andrea Yates case: Yates found not guilty by reason of insanity. (2006). *CNN*. Retrieved from www.cnn.2007/US/law/12/11/court.archive.yates8/.

Andrews, D. (2001). Principles of effective correctional programs. In L. Motiuk & R. Serin (Eds.), *Compendium 2000 on effective correctional programming* (pp. 9–17). Ottawa, ON: Correctional Service Canada.

Andrews, D.A., Bonta, J. & Wormith, J.S. (2011). The risk-needs-responsivity (RNR) model: Does adding the good lives model contribute to effective crime prevention? *Criminal Justice & Behavior, 38*, 735–755.

Andrews, D., Robblee, M., & Saunders, R. (1984). *The sentencing factors inventory*. Toronto, ON: Ontario Ministry of Correctional Services.

Andrews, D.A., & Bonta, J. (1995). *LSI-R: The level of service inventory-revised user's manual*. Toronto, ON: Multi-Health Systems.

Andrews, D.A., & Bonta, J. (2006). *The psychology of criminal conduct* (4th ed.). Cincinnati, OH: Anderson.

Andrews, D.A., & Bonta, J. (2010). *The psychology of criminal conduct* (5th ed.). New Providence, NJ: Matthew Bender & Company.

Andrews, D.A., Bonta, J., & Wormith, J.S. (2004). *The Level of Service/Case Management Inventory*. Toronto, ON: MultiHealth Systems.

Andrews, D.A., & Dowden, C. (2006). Risk principle of case classification in correctional treatment. *International Journal of Offender Therapy and Comparative Criminology, 50*, 88–100.

Andrews, D.A., Guzzo, L., Raynor, P., Rowe, R.C., Rettinger, L.J., Brews, A., & Wormith, J.S. (2012). Are the major risk/need factors predictive of both female and male reoffending? A test with the eight domains of the Level of Service/Case Management Inventory. *International Journal of Offender Therapy and Comparative Criminology, 56*, 113–133.

Andrews, D.A., Zinger, I., Hoge, R.D., Bonta, J., Gendreau, P., & Cullen, F.T. (1990). Does correctional treatment work? A clinically relevant and psychologically informed meta-analysis. *Criminology, 28*, 369–404.

Angus Reid. (2013). Three-in-five Canadians would bring back death penalty. Retrieved from www.angus-reid.com/wp-content/uploads/2013/03/2013.03.20_Death_CAN.pdf.

Annell, S., Lindfors, P., Sverke, M. (2015). Police selection – implications during training and early career. *Policing: An International Journal of Police Strategies & Management, 38*(2), 221–238.

Anshel, M.H. (2000). A conceptual model and implications for coping with stressful events in police work. *Criminal Justice and Behavior, 27,* 375–400.

Anson, R.H., & Bloom, M.E. (1988). Police stress in an occupational context. *Journal of Police Science and Administration, 16,* 229–235.

Appleby, S.C., Hasel, L.E., & Kassin, S.M. (2013). Police-induced confessions: An empirical analysis of their content and impact. *Psychology, Crime & Law, 19,* 111–128.

Archer, J. (2002). Sex differences in physically aggressive acts between heterosexual partners: A meta-analytic review. *Aggression and Violent Behavior, 7,* 313–351.

Archer, J. (2004). Sex differences in aggression in real-world settings: A meta-analytic review. *Review of General Psychology, 8,* 291–322.

Archer, R.P., Buffington-Vollum, J.K., Stredny, R.V., & Handel, R.W. (2006). A survey of psychological test use patterns among forensic psychologists. *Journal of Personality Assessment, 87,* 84–94.

Arnetz, B.B., Arble, E., Backman, L., Lynch, A., & Lublin, A. (2013). Assessment of a prevention program for work-related stress among urban police officers. *International Archives of Occupational and Environmental Health, 86,* 79–88.

Arnetz, B.B., Nevedal, D. C., Lumley, M.A., Backman, L., & Lublin, A. (2009). Trauma resilience training for police: Psychophysiological and performance effects. *Journal of Police and Criminal Psychology, 24,* 1–9.

Ascione, F.R. (1998). Battered women's reports of their partners' and their children's cruelty to animals. *Journal of Emotional Abuse, 1,* 119–133.

Ascione, F.R., Weber, C.V., Thompson, T.M., Heath, J. Maruyama, M., & Hayashi, K. (2007). Battered pets and domestic violence: Animal abuse reported by women experiencing intimate violence and by nonabused women. *Violence Against Women, 13,* 354–373.

Astwood Strategy Corporation. (2003, December). *Results of the 2002 Canadian Police Survey on Youth Gangs.* Ottawa, ON: Minister of Public Safety and Emergency Preparedness. Retrieved from www.astwood.ca/assets/gangs_e.pdf.

Atkinson, J.L. (1996). Female sex offenders: A literature review. *Forum on Corrections Research, 8,* 39–43.

AuCoin, K. (2005). Family violence in Canada: A statistical profile. Ottawa, ON: Statistics Canada.

Austin, J. (2006). How much risk can we take? The misuse of risk assessment in corrections. *Federal Probation, 70,* 58–63.

Azpiri, J. (2008). Judge sentences hip-hop fan to listen to classical music. *NowPublic.* Retrieved from www.nowpublic.com/strange/judge-sentences-hip-hop-fan-listen-classical-music.

Babchishin, K.M., Blais, J., & Helmus, L. (2012). Do static risk factors predict differently for Indigenous sex offenders? A multi-site comparison of the original and revised Static-99 and Static-2002 scales. *Canadian Journal of Criminology and Criminal Justice, 54,* 1–43.

Babcock, J.C., Green, C.E., & Robie, C. (2004). Does batterers' treatment work? A meta-analytic review of domestic violence treatment. *Clinical Psychology Review, 23,* 1023–1053.

Babcock, J.C., Miller, S.A., & Siard, C. (2003). Toward a typology of abusive women: Differences between partner-only and generally violent women in the use of violence. *Psychology of Women Quarterly, 27,* 153–161.

Babiak, P. (1995). When psychopaths go to work: A case study of an industrial psychopath. *Applied Psychology: An International Review, 44,* 171–188.

Babiak, P. (2000). Psychopathic manipulation at work. In C.B. Gacono (Ed.), *Clinical and forensic assessment of psychopathy: A practitioner's guide* (pp. 287–311). Mahwah, NJ: Lawrence Erlbaum Associates.

Babiak, P., Neumann, C.S., & Hare, R.D. (2010). Corporate psychopathy: Talking the walk. *Behavioral Sciences and the Law, 28,* 174–193.

Baer, R.A., Wetter, M.W., & Berry, D.T.T. (1995). Sensitivity of MMP-2 validity scales to underreporting of symptoms. *Psychological Assessment, 7,* 419–423.

Bagby, R.M., Nicholson, R.A., Bacchiochi, J.R., Ryder, A.B., & Bury, A.S. (2002). The predictive capacity of MMPI-2 and PAI validity scales and indexes of coached and uncoached feigning. *Journal of Personality Assessment, 78,* 69–86.

Baggot, M. (2014). *Stressed police officers took 250,000 sick days last year – and blame pressure of staff cuts.* Retrieved March 4, 2016 from http://www.mirror.co.uk/news/uk-news/police-sick-days-stressed-police-3132506.

Bailey, I. (2013, April 7). Training sessions change dialogue between B.C. police and mentally ill individuals. *The Globe and Mail.* Retrieved from www.theglobeandmail.com/news/british-columbia/training-sessions-change-dialogue-between-bc-police-and-mentally-ill-individuals/article10839919/.

Baillargeon, J., Binswanger, I., Penn, J., Williams, B., & Murray, O. (2009). Psychiatric disorders and repeat incarcerations: The revolving prison door. *American Journal of Psychiatry, 166,* 103–109.

Baillargeon, J., Williams, B., Mellow, J., Harzke, A., Hoge, S., Baillargeon, G., & Greifinger, R. (2009b). Parole revocation among prison inmates with psychiatric and substance use disorders. *Psychiatric Services* (Washington, D.C.), *60,* 1516–1521.

Bala, N. (1999). Child witnesses in the Canadian criminal courts. *Psychology, Public Policy, and Law, 5,* 323–354.

Bala, N., Lee, K., Lindsay, R.C.L., & Talwar, V. (2010). The competency of children to testify: Psychological research informing Canadian law reform. *International Journal of Children's Rights, 18,* 53–77.

Bandura, A. (1965). Influence of models' reinforcement contingencies on the acquisition of imitative responses. *Journal of Personality and Social Psychology, 1,* 589–595.

Bandura, A. (1973). *Aggression: A social learning analysis.* Englewood Cliffs, NJ: Prentice-Hall.

Banerjee, S. (2012). *Three dead Quebec siblings: Mother charged with first degree murder.* Retrieved April 4, 2016 from http://www.montrealgazette.com/Three+dead+Quebec+siblings+mother+charged+with+first+degree+murder/7659739/story.html.

Banning, A. (1989). Mother–son incest: Confronting a prejudice. *Child Abuse and Neglect, 13,* 563–570.

Baratta, A., Javelot, H., Morali, A., Halleguen, O., & Weiner, L. (2012). The role of antidepressants in treating sex offenders. *Sexologies, 21,* 106–108.

Barbaree, H. (1997). Evaluating treatment efficacy with sexual offenders: The insensitivity of recidivism studies to treatment effects. *Journal of Research and Treatment, 9,* 111–128.

Barbaree, H.E. (1991). Denial and minimization among sex offenders: Assessment and treatment outcome. *Forum on Corrections Research, 3,* 300–333.

Barbaree, H.E., Seto, M.C., Langton, C.M., & Peacock, E.J. (2001). Evaluating the predictive accuracy of six risk assessment instruments for adult sex offenders. *Criminal Justice and Behavior, 28,* 490–521.

Barbaree, H.E., Seto, M.C., Serin, R., Amos, N., & Preston, D. (1994). Comparisons between sexual and nonsexual rapist subtypes: Sexual arousal to rape, offense precursors, and offense characteristics. *Criminal Justice and Behavior, 21,* 95–114.

Barefoot *v.* Estelle, [1983] 463 U.S. 880.

Baron, R.A., & Bryne, D. (1991). *Social psychology: Understanding human interaction* (6th ed.). Toronto, ON: Allyn & Bacon.

Barthlow, B.D., Bushman, B.J., & Sestir, M.A. (2006). Chronic violent video game exposure and desensitization to violence: Behavioral and event-related brain potential data. *Journal of Experimental Social Psychology, 42,* 532–539.

Bartlett, C., Branch, O., Rodeheffer, C., & Harris, R. (2009). How long do the short-term violent video game effects last? *Aggressive Behavior, 35,* 225–236.

Bartol, C.R., & Bartol, A.M. (1994). *Psychology and law* (2nd ed.). Pacific Grove, CA: Brooks/Cole.

Bartol, C.R., & Bartol, A.M. (2013). History of forensic psychology. In I.B. Weiner and R.K. Otto (Eds.), *The Handbook of Forensic Psychology* (4th Edition) (pp. 3–34). Hoboken, NJ: John Wiley and Sons, Inc.

Baxstrom *v.* Herald, [1966] 383 U.S. 107.

Beauregard, E., & Field, J. (2008). Body disposal patterns of sexual murderers: Implications for offender profiling. *Journal of Police and Criminal Psychology, 23,* 81–89.

Beauregard, E., & Martineau, M. (2013). A descriptive study of sexual homicide in Canada: Implications for police investigation. *International Journal of Offender Therapy and Comparative Criminology, 57,* 1454–1476.

Beauregard, E., & Proulx, J. (2002). Profiles in the offending process of nonserial sexual murderers. *International Journal of Offender Therapy and Comparative Criminology, 46,* 386–399.

Beck, K.A., & Ogloff, J.R.P. (1995). Child abuse reporting in British Columbia: Psychologists' knowledge of and compliance with the reporting law. *Professional Psychology: Research and Practice, 26,* 245–251.

Beck, N.C., Menditto, A.A., Baldwin, L., Angelone, E., & Maddox, M. (1991). Reduced frequency of aggressive behavior in forensic patients in a social learning program. *Hospital and Community Psychiatry, 42,* 750–752.

Beck, V.S., Boys, S., Rose, C., & Beck, E. (2012). Violence against women in video games: A prequel or sequel to rape myth acceptance? *Journal of Interpersonal Violence, 27,* 3016–3031.

Becker, H.S. (1963). *Outsiders: Studies in the sociology of deviance.* London, England: Macmillan.

Behrman, B.W., & Davey, S.L. (2001). Eyewitness identification in actual criminal cases: An archival analysis. *Law and Human Behavior, 25,* 475–491.

Benaquisto, L. (2000). Inattention to sanctions in criminal conduct. In R. Silverman, T. Teevan, & V. Sacco (Eds.), *Crime in Canadian society* (pp. 203–215). Toronto, ON: Harcourt Brace and Co.

Benda, B.B. (2005). Gender differences in life-course theory of recidivism: A survival analysis. *International Journal of Offender Therapy and Comparative Criminology, 49,* 325–342.

Benia, L.R., Hauck-Filho, N., Dillenburg, M., & Stein, L.M. (2015). The NICHD investigative protocol: A meta-analytic review. *Journal of Child Sexual Abuse, 24*(3), 259–279.

Bennell, C., Bloomfield, S., Emeno, K., & Musolino, E. (2013). Classifying serial sexual murder/murderers: An attempt to validate Keppel and Walter's (1999) model. *Criminal Justice and Behavior, 40,* 5–25.

Bennell, C., Jones, N.J., Taylor, P.J., & Snook, B. (2006). Validities and abilities in criminal profiling: A critique of the studies conducted by Richard Kocsis and his colleagues. *International Journal of Offender Therapy and Comparative Criminology, 50,* 344–360.

Bennell, C., Mugford, R., Ellingwood, E., & Woodhams, J. (2014). Linking crimes using behavioural clues: Current levels of linking accuracy and strategies for moving forward. *Journal of Investigative Psychology and Offender Profiling, 11,* 29–56.

Bennell, C., Snook, B., MacDonald, S., House, J., & Taylor, P.J. (2012). Computerized crime linkage systems: A critical review and research agenda. *Criminal Justice and Behavior, 39,* 620–634.

Bennett, L.W., Stoops, C., Call, C., & Flett, H. (2007). Program completion and re-arrest in a batterer intervention system. *Research on Social Work Practice, 17*(1), 42–54.

Ben-Porath, Y.S. (1994). The ethical dilemma of coached malingering research. *Psychological Assessment, 6,* 14–15.

Ben-Porath, Y.S., & Tellegen, A. (2008). *MMPI-2-RF (Minnesota Multiphasic Personality Inventory-2 Restructured Form): Manual for administration, scoring, and interpretation.* Minneapolis: University of Minnesota Press.

Ben-Shakhar, G., & Elaad, E. (2003). The validity of psychophysiological detection of information with the guilty knowledge test: A meta-analytic review. *Journal of Applied Psychology, 88,* 131–151.

Ben-Shakhar, G., & Furedy, J.J. (1990). *Theories and applications in the detection of deception: Psychophysiological and cultural perspectives.* New York, NY: Springer-Verlag.

Benton, T., Ross, D.F., Bradshaw, E., Thomas, W., & Bradshaw, G. (2006). Eyewitness memory is still not common sense: Comparing jurors, judges, and law enforcement to eyewitness experts. *Applied Cognitive Psychology, 20,* 115–130.

Berg, J.M., Smith, S.F., Watts, A.L., Ammirati, R., Green, S.E., & Lilienfeld, S.O. (2013). Misconceptions regarding psychopathic personality: Implications for clinical practice and research. *Neuropsychiatry, 3,* 63–74.

Bergen, P., Tiedemann, K., & Lebovich, A. (2011, January 11). How many Gitmo alumni take up arms? *Foreign Policy.* Retrieved from www.foreignpolicy.com/articles/2011/01/11/how_many_gitmo_alumni_take_up_arms.

Bergstrøm, H., Forth, A., & Farrington, D.P. (2016). The psychopath: Continuity or change? Stability of psychopathic traits and predictors of stability. In A. Kapardis & D. Farrington (Eds.), *The psychology of crime, policing, and courses* (pp. 94-116). New York, NY: Rutledge.

Berko, A., Erez, E., & Globokar, J. (2010). Gender, crime and terrorism: The case of Arab/Palestinian women in Israel. *British Journal of Criminology, 50,* 670–689.

Bernat, D.H., Oakes, J.M., Pettingell, S.L., & Resnick, M. (2012). Risk and direct protective factors for youth violence: Results from the national longitudinal study of adolescent health. *American Journal of Preventive Medicine, 43*(2), S57–S66.

Berry, D.T.R., & Nelson, N.W. (2010). DSM-5 and malingering: A modest proposal. *Psychological Injury and Law, 3,* 295–303.

Bhui, K., Warfa, N., & Jones, E. (2014). Is violent radicalisation associated with poverty, migration, poor self-reported health and common mental disorders? *PLOS One, 9*(3), 1–10.

Binet, A. (1900). *La suggestibilité.* Paris, France: Schleicher Freres.

Bjerregaard, B. (2002). An empirical study of stalking victimization. In K.E. Davis, I.H. Frieze, & R.D. Maiuro (Eds.), *Stalking: Perspectives on victims and perpetrators* (pp. 112–137). New York, NY: Springer.

Blacker, J., Beech, A.R., Wilcox, D.T., & Boer D.P. (2011). The assessment of dynamic risk and recidivism in a sample of special needs sexual offenders. *Psychology, Crime and Law, 17,* 75–92.

Blair, R.J.R. (2006). The emergence of psychopathy: Implications for the neuropsychological approach to developmental disorders. *Cognition, 101,* 414–442.

Blair, R.J.R. (2008). The cognitive neuroscience of psychopathy and implications for judgments of responsibility. *Neuroethics, 1,* 149–157.

Blair, R.J.R., Budhani, S., Colledge, E., & Scott, S. (2005). Deafness to fear in boys with psychopathic tendencies. *Journal of Child Psychology and Psychiatry, 46,* 327–336.

Blais, J., & Forth, A. (2013). Potential labeling effects: Influence of psychopathy diagnosis, defendant age, and defendant gender on mock jurors' decisions. *Psychology, Crime & Law.*

Blais, J., & Forth, A. E. (2014). Prosecution-retained versus court-appointed experts: Comparing and contrasting risk assessment reports in preventative detention hearings. *Law and Human Behavior, 38,* 531–543.

Blais, J., Solodukhin, E., & Forth, A.E. (2014). A meta-analysis exploring the relationship between psychopathy and instrumental versus reactive violence. *Criminal Justice and Behavior, 41,* 797–821.

Blanchette, K.D., & Brown, S. L. (2006). *The assessment and treatment of women offenders: An integrative perspective.* Chichester, England: John Wiley & Sons.

Bland, R.C., & Orn, H. (1986). Family violence and psychiatric disorder. *Canadian Journal of Psychiatry, 31,* 129–137.

Bland, R.C., Newman, S.C., Dyck, R.J., & Orn, H. (1990). Prevalence of psychiatric disorders and suicide attempts in a prison population. *Canadian Journal of Psychiatry, 35,* 407–413.

Blandon-Gitlin, I., Pezdek, K., Rogers, M., & Brodie, L. (2005). Detecting deception in children: An experimental study of the effect of event familiarity on CBCA ratings. *Law and Human Behavior, 29*(2), 187–197.

Blonigen, D.M., Hicks, B.M., Krueger, R.F., Patrick, C.J., & Iacono, W.G. (2006). Continuity and change in psychopathic traits as measured via normal-range personality: A longitudinal-biometric study. *Journal of Abnormal Psychology, 115,* 95–95.

Bloom, H., & Schneider, R.D. (2007). *Mental health courts: Decriminalizing the mentally ill.* Toronto, ON: Irwin Law.

Blumstein, A., & Cohen, J. (1987). Characterizing criminal careers. *Science, 237,* 985–991.

Boccaccini, M.T., Murrie, D.C., & Duncan, S.A. (2006). Screening for malingering in a criminal-forensic sample with the Personality Assessment Inventory. *Psychological Assessment, 18,* 415–423.

Boccaccini, M.T., Murrie, D.C., Caperton, J.D., & Hawes, S.W. (2009). Field validity of the Static-99 and MnSORT-R among sex offenders evaluated for civil commitment as sexually violent predators. *Psychology, Public Policy, and Law, 15,* 278–314.

Boccaccini, M.T., Murrie, D.C., Rufino, K.A., & Gardner, B.O. (2014). Evaluator differences in psychopathy checklist-revised factor and facet scores. *Law and Human Behavior, 38,* 337–345.

Boddy, C.R. (2014). Corporate psychopaths, conflict, employee affective well-being and counterproductive work behaviour. *Journal of Business Ethics, 121,* 107–121.

Bonazzoli, M.J. (1998). Jury selection and bias: Debunking invidious stereotypes through science. *Quinnipiac Law Review, 18,* 247–305.

Bond, C.F., & DePaulo, B.M. (2006). Accuracy of deception judgments. *Personality and Social Psychology Review, 10,* 214–234.

Bond, C.F., & DePaulo, B.M. (2008). Individual differences in judging deception: Accuracy and bias. *Psychological Bulletin, 134,* 477–492.

Bond, C.F., & Uysal, A. (2007). On lie detection "Wizards." *Law and Human Behavior, 31,* 109–115.

Bongers, I.L., Koot, H.M., van der Ende, J., & Verhulst, F.C. (2004). Developmental trajectories of externalizing behaviors in childhood and adolescence. *Child Development, 75,* 1523–1537.

Bonnie, R.J., & Grisso, T. (2000). Adjudicative competence and youthful offenders. In T. Grisso & R.G. Schwartz (Eds.), *Youth on trial: A developmental perspective on juvenile justice* (pp. 73–103). Chicago, IL: University of Chicago Press.

Bonta, J., Blais, J., & Wilson, H.A. (2014). A theoretically informed meta-analysis of the risk for general and violent recidivism for mentally disordered offenders. *Aggression and Violent Behavior, 19,* 278–287.

Bonta, J., Law, M., & Hanson, K. (1998). The prediction of criminal and violent recidivism among mentally disordered offenders: A meta-analysis. *Psychological Bulletin, 123,* 123–142.

Book, A., Costello, K., & Camilleri, J.A. (2013). Psychopathy and victim selection: The use of gait as a cue to vulnerability. *Journal of Interpersonal Violence, 28,* 2365–2383.

Book, A., Methot, T., Bauthier, N., Hosker-Field, A., Forth, A., Quinsey, V., & Molnar, D. (2015). The mask of sanity revisited: Psychopathic traits and affective mimicry. *Evolutionary Psychological Science, 1,* 91–102.

Boothby, J., & Clements, C.B. (2000). A national survey of correctional psychologists. *Criminal Justice and Behavior, 27,* 715–731.

Bornstein, B.H., & Greene, E. (2011). Jury decision making: Implications for and from psychology. *Current Directions in Psychological Science, 20,* 63–67.

Borum, R. (1996). Improving the clinical practice of violence risk assessment: Technology, guidelines and training. *American Psychologist, 51,* 945–956.

Borum, R. (2011). Understanding terrorist psychology. In A. Silke (Ed.), *The psychology of counter-terrorism* (pp. 19–33). London, England: Routledge.

Borum, R. (2015). Assessing risk for terrorism involvement. *Journal of Threat Assessment and Management, 2*(2), 63–87.

Borum, R., Bartel, P. A., & Forth, A.E. (2002). *Manual for the structured assessment of violent risk in youth (SAVRY), Consultation edition, Version 1.* Tampa: University of South Florida.

Borum, R., Otto, R., & Golding, S. (1993). Improving clinical judgment and decision making in forensic evaluation. *Journal of Psychiatry and Law, 21,* 35–76.

Bottoms, B., Peter-Hagene, L., Stevenon, M., Wiley, T., Mitchell, T., & Goodman, S. (2014). Explaining gender differences in jurors' reactions to child sexual assault cases. *Behavioral Sciences and the Law, 32,* 789–812.

Bourke, M.L., Fragomeli, L., Detar, P.J., Sullivan, M.A., Meyle, E., & O'Riordan, M. (2015). The use of tactical polygraph with sex offenders. *Journal of Sexual Aggression, 21*(3), 354–367.

Bowen, E., & Gilchrist, E. (2006). Predicting dropout of court-mandated treatment in a British sample of domestic violence offenders. *Psychology, Crime and Law, 12,* 573–587.

Boyce, J. (2015). *Police-reported crime statistics in Canada, 2014.* Canadian Centre for Justice Statistics. Retrieved April 4, 2016 from Statistics Canada website at http://www.statcan.gc.ca/pub/85-002-x/2015001/article/14211-eng.pdf.

Bradfield, A., & McQuiston, D. (2004). When does evidence of eyewitness confidence inflation affect judgments in a criminal trial? *Law and Human Behavior, 28,* 369–387.

Bradfield, A.L., Wells, G.L., & Olson, E.A. (2002). The damaging effect of confirming feedback on the relation between eyewitness certainty and identification accuracy. *Journal of Applied Psychology, 87,* 112–120.

Brainerd, C., & Reyna, V. (1996). Mere testing creates false memories in children. *Developmental Psychology, 32,* 467–476.

Brainerd C.J., & Reyna, V.F. (2004). Fuzzy-trace theory and memory development. *Developmental Review, 24,* 396–439.

Brandl, S.G., & Smith, B.W. (2012). An empirical examination of retired police officers' length of retirement and age at death: A research note. *Police Quarterly, 16,* 113–123.

Brennan, S. (2011). Family violence in Canada: A statistical profile (Statistics Canada Catalogue no. 85-224-X). *Juristat.*

Breslin, N.A. (1992). Treatment of schizophrenia: Current practice and future promise. *Hospital and Community Psychiatry, 43,* 877–885.

Brewer, N., Potter, R., Fisher, R.P., Bond, N., & Luszcz (1999). Beliefs and data on the relationship between consistency and accuracy of eyewitness testimony. *Applied Cognitive Psychology, 13,* 297–313.

Brigham, J.C. (1999). What is forensic psychology, anyway? *Law and Human Behavior, 23,* 273–298.

Brink, J.H., Doherty, D., & Boer, A. (2001). Mental disorder in federal offenders: A Canadian prevalence study. *International Journal of Law & Psychiatry, 24,* 339–356.

Brodsky, S. (1991). *Testifying in court: Guidelines and maxims for the expert witness.* Washington, DC: American Psychological Association.

Brodsky, S. (1999). *The expert witness: More maxims and guidelines for testifying in court.* Washington, DC: American Psychological Association.

Broidy, L.M., Nagin, D.S., Tremblay, R.E., Bates, J.E., Brame, B., Dodge, K.A., Fergusson, D., Horwood, J.L., Loeber, R., Laird, R., Lynam, D. R., Moffitt, T.E., Pettit, G.S., Vitaro, F. (2003). Developmental trajectories of childhood disruptive behaviors and adolescent delinquency: A six-site, cross national study. *Developmental Psychology, 39,* 222–245.

Bronitt, S., & Stenning, P. (2011). Understanding discretion in modern policing. *Criminal Law Journal, 35,* 319–332.

Brooks, N. (1983). *Police guidelines: Pretrial identification procedures.* Ottawa, ON: Law Reform Commission.

Brown v. Mississippi, [1936] 297 U.S. 278.

Brown, D., & Pipe, M-E. (2003). Variations on a technique: Enhancing children's recall using narrative elaboration training. *Applied Cognitive Psychology, 17,* 377–399.

Brown, D., Pipe, M-E., Lewis, C., Lamb, M. E., & Orbach, Y. (2012). How do body diagrams affect the accuracy and consistency of children's reports across repeated interviews. *Applied Cognitive Psychology, 26*(2), 174–181.

Brown, D., Scheflin, A.W., & Hammond, D.C. (1998). *Memory, trauma treatment, and the law.* New York, NY: Norton.

Brown, G.R. (2004). Gender as a factor in the response of the law-enforcement systems to violence against partners. *Sexuality and Culture, 9,* 1–87.

Brown, J.M., & Campbell, E.A. (1994). *Stress and policing: Sources and strategies.* New York, NY: John Wiley & Sons.

Brown, S., Serin, R., Forth, A., Nunes, K., Bennell, C., & Pozzulo, J. (2016). *Psychology of criminal behaviour: A Canadian perspective.* Don Mills, ON: Pearson Canada, Inc.

Brown, S.L., & Forth, A.E. (1997). Psychopathy and sexual assault: Static risk factors, emotional precursors, and rapist subtypes. *Journal of Consulting and Clinical Psychology, 65,* 848–857.

Browne, A., & Finkelhor, D. (1986). Impact of child sexual abuse: A review of the research. *Psychological Bulletin, 99,* 66–77.

Bruck, M., & Ceci, S.J. (1999). The suggestibility of children's memory. *Annual Review of Psychology, 50,* 419–439.

Bruck, M., Ceci, S.J., & Francoeur, E. (2000). Children's use of anatomically detailed dolls to report genital touching in a medical examination: Developmental and gender comparisons. *Journal of Experimental Psychology: Applied, 6*(1), 74–83.

Bruck, M., & Melnyk, L. (2004). Individual differences in children's suggestibility: a review and synthesis. *Applied Cognitive Psychology 18*(8), 947–996.

Bruni, F. (1998, November 22). Behind the jokes, a life of pain and delusion; for Letterman stalker, mental illness was family curse and scarring legacy. *The New York Times.* Retrieved from www.nytimes.com/1998/11/22/nyregion/behind-jokes-life-pain-delusion-for-letterman-stalker-mental-illness-was-family.html?pagewanted=all&src=pm.

Brzozowski, J., Taylor-Butts, A., & Johnson, S. (2006). Victimization and offending among the Aboriginal population in Canada. *Juristat, 26.*

Buck, S.M., Warren, A.R., Betman, S., & Brigham, J.C. (2002). Age differences in Criteria-Based Content Analysis scores in typical child sexual abuse interviews. *Journal of Applied Developmental Psychology, 23,* 267–283.

Bucolo, D., & Cohn, E. (2010). Playing the race card: Making race-salient in defence opening and closing statements. *Legal and Criminological Psychology, 15,* 293–303.

Bull, R., & Clifford, B.R. (1984). Earwitness voice recognition accuracy. In G. Wells & E. Loftus (Eds.), *Eyewitness testimony: Psychological perspectives* (pp. 92–123). Cambridge, England: Cambridge University Press.

Bumby, K.M., & Hansen, D.J. (1997). Intimacy deficits, fear of intimacy, and loneliness among sexual offenders. *Criminal Justice and Behavior, 24,* 315–331.

Burczycka, M. (2016). Family violence in Canada: A statistical profile, 2014 (Statistics Canada catalogue no. 85-002-X). *Juristat.*

Burgess, A.W., Hartman, C.R., Ressler, R.K., Douglas, J.E., & McCormack, A. (1986). Sexual homicide: A motivational model. *Journal of Interpersonal Violence, 1,* 251–272.

Burgess, A.W., & Holmstrom, L.L. (1974). Rape trauma syndrome. *American Journal of Psychiatry, 131,* 981–986.

Burgmann, T. (2016). Kelly Ellard denied parole despite finally admitting blame in teen's 1997 death. Retrieved May 4, 2016 from http://news.nationalpost.com/news/kelly-ellard-denied-parole-board-calls-rationale-for-release-very-entitled.

Burke, J.D., & Loeber, R. (2014). The effectiveness of the Stop Now and Plan (SNAP) program for boys at risk for violence and delinquency. *Prevention Science, 16,* 242–253.

Burke, J.D., Waldman, I., & Lahey, B.B. (2010). Predictive validity of childhood oppositional defiant disorder and conduct disorder: implications for the DSM-V. *Journal of Abnormal Psychology, 4,* 739–751.

Burkhart, B. (1980). Conceptual issues in the development of police selection procedures. *Professional Psychology, 11,* 121–129.

Burns, P.J., Hiday, V.A., & Ray, B. (2013). Effectiveness 2 years post exit of a recently established mental health court. *American Behavioral Scientist, 57,* 189–208.

Burt, A.S., & Klump, K.L. (2012). Etiological distinctions between aggressive and non-aggressive antisocial behavior: Results from a nuclear twin family model. *Journal of Abnormal Child Psychology, 40,* 1059–1071.

Burt, M.R. (1980). Cultural myths and supports for rape. *Journal of Personality and Social Psychology, 38,* 217–230.

Burt, S.A. (2009). Are there meaningful etiological differences within antisocial behavior? Results of a meta-analysis. *Clinical Psychology Review, 29,* 163–178.

Bushman, B.J., & Anderson, C.A. (2001). Media violence and the American public: Scientific facts versus media misinformation. *American Psychologist, 56,* 477–489.

Buss, D.M., & Duntley, J.D. (2011). The evolution of intimate partner violence. *Aggression and Violent Behavior, 16,* 411–419.

Buss, D.M., & Shackelford, T.K. (1997). Human aggression in evolutionary psychological perspective. *Clinical Psychology Review, 17,* 605–619.

Butcher, J.N., Dahlstrom, W.G., Graham, J.R., Tellegen, A., & Kaemmer, B. (1989). *MMPI-2: Manual for administration and scoring.* Minneapolis, MN: University of Minnesota Press.

Cadoret, R.J., & Cain, C. (1980). Sex differences in predictors of antisocial behavior in adoptees. *Archives of General Psychiatry, 37,* 1171–1175.

Caldwell, M.F., McCormick, D.J., Umstead, D., & Van Rybroek, G.J. (2007). Evidence of treatment progress and therapeutic outcomes among adolescents with psychopathic features. *Criminal Justice and Behavior, 34,* 573–587.

Caldwell, M.F., Skeem, J., Salekin, R., & Van Rybroek, G. (2006). Treatment response of adolescent offenders with psychopathy-like features. *Criminal Justice and Behavior, 33, 5,* 571–596.

Caldwell, R.M., Silverman, J., Lefforge, N., & Silver, N.C. (2004). Adjudicated Mexican American adolescents: The effects of familial emotional support on self-esteem, emotional well-being, and delinquency. *The American Journal of Family Therapy, 32,* 55–69.

Call, C., Cook, A., Reitzel, J., & McDougle, R. (2013). Seeing is believing: The CSI effect among jurors in malicious wounding cases. *Journal of Social, Behavioral, and Health Sciences, 7,* 52–66.

Campbell, A. (1996, June). *Bernardo Investigation Review: Report of Mr. Justice Archie Campbell.* Ottawa, ON: Ministry of the Solicitor General and Correctional Services.

Campbell, C. (1976). Portrait of a mass killer. *Psychology Today, 9,* 110–119.

Campbell, J.C., Webster, D., & Koziol-McLain, J. (2003). Risk factors for femicide in abusive relationships: Results from a multisite case control study. *American Journal of Public Health, 93,* 1089–1097.

Campbell, M.A., Canales, D., Wie, R., Totten, E., Macaulay, W., & Wershler, J. (2015). Multidimensional evaluation of a mental health court: Adherence to the risk-need responsivity model. *Law and Human Behavior, 39,* 489–502.

Campbell, M.A., French, S., & Gendreau, P. (2009). The prediction of violence in adult offenders: A meta-analytic comparison of instruments and methods of assessment. *Criminal Justice and Behavior, 36(6),* 567–590.

Campbell, R., Sefl, T., & Ahrens, C.E. (2003). The physical health consequences of rape: Assessing survivors' somatic symptoms in a racially diverse population. *Women's Studies Quarterly, 31(1/2),* 90–104.

Canada v. Ewert, [2016] FCA 203 (CanLII).

Canadian Centre for Justice Statistics. (1997, February). Sentencing in adult provincial courts—A study of nine Canadian jurisdictions. *Juristat, 17.*

Canadian Foundation for Children, Youth, and the Law v. The Attorney General in Right of Canada, [2004] 1 S.C.R. 76, 2004 SCC 4.

Canadian Psychological Association (CPA). (2016). *Provincial and territorial licensing requirements.* Retrieved March 3, 2016 from http://www.cpa.ca/accreditation/PTlicensingrequirements/.

Candel, I., Hayne, H., Strange, D., & Prevoo, E. (2009). The effect of suggestion on children's recognition memory for seen and unseen details. *Psychology, Crime, & Law, 15(1),* 29–39.

Canter, D.V. (1994). *Criminal shadows.* London, England: HarperCollins.

Canter, D.V. (2000). Offender profiling and criminal differentiation. *Legal and Criminological Psychology, 5,* 23–46.

Canter, D.V., Alison, L.J., Alison, E., & Wentink, N. (2004). The organized/disorganized typology of serial murder: Myth or model? *Psychology, Public Policy, and Law, 10,* 293–320.

Canter, D.V., Coffey, T., Huntley, M., & Missen, C. (2000). Predicting serial killers' home base using a decision support system. *Journal of Quantitative Criminology, 16,* 457–478.

Canter, D.V., & Wentink, N. (2004). An empirical test of Holmes and Holmes's serial murder typology. *Criminal Justice and Behavior, 31,* 489–515.

Canter, D.V., & Youngs, D. (2009). *Investigative psychology: Offender profiling and the analysis of criminal action.* Chichester, England: Wiley.

Caprara, G.V., Barbaranelli, C., & Pastorelli, C. (2001). Facing guilt: Role of negative affectivity, need for reparation, and fear of punishment in leading to prosocial behaviour and aggression. *European Journal of Personality, 15,* 219–237.

Carlson, C.A., & Carlson, M.A. (2012). A distinctiveness-driven reversal of the weapon-focus effect. *Applied Psychology in Criminal Justice, 8*(1), 36–53.

Carney, M., Buttell, F., & Dutton, D. (2007). Women who perpetrate intimate partner violence: A review of the literature with recommendations for treatment. *Aggression and Violent Behavior, 12,* 108–115.

Carter, A.J., & Hollin, C.R. (2010). Characteristics of non-serial sexual homicide offenders: A review. *Psychology, Crime & Law, 16,* 25–45.

Cassell, P.G. (1998). Protecting the innocent from false confessions and lost confessions—and from Miranda. *Journal of Criminal Law and Criminology, 88,* 497–556.

Castillo, E.D., & Alarid, L.F. (2011). Factors associated with recidivism among offenders with mental illness. *International Journal of Offender Therapy and Comparative Criminology, 55*(1), 98–117.

Cattell, J.M. (1895). Measurements of the accuracy of recollection. *Science, 2,* 761–766.

Cavanaugh, M.M., & Gelles, R.J. (2005). The utility of male domestic violence offender typologies: New directions for research, policy, and practice. *Journal of Interpersonal Violence, 20,* 155–166.

CBC. (2015). *Sonia Blanchette, Quebecer, accused of killing her 3 kids, dies.* Retrieved April 4, 2016 from http://www.huffingtonpost.ca/2015/01/16/sonia-blanchette-montreal-killing-children_n_6486466.html.

Ceci, S.J., & Bruck, M. (1993). The suggestibility of the child witness: A historical review and synthesis. *Psychological Bulletin, 113,* 403–439.

Cervone, D., & Shoda, Y. (Eds.). (1999). *The coherence of personality: Social-cognitive bases of consistency, variability and organization.* New York, NY: Guilford Press.

Chadee, D. (1996). Race, trial evidence and jury decision making. *Caribbean Journal of Criminology and Social Psychology, 1,* 59–86.

Chae, Y., Ogle, C.M., & Goodman, G. (2009). Remembering traumatic childhood events: An attachment theory perspective. In J.A. Quas & R. Fivush (Eds.), *Emotion and memory development* (pp. 3–27). New York, NY: Oxford University Press.

Chaiken, J.M, & Chaiken, M.R. (1983). Crime rates and the active offender. In J.Q. Wilson (Ed.), *Crime and public policy* (pp. 203–229). New Brunswick, OH: Transaction Books.

Chan, H.C., Heide, K.M., & Myers, W.C. (2013). Juvenile and adult offenders arrested for sexual homicide: An analysis of victim-offender relationship and weapon used by race. *Journal of Forensic Sciences, 58,* 85–89.

Chan, H.C., Myers, W.C., & Heide, K.M. (2010). An empirical analysis of 30 years of U.S. juvenile and adult sexual homicide offender data: Race and age differences in the victim-offender relationship. *Journal of Forensic Sciences, 55,* 1282–1290.

Chan, K.L., Strauss, M.R., Brownridge, D.A., Tiwari, A., & Leung, W.C. (2008). Prevalence of dating partner violence and suicidal ideation among male and female university students worldwide. *Journal of Midwifery & Women's Health, 53,* 529–537.

Chandler, R.K., Peters, R.H., Field, G., & Juliano-Bult, D. (2004). Challenges in implementing evidence-based treatment practices for co-occurring disorders in the criminal justice system. *Behavioral Science and the Law, 22,* 431–448.

Chapman, L.J., & Chapman, J.P. (1967). Genesis of popular but erroneous psychodiagnostic observations. *Journal of Abnormal Psychology, 74,* 193–204.

Charette, Y., Crocker, A., Seto, M., Salem, L., Nicholls, T., & Caulet, M. (2015). The national trajectory project of individuals found not criminally responsible on account of mental disorder in Canada, Part 4: Criminal recidivism. *Canadian Journal of Psychiatry, 60,* 127–134.

Cheung, P.T.K. (1986). Maternal filicide in Hong Kong. *Medicine, Science, and Law, 26,* 185–192.

Chibnall J.T., & Detrick P. (2003). The NEO PI-R, Inwald Personality, Inventory, and MMPI-2 in the prediction of police academy performance: A case of incremental validity. *American Journal of Criminal Justice, 27,* 224–233.

Christianson, S.A., Azad, A., Leander, L., & Selenius, H. (2013). Children as witnesses to homicidal violence: What they remember and report. *Psychiatry, Psychology, and Law, 20*(3), 366-383.

Chu, C.M., Daffern, M., Thomas, S., & Lim, J.Y. (2012). Violence risk and gang affiliation in youth offenders: A recidivism study. *Psychology, Crime & Law, 18*(3), 299–315.

Chu, C.M., Daffern, M., Thomas, S.D.M., & Lim, J.Y. (2011). Elucidating the treatment needs of gang-affiliated youth offenders. *Journal of Aggression, Conflict and Peace Research, 3*(3), 129–140. Retrieved April 4, 2016 from http://search.proquest.com/docview/894163466?accountid=9894.

Clark, S.E. (2005). A re-examination of the effects of biased lineup instructions in eyewitness identification. *Law and Human Behavior, 29,* 575–604.

Cleckley, H.R. (1976). *The mask of sanity* (5th ed.). St. Louis, MO: Mosby.

Clifford, B.R. (1980). Voice identification by human listeners: On earwitness reliability. *Law and Human Behavior, 4,* 373–394.

Cochrane, R.E., Tett, R.P., & Vandecreek, L. (2003). Psychological testing and the selection of police officers: A national survey. *Criminal Justice and Behavior, 30,* 511–537.

Cocozza, J.J., Melick, M.E., & Steadman, H.J. (1978). Trends in violent crime among ex-mental patients. *Criminology: An Interdisciplinary Journal, 16,* 317–334.

Cocozza, J.J., & Steadman, H.J. (1978). Prediction in psychiatry: An example of misplaced confidence in experts. *Social Problems, 25,* 265–276.

Cohen, A.J., Adler, N., Kaplan, S.J., Pelcovitz, D., & Mandel, F.G. (2002). Interactional effects of marital status and physical abuse on adolescent psychopathology. *Child Abuse and Neglect, 26,* 277–288.

Cohen, J., & Tonry, M.H. (1983). Sentencing reforms and their impacts. In A. Blumstein, J. Cohen, S.E. Martin, & M.H. Tonry (Eds.), *Research on sentencing: The search for reform* (pp. 305–459). Washington, DC: National Academy Press.

Cohn, E.S., Buccolo, D., Pride, M., & Sommers, S.R. (2009). Reducing White juror bias: The role of race salience and racial attitudes. *Journal of Applied Social Psychology, 39,* 1953–1973.

Coid, J., Yang, M., Ullrich, S., Roberts, A., & Hare, R.D. (2009). Prevalence and correlates of psychopathic traits in the household population of Great Britain. *International Journal of Law and Psychiatry, 32,* 65–73.

Coie, J.D., Belding, M., & Underwood, M. (1988). Aggression and peer rejection in childhood. In B.B. Lahey & A.E. Kazdin (Eds.), *Advances in clinical child psychology* (Vol. II, pp. 125–158). New York, NY: Plenum.

Coie, J.D., Lochman, J.E., Terry, R., & Hyman, C. (1992). Predicting early adolescent disorder from childhood aggression and peer rejection. *Journal of Consulting and Clinical Psychology, 60,* 783–792.

Cole, W.G., & Loftus, E.F. (1979). Incorporating new information into memory. *American Journal of Psychology, 92,* 413–425.

Collins, P.I., Johnson, G.F., Choy, A., Davidson, K.T., & Mackay, R.E. (1998). Advances in violent crime analysis and law enforcement: The Canadian violent crime linkage analysis system. *Journal of Government Information, 25,* 277–284.

Conners, A.D., Mills, J.F., & Gray, A.L. (2012). An evaluation of intimate partner violence intervention with incarcerated offenders. *Journal of Personal Violence, 27,* 1176–1196.

Connolly, D.A., & Read, J.D. (2006). Delayed prosecutions of historic child sexual abuse: Analyses of 2064 Canadian criminal complaints. *Law and Human Behavior, 30,* 409–434.

Cook, S., & Wilding, J. (1997). Earwitness testimony 2: Voices, faces, and context. *Applied Cognitive Psychology, 11,* 527–541.

Cooke, D.J., & Michie, C. (2001). Refining the construct of psychopathy: Towards a hierarchical model. *Psychological Assessment, 13,* 171–188.

Cooper, B.R., & Lanza, S.T. (2014). Who benefits the most from head start? Using latent class moderation to examine differential treatment effects. *Child Development, 85,* 2317–2338.

Corder, B.F., Ball, B.C., Haizlip, T.M., Rollins, R., & Beaumont, R. (1976). Adolescent parricide: A comparison with other adolescent murder. *American Journal of Psychiatry, 133,* 957–961.

Cornell, D.G., Benedek, E.P., & Benedek, D.M. (1987). Characteristics of adolescents charged with homicide: Review of 72 cases. *Behavioral Sciences and the Law, 5,* 11–23.

Cornell, D.G., & Hawk, G.L. (1989). Clinical presentation of malingerers diagnosed by experienced forensic psychologists. *Law and Human Behavior, 13,* 374–383.

Cornell, D.G., Warren, J., Hawk, G., Stafford, E., Oram, G., & Pine, D. (1996). Psychopathy in instrumental and reactive violent offenders. *Journal of Consulting and Clinical Psychology, 64,* 783–790.

Corrado, R.R., Vincent, G.M., Hart, S.D., & Cohen, I.M. (2004). Predictive validity of the Psychopathy Checklist: Youth Version for general and violent recidivism. *Behavioral Sciences and the Law, 22,* 5–22.

Correctional Service Canada. (1989). *Mental health survey of federally sentenced female offenders at Prison for Women.* Unpublished raw data.

Correctional Service of Canada (CSC). (2013). *A profile of Aboriginal sex offender in Canadian federal custody.* Correctional Service of Canada: Ottawa, ON.

Correctional Service of Canada (CSC). (2013). *Adult correctional statistics in Canada, 2013/2014.* Statistics Canada. Retrieved from http://www.statcan.gc.ca/pub/85-002-x/2015001/article/14163-eng.htm.

Cortina, J.M., Goldstein, N.B., Payne, S.C., Davison, H.K., & Gilliland, S.W. (2000). The incremental validity of interview scores over and above cognitive ability and conscientiousness scores. *Personnel Psychology, 53,* 325–351.

Cortoni, F., Hanson, R.K., & Coache, M.E. (2010). The recidivism rates of female sexual offenders are low: A meta-analysis. *Sexual Abuse: Journal of Research and Treatment, 22,* 387–401.

Cottle, C.C., Lee, R.J., & Heilbrun, K. (2001). The prediction of criminal recidivism in juveniles: A meta-analysis. *Criminal Justice and Behavior, 28,* 367–394.

Cotton, D., & Coleman, T. (2008). *Contemporary policing guidelines for working with the mental health system.* Retrieved from Canadian Association of Chiefs of Police website: www.cacp.ca/media/committees/efiles/2/458/Guidelines_for_Police_-_2008_(2).pdf.

Cox, L. (2012). Mother's fury after judge forces her to cut off 13-year-old daughter's ponytail in court after her girl attacked a toddler with pair of scissors. Retrieved May 2, 2016 from http://www.dailymail.co.uk/news/article-2163723/Judge-orders-mom-chop-daughters-hair-punish-girl-hacking-chunks-toddlers-locks.html.

Coy, E., Speltz, M.L., DeKlyen, M., & Jones, K. (2001). Social-cognitive processes in preschool boys with and without oppositional defiant disorder. *Journal of Abnormal Child Psychology, 29,* 107–119.

Crawford, M., & Gartner, R. (1992). *Women killing: Intimate femicide in Ontario, 1974–1990.* Women's Directorate, Ministry of Social Services, Toronto, ON.

Crick, N.R., & Dodge, K.A. (1994). A review and reformulation of social information-processing mechanisms in children's social adjustment. *Psychological Bulletin, 115,* 74–101.

Crocker, A.G., Braithwaite, E., Côté, G., Nicholls, T.L., & Seto, M.C. (2011). To detain or to release? Correlates of dispositions for individuals declared not criminally responsible on account of mental disorder. *The Canadian Journal of Psychiatry / La Revue canadienne de psychiatrie, 56*(5), 293–302. Retrieved from http://search.proquest.com/docview/883436102?accountid=9894.

Crocker, A.G., Hartford, K., & Heslop, L. (2009). Gender differences in police encounters among persons with and without serious mental illness. *Psychiatric Services, 60,* 86–93.

Cross, J.F., Cross, J., & Daly, J. (1971). Sex, race, age, and beauty as factors in recognition of faces. *Perception and Psychophysics, 10,* 393–396.

Cross, T.P., & Saxe, L. (2001). Polygraph testing and sexual abuse: The lure of the magic lasso. *Child Maltreatment: Journal of the American Professional Society of the Abuse of Children*, 6, 195–206.

Cullen, F., & Gendreau, P. (2000). Assessing correctional rehabilitation: Policy, practice, and prospects. In J. Horney (Ed.), *NIJ Criminal justice 2000: Changes in decision-making and discretion in the criminal justice system* (pp. 109–175). Washington, DC: U.S. National Institute of Justice.

Cummings, E.M., Davies, P.T., & Campbell, S.B. (2000). *Developmental psychopathology and family process: Theory, research, and clinical implications*. New York, NY: The Guilford Press.

Cutler, B., & Bull Kovera, M. (2011). Expert psychological testimony. *Current Directions in Psychological Science*, 20, 53–57.

Cutler, B.L., & Penrod, S.D. (1989a). Forensically relevant moderators of the relationship between eyewitness identification accuracy and confidence. *Journal of Applied Psychology*, 74, 650–652.

Cutler, B.L., & Penrod, S.D. (1989b). Moderators of the confidence-accuracy relation in face recognition: The role of information processing and base rates. *Applied Cognitive Psychology*, 3, 95–107.

Cutler, B.L., Fisher, R.P., & Chicvara, C.L. (1989). Eyewitness identification from live versus videotaped lineups. *Forensic Reports*, 2, 93–106.

da Silva, D.R., Rijo, D., & Salekin, R.T. (2013). Child and adolescent psychopathy: Assessment issues and treatment needs. *Aggression and Violent Behavior*, 18, 71–78.

Dadds, M.R., Allen, J.L., McGregor, K., Woolgar, M., Viding, E., & Scott, S. (2014). Callous-unemotional traits in children and mechanisms of impaired eye contact during expressions of love: A treatment target? *Journal of Child Psychology and Psychiatry*, 55(7), 771–780.

Dadds, M.R., Allen, J.L., Oliver, B.R., Faulkner, N., Legge, K., Moul, C., Woolgar, M., & Scott, S. (2012). Love, eye contact and the developmental origins of empathy v. psychopathy. *The British Journal of Psychiatry*, 200(3), 191–196.

Daftary-Kapur, T., Dumas, R., & Penrod, S.D. (2010). Jury decision-making biases and methods to counter them. *Legal and Criminological Psychology*, 15(1), 133–154.

Dakil, S.R., Cox, M., Lin, H., & Flores, G. (2012). Physical abuse in U.S. children: Risk factors and deficiencies in referrals to support services. *Journal of Aggression, Maltreatment & Trauma*, 21(5), 555–569.

Dalby, J.T. (2006). The case of Daniel McNaughton: Let's get the story straight. *American Journal of Forensic Psychiatry*, 27, 17–32.

Dalley, M.L. (2008). *The killing of Canadian children by a parent(s) or guardian(s): Characteristics and trends 1990–1993*. Retrieved from www.rcmp-grc.gc.ca/pubs/omc-ned/kill-tuer-eng.htm#9.

Daly, M., & Wilson, M. (1988). Evolutionary social psychology and family homicide. *Science*, 242, 519–524.

Daly, M., & Wilson, M.I. (1982). Homicide and kinship. *American Anthropologist*, 84, 372–378.

Dando, C., Wilcock, R., & Milne, R. (2009). The cognitive interview: The efficacy of a modified mental reinstatement of context procedure for frontline police investigators. *Applied Cognitive Psychology*, 23, 138–147.

Darby, P.J., Allan, W.D., Kashani, J.H., Hartke, K.L., & Reid, J.C. (1998). Analysis of 112 juveniles who committed homicide: Characteristics and a closer look at family abuse. *Journal of Family Violence*, 13, 365–375.

Daubert v. Merrell Dow Pharmaceuticals Inc., 509 U.S. 579 (1993).

Daubney, D. (1988). *Taking responsibility: Report of the Standing Committee on Justice and Solicitor General on its review of sentencing, conditional release, and related aspects of corrections*. Ottawa, ON: Canadian Government Publishing Centre, Supply and Services Canada.

Davidson, W.S., & Redner, R. (1988). Prevention of juvenile delinquency: Diversion from the juvenile justice system. In R.H. Price, E.L. Cowen, R.P. Lorion, & J. Ramos-McKay (Eds.), *Fourteen ounces of prevention: A casebook for practitioners* (pp. 123–137). Washington DC: American Psychological Association.

Davies, G., Tarrant, A., & Flin, R. (1989). Close encounters of the witness kind: Children's memory for a simulated health inspection. *British Journal of Psychology*, 80, 415–429.

Davies, G.M., Stevenson-Robb, Y., & Flin, R. (1988). Telling tales out of school: Children's memory for an unexpected event. In M. Gruneberg, P. Morris, & R. Sykes (Eds.), *Practical aspects of memory* (pp. 122–127). Chichester, England: John Wiley & Sons.

Davis, G.E., & Leitenberg, H. (1987). Adolescent sex offenders. *Psychological Bulletin*, 101, 417–427.

Davis, K.E., & Frieze, I.H. (2000). Research on stalking: What do we know and where do we go? *Violence and Victims*, 15, 473–487.

Dawson, M. Canadian trends in filicide by gender of the accused, 1961–2011. *Child Abuse & Neglect*, 47, 162–174.

Dayan, K., Fox, S., & Kasten, R. (2008). The preliminary employment interview as a predictor of assessment center outcomes. *International Journal of Selection and Assessment*, 16, 102–111.

de Mesquita, E.B. (2005). The quality of terror. *The American Journal of Political Science*, 49, 515–530.

Decker, P. (1986). Social learning theory and leadership. *Journal of Management Development*, 5, 46–58.

Deffenbacher, K.A., Bornstein, B.H., Penrod, S.D., & McGorty, E.K. (2004). A meta-analytic review of the effects of high stress on eyewitness memory. *Law and Human Behavior*, 28(6), 686–706.

Deitz, S.R., Blackwell, K.T., Daley, P.C., & Bentley, B.J. (1982). Measurement of empathy toward rape victims and rapists. *Journal of Personality and Social Psychology*, 43, 372–384.

Dekovic, M. (1999). Risk and protective factors in the development of problem behavior during adolescence. *Journal of Youth and Adolescence*, 28, 667–685.

Delean, P. (2016, April 19). Karla Homolka's return to Châteauguay sends shock waves through Quebec community. *The National Post*. Retrieved from http://bit.ly/1SUTRx5.

DeLisi, M. (2006). Zeroing in on early arrest onset: Results from a population of extreme career criminals. *Journal of Criminal Justice*, 34, 17–26.

DeMatteo, D., & Edens, J.F. (2006). The role and relevance of the Psychopathy Checklist-Revised in court: A case law survey of U.S. courts (1991–2004). *Psychology, Public Policy, and Law*, 12, 214–241.

DeMatteo, D., & Marczyk, G. (2005). Risk factors, protective factors, and the prevention of antisocial behavior among juveniles.

In K. Heilbrun, N. Goldstein, & R. Redding (Eds.), *Juvenile delinquency: Prevention, assessment, and intervention* (pp. 19–44). New York, NY: Oxford University Press.

DeMatteo, D., Edens, J. F., Galloway, M., Cox, J., Smith, S. T., Koller, J. P., & Bersoff, B. (2014). Investigating the role of the Psychopathy Checklist–Revised in United States case law. *Psychology, Public Policy, and Law, 20*, 96–107.

DeMatteo, D., Heilbrun, K., & Marczyk, G. (2005). Psychopathy, risk of violence, and protective factors in a noninstitutionalized and noncriminal sample. *International Journal of Forensic Mental Health, 4*, 147–157.

Dempsey, J.L., & Pozzulo, J.D. (2008). Identification accuracy of eyewitnesses for a multiple perpetrator crime: Examining the simultaneous and elimination lineup procedures. *American Journal of Forensic Psychology, 26*, 67–81.

Denham, S., & Almeida, M. (1987). Children's social problem solving skills, behavioral adjustment, and interventions: A meta-analysis evaluating theory and practice. *Journal of Applied Developmental Psychology, 8*, 391–409.

Department of Justice (DOJ). (2015). *Canada's system of justice.* Retrieved April 29, 2016 from http://canada.justice.gc.ca/eng/csj-sjc/just/img/courten.pdf.

DePaulo, B.M., & Kashy, D.A. (1998). Everyday lies in close and casual relationships. *Journal of Personality and Social Psychology, 74*(1), 63–79.

DePaulo, B.M., & Kirkendol, S.E. (1989). The motivational impairment effect in the communication of deception. In Y.C. Yuille (Ed.), *Credibility assessment* (pp. 51–70). Dordrecht, the Netherlands: Kluwer.

DePaulo, B.M., & Pfeifer, R.L. (1986). On-the-job experience and skill at detecting deception. *Journal of Applied Social Psychology, 16*, 249–267.

DePaulo, B.M., Charlton, L., Cooper, H., Lindsay, J.J., & Muhlenbruck, L. (1997). The accuracy-confidence correlation in the detection of deception. *Personality and Social Psychology Review, 1*, 346–357.

DePaulo, B.M., Kashy, D.A., Kirkendol, S.E., Wyer, M.M., & Epstein, J.A. (1996). Lying in everyday life. *Journal of Personality and Social Psychology, 70*, 979–995.

DePaulo, B.M., Lassiter, G.D., & Stone, J.I. (1982). Attentional determinants of success at detecting deception and truth. *Personality and Social Psychology Bulletin, 8*, 273–279.

DePaulo, B.M., Lindsay, J.J., Malone, B.E., Muhlenbruck, L., Charlton, K., & Cooper, H. (2003). Cues to deception. *Psychological Bulletin, 129*, 74–118.

Deregowski, J.B., Ellis, H.D., & Shepherd, J.W. (1975). Descriptions of white and black faces by white and black subjects. *International Journal of Psychology, 10*, 119–123.

Dern, H., Dern, C., Horn, A., & Horn, U. (2009). The fire behind the smoke: A reply to Snook and colleagues. *Criminal Justice and Behavior, 36*, 1085–1090.

Desmarais, S.L., Nicholls, T.L., Read, D., & Brink, J. (2010). Confidence and accuracy in assessments of short-term risks presented by forensic psychiatric patients. *The Journal of Forensic Psychiatry & Psychology, 21*, 1–22.

Devine, D.J. (2012). *Jury Decision Making: The State of the Science.* New York, NY: New York University Press.

Devine, D.J., & Caughlin, D.E. (2014). Do they matter? A meta-analytic investigation of individual characteristics of guilt judgments. *Psychology, Public Policy, and Law, 20*, 109–134.

Devine, D.J., Clayton, L.D., Dunford, B.B., Seying, R., & Pryce, J. (2001). Jury decision making: 45 years of empirical research on deliberating groups. *Psychology, Public Policy, and Law, 7*, 622–727.

Devine, D.J., Olafson, K., Jarvis, L., Bolt, J., Clayton, L., & Wolfe, J. (2004). Explaining jury verdicts: Is leniency bias for real? *Journal of Applied Social Psychology, 34*, 2069–2098.

Devlin, K., & Lorden, G. (2007). *The numbers behind numb3rs: Solving crime with mathematics.* New York, NY: Plume.

DeWall, C.N., Anderson, C.A., & Bushman, B.J. (2011). The general aggression model: Theoretical extensions to violence. *Psychology of Violence, 1*, 245–258.

Diamond, S. (2008). *Sympathy for the devil: What made her do it?* Retrieved from www.psychologytoday.com/blog/evil-deeds/200805/sympathy-the-devil.

Dickinson, J., Poole, D., & Bruck, M. (2005). Back to the future: A comment on the use of anatomical dolls in forensic interviews. *Journal of Forensic Psychology Practice, 5*, 63–74.

Dietz, T.L. (1998). An examination of violence and gender role portrayals in video games: Implications for gender socialization and aggressive behavior. *Sex Roles, 38*, 425–442.

Dipboye, R.L., Macan, T., & Shahani-Denning, C. (2012). The selection interview from the interviewer and applicant perspectives: Can't have one without the other. In N. Schmitt (Ed.), *The Oxford Handbook of Personnel Assessment and Selection* (pp. 323–352). Oxford, UK: Oxford University Press.

Dixon v. Attorney General of the Commonwealth of Pennsylvania, [1971] 325 F. Supp. 966.

Doan, B., & Snook, B. (2008). A failure to find empirical support for the homology assumption in criminal profiling. *The Journal of Police and Criminal Psychology, 23*, 61–70.

Dobash, R., & Dobash, R.E. (1979). *Violence against women.* New York, NY: Free Press.

Dobash, R.E., Dobash, R.P., Cavanagh, K., & Lewis, R. (2004). Not an ordinary killer—just an ordinary guy: When men murder an intimate woman partner. *Violence Against Women, 10*, 577–605.

Dobash, R.P., Dobash, E.R., Wilson, M., & Daly, M. (1992). The myth of sexual symmetry in marital violence. *Social Problems, 39*(1), 71–91.

Dodge, K.A. (1991). The structure and function of reactive and proactive aggression. In D. Pepler & K. Rubin (Eds.), *The development and treatment of childhood aggression* (pp. 201–218). Hillsdale, NJ: Earlbaum.

Dodge, K.A. (2000). Conduct disorder. In A.J. Sameroff, M. Lewis, & S.M. Miller (Eds.), *Handbook of developmental psychopathology* (2nd ed., pp. 447–463). New York, NY: Kluwer Academic/Plenum.

Dodge, K.A., Lochman, J.E., Harnish, J.D., Bates, J.E., & Pettit, G.S. (1997). Reactive and proactive aggression in school children and psychiatrically impaired chronically assaultive youth. *Journal of Abnormal Psychology, 106*, 37–51.

Dodson, C.S., & Dobolyi, D.G. (2016). Confidence and eyewitness identifications: The cross-race effect, decision time and accuracy. *Applied Cognitive Psychology, 30*(1), 113–125.

Dolan, M., & Völlm, B. (2009). Antisocial personality disorder and psychopathy in women: a literature review on the reliability and validity of assessment instruments. *International Journal Law Psychiatry, 32*(1), 2–9.

Doob, A.N. (2011). The unfinished work of the Canadian sentencing commission. *Canadian Journal of Criminology and Criminal Justice, 53,* 279–287.

Doob, A.N., & Beaulieu, L.A. (1992). Variation in the exercise of judicial discretion with young offenders. *Canadian Journal of Criminal Justice, 34,* 35–50.

Douglas, J. (2010). *John Douglas.* Retrieved from www.johndouglasmindhunter.com/bio.php.

Douglas, J.E., Burgess, A.W., Burgess, A.G., & Ressler, R.K. (1992). *Crime classification Manual.* New York, NY: Lexington Books.

Douglas, J.E., Ressler, R.K., Burgess, A.W., & Hartman, C.R. (1986). Criminal profiling from crime scene analysis. *Behavioral Sciences and the Law, 4,* 401–421.

Douglas, K.S., Guy, L.S., & Hart, S.D. (2009). Psychosis as a risk factor for violence to others: A meta-analysis. *Psychological Bulletin, 135,* 679–706.

Douglas, K.S., & Skeem, J.L. (2005). Violence risk assessment: Getting specific about being dynamic. *Psychology, Public Policy, and Law, 11,* 347–383.

Douglass, A.B., & Pavletic, A. (2011). Eyewitness confidence malleability: Why it occurs and how it contributes to wrongful convictions. In B.L. Cutler (Ed.), *Conviction of the innocent: Lessons from psychological research* (pp. 149–165). Washington, DC: American Psychological Association Press.

Douglass, A.B., & Steblay, N. (2006). Memory distortion in eyewitnesses: A meta-analysis of the post-identification feedback effect. *Applied Cognitive Psychology, 20,* 859–869.

Dowden, C., & Brown, S.L. (2002). The role of substance abuse factors in predicting recidivism: A meta-analysis. *Psychology, Crime, and Law, 8,* 243–264.

Doyle, A. (2003). *Arresting images: Crime and policing in front of the television camera.* Toronto, ON: University of Toronto Press.

Dube, S.R., Anda, R.F., Whitfield, C.L., Brown, D.W., Felitti, V.J., Dong, M., & Giles, W. (2005). Long-term consequences of childhood sexual abuse by gender of victim. *American Journal of Preventive Medicine, 28,* 430–438.

Dupree, L., Patterson, D.A., Nugent, W.R., & White, S.F. (2016). How children verbally reported their experiences of a genital exam. *Journal of Human Behavior in the Social Environment, 26*(1), 110–118.

Dutton, D.G. (1995). *The domestic assault of women: Psychological and criminal justice perspectives.* Vancouver, BC: University of British Columbia Press.

Dutton, D.G. (2008). My back pages: Reflections on thirty years of domestic violence research. *Trauma, Violence and Abuse, 9,* 131–143.

Dutton, D.G., & Corvo, K. (2006). Transforming a flawed policy: A call to revive psychology and science in domestic violence research and practice. *Aggression and Violent Behavior, 11,* 457–483.

Duxbury, L., & Higgins, C. (2012, March). *Caring for and about those who serve: Work-life conflict and employee well-being within Canada's police departments.* Retrieved from http://sprott.carleton. co/wp-content/files/Duxbury-Higgins-Police2012_fullreport. pdf.

Dysart, J.E., Lindsay, R.C.L., & Dupuis, P. (2006). Showups: The critical issue of clothing bias. *Applied Cognitive Psychology, 20,* 1009–1023.

Easterbrook, J.A. (1959). The effect of emotion on cue utilization and the organization of behavior. *Psychological Review, 66,* 183–201.

Eastwood, J., & Snook, B. (2010). Comprehending Canadian police cautions: Are the rights to silence and legal counsel understandable? *Behavioral Sciences and the Law, 28,* 366–377.

Eastwood, J., Snook, B., & Luther, K. (2014). On the need to ensure better comprehension of interrogation rights. *Canadian Criminal Law Review, 18,* 171–181.

Eastwood, J., Snook, B., & Luther, K. (2015). Measuring the reading complexity and oral comprehension of Canadian youth waiver forms. *Crime and Delinquency, 61,* 798–828.

Ebata, A.T., Peterson, A.C., & Conger, J.J. (1990). The development of psychopathology in adolescence. In J. Rolf, A.S. Masten, D. Cicchetti, K. Nuechterlein, & S. Weintraub (Eds.), *Risk and protective factors in the development of psychopathology* (pp. 308–333). Cambridge, MA: Cambridge University Press.

Ebbesen, E.G., & Konecni, V.J. (1997). Eyewitness memory research: Probative versus prejudicial value. *Expert Evidence, 5,* 2–28.

Eberhardt, J.L., Davies, P.G., Purdie-Vaughns, V.J., & Johnson, S.L. (2006). Looking deathworthy: Perceived stereotypicality of black defendants predicts capital-sentencing outcomes. *Psychological Science, 17,* 383–386.

Edens, J.F., & Cox, J. (2012). Examining the prevalence, role and impact of evidence regarding Antisocial Personality, sociopathy, and psychopathy in capital cases: A survey of defense team members. *Behavioral Sciences and the Law, 30,* 239–255.

Edens, J.F., Colwell, L.H., Desforges, D.M., & Fernandez, K. (2005). The impact of mental health evidence on support for capital punishment: Are defendants labeled psychopathic considered more deserving of death. *Behavioral Sciences and the Law, 23,* 603–625.

Edens, J.F., Cox, J., Smith, S.T., DeMatteo, D., & Sörman, K. (2015). How reliable are psychopathy Checklist–Revised scores in Canadian criminal trials? A case law review. *Psychological Assessment, 27,* 447–456.

Edens, J.F., Davis, K.M., Fernandez Smith, K., & Guy, L.S. (2013). No sympathy for the devil: Attributing psychopathic traits to capital murderers also predicts support for executing them. *Personality Disorders: Theory, Research, and Treatment, 4,* 175–181.

Edens, J.F., Guy, L.S., & Fernandez, K. (2003). Psychopathic traits predict attitudes toward a juvenile capital murderer. *Behavioral Sciences & the Law, 21,* 807–828.

Edens, J.F., Poythress, N.G., & Watkins-Clay, M.M. (2007). Detection of malingering in psychiatric unit and general population prison inmates: A comparison of the PAI, SIMS, and SIRS. *Journal of Personality Assessment, 88,* 33–42.

Edens, J.F., Skeem, J.L., Cruise, K.R., & Cauffman, E. (2001). Assessment of "Juvenile Psychopathy" and its association with violence: A critical review. *Behavioral Sciences and the Law, 19,* 53–80.

Egeth, H.E. (1993). What do we not know about eyewitness identification. *American Psychologist, 48*, 577–580.

Egger, S.A. (2002). *The serial killers among us: An examination of serial murder and its investigation* (2nd ed.). Upper Saddle River, NJ: Prentice Hall.

Eglin, P., & Hester, S. (2003). *The Montreal massacre: A story of membership categorization analysis*. Waterloo, ON: Wilfrid Laurier University Press.

Eigenberg, H., McGuffee, K., Iles, G.D., & Garland, T.S. (2012). Doing justice: Perceptions of gender neutrality in the jury selection process. *American Journal of Criminal Justice, 37*(2), 258–275.

Eisen, M.L., Goodman, G.S., Qin, J., Davis, S., & Crayton, J. (2007). Maltreated children's memory: Accuracy, suggestibility, and psychopathology. *Developmental Psychology, 43*(6), 1275–1294.

Eisendrath, S.J. (1996). Current overview of physical factitious disorders. In M.D. Feldman & S.J. Eisendrath (Eds.), *The spectrum of factitious disorders* (pp. 21–36). Washington DC: American Psychiatric Association.

Ekman, P. (1992). *Telling lies: Clues to deceit in the marketplace, politics, and marriage*. New York, NY: W. W. Norton.

Ekman, P., & Friesen, W.V. (1974). Detecting deception from the body or face. *Journal of Personality and Social Psychology, 29*, 288–298.

Ekman, P., & O'Sullivan, M. (1991). Who can catch a liar? *American Psychologist, 46*, 913–920.

Elaad, E. (1990). Detection of guilty knowledge in real-life criminal applications. *Journal of Applied Psychology, 75*, 521–529.

Elaad, E., Ginton, A., & Jungman, N. (1992). Detection measures in real-life criminal guilty knowledge tests. *Journal of Applied Psychology, 77*, 757–767.

Elbogen, E.B. (2002). The process of violence risk assessment: A review of descriptive research. *Aggression and Violent Behavior, 7*, 591–604.

Elkins, I.J., Iacono, W.G., Doyle, A.E., & McGue, M. (1997). Characteristics associated with the persistence of antisocial behavior: Results from recent longitudinal research. *Aggression and Violent Behavior, 2*, 102–124.

Ellerby, L.A., & MacPherson, P. (2002). *Exploring the profiles of Aboriginal sexual offenders: Contrasting Aboriginal and non-Aboriginal sexual offenders to determine unique client characteristics and potential implications for sex offender assessment and treatment strategies*. Research report no. R-122. Ottawa: Correctional Service of Canada.

Elliott, D. (1994). Serious violent offenders: Onset, development course, and termination. The American Society of Criminology 1993 presidential address. *Criminology, 32*, 1–21.

Ellis, H.D., Shepherd, J.W., & Davies, G.M. (1980). The deterioration of verbal descriptions of faces over different delay intervals. *Journal of Police Science and Administration, 8*, 101–106.

Ellsworth, P.C., & Mauro, R. (1998). Psychology and law. In D.T. Gilbert, S.T. Fiske, & G. Lindzey. *The handbook of social psychology* (pp. 684–732). New York, NY: Aronson.

Elsayed, Y.A., Al-Zahrani, M., & Rashad, M.M. (2010). Characteristics of mentally ill offenders from 100 psychiatric court reports. *Annals of General Psychiatry, 9*(4).

Elwyn, L., & Smith, C. (2013). Child maltreatment and adult substance abuse: The role of adult memory. *Journal of Social Work Practice in the Addictions, 13*(3), 269–294.

Embry, R., & Lyons, P.M. Jr. (2012). Sex-based sentencing: Sentencing discrepancies between male and female sex offenders. *Feminist Criminology, 7*(2), 146–162.

Emeno, K., Bennell, C., Snook, B., & Taylor, P.J. (in press). Geographic profiling survey: A preliminary examination of geographic profilers' views and experiences. *International Journal of Police Science & Management*.

Engelhardt, C.R., Bartholow, B.D., Kerr, G.T., & Bushman, B.J. (2011). This is your brain on violent video games: Neural desensitization to violence predicts increased aggression following violent video game exposure. *Journal of Experimental Social Psychology, 47*, 1033–1036.

Ennis, A., McLeod, P., Watt, M., Campbell, M., Adams-Quackenbush, N. (2016). The role of gender in mental health court admission and completion. *Canadian Journal of Criminology and Criminal Justice, 58*, 1–30.

Ennis, B.J., & Litwack, T.R. (1974). Psychiatry and the presumption of expertise: Flipping coins in the courtroom. *California Law Review, 62*, 693–752.

Erickson, P.G., & Butters, J.E. (2006). Youth, weapons, and violence in Toronto and Montreal. Report prepared for Public Safety and Emergency Preparedness Canada, Ottawa, ON.

Erickson, W.B., Lampinen, J.M., & Moore, K.N. (July 25 2015). *Journal of Police and Criminal Psychology*.

Estelle *v*. Smith, [1981] 451 U.S. 454.

Everly, G.S., & Boyle, S.H. (1999). Critical incident stress debriefing (CISD): A meta-analysis. *International Journal of Emergency Mental Health, 3*, 165–168.

Everly, G.S., Boyle, S.H., & Lating, J.M. (1999). The effectiveness of psychological debriefing with vicarious trauma: A meta-analysis. *Stress Medicine, 15*, 229–233.

Everly, G.S., Flannery, R.B., & Mitchell, J. (2000). Critical incident stress management (CISM): A review of the literature. *Aggression and Violent Behaviour, 5*, 23–40.

Ewert *v*. Canada, [2015] FC 1093.

Ewing, C.P., & Aubrey, M. (1987). Battered woman and public opinion: Some realities about the myths. *Journal of Family Violence, 2*, 257–264.

Eysenck, H.J. (1964). *Crime and personality* (1st ed.). London, England: Methuen.

Fagan, A.A. (2005). The relationship between adolescent physical abuse and criminal offending: Support for an enduring and generalized cycle of violence. *Journal of Family Violence, 20*, 279–290.

Fagot, B.I., & Kavanagh, K. (1990). The prediction of antisocial behavior from avoidant attachment classifications. *Child Development, 61*, 864–873.

Fahsing, I.A., Ask, K., & Granhag, P.A. (2004). The man behind the mask: Accuracy and predictors of offender descriptions. *Journal of Applied Psychology, 89*(4), 722–729.

Faller, K.C., Grabarek, M., Nelson-Gardell, D., & Williams, J. (2011). Techniques employed by forensic interviewers conducting extended assessments: Results from a multi-site study. *Journal of Aggression, Maltreatment & Trauma, 20*(3), 237–259.

Farah, M.J., Hutchinson, J.B., Phelps, E.A., & Wagner, A.D. (2014). Functional MRI-based lie detection: Scientific and societal challenges. *Nature Reviews Neuroscience, 15*(2), 123–131.

Farrington, D. (2006). Family background and psychopathy. In C.J. Patrick (Ed.), *Handbook of psychopathy* (pp. 229–250). New York, NY: Guilford Press.

Farrington, D.P. (1991). Psychological contributions to the explanation of offending. *Issues in Criminological and Legal Psychology, 1,* 7–19.

Farrington, D.P. (1995). The development of offending and antisocial behavior from childhood: Key findings from the Cambridge Study in Delinquent Development. *Journal of Child Psychology and Psychiatry, 36,* 929–964.

Farrington, D.P. (2007). Advancing knowledge about desistance. *Journal of Contemporary Criminal Justice, 23,* 125–134.

Farwell, D. (2012). Brain fingerprinting: A comprehensive tutorial review of detection of concealed information with event-related brain potentials. *Cognitive Neurodynamics, 6,* 115–154.

Farwell, L.A., & Donchin, E. (1991). The truth will out: Interrogative polygraphy ("lie detection") with event-related brain potentials. *Psychophysiology, 28,* 531–547.

Faver, C.A., & Strand, E.B. (2003). To leave or to stay? Battered women's concern for vulnerable pets. *Journal of interpersonal violence, 18,* 1367–1377.

Fawcett, J.M., Russell, E.J., Peace, K.A., & Christie, J. (2013). Of guns and geese: A meta-analytic review of the "'weapon focus'" literature. *Psychology, Crime and Law, 19,* 35–66.

Fazel, S., & Grann, M. (2006). The population impact of severe mental illness on violent crime. *American Journal of Psychiatry, 163,* 1397–1403.

Fazel, S., Wolf, A., Palm, C., & Lichtenstein, P. (2014). Violent crime, suicide, and premature mortality in patients with schizophrenia and related disorders: A 38-year total population study in Sweden. *The Lancet Psychiatry, 1,* 44–54.

Febres, J., Brasfield, H., Shorey, R.C., Elmquist, J., Ninnemann, A., Schonbrun, Y.C., Temple, J.R., Recupero, P.R., & Stuart, G.L. (2014). Adulthood animal abuse among men arrested for domestic violence. *Violence Against Women, 20,* 1059–1077.

Feinman, S., & Entwisle, D.R. (1976). Children's ability to recognize other children's faces. *Child Development, 47,* 506–510.

Ferguson, C.J., & Rueda, S.M. (2010). The hitman study: Violent video game exposure effects on aggressive behavior, hostile feelings, and depression. *European Psychologist, 15,* 99–108.

Fergusson, D.M., & Horwood, L.J. (1996). The role of adolescent peer affiliations in the continuity between childhood behavioral adjustment and juvenile offending. *Journal of Abnormal Child Psychology, 24,* 205–221.

Fergusson, D.M., & Horwood, L.J. (1998). Early conduct problems and later life opportunities. *Journal of Child Psychology and Psychiatry, 39,* 1097–1108.

Fergusson, D.M., & Lynskey, M.T. (1997). Early reading difficulties and later conduct problems. *Journal of Child Psychology and Psychiatry, 38,* 899–907.

Fergusson, D.M., & Woodward, L.J. (2000). Educational, psychological, and sexual outcomes of girls with conduct problems in early adolescence. *Journal of Child Psychology and Psychiatry, 41,* 779–792.

Feshbach, S. (1964). The function of aggression and the regulation of aggressive drive. *Psychological Review, 71,* 257–272.

Fiedler, K., & Walka, I. (1993). Training lie detectors to use nonverbal cues instead of global heuristics. *Human Communication Research, 20,* 199–223.

Fiedler, M.L. (2011). *Officer Safety and Wellness: An Overview of the Issues.* Washington, DC: U.S. Department of Justice.

Finkel, N.J., Burke, J.E., & Chavez, L.J. (2000). Commonsense judgments of infanticide: Murder, manslaughter, madness, or miscellaneous? *Psychology, Public Policy, and Law, 6,* 1113–1137.

Finkelhor, D. (1984). *Child sexual abuse: New theory and research.* New York, NY: Free Press.

Finkelhor, D., Hotaling, G., Lewis, I.A., & Smith, C. (1990). Sexual abuse in a national survey of adult men and women: Prevalence, characteristics, and risk factors. *Child Abuse and Neglect, 14,* 19–28.

Finkelhor, D., Turner, H.A., Shattuck, A., & Hamby, S.L. (2013). Violence, crime and abuse exposure in a national sample of children and youth. *JAMA Pediatrics, 167*(7), 614–621.

Finn, P., & Tomz, J.E. (1996). *Developing a law enforcement stress program for officers and their families.* Washington, DC: U.S. Department of Justice.

Firestone, P., Bradford, J.M., Greenberg, D.M., & Larose, M.R. (1998). Homicidal sex offenders: Psychological, phallometric, and diagnostic features. *Journal of the American Academy of Psychiatry and the Law, 26,* 537–552.

Fisher, B.S., Cullen, F.T., & Turner, M.G. (2002). Being pursued: Stalking victimization in a national study of college women. *Criminology and Public Policy, 1,* 257–308.

Fisher, N.L., & Pina, A. (2013). An overview of the literature on female-perpetrated adult male sexual victimization. *Aggression and Violent Behavior, 18,* 54–61.

Fisher, R.P. (1995). Interviewing victims and witnesses of crime. *Psychology, Public Police, and Law, 1,* 732–764.

Fisher, R.P., & Geiselman, R.E. (1992). *Memory-enhancing techniques for investigative interviewing.* Springfield, IL: Charles C. Thomas.

Fisher, R.P., Geiselman, R.E., & Raymond, D.S. (1987). Critical analysis of police interviewing techniques. *Journal of Police Science and Administration, 15,* 177–185.

Fite, P.J., Raine, A., Stouthamer-Loeber, M., Loeber, R., & Pardini, D.A. (2010). Reactive and proactive aggression in adolescent males: Examining differential outcomes 10 years later in early adulthood. *Criminal Justice and Behavior, 37,* 141–157.

Fitzgerald, R. J. & Price, H. L. (2015). Eyewitness identification across the lifepan: A meta-analysis of age differences. *Psychological Bulletin, 141,* 1228–1265.

Fitzgerald, R.J., & Price, H.L. (2015, May 25). Eyewitness Identification Across the Life Span: A Meta-Analysis of Age Differences. *Psychological Bulletin.* Advance online publication.

Fitzpatrick, K.M. (1997). Fighting among America's youth: A risk and protective factors approach. *Journal of Health and Social Behavior, 38,* 131–148.

Flannery, D.J., & Williams, L. (1999). Effective youth violence prevention. In T. Gullotta & S.J. McElhaney (Eds.), *Violence in homes and communities: Prevention, intervention, and treatment.* Thousand Oaks, CA: Sage.

Flynn, C.P. (2000). Woman's best friend: Pet abuse and the role of companion animals in the lives of battered women. *Violence against women, 6*, 162–177.

Foa, E.B., & Rothbaum, B.O. (1998). *Treating the trauma of rape: Cognitive-behavioral therapy for PTSD*. New York, NY: Guilford.

Fontaine, R.G., Burks, V.S., & Dodge, K.A. (2002). Response decision processes and externalizing behavior problems in adolescents. *Development and Psychopathology, 14*, 107–122.

Forero, C.G., Gallardo-Pujol, D., Maydeu-Olivares, A., & Andres-Pueyo, A. (2009). A longitudinal model for predicting performance of police officers using personality and behavioral data. *Criminal Justice and Behavior, 36*, 591–606.

Forth, A.E., Hart, S.D., & Hare, R.D. (1990). Assessment of psychopathy in male young offenders. *Psychological Assessment: A Journal of Consulting and Clinical Psychology, 2*, 342–344.

Forth, A.E., Kosson, D.S., & Hare, R.D. (2003). *The Psychopathy Checklist: Youth Version manual*. Toronto, ON: Multi-Health Systems.

Fougere, A., & Daffern, M. (2011). Resilience in young offenders. *The International Journal of Forensic Mental Health, 10*(3), 244–253.

Fox, J.A., & Levin, J. (2012). *Extreme killing: Understanding serial and mass murder*. Thousand Oaks, CA: Sage.

Frank, M.G., & Feeley, T.H. (2003). To catch a liar: Challenges for research in lie detection training. *Journal of Applied Communication Research, 31*, 58–75.

Franke, W.D., Collins, S.A., & Hinz, P.N. (1998). Cardiovascular disease morbidity in an Iowa law enforcement cohort, compared with the general population. *Journal of Occupational and Environmental Medicine, 40*, 441–444.

Franke, W.D., Ramey, S.L., & Shelley, M.C. (2002). Relationship between cardiovascular disease morbidity, risk factors, and stress in a law enforcement cohort. *Journal of Occupational and Environmental Medicine, 44*, 1182–1189.

Frederick, R.I., Crosby, R.D., & Wynkoop, T.F. (2000). Performance curve classification of invalid responding on the Validity Indicator Profile. *Archives of Clinical Neuropsychology, 15*, 281–300.

Freedman, J.L., & Burke, T.M. (1996). The effect of pretrial publicity: The Bernardo case. *Canadian Journal of Criminology 38*(3), 253–270.

Fremouw, W.J., Westrup, D., & Pennypacker, J. (1997). Stalking on campus: The prevalence and strategies for coping with stalking. *Journal of Forensic Science, 42*, 666–669.

Frick, P.J. (1994). Family dysfunction and the disruptive disorders: A review of recent empirical findings. In T.H. Ollendick & R.J. Prinz, (Eds.), *Advances in clinical child psychology* (Vol. 16). New York, NY: Plenum Press.

Frick, P.J., & Hare, R.D. (2001). *Antisocial Process Screening Device*. Toronto, ON: Multi-Health Systems.

Frick, P.J., & Nigg, J.T. (2012). Current issues in the diagnosis of attention deficit hyperactivity disorder, oppositional defiant disorder, and conduct disorder. *Annual Review of Clinical Psychology, 8*, 77–107.

Frick, P.J., Bodin, S.D., & Barry, C.T. (2000). Psychopathic traits and conduct problems in community and clinic-referred samples of children: Further development of the Psychopathy Screening Device. *Psychological Assessment, 12*, 382–393.

Frick, P.J., Kimonis, E.R., Dandreaux, D.M., & Farell, J.M. (2003). The 4 year stability of psychopathic traits in non-referred youth. *Behavioral Sciences and the Law, 21*, 713–736.

Frick, P.J., Lahey, B.B., Loeber, R., Stouthamer, M., Christ, M.A.G., & Hanson, K. (1992). Familial risk factors to oppositional defiant disorder and conduct disorder: Parental psychopathology and maternal parenting. *Journal of Consulting and Clinical Psychology, 60*, 49–55.

Friedman, S.H., Cavney, J., & Resnick, P.J. (2012). Child murder by parents and evolutionary psychology. *Psychiatric Clinics of North America, 35*, 781–795.

Friedrich, W.N., & Luecke, W.J. (1988). Young school-age sexually aggressive children. *Professional Psychology: Research and Practice, 19*, 155–164.

Fritz, G., Stoll, K., & Wagner, N. (1981). A comparison of males and females who were sexually molested as children. *Journal of Sex and Marital Therapy, 7*, 54–58.

Frost, E.L., de Camara, R.L., & Earl, T.R. (2006). Training, certification, and regulation of forensic evaluators. *Journal of Forensic Psychology Practice, 6*, 77–91.

Frye v. United States, [1923] 293 F. 1013.

Fulero, S.M., & Everington, C. (2004). Mental retardation, competency to waive Miranda rights, and false confessions. In G.D. Lassiter (Ed.), *Interrogations, confessions, and entrapment* (pp. 163–179). New York, NY: Kluwer Academic.

Fyfe, J.J. (1979). Administrative interventions on police shooting discretion: An empirical examination. *Journal of Criminal Justice, 7*, 309–324.

Gallagher, C.A., Wilson, D.B., Hirschfield, P., Coggeshall, M.B., & MacKenzie, D.L. (1999). A quantitative review of the effects of sex offender treatment of sexual reoffending. *Corrections Management Quarterly, 3*, 19–29.

Gamer, M., Rill, H.-G., Vossel, G., & Gödert, H.W. (2005). Psychophysiological and vocal measures in the detection of guilty knowledge. *International Journal of Psychophysiology, 60*, 76–87.

Ganis, G., Kosslyn, S.M., Stose, S., Thompson, W.L., & Yurgelun-Todd, D.A. (2003). Neural correlates of different types of deception: An fMRI investigation. *Cerebral Cortex, 13*, 830–836.

Ganis, G., Rosenfeld, J.P., Meixner, J., Kievit, R.A., & Schendan, H.E. (2011). Lying in the scanner: Covert countermeasures disrupt deception detection by functional magnetic resonance imaging. *NeuroImage, 55*(1), 312–319.

Gao, Y., Raine, A., Chan, F., Venables, P.H., & Mednick, S.A. (2010). Early maternal and parental bonding, childhood physical abuse and adult psychopathic personality. *Psychological Medicine: A Journal of Research in Psychiatry and the Allied Sciences, 40*, 1007–1016.

Garber, C. (1947). Eskimo infanticide. *Scientific Monthly, 64*, 98.

Garcia, F.D., & Thibaut, F. (2011). Current concepts in pharmacotherapy of paraphilias. *Drugs, 71*(6), 771–790.

Garmezy, N. (1985). Stress-resistant children: The search for protective factors. In J.E. Stevenson (Ed.), *Recent research in developmental psychopathology* (pp. 213–233). New York, NY: Pergamon.

Garmezy, N. (1991). Resilience in children's adaptation to negative life events and stressed environments. *Pediatric Annuals, 20*, 460–466.

Glueck, S., & Glueck, E.T. (1968). *Delinquents and nondelinquents in perspective*. Cambridge, MA: Harvard University Press.

Gauce, A.M., Cormer, J.P., & Schwartz, D. (1987). Long term effects of a systems oriented school prevention program. *American Journal of Orthopsychiatry, 57*, 125–131.

Geiselman, R.E., & Padilla, J. (1988). Cognitive interviewing with child witnesses. *Journal of Police Science & Administration, 16*(4), 236–242. Retrieved from http://search.proquest.com/docview/617758899?accountid=9894.

Geiselman, R.E., Fisher, R.P., Firstenberg, I., Hutton, L.A., Sullivan, S., Avetissian, I., & Prosk, A. (1984). Enhancement of eyewitness memory: An empirical evaluation of the cognitive interview. *Journal of Police Science and Administration, 12*, 74–80.

Geiselman, R.E., Fisher, R.P., MacKinnon, D.P., & Holland, H.L. (1985). Eyewitness memory enhancement in the police interview: Cognitive retrieval mnemonics versus hypnosis. *Journal of Applied Psychology, 70*, 401–412.

Geller, W., & Scott, M.S. (1992). *Deadly force: What we know*. Washington, DC: Police Executive Forum.

Gendreau, P., Goggin, C., Cullen, F., & Andrews, D. (2001). The effects of community sanctions and incarceration of recidivism. In L. Motiuk & R. Serin (Eds.), *Compendium 2000 on effective correctional programming* (pp. 18–21). Ottawa, ON: Correctional Service Canada.

Gendreau, P., Little, T., & Goggin, C. (1996). A meta-analysis of the predictors of adult offender recidivism: What works! *Criminology, 34*, 575–607.

Ghetti, S., Edelstein, R.S., Goodman, G.S., Cordon, I.M., Quas, J.A., Alexander, K.W., Redlich, A.D., & Jones, D.P. (2006). What can subjective forgetting tell us about memory for childhood trauma? *Memory & Cognition, 34*(5), 1011–1025.

Giancola, P.R., Parrott, D.J., & Roth, R.M. (2006). The influence of difficult temperament on alcohol-related aggression: Better accounted for by executive functioning? *Addictive Behaviors, 31*, 2169–2187.

Gibbs, J.L., Ellison, N.B., & Heino, R.D. (2006). Self-presentation in online personals: The role of anticipated future interaction, self-disclosure, and perceived success in Internet dating. *Communication Research, 33*, 1–25.

Gidycz, C.A., Dardis, C.M. (2014). Feminist self-defense and resistance training for college students: A critical review and recommendations for the future. *Trauma, Violence, and Abuse, 15*(4), 322–333.

Glazebrook, S. (2010). Risky business: Predicting recidivism. *Psychiatry, Psychology, & Law, 17*, 88–120.

Global Deception Research Team. (2006). A world of lies. *Journal of Cross-Cultural Psychology, 37*, 60–74.

Gobeil, R., & Serin, R. (2009). Preliminary evidence of adaptive decision making techniques used by parole board members. *International Journal of Forensic Mental Health, 8*, 97–104.

Gobeil, R., & Serin, R.C. (2010). Parole decision-making: Contributions from research. In J. Brown & E. Campbell (Eds.), *Cambridge handbook of forensic psychology* (pp. 251–258). Cambridge, England: Cambridge University Press.

Gobeil, R., Scott, T.L., Serin, R.C., & Griffith, L. (2007, June). *A structured model of parole decision-making*. Poster session presented at the North American Corrections and Criminal Justice Psychology Conference, Ottawa, ON.

Golan, T. (2004). *Laws of man and laws of nature: A history of scientific expert testimony*. Cambridge, MA: Harvard University Press.

Golding, S.L. (1993). *Training manual: Interdisciplinary fitness interview revised*. Department of Psychology, University of Utah.

Golding, S.L., Roesch, R., & Schreiber, J. (1984). Assessment and conceptualization of competency to stand trial. Preliminary data on the interdisciplinary fitness interview. *Law and Human Behavior, 8*, 321–334.

Goldstein, A.G. (1979). Race-related variation of facial features: Anthropometric data I. *Bulletin of the Psychonomic Society, 13*, 187–190.

Gondolf, E., & Fisher, E. (1988). *Battered women as survivors: An alternative to treating learned helplessness*. Lexington, MA: Lexington Books.

Gondolf, E.W. (1985). *Men who batter: An integrated approach for stopping wife abuse*. Holmes Beach, CA: Learning Publications.

Gonzalez, R., Ellsworth, P., & Pembroke, M. (1993). Response biases in lineups and showups. *Journal of Personality and Social Psychology, 64*, 525–537.

Goodman, G.S., Pyle-Taub, E.P., Jones, D.P.H., England, P., Port, L.K., Rudy, L., & Prado, L. (1992). Testifying in court: The effects on child sexual assault victims. *Monographs of the Society for Research in Child Development, 57*(Serial No. 229), 1–163.

Goodman, G.S., Quas, J.A., Batterman-Faunce, J.M., Riddlesberger, M., & Kuhn, J. (1997). Children's reactions to and memory for a stressful event: Influences of age, anatomical dolls, knowledge, and parental attachment. *Applied Developmental Science, 1*, 54–75.

Goodwill, A.M., & Alison, L.J. (2007). When is profiling possible? Offence planning and aggression as moderators in predicting offender age from victim age in stranger rape. *Behavioral Sciences and the Law, 25*, 823–840.

Goodwill, A.M., Alison, L.J., & Beech, A.R. (2009). What works in offender profiling? A comparison of typological, thematic and multivariate models. *Behavioral Sciences and the Law, 27*, 507–529.

Goodwill, A.M., Lehmann, R.J.B., Beauregard, E., & Andrei, A. (2016). An action phase approach to offender profiling. *Legal and Criminological Psychology 21*(2), 229–250. doi: 10.1111/lcrp.12069.

Goodwill, A.M., Stephens, S., Oziel, S., Sharma, S., Allen, J., Bowes, N., & Lehmann, R. (2013). Advancement of criminal profiling methods in faceted multidimensional analysis. *Journal of Investigative Psychology and Offender Profiling, 10*, 71–95.

Gorey, K., & Leslie, D. (1997). The prevalence of child sexual abuse: Integrative review adjustment for potential response and measurement bias. *Child Abuse and Neglect, 21*, 391–398.

Gottfredson, M.R., & Hirschi, T. (1990). *A general theory of crime*. Palo Alto, CA: Stanford University Press.

Gowan, M.A., & Gatewood, R.D. (1995). Personnel selection. In N. Brewer & C. Wilson (Eds.), *Psychology and policing* (pp. 177–204). Hillsdale, NJ: Lawrence Erlbaum Associates.

Granger, C. (1996). *The criminal jury trial in Canada*. Toronto, ON: Carswell.

Granhag, P.A., Ask, K., Rebelius, A., Öhman, L., & Giolla, E.M. (2013). 'I saw the man who killed Anna Lindh': An archival study of witnesses' offender descriptions. *Psychology, Crime, & Law, 19*(10), 921–931.

Grann, M., Belfrage, H., & Tengström, A. (2000). Actuarial assessment of risk for violence: Predictive validity of the VRAG and the historical part of the HCR-20. *Criminal Justice and Behavior, 27*, 97–114.

Graves, S.L., Blake, J., & Kim, E. (2012). Differences in parent and teacher ratings of preschool problem behavior in a national sample: The significance of gender and SES. *Journal of Early Intervention, 34*, 151–165.

Gray, J.E., & O'Reilly, R.L. (2009). Supreme Court of Canada's "Beautiful Mind" case. *International Journal of Law and Psychiatry, 32*(5), 315–322.

Greco, C.M., & Cornell, D.G. (1992). Rorschach object relations of adolescents who committed homicide. *Journal of Personality Assessment, 59*, 574–583.

Greely, H.T., & Illes, J. (2007) Neuroscience-based lie detection: The urgent need for regulation. *American Journal of Law & Medicine, 33*, 377–421.

Green, D., & Rosenfeld, G. (2011). Evaluating the gold standard: A review and meta-analysis of the Structured Interview of Reported Symptoms. *Psychological Assessment, 23*, 95–107.

Green, D., Rosenfeld, B., & Belfi, B. (2013). New and improved? A comparison of the original and revised versions of the structured interview of reported symptoms. *Assessment, 20*(2), 210–218.

Greene, E., Raitz, A., & Lindblad, H. (1989). Jurors' knowledge of battered women. *Journal of Family Violence, 4*, 105–125.

Greitmeyer, T., & Mügge, D.O. (2014). Video games do affect social outcomes: A meta-analytic review of the effects of violent and prosocial video game play. *Personality and Social Psychology Bulletin, 40*, 578–589.

Gretton, H.M., Hare, R.D., & Catchpole, R.E.H. (2004). Psychopathy and offending from adolescence to adulthood: A 10-year follow-up. *Journal of Consulting and Clinical Psychology, 72*, 636–645.

Greyhound suspect whispers "please kill me" [Video file]. (2008, August 5). Retrieved from www.ctvnews.ca/greyhound-suspect-whispers-please-kill-me-1.313729.

Groscup, J., & Tallon, J. (2009). *Theoretical models of jury decision-making.* Burlington, VT: Ashgate. Retrieved from http://search.proquest.com/docview/622118100?accountid=9894.

Gross, A. (2004). Dangerous predictions: The case of Randall Dale Adams. *The Forensic Examiner, 13*(4). Retrieved from www.biomedsearch.com/article/Dangerous-predictions-case-Randall-Dale/125957151.html.

Grossman, F.K., Beinashowitz, J., Anderson, L., Sakurai, M., Finnin, L., & Flaherty, M. (1992). Risk and resilience in young adolescents. *Journal of Youth and Adolescence, 21*, 529–550.

Groth, A.N. (1979). *Men who rape: The psychology of the offender.* New York, NY: Plenum.

Groth, A.N., Burgess, A.W., & Holmstrom, L.L. (1977). Rape: Power, anger, and sexuality. *American Journal of Psychiatry, 134*, 1239–1243.

Groth, A.N., Hobson, W.F., & Gary, T.S. (1982). The child molester: Clinical observations. *Journal of Social Work and Human Sexuality, 1*, 129–144.

Grove, W., & Meehl, P (1996). Comparative efficiency of informal (subjective, impressionistic) and formal (mechanical, algorithmic) prediction procedures: The clinical-statistical controversy. *Psychology, Public Policy and Law, 2*, 293–323.

Grove, W.M., Zald, D.H., Lebow, B.S., Snitz, B.F., & Nelson, C. (2000). Clinical versus mechanical prediction: A meta-analysis. *Psychological Assessment, 12*, 19–30.

Grunwald, H.E., Lockwood, B., Harris, P.W., & Mennis, J. (2010). Influences of neighborhood context, individual history and parenting behavior on recidivism among juvenile offenders. *Journal of Youth and Adolescence, 39*(9), 1067–1079.

Gudjonsson, G.H. (1992). Interrogation and false confessions: Vulnerability factors. *British Journal of Hospital Medicine, 47*, 597–599.

Gudjonsson, G.H. (2003). *The psychology of interrogations, confessions, and testimony.* Chichester, England: John Wiley & Sons.

Gudjonsson, G.H., & MacKeith, J.A.C. (1988). Retracted confessions: Legal, psychological and psychiatric aspects. *Medicine, Science, and the Law, 28*, 187–194.

Gudjonsson, G.H., & Sigurdsson, J.F. (1994). How frequently do false confessions occur? An empirical study among prison inmates. *Psychology, Crime and Law, 1*, 21–26.

Gul, S.K., & O'Connell, P.E. (2013). *Police Performance Appraisals: A Comparative Perspective.* Boca Raton, FL: CRC Press.

Gunnell, J.J., & Ceci, S.J. (2010). When emotionality trumps reason: A study of individual processing style and juror bias. *Behavioral Sciences & the Law, 28*(6), 850–877.

Gutierrez, L., Wilson, H.A., Rugge, T., & Bonta, J. (2013). The prediction of recidivism with Aboriginal offenders: A theoretically informed meta-analysis. *Canadian Journal of Criminology and Criminal Justice, 55*(1), 55–99.

Guy, L.S., Edens, J.F., Anthony, C., & Douglas, K.S. (2005). Does psychopathy predict institutional misconduct among adults? A meta-analytic investigation. *Journal of Consulting and Clinical Psychology, 73*, 1056–1064.

Gylys, J.A., & McNamara, J.R. (1996). Acceptance of rape myths among prosecuting attorneys. *Psychological Reports, 79*, 15–18.

Haggard, U., Gumpert, C.H., & Grann, M. (2001). Against all odds: A qualitative follow-up study of high-risk violent offenders who were not reconvicted. *Journal of Interpersonal Violence, 16*, 1048–1065.

Hall, C., & Votova, K. (2013). *Prospective Analysis of Police Use of Force in Four Canadian Cities: Nature of Events and their Outcomes.* Ottawa, ON: Defence R&D Canada.

Hall, G.C. (1995). Sexual offender recidivism revisited: A meta-analysis of recent treatment studies. *Journal of Consulting and Clinical Psychology, 63*, 802–809.

Hamby, S., Finkelhor, D., & Turner, H. (2013). Perpetrator and victim gender patterns for 21 forms of youth victimization in the National Survey of Children's Exposure to Violence. *Violence and Victims, 28*, 915–939.

Hamilton Police Service. (2016). *Essential competencies.* Retrieved March 4, 2016 from https://hamiltonpolice.on.ca/sites/default/files/essentialcompetencies.pdf.

Hammond, E.M., Berry, M.A., & Rodriguez, D.N. (2011). The influence of rape myth acceptance, sexual attitudes, and belief in a just world on attributions of responsibility in a date rape scenario. *Legal and Criminological Psychology, 16*(2), 242–252.

Haney, C. (1980). Psychology and legal change: On the limits of a factual jurisprudence. *Law and Human Behavior, 17*, 371–398.

Hannah-Moffat, K., & Maurutto, P. (2003). *Youth risk/need assessment: An overview of issues and practices.* Ottawa, ON: Department of Justice Canada, Research and Statistics Division.

Hans, V.P., & Doob, A.N. (1976). Section 12 of the Canada Evidence Act and the deliberation of simulated juries. *Criminal Law Quarterly, 18*, 235–253.

Hanson, R. K., & Thornton, D. (2003). Notes on the development of Static-2002. (Corrections Research User Rep. No. 2003-01). Ottawa, ON: Department of the Solicitor General of Canada

Hanson, R.K. (1990). The psychological impact of sexual assault on women and children: A review. *Annuals of Sex Research, 3*, 187–232.

Hanson, R.K., & Bussière, M.T. (1998). Predicting relapse: A meta-analysis of sexual offender recidivism studies. *Journal of Consulting and Clinical Psychology, 66*, 348–362.

Hanson, R.K., Gordon, A., Harris, A.J.R., Marques, J.K., Murphy, W., Quinsey, V.L., & Seto, M.C. (2002). First report of the collaborative outcome data project on the effectiveness of psychological treatment for sex offenders. *Sexual Abuse: A Journal of Research and Treatment, 14*, 169–194.

Hanson, R.K., & Morton-Bourgon, K.E. (2005). The characteristics of persistent sexual offenders: A meta-analysis of recidivism studies. *Journal of Consulting and Clinical Psychology, 73*, 1154–1163.

Hanson, R.K., & Morton-Bourgon, K.E. (2009). The accuracy of recidivism risk assessments for sexual offenders: A meta-analysis of 118 prediction studies. *Psychological Assessment, 21*, 1–21.

Hanson, R.K., & Scott, H. (1995). Assessing perspective-taking among sexual offenders, nonsexual criminals, and offenders. *Sexual Abuse: Journal of Research and Treatment, 7*, 259–277.

Hanson, R.K., & Thornton, D. (1999). *Static-99: Improving actuarial risk assessment for sexual offenders.* Ottawa, ON: Department of Solicitor General.

Hanson, R.K., & Thornton, D. (2000). Improving risk assessments for sex offenders: A comparison of three actuarial scales. *Law and Human Behavior, 24*, 119–136.

Hardy, C.L., & Van Leeuwen, S.A. (2004). Interviewing young children: Effects of probe structures and focus of rapport-building talk on the qualities of young children's eyewitness statements. *Canadian Journal of Behavioural Science/Revue canadienne des sciences du comportement, 36*(2), 155–165.

Hare, R.D. (1991). *The Hare Psychopathy Checklist–Revised.* Toronto, ON: Multi-Health Systems.

Hare, R.D. (1993). *Without conscience: The disturbing world of the psychopaths among us.* New York, NY: Pocket Books.

Hare, R.D. (2003). *The Hare Psychopathy Checklist–Revised.* (2nd ed.). Toronto, ON: Multi-Health Systems.

Hare, R.D. (2007). Forty years aren't enough: Recollections, prognostications, and random musings. In H. Hervé & J.C. Yuille (Eds.), *The psychopath: Theory, research and practice* (pp. 3–28). Mahway, NJ: Erlbaum.

Hare, R.D. (2016). Psychopathy, the PCL-R, and criminal justice: Some new findings and current issues. *Canadian Psychology, 57*(1), 21–34.

Hare, R.D., & Neumann, C.S. (2008). Psychopathy as a clinical and empirical construct. *Annual Review of Clinical Psychology, 4*, 217–246.

Hare, R.D., Clark, D., Grant, M., & Thornton, D. (2000). Psychopathy and the predictive validity of the PCL-R: An international perspective. *Behavioral Sciences and the Law, 18*, 623–645.

Hare, R.D., Forth, A.E., & Strachan, K.E. (1992). Psychopathy and crime across the life span. In R.D. Peters & R.J. McMahon (Eds.), *Aggression and violence throughout the life span* (pp. 285–300). Thousand Oaks, CA: Sage.

Hare, R.D., Harpur, T.J., Hakstian, A.R., Forth, A.E., Hart, S.D., & Newman, J.P. (1990). The Revised Psychopathy Checklist: Reliability and factor structure. *Psychological Assessment: A Journal of Consulting and Clinical Psychology, 2*, 338–341.

Hargrave, G.E., & Hiatt, D. (1987). Law enforcement selection with the interview, MMPI, and CPI: A study of reliability and validity. *Journal of Police Science and Administration, 15*, 110–117.

Harkins, L., Beech, A.R., & Goodwill, A.M. (2010). Examining the influence of denial, motivation, and risk on sexual recidivism. *Sexual Abuse: A Journal of Research and Treatment, 22*, 78–94.

Harrington *v.* State, [2003] 659 N.W.2d 509.

Harris, G.T., Hilton, N.Z., Rice, M.E., & Eke, A.W. (2007). Children killed by genetic parents versus stepparents. *Evolution and Human Behavior, 28*, 85–95.

Harris, G.T., Lalumière, M., Seto, M.C., & Chaplin, T.C. (2012). Explaining the erectile responses of rapists to rape stories: The contributions of sexual activity, non-consent, and violence with injury. *Archives of Sexual Behaviour, 41*(1), 221–229.

Harris, G.T., Rice, M.E., & Quinsey, V.L. (1993). Violent recidivism of mentally disordered offenders: The development of a statistical prediction instrument. *Criminal Justice and Behavior, 20*, 315–335.

Harrison, L.A., & Esqueda, C.W. (1999). Myths and stereotypes of actors involved in domestic violence: Implications for domestic violence culpability attributions. *Aggression and Violent Behavior, 4*, 129–138.

Harrison, S. (1993). *Diary of Jack the Ripper: The discovery, the investigation, the debate.* New York, NY: Hyperion.

Hart, S.D. (1998). The role of psychopathy in assessing risk for violence: Conceptual and methodological issues. *Legal and Criminological Psychology, 3*, 121–137.

Hart, S.D., Cox, D.N., & Hare, R.D. (1995). *Manual for the Psychopathy Checklist: Screening Version (PCL: SV).* Toronto, ON: Multi-Health Systems.

Hart, S.D., Michie, C., & Cooke, D. J. (2007). Precision of actuarial risk assessment instruments: Evaluating the "margins of error" of group v. individual predictions of violence. *British Journal of Psychiatry, 190*, 60–65.

Hartford, K., Heslop, L., Stitt, L., & Hoch, J. (2005). Design of an algorithm to identify persons with mental illness in a police administrative database. *International Journal of Law and Psychiatry, 28*(1), p. 1–11.

Hartley, T.A., Violanti, J.M., Fekedulegn, D., Andrew, M.E., & Burchfiel, C.M. (2007). Associations between major life events, traumatic incidents, and depression among Buffalo police officers. *International Journal of Emergency Mental Health, 9*, 25–35.

Hartwig, M., & Bond, C. (2011). Why do lie-catchers fail? A lens model meta-analysis of human lie judgements. *Psychological Bulletin, 137,* 643–659.

Harvey, E.A., Breaux, R.P., & Lugo-Candelas, C.I. (2016). Early development of comorbidity between symptoms of attention-deficit/hyperactivity disorder (ADHD) and oppositional defiant disorder (ODD). *Journal of Abnormal Psychology, 125,* 154–167.

Hasham, A. (2016). *Forcillo guilty of attempted murder in shooting death of Sammy Yatim.* Retrieved March 4, 2016 from http://www.thestar.com/news/crime/2016/01/25/jury-returns-in-murder-trial-for-const-james-forcillo-charged-in-shooting-death-of-sammy-yatim.html.

Hastie, R., Penrod, S.D., & Pennington, N. (1983). *Inside the jury.* Cambridge, MA: Harvard University Press.

Havard, C., & Memon, A. (2009). The influence of face age on identification from a video line-up: A comparison between older and younger adults. *Memory, 17*(8), 847–859.

Havard, C., Memon, A., Clifford, B., & Gabbert, F. (2010). A comparison of video and static lineups with child and adolescent witnesses. *Applied Cognitive Psychology, 24*(9), 1209–1221.

Hawes, S.W., Boccaccini, M.T., & Murrie, D.C. (2013). Psychopathy and the combination of psychopathy and sexual deviance as predictors of sexual recidivism: Meta-analytic findings using the Psychopathy Checklist-Revised. *Psychological Assessment, 25,* 233–243.

Hayes-Smith, R., & Levett, L.M. (2011). Jury's still out: How television and crime show viewing influences jurors' evaluations of evidence. *Applied Psychology in Criminal Justice, 7*(1), 29–46. Retrieved from http://search.proquest.com/docview/928990929?accountid=9894.

Hazelwood, R.R., & Douglas, J.E. (1980). The lust murderer. *FBI Law Enforcement Bulletin, 50,* 18–22.

Health Canada. (2003). *The consequences of child maltreatment: A reference guide for health practitioners.* Report prepared by Jeff Latimer. Ottawa, ON: Health Canada.

Heinrick, J. (2006, Fall). *Everyone's an expert: The CSI effect's negative impact on juries.* Arizona State University: The Triple Helix.

Helmus, L., Babchishin, K.M., Camilleri, J., & Olver, M. (2011). Forensic psychology opportunities in Canadian graduate programs: An update of Simourd and Wormith's (1995) survey. *Canadian Psychology/Psychology Canadienne, 52,* 122–127.

Helmus, L., Hanson, R.K., Babchishin, K.M., & Mann, R.E. (2013). Attitudes supportive of sexual offending predict recidivism: A meta-analysis. *Trauma, Violence, and Abuse, 14*(1), 34–53.

Helmus, L., Thornton, D., Hanson, R. K., & Babchishin, K. M. (2012). Improving the predictive accuracy of Static-99 and Static-2002 with older sex offenders: Revised age weights. *Sexual Abuse: Journal of Research and Treatment, 24,* 64–101.

Henggeler, S.W. (2011). Efficacy studies to large-scale transport: The development and validation of multisystemic therapy programs. *Annual Review of Clinical Psychology, 7,* 351–381.

Henggeler, S.W., & Borduin, C.M. (1990). *Family therapy and beyond: A multisystemic approach to treating the behavior problems of children and adolescents.* Pacific Grove, CA: Brooks/Cole.

Henggeler, S.W., Melton, G.B., & Smith, L.A. (1992). Family preservation using multisystemic therapy: An effective alternative to incarcerating serious juvenile offenders. *Journal of Consulting and Clinical Psychology, 60,* 953–961.

Henggeler, S.W., Schoenwald, S.K., Borduin, C.M., Rowland, M.D., & Cunningham, P.B. (1998). *Multisystemic treatment of antisocial behavior in children and adolescents.* New York, NY: Guilford Press.

Henggeler, S.W., Schoenwald, S.K., & Pickrel, S.A.G. (1995). Multisystemic therapy: Bridging the gap between university and community based treatment. *Journal of Consulting and Clinical Psychology, 63,* 709–717.

Herrenkohl, T.I., Tajima, E.A., Whitney, S., & Huang, B. (2005). Protection against antisocial behavior in children exposed to physically abusive discipline. *Journal of Adolescent Health, 36,* 457–465.

Hershkowitz, I., Lamb, M. E., & Katz, C. (2014). Allegation rates in forensic child abuse investigations: Comparing the revised and standard NICHD protocols. *Psychology, Public Policy, and Law, 20*(3), 336–344.

Hess, A. K. (2006). Defining forensic psychology. In I.B. Weiner and A.K. Hess (Eds.), *The Handbook of Forensic Psychology* (3rd Edition) (pp. 28–58). New York, NY: John Wiley and Sons, Inc.

Heuer, L., & Penrod, S. (1994). Juror note taking and question asking during trials: A national field experiment. *Law and Human Behavior, 18,* 121–150.

Hickey, E.W. (2006). *Serial murderers and their victims.* Belmont, CA: Wadsworth.

Hicks, S.J., & Sales, B.D. (2006). *Criminal profiling: Developing an effective science and practice.* Washington, DC: American Psychological Association.

Hildebrand, M., de Ruiter, C., & de Vogel, V. (2004). Psychopathy and sexual deviance in treated rapists: Association with sexual and nonsexual recidivism. *Sexual Abuse: A Journal of Research and Treatment, 16,* 1–24.

Hill, C., Memon, A., & McGeorge, P. (2008). The role of confirmation bias in suspect interviews: A systematic evaluation. *Legal and Criminological Psychology, 13,* 357–371.

Hillbrand, M. (1995). Aggression against self and aggression against others in violent psychiatric patients. *Journal of Consulting and Clinical Psychology, 63,* 668–671.

Hilliar, K.F., Kemp, R.I., & Denson, T.F. (2010). Now everyone looks the same: Alcohol intoxication reduces the own-race bias in face recognition. *Law and Human Behavior, 34*(5), 367–378.

Hilton, N.Z., & Simmons, J.L. (2001). The influence of actuarial risk assessment in clinical judgments and tribunal decisions about mentally disordered offenders in maximum security. *Law and Human Behavior, 25,* 393–408.

Hilton, N.Z., Carter, A.M., Harris, G.T., & Sharpe, A.J.B. (2008). Does use of nonnumerical terms to describe risk aid violence risk communication? Clinician agreement and decision making. *Journal of Interpersonal Violence, 23,* 171–188.

Hilton, N.Z., Harris, G.T., Rawson, K., & Beach, C.A. (2005). Communicating violence risk information to forensic decision makers. *Criminal Justice and Behavior, 32,* 97–116.

Hinshaw, S.P., Lahey, B.B., & Hart, E.L. (1993). Issues of taxonomy and comorbidity in the development of conduct disorder. *Development and Psychopathology, 5,* 31–49.

Hirschell, D., & Buzawa, E. (2002). Understanding the context of dual arrest with directions for future research. *Violence Against Women, 8*, 1449–1473.

Hirschell, D.J., Hutchison, I.W., & Dean, C.W. (1990). The failure of arrest to deter spouse abuse. *Journal of Research in Crime and Delinquency, 29*, 7–33.

Hirsh, H.R., Northrop, L.C., & Schmidt, F.L. (1986). Validity generalization for law enforcement occupations. *Personnel Psychology, 39*, 399–420.

Hlavka, H. R., Olinger, S. D., & Lashley, J. L. (2010). The use of anatomical dolls as a demonstration aid in child sexual abuse interviews: A study of forensic interviewer's perceptions. *Journal of Child Sexual Abuse, 19*(5), 519–553.

Ho, T. (1999). Assessment of police officer applicants and testing instruments. *Journal of Offender Rehabilitation, 29*, 1–23.

Hoaken, P.N.S., & Stewart, S.H. (2003). Drugs of abuse and elicitation of human aggressive behavior. *Addictive Behaviors, 28*, 1533–1554.

Hoch, J.S., Hartford, K., Heslop, L., & Stitt, L. (2009). Mental illness and police interactions in a mid-sized Canadian city: What the data do and do not say. *Canadian Journal of Community Mental Health, 28*, 49–66.

Hogarth, J. (1971). *Sentencing as a human process*. Toronto, ON: University of Toronto Press.

Hoge, R.D. (1999). *Assessing adolescents in educational, counselling, and other settings*. Mahwah, NJ: Lawrence Erlbaum Associates.

Hoge, R.D., & Andrews, D.A. (2002). *Youth level of service/case management inventory (YLS/CMI) user's manual*. North Tonawanda, NY: Multi-Health Systems.

Hoge, R.D., Andrews, D.A., & Lescheid, A.W. (1996). An investigation of risk and protective factors in a sample of youthful offenders. *Journal of Child Psychology and Psychiatry and Allied Disciplines, 37*, 419–424.

Hoge, S., Poythress, N., Bonnie, R., Monahan, J., Eisenberg, M., & Feucht-Haviar, T. (1997). The MacArthur Adjudication Competence Study: Diagnosis, psychopathology, and adjudicative competence-related abilities. *Behavioral Sciences and the Law, 15*, 329–345.

Hoge, S.K., Bonnie, R.J., Poythress, N., & Monahan, J. (1992). Attorney–client decision-making in criminal cases: Client competence and participation as perceived by their attorneys. *Behavioral Sciences and the Law, 10*, 385–394.

Holliday, R.E., & Albon, A. (2004). Minimizing misinformation effects in young children with cognitive interview mnemonics. *Applied Cognitive Psychology, 18*, 263–281.

Holmes, R., & DeBurger, J. (1988). *Serial murder*. Beverly Hills, CA: Sage Publications.

Holmes, R.M., & Holmes, S.T. (1998). *Serial murder* (2nd ed.). Thousand Oaks, CA: Sage.

Holmes, R.M., & Holmes, S.T. (2002). *Profiling violent crimes: An investigative tool* (3rd ed.). Thousand Oaks, CA: Sage.

Holmes, R.M., & Holmes, S.T. (2009). *Serial murder* (3rd ed.). Thousand Oaks, CA: Sage.

Holtzworth-Munroe, A., & Stuart, G.L. (1994). Typologies of male batterers: Three subtypes and the differences among them. *Psychological Bulletin, 116*, 476–497.

Homant, R.J., & Kennedy, D.B. (1998). Psychological aspects of crime scene profiling: Validity research. *Criminal Justice and Behavior, 25*, 319–343.

Honts, C.R., & Raskin, D.C. (1988). A field study of the validity of the directed lie control question. *Journal of Police Science and Administration, 16*, 56–61.

Honts, C.R., Raskin, D.C., & Kircher, J.C. (1994). Mental and physical countermeasures reduce the accuracy of polygraph tests. *Journal of Applied Social Psychology, 79*, 252–259.

Honts, C.R., & Schweinle, W. (2009). Information gain of psychophysiological detection of deception in forensic and screening settings. *Applied Psychophysiology Biofeedback, 34*, 161–172.

Horner, J.J. (2007). *Canadian law and the Canadian legal system*. Toronto, ON: Pearson Canada.

Horowitz, I.A., Kerr, N.L., Park, E.S., & Gockel, C. (2006). Chaos in the courtroom reconsidered: Emotional bias and juror nullification. *Law and Human Behavior, 30*(2), 163–181.

Horry, R., Memon, A., Wright, D.B., & Milne, R. (2012). Predictors of eyewitness identification decisions from video lineups in England: A field study. *Law and Human Behavior, 36*, 257–265.

Horselenberg, R., Merckelbach, H., & Josephs, S. (2003). Individual differences and false confessions: A conceptual replication of Kassin and Kiechel (1996). *Psychology, Crime & Law, 9*, 1–8.

Houston, K., Hope, L., Memon, A., & Read, J. (2013). Expert testimony on eyewitness evidence: In search of common sense. *Behavioral Sciences and the Law, 31*, 637–651.

Howitt, D. (2002). *Forensic and criminal psychology*. London, England: Prentice Hall.

Hubbard, K.L., Zapf, P.A., & Ronan, K.A. (2003). Competency restoration: An examination of the differences between defendants predicted restorable and not restorable to competency. *Law and Human Behavior, 27*, 127–139.

Huesmann, L.R., Eron, L.D., Lefkowitz, M.M., & Walder, L.O. (1984). Stability of aggression over time and generations. *Developmental Psychology, 20*, 1120–1134.

Huffington Post. (2012). Melissa Todorovic, Teen Murderer, Moving to Adult Jail. Retrieved from http://www.huffingtonpost.ca/2011/12/22/melissa-todorovic-teen-murderer_n_1166461.html.

Hughes, M., & Grieve, R. (1980). On asking children bizarre questions. *First Language, 1*, 149–160.

Humm, D.G., & Humm, K.A. (1950). Humm-Wadsworth temperament scale appraisals compared with criteria of job success in the Los Angeles Police Department. *The Journal of Psychology, 30*, 63–57.

Hunter, E. C. M., & Andrews, B. (2002). Memory for autobiographical facts and events: A comparison of women reporting childhood sexual abuse and non-abused controls. *Applied Cognitive Psychology, 16*(5), 575–588.

Hunter, S., & Baron, E. (2006, December). A daunting task for Pickton jury. *Ottawa Citizen*, p. A3.

Huss, M.T., & Ralston, A. (2008). Do batterer subtypes actually matter? Treatment completion, treatment response, and recidivism across a batterer typology. *Criminal Justice and Behavior, 35*, 710–723.

Iacono, W.G. (2008). Effective policing: Understanding how the polygraph tests work and are used. *Criminal Justice and Behavior*, 35, 1295–1308.

Iacono, W.G. (2009). Psychophysiological detection of deception and guilty knowledge. In J.L. Skeem, K. Douglas, & S.O. Lilienfeld (Eds.), *Psychological science in the courtroom: Consensus and controversy* (pp. 224–241). New York, NY: Guilford.

Iacono, W.G., & Lykken, D.T. (1997). The validity of the lie detector: Two surveys of scientific opinion. *Journal of Applied Psychology*, 82, 426–433.

Iacono, W.G., & Patrick, C. J. (1988). Polygraphy techniques. In R. Rogers (Ed.), *Clinical assessment of malingering and deception* (2nd ed., pp. 252–281). New York, NY: Guilford Press.

Iacono, W.G., & Patrick, C.J. (1999). Polygraph ("lie detector") testing: The state of the art. In A.K. Hess & I.B. Weiner (Eds.), *The handbook of forensic psychology* (2nd ed., pp. 440–473). New York, NY: John Wiley & Sons.

Iacono, W.G., & Patrick, C.J. (2006). Polygraph ("lie detector") testing: Current status and emerging trends. In I.B. Weiner & A. Hess (Eds.), *Handbook of forensic psychology* (3rd ed., pp. 552–588). New York, NY: John Wiley & Sons.

Iacono, W.G., Cerri, A.M., Patrick, C.J., & Fleming, J.A.E. (1992). Use of antianxiety drugs as countermeasures in the detection of guilty knowledge. *Journal of Applied Psychology*, 77, 60–64.

Ibrahim, D. (2016). Family violence in Canada: A statistical profile, 2014 (Statistics Canada catalogue no. 85-002-X). *Juristat*.

Inbau, F.E., Redi, J.E., Buckley, J.P., & Jayne, B.C. (2013). *Criminal interrogation and confessions*. Burlington, MA: Jones & Bartlett Learning.

Inciardi, J.A. (1986). Getting busted for drugs. In G. Beschner & A.S. Friedman (Eds.), *Teen drug use* (pp. 63–83). Lexington, MA: Lexington Books.

Inwald, R.E. (1992). *Inwald Personality Inventory technical manual* (Rev. ed.). Kew Gardens, NY: Hilson Research.

Inwald, R.E., & Shusman, E.J. (1984). The IPI and MMPI as predictors of academy performance for police recruits. *Journal of Police Science and Administration*, 12, 1–11.

Iverson, K.M., King, M.W., Cunninghamn, K., & Resick, P.A. (2015). Rape survivors' trauma-related beliefs before and after cognitive processing therapy: Associations with PTSD and depressive symptoms. *Behaviour Research and Therapy*, 66, 49–55.

Izzett, R.R., & Leginski, W. (1974). Group discussion and the influence of defendant characteristics in a simulated jury setting. *The Journal of Social Psychology*, 93, 271–279.

Jackiw, L.B., Arbuthnott, K.D., Pfeifer, J.E., Marcon, J.L., & Meissner, C.A. (2008). Examining the cross-race effect in lineup identification using Caucasian and First Nations samples. *Canadian Journal of Behavioural Science*, 40, 52–57.

Jackson v. Indiana, [1972] 406 U.S. 715.

Jackson, J.L., Sijlbing, R., & Thiecke, M.G. (1996). The role of human memory processes in witness reporting. *Expert Evidence*, 5, 98–105.

Jacobs, P.A., Brunton, M., Melville, M.M., Brittain, M.M., & McClemont, W.F. (1965). Aggressive behaviour, mental subnormality and the XYY male. *Nature*, 208, 351–1352.

Jaffe, P., Hastings, E., Reitzel, D., & Austin, G. (1993). The impact of police laying charges. In Z. Hilton (Ed.), *Legal responses to wife assault: Current trends and evaluation* (pp. 62–95). Newbury Park, CA: Sage.

Jaffee, S.R., Moffitt, T.E., Caspi, A., & Taylor, A. (2003). Life with (or without) father: The benefits of living with two biological parents depend on the father's antisocial behavior. *Child Development*, 74, 109–126.

James, D.J., & Glaze, L.E. (2006). U.S. Department of Justice, Bureau of Justice Statistics: Mental health problems of prison and jail inmates (Report No. NCJ 2136000). Washington, D.C.: U.S. Government Printing Office.

Janoff-Bulman, R. (1979). Characterological versus behavioral self-blame: Inquiries into depression and rape. *Journal of Personality and Social Psychology*, 37, 1798–1809.

Jarey, M.L., & Stewart, M.A. (1985). Psychiatric disorder in the parents of adopted children with aggressive conduct disorder. *Neuropsychobiology*, 13, 7–11.

Jeffries, S., & Bond, C. (2012). The impact of indigenous status on adult sentencing: A review of the statistical research literature. *Journal of Ethnicity in Criminal Justice*, 10, 223–243.

Jeffries, S., & Stenning, P. (2014). Sentencing Aboriginal Offenders: Law, Policy and Practice in Three Countries. *Canadian Journal of Criminology and Criminal Justice*, 56, 447–494.

Jenkins v. United States, [1962] 307 F.2d 637.

Jessor, R., Turbin, M.S., & Costa, F. (1998). Risk and protection in successful outcomes among disadvantaged adolescents. *Applied Developmental Science*, 2, 194–208.

Jewell, L.M., & Wormith, J.S. (2010). Variables associated with attrition from domestic violence treatment programs targeting male batterers: A meta-analysis. *Criminal Justice and Behavior*, 37, 1086–1113.

John Howard Society. (1999). *Sentencing in Canada*. Toronto, ON: John Howard Society.

John W. Hinckley, Jr., a biography. (n.d.). University of Missouri-Kansas City School of Law. Retrieved from http://law2.umkc.edu/faculty/projects/ftrials/hinckley/hbio.htm.

Johnson, H. (1996). *Dangerous domains: Violence against women in Canada*. Scarborough, ON: Nelson.

Johnson, H., & Hotton, T. (2003). Losing Control: Homicide risk in estranged and intact intimate relationships. *Homicide Studies*, 7, 58–84.

Johnson, S.L., & Grant, B. (2000). Release outcomes on long-term offenders. *FORUM on Corrections Research*, 12, 16–20.

Jokinen, A., Santilla, P., Ravaja, N., & Puttonen, S. (2006). Salience of guilty knowledge test items affects accuracy in realistic mock crimes. *International Journal of Psychophysiology*, 62, 175–184.

Jolliffe, D., & Farrington, D.P. (2007) *A systematic review of the national and international evidence on the effectiveness of interventions with violent offenders* (Research Series 16/07). Retrieved from Ministry of Justice website: www.justice.gov.uk/docs/review-evidence-violent.pdf.

Jones, A.B., & Llewellyn, J. (1917). *Malingering*. London, England: Heinemann.

Jones, N.J., Brown, S.L., & Zamble, E. (2010). Predicting criminal recidivism in adult male offenders: Researcher versus parole officer assessment of dynamic risk. *Criminal Justice and Behavior, 37*, 860–882.

Jung, S., & Daniels, M. (2012). Conceptualizing sex offender denial from a multifaceted framework: Investigating the psychometric qualities of a new instrument. *Journal of Addictions and Offender Counseling, 33*, 2–17.

Justice Institute of British Columbia. (2016). *Assessment centre.* Retrieved March 4, 2016 from http://www.jibc.ca/programs-courses/schools-departments/school-criminal-justice-security/police-academy/assessment-centre.

Kahneman, D., & Tversky, A. (1982). Variants of uncertainty. *Cognition, 11*, 143–157.

Kalmuss, D.S. (1984). The intergenerational transmission of marital aggression. *Journal of Marriage and the Family, 46*, 11–19.

Kalvern, H., & Zeisel, H. (1966). *The American jury.* Boston, MA: Little, Brown.

Kanas, N., & Barr, M.A. (1984). Self-control of psychotic productions in schizophrenics [Letter to the editor]. *Archives of General Psychiatry, 41*, 919–920.

Karl, S. (2009, December 21). On memory: Hypnotically refreshed memory. *National Post.* Retrieved from www.nationalpost.com/story.html?id=2368653.

Kask, K., Bull, R., & Davies, G. (2006). Trying to improve young adults' person descriptions. *Psychiatry, Psychology, and Law, 13*, 174–181.

Kassin, S.M. (1997). The psychology of confession evidence. *American Psychologist, 52*, 221–233.

Kassin, S.M. (1998). Eyewitness identification procedures: The fifth rule. *Law and Human Behavior, 22*, 649–653.

Kassin, S.M. (2007). Internalized false confessions. In M.P. Toglia, J.D. Read, D.F. Ross, & R.C.L. Lindsay (Eds.), *The handbook of eyewitness psychology, Vol. 1: Memory for events* (pp. 175–192). Mahwah, NJ: Lawrence Erlbaum Associates Publishers.

Kassin, S.M. (2014). False confessions: Causes, consequences, and implications for reform. *Policy Insights from the Behavioral and Brain Sciences, 1*, 112–121.

Kassin, S.M. (2015). The social psychology of false confessions. *Social Issues and Policy Review, 9*, 25–51.

Kassin, S.M., & Gudjonsson, G.H. (2004). The psychology of confessions: A review of the literature and issues. *Psychological Science in the Public Interest, 5*, 33–67.

Kassin, S.M., & Kiechel, K.L. (1996). The social psychology of false confessions: Compliance, internalization, and confabulation. *Psychological Science, 7*, 125–128.

Kassin, S.M., & Sommers, S.R. (1997). Inadmissible testimony, instructions to disregard, and the jury: Substantive versus procedural considerations. *Personality and Social Psychology Bulletin, 23*, 1046–1054.

Kassin, S.M., & Sukel, H. (1997). Coerced confessions and the jury: An experimental test of the "harmless error" rule. *Law and Human Behavior, 21*, 27–46.

Kassin, S.M., & Wrightsman, L.S. (1985). Confession evidence. In S.M. Kassin & L.S. Wrightsman (Eds.), *The psychology of evidence and trial procedures* (pp. 67–94). London, England: Sage.

Kassin, S.M., Bogart, D., & Kerner, J. (2012). Confessions that corrupt: Evidence from the DNA exoneration case files. *Psychological Science, 23*, 41–45.

Kassin, S.M., Ellsworth, P., & Smith, V.L. (1989). The "general acceptance" of psychological research on eyewitness testimony. *American Psychologist, 49*, 878–893.

Kassin, S.M., Goldstein, C.C., & Savitsky, K. (2003). Behavioral confirmation in the interrogation room: On the dangers of presuming guilt. *Law and Human Behavior, 27*, 187–203.

Kassin, S.M., Leo, R.A., Meissner, C.A., Richman, K.D., Colwell, L.H., Leach, A-M., & La Fon, D. (2007). Police interviewing and interrogation: A self-report survey of police practices and beliefs. *Law and Human Behavior, 31*, 381–400.

Kassin, S.M., Meissner, C.A., & Norwick, R.J. (2005). "I'd know a false confession if saw one": A comparative study of college students and police investigators. *Law and Human Behavior, 29*, 211–227.

Kassin, S.M., Tubb, V., Hosch, H.M., & Memon, A. (2001). On the "general acceptance" of eyewitness testimony research. *American Psychologist, 56*, 405–416.

Katz, C., & Hershkowitz, I. (2012). The effect of multipart prompts on children's testimonies in sexual abuse investigations. *Child Abuse & Neglect, 36*(11–12), 753–759.

Kaufman, J., & Zigler, E. (1987). Do abused children become abusive parents? *American Journal of Orthopsychiatry, 57*, 186–192.

Kazdin, A.E. (1996). *Conduct disorders in childhood and adolescence* (2nd ed.). Thousand Oaks, CA: Sage.

Kebbell, M.R., & Wagstaff, G.F. (1998). Hypnotic interviewing: The best way to interview eyewitnesses. *Behavioural Sciences and the Law, 16*, 115–129.

Kendall, T., Pilling, S., Tyrer, P., Duggan, C., Burbeck, R., Meader, N., & Taylor, C. (2009). Borderline and antisocial personality disorders: Summary of NICE guidance. *British Medical Journal, 338*, 293–295.

Kendall-Tackett, K.A., Williams, L.M., & Finkelhor, D. (1993). Impact of sexual abuse in children: A review and synthesis of recent empirical studies. *Psychological Bulletin, 113*, 164–180.

Keogh, A. (2007). Rape trauma syndrome – Time to open the floodgates? *Journal of Forensic and Legal Medicine, 14*, 221–224.

Keppel, R.D., & Walter, R. (1999). Profiling killers: A revised classification model for understanding sexual murder. *International Journal of Offender Therapy and Comparative Criminology, 43*, 417–437.

Kerr, N.L., Boster, F.J., Callen, C.R., Braz, M.E., O'Brien, B., & Horowitz, I. (2008). Jury nullification instructions as amplifiers of bias. *International Commentary on Evidence, 6*.

Kershner, R. (1996). Adolescent attitudes about rape. *Adolescence, 31*, 29–33.

Kersholt, J.H., Jansen, N.J.M., Van Amelsvoort, A.G., & Broeders, A.P.A. (2006). Earwitnesses: Effects of accent, retention, and telephone. *Applied Cognitive Psychology, 20*, 187–197.

Key events in the Bernardo/Homolka case. (2010, June 17). *CBC News.* Retrieved from www.cbc.ca/news/canada/key-events-in-the-bernardo-homolka-case-1.933128.

Khurana, A., & Gavazzi, S.M. (2011). Juvenile delinquency and adolescent fatherhood. *International Journal of Offender Therapy and Comparative Criminology, 55*(5), 756–770.

Killer of actress stabbed in prison. (2007, July 28). *USA Today.* Retrieved from http://usatoday30.usatoday.com/life/television/2007-07-28-2301673642_x.htm.

Kilpatrick, D.G., Saunders, B.E., Veronen, L.J., Best, C.L., & Von, J.M. (1987). Criminal victimization: Lifetime prevalence, reporting to police, and psychological impact. *Crime and Delinquency, 33,* 479–489.

Kim, J., & Gray, K.A. (2008). Leave or stay? Battered women's decision after intimate partner violence. *Journal of Interpersonal Violence, 23,* 1465–1482.

Kim, Y.S., Barak, G., & Shelton, D.E. (2009). Examining the CSI-effect in the cases of circumstantial evidence and eyewitness testimony: Multivariate and path analyses. *Journal of Criminal Justice, 37,* 452–460.

Kimonis, E.R., Cross, B., Howard, A., & Donoghue, K. (2013). Maternal care, maltreatment and callous-unemotional traits among urban male juvenile offenders. *Journal of Youth and Adolescence, 422,* 165–177.

Kind, S.S. (1987). Navigational ideas and the Yorkshire ripper investigation. *Journal of Navigation, 40,* 385–393.

King, L., & Snook, B. (2009). Peering inside the Canadian interrogation room: An examination of the Reid model of interrogation, influence tactics, and coercive strategies. *Criminal Justice and Behavior, 36,* 674–694.

Kingsbury, S.J., Lambert, M.T., & Hendrickse, W. (1997). A two-factor model of aggression. *Psychiatry: Interpersonal and Biological Processes, 60,* 224–232.

Kirk, E., Gurney, D., Edwards, R., & Dodimead, C. (2015). Handmade memories: The robustness of the gestural misinformation effect in children's eyewitness interviews. *Journal of Nonverbal Behavior, 39*(3), 259–273.

Kirkman, C.A. (2005). From soap opera to science: Towards gaining access to the psychopaths who live amongst us. *Psychology and Psychotherapy: Theory, Research and Practice, 78,* 379–396.

Klassen, D., & O'Connor, W.A. (1989). Assessing the risk of violence in released mental patients: A cross-validation study. *Psychological Assessment, 1,* 75–81.

Klassen, D., & O'Connor, W.A. (1994). Demographic and case history variables in risk assessment. In J. Monahan & H.J. Steadman (Eds.), *Violence and mental disorder: Developments in risk assessment* (pp. 229–257). Chicago, IL: University of Chicago Press.

Kleinmuntz, B., & Szucko, J.J. (1984). Lie detection in ancient and modern times: A call for contemporary scientific study. *American Psychologist, 39,* 766–776.

Klenowski, P.M., Bell, K.J., & Dodson, K.D. (2010). An empirical evaluation of juvenile awareness programs in the United States: Can juveniles be "scared straight"? *Journal of Offender Rehabilitation, 49,* 254–272.

Klettke, B., Graesser, A.C., & Powell, M.B. (2010). Expert testimony in child sexual abuse cases: The effects of evidence, coherence and credentials on juror decision making. *Applied Cognitive Psychology, 24*(4), 481–494. Retrieved from http://search.proquest.com/docview/742978220?accountid=9894.

Knight, R.A. (1999). Validation of a typology for rapists. *Journal of Interpersonal Violence, 14,* 303–330.

Knight, R.A., & Guay, J.P. (2006). The role of psychopathy in sexual coercion against women. In C.J. Patrick (Ed.), *Handbook of psychopathy* (pp. 512–532). New York, NY: Guilford.

Knight, R.A., & Prentky, R.A. (1990). Classifying sexual offenders: The development and corroboration of taxonomic models. In W.L. Marshall & D.R. Laws (Eds.), *Handbook of sexual assault: Issues, theories, and treatment of the offender* (pp. 23–52). New York, NY: Plenum Press.

Kocsis, R.N. (2003). Criminal psychological profiling: Validities and abilities. *International Journal of Offender Therapy and Comparative Criminology, 47,* 126–144.

Kocsis, R.N., Middledorp, J., & Karpin, A. (2008). Taking stock of accuracy in criminal profiling: The theoretical quandary for investigative psychology. *Journal of Forensic Psychology Practice, 8,* 244–261.

Köehnken, G. (1995). Interviewing adults. In R. Bull & D. Carson (Eds.), *Handbook of psychology in legal contexts* (pp. 215–233). Toronto, ON: John Wiley & Sons.

Kohnken, G., Milne, R., Memon, A., & Bull, R. (1999). The cognitive interview: A meta-analysis. *Psychology, Crime & Law, 5,* 3–27.

Konecni, V.J., & Ebbesen, E.B. (1984). The mythology of legal decision making. *International Journal of Law and Psychiatry, 7,* 5–18.

Kong, R., & AuCoin, K. (2008). Female offenders in Canada (Statistics Canada Catalogue no. 85-022-XIE). *Juristat.*

Koocher, G.P., Goodman, G.S., White, C.S., Friedrich, W.N., Sivan, A.B., & Reynolds, C.R. (1995). Psychological science and the use of anatomically detailed dolls in child sexual-abuse assessments. *Psychological Bulletin, 118,* 199–222.

Korsch, F., & Petermann, F. (2014). Agreement between parents and teachers on preschool children's behavior in a clinical sample with externalizing behavioral problems. *Child Psychiatry and Human Development, 45,* 617–627.

Koss, M.P. (1993). Detecting the scope of rape: A review of the prevalence research methods. *Journal of Interpersonal Violence, 8,* 198–222.

Kosson, D.S., Cyterski, T.D., Steuerwald, B.L., Neumann, C.S., & Walker-Matthews, S. (2002). Reliability and validity of the Psychopathy Checklist: Youth Version (PCL:YV) in nonincarcerated adolescent males. *Psychological Assessment, 14,* 97–109.

Kozel, F.A., Johnson, K.A., Mu, Q., Grenesko, E.L., Laken, S.J., & George, M.S. (2005). Detecting deception using functional magnetic resonance imaging. *Biological Psychiatry, 58,* 605–613.

Kraanen, F.L., & Emmelkamp, P.M. (2011). Substance misuse and substance use disorders in sex offenders: a review. *Clinical Psychology Review, 31*(3), 478–489.

Kramer, J.H., & Lubitz, R. (1985). Pennsylvania's sentencing reform: The impact of commission-established guidelines. *Crime & Delinquency, 31,* 481–500.

Kratzer, L., & Hodgins, S. (1999). A typology of offenders: A test of Moffitt's theory among males and females from childhood to age 30. *Criminal Behaviour and Mental Health, 9,* 57–73.

Krienert, J.L., Walsh, J.A., Matthews, K., & McConkey, K. (2012). Examining the nexus between domestic violence and animal abuse in a national sample of service providers. *Violence and Victims, 27,* 280–295.

Kroes, W.H., Margolis, B.L., & Hurrell, J.J. (1974). Job stress in policemen. *Journal of Police Science and Administration, 2,* 145–155.

Kropp, R., Hart, S., & Lyon, D. (2002). Risk assessment of stalkers: Some problems and potential solutions. *Criminal Justice and Behavior, 29,* 590–616.

Kumpfer, K.L., & Alvarado, R. (2003). Family-strengthening approaches for the prevention of youth problem behaviors. *American Psychologist, 58*, 457–465.

Laboratory of Community Psychiatry, Harvard Medical School. (1973). *Competency to stand trial and mental fitness* (DHEW Pub. No. ADM-77-103). Rockville, MD: Department of Health, Education, and Welfare.

Lafortune, D. (2010). Prevalence and screening of mental disorders in short-term correctional facilities. *International Journal of Law and Psychiatry, 33*(2), 94–100.

Lahey, B.B., Waldman, I.D., & McBurnett, K. (1999). The development of antisocial behaviour: An integrative causal model. *Journal of Child Psychology and Psychiatry, 40*, 669–682.

Laird, R.D., Jordan, K.Y., Dodge, K.A., Petit, G.S., & Bates, J.E. (2001). Peer rejection in childhood, involvement with antisocial peers in early adolescence and the development of externalizing behavior problems. *Development and Psychopathology, 13*, 337–354.

Lalumière, M., Harris, G., Quinsey, V., & Rice, M. (2005). *The causes of rape: Understanding individual differences in male propensity for sexual aggression*. Washington, DC: American Psychological Association.

Lamb, M., Hershkowitz, I., Orbach, Y., & Esplin, P. (2008). *Tell me what happened: Structured investigative interviews of child victims and witnesses*. West Sussex, England: John Wiley and Sons.

Lamphear, V.S. (1985). The impact of maltreatment on children's psychosocial adjustment: A review of the research. *Child Abuse and Neglect, 9*, 251–263.

Langevin, R., Handy, L., Paitich, D., & Russon, A. (1985). A new version of the Clarke Sex History Questionnaire for Males. In R. Langevin (Ed.), *Erotic preference, gender identity, and aggression in men: New research studies* (pp. 287–306). Hillsdale, NJ: Erlbaum.

Larimer, M.E., Lydum, A.R., Anderson, B.K., & Turner, A.P. (1999). Male and female recipients of unwanted sexual content in a college student sample: Prevalence rates, alcohol use, and depression symptoms. *Sex Roles, 40*, 295–308.

Larsson, A.S., & Lamb, M.E. (2009). Making the most of information-gathering interviews with children. *Infant and Child Development, 18*, 1–16.

Larsson, H., Andershed, H., & Lichtenstein, P. (2006). A genetic factor explains most of the variation in the psychopathic personality. *Journal of Abnormal Psychology, 115*, 221–230.

Latimer, J., & Lawrence, A. (2006). *The Review Board systems in Canada: An overview of results from the mentally disordered accused data collection study*. Ottawa, ON: Research and Statistics Division, Department of Justice.

Law Courts Education Society of British Columbia. (2009). *Gladue and Aboriginal sentencing*. Retrieved from www.justiceeducation.ca/research/aboriginal-sentencing/gladue-sentencing.

Law Reform Commission of Canada. (1976). *Our criminal law*. Ottawa, ON: Author.

Leach, A.-M., Talwar, V., Lee, K., Bala, N., & Lindsay, R.C.L. (2004). "Intuitive" lie detection of children's deception by law enforcement officials and university students. *Law and Human Behavior, 28*, 661–685.

Leadbeater, B.J., Kuperminc, G.P., Blatt, S.J., & Hertzog, C. (1999). A multivariate model of gender differences in adolescents' internalizing and externalizing problems. *Developmental Psychology, 35*, 1268–1282.

Leblanc, M. (1993). Late adolescent deceleration of criminal activity and development of self- and social control. *Studies on Crime and Crime Prevention, 2*, 51–68.

Lee, M.Y., Uken, A., & Sebold, J. (2007). Role of self-determined goals in predicting recidivism in domestic violence offenders. *Research on Social Work Practice, 17*, 30–41.

Lee, T.M.C., Au, R.K.C., Liu, H., Ting, K.H., Huang, C., & Chan, C.C.H. (2009). Are errors differentiable from deceptive responses when feigning memory impairment? an fMRI study. *Brain and Cognition, 69*(2), 406–412.

Lee, T.M.C., Lieu, H.-L., Chan, C.C.H., Ng, Y.-B., Fox, P.T., & Gao, J.-H. (2005). Neural correlates of feigned memory impairment. *Neuroimage, 28*, 305–313.

Leinwand, D. (2004). Judges write creative sentences. *USA Today*. Retrieved from www.usatoday.com/news/nation/2004-02-24-oddsentences_x.htm.

Leippe, M.R. (1995). The case for expert testimony about eyewitness memory. *Psychology, Public Policy, and Law, 1*, 909–959.

Leistedt, S.J., & Linkowski, P. (2014). Psychopathy and the cinema: Fact or fiction? *Journal of Forensic Sciences, 59*, 167–174.

Leistico, A.M., Salekin, R.T., DeCoster, J., & Rogers, R. (2008). A large-scale meta-analysis relating the hare measures of psychopathy to antisocial conduct. *Law and Human Behavior, 32*, 28–45.

Lemmon, J.H. (2006). The effects of maltreatment recurrence and child welfare services on dimensions of delinquency. *Criminal Justice Review, 31*, 5–32.

Leo, R.A. (1992). From coercion to deception: The changing nature of police interrogation in America. *Crime, Law and Social Change, 18*, 35–39.

Leo, R.A. (1996). Inside the interrogation room. *Journal of Criminal Law and Criminology, 86*, 266–303.

Leo, R.A., & Ofshe, R.J. (1998). The consequences of false confessions: Deprivations of liberty and miscarriages of justice in the age of psychological interrogation. *The Journal of Criminal Law and Criminology, 88*, 429–496.

Leschied, A.W., & Cunningham, A. (2002). *Seeking effective interventions for serious young offenders: Interim results of a four-year randomized study of multisystemic therapy in Ontario, Canada*. London, ON: Centre for Children and Families in the Justice System.

Leve, L.D. Kim, H.K., & Pears, K.C. (2005). Childhood temperament and family environment as predictors of internalizing and externalizing trajectories from ages 5 to 17. *Journal of Abnormal Child Psychology, 33*, 505–520.

Levine, T.R., Shaw, A., & Shulman, H.C. (2010). Increasing deception detection accuracy with strategic questioning. *Human Communication Research, 36*, 216–231.

Lev-Wiesel, R., & Sternberg, R. (2012). Victimized at home revictimized by peers: Domestic child abuse a risk factor for social rejection. *Child & Adolescent Social Work Journal, 29*(3), 203–220. doi:10.1007/s10560-012-0258-0

Leyton, E. (2005). *Hunting humans: The rise of the modern multiple murderer*. Toronto, ON: McClelland & Stewart.

Lieberman, J.D., & Sales, B.D. (1997). What social science teaches us about the jury instruction process. *Psychology, Public Policy, and Law, 3,* 589–644.

Lilienfeld, S.O., & Andrews, B.P. (1996). Development and preliminary validation of a self-report measure of psychopathic personality traits in noncriminal populations. *Journal of Personality Assessment, 66,* 488–524.

Lilienfeld, S.O., & Fowler, K.A. (2006). The self-report assessment of psychopathy: Problems, pitfalls, and promises. In C.J. Patrick (Ed.), *Handbook of psychopathy* (pp. 107–132). New York, NY: Guilford Press.

Lilienfeld, S.O., & Widows, M. (2005). *Professional manual for the Psychopathic Personality Inventory-Revised (PPI-R).* Lutz, FL: Psychological Assessment Resources.

Lindberg, M., Chapman, M.T., Samsock, D., Thomas, S.W., & Lindberg, A. (2003). Comparisons of three different investigative interview techniques with young children. *The Journal of Genetic Psychology, 164,* 5–28.

Lindsay, D.S. (1994). Memory source monitoring and eyewitness testimony. In D.F. Ross, J.D. Read, & M.P. Toglia (Eds.), *Adult eyewitness testimony: Current trends and development* (pp. 27–55). New York, NY: Cambridge University Press.

Lindsay, D.S., & Read, J.D. (1995). "Memory work" and recovered memories of childhood sexual abuse: Scientific evidence and public, professional, and personal issues. *Psychology, Public Policy, and Law, 1,* 846–909.

Lindsay, P.S. (1977). Fitness to stand trial in Canada: An overview in light of the recommendations of the law reform commission of Canada. *Criminal Law Quarterly, 19,* 303–348.

Lindsay, R.C.L., & Wells, G.L. (1985). Improving eyewitness identification from lineups: Simultaneous versus sequential lineup presentations. *Journal of Applied Psychology, 70,* 556–564.

Lindsay, R.C.L., Lea, J.A., & Fulford, J.A. (1991). Sequential lineup presentation: Technique matters. *Journal of Applied Psychology, 76,* 741–745.

Lindsay, R.C.L., Martin, R., & Webber, L. (1994). Default values in eyewitness descriptions: A problem for the match-to-description lineup foil selection strategy. *Law and Human Behavior, 18,* 527–541.

Lindsay, R.C.L., Wallbridge, H., & Drennan, D. (1987). Do clothes make the man? An exploration of the effect of lineup attire on eyewitness identification accuracy. *Canadian Journal of Behavioural Science, 19,* 463–478.

Lindsay, R.C.L., Wells, G.L., & O'Connor, F.J. (1989). Mock-juror belief of accurate and inaccurate eyewitnesses: A replication and extension. *Law and Human Behavior, 13,* 333–339.

Lipsey, M.W. (1992). Juvenile delinquency treatment: A meta-analytic inquiry into the variability of effects. In T.D. Cook, H. Cooper, D.S. Corday, H. Hartmann, L.V. Hedges, R.J. Light, Hedges, R.J. Light, T.A. Louis & F. Mosteller (Eds.), *Meta-analysis for explanation* (pp. 83–127). New York, NY: Sage.

Lipsey, M.W. (2009). The primary factors that characterize effective interventions with juvenile offenders: a meta-analytic overview. *Victims and Offenders, 4,* 124–147.

Lipsey, M.W., & Derzon, J.H. (1998). Predictors of violent or serious delinquency in adolescence and early adulthood: A synthesis of longitudinal research. In R. Loeber & D.P. Farrington (Eds.), *Serious and violent juvenile offenders: Risk factors and successful interventions* (pp. 86–105). Thousand Oaks, CA: Sage.

Lipsitt, P.D., Lelos, D., & McGarry, L. (1971). Competency to stand trial: A screening instrument. *American Journal of Psychiatry, 128,* 104–109.

Lisak, D., & Roth, S. (1988). Motivational factors in nonincarcerated sexually aggressive men. *Journal of Personality and Social Psychology, 55,* 795–802.

Lloyd, C.D., Clark, H.J., & Forth, A.E. (2010). Psychopathy, expert testimony and indeterminate sentences: Exploring the relationship between Psychopathy Checklist-Revised testimony and trial outcome in Canada. *Legal and Criminological Psychology, 15,* 323–339.

Lochman, J.E., Whidby, J.M., & Fitzgerald, D.P. (2000). Cognitive-behavioural assessment and treatment with aggressive children. In P. Kendall (Ed.), *Child and adolescent therapy: Cognitive behavioural procedures* (2nd ed., pp. 31–87). New York, NY: Guilford Press.

Loeber, R., & Farrington, D.P. (1998a). Never too early, never too late: Risk factors and successful interventions for serious and violent juvenile offenders. *Studies on Crime and Crime Prevention, 7,* 7–30.

Loeber, R., & Farrington, D.P. (1998b). *Serious and violent juvenile offenders: Risk factors and successful interventions.* Thousand Oaks, CA: Sage.

Loeber, R., & Farrington, D.P. (2000). Young children who commit crime: Epidemiology, developmental origins, risk factors, early interventions, and policy implications. *Development and Psychopathology, 12,* 737–762.

Loeber, R., Keenan, K., Lahey, B.B., Green, S.M., & Thomas, C. (1993). Evidence for developmentally based diagnoses of Oppositional Defiant Disorder and Conduct Disorder. *Journal of Abnormal Psychology, 100,* 379–390.

Lofthouse, R.E., Lindsay, W.R., Totsika, V., Hastings, R.P., Boer, D.P., & Haaven, L. (2013). Prospective dynamic assessment of risk of sexual reoffending in individuals with an intellectual disability and a history of sexual offending behavior. *Journal of Applied Research in Intellectual Disabilities, 26,* 394–403.

Loftus, E., & Palmer, J.C. (1974). Reconstructions of automobile destruction: An example of the interaction between language and memory. *Journal of Verbal Learning and Verbal Behavior, 12,* 585–589.

Loftus, E.F. (1975). Leading questions and the eyewitness report. *Cognitive Psychology, 7,* 560–572.

Loftus, E.F. (1979a). The malleability of human memory. *American Scientist, 67,* 312–320.

Loftus, E.F. (1979b). Reactions to blatantly contradictory information. *Memory and Cognition, 7,* 368–374.

Loftus, E.F., Altman, D., & Geballe, R. (1975). Effects of questioning upon a witness's later recollections. *Journal of Police Science and Administration, 3,* 162–165.

Loftus, E.G., Miller, D.G., & Burns, H.J. (1978). Semantic integration of verbal information into a visual memory. *Journal of Experimental Psychology: Human Learning and Memory, 4,* 19–31.

Loftus, E.F., & Zanni, G. (1975). Eyewitness testimony: The influence of the wording of a question. *Bulletin of the Psychonomic Society, 5,* 86–88.

Loo, R. (1994). Burnout among Canadian police managers. *The International Journal of Organizational Analysis, 2,* 406–417.

Loos, M.E., & Alexander, P.C. (1997). Differential effects associated with self-reported histories of abuse and neglect in a college sample. *Journal of Interpersonal Violence, 12,* 340–360.

Lösel, F., & Farrington, D.P. (2012). Direct protective and buffering protective factors in the development of youth violence. *American Journal of Preventative Medicine, 43,* S8–S23.

Lösel, F., & Schmucker, M. (2005). The effectiveness of treatment for sexual offenders: A comprehensive meta-analysis. *Journal of Experimental Criminology, 1,* 117–146.

Lough, J., & Von Treuer, K. (2013). A critical review of psychological instruments used in police officer selection. *Policing, 36,* 737–751.

Luther, K. & Snook, B. (2016). Putting the Mr. Big technique back on trial: A re-examination of probative value and abuse of process through a scientific lens. *Journal of Forensic Practice, 18*(2), 131–142. doi 10.1108/JFP-01-2015-0004

Luus, C.A.E., & Wells, G.L. (1991). Eyewitness identification and the selection of distractors for lineups. *Law and Human Behavior, 15,* 43–57.

Luus, C.A.E., & Wells, G.L. (1994). The malleability of eyewitness confidence: Co-witness and perseverance effects. *Journal of Applied Psychology, 79,* 714–723.

Lykken, D.L. (2006). Psychopathic personality: The scope of the problem. In C.J. Patrick (Ed.), *Handbook of psychopathy* (pp. 3–13). New York, NY: Guilford Press.

Lykken, D.T. (1960) The validity of the guilty knowledge technique: The effects of faking. *Journal of Applied Psychology, 44*(4), Aug 1960, 258–262.

Lykken, D.T. (1998). *A tremor in the blood. Uses and abuses of the lie detector.* New York, NY: Plenum.

Lynam, D.R., Caspi, A., Moffitt, T.E., Loeber, R., & Stouthamer-Loeber, M. (2007). Longitudinal evidence that psychopathy scores in early adolescence predict adult psychopathy. *Journal of Abnormal Psychology, 116,* 155–165.

Lyon, T.D., Scurich, N., Choi, K., Handmaker, S., & Blank, R. (2012). "How did you feel?": Increasing child sexual abuse witnesses' production of evaluative information. *Law and Human Behavior, 36*(5), 448–457. doi:10.1037/h0093986

Lytle, N., London, K., & Bruck, M. (2015). Young children's ability to use two-dimensional and three-dimensional symbols to show placements of body touches and hidden objects. *Journal of Experimental Child Psychology, 134,* 30–42.

MacCoun, R.J., & Kerr, N.L. (1988). Asymmetric influence in mock deliberation: Jurors' bias for leniency. *Journal of Personality and Social Psychology, 54,* 21–33.

MacDonald, R. (2000). Time to talk about rape. *British Medical Journal, 321,* 1034–1035.

MacMillan, H.L., Tanaka, M., Duku, E., & Vaillancourt, T. (2013). Child physical and sexual abuse in a community sample of young adults: Results from the Ontario child health study. *Child Abuse & Neglect, 37*(1), 14–21.

Maeder, E., Dempsey, J., & Pozzulo, J. (2012). Behind the veil of juror decision making: Testing the effects of Muslim veils and defendant race in the courtroom. *Criminal Justice and Behavior, 39*(5), 666–678.

Maeder, E.M., & Corbett, R. (2015). Beyond frequency: Perceived realism and the CSI effect. *Canadian Journal of Criminology and Criminal Justice, 57,* 83–114.

Maeder, E.M., Yamamoto, S., & Saliba, P. (2015). The influence of defendant race and victim physical attractiveness on juror decision-making in a sexual assault trial. *Psychology, Crime, and Law, 21,* 62–79.

Mahoney, T.H. (2011). *Homicide in Canada, 2010.* Ottawa, ON: Minister of Industry.

Malik, M.S.A., Sandholzer, M., Khan, M.Z., & Akbar, S. (2015). Identification of risk factors generating terrorism in Pakistan. *Terrorism and Political Violence, 27,* 537–556.

Malinosky-Rummell, R., & Hansen, D.J. (1993). Long-term consequences of childhood physical abuse. *Psychological Bulletin, 114,* 68–79.

Malpass, R.S., & Devine, P.G. (1981). Eyewitness identification: Lineup instructions and the absence of the offender. *Journal of Applied Psychology, 66,* 482–489.

Malpass, R.S., Tredoux, C.G., & McQuiston-Surrett, D. (2009). Response to Lindsay, Mansour, Beaudry, Leach, and Bertrand's Sequential lineup presentation patterns and policy. *Legal and Criminological Psychology, 14,* 25–30.

Mancini, D.E. (2011). The CSI effect reconsidered: Is it moderated by need for cognition? *North American Journal of Psychology, 13*(1), 155–174. Retrieved from http://search.proquest.com/docview/862788386?accountid=9894.

Mann, M. (2013). Incarceration and the Aboriginal offender: Potential impacts of the tackling violent crime act and the corrections review panel recommendations. In J.P. White and J. Bruhn (Eds.), *Aboriginal police research: Exploring the urban landscape* (pp. 233–253). Toronto, ON: Thompson Educational Publishing, Inc.

Mann, S., Ewens, S., Shaw, D., Vrij, A., Leal, S., & Hillman, J. (2013). Lying eyes: Why liars seek deliberate eye contact. *Psychiatry, Psychology and Law, 20*(3), 452–461.

Mann, S., Vrij, A., & Bull, R. (2004). Detecting true lies: Police officers' ability to detect suspects' lies. *Journal of Applied Psychology, 89,* 137–149.

Manson, A. (2006). Fitness to be sentenced: A historical, comparative and practical review. *International Journal of Law and Psychiatry, 29,* 262–280.

Manzoni, P., Brochu, S., Fischer, B., & Rehm, J. (2006). Determinants of property crime among illicit opiate users outside of treatment across Canada. *Deviant Behavior, 27,* 351–376.

Markey, P.M., Markey, C.N., & French, J.E. (2015). Violent video games and real-world violence: Rhetoric versus data. *Psychology of Popular Media Culture, 4,* 277–295.

Marlatt, G.A., & Gordon, J.R., eds. (1985). *Relapse Prevention: Maintenance Strategies in the Treatment of Addictive Behaviors.* New York: Guilford Press.

Marques, J.K. (1999). How to answer the questions "Does sexual offender treatment work?" *Journal of Interpersonal Violence, 14,* 437–451.

Marshall, W.L. (1999). Current status of North American assessment and treatment programs for sexual offenders. *Journal of Interpersonal Violence, 14,* 221–239.

Marshall, W.L., & Barbaree, H.E. (1988). An outpatient treatment program for child molesters. *Annals of the New York Academy of Sciences, 528,* 205–214.

Marshall, W.L., & Barbaree, H.E. (1990). An integrated theory of the etiology of sexual offending. In W.L. Marshall & D.R. Laws (Eds.), *Handbook of sexual assault: Issues, theories, and treatment of the offender* (pp. 257–275). New York, NY: Plenum Press.

Marshall, W.L., Anderson, D., & Champagne, F. (1997). Self-esteem and its relationship to sexual offending. *Psychology, Crime and Law, 3,* 161–186.

Marshall, W.L., Barbaree, H.E., & Fernandez, Y.M. (1995). Some aspects of social competence in sexual offenders. *Sexual Abuse: Journal of Research and Treatment, 7,* 113–127.

Marshall, W.L., Eccles, A., & Barbaree, H.E. (1991). The treatment of exhibitionists: A focus on sexual deviance versus cognitive and relationship features. *Behavior Research and Therapy, 29,* 129–135.

Marshall, W.L., & Fernandez, Y.M. (2003). Sexual preferences: Are they useful in the assessment and treatment of sexual offenders? *Aggression and Violent Behavior, 8,* 131–143.

Martin, M. (2007). Men who solicited sex ordered to wear chicken suits. *The Houston Chronicle.* Retrieved from www.chron.com/news/bizarre/article/Men-who-solicited-sex-ordered-to-wear-chicken-1555834.php.

Martineau, M., & Corey, S. (2008). Investigating the reliability of the violent crime linkage analysis system (ViCLAS) crime report. *Journal of Police and Criminal Psychology, 23,* 51–60.

Martinson, R. (1974). What works? Questions and answers about prison reform. *The Public Interest, 35,* 22–54.

Masip, J., Alonso, H., Garrido, E., & Herrero, C. (2008). Training to detect what? The biasing effects of training on veracity judgments. *Applied Cognitive Psychology, 23,* 1282–1296.

Masten, A., & Coatsworth, J. (1998). The development of competence in favorable and unfavorable environments: Lessons from research on successful children. *American Psychologist, 53,* 205–220.

Mathieu, C., Neumann, C., Babiak, P., & Hare, R.D. (2015). Corporate psychopathy and the full-range leadership model. *Assessment, 22*(3), 267–278.

Matsumoto, D., Hwang, H.S., Skinner, L., Frank, M.G. (2011). Evaluating truthfulness and detecting deception. *FBI Law Enforcement Bulletin,* June, 1–11.

Maume, M.O., Ousey, G.C., & Beaver, K. (2005). Cutting the grass: A reexamination of the link between marital attachment, delinquent peers and desistance from marijuana use. *Journal of Quantitative Criminology, 21,* 27–53.

Maxwell, A. (2015). *Adult criminal court statistics in Canada, 2013–2014.* Retrieved May 1, 2016 from http://www.statcan.gc.ca/pub/85-002-x/2015001/article/14226-eng.htm#a6.

May, J., Osmond, K., & Billick, S. (2014). Juvenile delinquency treatment and prevention: A literature review. *Psychiatric Quarterly, 85,* 295–301.

McCabe, D.P., & Castel, A.D. (2008). Seeing is believing: The effect of brain images on judgments of scientific reasoning. *Cognition, 107,* 343–352.

McCabe, D.P., Castel, A.D., & Rhodes, M.G. (2011). The influence of fMRI lie detection evidence on juror decision-making. *Behavioral Sciences and the Law, 29,* 566–577.

McCloskey, M., & Egeth, H. (1983). Eyewitness identification: What can a psychologist tell a jury? *American Psychologist, 38,* 550–563.

McCloskey, M., & Zaragoza, M. (1985). Misleading post event information and memory for events: Arguments and evidence against memory impairment hypothesis. *Journal of Experimental Psychology: General, 114,* 1–16.

McCormick, C.T. (1972). *Handbook of the law of evidence* (2nd ed.). St. Paul, MN: West.

McCornack, S.A., & Parks, M.R. (1990). What women know that men don't: Sex differences in determining the truth behind deceptive messages. *Journal of Social and Personal Relationships, 7*(1), 107–118.

McCoy, S.P., & Aamodt, M.G. (2010). A comparison of law enforcement divorce rates with those of other occupations. *Journal of Police and Criminal Psychology, 25,* 1–16.

McCraty, R., & Atkinson, M. (2012). Resilience training program reduces physiological and psychological stress in police officers. *Global Advances in Health and Medicine, 1,* 44–66.

McCraty, R., Tomasino, D., Atkinson, M., & Sundram, J. (1999). *Impact of the HeartMath self-management skills program on physiological and psychological stress in police officers.* Boulder Creek, CA: HeartMath Research Center, Institute of HeartMath.

McCreary, D.R., & Thompson, M.M. (2006). Development of two reliable and valid measures of stressors in policing: The Operational and Organizational Police Stress Questionnaires. *International Journal of Stress Management, 13,* 494–518.

McDaniel, D.D. (2012). Risk and protective factors associated with gang affiliation among high-risk youth: A public health approach. *Injury Prevention, 18*(4), 253–258.

McDaniel, M.A., Whetzel, D.L., Schmidt, F.L., & Maurer, S.D. (1994). The validity of employment interviews: A comprehensive review and meta-analysis. *Journal of Applied Psychology, 79,* 599–616.

McDougall, A., Campbell, M., Smith, T., Burbridge, A., Doucette, N., & Canales, D. (2012). An analysis of general public and professional's attitudes about Mental Health Courts: Predictors of a positive perspective. *International Journal of Forensic Mental Health, 11,* 203–217.

McElvaney, R. (2015). Disclosure of Child Sexual Abuse: Delays, non-disclosure and partial disclosure: What the research tells us and implications for practice. *Child Abuse Review, 24*(3), 159–169.

McFarlane, J., Campbell, J.C., & Watson, K. (2002). Intimate partner stalking and femicide: Urgent implications for women's safety. *Behavioral Sciences and the Law, 20,* 51–68.

McFatter, R.M. (1986). Sentencing disparity. *Journal of Applied Social Psychology, 16,* 150–164.

McGowan, M.G., & Helms, J.L. (2003). The utility of the expert witness in a rape case: Reconsidering rape trauma syndrome. *Journal of Forensic Psychology Practice, 3*(1), 51–60.

McIntosh, C. (2015). Final evaluation summary of the Multisystemic Therapy program. (Report No. 2015-R015). Retrieved from Public Safety Canada website https://www.publicsafety.gc.ca/cnt/rsrcs/pblctns/fnl-mltsystmc-thrpy-prgrm/index-en.aspx.

McIntyre, M. (2009, March 5). Victim's family incensed as beheading killer avoids jail time. *National Post.* Retrieved from www.nationalpost.com/related/topics/story.html?id=1356797.

McKenna, P.F. (2002). *Police powers*. Toronto, ON: Prentice Hall.

McKimmie, B., Masters, J., Masser, B., Schuller, R., & Terry, D. (2012). Stereotypical and counterstereotypical defendants: Who is he and what was the case against her? *Psychology, Public Policy, and Law, 19*(3), 343–354.

McLellan, F. (2006). Mental health and justice: The case of Andrea Yates. *The Lancet, 368*, 1951–1954.

McNiel, D.E., Sandberg, D.A., & Binder, R.L. (1998). The relationship between confidence and accuracy in clinical assessment of psychiatric patients' potential for violence. *Law and Human Behavior, 22*, 655–669.

McQuiston-Surrett, D., Malpass, R.S., & Tredoux, C.G. (2006). Sequential vs. simultaneous lineups: A review of methods, data, and theory. *Psychology, Public Policy, and Law, 12*, 137–169.

Meadow, R. (1977). Munchausen syndrome by proxy: The hinterland of child abuse. *Lancet, 2*, 343–345.

Medicine Hat teen killer sentence reviewed. (2012, October 1). *CBC News*. Retrieved from www.cbc.ca/news/canada/calgary/story/2012/10/01/calgary-jr-medicine-hat-murder-court.html.

Meehl, P.E. (1954). *Clinical vs. statistical prediction*. Minneapolis, MN: University of Minnesota Press.

Megreya, A.M., Bindemann, M., Havard, C., & Burton, M. (2012). Identity-lineup location influences target-selection: Evidence from eye movements. *Journal of Police and Criminal Psychology, 27*, 167–178.

Mehta, D. (2014). *Sammy Yatime shooting death on Toronto streetcar shown in court*. Retrieved March 4, 2016 from http://www.ctvnews.ca/canada/sammy-yatim-shooting-death-on-toronto-streetcar-shown-in-court-1.2620119.

Meissner, C.A., & Brigham, J.C. (2001). Thirty years of investigating the own-race bias in memory for faces: A meta-analytic review. *Psychology, Public Policy, and Law, 7*, 1–35.

Meissner, C.A., Brigham, J.C., & Pfeifer, J.E. (2003). Jury nullification: The influence of judicial instruction on the relationship between attitudes and juridic decision making. *Basic and Applied Social Psychology, 25*, 243–254.

Meissner, C.A., & Kassin, S.M. (2002). "He's guilty!": Investigator bias in judgments of truth and deception. *Law and Human Behavior, 26*, 469–480.

Meissner, C.A., & Russano, M.B. (2003). The psychology of interrogations and false confessions: Research and recommendations. *The Canadian Journal of Police and Security Services: Practice, Policy and Management, 1*, 53–64.

Meissner, D. (2000, March 5). Reena Virk murder trial set to begin this week. *Canadian Press*. Retrieved from Canoe website: http://acmi.canoe.ca/CNEWSLaw0003/13_virk6.html.

Melinder, A., Alexander, K., Cho, Y., Goodman, G., Thoresen, C., Konnum, K., & Magnussen, S. (2010). Children's eyewitness memory: A comparison of two interviewing strategies as realized by forensic professionals. *Journal of Experimental Child Psychology, 105*, 156–177.

Melnyk, L., & Bruck, M. (2004). Timing moderates the effects of repeated suggestive interviewing on children's eyewitness memory. *Applied Cognitive Psychology, 18*(5), 613–631.

Melnyk, L., Crossman, A., & Scullin, M. (2006). The suggestibility of children's memory. In M. Toglia, J.D. Read, D. Ross, & R.C.L. Lindsay (Eds.), *The handbook of eyewitness psychology: Vol I. Memory for events* (pp. 401–427). Mahwah, NJ: Lawrence Erlbaum Associates.

Meloy, J.R. (1997). Predatory violence during mass murder. *Journal of Forensic Sciences, 42*, 326–329.

Melton, G., Petrila, J., Poythress, N.G., & Slobogin, C. (1997). Competency to stand trial. In *Psychological evaluations for the court: A handbook for mental health professionals and lawyers* (2nd ed., pp. 119–155). New York, NY: Guilford Press.

Memon, A., & Bull, R. (1991). The cognitive interview: Its origins, empirical support, evaluation and practical implications. *Journal of Community and Applied Social Psychology, 1*, 291–307.

Memon, A., Holliday, R., & Hill, C. (2006). Pre-event stereotypes and misinformation effects in young children. *Memory, 14*, 104–114.

Memon, A., Meissner, C.A., & Fraser, J. (2010). The cognitive interview: A meta-analytic review and study space analysis of the past 25 years. *Psychology, Public Policy, and Law, 16*(4), 340–372.

Memon, A., Vrij, A., & Bull, R. (2003). *Psychology and law: Truthfulness, accuracy and credibility*. London, England: Jossey-Bass.

Menard, S., & Huizinga, D. (1989). Age, period, and cohort size effects on self-reported alcohol, marijuana, and polydrug use: Results from the National Youth Survey. *Social Science Research, 18*, 174–194.

Mental Health Law and Police Institute (MHLPI). (2016). Mental health law and policy institute. Retrieved March 3, 2016 from http://members.psyc.sfu.ca/labs/mhlpi/.

Merari, A. (2010). *Driven to death: Psychological and social aspects of suicide terrorism*. New York, NY: Oxford University Press.

Merton R.K. (1938). Social structure and anomie. *American Sociological Review, 3*, 672–682.

Messman-Moore, T.L., & Long, P.J. (2003). The role of childhood sexual abuse sequelae in the sexual revictimization of women: An empirical review and theoretical reformulation. *Clinical Psychology Review, 23*, 537–571.

Meston, C.M., & Frohlich, P.F. (2000). The neurobiology of sexual function. *Arch Gen Psychiatry, 57*(11), 1012–30.

Miethe, T.D., & Drass, K.A. (1999). Exploring the social context of instrumental and expressive homicides: An application of qualitative comparative analysis. *Journal of Quantitative Criminology, 15*, 1–21.

Miladinovic, Z., & Mulligan, L. (2015). *Homicide in Canada, 2014*. Retrieved April 1, 2016 from http://www.statcan.gc.ca/pub/85-002-x/2015001/article/14244-eng.htm.

Miller, M.K., Maskaly, J., Green, M., & Peoples, C.D. (2011). The effects of deliberations and religious identity on mock jurors' verdicts. *Group Processes & Intergroup Relations, 14*(4), 517–532.

Milligan, S. (2011). Criminal harassment in Canada, 2009 (Statistics Canada catalogue no. 85-005-X). *Juristat Bulletin*.

Millis, J.B., & Kornblith, P.R. (1992). Fragile beginnings: Identification and treatment of postpartum disorders. *Health and Social Work, 17*, 192–199.

Mills, J.F., & Kroner, D.G. (2006). The effect of base-rate information on the perception of risk for reoffense. *American Journal of Forensic Psychology, 24*, 45–56.

Milne, R., & Bull, R. (1999). *Investigative interviewing: Psychology and practice*. Chichester, UK: Wiley.

Miranda *v.* Arizona, [1966] 384 U.S. 436.

Mitchell, J.T. (1983). When disaster strikes … The critical incident stress debriefing process. *Journal of Emergency Medical Services*, 8, 36–39.

Mitchell, K.J., Finkelhor, D., & Wolak, J. (2001). Risk factors for and impact of online sexual solicitation of youth. *Journal of the American Medical Association*, 285, 3011–3014.

Mitchell, K.J., Livosky, M., & Mather, M. (1998). The weapon focus effect revisited: The role of novelty. *Legal and Criminological Psychology*, 3, 287–303.

Mitchell, T., Haw, R., Pfeifer, J., & Meissner, C. (2005). Racial bias in mock juror decision-making: A meta-analytic review of defendant treatment. *Law and Human Behavior*, 29, 621–637.

Mitte, K., Steil, R., & Nachtigall, C. (2005). Eine meta-analyse unter einsatz des random effects-modells zur effektivität kurzfristger psychologischer interventionen nach acuter traumatisierung. *Zeitschrift fur Klinische Psychologie und Psychotherapie*, 34, 1–9.

Moffitt, T.E. (1993). Adolescence-limited and life-course persistent antisocial behaviour: A developmental taxonomy. *Psychological Review*, 100, 674–701.

Moffitt, T.E., Caspi, A., Harrington, H., & Milne, B.J. (2002). Males on the life-course persistent and adolescence limited antisocial pathways: Follow-up at age 26 years. *Development and Psychopathology*, 14, 179–207.

Moffitt, T.E., & Henry, B. (1989). Neurological assessment of executive functions in self-reported delinquents. *Developmental and Psychopathology*, 1, 105–118.

Mohamed, F.B., Faro, S.H., Gordon, N.J., Platek, S.M., Ahmad, H., & Williams, J.M. (2006). Brain mapping of deception and truth telling about an ecologically valid situation: Functional MR imaging and polygraph investigation: Initial experience. *Radiology*, 238, 679–688.

Mokros, A., Osterheider, M., Hucker, S.J., & Nitschke, J. (2010). Psychopathy and Sexual Sadism. *Law and Human Behavior*. Retrieved from www.springerlink.com/content/121631662p604u2u/fulltext.html.

Monahan, J. (1981). *Predicting violent behavior: An assessment of clinical techniques*. Beverly Hills, CA: Sage.

Monahan, J. (2012). The individual risk assessment of terrorism. *Psychology, Public Policy, and Law*, 18, 167–207.

Monahan, J., & Steadman, H.J. (1994). *Violence and mental disorder: Developments in risk assessment*. Chicago, IL: University of Chicago Press.

Moore, C.A., & Miethe, T.D. (1986). Regulated and unregulated sentencing decisions: An analysis of first-year practices under Minnesota's felony sentencing guidelines. *Law & Society Review*, 20, 253–277.

Moran, R. (1985). The modern foundation for the insanity defense: The cases of James Hadfield (1800) and Daniel M'Naughten (1843). *Annals of the American Academy of Political and Social Science*, 477, 31–42.

Morgan, R.D., Flora, D.B., Kroner, D.G., Mills, J.F., Varghese, F., & Steffan, J.S. (2012). Treating offenders with mental illness: A research synthesis. *Law and Human Behavior*, 36(1), 37–50.

Morgan, R.K., & Kavanaugh, K.D. (2011). Student stalking of faculty: Results of a nationwide survey. *College Student Journal*, 45, 512–523.

Morley, K.I., Lynskey, M.T., Moran, P., Borschmann, R., & Winstock, A.R. (2015). Polysubstance use, mental health and high-risk behaviours: Results from the 2012 global drug survey. *Drug and Alcohol Review*, 34, 427–437.

Morton, R.J., & Hilts, M.A. (2008). *Serial murder: Multi-disciplinary perspectives for investigators*. Retrieved from www.fbi.gov/stats-services/publications/serial-murder.

Mossman, D. (1994). Assessing predictions of violence: Being accurate about accuracy. *Journal of Consulting and Clinical Psychology*, 62, 783–792.

Mother who killed son on subway dies of injuries. (2000, August 21). *CBC News*. Retrieved May 31, 2013 from www.cbc.ca/news/canada/story/2000/08/20/subway_000820.html.

Motiuk, L.L., & Porporino, F.J. (1991). *The prevalence, nature and severity of mental health problems among federal male inmates in Canadian penitentiaries* (Research Report No. 24). Ottawa, ON: Correctional Service of Canada.

Motiuk, L.L., & Serin, R.C. (2001). *Compendium 2000 on effective correctional programming*. Ottawa, ON: Correctional Service of Canada.

Mulvey, E. (2005). Risk assessment in juvenile justice policy and practice. In K. Heilbrun, N. Goldstein, & R. Redding (Eds.), *Juvenile delinquency: Prevention, assessment, and intervention* (pp. 209–231). New York, NY: Oxford University Press.

Mulvey, E.P., Arthur, M.W., & Reppucci, N.D. (1993). The prevention and treatment of juvenile delinquency: A review of the research. *Clinical Psychology Review*, 13, 133–167.

Munsterberg, H. (1908). *On the witness stand*. Garden City, NY: Doubleday.

Murphy, J.M. (1976). Psychiatric labelling in cross-cultural perspective: Similar kinds of behaviour appear to be labelled abnormal in diverse cultures. *Science*, 191, 1019–1028.

Murrie, D.C., Boccaccini, M.T., Caperton, J., & Rufino, K. (2012). Field validity of the Psychopathy Checklist–Revised in sex offender risk assessment. *Psychological Assessment* 24(2), 524–529.

Murrie, D.C., Boccaccini, M.T., Guarnera, L.A., & Rufino, K.A. (2013). Are forensic experts biased by the side that retained them? *Psychological Science*, 24, 1889–1897.

Murrie, D.C., Boccaccini, M.T., Johnson, J.T., & Janke, C. (2008). Does interrater (dis)agreement on Psychopathy Checklist score in sexually violent predator trials suggest partisan allegiance in forensic evaluations? *Law and Human Behavior*, 32, 352–362.

Murrie, D.C., Boccaccini, M.T., McCoy, W., & Cornell, D.G. (2007). Diagnostic labels in juvenile court: How do descriptions of psychopathy and conduct disorder influence judges? *Journal of Clinical Child and Adolescent Psychology*, 36, 288–291.

Murrie, D.C., Boccaccini, M.T., Turner, D., Meeks, M., Woods, C., & Tussey, C. (2009). Rater (dis)agreement on risk assessment measures in sexually violent predator proceedings: Evidence of adversarial allegiance in forensic evaluation? *Psychology, Public Policy, and Law*, 15, 19–53.

Murrie, D.C., Cornell, D.G., Kaplan, S., McConville, D., & Levy-Elkon, A. (2004). Psychopathy scores and violence among juvenile offenders: A multi-measure study. *Behavioral Sciences and the Law*, 22, 49–67.

Mustard, D.B. (2001). Racial, ethnic, and gender disparities in sentencing: Evidence from the U.S. federal courts. *Journal of Law and Economics, XLIV*, 285–314.

Myers, B., Latter, R., & Abdollahi-Arena, M.K. (2006). The court of public opinion: Lay perceptions of polygraph testing. *Law and Human Behavior, 30*, 509–523.

Myers, C. (2012). Sex selective abortion in India. *Global Tides, 6*(3). Retrieved from http://digitalcommons.pepperdine.edu/global-tides/vol6/iss1/3.

Myers, W.C., Hall, R.C.W., & Tolou-Shams, M. (2013). Prevalence and assessment of malingering in homicide defendants using the mini-mental state examination and the rey 15-item memory test. *Homicide Studies: An Interdisciplinary & International Journal, 17*(3), 314–328.

Nathanson, C., Paulhus, D.L., & Williams, K.M. (2006). Predictors of a behavioral measure of scholastic cheating: Personality and competence but not demographics. *Contemporary Educational Psychology, 31*, 97–122.

National Crime Prevention Centre. (2012). *A statistical snapshot of youth at risk and youth offending in Canada.* Public Safety Canada. Retrieved from https://www.publicsafety.gc.ca/cnt/rsrcs/pblctns/ststclsnpsht-yth/index-en.aspx#fn48.

National Crime Prevention Council. (1995). *Risk or threat to children.* Ottawa, ON: National Crime Prevention Council.

National Crime Prevention Council. (1997). *Preventing crime by investing in families and communities: Promoting positive outcomes in youth twelve to eighteen years old.* Ottawa, ON: National Crime Prevention Council.

National Research Council (2003). *The polygraph and lie detection.* Washington, DC: National Academies Press.

National Research Council. (2009). *Strengthening forensic science in the United States: A path forward.* Washington, DC: National Academic Press.

Navon, D. (1990). How critical is the accuracy of eyewitness memory? Another look at the issue of lineup diagnosticity. *Journal of Applied Psychology, 75*, 506–510.

Nazroo, J. (1995). Uncovering gender differences in the use of marital violence: The effect of methodology. *Sociology, 29*, 475–494.

Neil v. Biggers, [1972] 409 U.S. 188.

Nemeth, M. (1996, May 20). Joudrie not guilty. *Maclean's.* Retrieved from http://thecanadianencyclopedia.com/index.cfm?PgNm=TCE&Params=M1ARTM001067.

Neumann, C.S., & Hare, R.D. (2008). Psychopathic traits in a large community sample: Links to violence, alcohol use, and intelligence. *Journal of Consulting and Clinical Psychology, 76*, 893–899.

Neumann, C.S., Hare, R.D., & Newman, J.P. (2007). The superordinate nature of the Psychopathy Checklist-Revised. *Journal of Personality Disorders, 21*, 102–117.

Neumann, C.S., Schmitt, D.S., Carter, R., Embley, I., & Hare, R.D. (2012). Psychopathic traits in females and males across the globe. *Behavioral Sciences and the Law, 30*, 557–574.

Nevin, R. (2000). How lead exposure relates to temporal changes in IQ, violent crime, and unwed pregnancy. *Environmental Research, 83*, 1–22.

New Brunswick Ombudsman and Child and Youth Advocate. (2008, June). *The Ashley Smith Report.* Fredericton, NB: Author.

Newman, J.P., Brinkley, C.A., Lorenz, A.R., Hiatt, K.D., & MacCoon, D.G. (2007). Psychopathy as psychopathology: Beyond the clinical utility of the Psychopathy Checklist-Revised. In H. Hervé & J.C. Yuille (Eds.), *The psychopath: Theory, research and practice* (pp. 173–206). Mahway, NJ: Erlbaum.

Newman, J.P., Curtin, J.J., Bertsch, J.D., & Baskin-Sommers, A.R. (2010). Attention moderates the fearlessness of psychopathic offenders. *Biological Psychiatry, 67*, 66–70.

Ng, W., & Lindsay, R.C.L. (1994). Cross-race facial recognition: Failure of the contact hypothesis. *Journal of Cross-Cultural Psychology, 25*, 217–232.

Nicholls, T.L., Brink, J., Greaves, C., Lussier, P., & Verdun-Jones, S. (2009). Forensic psychiatric inpatients and aggression: An exploration of incidence, prevalence, severity, and interventions by gender. *International Journal of Law and Psychiatry, 32*(1), 23–30.

Nicholls, T.L., Ogloff, J.R.P., & Douglas, K.S. (2004). Assessing risk for violence among male and female civil psychiatric patients: The HCR-20, PCL:SV, and VSC. *Behavioral Sciences and the Law, 22*, 127–158.

Nichols, T.R., Graber, J.A., Brooks-Gunn, J., & Botvin, G.J. (2006). Sex differences in overt aggression and delinquency among urban minority middle school students. *Applied Developmental Psychology, 27*, 78–91.

Nicholson, R.A., & Kugler, K. (1991). Competent and incompetent criminal defendants: A quantitative review of comparative research. *Psychological Bulletin, 109*, 355–370.

Nilson, C., Jewell, L.M., Camman, C., Appell, R., & Wormith, J.S. (2014). Community-engaged scholarship: The experience of ongoing collaboration between criminal justice professionals and scholars at the University of Saskatchewan. *Criminal Justice Studies: A Critical Journal of Crime, Law and Society, 27*, 264–277.

Nisbett, R.E., & Wilson, T.D. (1977). Telling more than we can know: Verbal reports on mental processes. *Psychological Review, 84*, 231–259.

No DNA match, no JonBenet charges. (2006). Retrieved from www.cnn.com/2006/LAW/08/28/ramsey.arrest/.

Nock, M.K., Kazdin, A.E., Hiripi, E., & Kessler, R.C. (2007). Lifetime prevalence, correlates, and persistence of oppositional defiant disorder: Results from the National Comorbidity Survey replication. *Journal of Child Psychology and Psychiatry, 48*, 703–713.

Nose, I., Murai, J., & Taira, M. (2009). Disclosing concealed information on the basis of cortical activations. *NeuroImage, 44*(4), 1380–1386.

Nunes, K.L., Firestone, P., Wexler, A., Jensen, T.L., & Bradford, J.M. (2007). Incarceration and recidivism among sexual offenders. *Law and Human Behavior, 31*, 305–318.

Nuñez, J.M., Casey, B.J., Egner, T., Hare, T., & Hirsch, J. (2005). Intentional false responding shares neural substrates with response conflict and cognitive control. *Neuroimage, 25*, 267–277.

O'Hara, M.W. (1995). Childbearing. In M.W. O'Hara, R.C. Reiter, S.R. Johnson, A. Milburn, & J. Engeldinger (Eds.), *Psychological aspects of women's reproductive health* (pp. 26–48). New York, NY: Springer.

O'Keefe, M., & Schnell, M.J. (2007). Offenders with mental illness in the correctional system. *Mental Health Issues in the Criminal Justice System*, 45, 81–104. Retrieved from http://jor.haworthpress.com.

O'Malley, M., & Wood, O. (2003). Cruel & unusual: The law and Latimer. *CBC News*. Retrieved from www.cbc.ca/news/background/latimer.

O'Sullivan, M. (2008). Unicorns or Tiger Woods: Are lie detection experts myths or rarities? A response to *On lie detection "Wizards"* by Bond and Uysal. *Law and Human Behavior*, 31, 117–123.

O'Sullivan, M., & Ekman, P. (2004). The wizards of deception detection. In M. O'Sullivan & P. Ekman (Eds.), *The detection of deception in forensic contexts* (pp. 269–286). New York, NY: Guilford.

O'Toole, M. (2007). Psychopathy as a behavior classification system for violent and serial crime scenes. In H. Hervé & J.C. Yuille (Eds.), *The psychopath: Theory, research and practice* (pp. 301–325). Mahway, NJ: Erlbaum.

Odeh, M.S., Zeiss, R.A., & Huss, M.T. (2006). Cues they use: Clinicians' endorsement of risk cues in predictions of dangerousness. *Behavioral Sciences and the Law*, 24, 147–156.

Odgers, C.L., & Moretti, M.M. (2002). Aggressive and antisocial girls: Research update and challenges. *International Journal of Forensic Mental Health*, 1, 103–119.

Odgers, C.L., Moretti, M.M., Burnette, M.L., Chauhan, P., Waite, D., & Reppucci, N.D. (2007). A latent variable modeling approach to identifying subtypes of serious and violent female offenders. *Aggressive Behavior*, 33, 339–352.

Odgers, C.L., Moretti, M.M., & Reppucci, N.D. (2005). Examining the science and practice of violence risk assessment with female adolescents. *Law and Human Behavior*, 29, 7–27.

Odgers, C.L., Reppucci, N.D., & Moretti, M.M. (2005). Nipping psychopathy in the bud: An examination of the convergent, predictive, and theoretical utility of the PCL-YV among adolescent girls. *Behavioral Sciences and the Law*, 23, 743–763.

Odinot, G., Wolters, G., & van Giezen, A. (2013). Accuracy, confidence and consistency in repeated recall of events. *Psychology, Crime & Law*, 19(7), 629–642.

Office of the Correctional Investigator. (2012, October 22). *Spirit matters: Aboriginal people and the corrections and conditional release act*. Retrieved from www.oci-bec.gc.ca/cnt/rpt/oth-aut/oth-aut20121022-eng.aspx.

Offord, D.R., Lipman, E.L., & Duku, E.K. (2001). Epidemiology of problem behaviour up to age 12 years. In R. Loeber & D.P. Farrington (Eds.), *Child delinquents* (pp. 95–134). Thousand Oaks, CA: Sage.

Ofshe, R.J. (1989). Coerced confessions: The logic of seemingly irrational action. *Journal of Cultic Studies*, 6, 1–15.

Ogloff, J.R.P., & Cronshaw, S.F. (2001). Expert psychological testimony: Assisting or misleading the trier of fact. *Canadian Psychology*, 42, 87–91.

Ogloff, J.R.P., & Rose, V.G. (2005). The comprehension of judicial instructions. In N. Brewer and K.D. Williams (Eds.). *Psychology and law: An Empirical Perspective* (pp. 407–444). New York, NY: The Guilford Press.

Ogloff, J.R.P., Schweighofer, A., Turnbull, S., & Whittemore, K. (1992). Empirical research and the insanity defense: How much do we really know? In J.R.P. Ogloff (Ed.), *Psychology and law: The broadening of the discipline* (pp. 171–210). Durham, NC: Carolina Academic Press.

Ogloff, J.R.P., & Vidmar, N. (1994). The effect of pretrial publicity on jurors: A study to compare the relative effects of television and print media in a child sex abuse case. *Law and Human Behavior*, 18, 507–525.

Ogloff, J.R.P., Wallace, D.H., & Otto, R.K. (1991). Competencies in the criminal process. In D.K. Kagehiro & W.S. Laufer (Eds.), *Handbook of psychology and law* (pp. 343–360). New York, NY: Springer Verlag.

Ogrodnik, L. (2008). *Child and youth victims of police-reported violent crime, 2008*. Ottawa, ON: Minister of Industry. Retrieved from www.statcan.gc.ca/pub/85f0033m/85f0033m2010023-eng.pdf.

Öhman, L., Eriksson, A., and Granhag, P. A. (2011). Overhearing the planning of a crime: Do adults outperform children as earwitnesses? *Journal of Police and Criminal Psychology*, 26(2), 118–127.

Oliveira, M. (2010). Canada a hotbed of online dating. *The Globe and Mail*. Retrieved from http://www.theglobeandmail.com/technology/canada-a-hotbed-of-online-dating/article4312016/.

Olver, M.E., Lewis, K., & Wong, S.C.P. (2013). Risk reduction treatment of high-risk psychopathic offender: The relationship of psychopathy and treatment change to violence recidivism. *Personality Disorders: Theory, Research, and Treatment*, 4, 160–167.

Olver, M.E., Neumann, C.S., Wong, S.C.P., & Hare, R.D. (2013). The structural and predictive properties of the psychopathy Checklist–Revised in Canadian aboriginal and non-aboriginal offenders. *Psychological Assessment*, 25, 167–179.

Olver, M.E., Stockdale, K.C., & Wormith, J.S. (2011). A meta-analysis of predictors of offender treatment attrition and its relationship to recidivism. *Journal of Consulting and Clinical Psychology*, 79, 6–21.

Olver, M.E., & Wong, S.C.P. (2006). Psychopathy, sexual deviance, and recidivism among sex offenders. *Sexual Abuse: A Journal of Research and Treatment*, 18, 65–82.

Ontario Human Rights Commission. (2003). *Paying the price: The human cost of racial profiling*. Retrieved from www.ohrc.on.ca/en/paying-price-human-cost-racial-profiling.

Orchard, T.L., & Yarmey, A.D. (1995). The effects of whispers, voice-sample duration, and voice distinctiveness on criminal speaker identification. *Applied Cognitive Psychology*, 9, 249–260.

Orchowski, L.M., Gidycz, C.A., & Murphy, M.J. (2010). Preventing campus-based sexual violence. In K.L. Kaufman (Ed.), *The prevention of sexual violence: A practitioner's sourcebook* (pp. 415–447). Holyoke, MA: NEARI Press.

Ormerod, D. (1999). Criminal profiling: Trial by judge and jury, not criminal psychologist. In D.V. Canter & L.J. Alison (Eds.), *Profiling in policy and practice* (pp. 207–261). Aldershot, England: Ashgate.

Otgaar, H., Horselenberg, R., van Kampen, R., & Lalleman, K. (2012). Clothed and unclothed human figure drawings lead to more correct and incorrect reports of touch in children. *Psychology, Crime & Law*, 18(7), 641–653.

Otto, R., & Heilbrun, K. (2002). The practice of forensic psychology: A look toward the future in light of the past. *American Psychologist*, 57, 5–19.

Otto, R.K., Kay, S.L., & Hess, A.K. (2013). Testifying in court. In I.B. Weiner and R.K. Otto (Eds.), *The Handbook of Forensic Psychology* (4th Edition) (pp. 733–756). Hoboken, NJ: John Wiley and Sons, Inc.

Otto, R.K., & Ogloff, J.R.P. (2013). Defining forensic psychology. In I.B. Weiner and R.K. Otto (Eds.), *The Handbook of Forensic Psychology* (4th Edition) (pp. 35–56). Hoboken, NJ: John Wiley and Sons, Inc.

Ozbaran, B., Erermis, S., Bukusoglu, N., Bildik, T., Tamar, M., Ercan, E.S., Aydin, C., & Cetin, S.K. (2009). Social and emotional outcomes of child sexual abuse: A clinical sample in turkey. *Journal of Interpersonal Violence*, 24(9), 1478–1493.

Page, J.W., Asken, M.J., Zwemer, C.F., & Guido, M. (2015). Brief mental skills training improves memory and performance in high stress police cadet training. *Journal of Police and Criminal Psychology*, 1–5.

Paglia, A., & Schuller, R.A. (1998). Jurors' use of hearsay evidence: The effects of type and timing of instructions. *Law and Human Behavior*, 22, 501–518.

Palys, T.S., & Divorski, S. (1986). Explaining sentencing disparity. *Canadian Journal of Criminology*, 28, 347–362.

Paolucci, E., Genuis, M., & Violato, C. (2001). A meta-analysis of the published research on the effects of child sexual abuse. *Journal of Psychology*, 135, 17–36.

Parker, A.D., & Brown, J. (2000). Detection of deception: Statement Validity Analysis as a means of determining truthfulness or falsity of rape allegations. *Legal and Criminological Psychology*, 5, 237–259.

Parker, J. (1995). Age differences in source monitoring of performed and imagined actions. *Journal of Experimental Child Psychology*, 60, 84–101.

Parker, J.G., & Asher, S.R. (1987). Peer relations and later personal adjustment: Are low accepted children at risk? *Psychological Bulletin*, 102, 357–389.

Parole Board of Canada. (2014). *Performance monitoring report*. Ottawa, ON: Parole Board of Canada.

Parole Board of Canada (PBC). (2016a). *History of parole in Canada*. Retrieved May 2, 2016 from http://pbc-clcc.gc.ca/about/hist-eng.shtml.

Parole Board of Canada (PBC). (2016b). *Fact sheet: Types of release*. Retrieved May 2, 2016 from http://pbc-clcc.gc.ca/infocntr/factsh/rls-eng.shtml.

Parole Board of Canada (PBC). (2016c). *Parole decision-making: Myths and realities*. Retrieved May 2, 2016 from http://www.pbc-clcc.gc.ca/infocntr/myths_reality-eng.shtml.

Parole Board of Canada (PBC). (2016d). *Decision-making policy manual for board members*. Retrieved May 2, 2016 from http://www.pbc-clcc.gc.ca/infocntr/policym/polman-eng.shtml#p2.

Patrick, C.J., Bradley, M.M., & Lang, P.J. (1993). Emotion in the criminal psychopath: Startle reflex modulation. *Journal of Abnormal Psychology*, 102, 82–92.

Patrick, C.J., Fowles, D.C., & Krueger, R.F. (2009). Triarchic conceptualization of psychopathy: Developmental origins of disinhibition, boldness, and meanness. *Development and Psychopathology*, 21, 913–938.

Patrick, C.J., & Iacono, W.G. (1991). Validity of the control question polygraph test: The problem of sampling bias. *Journal of Applied Social Psychology*, 76, 229–238.

Patrick, C.P. (2007). Getting to the heart of psychopathy. In H. Hervé & J.C. Yuille (Eds.), *The psychopath: Theory, research and practice* (pp. 207–252). Mahway, NJ: Erlbaum.

Patry, M.W. (2008). Attractive but guilty: Deliberation and the physical attractiveness bias. *Psychological Reports*, 102, 727–733.

Patterson, G.R., Reid, J.B., & Dishion, T.J. (1998). *Antisocial boys*. Eugene, OR: Castalia.

Paul, G.L., & Lentz, R.J. (1977). *Psychosocial treatment of chronic mental patients: Milieu versus social learning programs*. Cambridge, MA: Harvard University Press.

Paulhus, D.L., Neumann, C.S., & Hare, R.D. (2016). *Manual for the Hare Self-Report Psychopathy scale*. Toronto, ON: Multi-Health Systems.

Paulhus, D.L., Williams, K.M., & Nathanson, C. (2002). *The Dark Triad revisited*. Presented at the 3rd annual meeting of the Society for Personality and Social Psychology, Savannah, GA.

Pavlidis, I., Eberhardt, N.L., & Levine, J.A. (2002). Seeing though the face of deception. *Nature*, 415, 35.

Payne, D.L., Lonsway, K.A., & Fitzgerald, L.F. (1999). Rape myth acceptance: Exploration of its structure and its measurement using the Illinois Rape Myth Acceptance Scale. *Journal of Research in Personality*, 33, 27–68.

Pearson, C., Janz, T., & Ali, J. (2013). *Health at a glance: Mental and substance use disorders in Canada* (No. 82-624-X). Retrieved from Statistics Canada: http://www.statcan.gc.ca/pub/82-624-x/2013001/article/11855-eng.pdf.

Pence, E., & Paymar, M. (1993). *Education groups for men who batter: The Duluth model*. New York, NY: Springer.

Pennington, N., & Hastie, R. (1986). Evidence evaluation in complex decision making. *Journal of Personality and Social Psychology*, 51, 242–258.

Penrod, S.D., & Heuer, L. (1997). Tweaking commonsense: Assessing aids to jury decision making. *Psychology, Public Policy, and Law*, 3, 259–284.

People v. Hawthorne, [1940] 293 Mich. 15.

Perez, D.A., Hosch, H.M., Ponder, B., & Trejo, G.C. (1993). Ethnicity of defendants and jurors as influences on jury decisions. *Journal of Applied Social Psychology*, 23, 1249–1262.

Pérez-Fuentes, G., Olfson, M., Villegas, L., Morcillo, C., Wang, S., & Blanco, C. (2012). Prevalence and correlates of child sexual abuse: A national study. *Comprehensive Psychiatry*, 54(1), 16–27.

Perfect, T., Wagstaff, G.F., Moore, D., Andrews, B., Cleveland, Newcombe, S., Brisbane, K.A., Brown, L. (2008). How can we help witnesses to remember more? It's an (eyes) open and shut case. *Law and Human Behavior*, 32, 314–324.

Perreault, S. (2009). *The incarceration of Aboriginal people in adult correctional services. Juristat*, 29(3). Retrieved from www.statcan.gc.ca/pub/85-002-x/2009003/article/10903-eng.htm.

Perreault, S. (2012). Homicide in Canada, 2011 (Statistics Canada Catalogue no. 85-002-X). *Juristat*. Retrieved from www.statcan.gc.ca/pub/85-002-x/2012001/article/11738-eng.htm.

Perreault, S. (2015). *Criminal victimization in Canada, 2014.* Statistics Canada: Ottawa, ON.

Perreault, S., & Mahoney, T. (2012). Criminal victimization in the territories, 2009 (Statistics Canada Catalogue no. 85-022-X). *Juristat.*

Perreaux, L. (2015). Quebec woman, accused of drowning her three kids, starves herself to death. Retrieved April 4, 2016 from http://www.theglobeandmail.com/news/national/quebec-mother-charged-will-killing-kids-has-starved-to-death-report/article22486442/.

Perri, F.S. (2011). The flawed interview of a psychopathic killer: What went wrong. *Journal of Investigative Psychology and Offender Profiling, 8,* 41–57.

Perusse, D. (2008). *Aboriginal people living off-reserve and the labour market: Estimates from the Labour Force Survey.* Ottawa, ON: Statistics Canada.

Pescosolido, B.A., Monahan, J., Link, B.G. Stueve, A., & Kikuzawa, S. (1999). The public's view of the competence, dangerousness, and need for legal coercion of persons with mental health problems. *American Journal of Public Health, 89,* 1339–1345.

Peterson, C., & Biggs, M. (1997). Interviewing children about trauma: Problems with "specific" questions. *Journal of Traumatic Stress, 10,* 279–290.

Peterson, I.T., Bates, J.E., Dodge, K.A., Lansford, J.E., & Pettit, G.S. (2015). Describing and predicting developmental profiles of externalizing problems from childhood to adulthood. *Development and Psychopathology, 27,* 791–818.

Pezdek K., Morrow A., Blandon-Gitlin I., Goodman G.S., Quas J.A., Saywitz K.J., Bidrose S., Pipe M.E., Rogers M., Brodie L. (2004). Detecting deception in children: Event familiarity affects criterion-based content analysis ratings. *Journal of Applied Psychology, 89,* 119–126.

Philippon, A. C., Randall, L. M., & Cherryman, J. (2013). The impact of laughter in earwitness identification performance. *Psychiatry, Psychology and Law, 20*(6), 887–898.

Phillips, H.K., Gray, N.S., MacCulloch, S.I., Taylor, J., Moore, S.C., Huckle, P., & MacCulloch, M.J. (2005). Risk assessment in offenders with mental disorders: Relative efficacy of personal demographic, criminal history and clinical variables. *Journal of Interpersonal Violence, 20,* 833–847.

Phillips, H.K., Gray, N.S., MacCulloch, S.I., Taylor, J., Moore, S.C., Huckle, P., & MacCulloch, M.J. (2005). Risk assessment in offenders with mental disorders: Relative efficacy of personal demographic, criminal history and clinical variables. *Journal of Interpersonal Violence, 20,* 833–847.

Pickel, K.L. (1998). Unusualness and threat as possible causes of weapon focus. *Memory, 6,* 277–295.

Pickel, K.L. (1999). The influence of context on the "weapon focus" effect. *Law and Human Behavior, 23,* 299–311.

Pickel, K.L., Karam, T.J., & Warner, T.C. (2009). Jurors' responses to unusual inadmissible evidence. *Criminal Justice and Behavior, 36,* 466–480.

Pickel, K.L., Ross, S.J., & Truelove, R.S. (2006). Do weapons automatically capture attention? *Applied Cognitive Psychology, 20,* 871–893.

Pickel, K.L., & Staller, J.B. (2012). A perpetrator's accent impairs witnesses' memory for physical appearance. *Law and Human Behavior, 36,* 140–150.

Pinizzotto, A.J., & Davis, E.F. (1992). *Killed in the line of duty.* Washington, DC: Department of Justice, FBI Uniform Crime Reporting Program.

Pinizzotto, A.J., & Finkel, N.J. (1990). Criminal personality profiling: An outcome and process study. *Law and Human Behavior, 14,* 215–233.

Piquero, A.R., Blumstein, A., Brame, R., Haapanen, R., Mulvey, E.P., & Nagin, D.S. (2001). Assessing the impact of exposure time and incapacitation on longitudinal trajectories of criminal offending. *Journal of Adolescent Research, 16,* 54–74.

Piquero, A.R., & Chung, H.L. (2001). On the relationships between gender, early onset, and the seriousness of offending. *Journal of Criminal Justice, 29,* 189–206.

Pirelli, G., Gottdiener, W., & Zapf, P. (2011). A meta-analytic review of competency to stand trial research. *Psychology, Public Policy, and Law, 17,* 1–53.

Pithers, W.D., Martin, G.R., & Cumming, G.F. (1989). Vermont Treatment Program for Sexual Aggressors. In R.D. Laws (Ed.), *Relapse prevention with sex offenders* (pp. 292–310). New York, NY: Guilford Press.

Platz, S.J., & Hosch, M. (1988). Cross-racial/ethnic eyewitness identification: A field study. *Journal of Applied Social Psychology, 18,* 972–984.

Plecas, D., Cohen, I.M., Mahaffy, A., & Burk, K. (2013). *Do judges take prior record into consideration? An analysis of the sentencing of repeat offenders in British Columbia.* Abbotsford, BC: University of the Fraser Valley.

Polanczyk, G.V., Salum, G.A., Sugaya, L.S., Caye, A., & Rhode, L.A. (2015). Annual research review: A meta-analysis of the worldwide prevalence of mental disorders in children and adolescents. *Journal of Child Psychology and Psychiatry, 56,* 345–365.

Polaschek, D.L.L., & Collie, R.M. (2004). Rehabilitating serious adult violent offenders: An empirical and theoretical stocktake. *Psychology, Crime & Law, 10,* 321–334.

Poole, D. A., & Bruck, M. (2012). Divining testimony? The impact of interview props on children's reports of touching. *Developmental Review, 32*(3), 165–180.

Poole, D. A., & Dickinson, J. J. (2011). Evidence supporting restrictions on uses of body diagrams in forensic interviews. *Child Abuse & Neglect, 35*(9), 659–669.

Pope, H.G., Jonas, J.M., & Jones, B. (1982). Factitious psychosis: Phenomenology, family history, and long-term outcome of nine patients. *American Journal of Psychiatry, 139,* 1480–1483.

Porporino, F.J., & Motiuk, L.L. (1995). The prison careers of mentally disordered offenders. *International Journal of Law and Psychiatry, 18,* 29–44.

Porter, S., & Birt, A.R. (2001). Is traumatic memory special? A comparison of traumatic memory characteristics with memory for other emotional life experiences. *Applied Cognitive Psychology, 15,* S101–S117.

Porter, S., Birt, A., & Boer, D.P. (2001). Investigation of the criminal and conditional release profiles of Canadian federal offenders as a function of psychopathy and age. *Law and Human Behavior, 25,* 647–661.

Porter, S., Fairweather, D., Drugge, J., Herve, H., Birt, A., & Boer, D.P. (2000). Profiles of psychopathy in incarcerated sexual offenders. *Criminal Justice and Behavior, 27*, 216–233.

Porter, S., Juodis, M., ten Brinke, L., Klein, R. & Wilson, K. (2010). Evaluation of a brief deception detection training program. *Journal of Forensic Psychiatry & Psychology, 21*, 66–76.

Porter, S., & ten Brinke, L. (2008). Reading between the lies: How do facial expressions reveal concealed and fabricated emotions? *Psychological Science, 19*, 508–514.

Porter, S., ten Brinke, L., & Wilson, K. (2009). Crime profiles and conditional release performance of psychopathic and nonpsychopathic offenders. *Legal and Criminological Psychology, 14*, 109–118.

Porter, S., Woodworth, M., & Birt, A. (2000). Truth, lies, and videotape: An investigation of the ability of federal parole officers to detect deception. *Law and Human Behavior, 24*, 643–658.

Porter, S., Woodworth, M., Earle, J., Drugge, J., & Boer, D. (2003). Characteristics of sexual homicides committed by psychopathic and nonpsychopathic offenders. *Law and Human Behavior, 27*, 459–470.

Powell, B. (2009, February 2). Order to take off niqab pits law against religion. TheStar.com. Retrieved from www.thestar.com/printarticle/580790.

Powell, M., Murfett, R., & Thomson, D.M. (2010). An analysis of police officers' decisions about whether to refer cases of child abuse for prosecution. *Psychology, Crime and Law, 16*(8), 715–724.

Poythress, N.G., Petrila, J., McGaha, A., & Boothroyd, R. (2002). Perceived coercion and procedural justice in the Broward mental health court. *International Journal of Law and Psychiatry, 25*, 517–533.

Pozzulo, J.D., & Balfour, J. (2006). The impact of change in appearance on children's eyewitness identification accuracy: Comparing simultaneous and elimination lineup procedures. *Legal and Criminological Psychology, 11*, 25–34.

Pozzulo, J.D., Dempsey, J., & Crescini, C. (2009). Preschoolers' person description and identification accuracy: A comparison of the simultaneous and elimination lineup procedures. *Journal of Applied Developmental Psychology, 30*, 667–676.

Pozzulo, J.D., Dempsey, J., Bruer, K., & Sheahan, C. (2012). The culprit in target-absent lineups: Understanding young children's false positive responding. *Journal of Police and Criminal Psychology, 27*(1), 55–62. doi:10.1007/s11896-011-9089-8

Pozzulo, J.D., Dempsey, J., Corey, S., Girardi, A., Lawandi, A., & Aston, C. (2008). Can a lineup procedure designed for child witnesses work for adults: Comparing simultaneous, sequential, and elimination lineup procedures. *Journal of Applied Social Psychology, 38*, 2195–2209.

Pozzulo, J.D., Dempsey, J., Maeder, E., & Allen, L. (2010). The effects of victim gender, defendant gender, and defendant age on juror decision making. *Criminal Justice and Behavior, 37*, 47–63.

Pozzulo, J.D., & Lindsay, R.C.L. (1998). Identification accuracy of children versus adults: A meta-analysis. *Law and Human Behavior, 22*, 549–570.

Pozzulo, J.D., & Lindsay, R.C.L. (1999). Elimination lineups: An improved identification procedure for child eyewitnesses. *Journal of Applied Psychology, 84*, 167–176.

Pozzulo, J.D., & Warren, K.L. (2003). Descriptions and identifications of strangers by youth and adult eyewitnesses. *Journal of Applied Psychology, 88*, 315–323.

Pratt, T.C., & Cullen, F.T. (2000). The empirical status of Gottfredsson and Hirschi's General Theory of Crime: A meta analysis. *Criminology, 38*, 931–964.

Prentky, R.A., Knight, R.A., Lee, A.F.S., & Cerce, D.D. (1995). Predictive validity of lifestyle impulsivity for rapists. *Criminal Justice and Behavior, 22*, 106–128.

Proctor, J. (2016). Convicted teen killer Kelly Ellard denied day parole. Retrieved May 4, 2016 from http://www.cbc.ca/news/canada/british-columbia/reena-virk-kelly-ellard-day-parole-1.3564981.

Proulx, J., Beauregard, E., Cusson, M., & Nicole, A. (2007). *Sexual murder: A comparative analysis and new perspectives.* Winchester, UK: Wiley.

Pryke, S., Lindsay, R.C.L., Dysart, J.E., & Dupuis, P. (2004). Multiple independent identification decisions: A method of calibrating eyewitness identifications. *Journal of Applied Psychology, 89*, 73–84.

Public Safety Canada. (2012). *Corrections and conditional release statistical overview 2012.* Ottawa, ON: Public Works and Government Services Canada.

Public Safety Canada (2015). Corrections and conditional release statistical overview: Annual report 2014. Ottawa, ON: Author.

Public Safety Canada Portfolio Corrections Statistics Committee. (2007). *Corrections and conditional release statistical overview.* Ottawa, ON: Public Works and Government Services Canada.

Public Safety Canada Portfolio Corrections Statistics Committee. (2014). *Corrections and conditional release statistical overview, 2014 annual report.* Retrieved from https://www.publicsafety.gc.ca/cnt/rsrcs/pblctns/2014-ccrs/2014-ccrs-eng.pdf.

Pugh, G. (1985a). The California Psychological Inventory and police selection. *Journal of Police Science and Administration, 13*, 172–177.

Pugh, G. (1985b). Situation tests and police selection. *Journal of Police Science and Administration, 13*, 31–35.

Putnam, F.W. (2003). Ten-year research update review: Child sexual abuse. *Journal of the American Academy of Child Adolescent Psychiatry, 42*, 269–278.

Pynes, J., & Bernardin, H.J. (1992). Entry-level police selection: The assessment centre as an alternative. *Journal of Criminal Justice, 20*, 41–52.

Quan, D. (2010, March 25). Stop isolating mentally ill inmates: Ombudsman. *Canwest News Service.* Retrieved from www.globalmontreal.com/health/Stop+isolaing+mentally+inmates+Ombudsman/2726481/story.html?hub=WFive.

Quann, N., & Trevethan, S. (2000). *Police-reported Aboriginal crime in Saskatchewan.* Ottawa, ON: Statistics Canada.

Quas, J., Schaaf, J., Alexander, K., & Goodman, G. (2000). Do you really remember it happening or do you only remember being asked about it happening. In K.P. Roberts & M. Blades (Eds.), *Children's source monitoring* (pp. 197–226). Mahwah, NJ: Lawrence Erlbaum Associates.

Quayle, J. (2008). Interviewing a psychopathic suspect. *Journal of Investigative Psychology and Offender Profiling, 5*, 79–91.

Quinsey, V.L., & Ambtman, R. (1979). Variables affecting psychiatrists' and teachers' assessments of the dangerousness of mentally ill offenders. *Journal of Consulting and Clinical Psychology, 47*, 353–362.

Quinsey, V.L., & Earls, C.M. (1990). The modification of sexual preferences. In W.L. Marshall & D.R. Laws, *Handbook of sexual assault: Issues, theories, and treatment of the offender* (pp. 279–295). New York, NY: Plenum Press.

Quinsey, V.L., Harris, G.T., Rice, M.E., & Cormier, C. (1998). *Violent offenders: Appraising and managing risk.* Washington, DC: American Psychological Association.

Quinsey, V.L., Harris, G.T., Rice, M.E., & Lalumière, M.L. (1993). Assessing the treatment efficacy in outcome studies of sex offenders. *Journal of Interpersonal Violence, 8*, 512–523.

Quinsey, V.L., Jones, G.B., Book, A.S., & Barr, K.N. (2006). They dynamic prediction of antisocial behavior among forensic psychiatric patients: A prospective field study. *Journal of Interpersonal Violence, 21*, 1539–1565.

Quinsey, V.L., Khanna, A., & Malcolm, P.B. (1998). A retrospective evaluation of the regional treatment centre sex offender treatment program. *Journal of Interpersonal Violence, 13*, 621–644.

Quinsey, V.L., & Lalumière, M. L. (1995). Evolutionary perspectives on sexual offending. *Sexual Abuse: Journal of Research and Treatment, 7*, 301–315.

Quinsey, V.L., & Maguire, A. (1983). Offenders remanded for a psychiatric examination: Perceived treatability and disposition. *International Journal of Law and Psychiatry, 6*, 193–205.

Quinsey, V.L., Rice, M.E., & Harris, G.T. (1995). Actuarial prediction of sexual recidivism. *Journal of Interpersonal Violence, 10*, 85–105.

R. v. Andrade, [1985] 18 CCC (3d) 41 (Ont CA).

R. v. Arcand, [2010] ABCA 363 (CanLII).

R. v. Arenburg, [1997] O.J. No. 2386.

R. v. Balliram, [2003] O.J. No. 784.

R. v. Beaudry, [2007] 1 S.C.R. 190, 2007 SCC 5.

R. v. Béland, [1987] 2 S.C.R. 398.

R. v. Brown, [2005] SKCA 7.

R. v. Budai, Gill, and Kim, [2001] BCCA 198.

R. v. Chapple, [2012] ABPC 229.

R. v. D.D., [2000] 2 S.C.R. 275.

R v. Darrach, [2000] 2 SCR 443.

R. v. Davey, [2012] SCC 75.

R. v. Daviault, [1994] 3 S.C.R. 63.

R. v. Demers, [2004] 2 S.C.R. 489, 2004 SCC 46.

R. v. Find, [2001] SCC 32.

R. v. Gayme, [1991] 2 SCR 577.

R. v. Gill, [2002] BCSC 977.

R. v. Gladue, [1999] 1 S.C.R. 688.

R. v. Gladue, [1999] 1 S.C.R. 688.

R. v. Guess, [1998] BCCA 602.

R. v. Hart, [2014] SCC 52, 2 S.C.R. 544.

R. v. Henderson, [2009] SKQB 449 (CanLII).

R. v. Hubbert, [1975] 29 C.C.C. (2d) 279.

R. v. Ipeelee, [2012] SCC 13, [2012] 1 S.C.R. 433.

R. v. Kliman, [1998] 15078 (BC SC).

R. v. L.T.H., [2008] 2 S.C.R. 739, 2008 SCC 49.

R. v. Latimer, [2001] 1 S.C.R. 3.

R. v. Lavallee, [1990] 1 S.C.R. 852.

R. v. Levogiannis, [1993] 4 S.C.R. 475.

R. v. Lyons, [1987] 2 S.C.R. 309.

R. v. M.J.S., [2000] A.J. 391.

R. v. Mack, [1988] 2 SCR 903.

R. v. McIntosh and McCarthy, [1997] 117 CCC (3d) 385 (Ont. CA).

R. v. McLeod, [2005] ABQB 842.

R. v. McNaughton, [1843] All ER Rep 229.

R. v. Mentuck, [2001] 3 SCR 442.

R. v. Mohan, [1994] 2 S.C.R. 9.

R. v. Moore v. the Queen, [1984] 1 SCR 195.

R. v. Morgentaler, [1988] 1 SCR 30, 44 DLR (4th) 385.

R. v. Nepoose, [1991] 5967 (AB QB).

R. v. NS, [2012] 3 SCR 726.

R. v. Oickle, [2000] 2 S.C.R. 3.

R. v. Oickle, [2000] 2 S.C.R. 3.

R. v. Parks, [1992] 2 S.C.R. 871.

R. v. Poulin, [2002] NSCA 91 (CanLII).

R. v. Prichard, [1836] 7 C. & P. 303.

R. v. Saphonow, [1984] 2 S.C.R. 524.

R. v. Seaboyer, [1991] 2 SCR 577.

R. v. Sherratt, [1991] 1 S.C.R. 509.

R. v. Sophonow (no. 2) [1986], 25 C.C.C. (3d) 415 (Man. C.A.).

R. v. Sterling, [1995] 4037 (SK CA).

R. v. Stone, [1999] 2 S.C.R. 290.

R. v. Swain, [1991] 1 S.C.R. 933.

R. v. Symes, [2005] O.J. No. 6041 (C.J.).

R. v. Taylor, [1992] 77 C.C.C. (3d) 551.

R. v. Williams, [1998] 1 S.C.R. 1128.

Rainbow, L. (2008). Taming the beast: The UK approach to the management of behavioural investigative advice. *Journal of Police and Criminal Psychology, 23*, 90–97.

Ramey, S., Downing, N., & Franke, W. (2009). Milwaukee police department retirees: Cardiovascular disease risk and morbidity among aging law enforcement officers. *AAOHN Journal, 57*, 448–453.

Ramsland, K. (n.d.-a). Marc Lépine's gendercide: The Montreal massacre. *Crime Library.* Retrieved from www.trutv.com/library/crime/notorious_murders/mass/marc_lepine/index.html.

Ramsland, K. (n.d.-b). Movies made me murder. *Crime Libr* Retrieved from www.trutv.com/library/crime/criminal_ psychology/movies_made_me_kill/14.html.

Raphael, B., & Wilson, J.P. (Eds.). (2000). *Psychological ge Theory, practice and evidence.* Cambridge, England: University Press.

Raskin, D.C., & Esplin, P.W. (1991). Statement ment: Interview procedures and content anal statements of sexual abuse. *Behavioral Asses* ...

Raskin, D.C., Honts, C.R., & Kircher, J.C. (19 tus of research on polygraph techniques

tests. In D.L. Faigman, D. Kaye, M.J. Saks, & J. Sanders (Eds.), *Modern scientific evidence: The law and science of expert testimony* (pp. 565–582). St. Paul, MN: West.

Rasmussen, L.A., Burton, J.E., & Christopherson, B.J. (1992). Precursors to offending and the trauma outcome process in sexually reactive children. *Journal of Child Sexual Abuse, 1*, 33–48.

Raudino, A., Fergusson, D.M., Woodward, J.L., & Horwood, L.J. (2013). The intergenerational transmission of conduct problems. *Social Psychiatry and Psychiatric Epidemiology, 48*, 465–476.

Read, J.D. (1999). The recovered/false memory debate: Three steps forward, two steps back? *Expert Evidence, 7*, 1–24.

Read, J.D., Connolly, D.A., & Welsh, A. (2006). An archival analysis of actual cases of historic child sexual abuse: A comparison of jury and bench trials. *Law and Human Behavior, 30*, 259–285.

Read, J.D., & Desmarais, S.L. (2009). Lay knowledge of eyewitness issues: A Canadian evaluation. *Applied Cognitive Psychology, 23*, 301–326.

Reiser, M. (1982). *Police psychology: Collected papers*. Los Angeles, CA: LEHI.

Reiser, M. (1989). Investigative hypnosis. In D. Raskin (Ed.), *Psychological methods in criminal investigation and evidence* (pp. 151–190). New York, NY: Springer.

Rengel killer sentenced to life. (2009, September 28). *CBC News*. Retrieved from www.cbc.ca/canada/toronto/story/2009/09/28/rengel-killer-sentencing265.html.

Rennie, C.E., & Dolan, M.C. (2010). The significance of protective factors in the assessment of risk. *Criminal Behaviour and Mental Health, 20*(1), 8–22.

Renzema, M., & Mayo-Wilson, E. (2005). Can electronic monitoring reduce crime for moderate to high-risk offenders? *Journal of Experimental Criminology, 1*, 215–237.

Resick, P.A. (1993). The psychological impact of rape. *Journal of Interpersonal Violence, 8*, 223–255.

Resnick, P.J. (1969). Child murder by parents: A psychiatric review of filicide. *American Journal of Psychiatry, 126*, 325–334.

Resnick, P.J. (1970). Murder of the newborn: A psychiatric review of neonaticide. *American Journal of Psychiatry, 126*, 1414–1420.

Resnick, P.J. (1997). Malingered psychosis. In R. Rogers (Ed.), *Clinical assessment of malingering and deception* (2nd ed., pp. 47–67). New York, NY: Guilford Press.

Ressler, R.K., Burgess, A.W., & Douglas, J.E. (1988). *Sexual homicide: Patterns and motives*. New York, NY: Free Press.

Ressler, R.K., Burgess, A.W., Douglas, J.E., Hartman, C.R., & D'Agostino, R.B. (1986). Sexual killers and their victims: Identifying patterns through crime scene analysis. *Journal of Interper-*
Real *Violence, 1*, 288–308.

P. (1995, July 25). Consider "9 days of deceit" prosecu-
Reute Smith jury. *Toronto Star*, p. A4.

Re). U.S. judge sentences men to dress as women.
sent om www.zipadeeday.com/story/103/u.s.-judge-
Reynolds, to-dress-as-women/.
Long-te
tional ac, J.A., Robertson, D., & Mann, E.A. (2001).
low-incom an early childhood intervention on educa-
Medical As juvenile arrest: A 15 year follow-up of
ublic schools. *Journal of the American*
339–2346.

Rice, M.E., & Harris, G.T. (1990). The predictors of insanity acquittal. *International Journal of Law and Psychiatry, 13*, 217–224.

Rice, M.E., & Harris, G.T. (1997a). Cross validation and extension of the Violence Risk Appraisal Guide with child molesters and rapists. *Law and Human Behavior, 21*, 231–241.

Rice, M.E., & Harris, G.T. (1997b). The treatment of mentally disordered offenders. *Psychology, Public Policy, and Law, 3*, 126–183.

Rice, M.E., Harris, G.T., & Cormier, C.A. (1992). An evaluation of a maximum security therapeutic community for psychopaths and other mentally disordered offenders. *Law and Human Behavior, 16*, 399–412.

Richards, H.J., Casey, J.O., & Lucente, S.W. (2003). Psychopathy and treatment response in response to incarcerated female substance abusers. *Criminal Justice and Behavior, 30*, 251–276.

Risin, L.I., & Koss, M.P. (1987). The sexual abuse of boys: Prevalence and descriptive characteristics of childhood victimizations. *Journal of Interpersonal Violence, 2*, 309–323.

Robert Baltovitch: Not guilty. (2008, April 22). *CBC News*. Retrieved from www.cbc.ca/news/background/baltovich_robert/.

Roberts, J.V. (1991). Sentencing reform: The lessons of psychology. *Canadian Psychology, 32*, 466–477.

Roberts, J.V. (2012). Structuring sentencing in Canada, England and Wales: A tale of two jurisdictions. *Criminal Law Forum, 23*, 319–345.

Roberts, J.V., & Bebbington, H. H. (2013). Sentencing reform in Canada: Promoting a return to principles and evidence-based policy. *Canadian Criminal Law Review, 17*, 327–348.

Roberts, J.V., & Melchers, R. (2003). The incarceration of Aboriginal offenders: Trends from 1978 to 2001. *Canadian Journal of Criminology and Criminal Justice, 45*, 211–242.

Roberts, R.E., Ramsay Roberts, C., & Xing, Y. (2007). Rates of DSM-IV psychiatric disorders among adolescents in a large metropolitan area. *Journal of Psychiatric Research, 41*, 959–967.

Robins, L.N. (1986). The consequences of conduct disorder in girls. In D. Olweus, J. Block, & M. Radke-Yarrow (Eds.), *Development of antisocial and prosocial behavior* (pp. 385–408). New York, NY: Academic Press.

Roe *v.* Wade, [1973] 410 U.S. 113.

Roebers, C.M., Bjorklund, D.F., Schneider, W., & Cassel, W.S. (2002). Differences and similarities in event recall and suggestibility between children and adults in Germany and the United States. *Experimental Psychology, 49*, 132–140.

Roesch, R., Eaves, D., Sollner, R., Normandin, M., & Glackman, W. (1981). Evaluating fitness to stand trial: A comparative analysis of fit and unfit defendants. *International Journal of Law and Psychiatry, 4*, 145, 157.

Roesch, R., Ogloff, J.R.P., Hart, S.D., Dempster, R.J., Zapf, P.A., & Whittemore, K.E. (1997). The impact of Canadian Criminal Code changes on remands and assessments of fitness to stand trial and criminal responsibility in British Columbia. *Canadian Journal of Psychiatry, 42*, 509–514.

Roesch, R., Zapf, P.A., Eaves, D., & Webster, C.D. (1998). *The Fitness Interview Test* (rev. ed.) [Interview test]. Burnaby, BC: Mental Health Law, and Policy Institute, Simon Fraser University.

Rogers, R. (1984). *Rogers Criminal Responsibility Assessment Scales*. Odessa, FL: Psychological Assessment Resources.

Rogers, R. (1986). *Conducting insanity evaluations*. New York, NY: Van Nostrand Reinhold.

Rogers, R. (1988). Structured interviews and dissimulation. In R. Rogers (Ed.), *Clinical assessment of malingering and deception* (1st ed., pp. 250–268). New York, NY: Guilford Press.

Rogers, R. (1990). Models of feigned mental illness. *Professional Psychology, 21*, 182–188.

Rogers, R. (1997). Structured interviews and dissimulation. In R. Rogers (Ed.), *Clinical assessment of malingering and deception* (2nd ed., pp. 301–327). New York, NY: Guilford Press.

Rogers, R. (2008). *Clinical assessment of malingering and deception* (3rd ed.). New York, NY: Guilford Press.

Rogers, R., Bagby, R.M., & Dickens, S.E. (1992). *Structured Interview of Reported Symptoms (SIRS) and professional manual*. Odessa, FL: Psychological Assessment Resources.

Rogers, R., & Ewing, C.P. (1992). The measurement of insanity: Debating the merits of the R-CRAS and its alternatives. *International Journal of Law and Psychiatry, 15*, 113–123.

Rogers, R., Gillard, N.D., Berry, D.T.R., & Granacher, R.P. (2011). Effectiveness of the MMPI-2-RF validity scales for feigned mental disorders and cognitive impairment: A known-groups study. *Journal of Psychopathology and Behavioral Assessment, 33*, 355–367.

Rogers, R., & Sewell, K.W. (1999). The R-CRAS and insanity evaluations: A reexamination of construct validity. *Behavioral Sciences and the Law, 17*, 181–194.

Rogers, R., Sewell, K.W., & Gillard, N.D. (2010). *SIRS-2: Structured Interview of Reported Symptoms: Professional manual*. Lutz, FL: Psychological Assessment Resources.

Rogers, R., Sewell, K.W., & Goldstein, A.M. (1994). Explanatory models of malingering: A prototypical analysis. *Law and Human Behavior, 18*, 543–552.

Rogers, R., Sewell, K.W., Martin, M.A., & Vitacco, J.J. (2003). Detection of feigned mental disorders: A meta-analysis of the MMPI-2 and malingering. Assessment, 10, 160–177.

Rogers, R., Ustad, K.L., & Salekin, R.T. (1998). Convergent validity of the Personality Assessment Inventory: A study of emergency referrals in a correctional setting. *Assessment, 5*, 3–12.

Rojas, E.Y., & Gretton, H.M. (2007). Background, offence characteristics, and criminal outcomes of Aboriginal youth who sexually offend: A closer look at Aboriginal youth intervention needs. *Sexual Abuse, 19*(3): 257–283.

Roma, P., Martini, P.S., Sabatello, U., Tatarelli, R., & Ferracuti, S. (2011). Validity of criteria-based content analysis (CBCA) at trial in free-narrative interviews. *Child Abuse & Neglect, 35*(8), 613–620.

Rose, V.G., Chopra, S.R., & Ogloff, J.P. (2001, June). *The perceptions and reactions of real Canadian jurors*. Paper presented at the annual convention of the Canadian Psychological Association, Ste.-Foy, Quebec.

Rosenbaum, M. (1990). The role of depression in couples involved in murder-suicide and homicide. *American Journal of Psychiatry, 147*, 1036–1039.

Rosenberg, D.A. (1987). A web of deceit: A literature review of Munchausen syndrome by proxy. *Child Abuse & Neglect, 11*, 547–563.

Rosenfeld, B. (2004). Violence risk factors in stalking and obsessional harassment: A review and preliminary meta-analysis. *Criminal Justice and Behavior, 31*, 9–36.

Rosenfeld, J.P., Angell, A., Johnson, M., & Qian, J. (1991). An ERP-based, control-question lie detector analog: Algorithms for discriminating effects within individuals' average waveforms. Psychophysiology, 38, 319–335.

Rosenfeld, J.P., Nasman, V.T., Whalen, R., Cantwell, B., & Mazzeri, L. (1987). Late vertex positivity in event-related potentials as a guilty knowledge indicator: A new method of lie detection. *Polygraph, 16*, 223–231.

Rosenhan, D.L. (1973). On being sane in insane places. *Science, 179*, 250–257.

Rossmo, D.K. (1995). Place, space and police investigations: Hunting serial violent criminals. In J.E. Eck & D. Weisburd (Eds.), *Crime and place* (pp. 217–235). Monsey, NY: Criminal Justice Press.

Rossmo, D.K. (2000). *Geographic profiling*. Boca Raton, FL: CRC Press.

Rothbaum, B.O., Foa, E.B., Riggs, D., Murdock, T., & Walsh, W. (1992). A prospective examination of post-traumatic stress disorder in rape victims. *Journal of Traumatic Stress, 5*, 455–475.

Rowe, R., Costello, E.J., Angold, A., Copeland, W.E., & Maughan, B. (2010). Developmental pathways in oppositional defiant disorder and conduct disorder. *Journal of Abnormal Psychology, 119*, 726–738.

Royal Canadian Mounted Police (RCMP). (2016). *Behavioural Sciences*. Retrieved March 31, 2016 from http://www.rcmp-grc.gc.ca/to-ot/cpcmec-ccpede/bs-sc/bs-sc-broch-eng.htm.

Royal Canadian Mounted Police (RCMP). (2016a). *How to apply*. Retrieved March 4, 2016 from http://www.rcmp-grc.gc.ca/en/how-to-apply.

Royal Canadian Mounted Police (RCMP). (2016b). *RCMP entrance exam*. Retrieved March 4, 2016 from http://www.rcmp-grc.gc.ca/en/rcmp-entrance-exam.

Royal Canadian Mounted Police (RCMP). (2016c). *Incident management/intervention model*. Retrieved March 4, 2016 from http://www.rcmp-grc.gc.ca/ccaps-spcca/cew-ai/imim-migi-eng.htm.

Royal Newfoundland Constabulary. (2010). *Report on police service activities (2009–2010)*. Retrieved from www.rnc.gov.nl.ca/publications/pdf/RNC_Report_on_Police_Service_Activities.pdf.

Ruby, C.L., & Brigham, J.C. (1997). The usefulness of the criteria-based content analysis technique in distinguishing between truthful and fabricated allegations: A critical review. *Psychology, Public Policy, and Law, 3*, 705–727.

Ruddell, R., Lithopoulos, S., & Jones, N.A. (2014). Crime, costs, and well-being: Policing Canadian Aboriginal communities. *Policing: An International Journal of Police Strategies and Management, 37*, 779–793.

Rudin, J. (2006). *Aboriginal peoples and the criminal justice system*. Retrieved April 29, 2016 from http://www.archives.gov.on.ca/en/e_records/ipperwash/policy_part/research/pdf/Rudin.pdf.

Rudin, J. (2008). Aboriginal over-representation and *R. v. Gladue*: Where we were, where we are and where we might be going. *Supreme Court Law Review, 40*, 687–713.

Rudin, J. (2013). There must be some kind of way out of here: Aboriginal over-representation, Bill-C-10, and the Charter of Rights. *Canadian Criminal Law Review, 17*, 349–363.

Rudolph, K.D., & Asher, S.R. (2000). Adaptation and maladaptation in the peer system: Developmental processes and outcomes. In A.J. Sameroff, M. Lewis, & S.M. Miller (Eds.), *Handbook of developmental psychopathology* (2nd ed., pp. 157–175). New York, NY: Kluwer Academic/Plenum Publishers.

Russano, M.B., Meissner, C.A., Narchet, F.M., & Kassin, S.M. (2005). Investigating true and false confessions within a novel experimental paradigm. *Psychological Science, 16*, 481–486.

Rutherford, M.J., Alterman, A.I., Cacciola, J.S., & McKay, J.R. (1997). Validity of the psychopathy checklist-revised in male methadone patients. *Drug and Alcohol Dependence, 44*, 143–149.

Rutter, M. (1979). Protective factors in children's responses to stress and disadvantage. In M.W. Kent & J.E. Rolf (Eds.), *Primary Prevention of Psychopathology, Vol. 3: Social Competence in Children* (pp. 49–74). Hanover, NH: University Press of New England.

Rutter, M. (1988). *Studies of psychosocial risk: The power of longitudinal data.* Cambridge, MA: Cambridge University Press.

Rutter, M. (1990). Psychosocial resilience and protective mechanisms. In J. Rolf, A.S. Masten, D. Cicchetti, K. Nuechterlein, & S. Weintraub (Eds.), *Risk and protective factors in the development of psychopathology* (pp. 181–214). Cambridge, MA: Cambridge University Press.

Ruva, C., Dickman, M., & Mayes, J. (2014). Exposure to both positive and negative pretrial publicity reduces or eliminates mock-juror bias. *International Journal of Psychology and Behavioral Sciences, 4*, 30–40.

Ruva, C., McEvoy, C., & Bryant, J. (2007). Effects of pre-trial publicity and jury deliberation on juror bias and source memory errors. *Applied Cognitive Psychology, 21*, 45–67.

Ruva, C.L., Guenther, C.C., & Yarbrough, A. (2011). Positive and negative pretrial publicity: The roles of impression formation, emotion, and predecisional distortion. *Criminal Justice and Behavior, 38*(5), 511–534.

Ruva, C.L., & McEvoy, C. (2008). Negative and positive pretrial publicity affect juror memory and decision making. *Journal of Experimental Psychology: Applied, 14*, 226–235.

Ryan, G., Miyoshi, T.J., Metzner, J.L., Krugman, R.D., & Fryer, G.E. (1996). Trends in a national sample of sexually abusive youths. *Journal of the American Academy of Child and Adolescent Psychiatry, 35*, 17–25.

Saks, M.J., & Marti, M.W. (1997). A meta-analysis of the effects of jury size. *Law and Human Behavior, 21*, 451–466.

Salbach-Andrae, H., Klinkowski, N., Lenz, K., & Lehmkuhl, U. (2009). Agreement between youth-reported and parent-reported psychopathology in a referred sample. *European Child Adolescent Psychiatry, 18*, 136–143.

Salbach-Andrae, H., Lenz, K., & Lehmkuhl, U. (2009). Patterns of agreement among parent, teacher and youth ratings in a referred sample. *European Psychiatry, 24*, 345–351.

Salekin, R.T. (2002). Factor-analysis of the Millon Adolescent Clinical Inventory in a juvenile offender population: Implications for treatment. *Journal of Offender Rehabilitation, 34*, 15–29.

Salekin, R.T., Lee, Z., Schrum Dillard, C.L., & Kubak, F.A. (2010). Child psychopathy and protective factors: IQ and motivation to change. *Psychology, Public Policy, and Law, 16*(2), 158–176.

Salekin, R.T., Lester, W.S., & Sellers, M.K. (2012). Mental sets in conduct problem youth with psychopathic features: Entity versus incremental theories of intelligence. *Law and Human Behavior, 36*, 283–292.

Salekin, R.T., Rogers, R., & Machin, D. (2001). Psychopathy in youth: Pursuing diagnostic clarity. *Journal of Youth and Adolescence, 30*, 173–195.

Salmon, K., Pipe, M.-E., Malloy, A., & MacKay (2012). Do nonverbal aids increase the effectiveness of 'best practice' verbal interview techniques? An experimental study. *Applied Cognitive Psychology, 26*(3), 370–380.

Sampson, R.J., & Laub, J.H. (2005). A life-course view of the development of crime. *Annals of the American Academy of Political and Social Science, 602*, 12–45.

Sanders, B.A. (2003). Maybe there's no such thing as a "good cop": Organizational challenges in selecting quality officers. *Policing: An International Journal of Police Strategies and Management, 26*, 313–328.

Sanders, B.A. (2008). Using personality traits to predict police officer performance. *Policing: An International Journal of Police Strategies and Management, 31*, 129–147.

Sapers, H. (2008, June 20). *A preventable death.* Ottawa, ON: Office of the Correctional Investigator.

Sarteschi, C.M., Vaughn, M.G., & Kim, K. (2011). Assessing the effectiveness of mental health courts: A quantitative analysis. *Journal of Criminal Justice, 39*, 12–20.

Saslove, H., & Yarmey, A.D. (1980). Long-term auditory memory: Speaker identification. *Journal of Applied Psychology, 65*, 111–116.

Sauerland, M., & Sporer, S.L. (2011). Written vs. spoken eyewitness accounts: Does modality of testing matter? *Behavioral Sciences & the Law, 29*(6), 846–857.

Saunders, D.G. (2001). Developing guidelines for domestic violence offenders: What can we learn from related fields and current research? In R.A. Geffner & A. Rosenbaum (Eds.), *Domestic violence offenders: Current interventions, research, and implications for policies and standards* (pp. 235–248). New York, NY: Haworth.

Saunders, D.G. (2002). Are physical assaults by wives and girlfriends a major social problem? A review of the literature. *Violence Against Women, 8*, 1424–1448.

Saunders, J. (2009). Memory impairment in the weapon focus effect. *Memory, 37*(3), 326–335.

Saunders, J.W.S. (2001). Experts in court: A view from the bench. *Canadian Psychology, 42*, 109–118.

Saunders, P., & Thompson, J. (2002, February 7). The missing women of Vancouver. *CBC News.* Retrieved from www.cbc.ca/news/features/bc_missingwomen.html.

Saywitz, K.J., & Snyder, L. (1996). Narrative elaboration: Test of a new procedure for interviewing children. *Journal of Consulting and Clinical Psychology, 64*, 1347–1357.

Schaeffer, P., Leventhal, J.M., & Asnes, A.G. (2011). Children's disclosures of sexual abuse: Learning from direct inquiry. *Child Abuse & Neglect, 35*, 343–352.

Schmidt, F., McKinnon, L., Chattha, H.K., & Brownlee, K. (2006). Concurrent and predictive validity of the Psychopathy Checklist: Youth Version across gender and ethnicity. *Psychological Assessment, 18*, 393–401.

Schmidt, F., McKinnon, L., Chattha, H.K., & Brownlee, K. (2006). Concurrent and predictive validity of the Psychopathy Checklist: Youth Version across gender and ethnicity. *Psychological Assessment, 18,* 393–401.

Schneider, R.D., Bloom, H., & Heerema, M. (2007). *Mental health courts: Decriminalizing the mentally ill.* Toronto, ON: Irwin Law.

Schuller, R.A. (1992). The impact of battered woman syndrome evidence on jury decision processes. *Law and Human Behavior, 16,* 597–620.

Schuller, R.A. (1995). Expert evidence and hearsay: The influence of "secondhand" information on jurors' decisions. *Law and Human Behavior, 19,* 345–362.

Schuller, R.A., & Hastings, P. (1996). Trials of battered women who kill: The impact of alternative forms of expert evidence. *Law and Human Behavior, 20,* 167–187.

Schuller, R.A., & Hastings, P.A. (2002). Complainant sexual history evidence: Its impact on mock jurors' decisions. *Psychology of Women Quarterly, 26,* 252–261.

Schuller, R.A., & Ogloff, J.R.P. (2001). *Introduction to psychology and law: Canadian perspectives.* Toronto, ON: University of Toronto Press.

Schuller, R.A., & Rzepa, S. (2002). Expert testimony pertaining to battered woman syndrome: Its impact on jurors' decisions. *Law and Human Behavior, 26,* 655–673.

Schuller, R.A., Smith, V.L., & Olson, J.M. (1994). Jurors' decisions in trials of battered women who kill: The role of prior beliefs and expert testimony. *Journal of Applied Social Psychology, 24,* 316–337.

Schuller, R.A., Terry, D., & McKimmie, B. (2005). The impact of expert testimony on jurors' decisions: Gender of the expert and testimony complexity. *Journal of Applied Social Psychology, 6,* 1266–1280.

Schwartz, D., Dodge, K.A., Coie, J.D., Hubbard, J.A., Cillessen, A.H.N., Lemerise, E.A., & Bateman, H. (1998). Social-cognitive and behavioral correlates of aggression and victimization in boys' play groups. *Journal of Abnormal Child Psychology, 26,* 431–440.

Scogin, F., Schumacher, J., Gardner, J., & Chaplin, W. (1995). Predictive validity of psychological testing in law enforcement settings. *Professional Psychology: Research and Practice, 26,* 68–71.

Seagrave, D., & Grisso, T. (2002). Adolescent development and the measurement of juvenile psychopathy. *Law and Human Behavior, 26,* 219–239.

Sear, L., & Williamson, T. (1999). British and American interrogation strategies. In D.V. Canter & L.J. Alison (Eds.), *Interviewing and deception* (pp. 67–81). Aldershot, England: Ashgate.

Sector-Turner, M., Garwick, A., Sieving, R., & Seppelt, A. (2014) Characteristics of violence among high-risk adolescent girls. *Journal of Pediatric Health Care, 28,* 227–233.

Sellbom, M., & Bagby, R. (2010). Detection of overreported psychopathology with the MMPI-S RF form validity scales. *Psychological Assessment, 22,* 757–767.

Sellbom, M., Fischler, G.L., & Ben-Porath, Y.S. (2007). Identifying MMPI-2 predictors of police officer integrity and misconduct. *Criminal Justice and Behavior, 34,* 985–1004.

Sellbom, M., Toomey, J., Wygant, D., Kucharski, L., & Duncan, S. (2010). Utility of the MMPI-S-RF (restructured form) validity scales in detecting malingering in a criminal forensic setting: A known-groups design. *Psychological Assessment, 22,* 22–31.

Seltzer, T. (2005). Mental health courts: A misguided attempt to address the criminal justice system's unfair treatment of people with mental illnesses. *Psychology, Public Policy, and Law, 11,* 570–586.

Semmler, C., Brewer, N., & Wells, G.L. (2004). Effects of postidentification feedback on eyewitness identification and nonidentification confidence. *Journal of Applied Psychology, 89*(2), 334–346.

Semrau, S., & Gale, J. (2002). *Murderous minds on trial: Terrible tales from a forensic psychiatrist's case book.* Toronto, ON: Dundurn Press.

Serin, R.C. (1991). Psychopathy and violence in criminals. *Journal of Interpersonal Violence, 6,* 423–431.

Serin, R.C., Gobeil, R., Lloyd, C.D., Chadwick, N., Wardrop, K., & Hanby, L. (2016). Using dynamic risk to enhance conditional release decisions in prisoners to improve their outcomes. *Behavioral Sciences & the Law, 34,* 321–336

Serin, R.C., Gobeil, R., & Preston, D. (2009). Evaluation of the persistently violent offender treatment program. *International Journal of Offender Therapy and Comparative Criminology, 53,* 57–73.

Serin, R.C., & Lloyd, C. (2009). Examining the process of offender change: The transition to crime desistance. *Psychology, Crime, & Law, 15,* 347–364.

Serota, K.B., Levine, T.R., & Boster, F.J. (2010). The prevalence of lying in America: Three studies of self-reported lies. *Human Communication Research, 36,* 2–25.

Seto, M.C., & Barbaree, H.E. (1999). Psychopathy, treatment behavior, and sex offender recidivism. *Journal of Interpersonal Violence, 14,* 1235–1248.

Seto, M.C., & Lalumière, M.L. (2010). What is so special about male adolescent sexual offending: A review and test of explanations through meta-analysis. *Psychological Bulletin, 136,* 526–575.

Sevecke, K., Pukrop, R., Kosson, D.S., & Krischer, M.K. (2009). Factor structure of the Hare Psychopathy Checklist: Youth version in German female and male detainees and community adolescents. *Psychological Assessment, 21,* 45–56.

Shackelford, T.K., Buss, D.M., & Peters, J. (2000). Wife killing: Risk to women as a function of age. *Violence and Victims, 15,* 273–282.

Shaw, D.S., Keenan, K., & Vondra, J.I. (1994). Developmental precursors of externalizing behaviour: Ages 1 to 3. *Developmental Psychology, 30,* 355–364.

Shaw, J., & Porter, S. (2015). Constructing Rich False Memories of Committing Crime. *Psychological Science 26*(3), 291–301.

Shaw, J.S., III. (1996). Increases in eyewitness confidence resulting from postevent questioning. *Journal of Experimental Psychology: Applied, 12,* 126–146.

Shaw, J.S., III, & McClure, K.A. (1996). Repeated postevent questioning can lead to elevated levels of eyewitness confidence. *Law and Human Behavior, 20,* 629–654.

Shaw, M. (1994). Women in prison: A literature review. *Forum on Corrections Research, 6,* 13–18.

Sheehan, P.W., & Tilden, J. (1984). Real and simulated occurrences of memory distortion in hypnosis. *Journal of Abnormal Psychology, 93,* 47–57.

Sheehan, R., & Cordner, G.W. (1989). *Introduction to police administration* (2nd ed.). Cincinnati, OH: Anderson.

Sheldon, D.H., & Macleod, M.D. (1991). From normative to positive data: Expert psychological evidence re-examined. *Criminal Law Review*, 811–820.

Sheldon, W.H. (1949). *Varieties of delinquent youths: A psychology of constitutional differences.* New York, NY: Harper & Row.

Shepherd, J.W., & Deregowski, J.B. (1981). Races and faces: A comparison of the responses of Africans and Europeans to faces of the same and different races. *British Journal of Social Psychology, 20*, 125–133.

Sheridan, M.S. (2003). The deceit continues: An updated literature review of Munchausen syndrome by proxy. *Child Abuse & Neglect, 27*, 431–451.

Sherman, L.W., & Berk, R.A. (1984). The specific deterrent effects of arrest for domestic assault. *American Sociological Review, 49*, 261–272.

Sherman, L.W., Schmidt, J.D., & Rogan, D.P. (1992). *Policing domestic violence: Experiments and dilemmas.* New York, NY: Free Press.

Shin, S.H., Miller, D.P., & Teicher, M.H. (2012). Exposure to childhood neglect and physical abuse and developmental trajectories of heavy episodic drinking from early adolescence into young adulthood. *Drug and Alcohol Dependence, 127*(1–3), 31–38.

Shorey, R.C., Stuart, G.L., & Cornelius, T.L. (2011). Dating violence and substance use in college students: A review of the literature. *Aggression and Violent Behavior, 16*, 541–550.

Shover, N., & Thompson, C.Y. (1992). Age differential expectations, and crime desistance. *Criminology, 30*, 89–104.

Silver, E. (2006). Understanding the relationship between mental disorder and violence: The need for a criminological perspective. *Law and Human Behavior, 30*, 685–706.

Simon, D., Snow, C., & Read, S. (2004). The redux of cognitive consistency theories: Evidence judgments by constraint satisfaction. *Journal of Personality and Social Psychology, 86*, 814–837.

Simon, L.M.M., Ellwanger, S.J., & Haggerty, J. (2010). Reversing the historical tide of iatrogenic harm: A therapeutic jurisprudence analysis of increases in arrests of domestic batterers and rapists. *International Journal of Law and Psychiatry, 33*, 306–320.

Simpson, J. (2008). Functional MRI lie detection: Too good to be true? *Journal of the American Academy of Psychiatry and the Law, 36*, 491–498.

Sinha, M. (2012). Family violence in Canada: A statistical profile (Statistics Canada Catalogue no. 85-002-X). *Juristat.* Retrieved from www.statcan.gc.ca/pub/85-002-x/2012001/article/11643-eng.htm.

Sinha, M. (2012). Family violence in Canada: A statistical profile (Statistics Canada Catalogue no. 85-002-X). *Juristat.* Retrieved from www.statcan.gc.ca/pub/85-002-x/2012001/article/11643-eng.htm.

Skeem, J.L., & Monahan, J. (2011). Current directions in violence risk assessment. *Current Directions in Psychological Science, 20*, 38–42.

Slone, A.E., Brigham, J.C., & Meissner, C.A. (2000). Social and cognitive factors affecting the own-race bias in Whites. *Basic and Applied Social Psychology, 22*, 71–84.

Smith v. Jones, [1999] 1 S.C.R. 455.

Smith, C., & Thornberry, T.P. (1995). The relationship between childhood maltreatment and adolescent involvement in delinquency. *Criminology, 33*, 451–481.

Smith, C.A., Ireland, T.O., & Thornberry, T.P. (2005). Adolescent maltreatment and its impact on young adult antisocial behavior. *Child Abuse & Neglect, 29*, 1099–1119.

Smith, D.W., Letourneau, E.J., Saunders, B.E., Kilpatrick, D.G., Resnick, H.S., & Best, C.L. (2000). Delay in disclosure of childhood rape: Results from a national survey. *Child Abuse & Neglect, 24*, 273–287.

Smith, P., Cullen, F.T., & Latessa, E.J. (2009). Can 14,373 women be wrong? A meta-analysis of the LSI-R and recidivism for female offenders. *Criminology and Public Policy, 8*, 183–208.

Smith, S.M., Patry, M., & Stinson, V. (2008). Is the CSI effect real? If it is, what is it? In G. Bourgon, R.K. Hanson, J.D. Pozzulo, K.E. Morton Bourgon, & C.L. Tanasichuk (Eds.), *Proceedings of the 2007 North American Correctional & Criminal Justice Psychology Conference* (User Report). Ottawa, ON: Public Safety Canada.

Smith, S.M., Stinson, V., & Patry, M.W. (2009). Using the "Mr. Big" technique to elicit confessions: Successful innovation or dangerous development in the Canadian legal system. *Psychology, Public Policy, and Law, 15*, 168–193.

Smith, S.M., Stinson, V., & Patry, M.W. (2010). High risk interrogation: Using the "Mr. Big" technique to elicit confessions. *Law and Human Behavior, 34*, 39–40.

Snook, B., Cullen, R.M., Bennell, C., Taylor, P.J., & Gendreau, P. (2008). The criminal profiling illusion: What's behind the smoke and mirrors? *Criminal Justice and Behavior, 35*, 1257–1276.

Snook, B., Eastwood, J., & Barron. T. (2014). The next stage in the evolution of interrogations: The PEACE model. *Canadian Criminal Law Review.*

Snook, B., Eastwood, J., Gendreau, P., & Bennell, C. (2010). The importance of knowledge cumulation and the search for hidden agendas: A reply to Kocsis, Middledorp, and Karpin (2008). *Journal of Forensic Psychology Practice, 10*, 214–223.

Snook, B., Eastwood, J., Gendreau, P, Goggin, C., & Cullen, R.M. (2007). Taking stock of criminal profiling: A narrative review and meta-analysis. *Criminal Justice and Behavior, 34*, 437–453.

Snook, B., Eastwood, J., Stinson, M., Tedeschini, J., & House, J.C. (2010). Reforming investigative interviewing in Canada. *Canadian Journal of Criminology and Criminal Justice, 52*, 203–217.

Snook, B., Haines, A., Taylor, P.J., & Bennell, C. (2007). Criminal profiling belief and use: A survey of Canadian police officer opinion. *Canadian Journal of Police and Security Services, 5*, 169–179.

Snook, B., Luther, K., House, J., Bennell, C., & Taylor, P.J. (2012). The violent crime linkage analysis system: A test of interrater reliability. *Criminal Justice and Behavior, 39*, 607–619.

Snook, B., Luther, K., Quinlan, H., & Milne, R. (2012). Let em talk! A field study of police questioning practices of suspects and accused persons. *Criminal Justice and Behavior, 39*, 1328–1339.

Snook, B., Zito, M., Bennell, C., & Taylor, P. J. (2005). On the complexity and accuracy of geographic profiling strategies. *Journal of Quantitative Criminology, 21*, 1–26.

Solomon, E., & Allen, R. (2009). *Out of trouble: Reducing child imprisonment in England and Wales—lessons from abroad*. London, England: Prison Reform Trust.

Sonkin, D.J., Martin, D., & Walker, I.E. (1985). *The male batterer: A treatment approach*. New York, NY: Springer.

Sourour, T. (1991). *Report of Coroner's Investigation*. Retrieved from www.diarmani.com/Montreal_Coroners_Report.pdf.

Spanos, N.P., DuBreuil, S.C., & Gwynn, M.I. (1991–1992). The effects of expert testimony concerning rape on the verdicts and beliefs of mock jurors. *Imagination, Cognition, and Personality*, *11*, 37–51.

Sparling, J., Wilder, D.A., Kondash, J., Boyle, M., & Compton, M. (2011). Effects of interviewer behavior on accuracy of children's responses. *Journal of Applied Behavior Analysis*, *44*(3), 587–592. Retrieved from http://search.proquest.com/docview/909292048?accountid=9894.

Spitzberg, B.H., & Cupach, W.R. (2007). The state of the art of stalking: Taking stock of the emerging literature. *Aggression and Violent Behavior*, *12*, 64–86.

Sporer, S.L. (1996). Psychological aspects of person descriptions. In S. Sporer, R. Malpass, & G. Köehnken (Eds.), *Psychological issues in eyewitness identification* (pp. 53–86). Mahwah, NJ: Erlbaum.

Sporer, S.L., & Schwandt, B. (2006). Paraverbal indicators of deception: A meta-analytic synthesis. *Applied Cognitive Psychology*, *20*, 421–446.

Sporer, S.L., Penrod, S.D., Read, D., & Cutler, B.L. (1995). Choosing confidence and accuracy: A meta-analysis of the confidence-accuracy relations in eyewitness identification studies. *Psychological Bulletin*, *118*, 315–327.

Stack, S. (1997). Homicide followed by suicide: An analysis of Chicago data. *Criminology*, *35*, 435–453.

Stahlkopf, C., Males, M., & Macallair, D. (2010). Testing incapacitation theory: youth crime and incarceration in California. *Crime and Delinquency*, *56*, 253–268.

Stanton, J., & Simpson, A. (2002). Filicide: A review. *International Journal of Law and Psychiatry*, *25*, 1–14.

Starr, S. B. (2012). Estimating gender disparities in federal criminal cases. *American Law and Economics Review*, *17*, 127–159.

Starson v. Swayze, [1999] SCC 32.

Starson v. Swayze, [2003] 1 S.C.R. 722, 2003 SCC 32.

Statistics Canada (2012). Adult correctional statistics in Canada, 2010/2011 (85-002-X). Ottawa, ON: Author.

Statistics Canada (2013). Indigenous Peoples in Canada: First Nations People, Métis and Inuit (99-011-X2011001). Ottawa, ON: Author.

Statistics Canada, Canadian Centre for Justice Statistics. (2013, June 5). Integrated Criminal Court Survey. Retrieved from www.statcan.gc.ca/pub/85-002-x/2012001/article/11645/tbl/tbl03-eng.htm.

Statistics Canada. (2015). *Family violence in Canada: A statistical profile*. Retrieved April 4, 2016 from http://www.statcan.gc.ca/pub/85-002-x/2014001/article/14114-eng.pdf.

Steadman, H.J. (2000). From dangerousness to risk assessment of community violence: Taking stock at the turn of the century. *Journal of the American Academy of Psychiatry and the Law*, *28*, 265–271.

Steadman, H.J., & Cocozza, J. (1974). Careers of the criminally insane. Lexington, MA: Lexington Books.

Steadman, H.J., McGreevy, M.A., Morrissey, J.P., Callahan, L.A., Robbins, P.C., & Cirincione, C. (1993). *Before and after Hinckley: Evaluating insanity defense reform*. New York, NY: Guilford Press.

Steadman, H.J., Monahan, J., Appelbaum, P.S., Grisso, T., Mulvey, E.P., Roth, L.H., Robbins, P.C., & D. Klassen. (1994). Designing a new generation of risk assessment research. In J. Monahan & H.J. Steadman (Eds.), *Violence and mental disorder: Developments in risk assessment* (pp. 297–318). Chicago, IL: University of Chicago Press.

Steadman, H.J., Mulvey, E.P., Monahan, J., Robbins, P.C., Appelbaum, P.S., Grisso, T., Roth, L.H., & Silver, E. (1998). Violence by people discharged from acute psychiatric inpatient facilities and by others in the same neighborhoods. *Archives of General Psychiatry*, *55*(5), 393–401.

Steadman, H.J., Silver, E., Monahan, J., Appelbaum, P.S., Robbins, P.C., Mulvey, E.P., Grisso, T., Roth, L.H., & Banks, S. (2000). A classification tree approach to the development of actuarial violence risk assessment tools. *Law and Human Behavior*, *24*(1), 83–100.

Steblay, N., Dysart, J., & Wells, G.L. (2011). Seventy-two tests of the sequential lineup superiority effect: A meta-analysis and policy discussion. *Psychology, Public Policy, and Law*, *17*, 99–139.

Steblay, N., Dysart, J.E., Fulero, S., & Lindsay, R.C.L. (2003). Eyewitness accuracy rates in police showup and lineup presentations: A meta-analytic comparison. *Law and Human Behavior*, *27*, 523–540.

Steblay, N., Hosch, H., Culhane, S., & McWethy, A. (2006). The impact of juror verdicts of judicial instruction to disregard inadmissible evidence: A meta-analysis. *Law and Human Behavior*, *30*, 469–492.

Steblay, N.M. (1992). A meta-analytic review of the weapon focus effect. *Law and Human Behavior*, *16*, 413–424.

Steblay, N.M. (1997). Social influence in eyewitness recall: A meta-analytic review of lineup instruction effects. *Law and Human Behavior*, *21*, 283–298.

Steblay, N.M., Besirevic, J., Fulero, S.M., & Jimenez-Lorente, B. (1999). The effects of pretrial publicity on juror verdicts: A meta-analytic review. *Law and Human Behavior*, *23*, 219–235.

Steblay, N.M., & Bothwell, R.B. (1994). Evidence for hypnotically refreshed testimony: The view from the laboratory. *Law and Human Behavior*, *18*, 635–651.

Steblay, N.M., Dysart, J., Fulero, S., & Lindsay, R.C.L. (2001). Eyewitness accuracy rates in sequential and simultaneous lineup presentations: A meta-analytic comparison. *Law and Human Behavior*, *25*, 459–474.

Stefan, A., Lindfors, P., & Sverke, M. (2015). Police selection–implications during training and early career. *Policing: An International Journal of Police Strategies & Management*, *38*, 221–238.

Stefanie Rengel case statement of facts. (2009, April 9). *CityNews*. Retrieved from www.citytv.com/toronto/citynews/news/local/article/10094—stefanie-rengel-case.

Stein, M., Koverola, C., Hanna, C., Torchia, M., & McClarry, B. (1997). Hippocampal volume in woman victimized by childhood sexual abuse. *Psychological Medicine*, *27*, 951–959.

Steinberg, L. (2007). Risk taking in adolescence: New perspectives from brain and behavioral science. *Current Directions in Psychological Science*, *16*, 55–59.

Steinberg, L. (2009). Adolescent development and juvenile justice. *Annual Review of Clinical Psychology, 5,* 459–485.

Stellar, M. (1989). Recent developments in statement analysis. In J.C. Yuille (Ed.), *Credibility assessment* (pp. 135–154). Dordrecht, the Netherlands: Kluwer.

Stellar, M., & Kohnken, G. (1989). Statement analysis: Credibility assessment of children's testimonies in sexual abuse cases. In D.C. Raskin (Ed.), *Psychological methods in criminal investigation and evidence* (pp. 217–245). New York, NY: Springer.

Stern, L.W. (1939). The psychology of testimony. *Journal of Abnormal and Social Psychology, 40,* 3–20.

Sternberg, K., Lamb, M., Esplin, P., Orbach, Y, & Hershkowitz, I. (2002). Using a structure interview protocol to improve the quality of investigative interviews. In M. Eisen, J. Quas, & G. Goodman (Eds.), *Memory and suggestibility in the forensic interview. Personality and clinical psychology series* (pp. 409–436). Mahwah, NJ: Lawrence Erlbaum Associates.

Stevens, D.J. (1994). Predatory rape avoidance. *International Review of Modern Sociology, 24(2),* 97–118.

Stewart, L., Gabora, N., Kropp, R., & Lee, Z. (2005). *Family violence programming: Treatment outcome for Canadian federally sentenced offenders.* Ottawa, ON: Correctional Service of Canada.

Stiles-Shields, C., & Carroll, R.A. (2015). Same-sex domestic violence: Prevalence, unique aspects, and clinical implications. *Journal of Sex & Marital Therapy, 41,* 636–648.

Stockdale, L., Tackett, S., & Coyne, S.M. (2013). Sex differences in verbal aggression use in romantic relationships: A meta-analytic study and review. *Journal of Aggression, Conflict and Peace Research, 5,* 167–178.

Storm, J., & Graham, J.R. (2000). Detection of coached general malingering on the MMPI-2. *Psychological Assessment, 12,* 158–165.

Stouthamer-Loeber, M., Wei, E., Loeber, R., & Masten, A.S. (2004). Desistance from persistent serious delinquency in the transition to adulthood. *Development and Psychopathology, 16,* 897–918.

Stovall v. Denno, [1967] 388 U.S. 293.

Strand, S., Belfrage, H., Fransson, G., & Levander, S. (1999). Clinical and risk management factors in risk prediction of mentally disordered offenders—more important than historical data? A retrospective study of 40 mentally disordered offenders assessed with the HCR-20 violence risk assessment scheme. *Legal and Criminological Psychology, 4,* 67–76.

Straus, M. (2012). Blaming the messenger for the bad news about partner violence by women: The methodological, theoretical, and value basis of the purported invalidity of the Conflict Tactics Scales. *Behavioral Sciences and the Law, 30,* 538–556.

Straus, M.A. (1979). Measuring family conflict and violence: The Conflict Tactics Scale. *Journal of Marriage and the Family, 41,* 75–88.

Straus, M.A., Gelles, R. J., & Steinmetz, S. (1980). *Behind closed doors: Violence in the American family.* Garden City, NY: Anchor/Doubleday.

Straus, M.A., Hamby, S.L., Boney-McCoy, S., & Sugarman, D.B. (1996). The revised Conflict Tactics Scales (CTS2): Development and preliminary psychometric data. *Journal of Family Issues, 17,* 283–316.

Strömwall, L.A., Hartwig, M., & Granhag, P.A. (2006). To act truthfully: Nonverbal behaviour and strategies during a police interrogation. *Psychology, Crime & Law, 12,* 207–219.

Sundby, S.E. (1997). The jury as critic: An empirical look at how capital juries perceive expert and lay testimony. *Virginia Law Review, 83,* 1109–1188.

Supreme Court of Canada (SCC). (2016a). *Creation and beginnings of the court.* Retrieved April 29, 2016 from http://www.scc-csc.ca/court-cour/creation-eng.aspx.

Supreme Court of Canada (SCC). (2016b). *About the judges.* Retrieved April 29, 2016 from http://www.scc-csc.ca/court-cour/judges-juges/about-apropos-eng.aspx.

Sussman, R.W., Cheverud, J.M., & Bartlett, T.Q. (1994). Infant killing as an evolutionary strategy: Reality or myth? *Evolutionary Anthropology, 3,* 149–151.

Sutherland, E.H. (1939). *Principles of criminology.* Philadelphia, PA: J.B. Lippincott Company.

Swanson, J.W. (1994). Mental disorder, substance abuse, and community violence: An epidemiological approach. In J. Monahan & H.J. Steadman (Eds.), *Violence and mental disorder: Developments in risk assessment* (101–137). Chicago, IL: University of Chicago Press.

Swanson, J.W., Holzer, C.E., Ganju, V.K., & Jono, R.T. (1990). Violence and psychiatric disorder in the community: Evidence from the epidemiologic catchment area surveys. *Hospital and Community Psychiatry, 41,* 761–770.

Sykes, J.B. (Ed.). (1982). *The Concise Oxford Dictionary* (7th ed.). Oxford: Oxford University Press.

Szymanski, L.A., Devlin, A.S., Chrisler, J.C., & Vyse, S.A. (1993). Gender role and attitudes toward rape in male and female college students. *Sex Roles, 29,* 37–57.

Talaga, T. (2013, September 28). "Systemic racism" toward natives in justice system, Frank Iacobucci finds. *Toronto Star.* Retrieved from www.thestar.com/news/canada/2013/02/26/systemic_racism_toward_natives_in_justice_system_frank_iacobucci_finds.html.

Tarescavage, A.M., & Glassmire, D.M. (2016). Differences between structured interview of reported symptoms (SIRS) and SIRS-2 sensitivity estimates among forensic inpatients: A criterion groups comparison. *Law and Human Behavior.*

Taylor, A., & Bennell, C. (2006). Operational and organizational police stress in an Ontario police department: A descriptive study. *Canadian Journal of Police and Security Services, 4,* 223–234.

Taylor, G.F. (2013). Chicago police torture scandal: A legal and political history. *The CUNY Law Review, 17,* 329–381.

Taylor, S.P., & Sears, J.D. (1988). The effects of alcohol and persuasive social pressure on human physical aggression. *Aggressive Behavior, 14,* 237–243.

Technical Working Group for Eyewitness Evidence. (1999). *Eyewitness evidence: A guide for law enforcement* (NCJ 178240). Washington, DC: United States Department of Justice, Office of Justice Programs. Retrieved from www.ojp.usdoj.gov.

Tellegen, A., & Ben-Porath, Y.S. (2008). *MMPI-2-RF (Minnesota Multiphasic Personality Inventory-2 Restructured Form): Technical manual.* Minneapolis: University of Minnesota Press.

Temrin, H., Nordlund, J., Rying, M., & Tullberg, B.S. (2011). Is the higher rate of parental child homicide in stepfamilies an effect of non-genetic relatedness? *Current Zoology, 57*, 253–259.

ten Brinke, L., & Adams, G. (2015) Saving face?: When emotion displays during public apologies mitigate damage to organizational performance. *Organizational Behavior and Human Decision Processes, 130*, 1–12.

ten Brinke, L., Lee, J. J., & Carney, D. (2015). The physiology of (dis)honesty: Does it impact health? Invited article in *Current Opinion in Psychology, 6*, 177–182.

ten Brinke, L., Liu, C. C., Keltner, D., & Srivastava, S. (2015). Virtues, vices, and political influence in the U.S. Senate. *Psychological Science, 27*, 85–93.

ten Brinke, L., & Porter, S. (2012). Cry me a river: Identifying the behavioral consequences of extremely high-stakes interpersonal deception. *Law and Human Behavior, 36*, 469–477.

ten Brinke, L., Porter, S., & Baker, A. (2012). Darwin the detective: Observable facial muscle contractions reveal emotional high-stakes lies. *Evolution and Human Behavior, 33*, 411–416.

Teplin, L.A. (1984). Criminalizing mental disorder: The comparative arrest rate of the mentally ill. *American Psychologist, 39*, 784–803.

Teplin, L.A. (2000, July). Keeping the peace: Police discretion and mentally ill persons. *National Institute of Justice Journal*, 8–15.

Terman, L.M. (1917). A trial of mental and pedagogical tests in a civil service examination for policemen and firemen. *Journal of Applied Psychology, 1*, 17–29.

Terrance, C.A., Plumm, K.M., & Kehn, A. (2014). Battered women who kill: Impact of expert testimony type and timing. *Psychiatry, Psychology, and Law, 21*, 1–15.

Territo, L., & Sewell, J.D. (2007). *Stress management in law enforcement* (2nd ed.). Durham, NC: Carolina Academic Press.

Test, M.A., (1992). Training in community living. In R.P Liberman (Ed.), *Handbook of psychiatric rehabilitation* (pp. 153–170). New York, NY: Macmillan.

Texas "Dr. Death" retires after 167 capital case trials. (2003, December 20). *The Washington Times*. Retrieved from www.washingtontimes.com/news/2003/dec/20/20031220-113219-5189r/?page=all.

The Canadian Press. (2016). Notorious teen killer Kelly Ellard denied parole for being 'too entitled.' Retrieved May 4, 2016 from http://www.torontosun.com/2016/05/03/notorious-teen-killer-kelly-ellard-denied-parole-for-being-too-entitled.

The Hinckley trial: Hinckley's communications with Jodie Foster. (n.d.). University of Missouri-Kansas City School of Law. Retrieved from http://law2.umkc.edu/faculty/projects/ftrials/hinckley/jfostercommun.HTM.

The Use of Anatomically Detailed Dolls in Forensic Evaluations. (2016). Retrieved February 1, 2016, from http://www.apa.org/about/policy/dolls.aspx.

Theurer, G., & Lovell, D. (2008). Recidivism of offenders with mental illness released from prison to an intensive community treatment program. *Journal of Offender Rehabilitation, 47*, 385–406.

Thibaut, F., De La Barra, F., Gordon, H., Cosyns, P., & Bradford, J.M. (2010). The World Federation of Societies of Biological Psychiatry (WFSBP) guidelines for the biological treatment of paraphilias. *World J Biol Psychiatry, 11*(4), 604–655.

Thorley, C., Baxter, R., & Lorek, J. (2015). The impact of note taking style and note availability at retrieval on mock jurors' recall and recognition of trial information. *Memory*. Advance Online Publication.

Thornberry, T.P., & J.E. Jacoby (1979). *The criminally insane: A community follow-up of mentally ill offenders*. Chicago: University of Chicago Press.

Thornhill, R., & Palmer, C.T. (2000). *A natural history of rape: Biological bases of sexual coercion*. Cambridge, MA: MIT Press.

Tiplady, C.M., Walsh, D.B., & Phillips, C.J.C. (2012). Intimate partner violence and companion animal welfare. *Australian Veterinary Journal, 90*, 48–53.

Tolan, P., & Thomas, P. (1995). The implications of age of onset for delinquency risk: II. Longitudinal data. *Journal of Abnormal Child Psychology, 23*, 157–181.

Tolman, R.M., & Weisz, A. (1995). Coordinated community intervention for domestic violence: The effects of arrest and prosecution on recidivism of woman abuse perpetrators. *Crime and Delinquency, 41*, 481–495.

Toma, C.L., & Hancock, J.T. (2010). Looks and lies: The role of physical attractiveness in online dating self-presentation and deception. *Communication Research, 37*(3), 335–351.

Toma, C.L., Hancock, J.T., & Ellison, N.B. (2008). Separating fact from fiction: An examination of deceptive self-presentation in online dating profiles. *Personality and Social Bulletin, 34*, 1023–1036.

Toomey, J.A., Kucharski, L.T., & Duncan, S. (2009). The utility of the MMPI-2 Malingering Discriminant Function Index in the detection of malingering: A study of criminal defendants. *Assessment, 16*, 115–121.

Townsend, E. (2007). Suicide terrorists: Are they suicidal? *Suicide and Life-Threatening Behavior, 37*, 35–49.

Trocmé, N., Fallon, B., MacLaurin, B., Sinha, V., Black, T., Fast, E., Felstiner, C., Hélie, S., Turcotte, D., Weightman, P., Douglas, J., & Holroyd, J. (2010). *Canadian Incidence Study of Reported Child Abuse and Neglect: Final report*. Ottawa, ON: Public Health Agency of Canada.

Turtle, J.W., Lindsay, R.C.L., & Wells, G.L. (2003). Best practice recommendations for eyewitness evidence procedures: New ideas for the oldest way to solve a case. *The Canadian Journal of Police and Security Services, 1*, 5–18.

Turvey, B. (2002). *Criminal profiling: An introduction to behavioral evidence analysis* (2nd ed.). San Diego, CA: Academic Press.

Tuvblad, C., Bezdjian, S., Raine, A., & Baker, L.A. (2014). The heritability of psychopathic personality in 14- to 15-year-old twins: A multirater, multimeasure approach. *Psychological Assessment, 26*, 704–716.

Tversky, A., & Kahneman, D. (1981). The framing of decisions and the psychology of choice. *Science, 211*, 453–458.

Tweed, R.G., & Dutton, D.G. (1998). A comparison of impulsive and instrumental subgroups of batters. *Violence and Victims, 13*, 217–230.

Uggen, C. (1999). Ex-offenders and the conformist alternative: A job quality model of work and crime. *Social Problems, 46*, 127–151.

Ullman, S.E., & Knight, R.A. (1993). The efficacy of women's resistance strategies in rape situations. *Psychology of Women Quarterly, 17*, 23–38.

Ulmer, J.T. (1997). *Social worlds of sentencing: Court communities under sentencing guidelines*. Albany, NY: State University of New York Press.

Underwood, R.C., Patch, P.C., Cappelletty, G.G., & Wolfe, R.W. (1999). Do sexual offenders molest when other persons are present? A preliminary investigation. *Sexual Abuse: Journal of Research and Treatment, 11*, 234–247.

Undeutsch, U. (1989). The development of statement reality analysis. In J.C. Yuille (Ed.), *Credibility assessment* (pp. 101–121). Dordrecht, the Netherlands: Kluwer Academic Publishers.

Uniform Crime Reporting Survey. (2015). Statistics Canada. Retrieved from http://www23.statcan.gc.ca/imdb/p2SV.pl?Function=getSurvey&SDDS=3302.

Valdes, S.G. (2005). Frequency and success: An empirical study of criminal law defense, federal constitution evidentiary claims, and plea negotiations. *University of Pennsylvania Law Review, 153*, 1709–1736.

van de Weijer, S.G.A., Bijleveld, C.C.H., & Blokland, A.A.J. (2014). The intergenerational transmission of violent offending. *Journal of Family Violence, 29*, 109–118.

van der Stouwe, T., Asscher, J.J., Stams, G.J.J.M., Deković, M., & van der Laan, P.H. (2014). The effectiveness of Multisystemic Therapy (MST): a meta-analysis. *Clinical Psychology Review, 34*, 468–481.

Van der Velden, P.G., Rademaker, A.R., Vermetten, E., Portengen, M.A., Yzermans, J.C., & Grievink, L. (2013). Police officers: A high-risk group for the development of mental health disturbances? A cohort study. *BMJ Open, 3*.

Van Domburgh, L., Loeber, R., Bezemer, D., Stallings, R., & Stouthamer-Loeber, M. (2009). Childhood predictors of desistance and level of persistence in offending in early onset offenders. *Journal of Abnormal Child Psychology, 37*, 967–980.

van Emmerik, A.A.P., Kamphuis, J.H., Hulsbosch, A.M., & Emmelkamp, P.M.G. (2002). Single session debriefing after psychological trauma: A meta-analysis. *The Lancet, 360*, 766–770.

Van Schellen, M., Poortman, A.R., & Nieuwbeerta, P. (2012). Partners in crimes? Criminal offending, marriage formation, and partner selection. *Journal of Research in Crime and Delinquency, 49*, 545–571.

Vance, J.P. (2001). Neurobiological mechanisms of psychosocial resiliency. In J.M. Richman & M.W. Fraser (Eds.), *The context of youth violence: Resilience, risk, & protection* (pp. 43–81). Westport, CN: Praeger.

Vancouver Police Department. (2016). *The job*. Retrieved March 4, 2016 from http://vancouver.ca/police/recruiting/police-officers/policing.html.

Varela, J.G., Boccaccini, M.T., Scogin, F., Stump, J., & Caputo, A. (2004). Personality testing in law enforcement employment settings: A meta-analytic review. *Criminal Justice and Behavior, 31*, 649–675.

Varendonck, J. (1911). Les temoignages d'enfants dans un proces retentisaant. *Archives de Psycholgie, 11*, 129–171.

Verschuere, B., Rosenfeld, J.P., Winograd, M.R., Labkovsky, E., & Wiersema, R. (2009). The role of deception in P300 memory detection. *Legal and Criminological Psychology, 14*, 253–262.

Victoroff, J., Adelman, J.R., & Matthews, M. (2012). Psychological factors associated with support for suicide bombing in the Muslim diaspora. *Political Psychology, 33*(6), 791–809.

Viding, E., Blair, R.J., Moffitt, T.E., & Plomin, R. (2005). Evidence for substantial genetic risk for psychopathy in 7-year-olds. *Journal of Child Psychology and Psychiatry and Allied Disciplines, 46*, 592–597.

Viljoen, J.L., MacDougall, E.A.M., Gagnon, N.C., & Douglas, K.S. (2010). Psychopathy evidence in legal proceedings involving adolescent offenders. *Psychology, Public Policy, and Law, 16*, 254–283.

Viljoen, J.L., McLachlan, K., & Vincent, G.M. (2010). Assessing violence risk and psychopathy in juvenile and adult offenders: A survey of clinical practices. *Assessment, 17*, 377–395.

Viljoen, J.L., Roesch, R., Ogloff, J.R.P., & Zapf, P.A. (2003). The role of Canadian psychologists in conducting fitness and criminal responsibility evaluations. *Canadian Psychology, 44*, 369–381.

Villeneueve, D.B., & Quinsey, V.L. (1995). Predictors of general and violent recidivism among mentally disordered inmates. *Criminal Justice and Behavior, 22*, 387–410.

Vincent, G.M., Odgers, C.L., McCormick, A.V., & Corrado, R.R. (2008). The PCL:YV and recidivism in male and female juveniles: A follow-up into young adulthood. *International Journal of Law and Psychiatry, 31*, 287–296.

Vingoe, F.J. (1995). Beliefs of British law and medical students compared to expert criterion group on forensic hypnosis. *Contemporary Hypnosis, 12*, 173–187.

Violanti, J.M., Marshall, J.R., & Howe, B. (1985). Stress, coping and alcohol use: The police connection. *Journal of Police Science and Administration, 31*, 106–110.

Violanti, J.M., Vena, J.E., & Marshall, J.R. (1986). Disease risk and mortality among police officers: New evidence and contributing factors. *Journal of Police Science and Administration, 14*, 17–23.

Vizard, E., & Trantor, M. (1988). Helping young children to describe experiences of child sexual abuse: General issue. In A. Bentovim, A., Elton, J. Hilderbrand, M. Tranter, & E. Vizard (Eds.), *Child sexual abuse within the family: Assessment and treatment* (pp. 84–104). Bristol, England: John Wright.

Vrij, A. (2000). *Detecting lies and deceits: The psychology of lying and the implications for professional practice*. Chichester, England: John Wiley & Sons.

Vrij, A. (2005). Criteria-based content analysis: A qualitative review of the first 37 studies. *Psychology, Public Policy, and Law, 11*, 3–41.

Vrij, A. (2008). *Detecting lies and deceit: Pitfalls and opportunities* (2nd ed.). Chichester, England: Wiley.

Vrij, A., Akenhurst, L., Soukara, S., & Bull, R. (2002). Will the truth come out? The effect of deception, age, status, coaching, and social skills on CBCA scores. *Law and Human Behavior, 26*, 261–284.

Vrij, A., & Mann, S. (2001). Who killed my relative? Police officers' ability to detect real-life high-stake lies. *Psychology, Crime, and Law, 7*, 119–132.

Vrij, A., Mann, S., Leal, S., Vernham, Z., & Vaughan, M. (2015). Train the trainers: A first step towards a science-based cognitive lie detection training workshop delivered by a practitioner. *Journal of Investigative Psychology and Offender Profiling, 13*(2), 110–130.

Vronsky, P. (2007). *Female serial killers: How and why women become monsters.* New York, NY: Berkley Publishing Group.

Waddell, C., Shepherd, C., Schwartz, C., & Barican, J. (2014). Child and youth mental disorders: Prevalence and evidence-based interventions. A research report for the British Columbia Ministry of Children and Family Development. Children's Health Policy Centre http://childhealthpolicy.ca/wp-content/uploads/2014/06/14-06-17-Waddell-Report-2014.06.16.pdf.

Wadsworth, M.E.J. (1976). Delinquency, pulse rates, and early emotional deprivation. *British Journal of Criminology, 16,* 245–256.

Wagstaff, G.F., MacVeigh, J., Boston, R., Scott, L., Brunas-Wagstaff, J., & Cole, J. (2003). Can laboratory findings on eyewitness testimony be generalized to the real world? An archival analysis of the influence of violence, weapon presence, and age on eyewitness accuracy. *The Journal of Psychology, 137,* 17–28.

Waite, S., & Geddes, A. (2006). Malingered psychosis leading to involuntary psychiatric hospitalization. *Australian Psychiatry, 14,* 419–421.

Wakefield, H., & Underwager, R. (1998). Coerced or nonvoluntary confessions. *Behavioral Sciences and the Law, 16,* 423–440.

Walker, L. (1979). *The battered woman.* New York, NY: Harper Perennial.

Walma, M.W., & West, L. (2002). *Police powers and procedures.* Toronto, ON: Emond Montgomery.

Walsh, T., & Walsh, Z. (2006). The evidentiary introduction of Psychopathy Checklist-Revised assessed psychopathy in U.S. Courts: Extent and appropriateness. *Law and Human Behavior, 30,* 493–507.

Walsh, Z., Swogger, M.T., & Kosson, D.S. (2009). Psychopathy and instrumental violence: Facet level relationships. *Journal of Personality Disorders, 23,* 416–424.

Waltz, J., Babcock, J.C., Jacobson, N.S., & Gottman, J.M. (2000). Testing a typology of batterers. *Journal of Consulting and Clinical Psychology, 68,* 658–669.

Ward, T., & Siegert, R. (2002). Rape and evolutionary psychology: A critique of Thornhill and Palmer's theory. *Aggression and Violent Behavior, 7,* 145–168.

Warick, J. (2003 July, 5). Saskatchewan considers racially balanced juries. *Ottawa Citizen,* p. A16.

Warmelink, L., Vrij, A., Mann, S., Leal, S., Forrester, D., & Fisher, D. (2011). Thermal imaging as a lie detection tool at airports. *Law and Human Behavior, 35,* 40–48.

Warmington, J. (2007, December 6). Schizophrenic killer wandering around unmonitored. *Toronto Sun.* Retrieved from Canoe website: http://cnews.canoe.ca/CNEWS/MediaNews/2007/12/06/4710576-sun.html.

Warren, J.L., Burnette, M., South, C.S., Chauhan, P., Bale, R., & Friend, R. (2002). Personality disorders and violence among female prison inmates. *Journal of the American Academy of Psychiatry and the Law, 30,* 502–509.

Waschbusch, D.A. (2002). A meta-analytic examination of comorbid hyperactive-impulsive-attention problems and conduct problems. *Psychological Bulletin, 128,* 118–150.

Wasserman, G.A., & Saracini, A.M. (2001). Family risk factors and interventions. In R. Loeber & D.P. Farrington (Eds.), *Child delinquents: Development, intervention, and service needs* (pp. 165–190). Thousand Oaks, CA: Sage.

Waterman, A., Blades, M., & Spencer, C. (2004). Indicating when you do not know the answer: The effect of question format and interviewer knowledge on children's 'don't know' response. *British Journal of Developmental Psychology, 22,* 135–148.

Weber-Stratton, C., Rinaldi, J., & Reid, J.M. (2011). Long-term outcomes of incredible years parenting program: Predictors of adolescent adjustment. *Child and Adolescent Mental Health, 16,* 38–46.

Webster, C.D., Douglas, K., Eaves, D., & Hart, S. (1997). *HCR-20: Assessing risk for violence, Version 2.* Burnaby, BC: Simon Fraser University and Forensic Psychiatric Services Commission of British Columbia.

Webster, C.D., & Jackson, M.A. (Eds.). (1997) *Impulsivity: Theory, assessment, and treatment.* New York, NY: Guilford.

Webster, C.D., Menzies, R.S., Butler, B.T., & Turner, R.E. (1982). Forensic psychiatric assessment in selected Canadian cities. *Canadian Journal of Psychiatry, 27,* 455–462.

Webster-Stratton, C. (1992). The incredible years: A trouble shooting guide for parents of children ages 3–8 years. Toronto, ON: Umbrella Press.

Webster-Stratton, C. (2001). The incredible years: parents, teachers, and children training series. *Residential Treatment for Children and Youth, 18,* 31–45.

Webster-Stratton, C., & Hammond, M. (1997). Treating children with early-onset conduct problems: A comparison of child and parenting training interventions. *Journal of Consulting and Clinical Psychology, 65,* 93–109.

Webster-Stratton, C., & Reid, M. J. (2010). The Incredible Years parents, teachers and children training series: A multifaceted treatment approach for young children with conduct problems. In J. Weisz & A. Kazdin (Eds.), *Evidence based psychotherapies for children and adolescents* (2nd ed.) (pp. 194–210). New York: Guilford Publications.

Weiler, B.L., & Widom, C.S. (1996). Psychopathy and violent behaviour in abused and neglected young adults. *Criminal Behaviour and Mental Health, 6,* 253–271.

Weinrath, M. (2007). Sentencing disparity: Aboriginal Canadian, drunk driving, and age. *Western Criminology Review, 8,* 16–28.

Weinrott, M.R., & Saylor, M. (1991). Self-report of crimes committed by sex offenders. *Journal of Interpersonal Violence, 6*(3), 286–300.

Weiss, P.A., Vivian, J.E., Weiss, W.U., Davis, R.D., & Rostow, C.D. (2013). The MMPI-2 L Scale, reporting uncommon virtue, and predicting police performance. *Psychological Services, 10,* 123–130.

Wells, G.L. (1978). Applied eyewitness-testimony research: System variables and estimator variables. *Journal of Personality and Social Psychology, 12,* 1546–1557.

Wells, G.L. (1993). What do we know about eyewitness identification? *American Psychologist, 48,* 553–571.

Wells, G.L., & Bradfield, A.L. (1998). "Good, you identified the suspect": Feedback to eyewitnesses distorts their reports of the witnessing experience. *Journal of Applied Psychology, 83,* 366–376.

Wells, G.L., Leippe, M.R., & Ostrom, T.M. (1979). Guidelines for empirically assessing the fairness of a lineup. *Law and Human Behavior, 3,* 285–293.

Wells, G.L., & Loftus, E.F. (2003). Eyewitness memory for people and events. In A.M. Goldstein (Ed.), *Handbook of psychology: Forensic psychology* (pp. 149–160). New York: Wiley.

Wells, G.L., Malpass, R.S., Lindsay, R.C.L., Turtle, J.W., & Fulero, S.M. (2000). From the lab to the police station: A successful application of eyewitness research. *American Psychologist, 55,* 581–598.

Wells, G.L., & Olson, E.A. (2003). Eyewitness testimony. *Annual Psychology Review, 54,* 277–295.

Wells, G.L., Rydell, S.M., & Seelau, E.P. (1993). On the selection of distractors for eyewitness lineups. *Journal of Applied Psychology, 78,* 835–844.

Wells, G.L., Small, M., Penrod, S., Malpass, R.S., Fulero, S.M., & Brimacombe, C.A.E. (1998). Eyewitness identification procedures: Recommendations for lineups and photo spreads. *Law and Human Behavior, 22,* 603–647.

Wells, G.L., & Turtle, J.W. (1986). Eyewitness identification: The importance of lineup models. *Psychological Bulletin, 99,* 320–329.

Wenden v. Trikha, (1991), 8 C.C.L.T. (2d) 138 (Alta. Q,B.); aff'd. (1993) 14 C.C.L.T. (2d) 225.

Werner, E.E., & Smith, R.S. (1992). *Overcoming the odds: High-risk children from birth to adulthood.* Ithaca, NK: Cornell University Press.

Wertz, J., Zavos, H.M.S., Matthews, T., Gray, R., Best-Lane, J., Pariante, C.M., Moffitt, T.E., & Arseneault, L. (2016). Etiology of pervasive versus situational antisocial behaviors: A multi-informant longitudinal cohort study. *Child Development, 87,* 312–325.

Wetmore, S.A., Neuschatz, J.S., Gronlund, S.D., Wooten, A., Goodsell, C.A., & Carlson, C.A. (2015). Effect of retention interval on showup and lineup performance. *Journal of Applied Research in Memory and Cognition, 4*(1), 8–14.

Wetter, M.W., & Corrigan, S.K. (1995). Providing information to clients about psychological tests: A survey of attorneys' and law students' attitudes. *Professional Psychology: Research and Practice, 26,* 474–477.

Wheeler, S., Book, A., & Costello, K. (2009). Psychopathic traits and perceptions of victim vulnerability. *Criminal Justice and Behavior, 36,* 635–648.

Whelan, C.W., Wagstaff, G., & Wheatcroft, J.M. (2015). High stakes lies: Police and non-police accuracy in detecting deception. *Psychology, Crime & Law, 21*(2), 127–138.

Whetzel, D.L., Rotenberry, P.F., & McDaniel, M.A. (2014). In-basket validity: A systematic review. International *Journal of Selection and Assessment, 22,* 62–79.

Whipple, G.M. (1909). The observer as reporter: A survey of "the psychology of testimony." *Psychological Bulletin, 6,* 153–170.

Whipple, G.M. (1910). Recent literature on the psychology of testimony. *Psychological Bulletin, 7,* 365–368.

Whipple, G.M. (1911). The psychology of testimony. *Psychological Bulletin, 8,* 307–309.

Whipple, G.M. (1912). The psychology of testimony and report. *Psychological Bulletin, 9,* 264–269.

White Burgess Langille Inman v. Abbott and Haliburton Co., 2015 SCC 23, [2015] 2 S.C.R. 182.

Widom, C., & Ames, M. (1994). Criminal consequences of childhood sexual victimization. *Child Abuse and Neglect, 18,* 303–318.

Widom, C.S. (1989a). The cycle of violence. *Science, 244,* 160–166.

Widom, C.S. (1989b). Does violence beget violence? A critical examination of the literature. *Psychological Bulletin, 106,* 2–28.

Widom, C.S., & Morris, S. (1997). Accuracy of adult recollections of childhood victimization: Part 2. childhood sexual abuse. *Psychological Assessment, 9*(1), 34–46.

Wigmore, J.H. (1909). Professor Munsterberg and the psychology of testimony. *Illinois Law Review, 3,* 399–434.

Wilkins, F. (2003). The death of Rebecca Schaeffer. *Reel Reviews.* Retrieved from www.franksreelreviews.com/shorttakes/shaeffer/shaeffer.htm.

Williams, C., South Richardson, D., Hammock, G.S., & Janit, A.S. (2012). Perceptions of physical and psychological aggression in close relationships: A review. *Aggression and Violent Behavior, 17,* 489–494.

Williams, L.M. (1994). Recall of childhood trauma: A prospective study of women's memories of child sexual abuse. *Journal of Consulting and Clinical Psychology, 62*(6), 1167–1176.

Williams, S.L., & Frieze, I.H. (2005). Patterns of violent relationship, psychological distress, and marital satisfaction in national sample of men and women. *Sex Roles, 52,* 771–785.

Williamson, S., Hare, R.D., & Wong, S. (1987). Violence: Criminal psychopaths and their victims. *Canadian Journal of Behavioural Science, 19,* 454–462.

Williamson, S., Harpur, T., & Hare, R. (1991). Abnormal processing of affective words by psychopaths. *Psychophysiology, 28,* 260–273.

Willing, J. (2009, September 9). Arenburg back in Canada. *Ottawa Sun.* Retrieved from www.ottawasun.com/news/ottawa/2009/09/08/10789686.html.

Wilson, C.M., Crocker, A.G., Nicholls, T.L., Charette, Y., & Seto, M.C. (2015). The use of risk and need factors in forensic mental health decision-making and the role of gender and index offense severity. *Behavioral Sciences & the Law, 33,* 19–38.

Wilson, H.A., & Gutierrez, L. (2014). Does one size fit all?: A meta-analysis examining the predictive ability of the Level of Service Inventory (LSI) with Indigenous offenders. *Criminal Justice and Behaviour, 41,* 196–219.

Wilson, M., & Daly, M. (1993). Spousal homicide risk and estrangement. *Violence and Victims, 8,* 3–16.

Wilson, M., Daly, M., & Daniele, A. (1995). Familicide: The killing of spouse and children. *Aggressive Behavior, 21,* 275–291.

Wilson, P., Lincoln, R., & Kocsis, R. (1997). Validity, utility and ethics of profiling for serial violent and sexual offenders. *Psychiatry, Psychology and Law, 4,* 1–12.

Winfield, L. (1994). *NCREL Monograph: Developing resilience in urban youth.* NCREL: Urban Education Monograph Series.

Winter, R.J., & Greene, E. (2007). Juror decision making. In F.T. Durso, R.S. Nickerson, S.T. Dumais, S. Lewandosky, & T.J.

Perfect (Eds.), *Handbook of Applied Cognition* (2nd ed., pp. 739–761). Chichester, UK: John Wiley & Sons.

Wixted, J.T., Mickes, L., Clark, S.E., Gronlund, S.D., & Roediger III, H.L. (2015). Initial eyewitness confidence reliably predicts eyewitness identification accuracy. *American Psychologist, 70*(6), 515–526.

Wolfe, D.A., Crooks, C.V., Lee, V., McIntyre-Smith, A., & Jaffe, P.G. (2003). The effects of children's exposure to domestic violence: A meta-analysis and critique. *Clinical Child and Family Psychology Review, 6,* 171–187.

Wong, S.C.P., & Gordon, A. (2006). The validity and reliability of the violence risk scale: A treatment-friendly violence risk assessment tool. *Psychology, Public Policy, and Law, 12,* 279–309.

Woodhams, J., & Bennell, C. (2015). *Crime linkage: Theory, research, and practice.* Boca Raton, FL: CRC Press.

Woodrow, A.C., & Bright, D.A. (2011). Effectiveness of a sex offender treatment programme: A risk band analysis. *International Journal of Offender Therapy and Comparative Criminology, 55*(1), 43–55.

Woodworth, M., & Porter, S. (1999). Historical foundations and current applications of criminal profiling in violent crime investigations. *Expert Evidence, 7,* 241–264.

Woodworth, M., & Porter, S. (2002). In cold blood: Characteristics of criminal homicides as a function of psychopathy. *Journal of Abnormal Psychology, 111,* 436–445.

Woodworth, M., Agar, A.D., & Coupland, R.B.A. (2013). Characteristics of Canadian youth-perpetrated homicide. *Criminal Justice and Behavior, 40,* 1009–1026.

Wooldredge, J.D. (1988). Differentiating the effects of juvenile court sentences on eliminating recidivism. *Journal of Research in Crime and Delinquency, 25,* 264–300.

Worling, J.R., & Curwen, T. (2000). Adolescent sexual offender recidivism: Success of specialized treatment and implications for risk prediction. *Child Abuse and Neglect, 24,* 965–982.

Wormith, J.S. (1984). Attitude and behavioral change or correctional clientele: A three-year follow-up. *Criminology, 22,* 595–618.

Wray, A.M., Hoyt, T., & Gerstle, M. (2013). Preliminary examination of a mutual intimate partner violence intervention among treatment-mandated couples. *Journal of Family Psychology, 27,* 664–670.

Wright, A.M., & Holliday, R.E. (2007). Enhancing the recall of young, young-old, and old-old adults with cognitive interviews. *Applied Cognitive Psychology, 21,* 19–43.

Wright, D.B., & Skagerberg, E.M. (2007). Postidentification feedback affects real eyewitnesses. *Psychological Science, 18*(2), 172–178.

Wrightsman, L.S. (2001). *Forensic psychology.* Belmont, CA: Wadsworth.

Yang, M., Wong, S.C.P., & Coid, J. (2010). The efficacy of violence prediction: A meta-analytic comparison of nine risk assessment tools. *Psychological Bulletin, 136*(5), 740–767.

Yang, S., & Mulvey, E.P. (2012). Violence risk: Re-defining variables from the first-person perspective. *Aggression and Violent Behavior, 17,* 198–207.

Yardley, J. (2002, March 16). Mother who drowned 5 children in tub avoids death sentence. *The New York Times.* Retrieved from www.nytimes.com/2002/03/16/us/mother-who-drowned-5-children-in-tub-avoids-a-death-sentence.html.

Yarmey, A.D. (2001). Expert testimony: Does eyewitness memory research have probative value for the courts? *Canadian Psychology, 42,* 92–100.

Yarmey, A.D., Jacob, J., & Porter, A. (2002). Person recall in field settings. *Journal of Applied Social Psychology, 32,* 2354–2367.

Yarmey, A.D., Yarmey, M.J., & Yarmey, A.L. (1996). Accuracy of eyewitness identifications in showups and lineups. *Law and Human Behavior, 20,* 459–477.

Yesberg, J.A., Scanlan, J.M., & Ploachek, D.L.L. (2014). Women on parole: Do they need their own DRAOR? *Practice: The New Zealand Corrections Journal, 2,* 20–25.

Yllo, K., & Straus, M. (1990). Patriarchy and violence against wives: The impact of structural and normative factors. In M. Straus & R. Gelles (Eds.), *Physical violence in American families* (pp. 383–399). New Brunswick, NJ: Transaction.

Yoshimasu, K., Barbaresi, W.J., Colligan, R.C., Voigt, R.G., Killian, J.M., Weaver, A.L., & Katusic, S.K. (2012). Childhood ADHD is strongly associated with a broad range of psychiatric disorders during adolescence: a population-based birth cohort study. *Journal of Child Psychology and Psychiatry, 53,* 1036–1043.

Youth Criminal Justice Act, S.C. 2002. c. 1, s. 38(2).

Yuille, J.C., Hunter, R., Joffe, R., & Zaparniuk, J. (1993). Interviewing children in sexual abuse cases. In G. Goodman & B. Bottoms (Eds.), *Child victims, child witnesses: Understanding and improving testimony* (pp. 95–115). New York, NY: Guilford Press.

Zajac, R., & Karageorge, A. (2009). The wildcard: A simple technique for improving children's target-absent lineup performance. *Applied Cognitive Psychology, 23*(3), 358–368.

Zamble, E., & Quinsey, V.L. (1997). *The criminal recidivism process.* Cambridge, England: Cambridge University Press.

Zanis, D.A., Mulvaney, F., Coviello, D., Alterman, A.I., Savitz, B., & Thompson, W. (2003). The effectiveness of early parole to substance abuse treatment facilities on 24-month criminal recidivism. *Journal of Drug Issues, 33,* 223–236.

Zapf, P., & Roesch, R. (1998). Fitness to stand trial: Characteristics of remands since the 1992 criminal code amendments. *Canadian Journal of Psychiatry, 43,* 287–293.

Zigler, E., Taussig, C., & Black, K. (1992). Early childhood intervention: A promising preventative for juvenile justice. *American Psychologist, 47*(8), 997–1006.

Zinger, I., & Forth, A.E. (1998). Psychopathy and Canadian criminal proceedings: The potential for human rights abuses. *Canadian Journal of Criminology, 40,* 237–276.

Zingraff, M.T., Leiter, J., Johnsen, M.C., & Myers, K.A. (1994). The mediating effect of good school performance on the maltreatment delinquency relationship. *Journal of Research in Crime and Delinquency, 31,* 62–91.

Zoucha-Jensen, J.M., & Coyne, A. (1993). The effects of resistance strategies on rape. *American Journal of Public Health, 83,* 1633–1634. Porter, S., Juodis, M., ten Brinke, L., Klein, R. & Wilson, K. (2010). Evaluation of a brief deception detection training program. *Journal of Forensic Psychiatry & Psychology, 21,* 66–76.

Case/Legislation Index

Note: An italicized "n" following a page reference indicates a source note.

Name Index

Note: An italicized "*f*" following a page reference indicates a figure, an italicized "*n*" following a page reference indicates a source note and an italicized "*t*" following a page reference indicates a table.

Subject Index

Note: Page numbers followed by *f* or *t* represent figures or tables respectively.

Canadian Mental Health Association, 252
Canadian Psychological Association, 144, 291, 324
Canadian Security Intelligence Service (CSIS), 96
capital punishment, 219, 278, 337
capping, 244
celebrity stalkers, 400
challenge for cause, 201–203
change of venue, 201
chaos theory, 203
Charter of Rights and Freedoms, 239
Chicago Child-Parent Center (CPC) program, 368
child abuse. *See* child maltreatment
child maltreatment, 184–190
    emotional maltreatment, 185–186
    hippocampal volume of abused child, 189
    in need of protection, 186
    neglect/failure, 184
    outcomes of, 189–190
    physical abuse, 184–185, 187–188
    risk factors, 187
    sexual abuse, 184, 187–189
Child Maltreatment Section (CMS) of Health Canada, 184
child molesters, 410
child molester/sexual offender against children, 408
Children's Aid Society, 291
child victims and witnesses, 161
    anatomically detailed dolls, 167–169
    changes to cognitive system, 167
    cognitive interview, 174
    competency inquiry, 182
    courtroom accommodations, 183–184
    describing a culprit, 178–180
    false-positive responses, 180, 182
    free recall *vs.* directed questioning, 164–166
    history, 162–163
    how to question, 166
    interview techniques, 169–174
    lineup procedure and identification rates, 180–182
    Martensville Babysitting case, 163
    narrative elaboration, 172–172
    National Institute of Child Health and Human Development (NICHD) protocol, 173–174
    propensity toward suggestibility, 166–167
    recall for events, 163–174
    recall for people, 178–180
    recall memory following a long delay, 174–177
    recognition, 180–182
    social compliance, 166–167
    step-wise interviewing, 171, 172t
    testifying in court, 182–184
    traumatic memories, 176
Christopher's Law, 411
chromosomal theory, 7
civil commitment, 291
classic trait model of personality, 87
clinical forensic psychologists, 13–14
clinical risk factors, 302, 306–307
clothing bias, 145
cluster analysis, 86
Code of Ethics for Psychologists, 291
coerced-compliant false confessions, 73–74

coerced-internalized false confession, 74–75
coercive interrogations, 58–59, 70
    investigative biases in, 68
    Mr. Big technique, 58–59
cognitive ability tests, 34–35
cognitive-behavioural therapy, 368, 394
cognitive distortions, 419
cognitive-experiential self-theory (CEST), 218
cognitive interview, 135–137, 174
    enhanced, 136–137
    meta-analysis of, 137
cognitive theories, 360–361
comfort serial murderer, 445
commission errors, 179
community-based programs, 369
community service, 271
community treatment order, 257
Comparison Question Test (CQT), 96–98, 103
    question series used in, 97t
competency inquiry, 182
Competency Screening Test (CST), 233
Competency to Stand Trial Assessment Instrument (CAI), 233–234
compliance, 76
computerized geographic profiling systems, 91–92, 92f
concealed information paradigm, 104–105
Concealed Information Test (CIT), 98–100, 102
    mock-crime laboratory studies, 99
conditional discharge, 244, 271
conditional sentence, 271
conduct disorder (CD), 355–356
conduct-disordered youth, 360
confabulation, 76
confessions
    admissibility of, 69
    coerced-compliant false, 73–74
    coerced-internalized false, 74–75
    disputed, 71
    evidence, 58
    false, 70–79
    in polygraph tests, 99
    retracted, 71
    voluntary false, 72–73
confidence–accuracy relationship, 147–149, 149f
Conflict Tactics Scale, revised (CTS2), 376, 377t
Conflict Tactics Scale (CTS), 376–377
conscientiousness, 29–30
constitutional theory, 7
contextual factors, and risk assessment, 302, 307
contextual risk factors, 302, 307
Control Question Test. *See* Comparison Question Test (CQT)
Coping-Relapse Model of Criminal Recidivism, 310
Cops, 2
correct identification (target-present lineups), 142–143
Correctional Service of Canada, 394
    National Family Violence Prevention Programs, 394–395
Correctional Service of Canada (CSC), 416
countermeasures, 100–102
court of appeal, 199

courts
    aboriginal, 265–267
    Canadian court system, 263–267
    "inferior," 264
    Tax Court of Canada, 265
courts, interrogations and, 68
crime, in TV, 2
crime, theories of
    biological theories, 7
    psychological theories, 7–8
    sociological theories, 7
crime scene behaviours, 85–86
    organized-disorganized model, 84–85, 85t
    of serial sex offenders, 86f
criminal harassment, 397
Criminal Interrogation and Confessions, 60
criminal investigative analysis, 81
criminal investigative analysts, 81
criminal justice system, 1, 14, 39, 41, 130, 162, 228, 232, 235, 243, 252–253, 256–257, 263, 265–267, 273, 312–313, 330, 346–347, 350, 350t, 369, 371, 387
criminal justice system stressors, 50t
criminal profiling, 3, 79–90
    application of, 80
    case of New York City's Mad Bomber, 82
    construction of, 83–87
    deductive, 84
    defined, 79–81
    early attempts at, 81–82
    empirical support for profiling assumptions, 88–89
    Federal Bureau of Investigation (FBI) and, 79, 82
    Hollywood depictions of, 80
    impact of ambiguous profiles, 89
    inductive, 84
    investigative psychology approaches, 82–83, 85–87
    of Jack the Ripper, 81
    organized-disorganized model, 84–85
    origins of, 81–83
    professional profilers, 89–90
criminal responsibility, 8, 10
criminogenic needs, 301
criminological model of malingering, 118
criterion-based content analysis (CBCA), 169–171, 170t
Critical Incident Stress Debriefing, 13, 55
cross-race effect, 150–152
Crown attorney, 195
cue-utilization hypothesis, 152
culturally-relevant risk factors, 314
cycle of abuse, 386

D

Daubert criteria, 21
day parole, 281
death penalty in Canada, 278
Death-penalty trials, 299
deception detection, 64
    detection of a killer from a 911 call, 110
    myths and realities, 108
    in online dating, 111
    potential verbal and nonverbal characteristics of deception, 109t
    professional lie catchers, 110–115, 113t
deception paradigms, 103–105

base rate problem, 294
childhood history of maltreatment, 305–306
in civil contexts, 291
clinical factors, 302, 306–307
contextual factors, 302, 307
in criminal contexts, 292–293
culturally-relevant risk factors, 314
current issues, 310–319
defined, 290–291
demographics, 303
desistance from crime, 318–319
dispositional factors, 302–305
gender differences in criminality, 311–312
historical factors, 302, 305–306
history of, 295–296
judgment error and biases, 297–298
likelihood of engaging in criminal behaviour, 311
limitations, 315–317
mental disorder, 307
methodological issues, 296–297
myths and realities, 308
personality characteristics, 303–305
prediction outcomes, types of, 293–294, 293t
prevent or reduce crime and, 318–319
protective factors, 315
psychologists and decision makers, use of, 317–318
risk-assessment instruments, 308–310
risk factors, 302–310
social support, lack of, 307
static and dynamic risk factors in female offenders, 311–312
structured professional judgment (SPJ), 300
sub-population of offenders, 311–315
substance use, 306–307
of terrorism, 304
types of risk factors, 300–302
unstructured clinical judgment, 298
violence-risk-assessment approaches, 300
risk factors for abuse, 187t
risk principle, 279
Rogers Criminal Responsibility Assessment Scales (R-CRAS), 243
Royal Canadian Mounted Police (RCMP), 81, 83
Incident Management/Intervention Model, 46–47, 47f
Police Aptitude Test, 29
RCMP Entrance Exam (RPAB), 30
RCMP Member Selection Interview (RMSI), 30
RCMP officer, selection of, 30
RCMP Police Aptitude Test (RPAT), 30

S

sadistic rapist, 410
same-sex battering, 379
schizophrenia, 122
school and labour regulations, 291
school-based prevention programs, 368–369
secondary intervention strategies, 371–373
second-degree murder, 428
selection interview, 33–34
selective pressure, 385

selective serotonin-reuptake inhibitors (SSRIs), 422
self-defence, 225
self-labelled profilers, 90
self-presentation in online dating profiles, 111
Self-Report Psychopathy Scale (SRP), 325
Self-Report Questionnaire, 124–125
sentencing guidelines, 275
sentencing in Canada, 267–280, 349
absolute discharge, 271
community service, 271
conditional discharge, 271
conditional sentence, 271
creative options, 272
death penalty, 278
decisions across five simulated cases, 275
disparity in, 273–276
factors that affect, 271–272
fine, 271
fundamental principle of sentencing, 269–270
general deterrence, 267
goals of, 276–279
imprisonment, 271
need principle, 279
options, 270–271
principles of effective correctional intervention, 279–280
responsivity principle, 279
restitution, 271
risk principle, 279
specific deterrence, 267
systematic disparity, 273
uniformity, 277
unsystematic disparity, 273
unwarranted sentencing disparity, 273
sequential lineup, 142
sequential superiority effect, 143
serial killers, 443
serial murderer, 442
characteristics of, 442–443
female, 443–444, 444t
hedonistic, 444–445
mission-oriented, 444–445
power/control, 445
serial murderers
comfort, 445
visionary, 444–445
serial sex offenders, 86–87
sexual assault
definition of, 405–406
myths, 407
psychological and physical consequences for victims, 406–407
sexual history information, 221
sexual homicides, 333
sexualized behaviour, 189
sexually deviant offender, 86
polygraph tests, 96
sexual offenders
aboriginal, 416–417
adolescent, 412
assessment and treatment of, 419–422
child molesters, 408, 410
classification of, 407–411
cognitive distortions, 419
denial, 419
deviant sexual interests, 421–422
effectiveness of treatment for, 422–425

empathy, 420–421
exhibitionists, 408
female, 412–414
influence of alcohol, 405, 410, 416
intra-familial child molesters, 408
male-accompanied, 414
male-coerced, 414
minimizations, 419
pedophile, 408
predisposed, 414
rapists, 408–410
relapse prevention with, 422–423, 423f
social skills, 421
substance-abuse problems, 421
teacher/lovers, 414
voyeurs, 407
sexual sadism, 333
sexual violence
child molesters, 410
classification of sexual offenders, 407–411
definition of sexual assault, 405–406
intra-familial child molesters, 408
nature and extent of, 404–405
pedophile, 408
psychological and physical consequences for victims, 406–407
rapists typologies, 408–410
resisting sex attack, 408
sexual assault myths, 407
short-term memory, 127
showup, 144
The Silence of the Lambs, 80, 332
simulation, 206
simulation design, 119–120
primary strength of, 119
simultaneous lineup, 142
situational risk factors, 302
situational test, 36
Six Factor Personality Questionnaire, 29–30
social/agency testimony, 225
social compliance, 166–167
social learning theory, 8, 361–362, 383
socially competent offender, 86
socially isolated offender, 87
sociological theories of crime, 7
sociopath, 326
sociopathy, 326
source misattribution hypothesis, 134
specific deterrence, 267
spousal violence. *See* intimate partner violence
spree murder, 442
stalking, 397–401
offenders, 398
victims, 398–399
Stanford-Binet Intelligence Test, 29
statement validity analysis (SVA), 169–171
Static-99, 308, 318
static risk factors, 301–302
statutory release, 282
step-wise interviewing, 171
cognitive interview, 135–137
Stop Now And Plan (SNAP) Under 12 Outreach Project (ORP), 369–371
strain theory, 7
Structured Assessment of Violence Risk in Youth (SAVRY), 358, 365